CONFERENCE ON ENERGY AND ENVIRONMENT IN EUROPEAN ECONOMIES IN TRANSITION

PRIORITIES AND OPPORTUNITIES FOR CO-OPERATION AND INTEGRATION

PROCEEDINGS

Prague, 17th-19th June 1992

INTERNATIONAL ENERGY AGENCY

ORGANISATION FOR ECONOMIC
CO-OPERATION AND DEVELOPMENT

CENTRE FOR CO-OPERATION WITH
EUROPEAN ECONOMIES IN TRANSITION

INTERNATIONAL ENERGY AGENCY
2, RUE ANDRÉ-PASCAL, 75775 PARIS CEDEX 16, FRANCE

The International Energy Agency (IEA) is an autonomous body which was established in November 1974 within the framework of the Organisation for Economic Co-operation and Development (OECD) to implement an international energy programme.

It carries out a comprehensive programme of energy co-operation among twenty-three* of the OECD's twenty-four Member countries. The basic aims of the IEA are:

i) co-operation among IEA participating countries to reduce excessive dependence on oil through energy conservation, development of alternative energy sources and energy research and development;

ii) an information system on the international oil market as well as consultation with oil companies;

iii) co-operation with oil producing and other oil consuming countries with a view to developing a stable international energy trade as well as the rational management and use of world energy resources in the interest of all countries;

iv) a plan to prepare participating countries against the risk of a major disruption of oil supplies and to share available oil in the event of an emergency.

* IEA participating countries are: Australia, Austria, Belgium, Canada, Denmark, Finland, France, Germany, Greece, Ireland, Italy, Japan, Luxembourg, the Netherlands, New Zealand, Norway, Portugal, Spain, Sweden, Switzerland, Turkey, the United Kingdom, the United States. The Commission of the European Communities takes part in the work of the IEA.

ORGANISATION FOR ECONOMIC CO-OPERATION AND DEVELOPMENT

Pursuant to Article 1 of the Convention signed in Paris on 14th December 1960, and which came into force on 30th September 1961, the Organisation for Economic Co-operation and Development (OECD) shall promote policies designed:

— to achieve the highest sustainable economic growth and employment and a rising standard of living in Member countries, while maintaining financial stability, and thus to contribute to the development of the world economy;

— to contribute to sound economic expansion in Member as well as non-member countries in the process of economic development; and

— to contribute to the expansion of world trade on a multilateral, non-discriminatory basis in accordance with international obligations.

The original Member countries of the OECD are Austria, Belgium, Canada, Denmark, France, Germany, Greece, Iceland, Ireland, Italy, Luxembourg, the Netherlands, Norway, Portugal, Spain, Sweden, Switzerland, Turkey, the United Kingdom and the United States. The following countries became Members subsequently through accession at the dates indicated hereafter: Japan (28th April 1964), Finland (28th January 1969), Australia (7th June 1971) and New Zealand (29th May 1973). The Commission of the European Communities takes part in the work of the OECD (Article 13 of the OECD Convention).

Foreword

Within the countries of central and eastern Europe there has been a growing recognition that current levels of pollution create serious environmental and health problems. Much of this pollution is related to energy production and consumption. Governments -- East and West -- agree that they must rapidly develop effective strategies to address this situation, made all the more difficult since all decisions will have to be taken in the context of severe capital scarcity and economic uncertainty. At the same time, major changes are required in the production, consumption and trade of energy to meet the demands of transition economies.

The Prague conference was planned with the aim of identifying approaches for the reconciliation of energy and environmental policy objectives under conditions of capital scarcity and economic uncertainty. It examined opportunities for integrating environmental and energy policies with the potential to increase effectiveness and reduce costs. The present period of economic transition presents a unique opportunity to advance these aims.

Participants were asked specifically to address questions of environmental priorities in the energy sector and the way the economic transition will affect these priority areas. They were asked to identify mechanisms that can most effectively implement policies and to explore how economic, environment and energy policies can be co-ordinated. Participants examined the sources and magnitude of finance available for investment in the sector and ways in which limited investment capital can be used most effectively. Priorities for financial and technical assistance programmes were discussed as were innovative approaches that could augment traditional sources of finance. The main points to emerge from participants' discussions are summarised in the conference rapporteur's report that opens these conference proceedings.

The conference contributed to the activities carried out in the preparation of an Environmental Action Programme for Central and Eastern Europe which will be considered at the April 1993 European Conference of Environment Ministers in Lucerne, Switzerland.

ACKNOWLEDGEMENTS

On behalf of the International Energy Agency (IEA) and the OECD's Centre for Co-operation with European Economies in Transition (CCEET), we would like to express our appreciation to the organisations and individuals that contributed to the success of this Conference organised by the Agency and the OECD Environment Directorate headed by Mr. Bill Long. We would like to thank former Minister Dlouhy of the Federal Ministry of Economy of the Czech and Slovak Federal Republic (CSFR), and former Minister Vavrousek, Chairman of the Federal Commission for Environment, who actively supported the Conference. We also would like to thank them and their colleagues in the Federal Ministry of Economy and the Federal Commission for Environment for their active co-operation and assistance. We appreciate the material and financial support provided by the UN Development Programme and the UN Economic Commission for Europe -- which designated the Conference as one of the activities contributing to its Energy Efficiency 2000 Programme -- and the contributions of other international institutions that presented their work to the Conference.

We also would like to thank many individuals whose hard work helped make the Conference a success. The authors of the three country papers provided advice on the key energy-environment issues confronting these economies in transition: for Hungary, Ian Brown and Bela Barner of Energiahatekonysagi Iroda; in Poland, Slawomir Pasierb of the Polish Energy Efficiency Foundation, and in the CSFR, Jaroslav Marousek of SEVEn, the Energy Efficiency Centre. We also thank Mr. Marousek and his staff for his assistance in organising the Conference.

The rapporteurs and workshop chairmen worked energetically to promote a productive exchange of ideas and to generate constructive conclusions. The chief rapporteur was Christoph Hilz of the EC PHARE Programme. There were four workshop sessions. For the workshop on Coal and Power, Mr. Laszlo Hunyadi of Vattenfall, Sweden, was chairman, and Mr. Ian Brown was rapporteur. Mr. Joris Al of the Netherlands Ministry of Environment chaired the workshop on Transport, and Mr. Michael Walsh, an independent consultant was rapporteur. Mr. Nowicki, former Minister for Environment of Poland, chaired the workshop on Energy-Intensive Industries, and the rapporteur was Mr. William Chandler of Battelle Pacific Northwest Laboratories, USA. Mr. Karel Mrazek of the Building Technical Institute in Prague chaired the session on the Residential and Commercial Sectors, for which Mr. Jim Skea of the University of Essex, United Kingdom, was rapporteur.

The Conference was part of the programmes of work of the IEA and the CCEET. The team that prepared the Conference was comprised of Brendan Gillespie, Paul Schwengels, Tony Zamparutti and Anne Cariou of the OECD Environment Directorate, and Paul Vlaanderen, Stephen Perkins and Ubaldo Bianchi of the IEA. Finally, we would like to thank the many participants of the Conference, from both east and west, and we hope they found its three days of work to be as productive and rewarding as we did.

S. Zecchini   G. Quincey Lumsden, Jr.
Assistant Secretary-General, OECD   Director
Director of the CCEET   International Energy Agency

TABLE OF CONTENTS

Issues and Strategies for Domestic Financing

V. THE INTERNATIONAL CONTEXT

Pan-European Initiatives

The Role of External Financing and Technical Assistance

1. Reports from Multilateral and Bilateral Institutions

2. Private Sector Perspectives

3. Innovative Opportunities for East-West Financing

ANNEX: ENERGY STATISTICS FOR THE CSFR, HUNGARY, AND POLAND

EXECUTIVE SUMMARY

EXECUTIVE SUMMARY

The *OECD/IEA Conference on Energy and Environment in European Economies in Transition* brought together a broad mix of experts and institutions with an interest in this issue: representatives of central and eastern European governments, of OECD Member countries and of international organisations, and executives from private companies and public utilities. Participants discussed the relationships between energy use and the environment in the region and considered ways to achieve energy and environmental goals concurrently.

A **major conclusion** of the Conference is that <u>central and eastern European countries should develop integrated policies for energy and the environment</u> that will address the major problems in both sectors effectively and efficiently. The transition process provides these countries with a <u>unique opportunity</u> to put in place such policies and to direct economic growth and changes in ways that lead to energy and environmental goals. An initial integrated policy need not be complex, and could be described as an agreement between key ministries on priority measures for environment and energy.

Within these policies, **specific actions** need to be taken to address issues of energy supply and demand, energy efficiency, and environmental protection.

- <u>Economic reforms</u>, as well as the move to <u>market-based energy prices</u>, should continue. These are necessary to encourage more efficient energy use and a diversification of fuels; trends that can reduce energy-related pollution and improve energy security.

- Economic reforms alone are not sufficient. Government initiatives are needed to resolve problems such as the responsibility for past environmental pollution, and should in particular address barriers to <u>energy efficiency</u>.

- Governments need to develop <u>realistic, effective environmental strategies</u> that are adapted to the transition process. In the short-term, severe health problems, such as high levels of local air pollution, should be priorities for action. At the same time, governments should work to set explicit long-term environmental goals, so that industry and power generators can have a clear policy framework within which they can make decisions on investment.

- <u>Greater ministerial co-operation</u> will be needed to coordinate energy, environment, and economic initiatives and reach common goals.

- Governments in the region also need to search for <u>innovative funding mechanisms</u> to foster energy and environmental improvements.

Although the major part of the resources to develop and implement integrated energy and environment policies will have to come from domestic sources, **multilateral and bilateral assistance** can also help. Integrated energy and environment policies will help direct foreign loans and assistance to priority projects. At present, however, the existing coordination of external assistance programmes needs to be further improved, especially in regards to implementation at the country and operational level. There is scope for assembling small-scale energy efficiency projects into packages of sufficient magnitude to attract financing from multilateral assistance programmes.

Technical assistance could play an important role in identifying critical policy issues, and in preparing energy efficiency projects and other urgent energy and environment projects, for consideration by western investors and official loan programmes.

High-priority areas where Conference participants recommended that technical assistance be strengthened include:

- providing analytical methodologies to help governments design integrated strategies appropriate to the current process of economic restructuring;

- strengthening the capacity of government administration, and especially local authorities, to implement energy efficiency and environmental policies in a market-oriented economy (particularly through training);

- promoting energy and environmental demonstration projects;

- and assisting the optimisation of resource use and the introduction of Demand-Side Management for energy industries.

RAPPORTEUR'S REPORT

RAPPORTEUR'S REPORT

The chief Rapporteur was Mr. Christoph Hilz of the Commission of the European Communities/PHARE Programme. The rapporteurs of the four Conference workshops were: Mr. Ian Brown of the Hungary-EC Energy Centre, Hungary; Mr. William Chandler of Battelle Pacific Northwest Laboratories, USA; Mr. Laszlo Hunyadi of Vattenfall, Sweden; and Mr. Michael Walsh, independent consultant.

I. INTRODUCTION

Energy production and use create some of the most severe environmental problems in central and eastern European countries. These countries are now in the midst of extensive reforms to develop democratic political systems and market-based economies. The transition process, though often difficult, provides the countries in the region with a unique opportunity to address their energy and environmental problems concurrently. Specifically, if governments can integrate their energy, environmental, and economic policies, they will be able to achieve their goals in the three areas concurrently, and at lowest costs.

Developing and implementing coordinated policies can be a difficult process. Nonetheless, working toward this goal is in the interest of the countries of central and eastern Europe, as well as the OECD Member countries and the international organisations that are assisting the region in its economic transition. The *OECD/IEA Conference on Energy and Environment in European Economies in Transition* was convened to engage interested parties in a dialogue to discuss energy and environment issues and explore ways of developing coordinated energy and environment policies for the transition. In plenary sessions and four workshops -- covering special issues regarding the coal and power sectors, energy-intensive industries, the residential and commercial sectors, and the transportation sectors -- participants were asked to identify priority problems and areas for domestic initiatives and western assistance. Presentations and background papers provided information and proposals for discussion.

Approximately 200 persons attended the Conference, including representatives from central and eastern European countries, from OECD Member countries, and from multilateral institutions, as well as executives from private companies and public utilities. Almost two-thirds of the attendees were from central and eastern Europe, including energy and environmental officials from Beloruss, Bulgaria, the Czech and Slovak Federal Republic, Estonia, Hungary, Poland, Romania, and Ukraine.

II. ENERGY AND ENVIRONMENTAL PRIORITIES

The presentations and discussion during the conference, together with the conference background papers, pinpointed key energy and environmental issues that are priorities for policy action. The Conference focused on common issues for countries in Central and Eastern Europe: the patterns of energy use and environmental damage arising from their common legacy of command economies. Conference participants nonetheless recognised that each country has its particular energy use issues and environmental problems (Box 1, on the opposite page, describes some of the similarities and differences between three countries in the region, Poland, Hungary, and the CSFR).

1. Energy Issues and Goals

The conference identified the <u>inefficient conversion and use of energy</u> as a central problem: countries in central and eastern Europe consume significantly higher amounts of energy per unit of GDP than OECD countries. This aggravates energy-related environmental problems in the region, and is also a burden on domestic resources and foreign exchange. One essential reason for inefficient energy conversion and use was that energy prices were, until recently, decoupled from the world market and were artificially low and did not reflect costs.

In many countries in the region, energy prices have risen drastically (as described in Box 1), yet <u>energy intensities</u> remain high. Price changes alone are not rapidly translating into energy efficiency improvements. Identifying and removing the obstacles to greater energy efficiency is a priority. One aspect of the problem is that much of the <u>energy infrastructure</u> in the region is obsolete, inefficient, and heavily polluting -- over the long term, much of this infrastructure will have to be replaced, requiring costly investments. In addition, support for inefficient industry continues to distort the transition process.

<u>Diversification</u> is another important energy goal in the region. Countries are seeking to reduce their dependance on imports of oil, gas, and electricity from the Republics of the former Soviet Union. At the same time, substitute fuels are being sought to replace low-quality, indigenous solid fuels. Overall, many countries in the region are searching for new ways of assuring <u>security of energy supplies</u>.

2. Environmental Issues and Priorities

Central and Eastern Europe suffers from many environmental problems, and simple criteria are needed to establish priorities for action. Conference presentations and background papers recommended that, as a basic approach, attention should focus on those environmental problems that pose the greatest threats to human health, or to the productivity of natural resources, or risk irreversible environmental damage.

By this criterion, <u>local air pollution</u> appears to be the highest priority environmental problem created by energy use. It can be particularly severe in urban areas and in industrial "hot spots." In particular, high ambient levels of particulates appear to present the greatest threat to human health -- especially in countries that are dependant on highly polluting, indigenous solid fuels for energy. Local air pollution originates not only from large power plants and industrial

Box 1. Energy and Environmental Comparisons: Hungary, Poland, and the CSFR

Reports to the Conference on energy and environmental problems in Poland, Hungary, and the CSFR showed that these three countries have many common problems, but also a number of important differences in their energy use patterns.

Primary Fuels. In both Poland and the CSFR, domestic solid fuels form a large share of total fuel consumption. Solid fuels provided about three-quarters of Poland's total primary energy supply in 1990, and over half of the CSFR's (in the CSFR this share was lower in 1991 as the use of solid fuels fell more sharply than that of other fuels.) In Poland hard coal makes up about two-thirds of the solid fuel used, whereas in the CSFR brown coal and lignite provide over 50% of solid fuel supplies. All three countries import oil and gas from the former Soviet Union, but Hungary is the most dependent, importing about half of its primary energy supply -- including oil, natural gas, and electricity -- from the former USSR. Nuclear power stations generate about half of Hungary's domestic electricity supply and about 30 percent of electricity in the CSFR; Poland has no operating nuclear power stations.

Energy-Related Environmental Problems. Local air pollution is a priority in all three countries. The use of low-quality coal for residential and commercial heating creates severe air pollution in cities in Poland and the CSFR, resulting in serious threats to human health; this problem is less severe in Hungary, where other fuels are used more widely for heating. In all three countries, heavy industry and fossil-fuel power generation also create severe local and regional air pollution problems. These problems are particularly harsh in highly industrialized areas, such as Upper Silesia in Poland and northern Bohemia in the CSFR. In Poland and the CSFR, underground mining results in water pollution due to saline runoff, and open-pit mining has left extensive land damage. In all three countries, road transport and motor vehicle emissions are a growing problem, particularly for urban air quality.

Industrial Structure. In all three countries, industry takes the highest share of total energy consumption: just over 50% in the CSFR, and slightly under 50% in Poland and Hungary in 1989 (compared to not more than 33% in most western European countries). All three countries had a high level of employment and production in energy-intensive industries -- such as metals processing, chemicals, and building materials. The CSFR has a particularly large heavy industry sector: for example, steel production per capita was the second-highest in Europe (after Belgium), and cement production per capita the highest. In the economic transition, though, industrial production has fallen in all three countries.

Energy Price Reforms. Energy prices have risen in all three countries. In Poland, coal, oil, and natural gas prices increased significantly, reaching levels near those of the world market by early 1992. Electricity price increases were also severe, and were greatest for the residential and commercial sector, which paid much lower prices than industry before the transition. District heating prices continue to be subsidised, and were about 40 percent of real current cost in the first half of 1992. In the CSFR as well, fuel and energy prices increased significantly, particularly in the second half of 1991, to close to market levels. In Hungary, most fuel prices have increased to market levels, although government subsidies for district heating continued in early 1992, and cross-subsidies existed between industrial and household electricity and gas prices.

sites, but also from small sources: district heating plants, residential boilers, and open hearths in many areas still use low-quality coal, whose combustion can create severe local air pollution. They are sources of high particulate emissions that are difficult to control. In some industrial areas, pollution from toxic air emissions presents a severe threat to health. In many urban areas, motor vehicle traffic is rising sharply, and motor vehicle emissions are a growing problem.

The contribution of air pollution to regional problems, such as trans-boundary air pollution, and global issues, such as climate change, is also an important concern, but not as urgent as local air pollution. These concerns are, however, important over the long-term and also in regional and global international relations, and need to be addressed in government strategies. Measures to reduce local air pollution can and should be devised to minimise regional and global problems at the same time.

Because of the specialised nature of the technology and investment issues, there was little specific discussion of nuclear safety risks and solutions in this conference. However, Conference participants did identify nuclear safety as an important concern within the region. They emphasised that measures to address these concerns should be devised within the framework of a coherent, overall energy and environmental policy.

Other important environmental issues arising from energy use were also identified, such as waste water (including saline mine runoff), land damage and loss from coal mining, and worker health and safety problems.

III. THE REFORM PROCESS:
IMPLICATIONS FOR ENERGY AND ENVIRONMENT

The current economic reform programmes underway in central and eastern European countries include the privatisation of most economic activities, macroeconomic stabilisation programmes, and price liberalisation. These reforms are transforming the role of the state and the functions of public institutions. The reforms are intended to establish functioning markets throughout the region's economies, including in the energy sector. Presentations in the Conference outlined how well-functioning markets can effect energy use and related environmental pollution, but also identified barriers that need to be overcome for markets to operate effectively.

1. Expectations for Long-Run Change

Market forces are expected to play an important role in fostering energy and environmental improvements. As energy prices are freed and rationalised -- a process underway in many countries of the region -- they should increase to levels similar to those in western European countries. Through privatisation of companies and property, energy users -- both individuals and private companies -- facing higher prices and hard budget constraints should reduce their excess energy consumption and seek greater energy efficiency. For example, industrial plants that continue in production will seek to replace current, inefficient and highly polluting capital stock with more modern and energy-efficient plant and equipment. Energy use per unit of GDP should decline and, as a result, energy-related pollution should also decrease.

In addition, higher energy prices and the opening of industry to international and domestic competition is expected to drive a structural shift in these economies away from energy-intensive industries, further reducing industrial energy intensity and pollution.

Changes in relative fuel prices, in particular as the prices of indigenous solid fuels rise in relation to the prices of oil and natural gas, will probably promote a shift away from the use of highly polluting solid fuels in industry, and the residential and commercial sector. This diversification of fuel use will yield significant air pollution reductions.

2. Barriers to Change

Presentations and discussions in the conference identified several barriers that impede the creation of functioning economic markets and the realisation of expected energy and environmental improvements.

For example, institutional barriers remain, even though domestic reforms and western assistance are working to overcome many of them. Privatisation of state-owned enterprises is moving slowly in many countries in the region. In addition, some governments have not yet made clear choices regarding the structure and roles of energy monopolies, such as electricity transmission; until these choices are set, energy users face uncertainties over future energy developments and energy suppliers are not able to develop long-term strategies. Government administrations, on both national and local levels, often lack skills and resources to implement energy and environmental policies effectively. In addition, western private investors at the Conference emphasized that uncertainty over energy and environmental policies discouraged investment in the region, as these uncertainties magnified risks.

There are also social and political uncertainties to the reform process. These include the problems of unemployment and regional decline that arise from industrial restructuring. In addition, there may be public resistance to the large increases in energy prices (though in several countries, citizens have so far accepted many-fold increases in energy prices resulting from recent economic reforms, even though they have yet to see the corresponding benefits).

There are many barriers to greater energy efficiency. One problem is that energy users -- both in OECD countries and in central and eastern Europe -- often consider only those energy efficiency investments with extraordinarily short pay-back periods, thus overlooking many other profitable energy efficiency opportunities. This problem is magnified by other barriers. Individual energy users lack access to information and technical expertise to make energy efficiency improvements, and often the resources to implement changes in their energy use. They often face conflicting incentives that hinder energy efficient choices: for example, many individuals do not own their apartments, so are not able to make energy efficiency improvements; in addition, many residences are not individually metered for heat and electricity use. There is also a lack of infrastructure, with few companies or individuals that can analyse the potential and the economic returns from energy efficiency measures, or provide products and services to improve industrial, commercial, or residential energy efficiency.

For all sectors of the economy, a critical constraint in central and eastern Europe is the lack of access to finance and investment. In most countries, government resources are very limited in all spheres. Similarly, private energy users -- both individuals and enterprises -- often lack the funds to undertake energy efficiency improvements or pollution reduction investments.

As a result of these and other obstacles, the expected energy and environmental benefits from economic reform are not yet evident.

IV. RECOMMENDATIONS FOR NATIONAL POLICIES:
WORKING TOWARD AN INTEGRATED APPROACH

The Conference presentations and discussion emphasized that governments in central and eastern Europe need to take policy initiatives to overcome the barriers to energy and environmental improvement. Specifically, governments in the region should develop integrated energy and environmental strategies, with broadly accepted, explicitly stated priorities, and clear programmes to achieve these priorities.

As financial resources are limited, countries in the region will have to seek the most cost-effective methods to reach energy and environmental goals. Over the past 20 years, OECD countries have learned that energy and environment policies developed independently of each other are often contradictory. The countries of Central and Eastern Europe can not afford to learn this lesson over again.

Energy and environment issues are closely interrelated in the region's economic transition. First, national energy and environmental policies will have to consider the effects of industrial restructuring and other market-influenced economic changes: otherwise, scarce resources could be wasted if they are devoted to improvements at facilities that will eventually close due to restructuring. Second, industrial restructuring will change energy use patterns and resulting environmental damage. Third, energy policy decisions, from freeing fuel prices to the restructuring of the energy sector, can play an important role in changing the extensive environmental effects of energy production, distribution, and use. Fourth, well-conceived environmental policy can in turn affect industrial restructuring, energy sector decisions, and investment in a positive manner.

Integrated policies are needed to establish priorities and to identify opportunities to work simultaneously toward energy, environmental, and economic goals. Energy efficiency initiatives provide one such opportunity. Clear and consistent policies will also help to reduce uncertainties and to establish a stable investment climate for foreign investors.

Experience from OECD countries demonstrates that there is no one model for integrated policies, and central and eastern European countries must each set their own goals and priorities. In addition, the Conference emphasized that the development of integrated policies should not delay countries from taking high-priority and low-cost actions. The Conference did, however, recommend that governments in the region incorporate several key elements into their energy and environment policies, outlined in Box 2 and described in greater detail in the pages that follow. Governments should consider the development of integrated energy and environment policies as a long-term, continuing process, starting with relatively simple analyses and programmes that lead to more sophisticated work over time. An initial integrated strategy could be defined as a written agreement between key ministries on priority investments and measures, or on the policy steps to determine these priorities. This will help direct limited domestic resources, as well as international finance, to the most important projects and needs.

As their strategies become more established, governments in the region should also look closely at the environmental and energy effects of policies in other fields. For example, developments in the transport sector will have a great influence on energy use and environmental damage -- Box 3 describes some of these issues, as well as initial recommendations for the transport sector from the Conference.

Box 2. Summary of Recommendations for Integrated National Policies

1. Continue Economic Reforms -- including the move to market prices, privatisation, and the development of stable institutions to support the market -- and policies to:
   - Address the social costs of reforms;
   - Resolve environmental liability issues;
   - Begin, where feasible, to include environmental goals in economic reforms.

2. Continue Energy Policy Reforms:
   - Move to rational, market-based energy prices (that will, inter-alia, reduce the use of low-grade solid fuels in heating and industry);
   - Restructure energy supply enterprises;
   - Encourage utilities to optimise their resource use, and to consider the use of Integrated Resource Planning and Demand-Side Management techniques.

3. Address Barriers to Improved Energy Efficiency (with specific programs targeted to different sectors of the economy):
   - Provide information programs and training;
   - Consider potential demonstration projects that can play a valuable role in training and technology transfer (external assistance can play an important role in this area);
   - Adopt appropriate energy efficiency standards;
   - The development of a service industry of firms and individuals that can evaluate energy efficiency opportunities and can provide improvements would complement government actions on energy efficiency.

4. Develop Effective Environmental Policies:
   - Focus, in the transition period, on creating effective implementation and enforcement mechanisms, and promoting low-cost and no-cost measures that reduce pollution;
   - Set environmental requirements in coordination with energy policies and economic transition;
   - Establish long-term goals and requirements so enterprises can plan ahead;
   - Adopt the polluter-pays principle as a guide for environmental policies.

5. Improve Government Coordination and Implementation Capacities:
   - Establish strong Ministerial co-operation to develop integrated policies;
   - Develop analytical capacities needed to design policy;
   - Incorporate public participation in decision-making on national policies and major projects;
   - Improve administrative capacities -- at national, regional, and local levels -- to implement energy and environmental policies.

6. Search for Innovative Domestic Financing Mechanisms.

1. Economic Reforms

Conference participants affirmed that continuing the economic transition is a necessary prerequisite for effective energy and environmental policy. The establishment of functioning economic markets will serve as a base on which other reforms will be built. Unless market economies can be made to function, the resources needed to address severe environmental problems and to revitalise energy systems will not be available. Key elements of the reform process include moving to market-based prices for most goods and services, including energy prices; privatisation; and the creation of stable public and private institutions to support the market. The success of these reforms is essential to developments in other fields, including energy and the environment. For example, the establishment of an efficient domestic banking and finance sector will help provide individuals, companies, and utilities with loans and finance for energy and environmental improvements.

In addition, governments will need to address the social costs of reform, which can be high, especially in the initial stages of the transition. Many energy-intensive industries will be restructured or closed down in the face of higher energy costs and the new patterns of market demand. Individuals will pay higher prices for their energy use, while unemployment will rise. Several speakers at the conference stressed that social and political resistance is building in many areas and could impede the reform process unless adequately addressed. This may include resistance to further increases in energy prices.

Box 3. Energy Use and Environmental Issues in the Transport Sector

In the transport sector, both energy use and pollutant emissions are likely to increase sharply as more individuals in Central and Eastern European countries purchase and use private motor vehicles, and as road freight transport increases. (In most countries of the region, transport uses less than 10 percent of total energy consumption, compared to about one-third in western Europe.) This trend will increase environmental problems in urban areas and increase energy import requirements, unless new government policies are developed. Conference participants noted the importance of maintaining and improving the effective public transport systems in the region, both for passenger and freight movement. (The OECD/IEA/ECMT Conference, "Public Transport and the Environment: New Technologies, Systems, and Financing Mechanisms," to be held in Budapest in June 1993 should help to clarify policy options in this area.)

Emissions from trucks and buses are an important source of local air pollution and are likely to grow rapidly; governments need to consider measures to control this source of pollution urgently. Participants at the Prague Conference also recommended that countries introduce emissions standards for new automobiles similar to those to be required in the EC, with adequate enforcement mechanisms to ensure these standards are respected.

The indirect effects of major investment choices also require attention: for example, building new highways will bring increased traffic, higher energy use, and hence greater air pollution -- operating, in effect, as a hidden subsidy for energy use and environmental problems. This does not imply that such investments should be stopped; rather, future costs in terms of energy consumption and environmental pollution need to be weighed in choosing between alternatives. Otherwise, as many OECD countries have found, unaccounted long-term costs of energy use patterns and environmental problems can be high.

Environmental and energy issues can directly affect the economic transition. For example, to speed privatisation and encourage foreign direct investment, governments need to resolve environmental liability issues, as private investors want to know how potential risks will be allocated, including costs related to the cleanup of past pollution and the reduction of ongoing emissions. These issues will be especially important for highly polluting, energy-intensive industries, which often need foreign investment to finance their modernisation. In addition, the strictness of environmental requirements and the cost of energy will play a role in industrial restructuring.

The transition process can provide opportunities to incorporate environmental goals into economic reforms, as mentioned above. For example, as tax mechanisms are redesigned, some may begin to incorporate environmental goals -- a tool that many OECD countries are introducing. Higher taxes could be placed on high-polluting fuels, such as those with high sulfur contents, in order to encourage individual and corporate users to switch to less polluting fuels. (OECD countries introducing these new taxes often try to ensure that they are balanced by tax reductions in other areas, so that the overall burden on consumers and private business is not increased.) Significant taxes on fuels should be placed only after their prices risen to full market levels. Nonetheless, governments in central and eastern Europe may wish to consider simple measures that promote environmental improvements, such as establishing a higher tax on gasoline containing lead to encourage the distribution and use of lead-free gasoline.

Foreign investment in the energy and manufacturing sectors also provides an opportunity to encourage energy efficiency and pollution reduction: governments should encourage western investors to introduce cleaner, more fuel-efficient production techniques, for example by setting clear long-term environmental requirements.

2. Energy Policy Reforms

In the energy sector, the centrepiece of reform should be the continuing adjustment of energy prices to rational and market-based levels, encouraging energy efficiency, fuel diversification, and greater energy security. A number of governments in the region have already allowed many fuel and energy prices to move toward market levels. Fuel prices should be set by the market, where markets exist, and elsewhere should be based on market levels prevailing in the region. Governments may retain a greater role in determining prices in some energy sectors (such as electricity and district heating). Here prices should rise to levels based on the long-term cost of these energy systems; generally, this implies prices similar to those in western Europe.

As part of this price reform, governments should try to identify and remove subsidies that encourage high energy use or the use of highly polluting fuels, such as subsidies for local district heating, for coal mining, and for low-quality, domestic brown coals and lignite.

One priority problem identified in the conference was the use of low-grade solid fuels for district heating plants and residential and commercial boilers, a leading cause of health-threatening pollution in local areas. Price signals will encourage a long-term shift to less-polluting fuels, but immediate actions need to be considered. Improving the maintenance and efficiency of small boilers is one initiative that can help reduce pollution in the short term. Coal preparation techniques to remove sulfur and ash can also help.

The restructuring of energy supply enterprises is another important factor. Conference participants felt that the restructuring of electricity generators and other energy enterprises should take a priority over ownership decisions. In restructuring, governments will have to make provisions to regulate monopoly elements. There is no one answer, and OECD countries use different forms of ownership and regulation (for electricity generators and transmission systems, district heating suppliers, etc.). Most OECD countries are, however, trying to increase the role of competition, and central and eastern European governments should consider opportunities for competition that encourage greater efficiency.

Restructuring of the energy sector should transfer the authority for operational and investment decisions from government to enterprise management and refocus attention on economic efficiency and profitability. Independent utilities are likely to make use of techniques to optimise resource use, such as Integrated Resources Planning and Demand-Side Management. Under Integrated Resources Planning, utilities consider all options -- both on the supply side and the demand side -- and choose the most cost-effective mix of investments and initiatives to meet their requirements. Environmental goals and social goals can be explicitly included in Integrated Resources Planning. There is not one single method for Integrated Resources Planning used in OECD countries, and central and eastern European governments should evaluate different models and develop systems that best adapted to their domestic conditions. Demand-Side Management refers to utility initiatives to reduce and restructure demand. There are many possible programmes, depending on the specific end-use sector. The next section discusses many energy efficiency initiatives that could be used in Demand-Side Management programmes.

3. Energy Efficiency

Energy efficiency should be a priority for energy and environmental policies, as it can provide least-cost paths to reach both energy and environmental goals. In addition, the poor energy efficiency of central and eastern European economies drains both their domestic resources and foreign exchanges. One long-term goal of the transition process needs to be a move toward energy efficiencies similar to those of western European countries.

There are significant opportunities for energy efficiency improvements in the residential, commercial, and industrial sectors, and governments need to identify efficiency potentials and targets, build these into national policies, and develop policies to overcome barriers that hinder energy users from adopting more efficient technologies and methods. In the past, energy conservation programmes established under command economies were often ineffective and their funds were abused. New energy efficiency policies need to be effective and counter this legacy. Newly established Energy Efficiency Centres in several countries of the region have helped study energy use problems and propose new initiatives for energy efficiency (assistance from the U.S. government and the E.C. PHARE Programme helped establish these centres).

OECD countries use a wide variety of government policies to encourage energy efficiency, many of which can provide models for Central and Eastern European countries. These include information programmes, which can range from public campaigns to energy audits for individual factories; training to promote effective energy efficiency services; the use of minimum energy-

Box 4. Energy Efficiency Initiatives for
the Industrial, and the Residential and Commercial Sectors

In the industrial sector, governments can encourage relatively low-cost energy audits for industrial plants -- such audits can identify "good housekeeping" measures, such as simple process improvements, that reduce energy consumption and operating costs. Training for plant workers and managers, access to information on energy efficiency options, and pilot projects demonstrating energy efficient technologies and management can be of value. External technical assistance can provide expertise from energy efficiency programs undertaken in OECD country industries. For example, experts in industrial energy efficiency could train local consultants to provide energy efficiency audits and feasibility studies.

Over the long-term, large energy efficiency improvements in energy-intensive industries depend on costly investments in new, more efficient plant processes. This implies that ownership issues need to be resolved quickly so that new investors can make long-term plans for restructuring and investment.

Barriers to the efficient operation of price signals and other market mechanisms are highest in the residential and commercial sector. Priorities for energy efficiency in Central and Eastern Europe include the need for metering for heat and electricity. Property privatisation can play an important role, so that owners and residents have incentives to renovate their buildings. Through information programs, individuals and companies will be able to learn about energy efficiency options. Training can help provide the know-how and technical skills for energy efficiency improvements. District heating -- which can be more efficient than individual heating -- is widespread in the region and there may be opportunities for expansion in some areas. There is great potential for district heating plants to improve their operating efficiency. Overall efficiency will also improve as heat prices are raised to reflect costs (and, where possible, market value) once metering and control systems are installed.

Most difficult to address, however, is the severe lack of finance, as both families and companies are hard-pressed by the current economic difficulties. Nonetheless, OECD experience has shown that government financial incentives for energy efficiency are often not effective unless extremely well-designed and managed.

The central government can best encourage energy efficiency in this sector by setting standards, such as efficiency requirements for heat and electricity in new buildings, and ensuring that these are implemented. Local governments may be best placed to implement energy efficiency policies for the residential and commercial sector. This, however, is a new role, and local government personnel would need training to develop and implement effective programs. Financing will be a difficult problem. The OECD's ongoing program on Urban Energy Management could provide local governments in the region with information on the experiences and lessons from cities in OECD countries.

efficiency standards, particularly for new buildings, new vehicles, and new appliances; and support for research and development, including small-scale demonstration or pilot projects that can test the feasibility and effectiveness of introducing technologies and techniques and provide training for local personnel. OECD countries have generally restricted the use of financial incentives for energy efficiency; most forms of incentives will not be appropriate for central and eastern European countries either, considering the scarcity of resources in the region. Specific programmes should be tailored for the needs of different sectors -- Box 4 describes some of the issues and possible initiatives for industry and for the residential and commercial sectors.

Private sector solutions, such as energy service companies that help customers reduce their energy expenses, can play an important role in promoting energy efficiency. In OECD experience, however, these methods are best suited for large plants and large commercial establishments.

In OECD countries, utilities are also taking a growing role in promoting energy efficiency through Demand-Side Management programmes, and, if given appropriate incentives and training, they could play an important role in Central and Eastern Europe in planning and implementing energy efficiency actions, including those mentioned above and in Box 4. Utilities should only undertake energy efficiency programmes that can provide them with a payback; the use of techniques such as Integrated Resources Planning can identify cost-effective demand-side options.

4. Effective Environmental Policies

Effective environmental policies and requirements are essential if the economic restructuring process is to proceed in a cleaner, sustainable direction. Both short-term and long-term policies are needed. In the current transition period, the highest priority should be given to developing effective implementation and enforcement mechanisms for realistic, achievable standards. In many countries of the region, strict legal requirements were never effectively enforced, undermining the credibility of regulatory authorities. Implementation and enforcement mechanisms -- to encourage compliance with environmental requirements -- should be essential parts of new environmental policies. (A number of bilateral assistance programmes are currently assisting governments improve policy implementation and enforcement.)

There also are opportunities to work immediately on low-cost and no-cost programmes that reduce industrial pollution. For example, environmental audits of industrial plants can identify simple process changes that reduce emissions and can also save money by improving plant efficiency. These environmental audits could be developed in concert with plant energy audits. Highest priority should be given to plants whose emissions pose the greatest risks to human health and that are likely to continue in operation for some time to come. Another opportunity is environmental impact assessments, commonly used in OECD countries to identify and mitigate the adverse environmental consequences of new projects. Extensive environmental impact assessments can require complex analyses; nonetheless, simple environmental reviews can, in the immediate term, be a useful tool to prevent future environmental problems.

New plants should be subject to stricter standards than existing ones. However, the standards for existing plants should be designed to avoid discouraging new investments. Explicit long-term goals and requirements should be set out detailing the evolution of standards for new and existing plants. Such a framework of standards needs to be published to provide investors with clear signals on future requirements. Within this framework compliance schedules for existing plant can be negotiated on a case-by-case basis.

Some governments in Central and Eastern Europe have declared their intention to move toward the standards set in EC Directives. There are many areas, however, where the EC has not set environmental requirements, and policies still vary between EC countries, as between all Member countries of the OECD. Central and eastern European governments need to weigh carefully different types of standards and other instruments for their environmental policies. OECD countries are increasingly using economic instruments in conjunction with standard-based regulations, and some countries in Central and Eastern Europe already have experience with environmental fees and fines.

Over the past 20 years, OECD countries have learned that private firms can meet environmental requirements most efficiently when they have the flexibility to develop their response over several years, choosing measures that are best adapted to their specific circumstances. Such flexibility can encourage investments in new, more efficient low-polluting processes rather than purchases of add-on pollution control equipment. Economic instruments can play an important role in supporting such developments.

Finally, The polluter-pays principle, adopted by all OECD countries (and some central and eastern European countries), provides one important guide for the design of environmental policies. Exceptions to this principle may be needed during economic transition, but it is important that polluters realise they will be directly responsible for meeting eventual environmental requirements without subsidies.

5. Improve Government Coordination and Implementation Capacities

Ministerial co-operation is necessary for effective policy integration. Ministries responsible for the environment, energy policy, and economic policy need to begin co-operative activities. It will be also important to involve finance ministries, in particular in regards to investment strategies and taxation issues. Initial steps for Ministerial co-operation could include sharing data and creating joint committees to discuss priorities and goals. Over time, governments should increase coordination and communication at the working levels -- and policy-making levels -- between different ministries, agencies, and between national, regional, and local levels of government. As part of this co-operation, governments need to anticipate conflicts between energy and environmental policies, particularly in implementation; develop ways of identifying and resolving these conflicts in advance; and to encourage different agencies and ministries to work actively together to reach national goals. This co-operation will allow different ministries to identify opportunities for resolving multiple problems through a single, coordinated policy or investment decision.

The policies and goals developed through this co-operation will need broad political and social support for successful implementation. For this, integrity is needed: policies should be based on sound analysis and on thorough consultation. Box 5 describes some of the types of analytical approaches available to governments.

Public participation is also very important in obtaining broad support. Governments need to actively promote public awareness and education on energy and environmental goals and strategies, and should consult with key groups such as industry, environmentalists, and labor, as

Box 5. Priorities for Analytical Work

Developing integrated policies will require governments to undertake analyses to identify cost-effective options, set priorities, and identify key barriers and issues for policy implementation. One important area of work will be developing scenarios of the effects that economic restructuring will have on energy demand and pollution emissions: these projections will be important in guiding effective policy decisions. Government analysis should be able to consider complex problems: environmental analyses should look at a range of environmental concerns, pollution media and geographic regions. Coordination between national, regional and local decision-making is also important.

Analytical methods developed in OECD countries can be of use. For example, life cycle analysis approaches can be used to compare alternative energy options. In addition, a number of OECD governments are working on domestic economic scenarios and their environmental consequences. The preparatory work for the Environmental Action Program for Central and Eastern Europe employs some of these methods (this Action Program is being prepared for the April 1993 European Conference of Environment Ministers). Central and eastern European governments need to acquire skills in many of these areas, and western technical assistance programs can provide specific help.

well as the general public. Consultation with all these different interests is important both to provide a broad base of social support for eventual policies and to encourage government bureaucracies to be more responsive to national goals and to the public. Integrated policies will be most effective when they enjoy the support of democratic institutions and Parliament in particular.

Government agencies in central and eastern Europe need to improve their management skills in order to implement policies effectively. The competence of government institutions -- national, regional, and local administrations -- needs to strengthened, particularly in areas such as: environmental policy development and enforcement; accounting and least-cost planning; and regulating energy utilities in a market economy. In addition, many countries in the region intend to devolve decision-making to local and regional administrations, which should be able to act better for local citizens' interests. These local administrations have a particular need for training to implement new government programmes. In all of these areas, technical assistance can play an important role in providing results and lessons from experience in OECD countries.

6. Innovative Domestic Financing Mechanisms

Participants recognised that the majority of finance for energy systems and environmental improvements will ultimately have to come from domestic sources in the region and domestic actions to attract long-term private investment.

Resources from official assistance programmes, including the multilateral development banks, can be an important source of capital, especially in the short-term, but these will supply only a fraction of long-term finance needs for energy and the environment. Private foreign investment can also provide significant funding but remains limited at present, partly due to the current high levels of uncertainty attached to energy and environment projects.

Innovative ways of financing energy and environmental investments may be of use to governments. For example, national environmental funds based on pollution charges can create revenues for environmental protection and energy efficiency investments. Such funds raise a number of questions, including their position outside regular national budgets, and the "earmarking" of national funds for specific priorities. Market-based and cost-related energy prices will be most significant in generating revenues that can provide for investments in cleaner plants and processes in the energy sector.

V. PRIORITIES FOR EXTERNAL ASSISTANCE

Foreign technical assistance programmes, official grants and loans, and private investment can all support the energy and environmental programmes of central and eastern European countries. Many important initiatives are underway, including: the PHARE Programme (for Central and Eastern Europe) and TACIS (for the CIS) of the Commission of the E.C.; the bilateral aid programmes of the G-24 (the Member countries of the OECD); the UN ECE's Energy Efficiency 2000 programme; the work of other UN agencies; and the loan programmes of the World Bank, the European Bank for Reconstruction and Development, and the EC's European Investment Bank. At the Conference, representatives of many of these of organisations described their work in the region. However, the Conference identified areas where external assistance can be improved, and in particular areas for improved technical assistance.

1. Improving the Coordination of International Assistance

First, coordination among assistance programmes should be improved and strengthened, especially at the operational level. At present, several forums, and most importantly that of the G-24 under E.C. chairmanship, provide policy coordination for foreign assistance to the region. Nevertheless, with respect to implementation, foreign donors and international agencies need to improve their coordination of assistance within countries and within specific sectors. Moreover, there is a need to better ensure that foreign assistance is targeted on priority problems. The development of national energy and environment policies would help donors coordinate their assistance programmes and direct resources to the highest priority problems in each country. In addition, new international initiatives could increase international agreement on assistance priorities. These initiatives include the European Energy Charter, currently under negotiation, and the Environmental Action Plan being prepared for the April 1993 European Conference of Environment Ministers in Switzerland. Efforts at improved co-operation should not delay assistance -- a number of participants noted that international assistance has been slow -- but instead make international programmes more effective.

Another important area for work is improving integration within individual aid programmes. In many bilateral agencies and multilateral organisations, there is not enough contact between the energy and environmental programmes for the region. Energy and environmental personnel within these institutions need to work together on coordinated projects and assistance. Again, integrated national policies can provide a focus for this coordination.

External grants and loans need to be better coordinated to meet recipient countries' needs. Grant assistance is best suited for financing capital projects that solve priority environmental problems, as well as demonstration projects and technical assistance programmes. External loans should be directed to projects that will have cash returns, as countries in the region can ill afford to increase their foreign currency debts. Where immediate returns are not to be expected, long-term loans should be envisaged.

The potential demand for project loans in the region remains high. One problem cited at the Conference is that there is a lack of energy and environment projects which have been analysed and presented in the terms necessary to be considered for loans -- particularly the financial aspects of project appraisal. Technical assistance grants could be used to prepare energy and environment projects for funding to ease this problem and to provide training in this area.

Conference participants also noted that multilateral banks have difficulty funding small projects and prefer to provide single, large loans. This can be a problem for energy efficiency projects, which are often small-scale and often do not show easily measurable results and payback criteria. Energy loans tend to focus on supply-side solutions. Multilateral banks, working with technical assistance programmes, need to find ways of "bundling" small loans (for example, for energy efficiency measures for residences and small private companies) into large, "bankable" packages. The World Bank and European Investment Bank already have experience with this technique. In addition, ministries and local agencies be trained to help prepare such packages.

Multilateral banks can also play a valuable role in supporting technical assistance programmes to encourage cost-effective strategies such as Integrated Resources Planning and Demand-Side Management. Energy sector loans could include measures to help remove some of the market barriers to energy and environmental improvements, and loans to electricity generators should, in addition to financing infrastructure improvements, also provide a basis for implementing Integrated Resources Planning measures.

Finally, coordination between bilateral agencies, multilateral institutions, and private western investors can be improved. Private finance and foreign investment can provide an important share of the resources for energy and environmental projects in the region. Project financing, when carefully designed, provides a mechanism in which private finance can work together with multilateral development banks and other official sources. Foreign investors emphasized in the Conference that they would only invest in projects that could yield for a stable stream of revenue for profits; nonetheless, the participation of private finance cannot be ruled out from any priority energy and environmental project. There may be many innovative ways to develop such a stream of revenues, even from pollution-control investments. The fundamental conditions necessary to provide stable revenue streams -- and acceptable risks -- for private investors are the prompt development of stable, predictable government policies and regulations and the pursuance of market-oriented economic reforms.

2. Innovative Mechanisms for Funding

There may be specific opportunities for co-operation with western countries and the E.C. on pollution reduction initiatives. Poland has concluded a debt-for-nature swap with the United States and is negotiating similar arrangements with other countries. The resources that otherwise would have been used to repay foreign debts are being used to tackle environmental problems that have a specifically international dimension. A Conference report on co-operation between Dutch and Polish electric utilities on emissions reduction projects in Poland -- which would help reduce acid precipitation in the Netherlands -- provides another innovative example of international co-operation. Through similar arrangements, OECD countries could invest in reducing CO_2 emissions in Central and Eastern Europe as part of their commitments to national action under the recently signed climate change convention. This could provide a mechanism for co-operative financing of energy efficiency improvements, and would reduce local and regional air pollution as well as greenhouse gas emissions.

3. Priorities for Technical Assistance

As was noted in the Conference, a great number of technical assistance projects are already underway in the region. The Conference identified a number of areas where technical co-operation is needed on a priority basis. In the past, it was difficult to establish the degree to which existing or planned projects addressed these needs. However, the OECD and the Commission of the European Communities, coordinator of G-24 assistance, have made considerable efforts to overcome these problems by establishing a project information system that catalogues assistance programmes. This will enable better coordination among the various parties concerned and improve the effectiveness of support. Improved coordination remains a key area for follow-on work to the Conference.

The Conference discussions noted several principles that can improve technical assistance programmes. First, technical assistance should be designed to assist more closely the actual implementation of programmes and projects. Technical assistance programmes have often not been able to reach the right people, have been out of phase with policy or investment decisions, or have, for other reasons, not resulted in follow-through and measurable results. Using technical assistance to prepare loan proposals is one mechanism to improve assistance programmes. Second, work should be undertaken, to the maximum possible degree, by local experts. This will help ensure that the activities lead to the development of local expertise and, as a result, ongoing benefits for the recipient countries.

The Conference identified several priorities for technical co-operation -- areas where ongoing programmes should be strengthened and better coordinated, and where new initiatives should be undertaken. These include:

a. Methodologies to Develop and Analyse Policy Strategies.

Governments in the region will have to undertake complex analyses in order to develop integrated policy and investment strategies that can meet their energy and environmental goals. Policy-makers and analysts in the region may not be familiar with techniques for analysing and designing government strategies for a dynamic market context. The transfer of expertise, including economic methods and techniques, from OECD countries could be helpful. There are several important areas for improving government analysis; one is in developing methodologies for the appraisal and evaluation of potential energy efficiency investments and programmes.

Evaluation of the Competitiveness of Industries. One important area for analysis is the ongoing structural change in the transition to a market economy. Assistance from western experts can help government analysts in the region use economic techniques that indicate which of their existing industries and facilities are likely to be viable in the long run. These trends will have a very important role in terms of future energy use and environmental pollution. It is important to stress that governments should not attempt to designate "winners and losers," but allow market processes to operate freely. Nonetheless, the analysis of these trends will help governments target scarce investment capital. A related issue is the role that environmental and energy policies can have on economic restructuring.

Design of Government Policies. The administrations of central and eastern European countries have been used to directing command economies; the tasks of administration in market economies are quite different. Here technical assistance programmes can provide government administrations with guidance. The development of long-term, integrated energy and environmental policies -- as well as the establishment long-term goals and the strategies to attain them -- will require techniques and methods new to administrations in the region. Experiences in OECD countries, such as the work of the Government of the Netherlands on critical loads and on long-term environmental strategies, can provide examples of how this can be done.

Evaluation of the Environmental Impacts of Sectoral Policies. OECD countries are increasingly realising the importance of sectoral policies and mechanisms -- from transport sector investments to industrial incentives to agricultural policy -- for both energy use and environmental effects in the long term. Central and eastern European governments need tools that can help them evaluate these long-term effects. OECD governments are becoming increasingly aware of these issues, and the OECD, along with many member governments, is working increasingly on this aspect of policy integration.

b. Programme Implementation.

Government institutions also need to be strengthened so they can better implement energy and environmental policies in a market-based system. In particular, government administrations need assistance in managing environmental and energy programmes, in monitoring and enforcing environmental requirements, and in promoting effective energy management and efficiency. There are many needs and opportunities for effective training. **Energy efficiency** is one area where governments in the region need assistance in planning and implementing effective programmes. These programmes will have to find the best means and implementing agencies for different sectors, from industry to the residential sector to the growing private commercial sector.

In particular, **local and regional authorities** are, throughout the region, taking greater roles in implementing environmental and energy policies; these levels of government often have the greatest needs for training to design and manage effective energy efficiency and environmental programmes. These needs differ from country to country and area to area, but include: environmental data collection; enforcement of environmental regulations; dissemination of energy efficiency information; the design of energy efficiency programmes for residences; and techniques for environmental and energy audits. In addition, in many areas of the region, local air pollution from the widespread use of low-grade solid fuels is a severe problem, and local governments need assistance in developing programmes to reduce emissions and encourage fuel switching.

As already noted, countries in the region also need assistance in preparing **project proposals** for international finance. Both multilateral banks and private investors need to see detailed financial analysis and projections before deciding whether to commit finance (though official and private finance can require somewhat different forms of analysis). Training and assistance in this field is needed not only for government administrations, but also for utilities and private enterprises in the region.

c. Demonstration Projects.

External support may be particularly effective in establishing demonstration projects that act as catalysts for local initiatives and programmes. Demonstration projects can also play an important role in providing training. A number of assistance programmes have begun or are considering useful demonstration projects. In addition, countries in the region may be interested in participating in the IEA's collaborative projects for research, development, and demonstration of energy-related technologies. Areas of work include electricity demand side management and the IEA Centre for the Analysis and Dissemination of Demonstrated Energy Technologies (CADDET); though the IEA, not being a funding agency, cannot provide financial assistance for this participation.

d. The Optimisation of Resource Use in the Energy Sector

OECD countries have developed innovative ways of encouraging utilities to promote energy efficiency -- which is often a least-cost alternative to investments in pollution reduction equipment or new electricity generating capacity. Technical assistance programmes can provide governments in Central and Eastern Europe with information on policies that provide utilities with incentives to use Integrated Resources Planning and Demand-Side Management. Utilities will need training on the practical application of these methods. Though the potential short-term gains may be limited, in the longer term Integrated Resource Planning and Demand-Side Management can achieve both energy and environmental goals.

4. The Next Steps

This Conference has reinforced the importance that the IEA and OECD attach to the integration of energy and environmental goals in national policies. In their future work in Central and Eastern Europe, IEA and OECD will try to encourage policy integration; IEA and OECD will strive to incorporate the recommendations of this Conference in this work, and urge other international organisations and bilateral programmes to consider the Conference recommendations in their assistance to the region. Governments in Central and Eastern Europe are also encouraged to consider and work toward to goals and recommendations outlined in this report.

ENERGY AND ENVIRONMENTAL POLICY INTEGRATION:

AN OVERVIEW OF OECD EXPERIENCE

ENERGY AND ENVIRONMENTAL POLICY INTEGRATION: AN OVERVIEW OF OECD EXPERIENCE

Joint OECD Environment Directorate and International Energy Agency
Background Paper, Coordinated by Tony Zamparutti

I. INTRODUCTION

The relationship between energy and the environment is fundamental and pervasive in modern economies. Fuel combustion is one of the main sources of air pollution, and energy production, transformation, and distribution can have major effects in terms of water pollution, land use, and other environmental dimensions (see Box 1 for an overview of these impacts).

Until recently, most governments of OECD Member countries have formulated their energy and environmental policies separately. OECD Member governments have intervened extensively in these areas, and the lack of policy coherence has often resulted in higher economic costs and less effective policies, both for energy and the environment. Based on this experience, OECD Member countries have recognized a common need to integrate energy, and environmental policies.

Policy integration requires, first, consideration of environmental effects and goals in energy policy, and second, consideration of energy goals and economic issues in the formulation of environmental policy. Policy integration should also mean a process of improved cooperation between agencies responsible for energy and the environment. This involves identifying and pursuing compatible energy and environmental objectives, searching for policies that achieve both energy and environmental goals simultaneously, as well as analyzing potential trade-offs between energy goals, environmental goals, and economic costs in making policy decisions and reaching consensus decisions for these tradeoffs.

There are often tensions between political choices and market processes in OECD Member countries. Nonetheless, there is a growing public, private, and government realization that, as OECD Environment Ministers affirmed in 1991, the *quality* of economic growth has become as important in OECD Member countries as the *quantity* of growth. Energy Ministers recognize that energy security cannot be divorced from a clean environment. So, the goals of economic growth, high quality of life, clean environment and energy security are linked.

Box 1. Energy/Environment Interactions

Air pollution -- in particular from the combustion of fossil fuels -- is the environmental consequence of energy use that has perhaps received the greatest attention. To a great extent, this paper focuses on OECD country policies to control air pollution, for these have often been among the most expensive. Nonetheless, environmental and energy policies need to consider all the interactions between energy and the environment. These include:

- Environmental accidents -- in fuel extraction, such as the risk of explosion from oil or gas production, or in mines; in transportation, such as for maritime oil tankers; and in energy production, including risks of radioactive releases and nuclear power plants or floods resulting from hydroelectric dam failures.

- Water Pollution -- from sources including oil exploration runoff, refinery and power plant effluents, current or abandoned mine drainage, and also thermal pollution from power plants that threaten aquatic life.

- Solid Waste Disposal -- The use of some fuels, especially coal, creates large amounts of solid wastes for disposal. In addition, add-on pollution control devices such as scrubbers and desulphurization devices create solid waste requiring disposal. Some of these power plant wastes are classified as hazardous, increasing costs for safe disposal.

- Land Use -- The siting of power plants (especially nuclear plants) and hydroelectric reservoirs have often created public controversies in OECD countries. Renewable energy systems, such as wind power and solar power, can also require large land areas. Finally, land use and disturbance is also very important in transportation for oil and gas pipelines and for roads, airports, and railways.

- Radiation -- Risks of radiation release can occur in the mining, transport, use, and disposal of nuclear energy fuels and materials. In many OECD Member countries there is a great controversy over the use of nuclear power. Some countries have renounced nuclear power, while others have greatly expanded its use in the past 20 years.

OECD countries are expanding environmental policies to control an increasing number of these areas; Annex 1 describes some of the current and emerging areas for environmental rules on energy activities.

Based on: IEA, Energy and the Environment: Policy Overview, OECD, Paris, 1989.

Nonetheless, OECD countries differ greatly in their approaches to energy policy, environmental requirements, and policy integration; this paper describes some of the mechanisms and processes that OECD Member countries have used to integrate national decision-making on energy and the environment, but it can only provide an introduction to this subject. It cannot describe the diversity of policy approaches in these fields.

Trends in Energy Use and Energy Policy

Over the past two decades, OECD Member countries have seen significant changes in their energy use; two major trends have been a steady increase in energy efficiency, and a diversification of energy sources.

The 1973 oil shock marked the end of a period of fast economic growth and low energy prices. A second shock to prices occurred in 1979. After initial adjustments to these price shocks, OECD economies shifted to a more efficient use of energy. Between 1973 and 1988, gross domestic product in OECD countries grew significantly while total energy requirements grew only modestly. The energy intensity (energy needed per unit of GDP) for the OECD as a whole declined by 23 percent during this period. In industry, production in OECD countries increased by 40 percent between 1973 and 1988, while energy use <u>decreased</u> by 6 percent.

The increase in energy prices played a central role in inducing industries and consumers to use energy more efficiently. In addition, governments enacted a variety of programs to encourage energy efficiency. The reduction in fuel used per unit of GDP was one major contributing factor to an important environmental result: a significant reduction in the level of most types of energy-related pollution emissions per unit GDP. In contrast, Central and Eastern European countries, largely insulated from the changes in world market prices, had no incentive to make these adjustments -- one of the reasons for the much higher energy intensities of their economies.

Regarding the diversification of fuel sources, for the whole OECD region the shares of coal, gas, and nuclear energy within total primary fuels have grown, while that of oil has declined. Electricity production almost doubled, displacing direct industrial, commercial, and residential use of fuels. This has meant that the control of energy-related environmental problems can focus more on one sector -- power generation -- and less on controlling small and medium energy sources. For power generation, the shares of nuclear energy and coal have increased, while those of oil, gas, and hydro all declined. Nonetheless, there are major differences in these patterns between countries. For example, some OECD Member countries greatly expanded nuclear power, while others have renounced its use.

Two main trends in energy policy are apparent. First, an overall reduction in government intervention in energy markets, and second, increased international cooperation.

OECD governments recognize that economic efficiency will be promoted if the level and pattern of energy use and production are, to a considerable extent, determined by market forces. At the same time, all OECD governments intervene in the energy sector for a number of policy reasons, including:

- the importance of secure and reasonably priced supplies of energy to the economy as a whole;
- the need to use indigenous energy resources to the best national advantage;
- the environmental, social and regional implications of the energy sector developments;
- the links between energy and foreign policy; and
- the monopoly characteristics of some of the energy industries; and
- the development of new energy technologies and new energy sources.

Three general types of approaches to intervention in energy markets can be identified: in some countries government-owned corporations play central roles in energy exploration, production, and distribution; other OECD countries have used extensive regulation of mostly private sector energy activities; and in a few, mostly small European countries, there has been strong cooperation (or co-ownership) between public authorities and private operators. Over the past decade, however, there has been an overall trend toward privatization of energy industries and toward regulations which increase elements of competition in energy markets.

Despite their different approaches, OECD countries, cooperating through several forums, including the IEA and the negotiations for a European Energy Charter, have agreed on basic common goals for energy policy -- energy security, and assuring energy supplies for long-term economic growth. In recent years, environmental concerns and the need for greater policy integration have also been recognized as an important area for energy policy. Energy efficiency has been identified as a key tool for promoting all of these goals - economic growth, energy security and reducing environmental impacts - simultaneously.

The Evolving Focus of Environmental Policies

OECD countries have witnessed a great evolution in environmental policies over the past decades, reflecting both advancing scientific understanding of the environment and a greater public concern over environmental problems. As a result, the focus of environmental policy has widened to include an ever-greater range of issues. Emphasis has shifted in response to successes in controlling some pollutants and evolving scientific understanding of new problems.

For example, efforts to control air pollution have moved from an initial focus on the most obvious, usually local, pollution to regional and global problems and to new environmental issues. Initial air pollution policies in the 1950s combatted particulate concentrations in cities such as London in the United Kingdom and Pittsburgh in the United States -- a problem that presented a great health risk to the local population. As a result, many OECD countries were able to reduce particulate concentrations significantly. As the health effects of other air pollutants, such as airborne lead, ozone, sulfur dioxide, and carbon monoxide, became better known, these too became a focus of pollution control efforts.

In the 1970s, the regional and international effects of air pollution gained recognition, and in particular the effect on forest and lake ecosystems of acid depositions created by emissions of sulphur and nitrogen oxides. Many OECD countries increased the controls on these pollutants in the 1980s, and, largely as a result, total OECD emissions of sulphur dioxide have fallen, while those of nitrogen oxides have remained stable. More recently, in addition to these "pervasive" air pollutants, concerted attention is being focused on a range of other hazardous air pollutants, sometimes called "air toxics." This includes a large number of specific chemical substances, usually released in smaller amounts, which can nonetheless have serious health and environmental effects. Finally, the potential for global warming has become of increasing concern for public opinion, national governments, and international organizations, prompting a search for ways to control and stabilize emissions of carbon dioxide and other greenhouse gases.

Within this broad pattern, OECD Member countries have chosen varying paths for their environmental policies and differ in the scope, stringency, and application of their environmental requirements. To some degree, international cooperation is reducing the differences between national policies, both through efforts at harmonization in forums such as the OECD and the United Nations Economic Commission for Europe (UNECE), and in the process of European integration coordinated by the European Community. The UN Conference on Environment and Development contributed to a new global consensus on environmental priorities.

One emerging area of consensus is the "precautionary principle" with regard to the threat of irreversible environmental damage. OECD Environment Ministers endorsed this principle in 1991. Where this potential exists, governments agree to take preventive action to ensure that risks are minimized until better scientific information is available. Details of implementation of this principle are, of course, complex and depend on the particular issue, the action of individual governments and agreements for international co-operation.

Another emerging area of consensus, reaffirmed by the UN Conference on Environment and Development, is the goal of "sustainable development." The precepts of sustainable development include a shift to renewable resource use and attention to the rates of non-renewable resource depletion; greater global equity in development; and a recognition of intergenerational equity, particularly in terms of keeping options open for future generations. Policies to encourage sustainable development require comprehensive analyses of environmental and economic links, and the integration of environmental considerations throughout economic policy. OECD Member countries are still far from achieving this goal, but some countries have begun to work seriously toward them.

The Search for Policy Integration

OECD governments have agreed, however, that the importance of environmental issues calls for much greater integration of environmental considerations throughout economic policies. For example, in 1989 OECD Finance Ministers "reaffirmed the critical importance of integrating more systematically and effectively environment and economic decision-making as a means of contributing to sustainable development." OECD Environment Ministers, in a 1991 statement, affirmed that integrating economic and environmental decision-making should be one of the main goals for their countries' environmental policies in the 1990s. And at the 1991 meeting of the IEA Governing Board, Energy Ministers also "reaffirmed their strong commitment to develop integrated policies which further the objectives of energy security, environmental protection and sustainable economic growth."

Several factors motivate this consensus. In the energy sector, there is a realization that traditional pollution control methods have often been costly or inefficient, while energy policies have on occasion created incentives that work against environmental goals. At the same time, governments have realized that energy and technology trends can have an important effect on the environment; for example, changes in fuel prices and advances in technology have, through fuel switching and improvements in energy efficiency, played a significant role in improving air quality in many OECD countries. Overall, OECD governments have realized that it is cheaper and more efficient to anticipate and prevent environmental problems. The extensive links between economic activities and the environment require comprehensive analysis and policy responses. Some environmental problems, such as growing concerns over global climate change, can only be tackled through comprehensive national policies (closely linked to economic decisions in all sectors), within a framework of international co-operation.

Policy integration requires, first, the proper function of markets and economic mechanisms. This involves the use of environmental policy instruments to correct "market failures" -- instances where environmental costs are not properly reflected in the market system. One basic mechanism endorsed by OECD Member governments is the "polluter pays principle" (see Box 2). Other areas for work include the desirability of incorporating full social costs of resource use into prices; a greater emphasis on economic instruments, which create incentives for cost-effective

---

Box 2. The Polluter Pays Principle

Twenty years ago, OECD Member governments agreed on the Polluter Pays Principle (PPP), which states that the polluter should bear the cost of pollution control and prevention measures decided upon by public authorities to ensure that the environment is in an "acceptable state." Generators of pollution should "internalize" the costs of the use or degradation of environmental resources, which otherwise would continue to be external to the market, and would be paid for by society at large in the form of health effects, environmental damage, and other ills.

In theory, the polluter should pay the full cost of damage caused by his activity, thus creating the economic incentive to reduce environmental damage, at least to the level where the cost of pollution reduction is equal to the marginal cost of the damage caused. In practice the extent of environmental damage is often very difficult to determine, and in effect polluters are usually made to pay for the cost of pollution control required to meet national pollution standards. Although the PPP is generally accepted, the stringency with which it is implemented varies between OECD Member countries. For example, many Member governments continue to provide some financial assistance for pollution control expenditures. Nonetheless, the low current levels of pollution control assistance (particularly in comparison to other remaining forms of industrial assistance) do not appear to distort international trade and investment patterns. The ongoing trends toward harmonization of environmental quality objectives and standards, and toward identification and removal of energy market distortions, also reduce the potential for trade concerns.

---

environmental protection in a number of areas; and the prevention of pollution through encouragement of inherently cleaner (e.g. more energy efficient) technologies; and the precautionary principle.

An important part of incorporating "full social costs" into resource prices is the identification and removal of subsidies and other government policies in various sectors that distort prices and increase environmental damage -- such as government distortions in energy prices. In environmental regulation, (consistent with the Polluter Pays Principle) this argues against subsidies for pollution control expenditures, although exceptions are acknowledged in specific cases, discussed in the next section.

Economic instruments are an important tool to incorporate environmental damage costs into price mechanisms. OECD Environment Ministers have called for expanded use of these mechanisms as a means of integrating environmental concerns more directly into economic and energy decision-making. The use of these mechanisms are discussed in detail in the next section.

A second element for policy integration is to address linkages between the economy and the environment in long term national policies. This includes a search for mechanisms that ensure both economic development and environmental protection -- for example, in the energy sector, policies that work simultaneously toward energy, environmental, and economic goals. In addition, governments need to identify areas where economic development and environmental goals involve trade-offs, and to reach agreement on resolving such conflicts.

One of the important motivations for the integration of environmental, energy and economic decisions is the recognition that the choice of basic production technologies can have major implications for environmental impacts. Economic instruments can encourage consideration of environmental implications at all points in the chain of investment and technology decisions. In addition, governments have recognized the importance of policies to directly encourage investment in pollution prevention through the adoption of cleaner industrial technologies and products. For the energy sector, a prime example of pollution prevention is the promotion of energy efficiency which avoids the creation of combustion related pollution which otherwise would have to be removed through control technology.

II. MECHANISMS FOR
ENERGY AND ENVIRONMENTAL POLICY INTEGRATION

1. Energy Policies

<u>Energy Prices</u>
Energy price signals play a central role in determining consumer choices of fuels and levels of fuel use -- choices that in turn determine environmental impacts. Energy price shocks in the 1970s and 1980s induced companies and individuals to improve their energy efficiency, while expectations of long-term changes in relative energy prices encouraged a shift to less-polluting fuels, such as natural gas. Both trends contributed greatly to reductions in air pollution in OECD countries.

OECD governments in the past intervened strongly in energy markets, but they have moved increasingly toward removing energy subsidies and price controls. In general, OECD countries now agree that energy prices should be based on world market prices, where these exist. In cases where there are not clear world market prices (such as power generation) energy prices should be based on the long-term marginal cost of maintaining the supply of the fuel concerned.

Taxes on Fuels and Energy

Many OECD governments place fiscal charges on various fuels, most notably gasoline (although the pre-tax prices are based on world market levels). These charges can have important effects: for example, higher gasoline taxes are among the factors that have led consumers in European OECD countries to choose more efficient automobiles, and use them less, than in North American OECD countries. OECD governments are increasingly realizing the importance of coordinating fiscal levies on fuels with energy and environmental policy goals. The mix of fiscal measures may also influence the choices consumers make between fuels, in particular encouraging a switch to less-taxed fuels. OECD governments are paying increasing attention to the environmental effects of these decisions, and there is increasing interest in the use of such economic instruments to promote environmental goals, such as encouraging the use of less-polluting fuels (this topic is covered further under "economic instruments" in the following section).

Correcting Counterproductive Government Policies

OECD governments are realizing that, in addition to policies directly determining energy prices, many other policies in fields such as energy, transport, industry, or agriculture have indirectly had negative environmental effects. Modifying these counterproductive interventions can contribute to achievement of environmental goals.

Many OECD Member countries have provided either direct or indirect subsidies for the exploitation of fossil fuels that help reduce fuel prices. These policies may contradict other government efforts to increase the use of alternative energy sources and to promote energy efficiency. Some policies try to promote domestic energy production and protect employment. German energy policy, for example, subsidizes the domestic coal industry and ensures that coal is widely used in domestic industry and electricity generation. These measures have high economic costs, (the IEA estimates that these subsidies cost the German economy an additional DM 11 billion in 1989, or DM 153 per metric ton of coal used) and also increase the cost of Germany's air pollution control program by restricting the ability of utilities to use cleaner fuels. The U.S., in the 1970s, protected the mining of high sulfur coal by requiring utilities to use add-on pollution control equipment rather than low-sulfur coal to meet emissions limits -- a choice that also increased environmental protection costs. (This choice cost, by one estimate, an additional $4.2 billion in utility costs, or at least $400,000 a year per mining job saved. Howe, 1991).

Increasingly, OECD Member governments realize that these sorts of policy interventions are overly costly. For example, Belgium, the United Kingdom and France, have made great progress in removing protection for the coal mining industry, instead financing economic restructuring programs for mining areas. Germany has also announced plans to move in this direction, closing some inefficient coal mines.

In the transport sector, many OECD countries have subsidized road construction and use over other transport investments, resulting in a heavy reliance on motor vehicles for transportation -- a mode with high energy and environmental impacts. In addition, a number of countries provide hidden subsidies for automobile use, such as corporate tax concessions for "company cars" or personal tax deductions to cover the cost of commuting by car. By encouraging automobile use, these transport policies not only increase energy consumption, but also contradict other national policy goals, such as to reduce environmental damages, to make large cities more livable, and to encourage public transport use.

OECD governments have often undertaken policies for employment and other social reasons which have had counter-productive impacts on environmental goals, increasing environmental damage and creating other, sometimes high economic costs. One important task of policy integration is to identify and remove counterproductive policies. The goal of policy integration efforts is to prevent future policy contradictions by defining a common framework for considering environmental effects when developing policies in all areas of economic activity.

2. Environmental Policy Instruments

Despite the different paths that OECD countries follow in their environmental policies, there are several common trends that can be identified. First, environmental rules and requirements are being established for an increasingly wide array of energy activities. Second, there is a long-term trend toward stricter environmental policies (although different OECD countries are still at very different levels in terms of the development and stringency of their environmental requirements). Third, there is a greater international harmonization of policy goals; for example, the European Community has set progressive national emission reduction requirements for all its member countries. Fourth, OECD countries are searching for more flexible and cost-effective ways of achieving environmental goals. OECD countries have found that overly rigid regulations may increase compliance costs and encourage the use of expensive, end-of-pipe controls, hindering the introduction of new, cleaner technologies and production processes that reduce pollution at the source. In general, there is a growing recognition that governments need to set clear medium and long-term objectives so that private industry can efficiently include environmental factors into its long-term investment strategies.

Overall, OECD governments are searching for greater flexibility in their environmental policies, reducing the costs to attain environmental goals, and working in particular with the process of economic and technological development.

In the array of policy instruments used, all OECD Member countries rely on direct regulatory instruments as the main mechanism for implementing environmental goals. Direct regulatory instruments are mandatory controls on activities that specify the environmental performance of polluters directly. In the simplest (and most common) forms, they leave little choice to polluters, who have to comply, or face penalties through judicial and administrative procedures. An increasing number of OECD countries are also introducing economic instruments for environmental policy. Economic instruments use financial mechanisms, such as pollution charges, to encourage market actors -- companies and individuals -- to make environmentally favorable choices. In addition, several countries have used voluntary agreements with industry to attain certain environmental goals. There is also increasing use of methods to consider environmental issues at the project level, including environmental impact statements and environmental audits. OECD governments also encourage and support research and development of cleaner and more energy efficient production technologies and products. Finally, there is also increasing attention being paid to assessing the environmental implications of government programs and policies in various economic sectors.

The OECD has identified a number of criteria for the choice of specific policy instruments, including:

Environmental effectiveness. Regulations and economic instruments need to be judged against overall objectives of environmental policy, usually set in terms of goals of protecting human health and the environment.

Economic efficiency. The most efficient methods are those which provide the greatest environmental benefits at the least cost. In addition, economic effects should be considered both for the short and the long-term, as environmental policies can have important effects on industrial structures and technological developments.

Distributive consequences. Policies have different effects on different economic sectors and on different actors within these sectors. Governments need to develop policies that are equitable.

Administrative feasibility and costs. Environmental policies need to be implemented and enforced effectively. This implies administrative costs for monitoring pollution discharges and acting against violations. The costs and difficulty of implementation and enforcement differ greatly depending on the type of instrument used and the type of economic sector affected.

Attainability and acceptability. Economic actors must be financially and technically able to meet environmental requirements. Overly costly or technically difficult requirements may simply be ignored. Overall, it is important that most members of an economic sector affected by new environmental policies accept them as fair and necessary. This implies both consulting with target groups (as well as the public) in the design of new policies and providing adequate information to help the sector concerned comply with environmental requirements.

Direct Regulations

Direct regulatory instruments remain the most important tools for implementing environmental policy in OECD countries. Regulations are often regarded as being relatively easy to formulate, implement, and enforce (though this depends greatly on the type of regulation and the sector concerned). Properly formulated and enforced, they establish feasible minimum requirements necessary to protect the environment.

OECD governments have relied on two main types of regulatory instruments, particularly for air pollution from stationary sources.

Ambient standards set acceptable levels of pollution monitored in the environment based on human health risks or environmental thresholds. These standards imply a two stage process as they do not directly place requirements on any particular sources of pollution. They must be achieved through the development of emissions standards for individual sources or classes of sources. Some countries that have emphasized ambient standards for specific environmental problems or regions in an effort to follow a least-cost approach, requiring the greatest pollution reductions from plants in highly polluted areas, and less reductions from plants in cleaner areas.

Emissions standards set specific pollution limits for a particular source or type of source. These can be developed in conjunction with ambient standards, or can be applied uniformly to specific classes of sources. Governments have emphasized uniform emissions standards in the interests of equity -- setting equal requirements for similar polluters. Also, uniform standards, can be much simpler to implement and enforce, especially for new sources, than individual emission standards derived from ambient standards. Application of uniform standards can result in controls in clean areas and thus can be more costly than a targeted approach.

Several other types of standards are also used in conjunction with these two principle regulatory instruments. Technology specific standards can be rigidly applied, requiring all pollutant sources of a certain type to apply a specific control technology (e.g. fabric filter particulate removal). This type of regulation is relatively rare in OECD countries. Another type of technology regulation is the requirement for application of "best available technology (BAT)" for a class of sources. This generally allows for more flexibility for source-by-source decisions about the best technology considering site characteristics and cost. Governments also use other types of regulations such as fuel or product quality regulations to achieve pollution reductions indirectly. These can be effective and more administratively efficient in some cases.

Governments need to consider the issues of efficiency, cost, and feasibility when setting regulations. OECD countries have taken a number of different routes, as shown by their different choices regarding the regulation of stationary combustion plants. There are examples of regulatory systems emphasizing generalized emissions standards -- such as the strict German emissions standards for combustion plants. However, almost all OECD countries have used combinations of these different approaches, depending on the pollutant and the sector regulated. The following are issues that governments need to consider when setting regulations, in particular those for stationary combustion plants.

Which sources to regulate? Most countries have adopted strict regulations for large plants, which are fewer in number and thus easier to control. However, this may not solve local air pollution problems stemming from residential, commercial, and small business sources which, because of their number, are more difficult to control. For smaller sources, fuel pricing, fuel-related regulations and economic instruments may be more effective. In addition, some governments have set strict regulations for new plants, leaving old plants with easier requirements. The U.S. found that this system (combined with other economic factors) encouraged industry to keep older, dirtier plants in operation and discouraged investment in new, cleaner plants. By contrast, the 1983 German air emissions regulations set equally strict standards for both new and existing large sources, but gave existing plants a longer time for compliance.

Regulations on other sources of air pollution can also play an important role. For example, most OECD governments have set or are introducing emissions standards for motor vehicles, which greatly reduce emissions per vehicle. Many countries have used fuel standards, such as restrictions on the levels of lead in gasoline or sulphur in diesel fuel, to reduce emissions of these pollutants from both mobile and stationary sources.

Flexibility. Many regulations have explicitly or implicitly specified the use of specific pollution control technologies. Rigid requirements reduce private actors' ability to choose least-cost forms of compliance, and hence the incentive to adopt innovative pollution reduction approaches. Regulations that require quick compliance also reduce flexibility. Many OECD governments are trying to establish more flexible and longer term policies that encourage greater introduction of new, clean technologies rather than investment in end-of-pipe pollution control equipment.

Enforcement. Governments need to set in place adequate monitoring systems and enforcement mechanisms to ensure that polluters comply with environmental requirements. In Germany and Sweden, for example, large combustion plants must install costly equipment for continuous monitoring of stack emissions. It is more difficult to monitor smaller, more numerous pollution sources. Overall, though, there must be adequate mechanisms for monitoring and clear rules for dealing with violations.

Economic Instruments

OECD countries' use of economic instruments for environmental policy has been limited, but is steadily growing. (Annex 1 describes the application of economic instruments in one OECD country, Sweden.) In general, economic instruments are used to supplement rather than replace existing regulations. Economic instruments have a number of advantages -- they allow polluters the flexibility to choose the most cost-effective means of pollution reduction; they provide an ongoing incentive to reduce pollution, below regulated levels; they increase administrative flexibility and can be easily adjusted by authorities; and they can provide a source of government revenue.

Nonetheless, economic instruments do not necessarily reduce the administrative requirements of implementation by government agencies, though they do change the nature of these requirements. They also can be more difficult to design, implement, and enforce than direct regulations, as there is uncertainty about the reaction of market actors and thus their eventual results. In order to operate properly, economic instruments require that target groups react efficiently to market signals -- that is, that they operate in a competitive market. Three types of economic instruments commonly used in the energy sector in OECD countries are product charges, emission charges, and marketable permits. (Two additional types of economic instruments are user charges, payments for the costs of collective treatment of effluent or waste; and deposit-refund systems, under which a deposit is paid when potentially polluting products are bought and is then refunded when their products or their wastes are returned for recycling or disposal. These have less relevance for energy-related problems, especially air pollution.)

Product charges. These are levied on products (or elements of products) that are harmful to the environment. They can be effective for products that are consumed in large quantities and in diffuse ways -- such as fuels -- in order to try to incorporate the external costs of pollution and environmental damage into prices. Product charges can be easy to introduce, particularly since many governments already have fiscal charges on fuels. Finland, the Netherlands, Norway, and Sweden have recently introduced comprehensive taxes on the sulfur content or carbon content of fuels. The Swedish tax system appears to be motivating energy users to switch to low sulphur fuel oils. Many European OECD countries have introduced simpler strategies, such as taxing unleaded gasoline at a lower rate to persuade motorists to switch from leaded gasoline.

Emissions charges. These may be most effective for stationary sources where abatement costs vary between polluters. Emissions charges need to be designed carefully in order to attain desired emissions reductions. In addition, since charges should be calculated on the basis of actual emissions, governments need to pay close attention to the monitoring and enforcement requirements of emissions charges. Germany has successfully used a hybrid system for water pollution regulation, in which emissions charges are combined with standards (companies pay a higher rate for discharges above the standard) -- this has resulted in considerable investment in pollution reduction equipment, while meeting the overall standard for one-third less cost than an equivalent strict regulatory system. France has taxed sulphur and nitrogen oxide emissions from large combustion plants. As yet, this tax has been too low to induce significant changes in emissions behavior, but the funds are used to subsidize pollution reduction investments. Sweden and a number of other countries are also studying or introducing emissions charges, in particular for stationary combustion plants.

Marketable-permit systems. These establish a market between polluters so they can trade pollution reduction requirements and attain least-cost emissions reductions. The U.S. has used such systems since the 1970s for highly polluted local areas, and introduced an extensive national trading scheme for air emissions in 1990. This approach can be easily combined with an existing direct regulatory structure to increase flexibility and reduce cost. Unlike charges, there is less uncertainty about the pollution levels which will result from this approach. Nonetheless, one possible difficulty of such trading schemes is high transaction costs for polluters (especially when markets are first developing). In addition, polluters will have difficulty valuing their total long-term costs under a tradeable permit system, as the value of permits will fluctuate.

In addition to these broadly applicable instruments, financial assistance can provide an economic incentive to encourage pollution control reduction, but is, except in a few specific cases, considered incompatible with the Polluter Pays Principle. Certain exceptions have been allowed, however, under which financial assistance could be made available to assisted industries or enterprises which are not able to afford pollution control investments because of severe economic difficulties and is given for a fixed period of time in a clearly defined program. This may be provided as direct financial assistance, but more often takes the form of tax concessions for pollution control investments. Overall, pollution control assistance in OECD countries is small compared to other government assistance programs to industry, such as regional development programs.

<u>Private Sector Cooperation</u>

A growing number of OECD governments are cooperating with the private sector to achieve environmental goals. This cooperation has included both greater consultation with industry (discussed below under Institutional Arrangements) and specific agreements with industry associations for pollution reduction. In addition, many large private companies have adopted corporate environment policies.

<u>Voluntary Agreements with Industry</u>. Voluntary agreements for pollution reduction give private companies greater flexibility to achieve environmental goals through least cost methods. (To some degree, these agreements are only in part "voluntary," as one motivation for private companies is to avoid the introduction of less flexible regulations). Where agreements are successful, they lower industry's compliance costs and government's administrative costs. Voluntary agreements have been made on both national and local levels. In the Netherlands, for example, the government set, in its National Environmental Policy Plan, ambitious goals for reducing pollution and improving environmental protection. Implementation requires negotiation with different "target groups"; thus far, the government has reached agreement with several industries on long-term energy efficiency goals, and negotiations on other elements of the plan continue. In Germany, industry associations, under government persuasion, are introducing a voluntary system to recover and recycle consumer product packaging. In Japan, local governments often negotiate with companies to obtain pollution reductions that exceed national requirements.

Several conditions, however, are needed for these agreements to work, and so far only a few OECD countries have used industry agreements. One requirement is the existence of a well-organized industry association that can negotiate for companies in its field and ensure that they meet the negotiated commitments. In addition, government negotiators need adequate information, resources, political support, and flexibility to bargain as an equal partner with industry. Overall, voluntary agreements require a new way of looking at environmental problems. As one industry executive has declared:

> "The use of Voluntary Commitments ... demands a certain mental climate. It requires for example a good relationship between authorities and industry. It also requires the awareness that environmental protection should be a common responsibility of authorities and industry." (L.J.G. Tummers, Shell International Petroleum Co., in Dubini, 1991)

<u>Corporate Environmental Policies</u>. Many companies are concerned about the environmental consequences of their actions, and have adopted corporate environmental policies. Several hundred multinational corporations have subscribed to the International Chamber of Commerce's "Business Charter for Sustainable Development," which calls for responsible corporate environmental actions. Chemical industry associations in Europe and North America are advising the adoption of the "Preventive Care" principle, under which chemical companies should work for continuing environmental improvements in their operations. Many multinational corporations have adopted internal environmental policies that call for strict standards in all their manufacturing plants worldwide, such as following home-country requirements even in host countries where national laws are less strict. One reason that corporations have adopted such policies is that they have found that pollution prevention is a wiser and less costly strategy as

national environmental requirements become more stringent. In addition, in some countries many corporations have had to pay large sums for environmental damages from either accidents or ongoing pollution, and these companies now try to avoid situations that might result in further environmental liabilities; in addition, in a number of countries banks and other private lenders have included environmental liability concerns in their lending policies. Finally, disclosure laws in the U.S., requiring large corporations to release information on all their discharges to the environment, have encouraged corporations to reduce their emissions beyond regulatory requirements.

The Commission of the E.C., working with private corporations, several European industry associations, and representatives from Central and Eastern Europe has developed the Budapest Guiding Principles on the Environment, Industry, and Investment Decisions in Central and Eastern Europe. These guidelines provide a bench mark against which the environmental actions of western corporations investing in the region can be judged.

Integrating Environmental Concerns in Project Planning

Several mechanisms are used in OECD countries to integrate environmental issues into project planning and plant operations.

Permitting is used most visibly for large electricity generation and industrial plants, and for large commercial buildings. The permitting process sets specific environmental requirements that a new facility must meet in its operations: the focus is on emissions requirements that need to be met in relation to national ambient objectives or emissions standards. Often, local governments or authorities are involved in permitting, and in an increasing number of OECD countries there is a role for public participation and comment in the permitting process.

Environmental impact assessments (EIAs) provide a mechanism to evaluate the environmental effects of large new projects before they are approved. In the U.S., companies and government authorities have been required to prepare such studies for over 20 years. Many OECD countries have adopted an EIA process, and the European Community now requires them for certain large projects. The EIA process differs from country to country, but usually the studies are released to the public and there is an opportunity for public review and comment. In addition, the results of these assessments may convince local or national authorities to modify or stop a project. More recently, a number of OECD countries undertake EIAs in bilateral assistance projects; OECD countries also have encouraged multilateral lenders such as the World Bank and regional development banks to require such assessments for major investment projects outside the OECD countries.

The experience in the U.S. and other countries provides a number of lessons. First, the results of environmental assessments have led to the cancellation of many projects, including energy projects, and the modification of others, often creating public controversies. Nonetheless, the requirement to prepare EIAs has resulted in increased public and private awareness of the potential effects of large projects on human health, natural areas, flora and fauna, and sites of archeological, historical, and cultural importance. The assessments usually focus on local environmental issues rather than regional or international effects.

Second, EIA requirements may create project delays. In the U.S., the EIA process has in cases led to long disputes and protracted court cases that have delayed projects, inflating their costs, and sometimes leading to the abandonment of projects whose environmental impacts are not actually severe. Thus, in designing EIA procedures, a government should carefully consider efficiency and develop its own balance between formality, openness and timeliness. The EIA process should encourage an integration of environmental issues -- for example, when EIAs are made early in project planning, they can help identify issues and problems that could lead to later conflict and delays. In addition, the EIA process should be coordinated with related requirements, such as permitting or local planning procedures, to avoid a duplication of effort.

Environmental audits are used voluntarily by many large corporations, to study the environmental performance of their existing plants. These audits study the environmental efficiency of the plants: many companies have used them to identify actions and investments to reduce pollution and environmental damages, often through greater production efficiency -- in many cases these improvements prove to be profitable. In addition, many corporations undertake or commission environmental audits of existing plants they are considering purchasing: these audits identify environmental problems at the plants, including potential environmental liabilities, that require costly corrections.

Research and Development

Scientific and technological research activities are central to environmental policy. All OECD countries sponsor basic research on the environment, and scientific work on effects of pollutants on human health and the environment have helped set priorities for environmental actions.

Many OECD governments also support the development and introduction of new technologies in energy production and energy efficiency, as well as research into cleaner processes and products. OECD governments cooperate on research and share information through a number of international forums, including the IEA. Government programs include both applied research into new technologies and demonstration projects to help test new methods and demonstrate their feasibility for market use. The U.S., for example, has supported a large program to research clean coal technologies -- new techniques such as fluidized bed combustion that reduce pollutant emissions without the need for add-on pollution control equipment. This clean coal program has supported several pilot plants to test new methods and demonstrate their feasibility for commercial use.

Energy efficiency research may take place on a more routine level. For example, some OECD governments have worked with their national building industry to develop more efficient buildings and encourage the introduction of energy efficiency improvements in new and existing buildings.

Finally, private industries play an important role in developing cleaner, more efficient technologies. Often companies engage in such research in reaction to new environmental policies or in anticipation of future stricter requirements. For example, several western automobile manufacturers have developed prototype very-low emissions vehicles to meet strict future standards, such as those planned for California in the U.S. Much of private industry research and development is, however, motivated by market factors; rising energy prices encouraged the development and introduction of more energy-efficient production processes in the steel industry, the pulp and paper industry, and many other sectors. OECD governments are paying increasing attention to policies that encourage and stimulate private industry's development of new, cleaner technologies, as well as to environmental requirements that encourage the introduction of cleaner production processes instead of the use of end-of-pipe pollution reduction systems.

III. ENERGY EFFICIENCY: ACHIEVING BOTH ENERGY AND ENVIRONMENTAL GOALS

Energy efficiency is a central area for the integration of energy and environmental policies. OECD economies have become much more efficient in their use of energy over the past 20 years, but studies have shown that there remain significant opportunities for further efficiency gains. A number of OECD governments, including the Netherlands, Denmark, and Sweden, have undertaken ambitious energy efficiency programs as part of national strategies to arrest or reduce carbon dioxide emissions. These programs often can also be justified on the basis of other environmental benefits.

Energy efficiency improvements generate important social benefits: they can improve national energy security and reduce environmental effects while contributing to economic growth. In many cases, energy efficiency improvements are the most cost effective method of reducing pollution. The emphasis on energy efficiency represents a renewed focus in energy policy. After the energy shocks of the 1970s, OECD countries revised energy policies to promote energy efficiency as well as supply options, to meet energy security and to ensure economic growth. During the 1980s, with lower energy prices, emphasis on efficiency declined. There is now renewed attention to the demand side of energy use, primarily for environmental reasons, and a growing recognition that energy efficiency improvements can replace costly supply-side investments.

Energy price signals play a central role in encouraging market actors to use energy efficiently, and a high priority for energy efficiency policy is to remove any remaining price controls and energy subsidies that have constrained these investments in the past. Nonetheless, OECD governments have found that price mechanisms alone are not sufficient to encourage cost-effective, and socially beneficial levels of investment in energy efficiency improvements. A number of barriers to the introduction of energy efficient products and measures exist, including:

- Lack of awareness on the part of both policy makers and market actors that energy efficiency can provide both national and private economic benefits.

- Individuals and many small businesses use very high implicit discount rates when considering energy efficiency improvements (that is, they tend to only make investments that yield quick and significant paybacks).

- Institutional or structural barriers, such as where buildings are owned and maintained by landlords who do not directly benefit from reduced energy consumption, and tenants pay for energy.

- Many companies and individuals are not aware of specific energy efficiency opportunities that could provide economic advantages.

- Technical problems -- new, energy efficient equipment may not be widely marketed, and may not integrate well with existing equipment.

Countries have used different mechanisms to promote energy efficiency. In some countries, national administrations have actively promoted energy efficiency; in others, regional and local governments have taken the initiative. In general, the most successful programs are those in which governments provide goals and information but leave detailed implementation to private actors.

Tools to Promote Energy Efficiency

Information Programs. These provide companies and individuals with information to make better energy and investment decisions. For example, energy efficiency labelling for appliances and heating equipment helps inform consumers about the energy consumption and long-run costs of different appliances and heating equipment choices. Energy efficiency information may be more difficult to provide for buildings. In Denmark, an energy inspection must be performed before the sale of any house or apartment, providing prospective customers with estimates of building heating costs. In industry, targeted programs can be effective, such as advising architects and engineers about specific energy efficient technologies and methods. The U.S. also provides public recognition for corporations that have adopted advanced energy efficiency programs through the Environmental Protection Agency's "green lights" program, encouraging greater diffusion of energy efficiency initiatives.

Energy Management Services. A number of governments and utilities provide energy audits, or funding for audits, to small companies and residential users, pinpointing energy efficient changes that can save them money. Private companies have also found a profitable role in promoting energy efficiency. So-called energy service companies (ESCOs) pay for energy audits and energy efficiency investments of private energy users (usually companies); they then take their profits from the reduction in the client's energy costs. ESCOs may be subsidiaries of utility companies. These companies so far played only a minor role in energy use and have operated mainly in the U.S., although their role is growing and spreading to other countries. One problem is that the transaction costs and risks are relatively high, at least in the initial stages.

Energy-efficiency Standards. All OECD countries have set standards for energy efficiency for new buildings and appliances. In Denmark, planned building codes would require new buildings to use about 25 percent less energy for heat than existing codes, with further improvements in the future. In addition, both new and existing buildings must undergo an energy efficiency inspection before sale. New building regulations in England and Wales are expected to save about 20 percent in space and water heating for new buildings. The United States has adopted a system of minimum efficiency standards for home appliances, such as refrigerators, air conditioners, and water heaters. This is expected to save about 9 GW in electricity power requirements by the year 2015. The U.S. has also adopted fuel efficiency requirements for new cars.

Financial Incentives. Many OECD countries have encouraged energy efficiency improvements through tax measures, grants or low interest loans. For example, Norway provides grants covering 20 percent of the costs of energy efficiency improvements in industry. The United Kingdom has a grant program to help low-income households install energy saving insulation.

In the past, financial incentives have often proven expensive and have tended to provide public funds to some energy consumers to do something that they would have otherwise done on their own. Moreover, those who received public incentives to conserve energy sometimes have used the increased disposable income to increase energy consumption elsewhere. For these reasons, financial incentive policies for energy efficiency need to be carefully designed. In fact, OECD governments have gradually reduced or phased out such policies as they have moved away from direct involvement in energy markets and energy subsidies.

With the increasing concern about global environmental problems linked to fossil energy consumption, some governments are showing renewed interest in incentive programs. The most effective incentive systems do not pay the total cost of investments, but provide initial funding to encourage users to make energy-efficient investments. If programs are carefully targeted, some of the difficulties and inefficiencies of financial incentives may be overcome.

Reducing Government Energy Use. There can be significant opportunities for reducing the energy use of national and local administrations. However, this sector often reacts very slowly to market mechanisms. Government departments rarely retain savings they make in energy use. Nonetheless, efforts to improve government energy efficiency should be part of national energy efficiency programs. In some OECD countries, governments have tried to take a leading role by adopting new, energy efficient equipment before widespread private use. Several governments have started programs to improve the efficiency of heating and lighting in their buildings.

Power Systems. Finally, there can also be important opportunities for greater efficiency in energy supply, transmission, and distribution systems. OECD countries have adopted policies to encourage greater use of combined heat and power systems (CHP) and other supply innovations that make use of excess industrial heat. Many countries are introducing greater competition into electricity production, such as regulations requiring utilities to purchase power from independent producers and industrial companies with excess power production at certain intervals, if costs are lower than the marginal cost of new generation. This element of competition encourages greater efficiency in energy production generally.

Integrated Resource Planning

Most energy efficiency programs are designed and implemented by national or local governments. One new method receiving increasing attention is to spur electric utility companies to promote energy efficiency. These policies try to shift the role of utilities from energy suppliers to energy service companies that look at both the demand and supply sides of electricity, using tools such as integrated resource planning (or least cost utility planning) and demand-side management programs. In the U.S., most electric utilities are privately owned but are closely regulated by state (i.e. regional) governments, many of whom have introduced new mechanisms under which private utilities can profit from investing in electricity conservation rather than increases in energy supply.

There are significant examples, however, of publicly owned utilities in North America (such as Ontario Hydro, the Bonneville Power Authority, and several municipally owned utilities) which have become leaders in the implementation of least cost planning and demand management programs. In a number of European countries, local municipalities own electric utilities and district heating companies. Many of these local utilities, encouraged by their municipal owners, have developed programs to encourage their users to increase energy efficiency and conservation. Other OECD countries are also studying the greater use of demand-side management.

IV. INSTITUTIONAL MECHANISMS FOR POLICY INTEGRATION

Effective integration of environmental issues into energy policy -- and throughout economic policy -- requires high-level commitments from both government and parliamentary leadership. Integration also requires improved coordination between government ministries. Environment ministries have not had adequate communication and influence on economic and sectoral ministries, including ministries with responsibility for energy policy. Many OECD governments have started to introduced formal mechanisms to increase cooperation between environment, economic, and sectoral ministries, to improve communication and policy coordination, and to develop integrated policies.

Regarding energy and environmental policy integration, these mechanisms can: encourage energy administrations to consider environmental issues in policy development; assist environmental ministries in understanding the objectives and parameters of energy policies; identify opportunities for energy and environmental policies to meet their respective objectives through common actions; and allow a full consideration of trade-offs involved in policy conflicts. In addition, energy and environmental integration needs to take account work in related sectors, and especially the effects of macroeconomic goals and policies.

Improving Ministerial Cooperation

Joint Ministries. Sweden briefly established a joint Ministry for Energy and the Environment. Swedish Ministries are, however, small policy-making organizations, and separate energy and environment agencies remained in charge of policy implementation.

Cabinet-level Committees for Energy and Environment. These have been created in a number of countries. In Canada, for example, a Ministerial Committee on Energy and Environment brought together the two federal ministers responsible for energy and the environment. This ministerial cooperation provided the basis for integrated policy work, and has encouraged greater coordination between the staffs of the two ministries.

Staff-level Committees and Working Groups. The participation of environmental and energy officials in staff-level committees or special task forces is necessary to work out the details of integrated policies. For example, the Netherlands extensively used such working groups with participation from several ministries to develop its 1989 National Environmental Policy Plan. A number of governments have tried to encourage ongoing contacts and cooperation between environmental and energy ministries in order to reduce the real and perceived barriers between officials. Another element for policy integration and interministerial communication can come from offices within Energy Ministries that focus on environmental issues, and energy offices within Environmental Ministries.

Joint Implementing Agencies. Some OECD governments use agencies separate from ministries to implement policy decisions. Several countries have created joint energy and environment agencies: these include NOVEM in the Netherlands, ADEME in France, and ENEA in Italy. In these cases, energy and environment ministries are usually both represented on the agencies' governing boards.

Better Analytical Tools

Effective integration of environmental and energy policies depends on informed decisions on policy trade-offs and options, requiring governments to analyze the effects, costs, and benefits of different policy options. Energy and environmental administrations need to evaluate the economic costs and benefits of new policies, as well as scientific information on the causes and effects of environmental damages, in this process. OECD governments have experience with a range of tools to provide greater information on the interaction between energy use, economic development, and the environment.

One example of an important analytic methodology that the OECD and many governments are developing is life-cycle (or full fuel cycle) analysis of energy systems. This technique evaluates an energy system from fuel production through fuel use to the final disposal of eventual wastes, examining environmental effects throughout the chain. This can be an extremely useful approach for policy development, and specific applications have been developed, although there is not yet a widely accepted standardized methodology for life-cycle analysis.

A number of OECD countries have used quantitative risk assessment methods to identify the most pressing problems for human health or the environment, and thus rank policy priorities. In addition, the OECD and many governments are trying to develop easily understandable environmental indicators that provide quick appraisals of environmental quality and of progress toward environmental goals.

An emerging approach to policy planning is to set long-term targets for specific pollution and environmental indicators, based on scientific analysis, and to measure environmental performance against these targets. This is analytically difficult and politically sensitive, but technically should improve the efficiency and effectiveness of environmental policies as methods evolve. Another important class of analytic tools is economic and technology oriented models for projecting future energy and environmental conditions and trends, and the potential impact of various policy options. Other important tools include data handling and analysis systems and technology costing and optimizing methods.

Coordination with Outside Groups

Parliamentary Oversight. In a number of OECD countries, Parliaments take an active role in examining the effectiveness and coordination of government policies, holding administrations accountable for proper implementation of laws and national goals. For example, the U.S. Congress has wide-ranging powers to investigate the actions and performance of the executive branch, and has on occasion encouraged speedier or stricter implementation of environmental laws. In addition, all OECD country parliaments have an important role evaluating the effectiveness of current policies and proposing new laws to solve ongoing national problems.

Coordination with Regional and Local Governments. The relations between national, regional, and local administrations differ greatly between OECD countries. Nonetheless, in nearly all OECD countries, regional and local governments are taking a greater role in formulating and implementing environmental policies; in many countries, there are important resource transfers between national and local governments for policy implementation. Communication and coordination is essential for effective implementation. In some cases, regional or local governments develop policy innovations that are later adopted nationally. For example, California, which has notable automobile-related pollution problems, has led the U.S. in adopting strict emissions requirements for motor vehicles.

Public and Industry Participation. Many OECD countries are seeking to increase public and industry participation in the development and implementation of environmental policies. Although the main route for democratic participation remains representation through parliamentary systems, the importance and complexity of environmental issues call for additional modes of participation. Several OECD countries have used advisory committees and other mechanisms to involve industry, environmental groups, and other sectors in the development of energy and environmental policies: Canada, for example, used a so-called "multi-stakeholder" consultation process to bring together different interests in a national advisory council sponsored by the Federal Government to examine energy prospects and options. In the U.S., there is a formal process for public comments on proposed regulations -- this provides an opportunity for interested parties to review and assess the specific mechanisms proposed to implement national legislation.

National Policy Strategies

Many OECD countries have recently used the development of national energy or environment strategies as a mechanism to improve policy integration. Depending on the country, these documents may set general, non-binding goals and targets for government programs, or, may propose specific requirements and actions.

Sweden, Denmark, Switzerland, and Austria are among the OECD countries that have recently prepared national energy plans which integrate environmental concerns into energy policy. These energy plans all contain initiatives to arrest or reduce national greenhouse gas emissions, and focus on energy efficiency as a central tool for achieving environmental and energy goals. In addition, both Denmark and Sweden's energy plans proposed the use of economic instruments. The U.S. produced, in 1990, a National Energy Strategy, which included environmental protection as one of its main goals. Canada prepared a "Green Plan" on environmental policy in 1990, and the United Kingdom presented a comprehensive national environmental statement, "This Common Inheritance" in the same year, both of which addressed the integration of environmental issues throughout government policy.

The Netherlands has undertaken the most ambitious effort yet, initiating a long-term planning process to integrate environmental considerations throughout the country's economic policy. The first stage in this process was a 1989 National Environmental Policy Plan (NEPP). The process reviewed interactions between government policy, the economy, and the environment, and proposed new policy initiatives effecting nearly all economic sectors. (See Annex 2 for a description of the NEPP process.) In addition to these OECD initiatives, in 1990 Poland produced a plan for sustainable development that proposed near-term, medium-term, and long-term goals for environmental policy; this was an innovative and useful exercise for a country just beginning its economic transition.

In developing most of these national plans and national strategies, governments relied on policy coordination involving ministerial cooperation and consultation with industry, environmental groups,consumers and other interest groups. Each OECD country has different government policy planning and decision-making methods, and uses national plans within the framework of its democratic process and government priorities. In some cases, national plans were submitted to Parliament for approval, even if they mainly set new goals rather than new laws (for example, in Sweden's case, the energy plan proposed ambitious goals for reducing carbon dioxide levels); in other cases, national plans led to government proposals for new legislation. Some provisions can be introduced without new legislation; in the Netherlands, some new initiatives were negotiated with relevant interest groups in the private sector.

The goal of these national policy strategy exercises is to develop coherent, integrated policies. Nonetheless, the success of the resulting government proposals, as with all environmental and energy policy, depends on inducing changes in the behavior of private actors.

VI. CONCLUSIONS: POLICY INTEGRATION IN OECD COUNTRIES

OECD Member countries have recognized the importance of integrating environmental objectives into planning and policy for the energy sector and, more broadly, for their economies generally. Separate energy and environmental policies have at times contradicted each other, have increased overall economic costs, and have made it more difficult to achieve respective policy objectives. OECD governments are improving policy integration measures within their countries and through international cooperation. This is an ongoing process and countries recognize that policies and policy integration tools could be further improved. However, the principles and importance of integrating energy and environmental policies are widely agreed, and a range of approaches is now available and in use.

Policy integration implies considering the interrelationships of environmental objectives (such as reductions in pollution-related health effects, or ambient air and water quality goals) and other energy and economic objectives. This should occur early in policy and decision-making processes, and should continue through program and project implementation. Policy development that systematically includes energy and environmental goals and develops broad strategies is needed.

Institutional mechanisms for policy development and integration vary considerably between countries. Mechanisms for inter-ministerial and inter-agency cooperation have been important in all successful programs. There is also a growing trend toward broadening policy discussions to include all interested parties (stakeholders) early in the process, including consultation with affected industries, other interested parties, and the public. There are many models of processes for involving stakeholders in policy formulation and implementation. These need to be considered carefully as there can be a tradeoff between level, timing, and cost of public involvement, and the speed and efficiency of decision-making. Approaches which incorporate public consultation early in the policy formulation process are generally more efficient and effective.

Implementation of complementary energy and environmental policies can be promoted through flexible policy approaches, reliance on the operation of the market wherever possible, and use of market-based policy tools. Experience in OECD countries, however, indicates that economic instruments are generally most effective when used in combination with direct regulatory instruments. Also, market-based approaches do not necessarily result in reduced implementation and administration requirements by governments relative to direct regulations alone. Thus, implementation requirements should be considered carefully in the design of environmental and energy policies.

Environmental standards must be set realistically (based on consultations between industry, government agencies, and other parties) and enforced effectively in order to be credible. Timing of compliance should consider tradeoffs and synergies with other capital investment requirements where possible to allow for the most cost-effective response. Flexibility in the application of environmental policies can be helpful in reducing costs. OECD countries have had some success in targeting actions on the highest priority risks, and phasing in other environmental objectives over time. An example is the application of more stringent standards or more rapid schedules in areas experiencing high ambient concentrations of pollution. The experience also shows, however, that it is essential to consider the long term implications of present policies to ensure that in dealing with priority objectives, other environmental problems are not worsened.

Some common elements of OECD Member country energy and environmental policies are apparent. First, a high priority is placed on removing subsidies and those policies that distort market prices for energy and natural resources, and identifying and removing other market barriers and constraints resulting from ineffective government policies. The removal of subsidies and other market barriers reflects a long term trend. Second, correcting ineffective policies is a critical step toward fulfilling environmental, energy and economic goals. However, removing existing policy constraints, and allowing prices to be set by markets are not sufficient to achieve energy and environmental policy goals. Thus, and third, positive government intervention is often needed to tackle externalities and address other inherent market distortions and barriers.

The need for positive government intervention to promote energy efficiency is especially clear. OECD governments have recognized that improvements in energy efficiency can play a central role both for improving energy security and in reducing environmental damages. In addition, energy efficiency investments can also have other direct economic benefits by creating jobs, improving international competitiveness, and reducing the sensitivity of national economies to disruptive price shocks. Even in most open market economies, however, many barriers and institutional constraints exist which discourage implementation of cost-effective, energy efficient investments. Government intervention to overcome these barriers can have major societal benefits.

The experience of OECD Member countries demonstrates a range of approaches for integrating energy and environmental policies. Variations depend on the existing institutional structures, cultures, political systems, and overall patterns of interaction between government and industry. These experiences provide a range of models for the countries of Central and Eastern Europe. OECD countries can assist by providing information, technical assistance and frank evaluations of their own experience with specific approaches.

Annex 1: The Use of Economic Instruments in Sweden

Sweden is one of the OECD countries that has in recent years increased its use of economic instruments in energy and environmental policy: the government has, over the past few years, strongly restructured energy taxes and charges to help promote environmental goals, including the reduction of emissions of sulphur and nitrogen oxides, carbon dioxide, and other pollutants. This brief description should provide an overview of the changes that Sweden is introduction.

Fuel taxes and charges. In 1991, Sweden introduced three basic changes in its tax system for fuels: original energy taxes were halved; a 25 percent value-added tax was introduced on fuels (and throughout the economy); and charges placed on the carbon dioxide and sulphur contents of fuels. These carbon and sulphur taxes are intended to encourage the use of cleaner fuels. The table below provides a calculation of the effects of these tax changes. Gasoline taxes did not change greatly; in fact, Sweden has since 1986 had lower taxes on unleaded gasoline to encourage its use over leaded gasoline. There are other exceptions: fuels for electricity use are not taxed (the separate charges on electricity are listed); biofuels, waste used for energy, and ethanol and methanol are also exempt; and there is a cap on the total energy and carbon dioxide payments that industry must pay, so that energy-intensive industries remain competitive in world markets (in 1992 the tax was set at 1.2 percent of the value of a manufacturing company's production).

Emissions charges. In January 1992 Sweden introduced a charge on the emissions of nitrogen oxides from large combustion plants. This effects about 200 plants, which were required to install measurement equipment to determine actual emissions. In addition, Sweden has taxed, since 1989, hydrocarbon and nitrogen oxide emissions from domestic air transport.

Vehicle charges. Diesel-powered vehicles must pay a kilometer tax, based on the type and weight of the vehicle: the tax effects passenger cars, trucks, and buses.

Sweden intends to introduce a tax system on new vehicles based on their emissions levels. All new cars will have to meet minimum emission standards. New cars, however, will be grouped into three classes: those that merely meet the minimum standard; those that meet a stricter standard (equivalent to the 1994 U.S. national requirements); and those that reach a still stricter emissions control level (the 1994 California requirements). The first class of vehicles, meeting only the minimum standard, will be taxed 2000 kroner; the second class will be exempt from this tax; and the third will receive a subsidy of 4000 kroner per vehicle. Trucks and buses will face a similar system based on their emissions levels. The revenues from the new taxes are expected to be offset by the subsidies on the cleanest vehicles and a reduction in the kilometer tax.

These various tax systems have only been introduced, and it is not yet clear how effective they will be in reducing emissions. Nonetheless, there is evidence that some district heating systems have switched from coal to untaxed biofuels, and that demand for light, low-sulfur fuel oil has increased, taking the place of heavier fuel oils. Finally, vehicle fuel consumption appears to have decreased in reaction to the new tax system.

Taxation (Excluding VAT) of Fuels and Electricity in Sweden:
Comparison of Old and New Taxation Systems

Sources: IEA, <u>Energy Policies of IEA Countries: 1991 Review</u>, OECD, Paris, 1992.

	December 1990	September 1991			
		Energy Tax	CO2 Tax	Sulphur Tax	Total
Light fuel oil, SKr/MWh	109	55	73	6 *	134
Heavy fuel oil, SKr/MWh	101	50	67	14 to 20 *	131 to 137
Coal, SKr/MW	61	31	83	24 **	138
Natural gas, SKr/MWh	32	16	50	-	66
LPG, SKr/MWh	16	8	59	-	67
Biofuels	0	0	0	**	**
Gasoline, SKr/litre					
leaded	(2.84)	2.68	0.58	-	3.26
unleaded	(2.64)	2.37	0.58	-	2.95
Ethanol, SKr/litre	0.80	0.80	-	-	0.80 ***
Electricity, SKr/MWh					
industry	50	50	-	-	50
other users	72	72	-	-	72
non-industry in designated places	20	20	-	-	20

Notes:

CO_2 tax, 250 SKr/metric ton

SKr = approx. $0.165 in this table

*   27 SKr per cubic metre of fuel oil and per percentage point of sulphur

**   30 SKr/kg sulphur

***   From 1st January 1991 there is no sulphur tax if the fuel is 100% ethanol.

The calculations are based on the following net calorific values:

Light fuel oil: 9.9 MWh/cubic metre

Heavy fuel oil: 10.7 MWh/cubic metre

Coal: 7.5 MWh/metric ton

Natural gas: 10.8 MWh/thousand cubic metres

LPG: 12.79 MWh/metric ton

Annex 2. The Dutch National Environmental Policy Plan (NEPP)

The Dutch National Environmental Policy Plan (NEPP), published in 1989, is the first part of a national strategy to implement the goals of "sustainable development" throughout the country's policy. The NEPP's program resulted in perhaps the first time that an OECD government has fallen over environmental policy.

The NEPP was prepared by task forces that brought together representatives of different government ministries -- Environment, Agriculture, Transport, and Economic Affairs (The Dutch Ministry of Economic Affairs is responsible for energy). These task forces studied the linkages between the economy and the environment in the Netherlands and formulated policies to promote sustainable economic growth; one novel feature of their work was the systematic use of economic forecasting techniques to estimate future effects of economic activities on the environment. In the course of this work, the task forces also asked industry, environmental groups, and other interests for their advice. The resulting NEPP report, published in 1989, described the integrated approach and listed over one hundred measures to be undertaken through new legislation, through national and local government action, and through negotiation with "target groups" -- different industry sectors, in particular -- to agree on mechanisms to achieve the strategy's overall goals.

Although the Dutch government approved the strategy, in Parliament one of the parties in the government coalition rejected the NEPP's financing provisions, in particular its increased charges and reduced tax benefits for automobile users. Elections were called, and a new government coalition that supported the NEPP emerged; this new government approved an amended version of the Plan, NEPP-Plus, which included stronger measures to reduce greenhouse gas emissions through both energy efficiency measures and carbon taxes.

The new government also began planning for the next major environment plan. The original strategy behind the NEPP envisioned a sequence of new environmental strategies every four years. The next plan should be published in 1993, and adopted by the government in 1994. Many of the provisions of the NEPP and NEPP-PLUS were elaborated in subsequent government policy documents on energy conservation, air pollution reduction, and climate change measures, and many elements have been enacted in legislation. There have, however, been delays in implementing the environmental plan. One problem identified with the NEPP was that it did not focus on implementation mechanisms; these are a priority in the new environment plan now being developed. Also, many of the NEPP's goals require government negotiations with industry. These negotiations are underway, but the question of allocating the costs of new environmental provisions has been a difficult issue. The government been successful in negotiating with industry over energy conservation targets: by early 1992, nine industrial sectors agreed to reach specific, multi-year energy conservation targets, and the government hopes to reach agreements with 80 percent of industry by the end of the year. On the other hand, proposals to introduce carbon taxes on fossil fuels have generated industry opposition and disagreements within the current government coalition.

The process to develop the NEPP required a large effort in terms of government resources. New analyses had to be made of economy/environment linkages, and these new methodologies are still under development. The plan required close cooperation between different ministries, and its implementation calls for further intergovernmental cooperation (including cooperation between national, regional, and local administrations). Government negotiations with industry depend on a tradition of cooperation between the public and private sectors in the Netherlands. One additional key to the success of this ambitious strategy has been strong public concern for the environment in the Netherlands.

ECONOMIC RESTRUCTURING, ENERGY,

AND THE ENVIRONMENT IN CENTRAL AND EASTERN EUROPE

Regional Perspectives on Economic Restructuring,

Energy, and the Environment

CLEAN AIR BUT NO JOBS?
Environmental priorities and policies
during the transition in Central and Eastern Europe[1]

Gordon Hughes
The World Bank

1. SETTING PRIORITIES

The economic transition poses many difficult choices for those responsible for shaping economic and social policies in Central and Eastern Europe (CEE) and the newly independent states of the former Soviet Union (NIS). Determining priorities for remedying the environmental damage caused by past careless and wasteful industrial growth ranks high on the list of unenviable responsibilities. Environmental concerns were an important focus for political opposition to the former regimes, so that environmental groups understandably feel that governments should partly be judged by the extent of their commitment to rectifying past mistakes. On the other hand, the sharp falls in national income that have accompanied the breakdown of central planning mean that resources to fund investments in controlling current emissions are very limited, while the costs of dealing with the effects of past pollution appear prohibitive.

Two criteria should be used to identify environmental problems that warrant immediate action in these circumstances. First, the resources available should be allocated to measures which generate the largest ratio of the benefits of reducing environmental damage to the total costs incurred in achieving the reduction. Second, it is essential to avoid certain types of (almost) irreversible damage to the environment such as the contamination of deep groundwater aquifers or the loss of unique biological or other environmental resources. This can be thought of as a special application of the first criterion in which the benefits of environmental protection are very high because of the value attached by the community to avoiding a permanent loss of particular natural assets.

---

1.   I am grateful to Richard Ackermann, Janusz Cofala, David Craig, David Newbery and Andrew Steer for suggestions and discussions which have shaped the ideas discussed here. I have also benefitted from the assistance of many individuals and organizations in Central and Eastern Europe in compiling the data which underpins the empirical results. However, I alone am responsible for the views expressed here. They do not in any way represent the position of the World Bank or of its member governments.

Setting aside the specific problems posed by irreversible environmental changes, the assessment of the benefits of reducing environmental damage rests upon three key elements:

A. A reduction in the damage to human health caused by prolonged or intermittent exposure to poor environmental conditions.

B. An increase in the working life or productivity of physical or natural capital as a result of lower exposure to corrosion or other forms of damage caused by air or water pollution.

C. The enhancement of the amenity value of natural resources for recreational, cultural and social purposes.

Lack of data and the price distortions associated with central planning mean that it is quite difficult to assess the specific benefits of various forms of environmental improvement in the CEE/NIS countries. However, analyses carried out for other countries with similar levels of pollution and income suggest that the damage to human health is likely to dominate the other two components in any estimate of the total costs of environmental damage in the region. Loss of productivity due to pollution is serious in some countries or regions -- for example, the effects of water salinity in Poland and Ukraine or of acid deposition in Czechoslovakia -- but, overall, damage to human health due to environmental causes is the central issue in all of the countries and has very similar profile in most of them. Many of the main causes of health damage, especially air pollution, are also associated with the amenity costs of environmental damage, so these amenity costs are unlikely to alter rankings based on health considerations.

A review of the epidemiological evidence relating to environmental causes of ill-health and excess mortality in Central and Eastern Europe suggests that the primary issues of concern are:

(a) Damage to the neurological development of children caused by exposure to lead, especially in areas close to lead smelters.

(b) Acute and chronic respiratory diseases (bronchitis, emphysema, asthma) caused by air pollution. Exposure to particulates is believed to be the most serious problem, but excessive exposure to sulphur dioxide exacerbates the effects of particulates and can be a problem on its own.

(c) Excessive levels of nitrates in regular drinking water supplies may threaten the health of newborn babies unless alternative pure water is provided. This is a significant problem in many rural districts of most CEE/NIS countries.

(d) Various health problems associated with heavy metal discharges -- either as dust or into rivers -- from non-ferrous metallurgy plants.

The first and last of these issues tend to be highly localised and require specific measures to deal with emissions from the non-ferrous metals sector. Once such measures to reduce smelter emissions are implemented, motor vehicles using leaded gasoline will be the main source of lead emissions. Children living close to busy urban roads are particularly affected by these emissions. The threat to their health with increase unless the effects of growing traffic volumes are offset by steps to reduce the lead content of fuels (including a gradual switch to the use of unleaded gasoline). The problem of nitrates in drinking water is primarily the consequence of poor agricultural and sanitary practices which result in the contamination of shallow groundwater sources used by those living in rural areas. Reductions in fertiliser use plus information programmes which highlight the need for adequate septic tanks which are separated from any wells used for domestic drinking water should reduce the magnitude of this problem.

Thus, attention must focus upon the widespread damage caused by exposure to excessive levels of particulates and sulphur dioxide, which dominates the total amount of ill-health linked to environmental causes. In particular, the populations of urban areas with a concentration of heavy industrial plants or which depend upon coal as the primary fuel for heating and for industry are the most severely affected by particulates and sulphur dioxide. Looking ahead, air pollution caused by vehicle emissions will be an increasingly important problem as the size and average use of the car fleet are both likely to grow quite rapidly over the next decade. Already, emissions from ill-maintained diesel trucks and buses are a significant source of particulates and other pollutants in some cities.

2. THE MAIN SOURCES OF ENERGY-RELATED AIR POLLUTION

The quality of the air in some towns and cities of Central and Eastern Europe -- such as Ostrava and Teplice in Czechoslovakia, Katowice in Poland and Magnitogorsk in Russia -- is deplorable, especially in the winter. It is little consolation to point out that many urban areas in China, India and Latin America experience similar or worse levels of air pollution. However, it is relevant to note that average air quality in many towns and cities in Western Europe was as bad or worse than similar urban centres in the CEE or NIS countries today. London today ranks as one of the best European cities in terms of exposure to particulates -- soot and smoke -- and to sulphur dioxide, but it was notorious for the frequency and severity of its smogs from 1850 to 1960. Systematic comparison of major European cities shows that Athens, Madrid and Milan had poorer air quality in the 1970s and early 1980s, in terms of the indices that matter for human health, than comparable CEE or NIS cities (see Hughes, 1991b).

Central and Eastern Europe is caught in an economic and industrial time-warp with many of the characteristics of the rich countries in the 1950s and early 1960s. The result is high levels of air pollution linked to the level and composition of energy use in industry, households and other sectors. Comparisons between the CEE and NIS countries and similar ones in Western Europe, Asia and Latin America highlight various factors which tend to increase levels of air pollution.

A. High levels of energy use per unit of output or consumption.

Detailed comparisons between patterns of industrial energy use in Bulgaria and those standard in Western Europe for the cement, chemicals, iron and steel, and paper industries have shown that energy consumption is typically 3 or even 4 times higher per tonne of output in Bulgaria than in western Europe. The gap between the average energy intensity of Bulgarian industries and best practice in the West is even higher. Similar comparisons have shown that households in the CEE and NIS region households spend on average the equivalent of 15 per cent of total personal consumption on energy products (if these are valued at world rather than domestic prices), whereas the share of energy in total personal consumption is typically 5 per cent for countries with similar real income levels and 6 to 8 per cent in the rich West European countries. After allowing for differences in average temperatures, the composition of national income, energy prices and other factors, an econometric study of energy consumption in a sample of middle income and rich countries that I carried out showed that central and eastern European countries had an average level of energy consumption per unit of real income that was over 50 per cent higher than that of West European countries with similar characteristics (see Hughes, 1991a).

B. Low and distorted levels of energy prices.

Comparisons between the energy prices paid by industry and households in the CEE and NIS countries and in Western Europe, using the overvalued pre-reform exchange rates, show that the average cost of energy to CEE and NIS users was well below that in Western Europe. Immediately before the collapse of central planning the median ratios of West European to domestic prices for industrial users in six CEE/NIS countries varied from 1.56 for oil products to 1.91 for electricity, while for households the range was from 1.78 for oil products to 4.9 for electricity. Relative prices favoured consumption of coal and electricity in industry and of gas and electricity by households.

C. High levels of coal use by households and the service sector.

Coal is easily the dirtiest of the major primary fuels. It is also the abundant source of domestic energy in the CEE and NIS countries other than Russia, so that a strong preference for domestic resources encouraged the use of coal rather than gas or oil wherever this was technically feasible. The resulting environmental problems were substantially exacerbated by the fact that many of these countries rely upon relatively poor quality brown coal and lignite with high ash and sulphur contents. However, the general bias in favour of coal is only part of the story. Analysis of energy consumption data shows that West European coal consumption is concentrated in power generation and a small number of industrial sectors. These burn coal in large boilers to which environmental controls can be fitted. In the CEE and NIS countries, a much higher share of coal consumption is accounted for by the household and service sectors, whose emissions from coal burning cannot easily be dealt with, other than by switching to much more expensive smokeless solid fuels. The point is illustrated in Figure 1, which compares the volumes of coal consumption per person (expressed in tonnes of coal equivalent) in the household and service sectors combined, the industrial sector, and the power generation and district heating sector in 1988 between CEE and the USSR and average for the European Community countries. Note that in addition to the much higher share of direct coal consumption in the former socialist countries, they have a much higher dependence upon district heating which is often produced in small or medium scale coal-fired units. The use of coal in households and small scale boilers is the major contributor to high ambient concentrations of particulates and of sulphur dioxide in the urban areas of Central and Eastern Europe.

Figure 1 - Coal use in Central and Eastern Europe
(kg of coal equivalent per person)

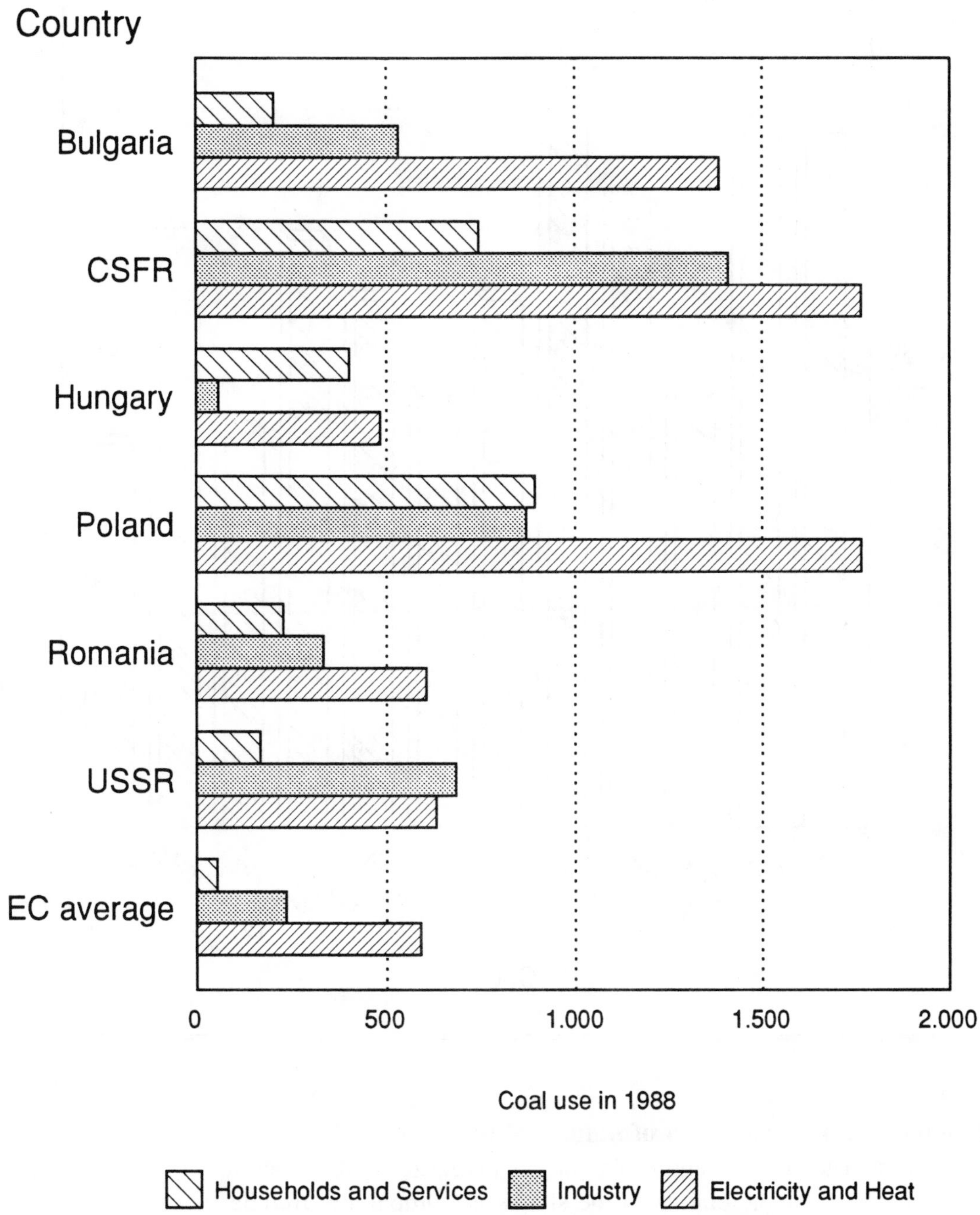

Coal use in 1988

◫ Households and Services ▦ Industry ▨ Electricity and Heat

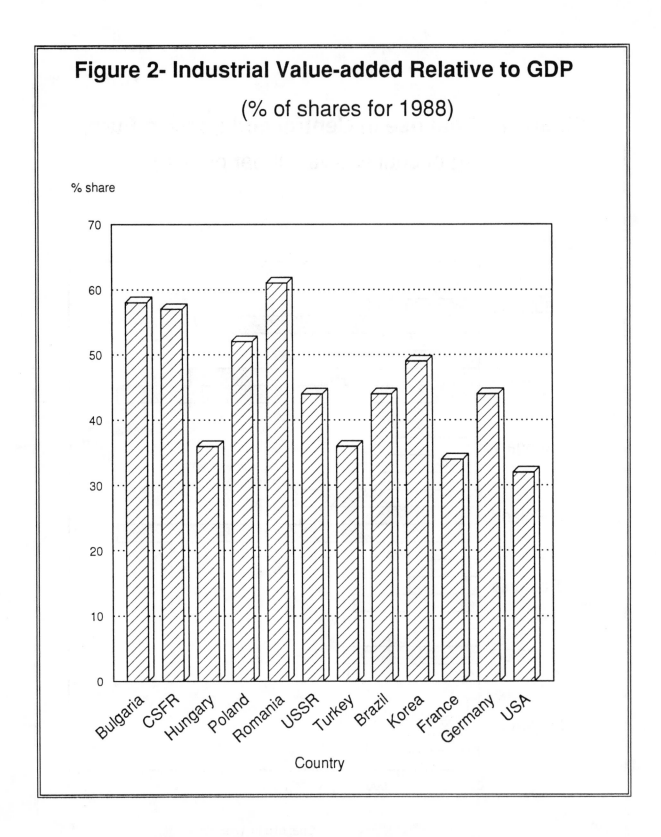

Figure 2- Industrial Value-added Relative to GDP

(% of shares for 1988)

% share

D. The level and composition of industrial production.

Another legacy of central planning is the large share of national income produced in the industrial sector relative to the shares in comparable middle income countries. Figure 2 shows that value-added in industry, mining and construction accounted for more than

50 per cent of GDP (measured on a consistent SNA basis) in Bulgaria, Czechoslovakia, Poland and Romania in 1988. Even for a highly industrialised middle income country such as Korea this share was only 49 per cent, while for most middle and high income countries it is less than 40 per cent. Further, the composition of industrial production in Central and Eastern Europe and the former USSR is biased towards industries such as building materials, ferrous and non-ferrous metallurgy, and machine-building which tend to be major sources of air pollution.

E. The age, technology and environmental controls of industrial plants.

Many steel mills in Central and Eastern Europe still rely upon old open-hearth furnaces which are cheap to operate provided that labour costs are low, but which emit much more air pollution than the basic oxygen or electric arc furnaces standard in richer countries. The region's non-ferrous metal smelters, especially for lead and aluminium, have primitive arrangements for filtering metal dusts from the exhaust gases coming from their furnaces by comparison with the options provided by modern technology. These and many other examples reflect two interrelated aspects of industrial capital in these countries. The average age of plants is much older than in Western Europe, and their technology and environmental controls have not been upgraded progressively over time in the way that is standard in market economies. As a consequence the environmental performance of most industrial plants is much worse than for plants of similar age in middle or high income countries. This basic weakness is reinforced by a tendency to neglect maintenance and renovation, especially of equipment that is not essential to keep up levels of production. Thus, dust filters often operate at levels of removal efficiency that are well below their design specifications.

These and related factors mean that the environmental problems of Central and Eastern Europe are closely linked to patterns of economic incentives and industrial development that were key aspects of the management of centrally planned economies. Indeed, similar features can be observed in countries which have followed a similar path, such as Algeria, China, North Korea and even India.

3. THE IMPACT OF THE ECONOMIC TRANSITION ON ENVIRONMENTAL PROBLEMS

The economic transformation of Central and Eastern Europe should make a large contribution to improving environmental quality by changing the incentives and structural features discussed in the previous section. First, it should lead to the elimination of explicit or implicit subsidies for the consumption of energy and other natural resources, thus encouraging energy conservation and the more careful utilization of other resource-based products. Second, it will bring about a restructuring of these countries' industrial sectors, leading to new investment that embodies technologies which reduce the amount of pollution per unit of output. These changes will take time, but their contribution to the improvement of air quality should be very large.

A gradual increase in energy prices to converge with the levels prevailing in Western Europe should reduce the energy intensity of economy activity by 30 to 50 per cent by the end of the century. At the same time, it will encourage the substitution of oil products and gas for coal and electricity in the industrial sector. Households, too, will tend to switch away from coal towards gas and other fuels once they are freed from the constraints imposed by central planners, though on grounds of convenience rather than changes in relative prices. Coal use will become concentrated in those sectors that are best placed to install environmental controls to reduce emissions of particulates and sulphur. A lessening of the preference for domestic resources will also lead to a shift away from brown coal and lignite towards hard coal, which should reduce total emissions per tonne of coal equivalent used for power generation or metallurgical production.

To analyse the impact of various components of economic reform on total emissions of the main pollutants in the CEE/NIS countries, an energy-environment projection model has been constructed for each of the countries in the region. It is based on a standardised 44 sector input-output framework plus 4 energy sectors obtained by aggregating detailed input-output tables. Energy prices influence both the total level and the composition of energy use per unit of output in each sector and for final demand. Changes in the relative prices of other material inputs have a similar effect on the material intensity of production, while it is assumed that there is scope for reducing overmanning and the wasteful use of raw materials, especially of agricultural products, in all industrial sectors. Then, given macroeconomic assumptions about the path of GDP and of the components of final demand such as personal consumption, investment, and net exports, it is possible to produce output projections up to the end of this century or beyond for various scenarios about the nature and speed of economic reforms. These projections are combined with a simple model of the manner in which electricity demand is met from a combination of trade, primary (nuclear and hydro) production and thermal generation to yield the total utilisation for primary energy and the total volume of emissions, assuming either fixed or changing emission coefficients. For most air pollutants the emission coefficients are linked to levels of energy consumption by sector, with a small adjustment for process emissions that are independent of energy use. This model has been used to generate the projections that are presented in the remainder of this section.

Governments in Central and Eastern Europe are all committed to eliminating energy subsidies and to ensuring that domestic energy prices are not less than comparable world prices by the end of an appropriate transitional period which, in most cases, will not extend beyond 1995. There are many non-environmental reasons for undertaking this reform, since high levels of energy consumption are economically inefficient and are a direct or indirect drain on government budgets. At the same time, significant environmental benefits should flow from a reduction in total energy use as well as from changes in the composition of energy consumption.

Figures 3A and 3B illustrate the potential impact of increasing real energy prices for the Central and Eastern European countries -- CEE -- (shown as solid lines for each set of assumptions) and for the republics of the former Soviet Union -- NIS -- (shown as dashed lines). Three scenarios are shown:

A.   Emissions if the real prices of energy are not increased. This projection is indicated by bars for each point and gives the highest level of emissions for each group of countries.

B.   Emissions if the real prices are increased to the level of prices in the U.S., which provides a good approximation to world market prices. This projection is indicated by squares for each point and is the middle line for each group of countries.

C. Emissions if the real prices of energy are increased to the level of typical prices in Western Europe (usually the OECD Europe an average or the German price when the average is distorted by extreme observations). This projection is indicated by * signs for each point and is the lowest line for each group of countries.

It is important to stress that these projections are not forecasts of the expected changes in emissions over the 1990s. They have been constructed to highlight the potential impact of increasing energy prices given a set of basic macroeconomic assumptions about changes in economic activity over the period. However, the actual path of emissions will depend upon how rapidly energy prices are increased to their assumed levels and on the time taken by enterprises and others to respond to the higher prices. If the full price increases had come

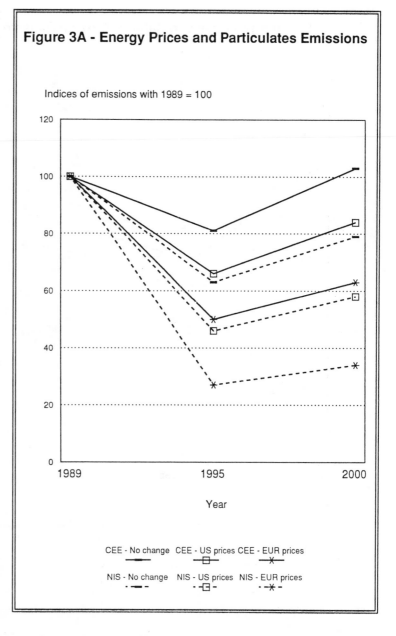

Figure 3A - Energy Prices and Particulates Emissions

into effect during 1991 and 1992 and enterprises had been subject to the kind of financial discipline that would have prompted them to economise on energy consumption as far as possible, then the projections for 1995 could be interpreted as forecasts, since they are based on reasonable estimates of the response of energy demand to prices. In practice, the process of adjustment will be much slower, so that the projections for 2000 provide a starting point for making a forecast of emissions for the end of the century. However, changes in economic structure and technology are likely to have an important impact on emissions after 1995, so the projections are designed to provide an insight into the potential contribution of raising energy prices to reducing emissions of air pollutants.

All of the countries in the region are expected to experience a fall in national income between 1989 and 1995, so that emissions of particulates and sulphur dioxide would fall by about 20 per cent for the CEE countries over this period without any increase in energy prices and by

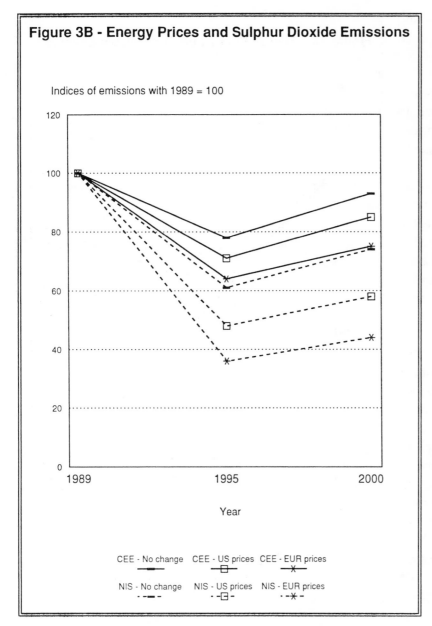

Figure 3B - Energy Prices and Sulphur Dioxide Emissions

Indices of emissions with 1989 = 100

Year

CEE - No change   CEE - US prices   CEE - EUR prices

NIS - No change   NIS - US prices   NIS - EUR prices

about 38 per cent for the NIS. The latter is much larger because it is expected to undergo a larger decline in total GDP combined with a greater decline in total GDP combined with a greater decline in the share of investment in GDP which means that demand for heavy, energy-intensive industrial goods will fall more sharply than GDP. Of course, as the decline in national income is reversed, emissions begin to increase after 1995-96, so that total emissions of particulates in the CEE countries are higher in 2000 than in 1989. Emissions of sulphur dioxide recover more slowly because large industries, which will be severely affected by the decline in investment spending, are relatively more important sources of sulphur emissions than of particulate emissions.

A temporary reduction in air pollution associated with the reduction in economic activity -- something that is clearly observable in the industrial cities of Upper Silesia -- is hardly a sustainable basis for improving environmental quality. When faced with choices between jobs and the environment, most governments in the region have clearly indicated that, with popular support, they will almost always opt for jobs. The figures, however, show that such a choice should not be necessary. Raising energy prices to world market levels, the minimum adjustment required to achieve economic efficiency, would result in emissions of particulates at least 20 per cent less than their equivalent "no real price change" levels in both the CEE countries and the NIS. Going further by imposing taxes which raise energy prices to West European levels would bring similar percentage reductions in particulate emissions. The reductions in sulphur dioxide emissions are not quite as great but they are still very substantial.

Figures 4A and 4B extend the analysis by contrasting the effects of a low response to higher energy prices (or, equivalently, of a delay in raising energy prices) with the impact of introducing better control technologies to reduce emissions. In these figures, the main projection is the lowest solid (CEE) or dashed (NIS) line which assumes that energy prices are raised to western European levels and that stricter environmental controls (to current western European standards) are applied to 50 per cent of the capital stock between 1995 and 2000. The top lines give the results for the projections in which demand for energy is little affected by higher prices but stricter environmental controls are applied after 1995. On the other hand, the middle lines show the impact of no improvement in environmental controls.

For particulates in the CEE countries, a limited response to higher energy prices or delays in raising prices leads to a substantially higher level of emissions than the main projection. By 2000, the projections show that stricter environmental controls just offset the smaller price response, so that the "no controls" and "low response" projections produce similar outcomes. For sulphur dioxide the impact of stricter environmental controls is larger than that of a low energy price response for the CEE countries because of their dependence upon relatively high sulphur coals. The share of coal in total energy consumption for the NIS is much smaller than for the CEE countries, so that stricter controls on sulphur emissions are less important than the overall response to higher prices. The main projections in both figures indicate that the impact of environmental controls between 1995 and 2000 should be sufficient to ensure that total emissions of particulates and sulphur dioxide do not increase even though economic activity and industrial production are rising quite rapidly -- at an average of 5 per cent per year over the period.

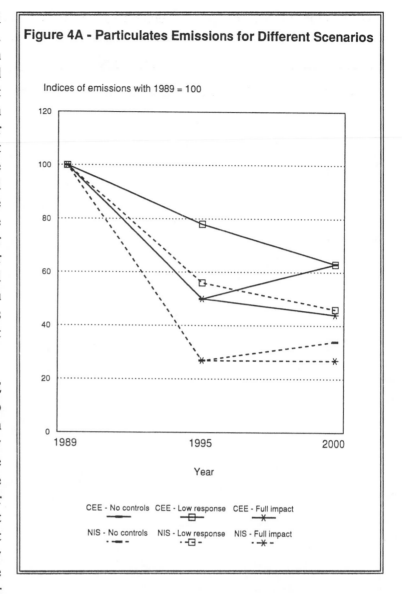

Figure 4A - Particulates Emissions for Different Scenarios

The projections demonstrate that a combination of higher energy prices plus stricter environmental controls linked to the replacement of old capital equipment should enable the CEE and NIS countries to achieve large falls in the average level of emissions of air pollutants per million dollars of GDP during the transition from central planning. Thus, they can make substantial improvements in ambient air quality even as their economies begin to recover from the recessions caused by the breakdown of the former economic system without imposing an unacceptable burden on private enterprises or the public budget. Indeed, the projections understate the extent of the environmental gains that should be achievable.

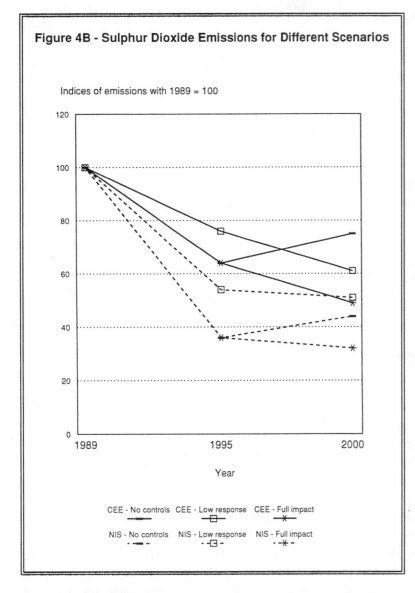

Figure 4B - Sulphur Dioxide Emissions for Different Scenarios

Indices of emissions with 1989 = 100

Year

CEE - No controls   CEE - Low response   CEE - Full impact

NIS - No controls   NIS - Low response   NIS - Full impact

More detailed, though still preliminary, analysis suggests that the recovery in the output of polluting industries such as cement, iron and steel, non-ferrous metals, and machinery will be much slower than that for industries such as food products, textiles, paper products and chemicals. Further, the growth in total industrial output will be much slower than that for national income as the relative under-provision of services is corrected. These changes in the structure of economic activity, which go beyond those implied by the decline in investment as a share of total GDP, mean that total emissions of air pollutants per million dollars of GDP will fall even more rapidly than the projections above envisage. However, the same structural changes imply a relative increase in the scale of industries which discharge water pollutants, so that measures will need to be taken to ensure that average water quality does not deteriorate. In view of the priority that should be given to air pollution, the net effect of these changes is clearly beneficial from an environmental point of view, especially as industrial emissions are a much lower share of total emissons for the main water pollutants than for the primary air pollutants.

4. COMPLEMENTARY ENVIRONMENTAL POLICIES

The environmental improvements discussed in the previous section will not be costless, nor will they be achieved as an automatic consequence of the transition to markets. Energy conservation induced by higher energy prices may be efficient in the sense that it increases national income, but it will involve real costs of adaption and investment for those enterprises, institutions and households which have to adjust. Without information and, in some cases, transitional assistance, they may be slow to respond to the new set of incentives. Thus, policies which encourage the rapid adoption of less energy-intensive methods or production or which enable households to control their energy use may yield substantial environmental benefits by accelerating the decline in emissions following the reform of energy prices.

This does not mean, however, that energy conservation should become a goal of policy for its own sake. A quite strict test should be applied to assess the economic return from policies or expenditures designed to promote energy conservation. Since higher energy prices will provide a strong incentive for enterprises and others to reduce their energy use, any evaluation of conservation programmes must focus on the benefits from cutting the lags between the implementation of energy price reforms and the realisation of feasible and efficient energy saving measures. In practice, this implies that such programmes should concentrate on low cost interventions -- for example, running information campaigns and funding demonstration projects -- which reinforce the economic incentives for energy users to switch to more energy efficient technologies or ways of working. Experience in the market economies following the oil shocks suggests that these policies can have a significant impact on the path of energy consumption following large price increases, though the ultimate decline in energy intensity depends primarily upon the scale of the increase in real prices. Note, however, that it is very important that governments not fall into the trap of establishing new subsidies designed to promote energy conservation, since these simply replace the old distortions with new ones. In the end it is energy prices that should govern the responses of enterprises and other consumers, not a panoply of subsidies and other conservation policies.

There are special considerations that apply to household energy consumption in Central and Eastern Europe for both environmental and economic reasons. As pointed out above, household and small scale commercial users of coal impose large environmental costs on the community because of the problem of particulate emissions. Environmental policy should, therefore, focus on replacing coal by other fuels as rapidly as possible in the household and service sectors. The natural alternative fuel is gas, which presents the problem of ensuring that gas distribution networks are developed to match the potential demand. In several countries the capacity of pipelines was designed to meet residential demand for cooking but not for heating, while in Bulgaria gas was only supplied to the industrial sector. Since the local distribution of gas is a classic natural monopoly requiring a large commitment to long-lived fixed assets, it is inevitable that the public sector will have to play a substantial role in facilitating and, probably, funding the investments required to make gas available to small scale users as a substitute for coal. The environmental benefits of fuel substitution suggest that, other things being equal, priority should be given to the distribution of gas in localities where exposure to particulates or sulphur dioxide is especially high, providing that household burning of coal is a major contribution to this air pollution.

Most small scale users of coal are very happy to switch to gas, even if it costs more, because of the convenience and the labour-saving that it brings. However, there are other kinds of energy conservation which may be economically efficient but are less attractive to households. There are two important reasons for such divergences of interest:

(a)   The well-known incentive to "free ride" in household energy consumption (that is, to use excess amounts) caused by the lack of meters to measure individual use of hot water or gas in many apartments and houses. This is combined with a similar lack of controls that would enable households and others to regulate heating levels. Pricing incentives can, at best, have only a limited impact on behaviour if the link between individual decisions and domestic heating or fuel bills is as weak as is implied by the present mechanisms for collective payment of energy charges by apartment building or housing complex. It is therefore essential to invest in the provision of individual meters and controls that provide both the means and the incentive for individual household controls over levels of energy consumption. The same applies, of course, to commercial and service premises which may currently operate on a similar basis in paying fuel bills.

(b)   Research has shown that households tend to apply very high rates of discount when deciding whether to invest in energy-saving measures or appliances. There can be many reasons for the divergence between the general social rate of discount and that used by households. In the CEE and NIS countries, the problem is exacerbated by the virtual non-existence of financial institutions that provide consumer loans together with the impact of recent high rates of inflation on household savings, both past and present. Such imperfections in the capital market are not easily remedied, since the task of establishing new institutions to take on the role of consumer lending is likely to be difficult and time-consuming. Government grants, which should probably amount to no more than 50 per cent of the cost of approved expenditures, may therefore be the only practical way of stimulating energy-saving investments to provide better insulation, more efficient energy utilisation and similar forms of energy conservation.

A focus on energy conservation is only one aspect of the policies required to reinforce the changes that will occur during the economic transition in Central and Eastern Europe. The replacement of outdated capital equipment will facilitate the introduction of stricter emission controls, but appropriate incentives will be required to speed up this process and to ensure that new investment does not lead to a deterioration in environmental conditions. Environmental policy should, therefore, be designed to reinforce the trends initiated by economic reform. A combination of regulatory and market-based instruments will be required in order to deal with the full range of environmental priorities, but energy-related pollution is particularly suitable for the application of marked-based instruments such as pollution charges and tradeable discharge permits (used for sulphur dioxide emissions in the US).

Most of the CEE and NIS countries in the region already had or have recently introduced systems of pollution charges covering the main air pollutants. These systems of fees and fines are equivalent to a non-linear pricing schedule in which discharges up to some permitted level are subject to a fixed fee per unit of emissions, while discharges above the permitted are penalised by a much higher fine per unit. While the system of fees and fines provides the basis for an effective set of incentives to reduce emissions, the actual levels of fees and fines have typically been too low to act as a serious deterrent and enforcement of payment of the sums due has been erratic. Until now the primary consideration in setting pollution charges has been to generate revenue for national or local Environmental Funds which have been established to finance environmental improvements. This may be an appropriate way of using the revenue from pollution charges, but the charges themselves should be set by reference to the damage caused by emissions in current or expected future circumstances.

The economic function of fees and fines is to "internalise" the costs of pollution by requiring that polluters face a charge on emissions that reflects the external costs (to the rest of the community) of their emissions. An efficient outcome will be achieved when the marginal cost of reducing pollution is set equal to the marginal damage caused by that pollution. This condition can be satisfied if the marginal pollution charge is set equal to the marginal damage at the level of pollution where the two are equal. However, there is no practical way of identifying the efficient charge when there is so much uncertainty about both the cost and damage functions. Frequent adjustments in the real level of charges may also be counter-productive because they engender uncertainty about the government's intentions and commitment. A practical approach is, therefore, to set pollution charges initially at (say) 50 per cent of the estimated damage caused by the emissions concerned and to announce that the real value of these charges will be revised every five years on the basis of trends in total emissions and of environmental damage.

Pollution charges can be applied to most energy-related emissions from large or medium industrial plants, since these can be monitored at reasonable cost. They could cover particulates, sulphur dioxide, nitrogen oxides, carbon monoxide and carbon dioxide. However, it is not practical to deal with emissions from small scale sources -- including vehicles -- in this manner. An alternative to direct pollution charges for small scale users is to impose indirect levies on different fuels in the form of refundable taxes at levels reflecting the average damage caused by burning each fuel. Refunds would be granted if users can show that they have installed environmental controls such as catalytic converters for cars which largely eliminate most emissions. The principle of differential charging for those who do and do not invest in environmental controls is important, since without refunds or some similar arrangement the incentive to improve environmental performance is limited to fuel conservation.

5. CONCLUSIONS

Central and Eastern Europe is certainly not the ecological disaster area that is the common image depicted in Western press and television commentaries. Nonetheless, its recent economic history has left a pattern of energy-related pollution which must be tackled as the main priority for environmental policy. The encouraging feature of the analysis outlined in this paper is that a combination of sensible economic reforms with appropriate environmental policies offers the prospect of substantial improvements in environmental conditions within a relative brief span of time, perhaps as little as 3-4 years. Current improvements in air quality have been achieved at a high cost in terms of lost jobs and income. That need not be the prospect for the future provided that effective systems of environmental incentives and regulations are implemented soon, so as to ensure that future economic recovery is accompanied by continuing improvements on the environmental front.

Higher energy prices, industrial restructuring and incentives to ensure that new investment meets higher environmental standards than the equipment it replaces should ensure that total emissions of particulates and sulphur dioxide fall over the remainder of this decade to less than one half (and perhaps as little as one quarter) of their pre-reform level. Emissions of nitrogen oxides will not fall as rapidly because of the growth in the size and use of the car fleet, but the gradual introduction of catalytic converters will ensure that these emissions fall in the longer term. Prospects for carbon dioxide emissions will depend upon whether countries are willing to impose some kind of carbon tax so as to reinforce the shift away from coal.

While these projections may seem rather optimistic, the example of London provides an indication of how much can be achieved within the period of 8 to 10 years. Between 1953 and 1960 the amount of smoke emitted from industrial premises in the city fell by 60 percent, and that from domestic premises by 20 percent. The average number of smogs per year fell from over 50 to less than 20 and the annual mean smoke concentration fell by one-half. This was before natural gas became available in Britain. In the following decade, as natural gas was spreading, the industrial smoke problem was effectively cured while domestic emissions of smoke fell by almost 60 percent and measures of air pollution fell by a further 50 to 60 percent. With the benefit of such past experience all of the countries in Central and Eastern Europe can set themselves a realistic target of reducing exposure to smoke and sulphur dioxide by 75 per cent over the next decade in all cities whose average exposures are more than twice the European Community guidelines. While reducing smoke does not have quite the aura of saving whales, this would be a noble goal worth the inspiration and commitment prompted by greener environmental objectives.

BIBLIOGRAPHY

Hughes, G.A. (1991a), "The energy sector and problems of energy policy in Eastern Europe," *Oxford Review of Economic Policy*, Vol. 7, No. 2, pp. 77-98.

Hughes, G.A. (1991b), "Are the costs of cleaning up Eastern Europe exaggerated? Economic reform and the environment," *Oxford Review of Economic Policy*, Vol. 7, No. 4, pp.106-136.

ENERGY AND ECONOMIC REFORM IN CENTRAL AND EASTERN EUROPE: A PERSPECTIVE ON POLAND

Henryka Bochniarz
President, Nicom Ltd

INTRODUCTION

The old economic system based on central planning has left a legacy of energy waste and environmental degradation in Central and Eastern Europe (CEE). The countries of the region have undertaken courageous reforms to reverse these problems. Governments have increasingly imposed hard budget constraints on energy enterprises while raising consumer prices to near Western European levels. These reforms, if continued, will help the region reduce the capital, economic, and environmental burdens associated with energy use, and thus help achieve both economic growth and environmental protection.

Energy sector restructuring to date, however, has been concentrated only on the supply side of the energy equation. This approach gives consumers the incentive to conserve energy through higher prices, but often leaves them without the means to increase their energy efficiency. A more balanced approach would help consumers adjust to higher prices by providing access to information, technical assistance, and financing. This approach has been used in all Western market economies to help overcome market failures and to protect consumers. Demand-side management, however, has not been a major emphasis of policymakers or international donors in Central and Eastern Europe. One of problem is that energy experts in the region were shaped by the notorious condition of excess demand for heavily subsidized energy, and they focused exclusively on the supply side of energy sector. In addition, neither political conditions nor cheap energy fostered independent organizations to protect the public interest in energy sector.

In the new political conditions, leadership is needed to implement demand-side measures and to protect consumers and the environment; leadership that is lacking throughout the region. Current governmental structures place energy policy in the hands of agencies historically associated with promoting the interests of the energy supply sector. It may not be possible to balance regional energy supply and demand policies within this framework. One solution would be to make energy efficiency the responsibility of consumer protection or environment agencies, arms of government that should higher interest in energy conservation. Restructuring governments to provide leadership in promoting energy efficiency and consumer protection should be a central feature of reform in Poland and elsewhere in Central and Eastern Europe.

ENERGY IN THE CURRENT ECONOMIC CONTEXT

The economies of most Central and Eastern European nations have fallen dramatically since 1989. This decline has generally been accompanied by reduced energy use, though this decline in many countries has been less than the drop in economic output.

In Poland, Gross Domestic Product (GDP) dropped roughly 20 per cent between 1989 and 1991. Polish energy use, however, has fallen faster than the economy, thus providing the first real reduction in energy intensity -- energy used per unit of economic output -- in over a decade. This change is already providing economic benefits: for example, the share of capital invested in energy production has dropped from almost 40 per cent of all industrial investment in 1988 to just over 20 per cent in 1990. This reduced requirement for the energy sector means that a larger share of available funds could be used to develop Poland's infrastructure -- improving the telephone service, upgrading health care facilities, and expanding public transportation -- as well as to satisfy the needs of a rapidly growing private sector.

Poland has won these gains the hard way -- in part by imposing an extremely rapid rate of adjustment to world prices on its citizens. Its policy represents extraordinary political courage. Consider the following changes in energy prices in Poland over the last two years:

- The price of residential natural gas has increased 1,600 per cent;
- The price of residential electricity has increased 1,000 per cent;
- The price of natural gas for Polish industry has reached U.S. levels.

Imagine trying to do that in the United States or in the European Community:

The price of residential electricity is now 5 cents per kilowatt hour, close to the actual cost and near the U.S. average, yet annual per capita income in Poland is less than one-fourth that of the United States. In two years, Poland has made the transition from highly subsidized energy to free prices. In comparison, the United States took 10 years to accomplish the same.

OPPORTUNITIES MISSED?

Central and Eastern Europe, despite its painful price reforms, is missing important opportunities in the energy sector that could improve the well-being of our citizens. Lack of capital and lack of government policies to overcome common market failures are limiting the adoption of clean, energy-efficient technologies and the pursuit of demand-side energy options.

For example, the Polish government in 1991 subsidized district heating by $1.8 billion. The government is moving to increase prices and reduce subsidies, but the limited ability of consumers to respond must be taken into account. Residential occupants whose buildings do not have heat meters, much less thermostats and insulation, cannot respond to price signals. Their behavior, which includes controlling room temperature by opening and closing windows, may continue as before. At the same time, they may be forced to allocate one-fifth or in many cases more of their income to pay their heating bills, which are based not on the heat used, but on the size of their dwellings.

All OECD countries have grappled with similar energy-related market failures of one type or another, including:

- Lack of information;
- Split incentives (for example, the different incentives for landlords and tenants);
- Natural monopolies; and
- Lack of capital for investment at the point of energy and use.

These problems are certainly found in Poland and throughout the region. Consider the information problem -- consumers cannot choose an energy-efficient refrigerator from among the products in the stores, as there are no labels indicating energy efficiency. Split incentives are a arise, for example, when landlords buy appliances and consumers pay the utility bills. The landlord will want to minimize initial costs, while the consumer will want the landlord to buy the more-efficient models.

The utility sectors, despite some efforts to create competition, will largely remain natural monopolies requiring government regulation. But our governments have limited ability to attract and keep qualified personnel to oversee the utilities when they are limited to paying salaries one-quarter or even less than those of the private sector. Lack of capital is an obvious problem in a region where real interest rates approach 20 percent.

Correcting these imbalances will take far longer and will be more costly than necessary if we do not adopt many of the energy efficiency policies that have developed and applied in the United States, Europe, and Japan over the past two decades.

Energy-efficiency opportunities in Eastern Europe include the use of better electric motors, motor speed controls, automation of industrial processes, combined cycle power cogeneration, more-sophisticated cars, improved lighting and refrigeration technologies, and thermal insulation in buildings. In the residential sector, specific opportunities include: installation of heat meters, installation of valves for controlling radiators, and the availability of more efficient appliances. In the transport sector, fuel economy remains low. The regional average is only 8.7 liters per 100 km in the typically small and low-power cars used in the region. Comparable vehicles used in the United States average less than 6 liters per 100 km. Increasing automobile fuel economy to cost-effective levels and converting the truck fleet from gasoline to diesel-powered engines can help reduce growth in transportation energy demand.

The commercial opportunities for selling, installing, and producing energy efficiency products is large. But this business is constrained in Poland by lack of access to technology and capital. The extent to which energy savings are actually captured depends not only on getting energy prices right, but also on attracting western firms to make investments and on helping consumers overcome the market failures that are barriers to energy efficiency in all market economies.

Energy policy must balance supply and demand measures to provide energy services for economic development while protecting consumers and the natural environment. A sustainable energy policy will promote economic development by:

1. Increasing industrial competitiveness by reducing net production costs;

2. Reducing net capital requirements by avoiding the need for new mines and power plants;

3. Improving overall productivity by promoting new technologies to increase labor and capital productivity while saving energy.

Such a balanced policy would help consumers cope with rising energy prices by giving them opportunities to save money through energy conservation.

AN ENERGY POLICY FOR SUSTAINABLE DEVELOPMENT

A number of policies can help central and eastern European countries move toward sustainable energy development. Energy policy is a means to an end, a set of strategies to achieve simultaneously national goals of economic development and environmental protection. Supply-side policies currently being applied in Poland include:

- Price reform and the removal of energy subsidies;
- Restructuring the energy supply sector;
- Decontrol of hard coal producers; and
- Privatization of energy suppliers.

To balance the supply side, countries in the region must develop demand-side policies to promote energy efficiency. Chief among these efforts should be the creation of:

- Energy-efficiency loan funds;
- Least-cost utility planning;
- Energy efficiency improvements in schools and government buildings;
- Environmental protection taxes;
- Product energy-efficiency labeling; and
- Improved domestic natural gas production and distribution.

Development of Integrated Resources Planning (IRP) for energy utilities would be particularly effective. With IRP, electric power and district heating distributors would be permitted to invest in energy savings just as they currently invest in energy supply. Distributors would be allowed to pay retail customers for saving energy -- either through one-time rebates for certain investments, or through lower rates. The utilities themselves would receive an incentive for participating in such energy-saving programs.

Providing consumers with access to capital is an important policy option. Energy-efficiency loan funds can be created for use by utilities and major industries through revenues from fuels taxes or loans from multi-lateral development banks. In the buildings sector, blocks of financing could be channeled to utilities for distribution to consumers through IRP programs. In the industrial sector, loans can be made available to enterprises for investments that increase energy efficiency in addition to output or productivity. Experience has shown that loans need to be accompanied by technical services, including:

- Energy audits for industry and buildings;
- IRP specialists to advise utilities;
- Loan processing training for banking, utility, and industrial organizations.

Consumer information -- in the form of appliance energy-efficiency labeling -- helps overcome a major market failure. New appliances can be labelled for energy efficiency, so that buyers can cut their future energy costs. The program fits within a philosophy of promoting market mechanisms because it promotes the availability of impartial and credible information, a legitimate activity for government. In the United States, most important energy-consuming appliances (including refrigerators, water heaters, furnaces, air conditioners, and lighting) must carry labels advising buyers of the energy cost of their operation. Many types of appliances also must meet standards for maximum rates of energy consumption. The European Community, led by Denmark, is actively considering energy-efficiency labeling. Some highly-efficient lighting products marketed in Europe already bear annual energy-cost labels. Labeling would help push manufacturers to produce competitive products, and ensure that inefficient products are not "dumped" on the region by foreign exporters.

One key point on implementing a balanced policy must be made clearly: creating balance is impossible within the current confines of government organization. This assertion means that energy bureaucracies in Central and Eastern Europe -- as elsewhere -- are captive to constituencies for energy supply. Promoting energy efficiency will require competition, and not just in the marketplace. It will require separation of responsibility of environmental agencies which have the motivation to promote it. However, in some cases, entirely new governmental machinery must be created.

INTERNATIONAL COOPERATION

OECD countries can benefit from helping Central and Eastern Europe overcome its energy and environmental problems in the following ways:

- Helping the region tackle the energy inefficiencies that constrain economic development, threatening the success of the vital experiments in democracy in central and eastern European countries;

- Create opportunities for OECD firms in providing environmental protection through energy efficiency improvements; and

- Help reduce the excessive energy sue that exacerbates Central and Eastern Europe's contribution to the risk of global warming and to regional air and water pollution problems.

The transition to democracy and markets will be difficult for the emerging democracies of Eastern Europe for some time to come. The mutual benefits we will share from this historic effort will make international assistance worthwhile.

The nature of the assistance provided, however, is very important. Cooperation on the part of multilateral and bilateral aid agencies has not been appropriate. Lending agencies have focused for the most part on the supply side of energy problems, ignoring the more difficult but more beneficial demand side. Second, **tied-aid -- which requires that most of the money provided be spent on foreign consultants and equipment -- is not very helpful.** And the largest portion of funds for assessing Poland's problems and designing solutions for them have by far flown not to Polish but to foreign experts. Local experts not only can but must contribute in order to design sensible approaches. A far better model is the type of approach taken by the U.S. Environmental Protection Agency in creating energy-efficiency centers in the region; these centers provide resources for local experts to solve our problems. This approach builds intellectual capital which will yield dividends for decades.

CONCLUSIONS

The sustainable development of Central and Eastern Europe cannot be achieved without significant new efforts in the energy sector. Past energy policy has seriously harmed the region's economic and environmental health by encouraging the development of expensive, polluting supply alternatives for providing energy services. However, by reorienting its policies to deliver cost-effective energy services through demand-side measures and, early in the next century, new renewable energy supply systems, CEE can achieve a healthier, more prosperous future. This strategy implies:

1. Improving energy efficiency in the short-term to maximum levels;

2. Satisfying new energy demand in the medium-term with natural gas, which is a far cleaner fuel than coal; and

3. Developing renewable supplies over the long-term.

The first element requires energy resources be priced to reflect both their replacement costs and their environmental impacts, and that governments act to overcome market failures that block energy efficiency. The second element requires careful development and use of natural gas resources in a way that will permit an easy transition to renewable energy carriers. The third element must rely on a combination of western research efforts and local measures to encourage market-based development and diffusion of new energy sources.

DIFFERENCES IN ENERGY EFFICIENCY BETWEEN EAST AND WEST: PROBLEMS AND OPPORTUNITIES

Dr. László Lengyel
Energy Division
United Nations
Economic Commission for Europe

A HISTORY OF ENERGY EFFICIENCY: EAST AND WEST

The energy intensities of the economies in the eastern and western parts of Europe differ significantly. This can be seen in Figure 1, which shows energy intensity patterns for three central and eastern European countries, the CSFR, Hungary, and Poland, and three western European countries, Austria, Denmark, and Italy.

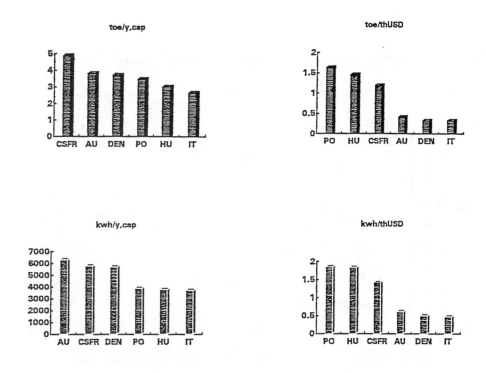

SPECIFIC ENERGY CONSUMPTIONS

Figure 1.

There are several reasons. During the sixties, up to the first oil shock, the main characteristics of the world energy development were:

- that in many countries a firm enhancement of supply took place,
- oil and gas grabbed a bigger and bigger share of the primary resources,
- many nuclear capacities came into operation and
- there was an easy access to very cheap resources worldwide so the energy world trade continuously strengthened.

These factors were more or less typical for Central and Eastern Europe and the Soviet Union, too: oil and gas production came into the forefront, grids and pipeline systems were developed to connect countries.

Then came the first oil shock and soon afterwards almost all industrialised countries revised and modified their energy policies and more or less their overall economic policies to achieve higher energy efficiency, to implement successful energy conservation policy, to identify the sectors of the economy having the greatest impact on energy consumption and identify the measures which can provide the greatest economic benefit. Energy consumption in these countries dropped back drastically, so while the primary energy consumption of the world had increased between 1960-1970 by 67%, the same figure for the period 1970-1980 was only 36%, and the process is still going on. Figure 2 shows the different energy intensity "histories" for the same six countries.

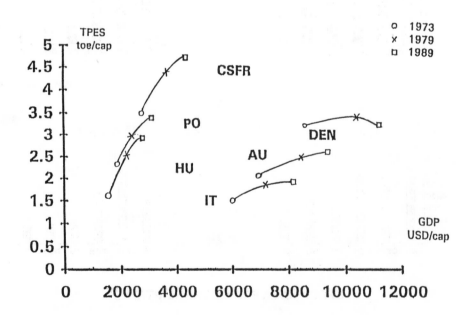

ENERGY CONSUMPTION AND ECONOMIC OUTPUT

Figure 2.

The restructuring of the economy and the shift forward to better energy efficiency were not typically strong in Central and Eastern Europe or the Soviet Union and all efforts needed to accomplish the aim of lower energy intensity were initiated and launched too late: there is almost a decade time gap between the industrialized countries and the region in this respect. Besides, measures and efforts were not too successful: energy intensity of the GDP production decreased by 10% in the Soviet Union and Central and Eastern Europe between 1973-1985 while in the industrialized countries 20% was achieved. The specific energy consumption in Eastern European countries per unit of national product is still considerably higher than in the West, approximately two times higher, although substantial progress has been made since 1983. The high energy intensity is a result of the fact that heavy industry accounts for a large share of the region's industrial output (Figure 3.) and because energy systems are operated and managed in a very inefficient manner. Figure 4. shows the relatively high share of industry in central and eastern European countries compared to OECD Europe countries.

In central and eastern European countries the mystique of smokestack industries persisted long after the first oil shock and the substantial restructuring of the Western economies. The inertia of the ideology of the 1950s was strong -- namely, to produce more heavy industrial goods than the capitalist economies. Energy was a very cheap production factor and at the beginning of the sixties in many countries in the region, official announcements declared energy as a cost-free commodity for the eighties. Figure 5 shows that, for example, in Hungary, "basic industries" used 50 per cent of industrial energy consumption but provided only about 15 per cent of industrial economic output, while in neighboring Austria the figures were 35 per cent and 20 per cent, respectively.

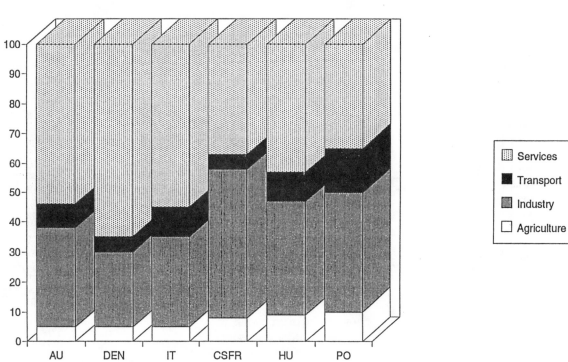

Figure 3.

FINAL ENERGY CONSUMPTION BY SECTORS
1989

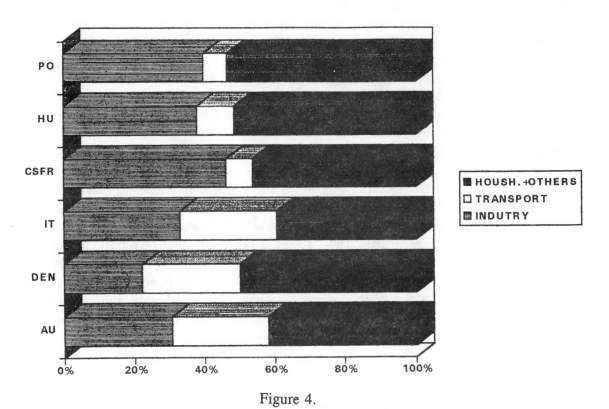

Figure 4.

STRUCTURE OF INDUSTRIAL ENERGY CONSUMPTION
(1989)

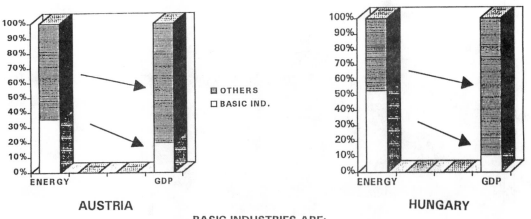

BASIC INDUSTRIES ARE:
IRON AND STEEL
NON-FERROUS METAL
CHEMICAL

Figure 5.

Even after the first oil shock in the mid-seventies, initiatives for energy conservation and improvement of energy efficiency were non-existent, the price-shock itself was regarded as beneficial, partly because it would destroy competitiveness of the western industries, increasing by that means the exportability of the "classical" heavy industrial export products of the East, and partly because the oil price upswing increased hard currency earnings in the USSR through direct oil exports.

The reaction to the price shock was so late, the changes of attitude were so slow, that in almost all Eastern European countries -- except the Soviet Union -- the share of oil had been increasing up to 1980 and the overall oil consumption reached 23% of the total primary energy consumption of these countries, against the 20% in 1970. Oil gained a bigger share, while solid fuels, i.e. mainly coal and lignite demand decreased from 68% in 1970 to 59% in 1980. Only between 1981 and 1985 can lower oil consumption be observed, the share of oil diminished to 21% in 1985 with a very modest, approximately 1% increase of the solid fuel consumption. To appreciate correctly these data it is useful to recall that the world oil consumption peaked in 1973 at 47% and went down to 41% in 1985, while the figures for the industrialized countries were 53% and 46%, respectively.

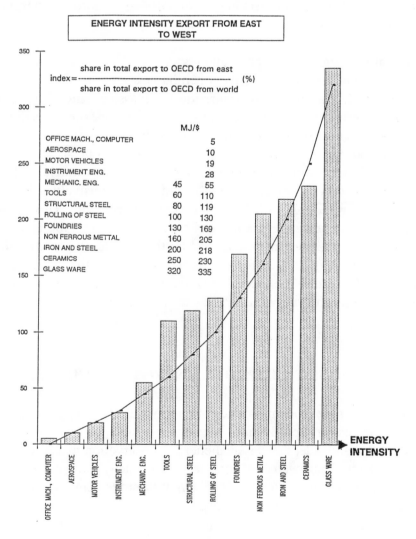

Figure 6.

To understand the relatively late and clumsy reaction of central and eastern European countries and the Soviet Union to world price changes, it is important to note that the region exported some 130 million tonnes in 1985 and accounted for 17% of intercontinental energy flows. Energy sales generated 50% of their total export earnings and covered 60% of their imports of goods and services. Energy-related trade is a primary source of foreign currency, therefore it plays a key role in the financial and economic balances of the countries in the region.

So, in the seventies the Soviet Union-dependent central and eastern European countries fell in the trap of the energy price gap: the profound need of these countries to earn hard currency drove economic policies to enhance and accelerate production of goods and commodities exportable to western markets. Due to the lack of sophisticated manufacturing techniques and upgrading capabilities the benefit of the export trade was greater when the energy intensity of the export product was higher. Figure 6 shows that there was a direct relationship between energy intensity and the exportability of the products of Eastern industries.

However, "intergovernmental" agreements set up between Soviet Union and its allies did not allow direct energy exports (cheap crude, gas and electricity) from central and eastern European countries to the West, so indirect energy exports, in the form of energy-intensive goods, increased.

In the seventies, parallel to the profound restructuring of the Western economies, shaping them to be less energy (and material) intensive, opening new areas for information techniques and developing new high-tech branches, de-glamorizing the classical smoke-stack industries, in the Eastern European countries, the economies moved in the opposite direction: they enhanced production capacities in smoke-stack industries, in many cases "modernizing" them, based on cheap Soviet energy and the exportability of these industrial products. The political stability of the central and eastern European countries mainly depended on how much hard currency earnings were produced by this hidden energy export and -- and, more decisively -- how consumer goods imported from the West were able to balance the social discontent. This very beneficial hard currency earnings of central and eastern European countries based on the favourable ruble-dollar conversion by this energy trade became dampened by the introduction of the Bucharest formula, which resulted in higher energy prices for the Soviet imports in the eighties, but were paid in "transferable" rubles. Therefore, the incentive to modernize and adapt their energy consuming sectors to use energy more efficiently was absent in these countries.

OPTIONS TO IMPROVE ENERGY EFFICIENCY

This history underlines the importance of energy efficiency improvements in Central and Eastern Europe -- in energy production, distribution and consumption. The efficiency improvement on the demand side, the classical energy conservation measures, will have a "back-rolling effect" producing "negawatts" -- not-needed capacity and energy. The pollution consequences of "negawatt" production, i.e. efficiency improvements, are positive, especially if the fuel mix used in the eastern region is also taken into consideration. The atmospheric pollution in Eastern Europe largely stems from the low grade solid fuels which have been available in the region, and the combustion techniques as they are used. The economic policy drive in the Eastern countries toward self-sufficient economies and these countries' very poor endowment with other forms of energy resources resulted in that these deposits have been heavily exploited. Further on, combustion inefficiency and low levels of desulphurisation and particulate trappers are in the heart of much of the Eastern European atmospheric pollution problem. An obvious option open to Eastern European countries, struggling to reduce energy-based environmental pollution, is to improve the fuel mix by importing better quality energy carriers. The problem is largely financial and economic, logistical and infrastructural, as well.

The energy efficiency improvement on the demand side not only means a pollution reduction by producing "negawatts", but also eases the problem of financial and economic character of the fuel mix change.

In the Eastern part of Europe, the potential for future energy conservation appears to be sizeable. The energy intensity of an economy (i.e. the level of energy consumption per unit of gross output produced) depends first of all on the country's level of economic development and its socio-economic structure, but it also depends on efficiency in energy utilization.

The low energy efficiency is partly explained by differences in the economic structure, as it has already been mentioned, since energy intensive industries account for a higher share of economic activity in the Eastern countries, which is another legacy of the factor-intensive heavy industrialization programmes pursued in the past. More importantly, however, the high energy intensity in the Eastern region can be attributed to inefficient use of energy. Another contributing factor is the inefficient energy mix resulting from their heavy reliance on brown coal, which has a low calorific content. The inefficiency of energy use in these countries appears to be particularly problematic in the industrial sector where the share of energy consumption is conspicuously high by international standards.

The solution is at hand, knowing that the fundamental impediment to rapid progress in energy conservation is the planning and incentive system governing the whole economy, which places far more emphasis on the requirement that enterprises meet their output targets, than on achievement of the cost efficiencies embodied in the input plan, including energy savings.

Reformist energy policy makers intend to introduce prices corresponding to economic costs, which are for tradeable products such as hydrocarbons, coals, etc. defined as the world market boarder price, while for electricity it is the long-run marginal cost of expanding power production (e.g. in most central and eastern European countries liquid petroleum products are already priced in accordance with this principle).

Nevertheless, there are still wide variances in prices from country to country in the region paid by different classes of producers and consumers for natural gas, different oil products and electricity. All governments are aware of the disadvantage of wrong-pricing structure, i.e. the prices of different fuels relative to each other, are distorted relative to the price structure in the international markets and in relation to supply and demand conditions in the country concerned due to subsidies, taxes, import duties and externalities.

While the governments appear to hold an overriding view that subsidies, particularly to households, should gradually be eliminated, they continue to face resistance to action needed to eliminate these subsidies during the period of official belt-tightening, recession period associated with tax policy reforms envisaged in most of the countries. The issue of appropriate levels of consumer energy prices involves a complex interaction of economic, social and political factors. Nevertheless, the available evidence suggests that the long-run benefits to the economy of raising consumer prices to their economic level are sufficiently large to justify the short-run social costs, and analysis shows that bringing consumer prices in line with producer prices would have only a limited effect on increased inflation, but would have a substantial impact on consumption levels over the long term.

As a component of new conservation policy in the countries concerned, energy contract management companies are under wider implementation; these manage energy use in enterprises by providing technical, managerial and financial resources for energy efficiency improvement, or for retrofit projects. They receive in return on their investment financial benefits from the achieved savings. The success of such companies is greatly influenced by the tax practices to be developed in the country.

As far as the capital shortage is concerned in some countries, a viable option would be to involve supply industries in conservation issues. Energy supply industries, e.g. power utilities can play an important role in providing energy conservation support. These activities need to be developed and initiated by the governments largely owing to the heavy financial burdens which utility companies or governments behind them, have to face today in the region to provide new capacity. These services fit in very well with a least-cost strategy which a utility company should pursue, and such a role and service, which needs to reshape the institutional building of the power sector in each Eastern country, can also bring relief to load management concerns a power company may have. The role of the supply company, within the frame of the new organization and institutional set-up, can best be decided in the light of specific national and local circumstances.

Influencing the success of conservation policies as a crucial part of the economic reform all laws and regulations pertinent to energy use must be reviewed . Laws affecting the economies of energy conservation projects must also be examined. Some laws and regulations will need amendments, new ones will need to be promulgated. The degree of intervention is directly dependent on the status of the economic reforms.

Another important consequence of the economic reforms in Eastern countries is the (re)privatisation of the energy producing, distributing and consuming enterprises, which will significantly lessen the number of government-owned enterprises. It involves a change of attitude of management, which is commonly more oriented towards increasing production than to improving efficiency. With motivated management, many companies will be able to do away with these roadblocks, taking into consideration that in case of an appropriate price system the pricing is not based on a cost-plus principle, so inefficiencies cannot be passed on to customers.

All these circumstances defined the strategy of the UN ECE's Energy Efficiency 2000 project and the actual policy making of the project is carefully considering the changes of these conditions and the work method is elaborated to suit these demands (see Box 1).

Box 1. The Energy Efficiency 2000 Project

The main aims of the UN ECE's EE 2000 project are:

- to establish business contacts between technology and know-how suppliers of western companies, private business or governmental institutions and the recipient eastern institutions, firms and enterprises. To overcome the problems generated by the price-deterioration in the eastern countries, special financial framework is to be provided for the actual project implementation;

- to develop demonstration projects, especially "Energy Efficiency Demonstration Zone" in which market economy energy conservation policies and technical improvements will produce measurable savings, stimulating in that way the implementation of the market forces in energy policy making;

- to analyse and identify key energy efficient technologies and management practices to determine their potential impact on energy savings and environmental quality in ECE economies in transition and development.

FINANCING ENERGY EFFICIENCY

The energy efficiency improvement in the European economies in transition represents many attractive business opportunities for various kinds of enterprises and investors. In many cases significant and profound energy efficiency improvement can be achieved by implementing management and/or organizational measures at enterprise level, these measures are to be determined by special consultancy or technical assistance provided by competent consulting companies.

Comprehensive analyses made in the European transition economies indicate that, contrary to the general opinion, the majority of energy conservation projects have mainly been no-cost or low-cost measures. The rate of implementation of projects during the past ten years in the countries in transition that do require significant investment has been much lower even with payback times less than two years. These facts support the conclusion that many energy conservation investments that are cost effective, are not being made or are having a long delay. The majority of the identified and implemented projects have payback times two years or less.

Energy conservation and efficiency improvement is a cheap, quick and relatively painless way to stretch energy supplies, slash energy costs, and save foreign exchange. The industrial and power sectors offer the largest and most easily captured energy conservation potential. Technically proven, cost-effective energy conservation techniques and processes can save transitional economies an estimated 10 to 30 percent of industrial sector energy consumption and 10 to 25 percent of power sector energy consumption.

Innovative Private Financing Mechanisms

Confronted with impediments to mobilizing capital for conservation investments, innovative financial arrangements recently implemented by some financiers and entrepreneurs in industrialized countries for the energy conservation related investments are recommended for application in the countries concerned. These arrangements are:

Shared-saving arrangements, which mean that a shared-savings firm identifies and evaluates the conservation investment opportunities at the energy user's facilities. This evaluation is usually undertaken at no cost to the energy user. However, the energy user will usually be liable for reimbursement of the cost of the detailed engineering and financial evaluation if the shared-savings firm identifies investment opportunities that it is willing to finance but the energy user refuses the firm's financing offer and undertakes the investments himself. On the basis of the evaluation the shared-savings firm and the energy user negotiate the shared-savings agreement. The agreement includes procedures for establishing the quantity and value of energy savings. With regard to a sharing formula, a common arrangement is for the share-savings firm to receive 60% of the value of savings for the five years after installation of an improvement and 40% for the second five years. In addition to receiving a share of the gross value of savings, the share-savings firm also usually receives any tax benefit associated with the investment. The agreement also addresses such matters as procedures for managing and maintaining the conservation improvement, because income to the shared-savings firm depends on the performance of the improvement, the shared-savings firm has a strong interest in ensuring that the improvement is maintained and operated efficiently.

Once the shared-savings firm and the energy user have negotiated the agreement, the firm finances and undertakes the conservation improvement. The firm may remain the sole owner/investor in the project and finance the improvement from its own financial resources. However, as an increasingly frequent alternative the firm may syndicate the investment as a limited partnership with other investors then providing the bulk of the investment funds. The typical financial structure of the shared-savings arrangement would be 30-40% equity leveraged with 60-70% debt. Occasionally, the debt may be project-secured.

After the improvement is completed the firm and the energy user operate under the negotiated agreement, sharing the value of energy savings according to the savings formula. In a shared-savings financing arrangement, the energy user is able to eliminate all or part of several important risk elements that it would otherwise bear in undertaking a conservation investment.

A joint venture between energy user and an external investor is essentially a special variation of the shared savings arrangement. An external investor provides most or all of the capital investment required to undertake an energy conservation project. The energy user provides the site the investment. However, in contrast to the shared-savings agreement, the investor and the energy user have more flexibility in tailoring the joint-venture arrangement to suit their specific risk/return objectives. The flexibility afforded by the joint-venture arrangement makes this financing arrangement attractive for large industrial projects where both the energy user and the external investor wish to control the construction and operation of the project.

In a joint venture arrangement the external investor and the energy user form a separate investor entity to manage the construction and operation of the conservation project. The investor entity might be a corporation, a general partnership, or a limited partnership. For example, in a limited partnership, the energy user may assume the role of general partner, with the external investor(s) acting as the limited partner(s). Under this arrangement, the energy user retains management control over the construction and operation of the conservation improvement, while the external investor/limited partner receives the tax benefits of project ownership.

The financial structure of a joint venture is usually similar to that of a shared-savings agreement, and typically consists of 30-40% equity and 60-70% debt. For some investments the debt may be project-secured. However, the debt will more generally need to be supported by the assets of the external investor or the energy user, or both.

The financing benefits of a joint venture depend on the terms of the specific agreement. Generally, the external investor is responsible for providing the bulk of the capital required for the conservation project. As such, the energy user will receive its share of the benefits of the conservation improvement with little or no front-end investment being required. Whether a joint venture will provide off-balance-sheet/off-credit financing will depend on the extent of the minimum payment and debt support obligations assumed by the energy user.

A joint-venture agreement specifies procedures for sharing the benefits of constructing and operating the conservation improvement. As in a shared-savings agreement, revenue of the joint venture is generally determined by first estimating the energy costs the user would have incurred in the absence of the conservation improvement, and then subtracting actual energy costs from the estimated costs.

An energy service agreement is similar to shared-savings financing arrangements in that an external investor provides the capital for conservation improvements at the facility of the energy user. As with the shared-savings agreement, the energy user makes no cash outlays and incurs no financial obligations in allowing the energy-related capital improvement to be installed. However, the agreement differs from the shared-savings agreement in the manner in which the energy service firm (and potential external investors) receives its financial return.

Under an energy service agreement, the energy service firm agrees to provide the energy user with specified energy services (e.g. heat and air-conditioning, hot water, lighting and refrigeration) at a fixed aggregate cost or unit price that is less than the cost the energy user would incur for the specified energy services in the absence of the conservation improvement. The aggregate cost or unit price will often be specified as a fraction (e.g. 80-90%) of the energy costs that would have been incurred in the absence of any energy-related investments.

The energy service firm installs those conservation improvements it has identified as being economically advantageous and necessary to earn an adequate return, given the pricing agreement for providing energy services. After installing the conservation improvements, the user firm generally receives the tax benefits (i.e. depreciation and investment tax credits), the user pays the energy service firm, and the energy service firm is responsible for all payments to utilities and fuel suppliers.

The energy service firm earns a return on its conservation investment by providing the specified energy services at a cost that is less than the amount paid by the energy user to the energy service firm for the energy services. In addition, the energy service firm generally receives the tax benefits (i.e. depreciation and investment tax credits) associated with ownership of the conservation improvement. The energy service firm may finance the conservation improvement from its own corporate resources, or may syndicate the investment to other investors (e.g. through a limited partnership).

As in a shared-savings agreement, the energy service firm is fully responsible for maintaining the conservation improvement during the term of the energy service agreement, which typically ranges from 6 to 12 years. At the end of the service agreement the energy user generally has the option of renewing the agreement or purchasing the conservation improvement.

A variable payment loan differs from the three preceding financing arrangements in that the external funds are provided through debt rather than through an equity-orientated financing, and ownership of the conservation improvement accordingly rests with the energy user.

The specific structure of a variable-payment loan depends on the willingness of a creditor to accept an uncertain debt retirement stream. Under a typical structure, the conservation financing organization or other creditor evaluates the conservation opportunities at an energy user's facility. For economically attractive opportunities the creditor extends a loan to cover a substantial share (e.g. 80-100%) of the cost of installing the conservation improvement. The creditor and energy user then agree on a formula for estimating the cost of energy that the energy user would incur without the improvement. The energy user agrees to pay the creditor a loan payment in each period equal to a fraction (e.g. 75%) of the energy cost savings in a period. The savings equal the difference between the projected energy costs without the improvement and the actual energy costs. In addition, the loan agreement specifies a minimum loan payment, which is usually the payment required to retire the loan in 1.5-2 times longer than the repayment period that would occur if the improvement performs to expectations in achieving energy savings.

A limited term, guaranteed-payback loan is similar to the variable payment loan. However, a key difference with the variable-payment loan, is that the creditor in a limited-term, guaranteed-payback loan accepts the risk that a conservation improvement may not achieve payback within a specified period. Thus, the creditor shares directly in the risk of the technical and economic performance of the project.

Third-party financing involves the packaging of both technical aid and the necessary funding for energy efficient investments by an outside company. This method is has been studied by international institutions such as the Commission of the European Communities. If the market potential for third party financing is as large as estimated by the Commission, to achieve the global energy saving target of 70% by 1995, endorsed by the EC Council of Ministers, would require an investment of US$ 50 billion in the industrial sector, and would save 42 million tonnes of oil.

When the improvements have been installed, the new level of energy consumption will be compared to the 'baseline' consumption previously agreed, and energy cost savings computed. How exactly these savings are used to repay the energy service company depends upon the exact nature of the arrangement used by the two parties. Common types of arrangements are shared-savings contracts; contracts where 100% of the savings go to the energy service company until the project is paid off; and arrangements where the energy user is given a guaranteed cost saving on the previous energy bill.

Normally the equipment installed through the energy performance contract remains the property of the energy service company until the contract period has ended. If the contract has been successfully concluded, the equipment can either be transferred at no cost, or in some cases, the ownership is transferred to the energy user from the outset.

The innovative financing arrangement described above could be one of the main market shares of the actual business partner by assisting countries in transition to flow the capital into conservation investments that might otherwise go unfunded.

However, using these financing arrangements requires that financial institutions be able to evaluate the technical and economic risks associated with energy-related investments. In addition, the institutions must be willing to assume certain risks associated with the innovative financing arrangements. In return for accepting these risks, the creditors can expect commensurately higher returns than might be obtained by offering conventional loans to finance energy-related investments. The government of the "target" country can play various roles in promoting the development of the necessary financial infrastructure and the use of these innovative financing arrangements.

Government Roles

The most direct public-sector role to assist in promoting use of innovative financing arrangements for energy-related investments would be to form a publicly-chartered finance corporation that would be authorized to engage in any of the financing activities discussed in the preceding section. This corporation would be initiated with public capital. However, after a period of start-up operations, the corporation would be able to gain access to private capital and perhaps become completely independent of government support.

Another government role would be to sponsor demonstration of the financing arrangements in the economies in transition. Such demonstrations would be conducted jointly by a public agency and a private organization (e.g. a commercial bank, investment bank, or utility firm). The public would provide technical assistance in identifying appropriate investment opportunities and in structuring the financing arrangements. The government might also guarantee the return of capital for the projects or provide other incentives if such incentives were needed to entice private sector participation in the demonstrations. Demonstration programs have been helpful in encouraging the use of energy-saving technologies and innovative methods for financing investments in conservation technologies.

Country Case Studies

ENERGY AND ENVIRONMENT:
THE PATH OF COEXISTENCE
FOR THE CSFR

Jaroslav MAROUŠEK
Executive Director,
SEVEn
The Energy Efficiency Center
Prague

1. FOREWORD

The Czech and Slovak Federal Republic (CSFR) is an industrialized country with nearly 16 million inhabitants and an area of 128,000 km^2. The country consists of two republics -- the Czech Republic and the Slovak Republic. (A brief Addendum to this paper, written after the Conference, outlines energy and environmental issues regarding the probable division of the CSFR into two sovereign republics.)

Unfortunately, the former system of central planning led to a poorly structured economy with a very high level of energy intensity. Industry was concentrated in heavy machinery. Steel production reached 1 ton per capita -- the second highest per capita production in Europe (after Belgium). In Communist ideology, the energy sector was denoted as a key strategic branch whose development had the highest priority. For every unit of generated GDP, the CSFR consumes twice as much energy as the average west European country. (Using current exchange rates, energy intensity in the CSFR appears to be four times higher than in west European countries. In this paper, comparisons are based on purchasing power parities. This method avoids distortions caused by the weak position of central and eastern European currencies.) In 1989, the CSFR consumed 3137 PJ of primary energy sources. This is equivalent to 200 GJ per capita, a figure that ranks among the highest in Europe.

2. ENVIRONMENTAL PROBLEMS RELATED TO ENERGY USE

The environmental devastation accompanying energy production in the CSFR is among the worst in Europe. The area with the greatest concentration of coal mines and coal-fired power plants, Northern Bohemia, is a wasteland, testament to the damage wrought by careless extraction and use of energy resources. The low quality of indigenous lignite and brown coal is to blame for the poor air quality in the area.   The many open cast coal mines have devastated the countryside.   The average life expectancy in the CSFR is 68 for men and 74 for women, significantly less than the west European average (72 and 79 years respectively).   The average lifetime of men in Northern Bohemia is about 63 years.   Studies of the health levels of the inhabitants of this area reveal an incidence of respiratory diseases 50 per cent higher than the national average.   While Northern Bohemia experiences the gravest environmental deterioration, there are many other damaged areas in the CSFR, such as the Ostrava region in Northern Moravia, the Vah River valley in Slovakia, as well as urban areas including Prague and Bratislava.

Specific Emissions t/km^2					
year	Solid particulates	SO_2	NO_x	CO	C_xH_x
Č S F R					
1985	10.7	21.8	7.8	9.7	1.5
1990	7.3	19.1	7.7	10.0	2.4
Czech republic					
1985	12.9	27.4	10.1	11.4	1.7
1990	8.0	23.8	9.4	11.3	2.9
Slovak republic					
1985	7.3	12.7	4.0	6.9	1.2
1990	6.2	11.1	5.0	8.2	1.6

Source: Životní prostředí FSÚ, ČSÚ a SSÚ, 1990 a ČHMÚ a SHMÚ, ČTIO, 1990

For the whole country, sulfur dioxide (SO_2) is one of the most important air pollutants; emissions grew sharply under central planning. Country-wide emissions went from 900,000 tons in 1950 to 3,150,000 tons in 1985. In 1988, emissions decreased slightly to about 2,800,000 tons, and have decreased further since. This fall, in part, has been the outcome of milder winters, which lowered coal consumption. More importantly, after 1989 the process of economic transformation led to a decline in industrial production, contributing strongly to decreased energy consumption. Expressed in kilograms, the CSFR currently emits about 102.3 kilograms of sulphur per person each year.

The main sources of SO_2 emissions are electric power plants and district heating plants burning solid fuels with a high sulphur content -- these combine to produce 79 per cent of total emissions. Home heating contributes about 7 per cent to the total, industry about 11 per cent, and vehicles with diesel motors burning high-sulphur oil add a further 3 per cent. Emissions are concentrated in cities and in areas with large power generating and industial plants. In Northern Bohemia, for example, emissions reach up to 117.6 tons/km^2.

Until the 1990s, only one large energy source in the CSFR was equipped with desulphurization equipment: the Soviet NIIOGAS system was installed at the Tušimice 2 electric power plant, but due to technical problems this system has never operated successfully. A dry additive system was installed last year at the Tisová 1 electric power plant (it should remove 30 to 40 per cent of SO_2 from the flue gas). The installation of desulfurization equipment is planned for more than ten other power plants under the Czech Energy Policy [4].

Sulphur dioxide emissions are by far the most commonly debated factor in atmospheric pollution. However, even though there is an unusually high concentration of sulphur dioxide, this factor in itself is not the most dangerous component of atmospheric pollution. Recent research has shown that the cumulative effect of exposing a living organism to several different hazardous materials is far more destructive than a simple total of the individual components would indicate. Thus, the biggest problem is the synergistic effect of many hazardous materials present in the CSFR's air. These include sulphur dioxide, nitrous oxide, carbon monoxide, hydrocarbons, and fly ash as well as air emissions of heavy metals and other toxic substances.

The emissions of particulates -- mainly fly ash -- were approximately 800,000 tons in 1950. Atmospheric pollution from solid emissions peaked in the 1970s (the level in 1970 is estimated to have been 1.94 million tons). During the 1980s, emissions levels decreased as filtering equipment was installed on many large sources and several of the most significant sources of solid emissions were retrofitted. In 1985, emissions were 1.37 million tons. However, this trend slowed after 1985 as existing filters began to wear out and their effectiveness decreased. The threat to the health of the CSFR's population by the most dangerous type of solid emissions -- fly ash -- remains, because plants mainly use electrostatic filters. Textile filters have only recently begun to be installed in small industrial sources.

Total nitrous oxide (NO_x) emissions for 1989 comprised roughly 1.1 million tons per year, or 73 kg per person (using NO_2 as a base for calculations). Nitrous oxide arises mainly from incineration at high temperatures, a process concentrated mainly in power production and energy (71 per cent), transport (22 per cent) and central and local heating (7 per cent). In the past two years, some statistics have shown an increase in these emissions, but estimates differ.

Total hydrocarbon emissions are estimated at 150,000 to 300,000 tons annually. The main sources are estimated to be industry (50 per cent), transport (30 per cent), and home heating (17 per cent). Polycyclical hydrocarbons are especially dangerous to human health because of their carcinogenic effects. Significant emissions come from chemical production and waste incineration when these processes are carried out at a sufficiently high temperature or where production facilities are not equipped with adequate waste gas treatment systems.

Carbon dioxide (CO_2) emissions -- arising mainly from burning low-quality solid fossil fuels -- amount to about 60.4 million tons annually (a figure based on fuel carbon content). the CSFR contributes approximately 1.1 per cent of total global CO_2 emissions, even though it comprises only 0.3 per cent of the world's population. These figures work out to approximately

4.1 tons per person each year, one of the world's highest levels. In comparison, the US and Canada emit about 4.4 tons per person annually, while in European countries (with the exception of former East Germany), the amount is much smaller -- 3.0 tons per person in Belgium, 2.9 tons in western Germany, 2.5 tons in the Netherlands, and 2.0 tons in France.

While the information available to Czechoslovak citizens about the state of their country's environment and the resultant effects upon public health has recently improved, it is still insufficient. The connection between energy production and global warming is still not presented as an important danger. The first study dealing with greenhouse gas reduction through energy efficiency in the CSFR was completed only in 1990 (and was funded by foreign assistance) [8].

Some air pollution originates in other countries. The former East Germany and Poland are probably the largest "exporters" of air pollution to the CSFR. For example, in the foothills of the Tatra Mountains almost 50 per cent of the acid depositions are estimated to come from foreign sources. Nonetheless, the CSFR is a significant "exporter" of hazardous emissions: total Czechoslovak "exports" are probably 20 to 60 per cent higher than "imports."

The CSFR has signed pan-European treaties to limit regional air pollution. In 1979, European countries signed the Convention on Long-Range Transboundary Air Pollution. One element was a Cooperative Programme for Monitoring and Evaluation of the Long-range Transmission of Air Pollutants in Europe, which established co-operative European air pollution monitoring. The 1985 Helsinki Protocol to the Convention committed countries to reduce SO_2 emissions by 30 per cent by 1993 from 1980 levels. The CSFR, however, may have difficulty reaching this target. The 1988 Sofia Protocol commits signatories to limit NO_x emissions to 1987 levels. It may be possible for the CSFR to fulfill this agreement if the share of automobiles with catalytic convertors increases.

3. ENERGY USE

Energy-related environmental problem stem primarily from the extensive use and poor quality of brown coal and lignite. Coal is the country's primary energy source -- in 1990, it made up 53 per cent of the Czechoslovak energy balance, compared with 18 per cent for oil, 15 per cent for natural gas, and the remainder from nuclear energy and hydroelectric energy.

Industry consumes half of all energy. Only one-third of energy is used for commercial and residential use. A comparison of energy consumption in industrial and non-industrial sectors shows the marked difference between the CSFR and western Europe: in western Europe, consumption centers on commercial and residential sectors. In the CSFR, industrial consumption dominates, and there is an even sharper difference regarding the consumption of electricity; industry alone consumes 60 per cent of electricity for end use.

The transition to a market-based economy has generated severe economic problems; as a result, domestic consumption of primary energy resources in the CSFR has been declining since the end of the 1980s. In 1990, consumption fell 3.7 per cent from 1989 levels, and in 1991 the decline continued by another 8.9 per cent.

GDP and Energy Trends: 1980 to 1991

	1980	1985	1989	1990	1991
GDP [bl.Kcs] (1984 prices)	...	664.8	730	727	611.4
GDP [bl US$] (purchasing power parities 1985 p.)	95.4	96.9	...	102.9	...
Primary Energy Sources - PES [PJ]	3015	3102	3137	3021	2752
- solid fuels	1870	1912	1792	1708	1152
- liquid fuels	793	684	633	553	447
- gaseous fuels	268	337	407	449	463
Gross Electricity Consumption [TWh]***	74.6	84.2	92	91.2	85.2
Energy Intensity PES/GDP [GJ/ths.Kcs]	...	4.67	4.3	4.16	4.5
Energy Intensity PES/GDP [GJ/ths.US$]	31.6	32	...	29.4	

*** This includes foreign imports and exports
Sources: Federal Statistical Office ČSFR, National Center for Economic Information Prague

The Structure of Electrical Energy Production

	1985		1989		1990		1991	
	TWh	%	TWh	%	TWh	%	TWh	%
Electricity TOTAL	80.6	100	89.2	100	86.7	100	83.4	100
Of that total:							56.5	56.4
Steam Plants	64.5	80.0	60.3	67.6	58.2	67.0	56.5	56.4
Hydro Plants	4.3	5.3	4.3	4.8	3.9	4.6	3.1	3.4
Nuclear Plants	11.8	14.6	24.6	27.6	24.6	28.3	23.8	29.4

Source: Electricity Dispatch Office of ČSFR, Prague

The future structure of electricity production is a subject of lively discussion in the CSFR. The right approach hinges on the question of how much energy will be necessary in the future. Obviously, improvements in electricity efficiency must be considered in conjunction with the question of energy production. In 1990, for the first time in many years, the CSFR experienced a decline in primary energy sources, accompanied by a decline in electricity consumption. The economic recession will lead to a continued decline. Most experts (including those working in the field of energy production) no longer contend that the CSFR is threatened by a shortage of electricity generation in the next decade.

The electricity sector must face a number of environmental issues. Those associated with the combustion of coal and lignite have already been described.

Another important issue is that the CSFR's nuclear power plants lack the containment equipment found at nuclear plants in Western Europe and North America. In addition, the storage of depleted radioactive fuel has recently become an problem. Formerly, the Soviet Union had agreed to collect spent fuel. The Russian Federation demands about US$ 1100 per kilogram of spent uranium collected for storage, which implies that US$ 60 million a year would be needed to send only the spent fuel of the Jaslovské Bohunice nuclear power plant. At this rate, the amount of spent fuel held in interim storage facilities would require US$ 565 million for disposal -- impossible to pay considering the CSFR's economic situation.

Another long-standing issue is the construction of a hydroelectric dam on the Danube River at Gabčikovo-Nagymaros on the Slovak-Hungarian border. The dam was originally envisioned as a joint project between the CSFR and Hungary. In 1977, the two countries signed an agreement to build the dam, and construction began in 1978. Hungary interrupted its part of the work in 1981, renewed it in 1983, questioned it again in 1988, and finally stopped its part of the project in May, 1989. For Hungarian environmentalists, this policy change was their first victory over the state's authority. In Slovakia, construction has continued and environmental opposition is weak. It is argued that stopping construction and dismantling the complex would not be feasible at this late stage -- "things done cannot be undone".

4. ENERGY POLICY AND LEGISLATION

The Czechoslovak Federal Energy Policy Principles set a goal of guaranteeing the dependable, economical, and environmentally sustainable supply of energy. Energy efficiency is mentioned in the second section of the principles, but a distinct priority is given to energy production and the deregulation of the energy sector in the spirit of the European Energy Charter. The Principles are not binding legislation, but a political document intended to serve as a guide for the energy sector, which is currently mostly government-owned. The ownership structure will be changed by the privatization process that commenced this year, but a decisive portion of shares in energy monopolies is likely to remain in government hands.

The price of energy in the CSFR has risen rapidly since 1989. In 1990 and 1991 there was a marked rise in wholesale energy prices, which reached levels close to the economic costs of production. Fuel and energy prices in CSFR Koruny (CSK) are shown below.

Prices for Fuel and Energy in
the Second Half of 1991 (for Industry)

Fuel Coal (including Ostrava)	932.7	CSK/t
Brown Fuel Coal	324.6	CSK/t
Coking Coal	1460.0	CSK/t
Coke	2058.0	CSK/t
Town Gas	1850.0	CSK/1000 cu.m.
Natural Gas	3350.0	CSK/1000 cu.m.
Heat (Average)	116.0	CSK/GJ
Electrical Energy (for Industry)	1470.0	CSK/MWh
Light Fuel Oil	4900.0	CSK/t
Heavy Fuel Oil	3000.0	CSK/t

The price the CSFR pays for imported fuel has also steadily increased in recent years. As of January 1, 1991, imports from Russia were based on global market prices and had to be paid for in convertible currencies (most importantly for crude oil).

One of the most important goals stated in the Energy Policy Principles is the elimination of all subsidies and other contributions to the energy sector (direct subsidies, indirect subsidies, and cross-subsidies between sectors) by 1995 at the latest. Beginning in 1993, all nuclear power plants will be required to begin to create a fund for the long-term storage of fuel and for the costs of their eventual decommissioning. The Principles also propose environmental charges on coal used for energy generation.

Price increases encourage energy efficiency, but additional measures are necessary. To support this objective, the Federal Ministery of Economy established a special department, the Federal Energy Agency, in 1991.

The Federal Principles provided a starting point for the formulation of individual Czech and Slovak Energy Policies. Each Republic has its own Energy Policy document, more detailed than the Federal Principles but generally based on them. Both Republics declare energy efficiency to be an important part of energy policy. However concrete proposals are focused primarily on investments for cleaner energy generation. The Czech Energy Policy has been influenced by the Czech Ministry for the Environment's suggestions for least cost planning, and state regulation of energy monopolies. The Policy, however, does not have the force of law. Slovak energy policy focuses on attaining energy supply self-sufficiency for Slovakia, and it is oriented more towards increased production.

In addition to the Federal Principles and Republics' Energy Policies, several new Federal laws are being prepared in the field of energy management:

- A comprehensive law for the energy sector. (This law sould create the basis for implementing energy policy, for establishing utility regulation, and for promoting energy efficiency.);
- A law on the production, distribution and consumption of electricity;
- A law on the production, distribution and consumption of gas;
- A law on the of production, distribution and consumption of district heating; and
- A set of laws to govern nuclear power.

Laws governing electricity, gas and district heating existed during the socialist period. The spirit of the new laws is remarkably similar to that of the old ones. For instance, the three new laws guarantee the legality of routing and constructing heating, electricity, and gas transmission systems on the property of third parties. They do not provide clear statements regarding the regulation of electric and gas utilities. It is quite likely that these laws will be discussed at length in Parliament.

5. ENERGY SUPPLY AND THE ENVIRONMENT

The current work of the Federal Committee for the Environment, the Czech Ministry of the Environment, and the Slovak Commission for the Environment, including preparing new legislation for environmental protection, represents substantial progress. Previously, activists in the environmental movement were imprisoned for making public information about the state of the environment. The Communist regime considered comprehensive information about the state of the environment and its effects on the health of the population to be state secrets.

As a result, the CSFR does not have any practical experience with environmental protection laws, even though they have existed formally for some time. For the effective use of legislation to protect the environment, it is necessary that laws meet two conditions:

- Laws must require sufficient reductions in environmental damages to protect the environment;
- The conditions set by law must be realistic and achievable in the time frame set.

The creation of the legislative framework for environmental protection was necessary, but it has in no way been sufficient to improve the relationship between the energy sector and the environment. Truly effective legislation can arise only by refining experience through an iterative approach to attaining policy goals.

The new legal limits for pollution emissions and discharges are similar to those in western Europe (a description of new environmental legislation can be found in Annex 1. Annex 2 details the air pollution limits).

One important issue to be resolved is level the of pollution fees and fines to be set in

Slovakia. A second issue is the clause granting a four-year grace period for adapting existing pollution sources to the limits stated in the new law. This exception should not be used as an opportunity for non-compliance. Legal pressure on environmental polluters has consisted mainly of a cost increase in those activities that are harmful to the environment. However, it is important that this pressure is not confined only to a rise in costs, such as those incurred in installing desulphurization equipment. The change in value relationships must start with a change in the very structure of economic activities. Moreover, this change can mean new opportunity for profits and consequent growth in the well-being of society.

At the beginning of the energy crisis in the 1970s, the phasing in of substitute sources of energy, mainly renewables, was seen as the path of the future. Analyses gauging the potential for renewable energy sources were conducted in the CSFR. Natural conditions exclude the large-scale use of wind power. Various estimates of the potential of solar collectors differed greatly. However, technicians now agree that only hydroelectric power and biomass energy can contribute to future energy demand in the CSFR, and each of these probably can provide only about one percent of the country's energy. Naturally, changes in energy prices and costs can lead to a reevaluation of these estimates. Nonetheless it is clear that renewable energy sources probably will not be a major alternative for the CSFR in the next twenty years.

One expected change that will reduce environmental damage is a shift in energy sources toward higher grade fossil fuels. The Federal Energy Policy estimates a rise in the share of natural gas up to 20 per cent in the year 2000, compared to 15 per cent in 1990, and a corresponding drop in coal consumption.

A significant step towards increasing efficiency in electricity production can be cogeneration of heat and power. In the past, extensive centralized district heating systems were constructed. Now, however, it will be necessary to minimalize losses in heat transmission and distribution networks. Greater decentralization of these systems can reduce the losses. Today's technology makes small cogeneration plants with a capacity of around 100 kW possible.

A great deal of effort has been and will be devoted to clean-coal technology. These efforts are hindered, however, by the extremely poor quality of domestic coal. As a result, the reliability of such technology is low, and it is expected that this technology will turn out to be quite expensive for our enterprises. Policy choices regarding coal use may also be influenced by commitments made under the Climate Change Convention signed at Rio.

6. PAST EXPERIENCES AND NEW OPPORTUNITIES FOR ENERGY EFFICIENCY

All energy use analyses of Central and Eastern Europe emphasize the low level of energy efficiency in the region. This is surprising considering the fact that, throughout the era of central planning, a lack of sufficient energy was considered to be hindering economic growth. Why were energy conservation measures not applied?

Under central planning, attention was focused on increasing energy production capacity rather than on conservation. Proposals to increase energy efficiency were not often implemented.

Energy conservation plans were established only when it was necessary to bridge the gap between energy demand and supply after all financial options for new energy sources had been exhausted. However, the sole reason for the existence of such plans was the need to show balanced energy flows in every five-year plan -- a requirement for each centrally planned economy. As a result, implementing energy conservation programs never had a high priority.

These experiences have influenced public opinion of energy conservation. The unsuccessful energy-saving programs that were announced in conjunction with every five-year plan since 1975 left a negative impression in people's minds. Under those programs, pressure was exacted from the center to implement the plans. This evoked a feeling in people that centralized dictates on energy were only a further means of strengthening control mechanisms and curtailing personal freedoms under the communist regime. People quickly learned to meet the demand for demonstrated savings by changing enterprise accounting reports rather than factory energy use, a phenomenon that further increased energy producers' conviction that energy savings programs were utterly useless.

The technical potential of energy savings is quite significant. As the table below illustrates, up-to-date energy efficient technologies could save a total of approximately 700 PJs if fully implemented. This is equivalent to approximately one-third of total end use consumption in 1990. Of course, energy efficiency measures need to be economically productive.

ENERGY SAVING POTENTIAL - TECHNICAL POSSIBILITIES IN INDUSTRY

	Savings (PJ/Year)
Switch from local coal heating to gas	30
Retrofitted boilers	10
Retrofitted furnaces	259
Non-iron metals	7
Iron Metallurgy	50
Construction materials	7
Paper and pulp industry	9
Glass industry	13
Chemical and petrochemical industry	46
Other industry	10
Secondary Energy Sources	350
TOTAL	701

Source: Energy saving potential in the CSFR's economy. SEVEn 1991

It remains as yet difficult to conduct an economic evaluation of energy efficiency potential because of changing prices.

Efficiency in electricity generation, distribution, and use needs to be emphasized. The significant potentials to reduce district heat and other types of fuel consumption are already widely recognized. However, it is generally assumed that current levels of electricity use must be maintained to ensure economic development. Thus, proponents of electricity savings are unjustly labelled as opponents of economic growth. Nevertheless, the potential for saving electricity is significant, especially in industry.

7. POLICIES FOR ENERGY CONSERVATION

The Federal government seems to be aware of the significance of energy efficiency, but it is difficult for energy policy to switch from a tradition of power plant construction to programs that encourage energy efficiency. Unfortunately, foreign assistance is very often focused on energy production, and efficient energy use is either a negligible part of these projects or is omitted.

The first foreign support for energy conservation was US AID's 1990 Energy Emergency Program for the CSFR. The focus of US AID's support, however, has been energy production, and its successful energy efficiency project has not been followed up. The PHARE Programme of the Commision of the European Communities has made important studies of the CSFR's energy sector, but the major subject has been the energy generation sector. This year, however, the PHARE Programme intends to devote about one-third of its energy funds to energy efficiency studies. The World Bank loans for the CSFR's energy sector (ENERGY I and II) are focused on clean energy production by installing scrubbers and refurbishing power plants, and have no component for end-use efficiency. Several other assistance programs are preparing energy projects, but none of these has energy efficiency improvement as a top priority.

Some domestic resources, however, have been available. The Federal government provided, in the spring of 1991, 500 million crowns for "State participation in the reduction of energy consumption in residential buildings." The project was intended to help citizens deal with the sharp increase in residential energy prices. There is no doubt the project was well designed and will be useful. Nonetheless, because they were managing such a project for the first time, the three government bodies implementing the project (the Federal, Czech and Slovak Energy Ministries) had difficulties apportioning the money in an optimal way. If the process could be repeated this year, the lessons from last year's experience would be invaluable. Unfortunately, government budget constraints are such that it is unlikely that the project will be repeated.

New approaches to overcoming financing and other economic barriers must be found. Least-cost planning, integrated resource planning, and similar techniques have recently begun to be considered. Least-cost planning enables energy producers to invest in energy conservation measures if they are to be more economical than supply-side measures. This approach could provide financing for energy efficiency, and studies for implementing this approach in the Czech and Slovak energy sectors are underway.

High European energy prices on the one hand and a high level of energy consumption on the other provide opportunities for the development of energy efficiency businesses. Recently, a new energy consulting industry has emerged. Energy service companies (ESCOs) have begun to identify energy saving opportunities in industrial plants and commercial buildings and propose equipment and process changes. In OECD countries, ESCOs finance the investments themselves, and take their profit from the energy costs saved at the plant. The CSFR needs a legislative base to enable ESCOs to undertake a similar role and share the profits resulting from investments in efficiency.

The most important condition for implementing energy efficiency is the removal of energy price subsidies and the calculation of externalities for various fuel sources. Energy prices for industry are close to western European levels. This is not the case for residential users, who pay a lower price. Nonetheless, these levels can encourage energy efficiency. Even though residential energy is priced two to three times lower than in Western countries, Czechoslovak salaries are at least 10 times lower that those in western Europe. Residential users are quite interested in improving their energy efficiency where possible.

One problem is that imported, energy-efficient appliances are very expensive for domestic consumers. If it were possible to produce such goods domestically, costs would be much lower. A potential solution would be joint ventures in producing energy efficient products.

8. CONCLUSIONS: AN ENERGY EFFICIENCY PATH

The road to sustainable development consists of many factors, but energy efficiency can play a key role in achieving both energy and environmental goals. Nonetheless, the required environmental policy and energy efficiency measures vary in the different sectors of the CSFR's economy.

Industry

An energy efficiency strategy should be built on several pillars:

- dissemination of information on energy efficient technologies;
- promotion of energy consultancy services;
- new methods for financing of energy efficiency (for example, energy savings and leasing);
- restructuring financial incentives so that investment in energy efficiency measures are not handicapped in comparison with energy production investment (as they can be with tax provisions that favor production investments); and
- support for research in energy efficient technologies.

We cannot predict what our industrial sector will look like ten years from now. However, we expect a significant shift in the industrial base towards less energy-intensive industry.

Transport

Now is the time to promote energy efficiency measures in this sector because transport infrastructure and motor vehicle use should grow quickly in the future. Thus,

- Public transportation should be supported in all areas where it can compete with private cars.

- Energy efficiency standards should be set, especially for automobiles. A general goal should be to adapt the "polluter pays" principle to transport. For example, low energy efficiency vehicles could be penalized by fees.

Residential and Commercial Sectors

The key barrier to energy efficiency investment in the residential area is the absence of home ownership. In this situation, the owner usually has no motivation to reduce energy consumption: energy costs are paid by the tenant. This landlord/tenant problem is found throughout the world. In the CSFR, it is compounded by the fact that the state, or state-owned enterprises, have owned most buildings. The privatization of apartments can begin to solve this problem, but this is only a start.

The measurement of heat consumption is critical to promoting energy savings. A regulation issued by the Czech Ministry of Economic Policy and Development in 1991 required meters for heat consumption in all buildings connected to district heating by the end of 1993, and in every apartment by 1996. The same measure was issued by the Slovak Ministry of Economy. There is, however, concern that the period for compliance is too short. On the other hand, there is no doubt that this measure will greatly encourage energy conservation by creating incentives for the consumer to use energy wisely.

Residential energy efficiency should also be supported by information and financing measures similar to those that support industrial conservation.

The transformation of the economy, the adoption of high-quality technology, the drafting of second legislation, and the privatization of the assets are challenges that the CSFR must meet. The most formidable barrier today is related to people's perceptions. The public is accustomed to a way of evaluating issues and to a way of behavior cultivated by the ideology of the omnipotence of science and technology and the absolute power of the state, an ideology which has led to the conviction that the individual has no real influence. This is related to the perception that the individual does not bear responsibility for future development.

As long as the average citizen persists in thinking that energy savings are an emergency measure for those who do not have enough money for energy, there is little hope for the success of energy conservation initiatives in any field. The increased use of energy savings technologies is not only something that must be undertaken by the CSFR, but also something that should be undertaken by all industrialised countries, in order to move toward sustainable development. No country has exhausted the possibilities for increasing energy efficiency. The CSFR is only an extreme case. If we succeed in reducing energy consumption as part of a transformation of society which encourages people to have an interest in and an appreciation of their environment, the CSFR could move to the opposite extreme.

We have to learn to preface every demand for new sources of energy with the question: "How are we using the energy that we already have? Do we really need more?" Every individual should cease to view energy efficiency as a symptom of poverty and see it instead as an approach that is synonymous with health, harmony, and a prestigious lifestyle. Other countries may currently have the luxury of choosing among different approaches. For the CSFR, however, the only hope for the future lies in the philosophy of energy conservation.

REFERENCES

1. *Principles of State Energy Policy.* Government of Czech and Slovak Federal Republic. Prague, 1991.

2. *Energy policy of Czech Republic.* Czech Ministry for Economic Policy and Development. Prague, 1992.

3. *Energy Plan for Slovak Republic through the Year 2005.* Slovak Ministry for Economy. Bratislava, 1991.

4. *Reconstruction Plan for Desulphurization in the Electricity Sector.* Czech Ministry for Economic Policy and Development. Prague, 1992.

5. *Principles of State Participation on Energy Conservation in Residential Area.* Federal Ministry of Economy. Prague, 1991.

6. Vrbová M. and Šimek J., *Law in Environment in CSFR.* Prague, 1992.

7. *State of the Environment in Czechoslovakia.* Federal Committee for the Environment. Prague, 1992.

8. Kolar S., Kostalova M., and Suk J., *Reducing Greenhouse Gases in Czechoslovakia.* Study sponsored by US Environmental Protection Agency. Washington, 1990.

9. Air Protection Law No. 309/1991. Federal Parliament. Prague 1991.

10. Law on Institutional Arrangement in Air Protection and Fees, No. 389/1991. Czech National Council. Prague, 1991.

11. *Czechoslovakia's Energy Balance for the Years 1989, 1990.* Federal Statistical Office. Prague, 1991 and 1992.

12. Law on Energy Economy (Proposal). Federal Ministry of Economy. Prague, 1992.

13. Proposal of Legal Principles for the Production, Distribution and Consumption of Electricity. Federal Ministry of Economy. Prague, 1992.

14. Proposal of Legal Principles for the Production, Distribution and Consumption of Gas. Federal Ministry of Economy. Prague, 1992.

15. Proposal of Legal Principles for the Production, Distribution and Consumption of Heat. Federal Ministry of Economy. Prague, 1992.

16. *International Economic Statistics.* National Information Center of Czech Republic. Prague, 1991.

17. Chandler W., Geller H. S., and Ledbetter M. R., *Energy Efficiency: A New Agenda.* Washington, 1988.

18. *Statistical yearbook 1991.* Federal Statistical Office. Prague, 1991

Annex 1. Legal Regulations in the Field of Environmental Protection in the CSFR

Environmental protection is specified by Article 21 of the National Constitution, which entrusts the Federal government with the following responsibilities:

- Legislation in Matters of Environmental Principles
- Legislation and State Inspection Responsibilities in Matters of Nuclear Safety
- The Creation of an Environmental Policy
- International Cooperation

The main government bodies involved in these duties are the Federal Committee for the Environment, the Czech Republic's Ministry of Environment, and the Slovak Republic's Commission for the Environment.

At the republic levels, State Funds for the Environment have been created. These funds are financed by environmental payments, fees, fines. They are used to implement projects and investments to protect the environment.

The main environmental laws affecting the energy sector are the "Law of the Federal Government on the Protection of the Environment" dated December 5th, 1991 and Federal Law 309/1991 Sb., on protecting the atmosphere against pollution.

The Law of Environmental Protection lists certain obligations to protect the environment. It declares that all actions on national territory must take into consideration potential environmental impacts. Persons who by their actions pollute or harm the environment or who use natural resources are obligated to ensure that environmental effects are monitored at their own expense and that possible consequences are known. There is an obligation to use caution in avoiding hazards and in minimizing the consequences of actions that affect the environment, to the extent of one's ability. Specific requirements in this regard will be administrated by the government.

The second piece of legislation -- Federal Law 309/1991 Sb. -- sets binding limits on air pollution levels for the entire country. While the two republics can make the limits stricter or decide to charge higher fines for pollution, they are not allowed to weaken the limits.
The principal difference between this law and the one it replaced is in the regulation of air pollution. The old law (35/1967 Sb.) was based on ambient standards. It allowed the use of high smoke stacks to reduce ambient pollution, and thus did not stop the growth of total emissions. In addition, the hazardous substances emitted from great heights (smoke stacks up to 300 m tall were constructed) were dispersed over great distances and deposited far from the Czechoslovak border. In contrast, the new law establishes binding emissions limits for different sources.

The new emissions limits should gradually halt the spread of air pollution over the next 5 years, during which requirements will be gradually tightened.

Federal legislation has set emissions limits for selected pollutants and sources. Table 1 shows the limits that apply to steady state systems for fuel combustion (electric power plants, heating plants, and heaters) with capacities greater than 5 MW. The general emissions regulations that are applied to other stationary sources are listed in Table 2.

Table 1: Emissions Limits for Selected Sources of Pollution

Type of Emission	Capacity [MW]	Emissions Limit [mg/m³]	Notes
Burning Solid Fuel			
Solid Materials	over 50	100	
SO_2	more than 300 50 - 300 5 - 50	500 1700 2500	w/out desulphur. 15% orig.emis. w/out desulphur. 30% orig.emis.
NO_x	more than 5	650 1100	calculated on NO_2 content <=For smelting boilers
CO	more than 50	250	
Organic materials	more than 5	50	calculated on the basis of carbon content
Burning Liquid Fuels			
Solid Materials	more than 50 5 - 50	50 100	
SO_2	more than 300 5 - 300	500 1700	w/out desulphur. 15% orig.emis.
NO_x	more than 5	450	calculated on the basis of NO_2
CO	more than 5	175	
Burning Gaseous Fuels			
Solid Materials	more than 5	100	
SO_2	more than 5	35	
NO_x	more than 5	200	calculated on NO_2 content
CO	more than 5	100	

Burning Municipal Waste[*]			
Solid Materials	w/ capacity up to 1 t. incinerated waste, limit on emissions applies to O_2 content of 17%	50	
Hydrogen Chloride		30	
Organic Compounds		20	calculated on C content
CO		100	
Solid Materials	w/ capacity over 1 t. incinerated waste, limit on emissions applies to O_2 content of 11%	30	
Hydrogen Chloride		30	
Organic Compounds		20	calculated on C content
SO_2		300	
NO_x		350	calculated on NO_2 content
Hydrogen Fluoride		2	
Heavy Metals		total 0,2 total 2,0 total 5,0	mercury, thalium, cadmium arsenic, nickel, chromium, cobalt lead, copper, manganese
CO		100	

[*] Special limits apply to the incineration of hazardous and other special wastes.

Table 2: Generally Applicable Emissions Limits

Type of emissions	Mass flow of polluting materials [kg/h]	Emissions limit [mg/m^3]	Notes
Solid Materials	less than 2,5 more than 2,5	200 150	
SO_2	more than 20	2.500	
NO_x	more than 10	500	calculated on NO_2 content; does not apply to select branches
CO	more than 5	800	does not apply to select branches

When burning several types of fuel, limits are applied on the basis of the dominant fuel in the mix.

Payments for polluting emissions are charged according to the Law of Legal and Physical Entities to sources of pollution that are classified as large, medium, or small. In the Czech republic, the amount paid by large sources of pollution (over 5 MW) is decided upon and collected by the Czech Environmental Inspectorate. The amount paid by medium-sized polluters (from .2 to 5 MW) is decided upon and collected by the regional government, and the amount paid by small polluters (under 0.2 MW) is decided upon and collected by governing bodies in the community.

According to the Czech National Committee's Law on the Administration of Atmospheric Protection and Payments, the annual payments for air pollution by the main hazardous substances are currently set as follows in CSFR korunys (CSKs):

Polluting Material	Rate [CSK/t]
Solid emissions	3,000
Sulphur Oxides	1,000
Nitrous Oxides	800
Carbon Oxides	600
Hydrocarbons	2,000

The basic payment is according to the quantity of the pollution released, based on data for the previous year, and the payment rate. The basic payment is increased by 50 per cent in the event that the source exceeds the emissions limits for a certain material.

Currently, there is a given period of time in which polluters are provided with an opportunity to install equipment to reduce hazardous emissions. The timetable for payments develops as follows:

30 % in 1992 and 1993;
60 % in 1994 and 1995;
80 % in 1996; and
100 % from 1997 on.

As long as the operator has begun to attempt to reduce hazardous emissions at the source, a 40 per cent payment rate will be allowed until the improvements are completed. Where specified conditions are not adhered to, air protection bodies will decide whether the operator should be held liable for the full amount of the payment, and can establish a time limit for compliance.

The annual amount of the payments for small air pollution sources will start at 10,000 CSK, and will increase in conjunction with the size of the source of pollution and the hazardousness of the pollution that it produces.

ADDENDUM
Energy and Environmental Issues and
the Imminent Division of the CSFR

The CSFR is going through turbulent political changes, which the elections in June 1992 accelerated. In the last two years, national feelings in Slovakia have increased, and the elections clearly revealed Slovak desires to transform the existing federation into a more open relationship between the two republics. In the end, the newly elected representatives of the Czech and Slovak Republics arrived at an agreement, in which it was established that the two republics would be independent as of January 1, 1993. As much as possible, the republics will attempt to preserve their economic ties, including a customs union and a common market with free movement of labor.

Splitting the country will not be easy, but it should not affect many of the economic activities proposed or in progress in the Czech and Slovak Federal Republic. Both of the republics have promised to assume all of the past obligations of the federation, and divide those obligations in a mutually agreeable manner, taking into consideration third party interests. In fact, most of the economic and administrative responsibilities have been transferred to the republic level over the last twenty years, and especially in the last two years. The federal government retains responsibility for only a small part of the country's administration.

This is also true for the energy sector. Federally owned power plants were transferred to the republic over the last two years, and all energy enterprises are now controlled at the republic level or have become independent. As already mentioned, the Federal Energy Policy Principles represent a political declaration, and it was up to the republics to decide whether they would follow them.

On the contrary, any Federal legislation that has been approved at the republic level will continue to be mandatory law. This means, for example, that the emissions limits described in Annex 2 will become law in the independent Czech Republic, because the Czech Parliament approved them last year.

The impending division of the country will neither provide easier solutions nor cause the relationship between energy and the environment to deteriorate further. Analyzing the current situation and proposing plans for sustainable development will remain an important issue for both independent republics. As many of the environmental issues have similar origins and histories, cooperation between the two independent states will be as useful in the future as it has been under the Federation.

Primary Energy Consumption
Per Capita in 1988

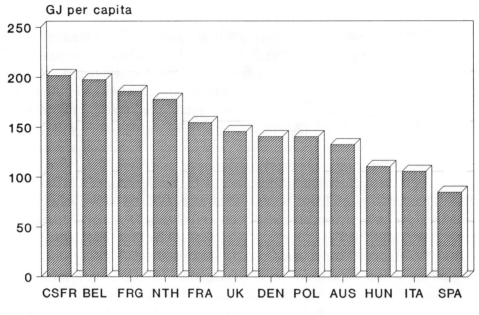

SEVEn

International Comparison of Energy
Intensity per GDP for the Year 1988

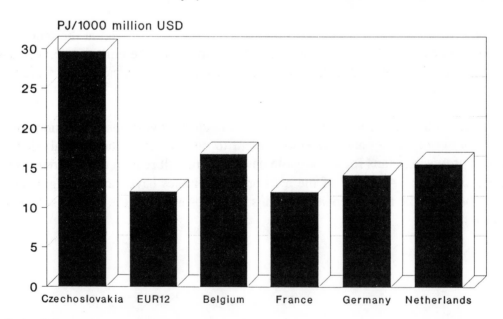

Note: GDP applies to constant prices
and purchasing power parity in 1985
EUR12 - European Community

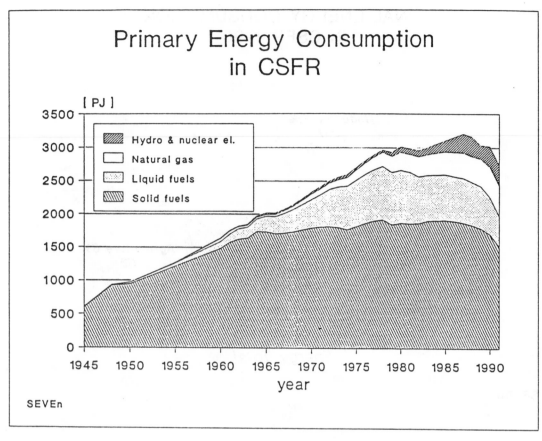

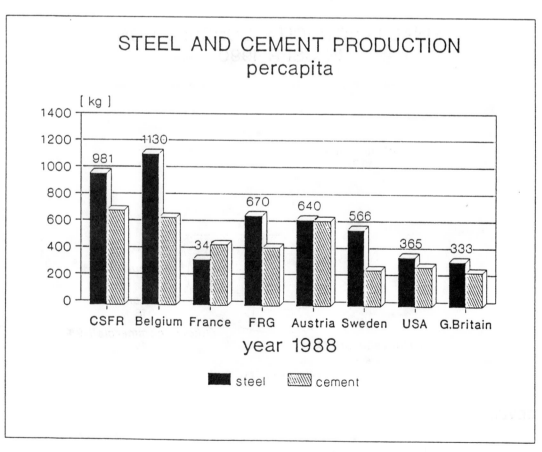

FINAL ENERGY CONSUMPTION
IN CSFR 1990

[PJ]

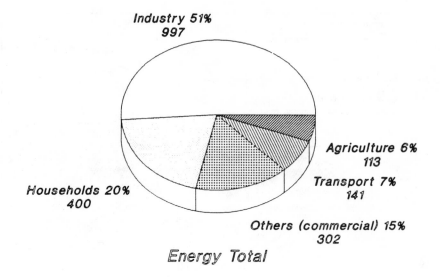

Industry 51%
997

Agriculture 6%
113

Transport 7%
141

Others (commercial) 15%
302

Households 20%
400

Energy Total

FINAL ELECTRICITY CONSUMPTION
IN CSFR 1990

[PJ]

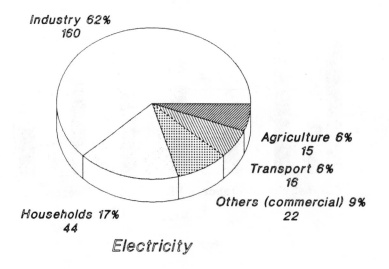

Industry 62%
160

Agriculture 6%
15

Transport 6%
16

Others (commercial) 9%
22

Households 17%
44

Electricity

PROSPECTS FOR ENERGY AND ENVIRONMENT POLICY INTEGRATION IN HUNGARY

Ian Brown
Béla Barner
Hungary-EC Energy Centre

INTRODUCTION

The purpose of this paper is to introduce the energy and environment situation in Hungary, and to describe the present outlines of the country's energy and environment policies.

This paper is not an "official" Hungarian paper, but the personal viewpoint of the authors. In addition, it is not comprehensive -- while we have strived to present all facts which we believe to be directly relevant for a background paper, this can only be a partial picture, for two reasons. First, this paper reflects the priorities and biases of the authors, and second, if the paper were comprehensive, it would have had to be as long as War and Peace. In the interests of readability, this paper is necessarily selective.

The paper is organised in three sections. Section one deals with the environmental situation and policies; section two considers the energy situation and policies; and section three focuses on the integration of energy and environmental policies in Hungary.

1. ENVIRONMENTAL PROBLEMS AND POLICIES

Hungary has a land area of 93 030 km^2, and a population of 10.6 million. The capital, Budapest, and its agglomeration account for 25 per cent of the total population. Hungary has inherited from the legacy of central planning an inefficient economy, and an environment that has, for most of the past 40 years, been neglected.

The State of the Environment

As in other countries of the region, energy-related environmental problems are a major source of concern in Hungary. Although water pollution, soil erosion, and solid waste are all serious environmental problems in Hungary, atmospheric pollution is the problem principally linked to energy use. Approximately 45 per cent of the population breathes polluted air, while 30 per cent breathe heavily polluted air. Air quality in approximately 12 per cent of the country falls far below World Health Organisation standards. High levels of major environmental problems. NO_x, SO_2, and particulate emissions to pose a threat to human health, especially in the heavily populated industrial area running from Lake Balaton northeast through Budapest to Miskolc.

The Ministry for Environment and Regional Policy has identified the following priority environmental problems:

- vehicle emissions;
- emissions of sulfur dioxide (SO2) and nitrogen oxides (NO_x) in highly industrialised areas; and
- emissions of SO_2 and NO_x from coal-fired power plants.

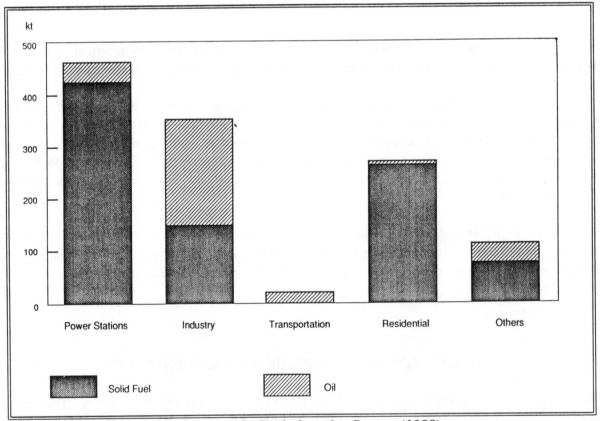

Figure 1. SO_2 Emissions by Sector (1988).
Source: IEA

In Hungary, SO_2 emissions are caused principally by the combustion of fossil fuels: 38 per cent of emissions are derived from electricity generation, 40 per cent from the services sector, and 22 per cent from the residential sector (see Figure 1). In the past 8 years SO_2 emissions have been reduced by 25 per cent as a result of a reduction in energy and electricity demand, due to the country's economic recession as well as structural changes in the economy.

Hungary has signed the Helsinki Protocol for the reduction of SO_2 emissions. This requires Hungary to reduce SO_2 emissions 30 per cent below the 1980 level (approximately 1.63 million tons), to about 1.14 million tons. In 1989, SO_2 emissions fell to 1.08 million tons, clearly below the limit.

The major contributors to NO_x emissions include: the transport sector (47 per cent of total

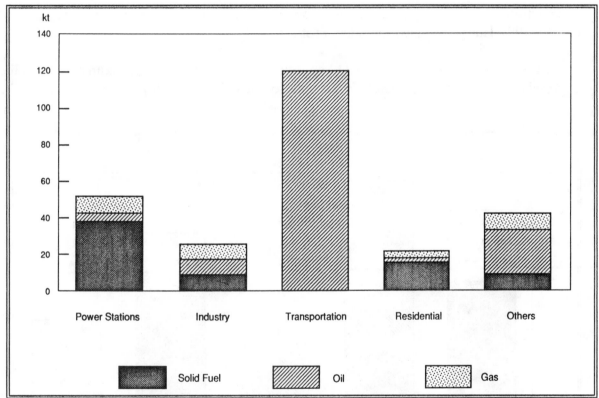

Figure 2. NO_x Emissions by Sector (1988)
Source: IEA

emissions) and heating and power stations (20 per cent) -- see Figure 2. Other industries and agriculture combined contribute about 20 per cent. Approximately 85 per cent of the transport related emissions are produced by road traffic. The principal sources of transport emissions are the poorly maintained diesel bus and truck engines, and the two-stroke engines of the Trabant and Wartburg cars manufactured in the former East Germany. Legislation promoting the use of catalytic converters on new cars and initiatives to reduce bus emissions have been introduced, but the expected market growth in private car ownership in the medium term is expected to raise

NO$_x$ emissions substantially.

Hungary has signed the Sofia Protocol, which specifies what NO$_x$ emissions be reduced to their 1987 level -- for Hungary, about 280,000 tons. In 1990 NO$_x$ emissions were 235,000 tons. Further decreases in emissions can be expected as more stringent domestic legislation is enacted. For example, the Government plans to require that all new western cars sold in the country be equipped with a catalytic converter.

Particulate emissions have dropped dramatically from 1980 to 1990 as a result of a programme to install electrofilters in power stations. Further emissions decreases are expected in 1992.

Volatile Organic Compound (VOC) emissions in Hungary were approximately 200,000 to 220,000 tons per year. Transport and oil refining activities are the main sources. The planned reconstruction of the country's largest oil refinery at Százhalombatta, should reduce emissions loads. In 1991 Hungary signed the VOC Protocol.

In 1990, total carbon dioxide (CO$_2$) emissions in Hungary were approximately 75 million tons, of which 38 per cent originated the combustion of solid fuels, 29 per cent from oil, and 20

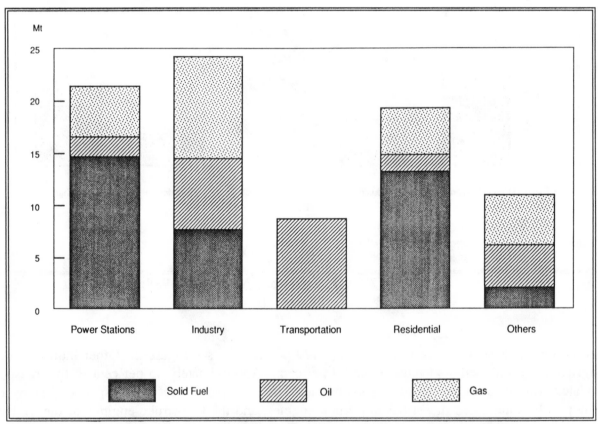

Figure 3. Carbon dioxide Emissions by Sector and Fuel (1988)
Source: IEA

per cent from natural gas.

Institutional Organisation

Environmental protection in the energy field is the joint responsibility of the Ministry for Environment and Regional Policy, and the Ministry of Industry and Trade. Within the Ministry of Environment, the Department of Air, Water and Soil Protection and the Department of Environmental Policy and Analysis are directly concerned with issues related to energy use and energy policy. Enforcement of regulations is the responsibility of the National Agency for Environmental Protection, which has 12 regional Environmental Inspectorates. The Ministry of Welfare is responsible for setting ambient air quality standards and monitoring air quality.

The Ministry of Industry and Trade (which oversees energy policy) has an environmental protection unit that is charged with integrating environmental considerations into energy and industrial policy.

Environmental Policies

Hungary's new environmental policy, developed by the Ministry for Environment and Regional Policy, has yet to be accepted by the Parliament. The Ministry's proposal is based on six principles:

1. Sustainable development

The long term goal of the government's environmental policy is to clean up the environmental problems left from the former centrally planned economic system, to improve air and water quality, to eliminate the soil degradation, and to relieve the current pressure on the environment and natural resources. Priority should be given to should reducing air pollution, managing toxic wastes, and developing waste water treatment capabilities. Under the policy, Hungary intends to start moving towards the goal of sustainable development in its medium term policies (however, the environment policy does not define "sustainable development"). For example, economic restructuring economy should follows paths that lead to environmental improvements.

2. Prevention of Environment Damage

High priority would be given to the prevention of environmental damage, with the widespread use of environmental impact assessment being promoted.

3. Integration of environmental concerns into economic policy

Environmental protection should be integrated into industrial and economic sector policy making.

4. International cooperation

As a result of the country's geographical position, the quality of the domestic environment is significantly affected by external produced pollution and high priority is given to international cooperation in environmental protection.

5. Government Responsibility to Ensure Environmental Protection

This is recognised as a responsibility of the State, and one which requires government intervention in market processes, where justified and necessary.

6. Public participation

Public participation in formulating and implementing environmental policy needs to be improved. Public awareness of the effects of environmental damage should be improved.

As in other countries of the region, the implementation of environmental policies is rather slower than their development. A key element needed is Parliamentary enactment of new environmental legislation -- Parliament is expected to pass a new environmental law in 1992. Clearly, this new law will not, by itself, solve Hungary's environmental problems, but it will provide a framework for environmental monitoring, regulation, and public participation.

2. ENERGY ISSUES AND POLICIES

Hungarian energy policy, as presented by the Government to the Parliament in June 1991, is based upon five strategic elements:

- diversification;
- improving energy efficiency;
- liberalisation of prices;
- environmental protection; and
- reorganisation and regulation.

These elements are described below in turn.

Diversification

Hungary has relied heavily on energy imports (see Table 1). In the past, energy imports from the former Soviet Union were priced below world market levels, and were paid for on a barter basis. The move to world market prices and payment in dollars has significantly increased the cost of energy imports from the CIS. For these reasons supply diversification is a cornerstone of the new Hungarian energy policy.

Oil Sector

Until 1990 all oil imports came from the Soviet Union, via the "Friendship pipeline." In 1989, Soviet crude oil imports accounted for 80 per cent of supplies, with domestic production accounting for the remaining 20 per cent. Because of both price increases and supply problems, in 1990 Hungary purchased around 10 per cent of its oil needs (0.8 million tons from a total

Table 1. Evolution of Total Primary Energy Supply (Mtoe)
Source: IEA

	1975	1980	1985	1989	1990
Indigenous Production	14.27	15.12	16.95	16.69	14.64
Coal	7.34	6.94	6.28	5.30	4.46
Crude Oil	2.00	2.03	1.96	1.91	1.88
Natural Gas	4.31	5.09	5.84	4.72	3.81
Nuclear	-	-	1.68	3.62	3.57
Other	0.62	1.06	1.19	1.14	0.92
Imports	11.68	15.36	15.35	16.23	15.49
Exports	0.57	1.30	1.76	2.25	1.69
Stock Building	-0.44	-0.45	-0.43	-0.27	-0.15
TPES	24.94	28.73	30.11	30.40	28.29
Import % of TPES	46.83%	53.46%	50.98%	53.39%	54.75%

consumption of around 8 million tons) from other sources, imported through the Adria pipeline from the Adriatic. In 1991, Hungary was expected to increase non-CIS oil purchases up to 2 million tons, but the war in Yugoslavia, and the consequent closing of the Adria pipeline, blocked this plan. Nonetheless, over the next several years, Hungary intends to diversify her oil supplies, and thus reduce reliance on imports from Russia.

Gas Sector

Hungarian imports of natural gas is diversifying previous dependence on the USSR to other suppliers. Natural gas consumption is forecast to increase, but domestic production has been declining, falling from a peak production of 7.5 billion cubic metres in 1985 to 4.9 billion in 1990. By 2000, it is estimated that imports will account for 75 per cent of natural gas supply, so diversifying suppliers is important to ensure security. These trends pose major risks for Hungary's security of supply. To diversify natural gas imports, the Government is considering several options for the construction of new pipelines. In the short term, the government is evaluating a link with Austria, which would connect the country to the western European gas transmission network.

Electricity Sector

Nuclear power has played an increasingly important role in Hungary's electricity production, and now accounts for over 48 per cent of power supply (See Table 2). Some of Hungary's nuclear-generated electricity comes from the CIS, although electricity imports have been substantially reduced in recent years: in 1990 imports totalled 11,147 GWh, or 28 per cent of Hungary's total demand, while in 1991 imports were only 6200 GWh. In addition, about one-quarter of Hungary's electricity production comes from the combustion of oil and natural gas, fuels the country imports. To diversify her electricity supplies, Hungary is actively pursuing connection with the UCPTE (Union for the Co-ordination of Production and Transmission of Electricity) electricity network of western Europe.

Table 2. Distribution of Fuel Inputs to the MVM System
(in Petajoules and percent of Total)

	1985	1986	1987	1988	1989	1990
Lignite	46.5	44.5	45.8	36.9	35.8	35.5
Brown Coal	75.4	77.6	79.2	79.3	75.3	72.8
Hard Coal By-products	14.8	18.7	18.3	17.5	16.7	16.1
Fuel Oil	59.8	59.8	48.4	26.3	20.4	18.6
Natural Gas	85.0	92.1	77.8	74.8	82.0	73.8
Nuclear	72.7	80.2	119.5	147.3	151.0	148.4
Total (PJ)	354.2	372.9	389.0	382.1	381.2	365.2
Lignite	13.1%	11.9%	11.8%	9.7%	9.4%	9.7%
Brown Coal	21.3%	20.8%	20.4%	20.8%	19.8%	19.9%
Hard Coal By-products	4.2%	5.0%	4.7%	4.6%	4.4%	4.4%
Fuel Oil	16.9%	16.0%	12.4%	6.9%	5.4%	5.1%
Natural Gas	24.0%	24.7%	20.0%	19.6%	21.5%	20.2%
Nuclear	20.5%	21.5%	30.7%	38.6%	39.6%	40.6%

Improving Energy Efficiency

Hungary's energy efficiency is considerably lower than that of western European countries. For example, in 1989, Hungary used nearly four times as much energy to produce a unit of output as OECD Europe (see Table 3). In general, Hungary's energy performance is characterised by inefficient production and energy use, low value-added outputs, and a high share

Table 3. Energy Intensity in Hungary and Other OECD Countries
(1989 Index, based on OECD Europe = 1.00)

	TPES/Capita	TPES/GDP
Hungary	0.86	3.91
OECD Europe	1.00	1.00
Western Germany	1.39	1.13
France	1.21	1.04
Italy	0.85	0.74
Austria	1.01	0.90
Portugal	0.49	0.86

Source: IEA

of energy intensive industries. There are substantial opportunities for energy efficiency improvements in the industrial and residential sectors.

Industrial Energy Use

This is characterised by the high share of energy intensive industries and by the low level of energy efficiency, a situation which is partly the result of the previous low energy prices. Other causes are the low levels of plant maintenance, and the lack of any incentives for industry either to use energy efficiently or to strive for energy efficiency improvements.

The energy efficiency of Hungarian industry in Hungary can be improved in two ways: first, by the restructuring of industry away from the old energy intensive basic industries towards less energy intensive, light industries and services, and second, by improving energy efficiency in industry.

Industry restructuring has commenced -- a consequence of the transition to a market economy. In 1990, production in heavy industry declined by 10 per cent, with particularly large declines in production from the very energy intensive metallurgical (-19 per cent) and fertiliser (-20 per cent) industries. This trend continued in 1991. Overall industrial output has been declining -- by 10 per cent in 1990 and 1991 -- leading to reductions in energy use.

The State Authority for Energy Safety (AEEF) has estimated that, in Hungary's transition to a market-based economy, two-thirds of the total reduction in energy intensity will be caused by industrial restructuring, and one third by increases in energy efficiency. It is this latter third which will be difficult to achieve, and where international assistance is required.

Previously, it was mandatory for industries to appoint energy managers. Energy efficiency was assisted, in theory, by this law, and by a scheme of grants and loans for energy efficiency, under which considerable sums were spent. Unfortunately, this law has hampered current efforts to improve energy efficiency. The number of energy managers has declined, and the combination of a misuse of the grant and loan funds and poor results of energy efficiency programs under the socialist regime has diminished the credibility of the government energy efficiency efforts. Experience in OECD countries suggests that the present policy -- which relies solely on pricing to bring about energy efficiency improvements -- is unlikely to succeed. A lack of access to capital and a lack of information are among the barriers that will likely restrict the response of industry to the higher prices.

Policies are required to address these barriers to energy efficiency. The Hungary-European Community Energy Centre plans to offer training for energy managers, revive a professional "energy managers movement," and offer information programmes. These efforts will be useful, but will not be sufficient. Improving access to finance is a key if energy efficiency in industry is to be improved. Third-party financing, where the savings are used to repay the investment costs, is one option to find energy efficiency investments. The EBRD and the World Bank could play important roles in this respect.

<u>Residential Energy Use</u>

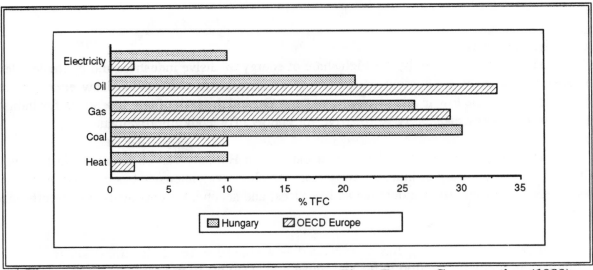

Figure 4. Residential and Commercial Sector Final Energy Consumption (1989)

The structure of energy use in the residential sector is considerably different from that in western Europe. Coal and particularly district heating provide a very high share and electricity use is low compared to western standards. Low ownership levels of domestic appliances, as compared to western Europe, and the smaller size of the electricity intensive commercial sectors are the main reasons for these differences. Figure 4 shows the final consumption by fuel type for Hungary as compared to OECD Europe.

The housing stock in Hungary is made up of 3.6 million dwellings, of which approximately 60 per cent are single family houses and 40 per cent are apartments. Most

Table 4. Energy Intensity in the Residential Sector (toe/000 m²)

	Total Final Consumption	Electricity Consumption
Hungary	24.2	2.5
United States	18.7	5.8
Italy	17.9	2.4
Sweden	21.3	8.0
United Kingdom	21.9	4.4

Source: IEA

apartments are connected to district heating networks - 635,000 in total, while another 170,000 have central heating within the building. A comparison of residential energy intensity is provided in Table 4.

There is a significant potential for improved energy efficiency in the residential sector, particularly in district heating systems and in apartment buildings. Around 1.2 million apartments were constructed between 1955 and 1985 (one third of the total housing stock as of 1990) -- many of these were built by the prefabricated "panel" method. A study evaluating the energy saving possibilities for panel housing concluded that savings of up to 35 per cent were possible, with a maximum payback of 10 years.

Most of the district-heated apartments of this panel-construction type have neither any form of metering nor any form of heat control. Heating costs are calculated on an average cost per cubic metre of the apartment, while the "thermostat" in such apartments is the window. In approximately 125,000 district-heated apartments, the heating is supplied by a single pipe system which does not allow for any form of temperature control. While significant energy savings could be made in this type of dwelling, it would require the wholesale transformation of the heating system, in which is not an option in the short term. The low cost of initial construction was the primary motivation for building panel type apartment buildings. Insulating such buildings can be expensive, with long payback times. The capital for such investments is unlikely to come from the individual apartment owners, and is not available from the Hungarian state.

There is also a significant potential for improved energy efficiency in the production of district heating. An assessment of district heating for industrial consumers in Budapest indicated that the network losses may be between 30 and 40 per cent. In Budapest, the district heating company is replacing the main distribution system. Considerable energy savings are likely if other district heating companies in Hungary followed suit.

There is also scope for increased efficiency in heat production through the upgrading of existing thermal plants and through the construction of combined heat and power plants. Plans under consideration by MVMT, the electricity board, suggest that new plants, including combined cycle gas turbines, could provide up to 700 MW in new capacity.

Price Liberalisation

One reason for Hungary's low level of energy efficiency is energy pricing. In the past, energy costs did not reflect the full economic cost of production, particularly for household consumers. In 1989, the prices of coal, electricity, and district heating for residential users accounted for only one-third of the real cost of production.

As part of the transition to a market economy, energy prices increased substantially in 1990 and in 1991, and subsidies were eliminated. For coal and oil products, prices are already at world market levels, while petrol prices are around the average level for Western Europe (but disposable incomes are much lower). Subsidies for gas and district heating were phased out in

Table 5. Energy End-Use Prices

	1987	1988	Nov-90	Nov-91
Households				
Natural Gas (Ft/m3)	2.9	3.2	5.1	7.8
Heating Oil (Ft/l)	8.0	8.0	11.0	21.5
Electricity-day (Ft/kWh)	1.27	1.60	2.45	3.70
Coal (Ft/t)	747	615	1,311	3,620
Coal briquettes (Ft/t)	1,137	1,089	2,004	6,460
Natural Gas (Ft/GJ)	87	94	150	230
Heating Oil (Ft/GJ)	228	230	316	617
Electricity-day (Ft/GJ)	353	447	681	1,028
Coal (Ft/GJ)	47	38	82	226
Coal briquettes (Ft/GJ)	57	55	102	302
Industry				
Gas(Ft/GJ)	144	148	359	281
Coal (Ft/t)	1,085	1,177	1,706	1,686
HFO (Ft/t)	4,340	4,280	8,950	7,606
Electricity (Ft/kWh)	2.47	2.82	3.80	5.06

April 1992. Further large increases in the tariffs for electricity and district heating for residential consumers are likely.

Environmental Protection

The Ministry of Environment and Regional Development and the Ministry of Industry and Trade are jointly responsible for common energy and environment matters. Hungary's Energy Policy states that "the minimisation of environmental damage" should be an achieved. The environmental protection unit of the Ministry of Industry and Trade is charged with the integration of environmental considerations into energy and industrial policy.

Restructuring and Regulation

As part of the move towards a market economy, efforts are underway to restructure the energy industries. Formerly, both oil and gas industries, (in all activities -- production, transmission, refining, distribution and marketing) were part of one giant "trust," the OKGT, which was the largest enterprise in Hungary in terms of sales. Similarly, the electricity industry was characterised by a single state-owned entity, the Hungarian electricity trust.

Both trusts have been reorganised into a number of joint stock companies. The reorganisation of the oil and gas industries is well underway. Several companies now undertake natural gas distribution, while remaining oil and gas activities have been reorganised, with a number of subsidiaries being established within the framework of a holding company, called MOL. A number of peripheral activities (machinery production and fabrication) have been separated from the holding company.

The electricity industry is now controlled by a two tier holding company. At present, the generating stations and the regional distribution companies are owned by the holding company, MVM, but act as individual companies. The transmission grid belongs directly to the holding company, including power despatch control. At least for the medium term, the national government plans to own most shares in MVM, but a proportion are being given to municipalities.

Privatisation is also being considered in the energy sector, although the issues of restructuring and privatisation are being handled separately. The government has decided that for industries of "strategic importance," including energy, the government will retain a minimum 51 per cent of shares.

Local government will play a much more important role in the ownership of energy industries than it has in the past. Shares in the electricity distribution companies will be given to municipalities, and the district heating companies are being transferred from central government to local government ownership.

Transparent regulation of the newly established energy companies is crucial. The Hungarian government has yet to formulate detailed plans, but it is an area whose importance is certainly recognised. The government intends to create a new regulatory regime to control monopolies operating in a market economy.

New legislation for the energy sector is being developed, based upon the framework of the 1991 Concession Law, which governs oil, gas, and coal exploration. The new Mining Law has already been submitted for approval by Parliament. A new Power Act is under final codification before its initial submission to the Government. It is envisaged that both of these substantial legal regulations will be enacted by Parliament this year. A new law for the natural gas sector is also under preparation.

3. POLICY INTEGRATION: DOES IT EXIST? IS IT POSSIBLE?

Several conclusions can be drawn from this brief review of environment and energy policies:

1. As the IEA report on Hungary has noted, "The Government lacks a coherent statement of environmental policy in the energy sector." The environmental policy is a good statement of general intentions, but it has yet to be implemented in substance.

2.   The establishment of a unit in the Ministry of Industry and Trade responsible for integrating environmental protection into energy policies is commendable, but institutional coordination is still weak. Environmental policies and energy policies have not been integrated at an early stage.

3.   Significant institutional and legal change is underway, but the focus of these changes, and the attention of energy policy makers, is on improving the supply side of the energy equation. Improving energy efficiency is a vital task for Hungary, yet the organisation of energy efficiency programmes remains weak.

The Hungarian economy is highly energy inefficient. Changes are needed both in technology and behavior. Improving energy efficiency requires government support, and a fundamental change in public attitudes. In Hungary, energy conservation is often regarded as being synonymous with poverty, and until the idea that energy efficiency is a part of an advanced economy takes hold, then progress in improving energy efficiency will be slow.

Energy security and organisational changes are the focus of the changes now being underway in the energy sector in Hungary. Policy makers are concentrating on supply issues without similar attention to demand management. There remains much to do to integrate energy and environment policies.

Policy integration between energy and environmental policies is neither a reality, nor is it impossible. In Hungary, efforts have been made to integrate these two policies, although more can be done. The success of some EC countries in integrating energy and environment policies -- for example, the Netherlands -- offers valuable lessons for Hungary.

A REVIEW OF
ENERGY AND ENVIRONMENTAL POLICIES
IN POLAND

Slawomir M. Pasierb

Executive Director
The Polish Foundation
for Energy Efficiency

1. INTRODUCTION

This paper aims to summarize current understanding and concerns about environmental and energy policy goals in Poland. It does not claim to be a comprehensive evaluation of energy and environmental policy. The paper is based on the author's own work and experiences: it may present personal interpretations open to argument, but the intention is to provide a basis for discussion by raising specific questions and issues.

2. POLAND'S ENVIRONMENTAL POLICY GOALS

Government Goals

The Government of Poland has prepared a national environmental policy, developed and coordinated by the Ministry of Environmental Protection, Natural Resources and Forestry (MEPNRF), to achieve significant improvements in environmental protection over the short, medium, and long term. These improvements are to achieved through the modernization of the economic sectors that present the greatest threats to the environment (specifically, energy production, industrial processes and transportation), as well as implementing measures to achieve sustainable development goals in sectors that directly use natural resources -- including mining, agriculture, forestry. The policy's energy-related objectives are listed in Box 1.

The environmental policy covers both specific and potential activities as the long neglect of environmental protection, together with the limited resources available, requires that priorities are set for environmental protection goals. The Ministry has divided policy actions into three time frames. Near-term priorities should be started as soon as possible and should begin to be achieved over the next three to four years. Medium-term priorities should begin to reverse degradation of the environment; their implementation by the year 2000 should move Poland closer

---

Box 1. Energy-Related Objectives of Poland's Environmental Policy

1. Reduce environmental impacts from energy production and use:
   - Increase energy efficiency in all sectors of the national economy, encouraged by market mechanisms, taxation policy and administrative regulations;
   - Improve coal quality through deep enrichment, the removal of pyrite and the production of smokeless fuel;
   - Modernize combustion techniques in coal-fueled power plants and switching to improved firing systems, such as fluidized bed boilers and low emission burners or utilizing emission-reducing additives in combustion;
   - Gradually change the current structure of prime energy carriers toward carriers less dangerous to the environment;
   - Installing dust and gas reduction equipment on power plants and maintaining the proper use of this equipment; and
   - Promote renewable sources of energy.

2. Encourage environmentally beneficial industrial restructuring that will:
   - Reduce industrial demand for energy, raw materials and water, with a commensurate reduction in pollution emissions;
   - Lead to the dissemination of cleaner technologies and of pollution prevention;
   - Create a domestic environmental protection equipment industry;
   - Install and maintain pollution control equipment where needed.

3. Reduce transport-related pollution:
   - Improve public transport systems and promote "clean" transportation;
   - Encourage the use of low-emissions motor vehicles;
   - Supply fuels that meet international standards for pollutant content;
   - Convert or remove engines requiring leaded petrol;
   - Manufacture lead-free petrol and introduce catalytic converters.

4. Improve water resources use and management:
   - Reduce allowable concentrations of pollutants discharged into surface and groundwaters and introduce progressively increased charges for waste discharge to improve the quality of surface and deep groundwaters;
   - Strengthen economic instruments in order to enforce efficient use of water, minimize water losses in the pipe network, and encourage the recirculation of water in industrial processes and in energy production.

5. Rationalize mining and the use of mineral resources:
   - Introduce a comprehensive geological and mining law that guarantees a rational management of non-renewable mineral resources;
   - Encourage the modernization of processing facilities and the introduction of new technologies to enrich and purify minerals.

---

to western European standards, and prepare the way for entry into the EC. (Poland's Near- and Medium-Term priorities are listed in Box 2). Long-term priorities, whose introduction may not take place until 2020, would move toward the goal of sustainable development; these are listed in Box 3.

Box 2. Poland's Near and Medium-Term Environmental Policy Priorities

Near Term Priorities

- The closure or change of the most dangerous manufacturing plants. This refers to the 80 highly polluting industrial plants included on a national list, as well as up to 500 other plants that will be identified by local governments;
- Implementation of a coal quality improvement program (pyrite removal from sulfur and increase in calorific value, and the adoption of world standards for coal used for domestic purposes;
- Energy efficiency improvements to reduce air pollution;
- Noticeable reduction in dust and gas emissions, particularly in Upper Silesia and in other regions where environment and public health is threatened.

Medium-Term Priorities

1. Air Quality

- Reduce SO_2 emissions by 30% by 2000 compared to 1980 levels (i.e. from 4.2 million tons per year, down to 2.9. million tons);
- Reduce NO_x emissions by 10% by 2000 (from 1980's level of 1.5. million tons per year);
- Reduce dust emissions by about 50% from industrial sources;
- Reduce emissions of volatile organic substances, hydrocarbons, heavy metals and other air pollutants;
- Take measures to counter global climate change (i.e. reduce emissions of CO_2 and other greenhouse gases, as well as ozone-destroying substances.

2. Water Resources

- Reduce pollutant discharges from industry and municipalities into rivers by 50 per cent -- reducing the levels of untreated industrial wastewater and municipal sewage from 0.5 billion and 1.2. billion m^3 respectively, at present, to 0.1 billion and 0.6 billion m^3 by the year 2000; and increasing the effectiveness of wastewater treatment systems (biological and chemical) in the overall sewage treatment from the present 48 per cent to 70 per cent in the year 2000;
- Reduce saline water discharges from coal mines into surface waters by 50 per cent.

3. Waste Management and Other Issues:

- Increase waste reutilization (ashes and slag from power and heat plants, metallurgical and chemical wastes);
- Adjust waste management regulations and organizational systems to match EC standards;
- Create a country-wide environmental monitoring system.

Box 3. Poland's Long-Term Environmental Priorities

- Full elimination of coal firing domestic stoves and boilers in urban agglomerations and in protected natural areas;

- Reduction of SO_2 and NO_x by 80% from current levels;

- Eliminate the use of chlorofluorocarbons (CFCs) and other ozone depleting chemicals;

- Reduce CO_2 emission to an internationally determined level;

- Reduce pollution loads into the Baltic Sea by 80% from current levels.

Priorities for Human Health

One priority for action that should receive greater emphasis in Poland's Environmental Policy is urban air pollution. The most serious threats to human health related to energy use occur in areas with high levels of urban air pollution. One problem is that many of Poland's major cities experience occasional pollution "emergencies" -- very high, intermittent ambient air pollution levels (usually much higher than average ambient level). There are a number of local "hot spots" where emissions from one or more highly polluting industrial plants are a significant cause of urban air pollution. Nonetheless, small and medium-sized coal-fired burners are the main cause of high air pollution in urban areas.

This implies that systems for dealing with urban air pollution emergencies, including programmes to reduce emissions from small and local sources, should have a higher priority than pollution controls on all emissions sources. This is directly related to energy policy, which should focus on reducing emissions from domestic coal stoves and coal-fired small and medium size heat boiler houses -- and encouraging conversion to cleaner fuels, such as natural gas -- as priorities.

3. POLAND'S ENERGY POLICY OBJECTIVES

The general objectives of Polish energy policy, which is developed and coordinated by the Ministry of Industry and Trade, include achieving an efficient and secure energy supply; improving energy efficiency; changing the energy balance by reducing dependence on coal and increasing the share of gas and oil in the energy supply; and reducing pollution through these measures as well as specific action targeted at environmental protection.

The Polish Government sees the main means of achieving these objectives as being the establishment of market systems in the energy sector -- one of the changes in the country's overall transition to a market-based economy. Initial priorities include pricing and institutional changes to enhance the role of the market in the energy sector. Energy prices are being increased both in absolute terms and relative to other production factors such as capital, labor, and raw materials.

Four near and medium term actions have been articulated to implement this strategy: market pricing of energy supplies; restructuring and removal of controls on the energy supply sector; commercialization and privatization of the energy supply sector; and the development of a regulatory system that promotes efficient exploitation of natural resources, competition in the sector, anti-monopoly regulations, and compliance with environmental standards.

Specific targets have been established to implement these actions:

- Price reform and liberalization, including: the liberalization of coal prices and elimination of coal export quotas; parity in prices between household and industrial consumers of natural gas and electricity; natural gas prices based on western European levels for industrial users; the removal of controls on oil and gas development; equal tariffs for household and industrial consumers of district heating; partial removal of controls on electricity, natural gas and district heat networks.

- Elimination of energy subsidies, including government subsidies for coal, heat and electricity producers and the cross-subsidies under which households paid less than industrial users for gas, electric and district heating and hot water.

- Sector restructuring. Coal mines are to be commercialized and then privatized. Lignite mines, together with lignite-fueled power plants located at mine sites, will be restructured and commercialized. A national electric transmission grid company, PSENN, will be created. Electric and heat generating companies will be reorganized (and new companies will be created; these companies will then bid to supply power to PSENN and to district heating networks). In addition, electric power, gas and heat distributors will be commercialized.

- Regulatory reforms will include anti-monopoly rules for electricity, gas and heat transmission and distribution, and overall the promotion of competition in the electricity, gas and heat sectors.

The government has not yet determined an energy efficiency policy or any particular energy conservation program to address Poland's large potential for improved energy efficiency. The energy efficiency strategy has been limited to macroeconomic and price reform, which in the opinion of energy policy decisionmakers should provide important incentives to take energy saving measures. As yet no actions to support market mechanisms and to help overcome market barriers have been undertaken.

Several priority actions have been implemented to reduce energy-related pollution. In the hard coal industry, measures have been taken to desalinize mine water runoff and to treat coal to reduce its sulfur content and increase its calorific value. In the electricity and district heat sector, the focus is on reducing SO_2, NO_x, and particulate emissions.

4. EVALUATING POLAND'S ENERGY AND ENVIRONMENTAL OBJECTIVES

The environmental protection goals of the two policies have many common points: both focus on reducing pollutant emissions to the air, water, and soil; changing the structure of energy use by switching from consumption of coal to oil and gas; improving energy efficiency throughout the economy; and eliminating highly polluting industrial plants, including energy producers.

Energy Policy

Poland's energy policy focuses mainly on supply side measures, in particular organizational and ownership changes, new investment, and energy price reform, as well as commensurate legislative changes. Demand-side changes are expected to occur through the influence of market mechanisms, especially the liberalization of energy prices. Apart from this, no short or medium term priorities and activities for energy efficiency were defined.

The following questions arise when reviewing energy policy:

1. To what extent does energy policy integrate supply and demand side activities?

2. Is this policy a change from the former socialist strategy that strived to satisfy the energy supply for each increase in demand? This resulted in a national energy intensity two to four times greater than western Europe, as well as significant environmental degradation.

3. Are the energy policies consistent with a transition to a market-based economy? Will energy price increases result in greater efficiency on the part of energy users, and cost reductions and increased competitiveness among energy producers?

4. Is it sufficient to limit the energy efficiency policy to energy price reform during the transition period? Will market responses be sufficient to change Poland's energy intensive economy?

5. Which institutions and what regulatory mechanisms will implement policy?

Areas of Policy Conflict

There are inconsistencies between the objectives of Poland's energy and environmental policies. These differences concern the emphasis of policy objectives. Environmental policy focuses on improving the efficiency of natural resource use, including energy use, rather than developing new energy sources. Energy policy favours the latter as its primary objective. Neither policy, takes due account of the constraints and changes in the current economic transition.

In addition, there may be inconsistencies in the implementation and enforcement of energy and environmental policy objectives. In energy policy, only energy price liberalization and the restructuring and commercialization of the sector were identified as policy tools. Hence there is little opportunity to evaluate differences between these policies.

The following example shows that conflicts in implementation can occur. Energy policy is seeking to improve the competitiveness of energy producers through restructuring and commercialization of public power stations. On the other hand, environmental policy requires power plants to limit their SO_2 and NO_x emissions. This will increase the energy costs of those producers that first install expensive Flue Gas Desulfurization (FGD) devices. Newly built power plants, under increased environmental and social pressures, need to install pollution control equipment before commissioning (as, for example, in the case of the Opole plant). This could, however, increase their electricity costs up to 20 percent, reducing their competitiveness. Fees and fines for SO_2 emission are at present only a small fraction of the energy costs and are weak motives for the wide installation of FGD equipment. If fees and fines were increased to match the cost of FGD installation, the electricity costs of all producers would rise. This would lower the international competitiveness of the large energy-intensive part of Polish industry.

Thus, further questions can be raised. Is competition between power plants possible during the transition period? What role should be played by regulatory and anti-monopoly agencies?

The problems of compatibility between energy and environmental policies will be considered again later in this paper, when introducing proposed solutions for these policy problems.

The Feasibility of Poland's Environmental Policy Goals

Poland's environmental policy is characterized by a wide set of principal ideas, objectives, priorities, and program declarations that represent a major change in the approach toward environmental protection. The main question that arises when considering government policy is: Are these ambitious goals feasible in the transition period, which is characterized, at least at this moment, by a deep economic recession?

This question is particularly relevant for air pollution requirements, which are meant to reach European Community levels in the medium and long term. For example, by 1997 permitted SO_2 emissions for combustion processes (hard and brown pulverised coal boilers) will be 200g/GJ, close to the EC standard of 180g/GJ.

The government has estimated that achieving the long term goals of Poland's environmental protection will cost about US$ 260 billion.[10] This is, however, a very general estimate. Nonetheless, according to our calculations, meeting the specific air emission requirements for 1997 (SO_2 and NO_x only) -- reducing SO_2 emissions by 80 to 90 per cent and NO_x emissions by 50 to 80 per cent in public, industrial, communal power and heat plants -- will cost about US$ 17.4 billion (at the present exchange rate, equivalent to about 235 trillion zlotys). This estimate assumes the purchase of new technical equipment: post-combustion flue gas desulfurization (FGD) equipment to reduce SO_2 emissions, co-firing and gas reburning for No_x reduction, and the introduction of fluidized bed combustion in many plants.

What are the financial sources for environmental protection measures? In 1990, Poland spent about US$ 437 million -- about 1.1 per cent of Poland's GDP -- on investments for environmental protection, of which US$ 144 million were spent to reduce air emissions. Expenditures in 1991 were greater than this. Nonetheless, if the investments to reduce air emission in the energy sector were to reach US$ 0.5 to 1 billion per year, the air protection standards for 1997 would be achieved in between 17 and 34 years. Perhaps the options of FGD and denitrification will be less expensive; however, this does not change at all the financial problem. Even if the recession ends in 1992 and there is slow economic growth in 1993, spending such an immense sum on environmental protection seems unrealistic.

In 1990, the National Fund for Environmental Protection collected US$ 42.1 million, two thirds of which came from fees and fines for environmental pollution. If pollution fees and fines are to increase to meet the estimated expenses for pollution abatement equipment for the 1997 requirements, energy costs would increase up to 25 per cent. If this were the case, one can ask whether Poland's industrial goods would be competitive on world markets, and what the social costs of further energy price increases would be?

Overall, where would Poland's limited financial resources be best invested -- to tackle the causes of pollution, through economic restructuring or to tackle end-of-pipe emissions? Do present energy and environmental policies encourage investment optimization?

5. THE IMPACT OF ECONOMIC REFORM

Upon assuming power in September 1989, Poland's new government started planning wide-ranging economic reforms. The stabilization program, launched on January 1, 1990 aimed at: reducing the fiscal deficit; restraining credit and money supply; achieving a positive real interest rate; reducing government subsidies; and freeing prices, international trade, and the exchange rate.

This drastic program has had some success. The annual rate of inflation, which had reached about 2000 per cent in the second half of 1989, fell to 250 per cent in 1990 and 60 per cent in 1991. For most market goods and services, there was a supply and demand equilibrium. The state budget was balanced in 1990, while in 1991 the deficit was under 4% of GDP. Real interest rates were positive in 1990 and 1991. Poland had a trade surplus of US$ 3.77 billion in 1990, and a small trade deficit (about 0.2%) in 1991. The black market for foreign exchange was almost totally eliminated.

In addition, by 1991 the private sector accounted for 45 per cent of employment. Most of the retail business is in private hands, and 24 per cent of total industrial production comes from private firms.

There has also, however, been a deep recession. Gross domestic product (GDP) fell 12 per cent in 1990 and an additional 7 to 8 per cent last year. Industrial production fell 24 per cent in 1990 and a further 14 percent in 1991. Real wages declined 35 per cent in 1990 (although they increased 2 per cent in 1991). Unemployment jumped to 8 per cent of the labor force in 1990 and to 11.4 per cent in 1991 (or about 2 million workers). Domestic investment fell drastically (although foreign investment has grown). In 1991, the profit of all firms was negative, about -1.3%.

Increases in Energy Prices

The economic transformation has had significant effects on energy use and the environment. The Polish government was determined to increase energy prices and eliminate subsidies to the energy sector. In 1990 and 1991 energy prices were increased substantially. In dollar terms, natural gas prices increased 18.8 times for households and 2.3 times for industry (see Fig. 1). Electricity prices increased 12.6 times for households and 3.4 times for industry (Fig. 2). The prices of coal for industry increased 3.8 times (Fig. 3), and district heat and hot water for households rose 20.5 times (Fig. 4).

The prices for natural gas, electricity, and coal are now close to "real, current" costs. The district heating prices for households cover about 40 per cent of "real, current" cost. Further increases in energy prices would meet social and political resistance, due to the mismatch between the current average incomes and energy prices (the average salary in Poland is at present US$ 185 per month). For example, at the end of 1989 the average monthly salary was equivalent to 8035 kWh of electricity or 7441 m^3 of natural gas (at the prices charged households), while it now purchases only 3571 kWH of electricity or 1106 m^3 of natural gas. The cost of district heat (for a 60 m^2 apartment) increased from 2.1 per cent of an average salary to 10.4 per cent (and district heat prices are still subsidized).

Nonetheless, government budgetary constraints require continued liberalization of energy prices. The subsidies for hard coal production were reduced by 34 per cent in 1990 (or US$ 958 million), and 13 per cent in 1991 (US$ 518 million). In 1992 they should fall a further 1.3 per cent (US$ 58 million). This means that hard coal prices will be liberated soon.

Primary energy consumption has declined since 1987 (Fig.5). Over the first year of transition, primary energy consumption fell rapidly: from 5097 PJ in 1989 to 4229 in 1990. This was greater than the decline in GDP. In other words, the energy intensity of GDP decreased (Figs. 5 and 6). In 1991, primary energy consumption declined slower than GDP, so energy intensity increased for the first time in a decade.

The increase in energy prices and elimination of subsidies have been carried out quickly during the last two years. This process is continuing. It is difficult to determine explicitly whether prices have been effective as an incentive and market signal for producers and consumers. The important question is, what is the price elasticity of energy demand? Which of the end-use energy consumers -- industry, transport, residential and commercial sectors -- are most sensitive to price signals? Does this signal reach all energy consumers?

In 1989 and 1990, the changes in final energy consumption (Figs. 7 & 8) were as follows:

- Industrial energy consumption fell by about 19.4%, greater than the overall national decline of 15.1%;

- Transport sector energy consumption fell 14%, similar to the overall decline;

- The most dramatic drop occurred in the residential, commercial, and other sectors, where final energy consumption fell 31.1%.

An Evaluation of the Changes in Energy Consumption

In <u>industry</u> (Fig.9) final energy consumption fell 91.3 PJ in 1989 and by 317.9 PJ in 1990. Figures 10a and 10b show the trends in energy intensity for selected industries. An analysis of energy-intensity changes reveals the following structure.

In 1989, the decline in final energy consumption was greater than production. The total decline in the final energy consumption (91.3 PJ) was composed of:

- A 26.1 PJ decrease in energy use due to the decline of industrial production (28.6 per cent of the total);

- A 10.7 PJ decrease due to an increased share of production in less energy-intensive industries (11.7 per cent); and

- A decline of 54.5 PJ due to an improvement of energy- intensity throughout all industrial branches (59 per cent of the total decrease).

In 1989, despite the decline of production in industry, an improvement in energy efficiency took place. This was achieved through both better utilization of energy by industrial branches and the declining share of heavy industry in total industrial production.

In 1990, the percentage decrease in final energy consumption was lower that of industrial production. The decrease in energy consumption (317.9 PJ) was composed of:

- A fall of 443.1 PJ due to the decline of total industrial production (or 139.4 per cent of the total energy consumption decrease);

- An increase of 40.9 PJ due to the increased share of energy-intensive industries in total industrial output (12.9 per cent of the total change);

- An increase of 84.3 PJ due to the increase of overall industrial energy-intensity (26.5 per cent).

Thus, in 1990 the energy efficiency in industry worsened due to both less efficient energy use in industrial branches, and an increased share of heavy industrial branches contributing to total industrial output. There are two main reasons for this.

First, industrial production fell 27 per cent between 1989 and 1990, while capacity remained unchanged (enterprise bankruptcies or liquidations were rare) -- this probably caused an increase in production costs, including an increase of energy use per unit of output. Low cost investments compensated for this production drop.

Second, the process of restructuring and privatization of state-owned enterprises is progressing slowly, while the recession continues. Thus, it can be assumed that the period required for short-term adjustment of industrial energy consumption to new, higher energy prices has been extended from one year to three or four years, perhaps longer.

In the public transport sector (see Figs. 7 and 11), the fall in energy consumption from 1988 to 1990 was sharply higher than the fall in cargo and passenger transport. Current Polish statistics categorise the energy consumption by private transport into residential, commercial and other sectors. Despite the recession, private transport of goods and passengers has increased (see Fig. 12). However, the rising prices of motor fuels and the fall of the real income of households reduced the consumption of fuels, especially by private car owners.

In the residential, commercial and other sectors (see Figs. 7 and 8), energy consumption -- including motor fuel consumption and end-use consumption -- fell from 1759 PJ in 1989 to 1149 PJ in 1990, or a reduction of one- third. During this period, the prices for most household fuels and energy increased from 12.6 to 20.5 times (Figs 1 to 4).

The decrease in energy consumption was less than may have been expected from these multifold price increases. There are several reasons. First, almost none of the 5.3 million apartments heated by district heating systems have any incentive to save hot water or heat. There are no meters for heat or hot water use. The occupant pays according to the size of the apartment (i.e. in zlotys per square meter of heated area, as shown in Fig. 4), not the thermal energy used. Second, there is no well organized system of public information or public education to promote household energy efficiency. Third, the infrequent readings of electricity and gas meters -- either annually or prior to rate changes -- do not provide sufficient information on energy consumption and on the actual or potential impact of installed improvements.

Economic Restructuring: Its Environmental Impact

What was the impact of the first two years of economic reform and the reduction of energy production and consumption on environmental conditions? Changes in air emissions were significant. Emissions of gases like CO_2, SO_2, No_x (see Figs. 13 to 15) are strongly related to primary energy consumption. From 1988 to 1991, primary energy consumption decreased by 22.5 per cent; emissions of CO_2, SO_2 fell 25 per cent, and emissions of NO_x, 18.8 per cent. Emissions of particulates (Fig. 16) declined 44.2 per cent, due not only to the reduction of energy production and consumption but also to new equipment for removing particulates from stackgases. The present level of NO_x emissions is lower than Poland's medium term priority goal for the year 2000, and the level of SO_2 and dust emissions are close to the medium-term goals (see Figs. 14 and 16).

6. EVALUATING ENERGY POLICY PROPOSALS AND OPPORTUNITIES

The Coal and Power Sectors

Poland's Ministry of Industry and Trade has elaborated the following major institutional and legal reforms for energy sector restructuring to be carried out in 1992 and 1993:

- Introduction of a new energy law;
- Development of restructuring programmes;
- Establishment of administrative units to undertake restructuring programmes;
- Establishment of regulatory principles for the energy sector and the creation of appropriate regulatory bodies;
- Continued fuels and energy price reform, including the introduction of market-based regulation of prices;
- Privatization and commercialization of the energy sector.

Poland's experience thus far in energy sector reform has not been satisfactory. The slow pace of reform and the existing institutional limits demonstrate the need for:

- The creation of a well-staffed, financially stable institution (or specific agencies) to carry out these reforms. Financing may be the most important issue as existing energy companies could be partly utilized.

- The reform of national offices charged with supervising the operation and restructuring of the energy sector and for implementing energy efficiency. At present, six ministries share authority in these fields.

- Innovations in financial policy and banking so that long-term credit lines for plant modernization, environmental protection and improved energy efficiency can be provided. At present, private foreign banks mostly grant short-term loans, usually with a two-year repayment period, or less. The majority of Polish banks grant loans that must be repaid within one-half or one year.

- Feasibility studies of government energy and environmental priorities, to verify the ordering of these priorities. Action programmes for these priorities, based on least-cost strategies should then be developed. It should be clearly recognized that the choice of environmental standards represents a political decision, involving trade-offs between economic constraints and environmental objectives and between cost-effective and politically chosen approaches. There is a need to integrate investment choices and organization responsibilities for environmental and energy policies.

- There is a need for further study and for legal and economic solutions regarding the following questions: How can energy and fuel producers compete if they must account for real capital costs and environmental costs? Can the system of fees and fines for environmental pollution compensate the significant differences in production costs, due to differences in pollution controls? What role will regulatory agencies play in energy pricing policy? Will these agencies include representatives from environmental offices?

The Transport Sector

The near term objectives of energy and environmental policy within the transport sector should concentrate on two areas: promoting low-lead and unleaded motor fuels (through lower prices); and promoting the purchase and use of fuel-efficient and low-emissions automobiles through road taxes, customs duties, and other incentives. In addition, public information programmes are necessary to communicate the reasons and goals of these reforms.

Energy-Intensive Industries

Experience from the first years of economic transition indicate that it is impossible to achieve the reconstruction of state-owned industries through market mechanisms only. Market mechanisms are not yet fully developed, a strong connection between industry and the state budget remains, and social issues, such as unemployment, must be considered. If strong state intervention in the transition period continues, in order to restructure and rationalise energy-intensive industry, then clear objectives must be set.

For all central and eastern European countries, the following is the key problem: To what extent are strong state interventions needed in order to change the structure of the previous centrally planned system and promote the creation of market mechanisms? For example, the Polish government currently gives credit guarantees to retrofit large plants with pollution control equipment. This, *de facto*, influences industrial restructuring. During the transition and recession period, a policy for better energy efficiency, along with action plans to implement it, should be formulated. The following policy tools are needed:

- Information programs;
- Targeting and monitoring;
- Financial incentives;
- Regulation and standards;
- Research, development and demonstration.

In the near future our government is going to create an Energy Conservation Agency (Agencja Poszanowania Energii). To be effective, this Agency needs adequate financial and political support. There is, however, the possibility that the institutional separation between agencies overseeing energy supply and demand will deepen the traditional incoherence of energy policy. How will demand and supply side initiatives be reconciled? One solution would be to make the Energy Conservation Agency an interministerial agency comprising the Ministry of Industry and Trade and the Ministry of Environmental Protection (and, in the future, the Ministry of Economy). The Ministry of Environmental Protection could then influence other ministries to include energy efficiency in national economic policy.

The Residential and Commercial Sectors

These sectors together make up the biggest share of energy consumption (Fig. 7). At present energy use in this sector is influenced only by prices and by the standardization of household appliances. This sector could react very quickly to price signals if it were supported by an appropriate energy efficiency policy. There is no institution representing this sector in energy management. This role can be fulfilled by the Energy Conservation Agency. There is an urgent need for improvements in the balance of investments between the supply and demand side of energy. The World Bank loan for the retrofit and regulation of district heating networks and the modernization of local boilerhouses, without any provision for improvement of energy efficiency in buildings, is an example of the problem. One short and medium term priority should be the installation of heat meters, thermostatic valves, and other measurement devices in the 110,000 buildings connected to district heating systems. The investment cost would be about US$ 900 million, and the estimated payback period about 2 years. The reduction in energy consumption and related air emission would be about 15 percent. Public information and education programmes are needed to support such an initiative. Specific actions should be formulated within the scope of local programs to reduce emissions.

7. CONCLUSIONS: PRIORITIES FOR ACTION

The poor condition of Poland's natural environment prompted the new democratic government to set ambitious environmental goals, affecting the energy sector and others. The feasibility of achieving these goals within the specified period of time should be analyzed, especially considering the problems of current economic transition. Verified goals, and action plans to achieve them, should be based on least-cost strategies.

Environmental policy is strengthening the role of regional and local authorities. These authorities should play the major role in creating local action plans to improve environmental protection in connection with energy production and consumption. At this level there will be an opportunity to implement Integrated Resource Planning to meet energy needs, taking into consideration environmental costs and the economic and social development of the region. Here there will be the opportunity to compare local priorities with overall national means, and to focus on the most threatened areas and the most effective actions, such as limiting emissions from small urban sources and highly polluting industries. Local regulatory agencies will have to be created and financed. On the local and regional level, in addition to the national level, energy supply policies will have to be integrated with environmental protection goals.

Central and eastern European countries are entering the economic transition with excessive energy intensities (two to four times higher per unit of GDP than western European countries). Improving energy efficiency provides the best means of strengthening economic development and improving the environment. Energy efficiency does not happen on its own. Pricing policy and economic restructuring are the main market barriers to be removed. But the government has to take initiatives to develop the necessary programs and policies. Integrated Resource Planning should determine the optimum allocation of investments between the demand and supply sides. A specific agency is needed to sponsor energy efficiency, with the resources to implement action plans. When such an agency does not exist, faulty decisions can be made, such as the allocation of the World Bank's largest loan for the energy sector solely to investments for district heat supply and distribution. Significant energy savings and emissions reduction can be achieved through low and medium cost improvements in building energy efficiencies.

Finally, central and eastern European countries need greater international assistance for:

- The creation of financial, legal and commercial institutions to implement energy and environmental policies;

- Access to information on energy efficient technologies, and environmentally sound technologies related to energy production and consumption; and

- The creation of common programs for research, analysis and demonstration projects, as well as training and education. There is a fear that in the transition period many research programs will be curtailed and research and development institutes will go bankrupt.

REFERENCES

1. Główny Urząd Statystyczny. *Rocznik statystyczny: 1989,1990,1991*. Warszawa.

2. Główny Urząd Statystyczny. *Gospodarka Paliwowo - Energetyczna w latach: 1988 - 1989, 1989 - 1990*. Warszawa.

3. Główny Urząd Statystyczny. *Ochrona Środowiska: 1989,1990,1991*. Warszawa.

4. International Energy Agency. *Energy Policies: Poland 1990 Survey*. OECD, Paris 1991.

5. Ministerstwo Przemysłu i Handlu. "Informacja o zamierzeniach w dziedzinie gospodarki paliwowo - energetycznej na lata 1991 - 1992." Warszawa, lipiec 1991.

6. Ministry of Industry and Trade. Heat supply Restructuring and Conservation Project. Letter of Sector Development Policy.

7. Centralny Urząd Planowania. Założenia polityki energetycznej w latach 1992 i 1992 -1994. Warszawa, styczeń 1992 (projekt).

8. Ministerstwo Przemysłu i Handlu. Propozycje w sprawie programów restrukturyzacji górnictwa węgla kamiennego i brunatnego, gazownictwa, elektroenergetyki, ciepłownictwa i przemysłu paliw ciekłych. Warszawa, luty 1992.

9. Ministry of Environmental Protection, Natural Resources and Forestry. *National Policy of Poland*. Warsaw, May 1991.

10. Ministry of Environmental Protection, Natural Resources and Forestry. *National Environmental Policy of Poland*, Warsaw, February 1992.

11. Coopers and Lybrand. *Restructuring of the Electricity/ Lignite and District Heating Sub-sectors*. Final Report. January 1991.

12. Bochniarz Z. and others. *Environmental and Development for Poland*. Hubert Humphrey Center, University of Minnesota, Minneapolis, September 1990.

13. Michna J., "Assesment of energy conservation policy in economy in transition." *IPIS PAN*. No 4/91.

14. Pasierb S. and Guła A. "Energy Efficiency in Economy in Transition." International Conference on Environmentally Sound Coal Technologies. Madras. January 1992.

15. Pasierb, S. "Structural and technological changes of industrial energy intensity in the years 1960 - 1987." *Gospodarka Paliwami i energią* No.4/1990.

16. Kumanowski M. and others. *Energy economic characteristics of industrial branches*. MP i H, CIE. Warsaw, November 1991.

17. Szpumar C.B. and others. "Poland: Energy and Environmental Overview." Argonne National Laboratory, Argonne, Illinois. October 1990.

18. Cofała J. "Energy pricing and transition from command to a market economy in Central/Eastern Europe and the Soviet Union." Polish Academy of Sciences. Institute of Fundamental Technological Research. Warsaw.

19. Mac Innes G. "Development of energy conservation programmes in IEA Member Countries. The Role of Governments and Producers." UNIDO/WB. Warsaw. October 1990.

20. Hughes G. "Are the costs of cleaning up Eastern Europe exaggerated? Economic reform and the environment." *Oxford Review of Economic Policy*. Vo. 7. No 4.

FIGURES

FIG.1. PRICES OF NATURAL GAS

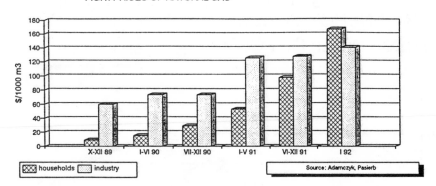

FIG.2. PRICES OF ELECTRICITY

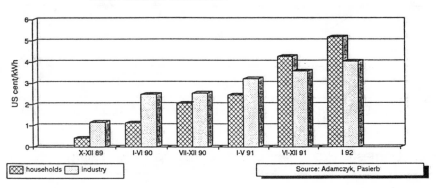

FIG.3. PRICES OF STEAM COAL FOR POWER

Source: Adamczyk, Pasierb

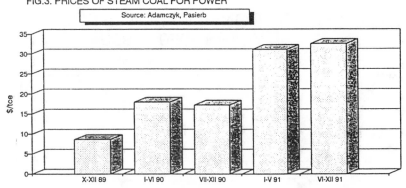

FIG.4. PRICES OF HEAT (households)

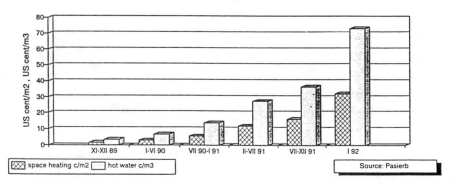

- 155 -

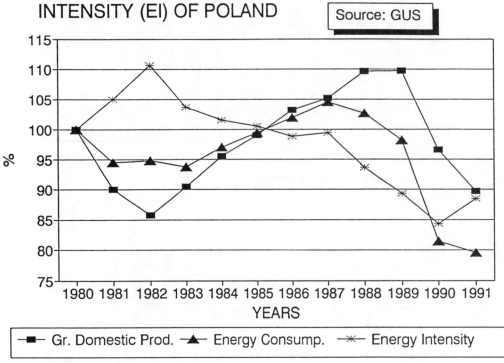

FIG.5. GROSS DOMESTIC PRODUCT (GDP), FINAL ENERGY CONSUMPTION (FEC), ENERGY INTENSITY (EI) OF POLAND

Source: GUS

—■— Gr. Domestic Prod.   —▲— Energy Consump.   —※— Energy Intensity

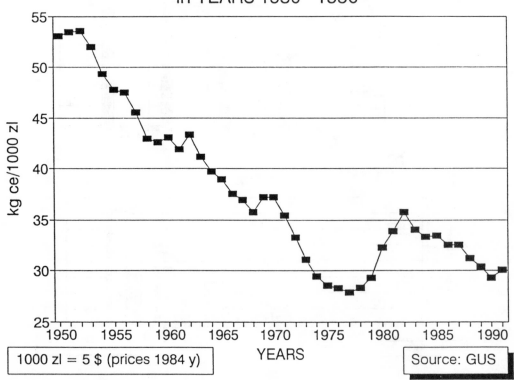

FIG.6. ENERGY CONSUMPTION of POLISH GDP in YEARS 1950 - 1990

1000 zl = 5 $ (prices 1984 y)

Source: GUS

FIG.7. FINAL ENERGY CONSUMPTION (FEC) IN SECTORS IN YEARS 1988-1990.

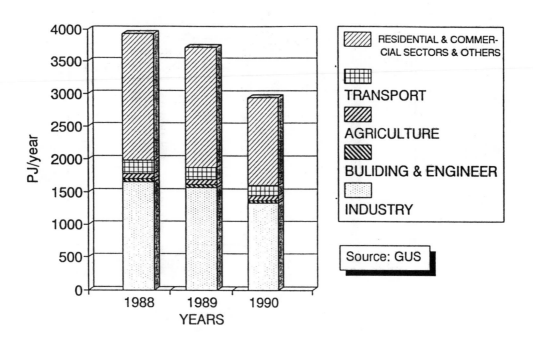

FIG.8.CHANGES FINAL ENERGY CONSUMPTION (FEC) IN SECTORS IN YEARS 1988-1990.

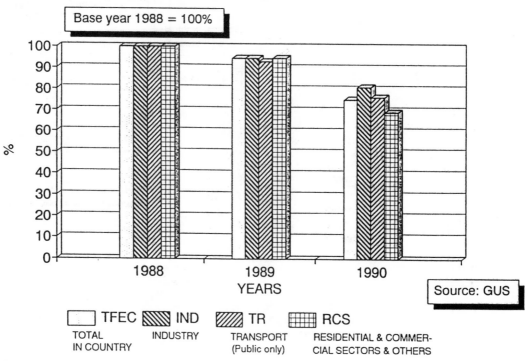

FIG.9. CHANGES OF FINAL ENERGY CONSUMP. (FEC) IN INDUSTRY DURING 1988-1990

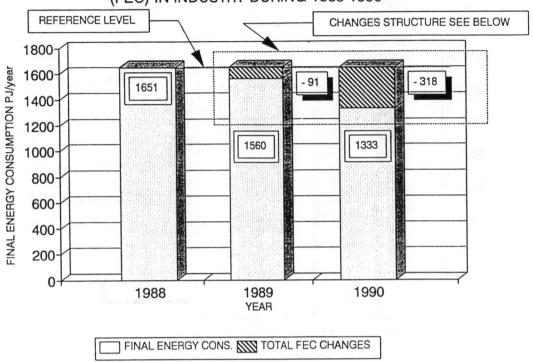

REFERENCE LEVEL

CHANGES STRUCTURE SEE BELOW

1651

1560

1333

- 91

- 318

FINAL ENERGY CONSUMPTION PJ/year

YEAR

1988   1989   1990

☐ FINAL ENERGY CONS.   ▧ TOTAL FEC CHANGES

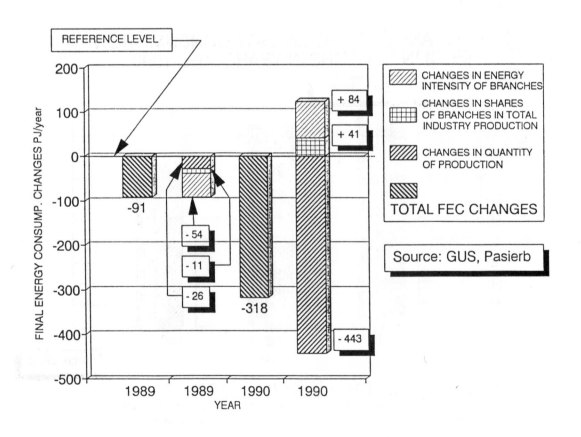

REFERENCE LEVEL

-91

- 54

- 11

- 26

-318

- 443

+ 84

+ 41

FINAL ENERGY CONSUMP. CHANGES PJ/year

YEAR

1989   1989   1990   1990

▧ CHANGES IN ENERGY INTENSITY OF BRANCHES

▦ CHANGES IN SHARES OF BRANCHES IN TOTAL INDUSTRY PRODUCTION

▨ CHANGES IN QUANTITY OF PRODUCTION

▩ TOTAL FEC CHANGES

Source: GUS, Pasierb

FIG.10a. EI - THE MOST FEC SELECTED PRODUCTS

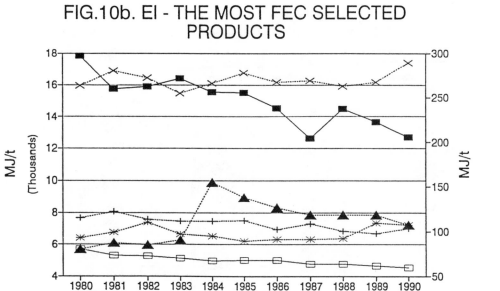

Source: GUS

FIG.10b. EI - THE MOST FEC SELECTED PRODUCTS

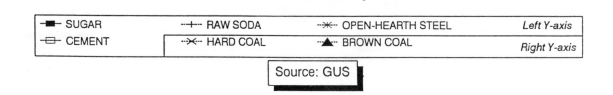

Source: GUS

FIG.11. PUBLIC TRANSPORT INDEXES IN YEARS 1988-1990.

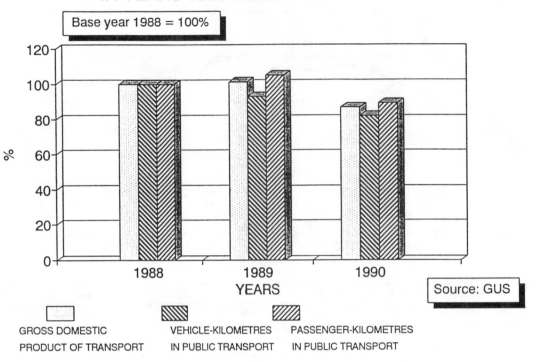

Base year 1988 = 100%

Source: GUS

GROSS DOMESTIC PRODUCT OF TRANSPORT

VEHICLE-KILOMETRES IN PUBLIC TRANSPORT

PASSENGER-KILOMETRES IN PUBLIC TRANSPORT

FIG.12. PRIVATE TRANSPORT INDEXES IN YEARS 1988-1990.

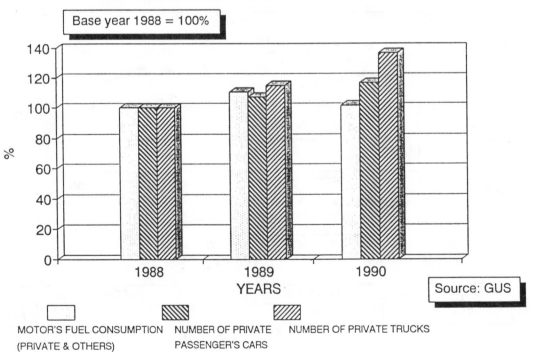

Base year 1988 = 100%

Source: GUS

MOTOR'S FUEL CONSUMPTION (PRIVATE & OTHERS)

NUMBER OF PRIVATE PASSENGER'S CARS

NUMBER OF PRIVATE TRUCKS

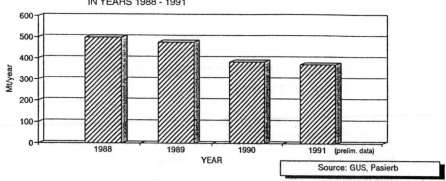

FIG.13. EMISSION OF CO2 IN POLAND
IN YEARS 1988 - 1991

Source: GUS, Pasierb

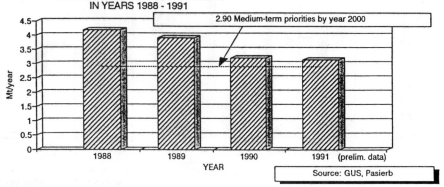

FIG.14. EMISSION OF SO2 IN POLAND
IN YEARS 1988 - 1991

2.90 Medium-term priorities by year 2000

Source: GUS, Pasierb

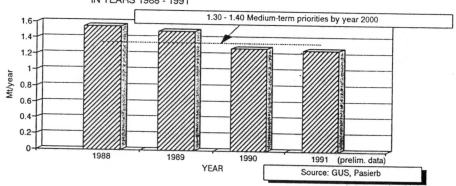

FIG.15. EMISSION OF NOx IN POLAND
IN YEARS 1988 - 1991

1.30 - 1.40 Medium-term priorities by year 2000

Source: GUS, Pasierb

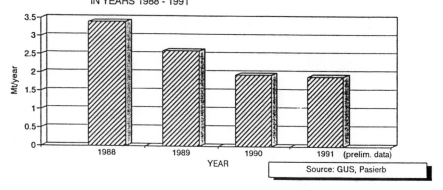

FIG.16. EMISSION OF DUST IN POLAND
IN YEARS 1988 - 1991

Source: GUS, Pasierb

FIG.17. DEVELOPMENT OF ENVIRONMENTAL PROTECTION INVESTMENTS

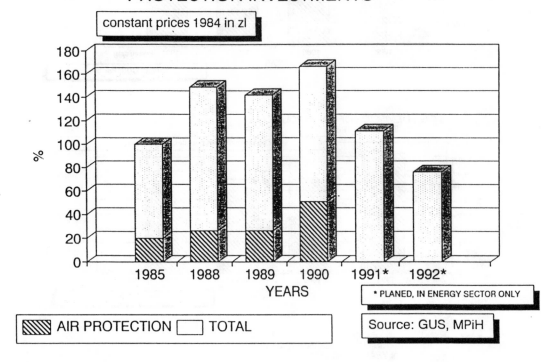

constant prices 1984 in zl

AIR PROTECTION   TOTAL

* PLANED, IN ENERGY SECTOR ONLY

Source: GUS, MPiH

Issues and Strategies for Domestic Financing

**Energy and Environmental Policy Integration:
A Survey of the Activities of the
Czech Power Company (CEZ)**

Mr. Miroslav Vlcek
CEZ

I. Introduction

The Czech and Slovak Federal Republic launched a wide-ranging economic reform program in September 1990. The structural changes resulting from the country's economic transition will have a profound impact on the development and operation of the energy sector.

For forty years, energy sector development was controlled by the central authorities. The primary goal was to meet pre-established performance and/or production goals. The energy sector now faces a number of problems that are legacies from the previous system, such as:

- Heavy dependence on domestically produced coal and lignite in the industrial and power sectors;

- An almost complete dependence on the former USSR for oil and gas imports;

- Low energy efficiencies (due to misguided industrial policies and heavily subsidized energy prices);

- a poorly developed regulatory system for natural and/or institutional monopolies; and

- severe environmental problems related to use of poor quality coal and lignite (such as high levels of air pollution).

In addition, the power sector is at present handicapped by financial difficulties, because of the limited availability of domestic or foreign capital.

One important development that should help the energy sector is a 1991 agreement between the CSFR and the PHARE Programme of Commission of the European Communities. The activities to be undertaken should assist economic restructuring and enhance the development of a market based economy. The cooperative program is assisting the CSFR Government implement new energy policies in the following fields: (i) an integrated approach to energy planning, including demand forecasting, (ii) demand management programs, (iii) analysis of alternative supply options, (iv) regulation of natural monopolies, (v) pricing policy, supply diversification, and environmental protection, (vi) improvement of energy efficiency, and (vii) regional development strategies for three selected and heavily polluted areas.

II. Reorganisation of the Power Sector

As of May 1992, the Federal Ministry of Economy is responsible only for establishing national energy policy principles, proposing energy laws to the Federal Parliament, and overseeing certain activities concerning nuclear energy. All other energy sector activities are the responsibility of the governments of the Czech and Slovak Republics -- specifically, the Ministry for Economic Policy and Development in the Czech Republic and by the Ministry of Economy in the Slovak Republic. These authorities have prepared their respective energy policies, approved by each Republic's government.

The power sector consists of several national utilities. Power generation, transmission and distribution are organized in the following way:

- In the Czech Republic, the Czech Power Company (CEZ) is responsible for the greater part of power generation and transmission. A small share of electricity is produced by autoproducers, independent cogeneration plants, and the power plants owned by eight regional distribution companies (which are otherwise responsible mainly for distribution activities). These distribution companies deal directly with practically all energy consumers.

- In the Slovak Republic, the Slovak Power Company (SEP) is responsible for the majority of power generation and transmission. A smaller amount of electricity is produced by independent producers and by the power plants owned by three regional distribution companies.

A special organization -- the Czechoslovak Energy Dispatch Centre (established jointly by CEZ and SEP) -- coordinates power generation between the two Republics to best meet operational constraints and to generate and dispatch power to the national system economically. Bulk electricity supply is provided by CEZ and SEP through a 400 KV and 220 KV integrated power network. The CSFR network is connected with Austria, Germany, Poland, the CIS, and Hungary, and has import-export contracts and other arrangements to manage regular power exchanges.

Privatization of the power sector has started. The principal generating company in the Czech Republic -- CEZ -- was partially privatized at the beginning of May 1992, in the so-called first wave of voucher privatization. Through the voucher system, approximately 30 per cent of CEZ's equity was privatized. Simultaneously, several individual cogenerating and district heating companies were established as separate share companies. After privatization, CEZ continued to produce about 80 per cent of the total electricity generated in the Czech Republic. Both distribution companies and public power companies in the Slovak Republic are to be privatized as part of the second wave of privatization.

III. Electricity Generation and Consumption Trends

In 1991, gross domestic consumption of electricity was 85.2 TWh (about 7 per cent less than in 1989), with a peak demand of 13.3 GW. Total electricity generation was 83.4 TWh. The total installed capacity of 21.3 GW consists of: thermal power plants (12.1 GW); hydroelectric plants (3.0 GW); nuclear power plants (3.5 GW); and autoproducers (2.7 GW). About 56 per cent of electricity was generated from coal, of which 80 per cent was sourced from lignite-fired power plants.

Two nuclear plants (Temclin: 2x1000 MW, Mochovce: 4x440 MW) are under construction, both scheduled for completion between 1993 and 1996. In addition, one pumped storage hydro plant (Dlouhe Strane: 2x325 MW) and one hydroelectric plant (Gabcikovo) are also under construction. Neither CEZ nor SEP are planning any other new power plant construction before 1996. However, several existing coal-fired power plants will be retrofitted in order to meet new environmental limits stipulated by the Federation Air Pollution Act (based on "best available technology").

Air pollution from coal-fired plants causes severe health and environmental damage (especially in Northern Bohemia). Reducing air pollution, and in particular SO_2 and dust emissions, is highly expensive. For example, CEZ's Power and Environmental Project, supported by a World Bank loan, will represent the largest environmental project in the Bank's history. Nevertheless, the loan will cover only a small part of the CEZ's power capacity that needs to be "cleaned."

In the 1980's, electricity demand grew by about 3 per cent annually. The growth rate for small consumers (mostly households) was about 4.5 per cent per year, while large consumers increased their purchases only around 2.5 per cent annually. Nonetheless, industry still takes the largest share, about 60 per cent of final consumption. Daily load curves are relatively flat and the load factor (promoted by low off-peak tariffs) is high (about 73 per cent).

It is expected that the future electricity demand and growth patterns will be influenced by structural economic changes, such as: a strong decline in outputs from heavy industry, an overall decrease in GDP for several years, followed by gradual economic recovery and a restructured industry sector. Household and tertiary sector electricity consumption is expected to steadily grow. We estimate that the total electricity consumption in 1990 -- 91.2 TWh -- will only be exceeded by the end of this century (sometime between 1998 and 2002).

IV. The Power Sector Least-Cost Study

One of the projects financed by the EC's PHARE Programme is a Power Sector Least-Cost Development Study, whose goals are to establish, analyze and evaluate feasible alternative power development scenarios, and to optimize generation and transmission systems by 2010. The least-cost objectives reflect resource constraints, including financial constraints and fuel availability, but the study also takes into account emissions limits that will have to be met. The potential for demand side management will be integrated into this least-cost analysis.

The LCP study is to completed by the end of 1992, and will contain a detailed program of actions for the medium term (up to the year 2000), principally a set of investment plans. The recommended development program will have to meet stringent economic criteria and will also need to be acceptable to the public. The study examines three major paths that will have to be pursued simultaneously: demand management; more efficient operation of existing supply systems; and the introduction of new sources. The analysis is not easy because there are a lot of uncertainties regarding future economic trends. To deal with these uncertainties, a wide variety of feasible solutions will be taken into account, and sensitivity analysis will be used to assess options. A relatively stable development program will then be defined.

The proposed power generation program will, together with demand management options, try to optimally serve load and other demand requirements. New generating technologies will be selected from cost-effective alternatives that can meet appropriate environmental standards. The upgrading or life extension of existing units will be evaluated in comparison with new generating units. Special attention will be devoted to nuclear units in operation or under construction and to candidate areas for new power plant installation. Special models shall be used for the assessment of power flow, stability and reliability analysis.

The estimate of long-run marginal costs will be very important as a basis for setting the future tariffs of electricity and for the evaluation of demand-side options. A financial analysis and evaluation of the environmental impacts of different development strategies is also being examined as a special part of LCP study. This contract is not financed by the PHARE Programme.

V. Environment and CEZ's Investment Programme

As mentioned above, whereas no construction of new power plants is planned before 1996, several coal-fired plants must be retrofitted before the end of 1996. In accordance with the 1991 Ambient Air Act, power plants will be able to operate after October 1996 only if they meet national air emissions limits. This implies that practically all existing power plants (including autoproducers and other generating units) will have to reduce their current air emissions. Emissions reduction requirements necessitate an expensive investment program, constrained by the short time period for compliance.

From 1991 to 1996, CEZ intends to carry out total investments of 130 to 140 billion Korunas. The three main areas for investment are:

- environmental improvement (approximately 47 per cent of total spending);

- completion of the Temelin nuclear power plant (approximately 33 per cent);

- other construction projects, including -- completion of the pumped-storage hydroelectric power plant at Dlouhe Strane, development of an interim used nuclear fuel storage facility at Dukovany, transmission system improvements (including connection to the UCPTE network, transformation capacity), power plant reconstruction, waste disposal work, and several small investments (approximately 20 per cent).

Between 1992 and 1996, about 80 per cent of CEZ's total investments will directly or indirectly reduce environmental impacts. Direct expenditures for pollution reduction include the installation of desulfurization equipment on a first set of thermal power plants whose total production is 3,600 MW: Prunerov II (1,050 MW), Prunerov J (440 MW), Pocorady (800 MW), Tusimiee II (800 MW) and Melnik III (500 MW). A World Bank loan has been approved for the foreign currency portion of the FGD investment for Prunerov II. Investments for desulphurization equipment will then be planned for a second set of power plants (whose installed capacity is about 3,100 MW). In addition, power plants with a total capacity about 1,400 MW will be decomissioned before the end of 1996 or during 1997 (NB. a total of 600 MW of power plant capacity has been closed).

VI. Financial Sources

There is a lot of uncertainty regarding the level of funds that will be available from domestic sources; this will depend on trends in electricity demand, electricity prices, fuel prices, and electricity export restrictions, as well as government policies regarding taxation and depreciation.

CEZ foresees a shortage of about 60 to 70 billion korunas in domestic financing for its 1992 to 1996 investment plans. At present, CEZ is negotiating with various government authorities for alternatives to meet its capital requirements, ensuring that the Air Pollution Act provisions can be met and the Czech power system can be improved. The following topics are under negotiation:

- **Electricity pricing policy** (prices for the residential sector will be increased in 1993 and 1994);

- **State taxation policy** (which at present allows no exceptions for the power industry);

- **Depreciation policy and the fixed assets revaluation** (favorable adjustments for the former are possible, but CEZ's requests in the latter area have only a small chance of being accepted);

- **State subsidies and use of the Czech Republic's environmental fund** (at present, CEZ cannot use these sources);

- **Foreign credits** (export credits for foreign equipment and loans from international financial institutions)

- **Emission of Debt Securities** (possibilities are being studied);

- **Electricity exports** (there is, however, opposition to exports of electricity);

- **Sale of a share of the energy sector to foreign investors.**

CEZ expects that the financial requirements for short and medium-term investments can be met through a combination of the measures listed above, as well as the provision of government guarantees to raise capital on international markets. The financial position of CEZ, measured by its credit rating, was assessed as BBB (in an analysis made by PlanEcon Capital group, using Standard & Poor's criteria); we hope that raising capital on international markets will be possible.

Financing Energy Efficiency and Environmental Protection: Poland's Environmental Funds

Prof. Boguslaw Fiedor
Department of Economics
Academy of Economics
Wroclaw, Poland

SOURCES FOR FINANCING ENVIRONMENTAL PROTECTION EXPENDITURES

There is a dire need for finance for environmental protection. By some estimates, the environmental situation in Poland is such that the country needs to spend about 4 per cent of yearly national income on environmental investments for at least 20 years; in contrast, spending in OECD countries does not exceed 1.5 to 2 per cent of national incomes. Nonetheless, the creation and growth of environmental funds has provided Poland with an important new resource for environmental protection. Finance from these funds could address the energy sector's emissions problems as well as the need for greater energy efficiency.

In 1989, the Government of Poland established the National Fund for Environmental Protection, whose revenues come mainly from emissions charges and non-compliance fines on polluters. In addition, each Voivodship (regional government) has an environment fund. In fact, environmental charges and fines are collected at the regional level; half goes to the national fund, and half to the regional fund (with some exceptions for specific pollutants).

In Poland, spending on environmental protection has greatly increased in recent years for two reasons. First, because of the radical growth of these national and regional funds due to major increases in the level of environmental fees and fines (in 1991, these increased 13 times in nominal terms, and 9 times in real times); and second, the greater stringency of environmental policy, such as improved enforcement of requirements for stationary sources. In 1991, the National Fund alone collected about 1.7 trillion zloty.

These funds are not, however, the sole source of financing for environmental protection expenditures. In 1991, the structure of expenditures was:

National Environment Fund	21 %
Voivodship Funds	23 %
Local government direct expenditures	14 %
National government direct expenditures	6 %
Enterprise investments in pollution control	30 %
Foreign aid	6 %

In 1991, expenditure on environmental protection reached 1.2 per cent of Poland's national income. By contrast, expenditure prior to 1983 was under 0.5 per cent of national income; this level rose slowly to about 0.8 per cent in the second half of the 1980s. It is estimated that 8.4 trillion zloty (approximately US$ 760 million) were spent on environmental protection in 1991. Of this amount, about one-half went to control water pollution, 40 per cent to control air pollution, and most of the remainder to control solid wastes and to restore contaminated cropland and forest areas.

The money resources collected in the National Fund can be transferred back to enterprises for environmental investments. Most of this financing is in the form of low-interest (soft) loans. Only about 25 per cent of the National Fund's financing are in the form of direct subsidies. By contrast, most of the financing from the Voivodship funds are in the form of direct subsidies.

In selecting which projects to finance, the National Fund tries to follow the priorities of Poland's National Environmental Policy.

In terms of external assistance, beyond the traditional forms of multilateral and bilateral assistance programs currently underway, there are hopes that Poland will be able to receive financing for environmental protection utilising debt for environment swaps. Under Poland's proposal to the Paris Club of official creditors, debts that Poland owes to 17 creditor countries could be converted into internal funds for environmental protection: this would provide about 30 trillion zlotys (overt US$ 2 billion in 1991 terms). It should be noted, however, that this sum would be spent over 18 years. Thus, these funds would provide only about 5 per cent of yearly environmental spending.

SHORT AND MEDIUM TERM ENERGY AND ENVIRONMENT ISSUES

There are no substantive opportunities to increase the revenues of the National Fund and Voivodship funds, because pollution charges, fees, and fines have already become a significant share of production costs in the mining and manufacturing sectors. It is estimated that in the first half of 1991 these charges comprised 5.5 per cent of industrial costs, while direct enterprise environmental expenditures added an additional 1.6 per cent. For power plants, pollution charges amounted to 12 per cent of costs, and direct expenditures 5.3 per cent (Poskrobko, 1991).

There is growing consensus within expressed the Ministry of Environmental Protection, Natural Resources, and Forestry about the need to decentralize the system of environmental fees and fines. This implies transferring the system to the voivodships, which would then have at their disposal the 50 per cent of funds presently transferred to the National Fund. (Only three types of fines would still go to the National Fund: those for SO_2 and NO_x emissions and for saline discharges from coal mines into rivers. The National Fund receives 100 per cent of these charges.)

Nonetheless, it seems indispensable to have a financing source that can continue to address nation-wide priorities in the National Environmental Policy, including meeting Poland's international environmental obligations. In order to offset the loss of funds from the planned decentralization of fees and fines, the Ministry of Environment is considering a system of product charges on fossil fuels (these would differ by fuel type, but would average approximately 5 per cent of their price). This would create another important source of financing for environmental protection.

The system of environmental fees and fines is principally one of revenue transfer, and not one of environmental incentives (that is, the fees are, by and large, still below either average or marginal abatement costs). To stimulate enterprises to undertake further environmental investments, another form of incentives is needed. I would like to suggest a broad system of income tax allowances for enterprises that make environmental investments -- especially for those in the energy sector, which is the main source of air and water pollution.

Although Poland has radically increased measures to improve the environment, the range and importance of the problems that need to be solved, especially in the short and medium-term, call for a least-cost oriented environmental policy. In addition, specific priorities and goals should also take into account the great regional differences in Poland's environmental conditions. The shortfall of funding compared to goals that need to be achieved also makes it indispensible to identify for new financing sources and, above all, to encourage greater financial commitments from the public (ie., households).

Electricity Generation

Because it is not really possible to substantially change the mix of fuels used in electricity generation in the next three to five years, actions should focus on coal-cleaning methods and on improving combustion efficiencies.

Coal-washing has been started at four mines where the hard coal extracted has a high sulphur content (about 2.5 per cent). This should remove much of the sulphur, reducing SO_2 emissions by about 200,000 tons per year; in addition, this process should increase the caloric value of the coal, increasing power generated by approximately 400 MW. Similar programs have been started in 14 other mines, which should reduce SO_2 emissions by a further 200,000 tons per year. The goal is to wash about 50 million tons of hard coal annually at these 18 mines, reducing SO_2 emissions by 400,000 tons, equivalent to about 10 per cent of Polands SO_2 emissions and about one-quarter of the emissions from the electricity generators. The total cost of this program will be about 4 trillion zloty (about US$ 300 million in 1991 terms), to be spent over four years.

Another example of cost-effective improvements in the electricity sector is the use of better combustion technologies and the broader use of electricity and heat cogeneration. Under a program proposed by the Ministry of Environment, the introduction of fluidized bed systems could reduce SO_2 emissions by 200,000 to 300,000 tons per year within ten years. In addition, NO_x emissions would be reduced by 60 to 80 per cent.

For power plants that use brown coal, the only way to significantly reduce their SO_2 emissions is the introduction of flue gas desulphurization. The Ministry of the Environment's program has the goal of reducing emissions by 500,000 tons per year by the year 2000, at a cost of 5 to 6 trillion zlotys.

The implementation of these environmental measures for the electricity generation sector should reduce Poland's sulphur dioxide emissions by one-quarter over the next few years.

Heat Generation

The most important actions to be taken in this area are:

- For individual households, switch from coal stove heating to gas heating or to gas-fired district heating systems. To promote these changes, it will probably be necessary to introduce, as in some western European countries (such as Germany), financial incentives -- for example, income tax reductions for households that install gas heating systems.

- For municipalities, cogeneration should switch from coal to gas-fired systems, especially in the most heavily polluted regions. Great expectations are placed on plans for the large-scale extraction of methane from hard coal deposits.

It should be noted that heat generation for households creates a high share of air pollution: approximately one-quarter of total SO_2 emissions, in addition to high levels of particulate emissions.

Energy Efficiency

One of the reasons for the Polish economy's high energy intensity has been the historically low prices for practically all forms of energy, and in particular for electricity. The transformation to a market-based economy has, as expected, resulted in a sharp increase in the prices of fuels and energy -- chiefly due to the reduction in subsidies for energy generation. For example, by mid-1991, electricity prices were 5.5 times higher for industrial plants and 22 times higher for households than their levels in 1989. Natural gas prices have increased 7.5 times for industry and 47 times for households. Compared to the increases in prices for most goods, energy prices rose between 3 and 10 times higher.

This huge increase in final energy prices has not yet resulted, as many analysts expected, in a reduction of the economy's energy intensity. Only the residential sector has clearly reacted to price signals: electricity consumption declined from 1989 to 1990 by about one-third. This is, however, a relatively small change, and further reductions in the short and medium term cannot be expected because of the higher power consumption of most home appliances in Polish households.

There is great potential for savings in the use of heat. However, changes in the prices of heat supplied by district heating systems have little effect, because most apartments supplied by district heating lack individual meters. The installation of meters on about 6.6 million apartments -- roughly estimated at a total cost of US$ 1 billion -- could result in a 20 per cent reduction in household heat consumption. This seems much more cost-effective than alternative proposals to provide energy efficient renovations of apartments and houses on district heat systems, a program that would cost approximately US$ 10 billion and would, under current plans, take about 30 years to complete. (This does not imply, however, that such a program, or the overall modernization of district heating networks should not be undertaken -- but they will take a long time to implement.)

CONCLUSIONS

The expectation that rapid increases in final energy prices would lead to a reduction in the energy intensity of Poland's economy in the short or medium-term has not materialized. Energy costs, calculated on the basis of purchasing power parities, are already approaching western European levels, but the gap between Poland and OECD countries remains practically unchanged. The main reason is that state-owned enterprises show relatively little sensitivity to market signals. (Though many of these enterprises, particularly those producing durable goods, are facing strong competition from imported goods.)

Privatization is clearly necessary to improve the efficiency of energy use. Nonetheless, the decrease in energy intensity also depends on an active government industrial and energy policy -- such a policy should also incorporate environmental goals. Since the first oil price shock many OECD countries have implemented active policies which have contributed to their low growth in energy use and improvements in energy intensity. In Poland, utopian views have often suggested that a national energy policy and national institutions to prepare and implement such a policy are not necessary in a market-based economy (see, for example, 1991 issues of Gospodarka Paliwami i Energia). My view is that an Energy Conservation Agency should be established in Poland, with responsibility for improving efficiency in energy production, distribution, transmission, and final use.

THE INTERNATIONAL CONTEXT

Pan-European Initiatives

ENVIRONMENT FOR EUROPE:
The Environmental Action Programme

Ambassador R. Jeker
Delegate of the Swiss Government for Trade Agreements

I would like to describe the objectives and the present status of the Environment for Europe programme, and explain how this Conference on Energy and Environment can contribute to the implementation of the Action Programme. The origin of the Environment for Europe programme goes back to an initiative taken by the Czeck and Slovak Federal Government in June 1991, when it hosted a Conference of European Environment Ministers at Dobris Castle, near Prague.

The Dobris Caste Conference and its subsequent follow-up process have had two main objectives:

- To give a political impulse for a coherent environment programme for the whole of Europe. Environmental problems are not restricted to borders. Measures are needed in all countries. Consequently, there is a need to harmonize such measures. Failure to do so will result in ineffective and uneconomic action as well as trade distortion.

- To emphasize right from the start the need to integrate environmental concerns in to the on-going economic and political transformation process in Central and Eastern Europe.

The process aims, therefore, to improve the state of environment in all of Europe but has a clear emphasis on Central and Eastern Europe, including measures to assist countries of the region achieve environmental improvements.

It is of interest to note that this initiative is -- after the creation of the European Bank of Reconstruction and Development -- the second truly pan-European initiative going well beyond regional integration agreements. The latest pan-European initiative is the European Energy Charter, which will be of substantive relevance for the environment in Central and Eastern Europe. The intention of work on the Charter is to conclude a legally binding Basic Agreement and various Protocols (on specific topics such as energy efficiency). Maybe similar legal developments might evolve out of the Environment for Europe programme. These initiatives -- and this is an important element I would like to stress -- do not exclude the participation of major non-European countries. All major countries and international organizations are associated with this work.

The Dobris Conference was only the first step of the Environment for Europe process. It gave a mandate to an Expert Group to coordinate the work, provide an inventory of problems and suggest appropriate solutions. The Expert Group is responsible for the final product to be submitted to the next Ministerial Conference, which will take place in Lucerne, Switzerland, in April 1993. The Expert Group, as a central coordinating body, has created various task forces and draws on work done by other organisations to support it in its preparatory process:

- There is first and foremost the Task Force for an Environment for Europe Action Programme, chaired by the Commission of the European Communities and assisted by the World Bank and the OECD.

- The UN ECE Advisors on Environment and Water Problems are to identify major long-term issues, assess the results of the UN Conference on Environment and Development in Rio, and draft elements for a strong political commitment in form of a Ministerial Declaration.

- A group under the direction of the EC Task Force for the European Environment Agency, in cooperation with UN ECE and other international organisations, is preparing a report on the State of the Environment in Europe. Preliminary findings will be presented at the Lucerne Conference.

- The Council of Europe is working on co-operative initiatives in the field of nature protection.

I will limit the rest of my remarks to the work of the Action Programme as presently pursued, in particular to the main substantive issues it addresses and the key principles by which it is guided.

Capital constraints, high indebtedness, and serious shortage of implementation capacity in central and eastern European countries highlight the urgent need to establish clear priorities. Not every problem can be tackled at the same time. <u>Measures that ensure the greatest benefits in the shortest time at the lowest cost</u> need to be chosen and implemented first.

This objective can be satisfactorily achieved only if the use of market instruments prevails over regulatory instruments in environmental policy. It is amply proven that the latter -- necessary in some circumstances -- achieve environmental objectives at higher cost. Concurrently, mechanisms need to be put in place to overcome environmental constraints to the transformation and privatization process and to encourage environmentally sound domestic and foreign investment.

The major emphasis of the on-going work is, therefore:

- to develop an agreed set of criteria to determine the priorities;
- to use these criteria to identify the highest, immediate priorities;
- to demonstrate how these proposed short-term actions fit into a longer-term strategy;
- to evaluate the cost and financing options.

To the extend the Action Programme is project-oriented, it is understood that it will focus on short-term priorities and concentrate on a limited number of highly polluted regions and "hot spots" throughout Central and Eastern Europe.

The analytical work is based on a double approach, addressing the problem from two different angles: first, establish what is economically feasible; and second, establish what is technically desirable. The latter is the ultimate objective -- identifying the desired environmental quality to be reached at a certain point in time. The first approach identifies the most cost-effective measures to improve environmental quality incrementally. The result is programme aiming at long term sustainability, building on economically feasible measures in the short and medium term.

The work programme addresses three distinct aspects of policy measures:

- non-environmental policy measures that have indirect effects on the environment;
- broad policies put in place for economic reasons (i.e. energy pricing) but with direct effects on the environment;
- and policies aimed directly at the environment, including incentives and regulations.

Transboundary and global issues are equally subject to examination. The transboundary and global component of the work programme has two principal aims: to help assess whether expensive investments to deal with the causes of acid rain are called for, and what could be done to minimize necessary investments; and to develop the outlines of a strategy for controlling ozone-depleting substances and greenhouse gases.

Enumerating the full and detailed list of issues to be addressed would go beyond the objective of a short introduction to the Action Programme. In fact, work is divided into 44 so-called modules. Each examines one particular aspect of environment issues. Together they make up the puzzle and should provide the basis for recommendations for action to the Ministerial Conference.

Energy policy is a major factor in the Action Programme, for both economic and environmental reasons. The region's inefficient use of energy wastes resources. Energy production and use are a major cause of environmental problems in Central and Eastern Europe -- air pollution in particular -- and the Action Programme needs to include a clear strategy for the energy sector. Restructuring this sector is necessary both for the economic transformation of the region and to improve its environment.

This Conference is an integral part of the Action Programme process: it has especially been organized to provide important information and conclusions on energy issues. I'm confident that we can live up to these expectations during the Conference.

THE EUROPEAN ENERGY CHARTER:
A Framework for Reshaping the Energy Industry in European Economies in Transition

Prof. Tamas Jaszay
Technical University of Budapest
Chairman, Working Group III, European Energy Charter

On December 17th, 1991, Ministers of 49 countries signed the European Energy Charter in the Hague, the Netherlands. This Charter aims to create a new model for long-term energy co-operation in Europe (and worldwide), based on a market economy framework and on mutual respect, confidence and assistance between nations.

The 49 countries that signed the Charter affirmed that broader energy co-operation between them is essential for economic progress, social development, and quality of life improvements. Taking advantage of the complementary energy sectors within Europe will benefit both European economies and the world economy. Because of the global nature of energy problems, the US, Japan, Canada and also Australia joined the Charter.

The Charter is a political declaration, and negotiations are now underway to draft a set of legally binding documents, including a Basic Agreement and several Protocols. Protocols on the following topics are now under negotiation: Energy Efficiency and Environmental Aspects of the Energy System; Hydrocarbons; Nuclear Energy; Coal; Electricity; and Renewable Energies.

Signatory countries intend to work together to improve the security of supply, the efficient management and use of energy resources, and the full potential for environmental improvement. This includes maximising the efficiency of energy production, conversion, transport, distribution, and use, enhancing safety, and minimising environmental impacts on an economic basis. They intend to promote the development of an efficient energy market throughout Europe and a better functioning global market, following the principles of non-discrimination and market-oriented price formation and taking due account of environmental concerns. This requires a climate favourable to the operation of private enterprises and to the flow of energy investments and technologies along market principles.

To create a broader European energy market and enhance the efficiency of the global energy market, the signatories pledged to undertake joint or co-ordinated action in the following areas:

- access to and development of energy resources;
- access to markets;
- liberalization of trade in energy;
- promotion and protection of investments;
- safety principles and guidelines;
- research and development and technology dissemination;
- energy efficiency and environmental protection;
- and education and training.

In implementing joint and co-ordinated work, the signatory countries will try to foster private initiative, making use of the capacities of enterprises, institutions, and financial sources, and facilitating market-based co-operation between enterprises and institutions from different countries.

The Charter's most relevant implications for central and eastern European countries can be summarized by citing action that has to be taken in the following three areas.

1. The Development of Energy Trade:

- establishment of an open and competitive market for energy products, materials equipment and services;
- access to energy resources, and exploration and development thereof on a commercial basis;
- access to local and international markets;
- removal of technical, administrative and other barriers to trade in energy and associated equipment, technologies and energy•related services;
- modernization, renewal and rationalization by industry of services and installations for the production, conversion, transport, distribution and use of energy;
- development and interconnection of energy transport infrastructure;
- promotion of the best possible access to capital particularly through appropriate existing financial institutions;
- access to energy transport infrastructure for international trade, in accordance with the objectives of the Charter;
- access on commercial terms to technologies for the exploration development and use of energy resources.

2. Energy Co-operation:

- co-ordination of energy policies;
- mutual access to technical and economic information;
- formulation of sable and transparent legal frameworks creating conditions for the development of energy resources;
- co-ordination and, where appropriate, harmonization of safety principles and guidelines for energy products and their transport, as well as for energy installations;
- exchange of technology information and know-how in the energy and environment fields, including training activities;
- research, technological development and demonstration projects.

3. Energy Efficiency and Environment Protection:

- the creation of mechanisms and conditions to ensure that energy is used as economically and efficiently as possible (including, as appropriate, regulatory and market-based instruments);
- promotion of an energy mix that minimizes negative environmental consequences in a cost-effective way through:

   (i)   market-oriented energy prices that more fully reflect environmental costs and benefits;
   (ii)   efficient and co-ordinated policy measures related to energy;
   (iii) the use of new and renewable energies and clean technologies.

- achievement of a high level of nuclear safety, and assuring effective international co-operation in this field.

The Charter's long-term goal is to create an integrated European energy market. It is obvious that at present the signatory countries are on considerably different levels of economic development. For this reason, the Charter will include transitionary arrangements that, in particular, take into account the specific circumstances facing some central and eastern European countries and newly independent states of the former Soviet Union. Considering these countries' transition to market-based economies, it will be possible for them to make a stage-by-stage adoption of provisions -- in the Charter, the Basic Agreement and the Protocols -- that they cannot yet fully implement. Specific arrangements for coming into full compliance with the Charter, the Basic Agreement, and the Protocols will be negotiated by each Party requesting transitional status, and progress towards full compliance will be subject to periodic reviews.

The European Energy Charter provides a framework for the reconstruction of the energy sectors of the European countries in transition, and it also represents a major step towards a establishing a sustainable global energy system.

The Role of External Financing and Technical Assistance

1. Reports from Multilateral and Bilateral Institutions

THE ASSISTANCE OF THE G-24 COUNTRIES

Andrea Fennesz[1]
G-24 Coordination Unit
Commission of the European Communities

INTRODUCTION

At their Paris summit meeting in July 1989, the Heads of State and Government of the seven principal industrialised countries (the G-7) and representatives of the European Community pledged to support the reform process underway in Poland and Hungary and to extend economic aid to help them transform their economies. They gave the Commission of the EC a mandate to co-ordinate aid to these two countries. Subsequently, 24 western countries became associated with this operation (now referred to as the G-24).

This co-ordinated assistance process has gradually widened its scope, and now nine countries of Central and Eastern Europe and the Baltic States are covered. Economic assistance to Yugoslavia, on the other hand, was suspended in November 1991. Eligibility for G-24 assistance is based on political and economic principles -- the recipient country must recognize the rule of law, respect for human rights, free and fair elections, and, in regards to its economy, a process of liberalisation to introduce a market-based system.

According to the G-24 Scoreboard, by the end of the first half of 1992, the G-24 countries had committed ECU 33.9 billion to Central and Eastern European countries. If the commitments of the international financial institutions are included, the total is ECU 46.9 billion.

In the co-ordination of assistance to Central and Eastern Europe, the Commission has co-operated with other international organisations whose mandates cover the region. Thus, the International Monetary Fund, the World bank, the European Bank for Reconstruction and Development, and OECD, as well as the Paris Club creditor nation co-ordination process, have become associated with the work of the G-24.

The G-24 co-ordination work has been aimed at ensuring coherence and complementarity of bilateral assistance, at reaching common strategies and guidelines for sector programmes, and

---

[1] The author is solely responsible for the content and views presented in this paper. This paper does not in any sense represent an official statement by the Commission of the European Communities.

at promoting joint actions. In its co-ordinating role, the Commission has defined priorities, carried out action plans, and developed strategies on behalf of the G-24 countries; these proposals have been submitted to the G-24 participants in regular and ad hoc meetings of senior officials and in the sectoral G-24 Working Groups.

The G-24 endeavours to adapt assistance to the changing needs of the central and eastern European countries, corresponding to their stage of transformation. National priorities and each country's absorptive capacity are taken into account. As the process of transition has advanced, G-24 assistance has changed from a form of "first-aid" to co-ordinated, longer term assistance to support economic reconstruction and economic reforms.

ASSISTANCE FOR ENERGY AND THE ENVIRONMENT

Environment has been a priority area for G-24 assistance from the beginning. Energy subsequently became a priority area as well, in recognition of the importance of energy sector supply and demand issues and environmental and safety problems.

Long-term investment needs for Central and Eastern Europe's energy and the environmental problems are considerable. These will have to be met primarily by domestic financing strategies in the countries of the region. Nonetheless, external assistance -- both financial assistance and technical assistance -- can play an important role, particularly in the early stages of economic transformation.

By the end of the second half of 1992, assistance from the G-24 countries in the energy and environment sectors reached ECU 781.4 million. If the assistance of the international financial institutions is included, the total is ECU 1.83 billion, or roughly 4 per cent of total assistance commitments.

Considering the magnitude of Central and Eastern Europe's investments needs in these two sectors, the bilateral aid of the G-24 countries, though important, can be considered only a contribution to the resolution of immediate problems. In the longer term, multilateral and domestic funding will have to play dominant roles.

If sustainable economic development is a common, long-term policy goal, then environmental issues need to be integrated into all sectoral policies; this includes, of course, western assistance to the countries of Central and Eastern Europe. For this Conference, it is useful to ask to what extent integration has already been reflected in bilateral (and also multilateral) assistance to the region, particularly in the energy sector, and what can be expected later for the economic restructuring process. This paper attempts to provide some information on the G-24 process that, hopefully, can help answer these questions.

STRATEGIES FOR THE ENERGY AND ENVIRONMENT SECTORS

There are separate G-24 Working Groups for the co-ordination of bilateral assistance in these two sectors. The purpose of the Working Groups is to guarantee, in regular meetings, a transparency of ongoing activities, an exchange of information to avoid the duplication of effort, an assessment of the most pressing needs of central and eastern European countries, and, related to this last point, an appraisal of assistance experience. To assist this work with adequate information on ongoing activities, the G-24 Co-ordination Unit has established the G-24 Project Database.

Due to the extent of the problems to be addressed and the limitation of donor country resources, a "shopping-list" approach to aid co-ordination was soon recognised to be inadequate. Consequently, the Commission, as co-ordinator of the G-24 process, prepared strategy papers in both energy and environmental sectors, in close contact with other international organisations working in these areas. These papers were subsequently discussed and approved by the G-24. These strategy papers have served as the framework for the co-ordination of G-24 assistance in the two sectors. They have defined guiding principles, needed actions, and bilateral assistance priorities.

The G-24 Environmental Strategy

The strategy's aim is to relate the bilateral financing facilities of the G-24 donors to the priority needs of the recipient governments through a limited number of policy, institutional, and investment priorities; projects and programmes should mitigate the most critical environmental problems and encourage environmentally sustainable development, including pollution prevention, resource conservation, and nature conservation.

Under this strategy, G-24 environmental assistance programmes should apply the following guiding principles and selection criteria:

- reflect the recipient country's priorities and pace and method of reform;
- use grant financing and minimise aid-tying practices;
- concentrate on key sectors or "core areas";
- follow an integrated programme rather than a "shopping-list" approach;
- do not use grants for projects with clear financial or commercial returns -- nonetheless, grants can be used to complement or prepare the loans of international financial institutions;
- reinforce the link between environmental reform and economic reform;
- encourage policies and regulations to provide economic incentives for pollution prevention;
- strengthen and expand institutional frameworks and capabilities;
- concentrate on support of the reform process, such as encouraging the introduction of new policies (regulatory changes, codes of conduct, etc.) and providing operational activities (training, feasibility studies, pilot projects) to foster new investments;
- focus on preventive rather than curative actions;

- give priority to the transfer of know-how, to least-cost technologies, to increased public awareness, and to low-cost options with a multiplier effect; and
- contribute to regional co-operation and the reduction of transboundary pollution.

Using these guidelines, G-24 environmental assistance programmes should concentrate on:

- Improving and strengthening institutions and policy-making through support for improved systems of environmental auditing; improved data collection, monitoring and analysis; policy studies; and training and technical assistance.

- Promoting information and awareness through generational information programmes, publication of data and baseline information, and assistance to NGOs.

- Undertaking feasibility studies of priority projects for possible financing by the donor community or by commercial investors.

- Providing direct investment where human health or natural resources are under severe and immediate threat.

- Promoting regional programmes.

The Energy Sector Strategy

Many of the problems identified in the energy sectors of central and eastern European countries -- fixed prices below world market levels, high dependency of many countries on one single foreign supplier, the neglect of environmental protection and nuclear safety -- are structural problems related to the legacy of a central planning system.

Considering this, the approved sectoral strategy, prepared by the Commission in co-operation with the IEA, the World Bank, and other international institutions, defined assistance criteria consistent with those for other sectors.

Three broad areas were defined as priorities for G-24 assistance:

- Policy formulation and the planning of energy strategies in central and eastern European countries, including developing market-oriented structures, realistic pricing mechanisms, supply and demand analyses, policy choice assessments, forecasting, and appropriate regulatory frameworks, as well as regional energy planning, through the following forms of assistance: country reviews; studies and workshops; data and information collection and management; and training and institution-building.

- Energy supply and demand issues, encompassing, in the shorter term, mainly measures for increasing energy efficiency and developing policies and options to restructure energy supplies;

- The introduction of greater environmental and safety awareness by means of technology transfer, establishing monitoring institutions, and setting regulatory standards and targets to control emissions of pollutants such as CO_2 and NO_x.

Environmental considerations also need to be incorporated into the process in two other areas, particularly relevant to policy planning and formulation: energy conservation and efficiency; and the switch to cleaner fuels.

Co-ordinated bilateral G-24 assistance has a short to medium-term orientation. The energy assistance strategy, particularly in reference to short-term priorities, clearly incorporates the integration of environmental issues.

An Initial Summary

- Co-ordinated bilateral G-24 assistance has been set up with a short to medium-term orientation.

- The energy assistance strategy, particularly with reference to shorter term priorities, clearly incorporates environmental issues.

- In both sectors, the priority areas identified by the two assistance strategies -- institutional strengthening and policy planning, and, in the energy sector particularly, environmental safety and awareness -- indicate the scope and necessity for co-operation and co-ordination, both for assistance programmes and for the governments in the region.

THE SCOPE OF G-24 ASSISTANCE IN THE ENERGY AND ENVIRONMENTAL SECTORS

Bearing in mind these points, it will now be interesting to look at the actual assistance programmes and projects for environment and energy -- at least, as far as they have been documented by the G-24 Project Database -- first with respect to the amount of financial commitments and second, to estimate the scope of integration of environmental issues.

Total Assistance for Energy and the Environment

As mentioned above, total assistance from the first quarter of 1990 through the second quarter of 1992 of the G-24 countries and of international financial institutions totals ECU 46.9 billion. Assistance from the G-24 makes up roughly 70% -- ECU 33.9 billion -- while that of the international financial institutions, ECU 13 billion.

Of the ECU 33.9 billion from the G-24 countries, roughly 1.47%, or ECU 501 million, were committed for environmental project assistance, of which over 95% were grant funds. The

G-24 countries committed 0.82% of their total assistance, or about ECU 280 million, for energy sector assistance. Just over 51% of energy sector assistance was in the form of grants.

Environmental commitments by the international financial institutions were ECU 209.6 million (of which, just over 1% were in the form of grants); commitments for the energy sector were ECU 846.4 million (of which, 1.3% in grants).

Pattern of Assistance

The collected project information in the G-24 Database show the following patterns in energy and environmental assistance:

Major Recipients. In environment, in terms of numbers of projects, the major recipients are the CSFR, Poland, and Hungary, followed by region-wide projects. In terms of grant totals, the CSFR ranks first, followed by region-wide projects and by Poland. In energy, the CSFR has received the largest number of projects, followed by Hungary, Romania, and Poland.

Largest Donors. In environment, in terms of numbers of projects, the largest donors are the EC, Denmark, the Netherlands, and then Sweden; in terms of total grant aid, the EC again comes first, followed by the U.S., Denmark, and the World Bank. In energy, a different pattern emerges, as generally there are fewer, more costly projects than in environment. The EC and the World Bank lead in terms of number of projects. In terms of financial commitments, the largest provider of loans is the World Bank, while the EC and the U.S. are the largest providers of grants.

Assistance Projects by Sub-sector. In environment, most assistance projects are apparently conducted in waste management, air pollution control, and environmental research, education, and information. In energy, most projects are in energy efficiency and conservation (projects for the building and housing sector, for energy efficiency and conservation programmes, for combined heat and power generation plants, and for SO_2 reduction), in the "general" sub-sector (policy development, energy management, etc.), and in electricity (including power sector programmes and power plant retrofits), followed by oil and gas (supply, storage, training, and sectoral studies), coal (substitution, retraining, and market adaption studies) and finally, in the field of renewables. This last topic includes training projects, feasibility studies, and pilot projects.

Type of Aid. In energy, technical co-operation is dominant (particularly for efficiency and conservation), followed by investments in efficiency and conservation, electricity, and oil and gas. In environment, technical co-operation is again dominant, particularly for waste management.

SUMMARY AND OUTLOOK

The majority of assistance projects in both sectors has so far been in technical assistance: training, studies, and support for policy making.

An analysis of environmental project assistance indicates that the amount of money spent or committed is not necessarily an indicator of the impact of the assistance. Donors such as the Netherlands and Denmark are not among the largest aid providers, but their projects often aim to achieve a demonstration effect (for pilot projects) or a multiplier effect (for training).

Environmental considerations seem by and large integrated into energy sector assistance projects, particularly projects for policy elaboration, demonstration projects, and technical assistance for energy efficiency.

On the whole it can be noted that in both sectors the G-24 strategies have largely been followed by the donor community. In future, with the progress of reforms, a shift to more investment-related assistance will be required, with a wider variety of assistance projects and improved operational co-ordination, particularly for implementation.

US Agency for International Development
Energy Sector Assistance:
Regional Strategy and Country Programs

Robert A. Archer
Energy and Infrastructure Division
Office of Development Resources
Bureau for Europe
US AID

Background

The United States Agency for International Development (USAID) is responsible for the administration of the US Central and East European Assistance Program under the guidance of the Department of State.

The USAID energy assistance program is based upon the recognition that the creation of efficient energy systems is a critical element in the transformation of the economies of Central and Eastern Europe to private sector-led market economies. The region's current inefficient energy systems are a major impediment to economic reform and improvements in the quality of life. Profound changes are occurring in these systems as a result of the internal economic reforms and in response to external factors that include: declining energy supplies from the former Soviet Union; the European Energy Charter dialogue; growing international concerns about the safety of Soviet-designed nuclear reactors; and the impact of energy generated emissions on the region and globally.

Strategic Framework

To carry out the energy assistance program we have established a Regional Strategic Framework with a focused country implementation approach. The Framework consists of five strategic objectives, which are:

1)   Rationalization of energy prices
2)   Promotion of energy efficiency, restructuring and privatization
3)   Promotion of US investment and technology transfer
4)   Reduction of environmental pollution and improvement of nuclear safety
5)   Promotion of regional cooperation and integration with western europe and international energy markets

Assistance Programming and Donor Coordination

Within this framework, assistance priorities were established through discussions between country officials and joint teams of representatives from USAID, the US Department of Energy, the US Environmental Protection Agency, and the US Department of State. The work program was developed and is being carried out in cooperation with the G-24 process, including cooperation with the World Bank, EBRD and the European Communities. US central and eastern European cooperation consists primarily of technical assistance and training activities and includes US$ 50 to 60 million annually in grant assistance for energy and environmental programmes.

Implementation

To implement the strategy a set of five projects have been put in place. Following are brief descriptions of some their activities.

The Regional Energy Efficiency Project. This major initiative, with an overall focus on improving energy system and end-use efficiencies, environmental impact and safety includes the following activities carried out by U.S. companies under contract, the US Energy Association, the US Nuclear Regulatory Commission and US Department of Energy.

US private companies provide assistance in three major areas:

1)   Energy efficiency, pricing and restructuring
2)   Electricity systems
3)   Oil and gas systems

Activities underway include: electricity tariff reform analysis; the development of plans for private power generation; the development and implementation of demand side management programs and integrated resource planning; support for private sector energy efficiency consulting capabilities; power sector restructuring, including environmental analysis; and institutional development for oil and gas concession organization and management.

Through the US Energy Association, a partnership program has been established linking US electric utilities and central and eastern European utilities. These partnerships are designed to introduce modern financial and management concepts necessary for utility reform. To date five partnerships have been established and three are in planning.

Technical cooperation activities for nuclear safety, energy efficiency, renewable energy and clean coal technology are supported by the Department of Energy and Nuclear Regulatory Commission. Grant funding is also provided to the International Energy Agency for energy policy work in Central and Eastern Europe.

Emergency Energy Project. This recently completed initiative was a quick-response one-year effort that identified and demonstrated the potential for low-cost and no-cost energy efficiency improvements in industrial facilities and refineries. It provided energy audits at 48 industrial plants in six countries as well as energy efficiency equipment to implement audit recommendations. For all the work, US engineering experts subcontracted with local engineers (in the private sector where possible). The lessons learned are: (a) low- and no-cost improvements, through better energy management and the installation of low-cost equipment, can usually save at least 15 percent of the energy consumed per plant (in some cases savings may reach 40 percent) -- "non-technical" management and organizational changes also promise significant energy savings; (b) energy pricing, restructuring and privatization are critical if energy efficiency is to become widespread, and private sector firms to provide energy efficiency services and equipment are to emerge. The Emergency Energy Project also supported energy pricing analysis and training in international oil procurement.

Krakow Power Plant Retrofit and Krakow Clean Fossil Fuels and Energy Efficiency Projects. The Krakow Power Plant Retrofit Project provides co-finances, with the Polish Government, the demonstration of an advanced desulphurization system at the Skawina Power Plant in Krakow, Poland. The Krakow Clean Fossil Fuels and Energy Efficiency Project identifies environmental pollution from small sources in Krakow and tries to commercialize cost-effective approaches to these emissions through demonstrations, testing, and commercial joint ventures between US and Polish companies. The two projects are being implemented by the US Department of Energy.

Hungary Energy Sector Grant. This US$ 10 million project provides balance of payments financing as part of World Bank Programme to support energy policy and pricing reform. USAID's grant supports the establishment of a local currency account that disburses funds to help low-income pensioners reduce the burden of tariff increases.

Capital Development Initiative. This initiative supports expanded Central and East European and US industry linkages related to energy infrastructure. It provides technical assistance to identify priority energy investment needs and supports project development costs for US and Central and East European partners.

The PHARE Programme of the
Commission of the European Communities

Dr. Christoph Hilz
PHARE Operational Service
Commission of the European Communities

The PHARE and TACIS Programmes

The overall objective of the PHARE programme is to support the countries of Central and Eastern Europe in the process of restructuring their previously centrally controlled economies to market oriented economies. The PHARE 1992 guidelines underline that assistance should be targeted to support specific investment activities while also mobilising local resources. The Commission's energy assistance tries to incorporate the goals of the European Energy Charter, which provides a common framework for energy sector cooperation.

The PHARE programme (originally, Poland and Hungary Assistance for Restructuring of the Economy) was initiated by the European Community in 1989 to provide ECU 300 million for technical assistance to support the economic and political reform process of these two countries and an additional ECU 200 million for Bulgaria, the CSFR, the former GDR, Romania and Yugoslavia. Since then, the PHARE programme has been extended to eleven countries and the budget has increased to ECU 800 million in 1991 and ECU 1 billion in 1992. The projections for the next years indicate that the programme should grow approximately 20 per cent per year. The PHARE budget may thus reach ECU 1.2 billion in 1993 and, over the following five years, double to ECU 2.4 billion in 1997.

Under a separate Commission programme for Technical Assistance for the Commonwealth of Independent States (TACIS), the Commission allocated ECU 400 million in 1991 and ECU 500 million in 1992 to assist the newly independent states of the former USSR.

PHARE's energy sector assistance has two budget lines: the national programmes and a regional energy programme that sponsors projects of relevance to all countries. The budget of the national energy programmes is approximately ECU 3 to 5 million per year for each country, and the regional programme receives about ECU 7 million per year. Currently the funds available for energy related assistance amount to approximately ECU 40 million for 1991 and 1992 combined. In addition, assistance for the environment sector totals approximately ECU 80 million per year.

In addition to the PHARE programme, two other assistance activities of the Commission in Central and Eastern Europe relating to energy should be mentioned. Under the TACIS programme, approximately ECU 50 million per year are available to support energy sector transformation activities in the former USSR. In addition, the Directorate General for Energy runs the THERMIE programme, which tries to introduce energy technologies within the European Community and in central and eastern European countries. Its budget for Central and Eastern Europe is ECU 5 to 6 million per year.

Energy and Environment

Two central goals of the PHARE programme are to assist the countries of Central and Eastern Europe develop a sound energy policy -- namely security and high reliability of supply, and moderate prices to allow industrial growth -- as well as an effective environmental policy to reduce the overall pollution and minimise risks for public health.

In order to achieve these objectives, PHARE projects range from assistance for policy formulation, education and training, management assistance and institutional support to concrete measures in energy saving activities. Clearly, improving energy efficiency is a priority. In 1991, there were about 50 projects in the energy sector. To provide a brief overview on scope and depth of these assistance programmes, a few selected projects can be mentioned:

- Least-Cost Planning studies have been undertaken for the energy sectors in Romania and the CSFR, in order to assist in energy policy formulation.

- Energy Centres or other activities to promote energy efficiency have been supported in all PHARE countries, providing training, public awareness campaigns, energy audits, and other initiatives to reduce energy consumption and increase energy efficiency.

- A Corporate Restructuring Study for Romania and a Regulatory Institutions Study for the CSFR will assist the reorganisation of these countries' energy sectors.

- Energy conservation projects for public buildings and for selected industries have been undertaken in all PHARE countries.

- In order to address issues and problems common to PHARE countries, a Regional Energy Programme was initiated for 1992 which covers electricity and gas interconnection, oil refining and transportation, and other sectors.

Cooperation

In order to facilitate the work of international banking institutions such as the EIB, EBRD, and WB, the PHARE energy sector programme closely cooperates with these institutions and also provides direct assistance. In this context, PHARE assistance could be interpreted as seed funding to attract international loans and private investments. One example is a project in cooperation with the EIB and EBRD to complete the Maritza East thermal power plant in

Bulgaria. Other examples include joint studies to identify energy sector investment options in the several countries.

Conclusion

This brief presentation shows how technical assistance by the Commission of European Community's PHARE programme is an important and effective component of the international aid programmes to support the restructuring of the central and eastern European countries' energy sectors as part of their transition towards market-based economies.

The European Investment Bank

Christopher Knowles
Unit for Operations in Eastern and Central Europe
European Investment Bank (EIB)

EIB Financing

The European Investment Bank (EIB) is the long-term finance bank of the European Communities. It was created in 1958 under the Treaty of Rome that established the European Economic Community.

In accordance with Article 130 of the Treaty of Rome, the EIB finances investments that contribute directly or indirectly to economic development in the EC in general, and that further:

- economic development of the Community's less-favoured regions;

- attainment of the Community's energy policy objectives, which include developing indigenous resources, promoting the rational use of energy, and diversifying imports away from oil;

- modernisation or conversion of enterprises, and the development of advanced technology to improve the competitiveness of Community industry and to foster co-operation between enterprises in different Member countries;

- improvement of communications between Member States, including transportation and telecommunications links.

- Other Community objectives, such as protection of the environment and implementation of the Community's co-operation policies.

In 1989, EIB was mandated to lend up to ECU 1 billion in Hungary and Poland, and in 1991 received an additional mandate to lend up to ECU 700 million in Bulgaria, the CSFR and Romania. So far, the Bank has lent ECU 650 million in these countries.

The Bank's involvement with environmental protection is also long standing -- systematic environmental assessments were introduced in 1972 (the year of the UN's Stockholm conference on the environment). The scope of environmental lending has progressively widened and now covers the full range of interventions -- improvements in water and air quality and in urban and natural environments.

A few figures serve to demonstrate the seriousness with which these policies are held. In the five years ending December 1991, EIB's total financing was almost ECU 60 billion, more or less equivalent to US$ 75 billion. Around ECU 10 billion primarily furthered energy policy objectives -- and about 30% of this went towards "rational energy usage". Over ECU 8 billion was lent for projects to improve the environment and quality of life. A further ECU 10 billion of regional development funding had energy and/or environmental benefits.

Future Assistance to Central and Eastern Europe

The question of the overall scope and magnitude of assistance is inevitably a delicate one which will not be decided by the EIB alone. One element that can be taken into consideration is the fact that ECU 1.1 billion of the existing mandates in five countries in the region remains to be committed before their expiration in 1993.

A further element is the fact that each of these five countries has negotiated or is in the process of negotiating an associate membership of the European Communities. These "European Agreements" include a protocol providing for financial cooperation embracing EIB lending. The amounts and timing of this lending remain to be fixed.

One last element is the fact that EIB's lending policy does not prescribe any minimum guaranteed lending amount to a given country or sector, nor any maximum other than that which may result from overall lending ceilings. On the other hand EIB's financing is limited to no more than half the costs of a given project. This means in turn that EIB's ability to lend is *inter alia* determined by the presence of conditions favourable to investment or co-financing and, considering the scarcity of financial resources in the region, perhaps more specifically the conditions which will encourage foreign investment, notably in the energy sector. There appear to be three main conditions, namely <u>favourable general economic circumstances, the promise of a sufficiently high rate of return, and an acceptable level of risk</u>.

The energy sector, together with its environmental implications, is recognised by the EIB as being of the greatest importance -- approximately one-third of our commitments so far in Central and Eastern Europe have been for this sector, and in each case have been accompanied by environmental goals. Though by no means a target, this current share could probably be regarded as some sort of floor for future energy sector lending.

Environmental goals and EIB lending

As a long-term project financing bank, the EIB ensures the effectiveness of its investments through detailed in-house appraisals. Projects have to be financially, economically, technically and environmentally viable. Where a project is deemed unsatisfactory from an environmental (or other) point of view the Bank simply refuses to finance.

Environmental awareness can be considered as a part of the Bank's culture, and in all projects within the European Communities (and indeed most outside projects) the application of national and/or EC regulations is required. Even where binding regulations are not yet in force, Bank staff try and raise environmental awareness of project promoters to ensure the adoption of environmentally optimal designs even where this is not required by law.

This applies to all categories of lending, but is particularly critical in the case of energy lending. Legislation or guidelines applicable by the Bank, depending on circumstances, includes the EC directive on emissions from large combustion plants as well as the transboundary targets of the Helsinki Agreement.

Environment projects can be financed by EIB within an energy loan, or in their own right, or possibly within the context of integrated regional development projects. Preparatory steps for this type of operation could be one result of the Baltic Sea initiative discussed below.

In general, EIB endeavours to respect the

```
╔══════════════════════════════════════════════╗
║               EIB Energy Projects            ║
║          In Central and Eastern Europe       ║
║                (as of June 1992)             ║
║                                              ║
║  A. Projects                    Financing*   ║
║                                              ║
║  1. Poland   -  Gas development       50     ║
║  2. Hungary  -  Power grid (ripple control  15║
║  3. Hungary  -  CC Gas turbine (district heating) 35║
║  4. Romania  -  Lignite plant rehabilitation  25║
║  5. Bulgaria -  Lignite plant completion,    ║
║                 flue gas desulphurisation    45 ║
║                                              ║
║                 TOTAL                 170    ║
║                                              ║
║  B. Studies                                  ║
║                                              ║
║  1. Hungary  -  Power interconnection        ║
║                 with Western Europe    0.4   ║
║  2. Romania  -  Least cost development       ║
║                 -- power sector        0.6   ║
║                                              ║
║              *in millions of ECU             ║
╚══════════════════════════════════════════════╝
```

priorities of its borrowers, always assuming that these conform to sound least cost and optimisation techniques. At the present moment, data and methodological problems make these techniques difficult to apply meaningfully in much of Central and Eastern Europe, to which must be added the considerable uncertainty surrounding future levels of energy demand. This fact leads to emphasis of two other aspects - flexibility of investment and risk analysis.

A high degree of uncertainty is probably inherent in the energy sector in that choices have to be made regarding the very long term, whereas we cannot be confident of judgements concerning periods so far ahead. The life time of power plants and energy transport infrastructure is often more than 25 years. It is therefore necessary to take a long term view, despite the uncertainties, but also desirable to hedge ones bets where possible -- for example by emphasising flexibility and a diversification of energy investment. This approach may even sometimes mean looking for options with relatively short lives and having a preference for phased projects.

Coordination with Other Financing Organisations

Environmental lending in particular is a field for appropriate coordination and cooperation. For many years there has been active cooperation between the Bank and the Commission of the European Communities regarding lending for EC countries and for elements of the EC's cooperation policy. EIB has maintained this tradition in becoming an active participant in the principal forum for coordinating of all assistance to Central and Eastern Europe, namely the various G-24 groups.

The EIB has also participated in various "cooperative" initiatives relevant to its operations in Central and Eastern Europe. In the energy sector the EIB has worked closely with the World Bank on its CEENERGY initiative, and with programmes of the Commission of the European Community and UNECE.

The EIB has recently joined the Baltic Sea regional programme, the initiative for which came form the CSFR and Poland in particular, and which involves, in addition to the states of the Baltic region, the Commission of the European Communities, the World Bank, EBRD and the Nordic Investment Bank. The EIB has supervised the execution of pre-feasibility studies in the Oder river basin, in parallel with other river basin studies supervised by other members of the initiative. The programme is expected to result in long term measures, including investments, to diminish pollution of the Baltic Sea and improve environmental conditions in the river basins, including the reduction of emissions from the energy sector.

Observations on the Conference Discussions

First, the importance of distinguishing between privatisation and restructuring in the energy sector should be underlined. Speaking from an EIB perspective, we work across the complete range of energy ownership and operating structures in the EC, and even after 35 years I would hesitate to make too many generalisations. Certainly we would not wish to export any particular doctrine, and in Central and Eastern Europe we have become very conscious of the political and operational complications of demanding privatisation simultaneously with profound restructuring.

In the interests of achieving any results and not further dashing expectations, however unwarranted they may be, it is, second, necessary to be very realistic about the conditions and/or concessions demanded.

Third, there is a paradoxical co-existence of major investment needs with large amounts of funds which are proving more difficult and slower to commit than most people expected. If the bottle-neck is not primarily one of finance, then it must be one of people. In the energy sector at least I am relatively impressed by the level and abundance of technical and engineering skills in the region, and therefore by process of elimination we arrive at a problem concerning non-technical (that is, government and managerial) skill levels. As a would be lender, the problem seems to be the difficulty in setting technically defined investment needs into an economically and financially rational context.

I am not sure that the problem is overcome by adding to the existing army of consultants. Whatever the means, what is needed is greater attention to least cost and optimisation types of analysis, and of course to the integration of the different fields of analysis. But all this has to be kept in perspective -- there is a temptation to go overboard with this type of work. Some early results are necessary in political as well as economic terms, and a measured degree of compromise in the investment planning process would be quite justified in achieving these ends.

EBRD's Approach to Energy and Environmental Funding

Dr. Erich Unterwurzacher
Economist,
Public Infrastructure, Energy and Environment Department
The European Bank for Reconstruction and Development

The Environmental Policy of the EBRD

The European Bank for Reconstruction and Development is directed by its founding agreement to "promote in the full range of its activities environmentally sound and sustainable development." This is the first time that an international financial institution has been given a clear mandate in its founding Charter for environmental protection and rehabilitation -- a recognition of the environmental deterioration in the EBRD's countries of operation. Economic growth and political and social stability in the region depend upon restoring the environment.

The EBRD pursues the following policies for promoting environmental improvements:

- assisting countries formulate environmental policy, including the development of effective legal and regulatory frameworks;

- promoting the use of economic instruments and the adoption of market-based techniques in environmental management;

- encouraging the development of domestic environmental goods and services industries;

- supporting studies and programmes that address regional and national environmental problems;

- following environmental assessment, management planning, audit, and monitoring procedures throughout EBRD activities and investments; and

- encouraging the dissemination of environmental information to all levels of government and to the public.

EBRD's procedures integrate environmental concerns into all parts of the project preparation and approval process. These procedures include environmental information on projects, an environmental review, the incorporation of environmental covenants into loan agreements, and supervision and monitoring of the environmental aspects of all projects. The procedures should ensure that the highest environmental standards are met in the Bank's operations. A potential project can be rejected when there are major environmental problems or when a project sponsor fails to handle environmental issues in a satisfactory manner.

These principles apply to all of EBRD's projects, not just to activities in the energy sector. The construction of motorways or the establishment of industrial or commercial enterprises would all have to undergo the same environmental review procedures.

The Bank's Energy Sector Priorities

EBRD's energy strategy is designed to respond to the most pressing needs of European economies in transition. The overall objective is to assist these countries reorient their energy sectors along more commercial lines and to use least-cost principles that give priority to the consideration of resource-use efficiency.

EBRD will assist countries enhance the efficiency of existing supply facilities, foster energy supply security, and promote regional energy connections where they are cost-effective and lead to gains in energy supply security, foreign exchange earnings, and a more open energy market. In line with EBRD's mandate to promote private sector development and market competition, energy activities should also stimulate foreign investment and the creation of domestic small and medium-sized enterprises. Measures to promote energy efficiency throughout the energy chain, from production to end use, will be a priority in energy sector operation -- these measures coincide closely with the Bank's environmental mandate. Over the next few years, EBRD will focus its energy operations on:

- repairing and rehabilitating existing energy supply facilities, such as power plants and oil and natural gas pipelines;

- completing existing high-priority projects, including transmission lines and power stations under construction that need continued or new financial assistance;

- assisting countries diversify their sources of energy supply (taking into account their energy security needs), for example through projects that provide improved access to international oil markets;

- encouraging private sector projects that liberalise energy supply and inject foreign capital, such as initiatives to bring oil and gas fields on stream;

- assisting with priority nuclear projects -- in particular those that improve the safety of existing nuclear plants -- when they can be brought fully in line with internationally accepted safety standards -- safety considerations and economic viability are the guiding principles of EBRD's potential involvement in nuclear projects.

In the immediate future, EBRD will also provide emergency energy sector technical assistance and emergency investments to help limit social hardships resulting from economic restructuring. In addition, short-term operations will concentrate on measures to alleviate the impact of energy shortages resulting from significant reductions in deliveries from the region's traditional supplier; short-term operations will also guard against spare-part supply disruptions that could jeopardise the reliability of the energy system.

Financing Mechanisms

As an international financial institution, the EBRD provides advice, loans, equity investments, and debt guarantees to qualified applicants. To ensure the most effective implementation, the Bank is organized into two parts, Merchant Banking and Development Banking. EBRD's Merchant Banking Vice-Presidency concentrates primarily on deals with private enterprises. The Development Banking Vice-Presidency includes a full range of financing, economic, and country experience, as well sectoral expertise in areas such as agriculture, communications, energy, and environment. Projects financed by the Development Banking Vice-Presidency usually require a state guarantee of the recipient country. Development Banking loans aim to replace, upgrade, rehabilitate, and construct countries' physical infrastructures. EBRD offers assistance in project identification, preparation, funding -- including the mobilization of co-financing from other official sources -- and support for project implementation, including procurement.

The majority of EBRD's energy operations are expected to finance fuel industries and public utilities. Operations will also involve private investment, either in joint venture with public utilities (such as Build-Operate-Transfer schemes) or in providing finance to newly privatised utilities or to private entrants in the utility sector. Most of these operations would provide loan finance, but EBRD could also take equity stakes. Projects that involve electricity generation or other regulated energy industries, such as heat production and distribution or gas transmission and distribution, are operations typically supported by EBRD's Development banking side.

The EBRD intends to provide financing for technical assistance and human resource development throughout its operations, but especially those involving public utilities and the restructuring of highly integrated, non-competitive energy sectors. Technical assistance projects may be financed through funds specifically provided by certain of the EBRD's member government (through the Technical Assistance Co-operation Funds Programme). These special co-operation funds provide significant financial resources.

Examples of Operations in the Energy and Environment Sectors

In the first year of operation since its inauguration in April 1991, EBRD has committed more than ECU 550 million of funding. So far, approximately 15% of EBRD's funds have been allocated to energy sector projects; the share within the Development Banking Vice-Presidency is even higher. The share of energy sector investments in the Bank's lending portfolio is likely to increase. Recently, EBRD approved a project to finance the modernization and rehabilitation of oil fields in Romania, and various sector projects are currently under review or in an early stage of identification.

Other energy sector projects which have been committed in the Bank's first year of operation include a loan for district heating supply in Poland. This project was co-financed with the World Bank. The loan was made to a Polish bank, which served as an intermediary and will disburse money to selected district heating companies. In April 1992 EBRD approved a loan for the completion of the Maritza lignite power plant in Bulgaria, including the installation of flue-gas desulphurization equipment at the plant. The European Investment Bank (EIB) and the National Electricity Company of Bulgaria co-financed this loan. Both projects have a strong environment component, in line with the Bank's mandate. The increased efficiency and extension of district heating systems in Poland will reduce the emissions of boiler stations and individual heating units, and the installation of flue-gas desulphurization equipment in Bulgaria will reduce power plant emissions.

The EBRD's technical assistance projects focus on identifying urgent needs -- investments that can avoid economically damaging shortfalls in country energy supplies, improve the efficiency of energy production and use to reduce country energy imports, and identify short-term options to diversify fuel supply and increase country energy security. Pre-investment technical assistance projects are being carried out in the Baltic States and Belorus. The technical assistance project in Belorus will also investigate the scope of emergency investments needed to upgrade the electricity and gas supply infrastructure for protection against contamination in areas affected by radioactive fall-out from Chernobyl. Other technical assistance activities assist governments in the region in project implementation and in the restructuring of their energy industries along commercial lines. For example, the oil rehabilitation project in Romania will be accompanied by technical assistance activities that will introduce computerised accounting systems, financial controls, and auditing arrangements in the oil industry.

In the area of environment, EBRD is carrying out studies on environmental standards and legislation in Central and Eastern Europe. The objective of these studies is to review existing environmental legislation and policies, including environmental assessment requirements, standards for emissions and discharges, and enforcement mechanisms, and explore developments over the next 10 to 15 years. The status and harmonization of environmental standards in western, central, and eastern European countries will also be assessed.

The EBRD's technical assistance pipeline include pre-investment activities as part of the Baltic Sea Environmental Programme, a co-operative initiative with the World Bank, EIB, Nordic Investment Bank, and Commission of the European Communities. Another co-operative activity with EBRD participation is the Danube River Basin Environmental Programme, whose activities are supported by a number of international agencies, most notably the EC Commission and the Global Environmental Facility, as well as NGOs and bilateral donors.

The Bank is also assisting the development of an energy master plan for the region of Karelia in Russia -- this master plan will guide government initiatives to rehabilitate and develop the inadequate energy infrastructure of this remote area. The study will include a least-cost analysis of various options to improve energy supply security and energy efficiency.

EBRD places great emphasis on the co-ordination, co-operation, and participation of competent local or foreign partners. In its investment operations, EBRD looks for co-financing possibilities and the participation of local agencies and industry. EBRD encourages international institutions, including the EC, the World Bank, and OECD, to engage in a dialogue on allocating lead responsibilities for different aspects of the policy dialogue with central and eastern European countries. This is essential to avoid duplication of effort and to optimize the use of public and human resources.

The World Bank Group's Energy Activities
In Central and Eastern Europe[1]

I. Evolution of World Bank Group Activities

As of December 31, 1991, World Bank cumulative lending commitments to Central and Eastern Europe amounted to US$ 14.4 billion -- of which US$ 5.4 billion were provided over the last three years. The largest Bank borrowers in the region have been Yugoslavia (US$ 6.2 billion), Hungary (US$ 3.1 billion), Romania (US$ 2.4 billion), and Poland (US$ 2.2 billion).

Before fiscal year 1990 (FY90), most World Bank lending to the region was project-specific, with the bulk of loans supporting investments in infrastructure, industry, and agriculture. With the political changes since 1989, countries in Central and Eastern Europe began to undergo comprehensive economic transformations. The World Bank has begun to implement substantial programs of assistance to facilitate the region's economic transition. In its 1989 fiscal year, Bank lending to the region was limited to Hungary and Yugoslavia and amounted to a little over US$ 500 million. In FY90, the Bank lent US$ 1.8 billion to Hungary, Poland, Yugoslavia, Bulgaria, and Romania.

Currently the Bank provides about 15% of the US$ 20 billion in yearly external financing needs of Central and Eastern Europe (this figure is based on World Bank estimates; it does not include the financing needs of the former USSR). Its assistance is part of a broader effort by the international community. The Bank has developed a close and effective cooperation with the EC's PHARE Programme. The Bank is also closely coordinating and collaborating with the IMF, and -- as a result -- the governments of central and eastern European countries have prepared medium-term economic reform frameworks based on joint input from IMF and Bank staff. Close coordination with other multilateral agencies (EBRD, EIB, and OECD) is also maintained through regular meetings to review programs of assistance, avoid overlap and thereby enhance the overall effectiveness of external support to Central and Eastern Europe.

The World Bank has co-financed a number of projects with other organizations, including the Japanese Export-Import Bank, the European Investment Bank, and the EBRD. Further cooperative operations with these institutions are expected in the future. The Bank is also closely coordinating a wide array of activities with bilateral donors (such as the U.K. Know-How Fund, USAID, and others) as well as with the Hexagonal group.

---

1. This is an abridged version of a paper prepared by Bernard Montfort and Harold E. Wackman of The World Bank.

II. The Transformation Process and World Bank Group Efforts

Energy sector transformation cannot be separated from the broader macroeconomic reform and industrial restructuring processes. The World Bank has undertaken substantial economic and sectoral analysis in support of the transformation process. Work includes: country economic memoranda that focus on macroeconomic issues (undertaken for most countries in the region, including new World Bank members such as Czechoslovakia and Bulgaria); trade analyses for Hungary and Poland, with an emphasis on regional issues; financial sector assessments for Hungary, Poland, Czechoslovakia and Yugoslavia; industrial sector work in Hungary and Yugoslavia; energy and environmental studies for Hungary, Czechoslovakia, Poland and Yugoslavia; and analyses of social sector issues in Hungary and Poland. Moreover, in Poland, a number of joint task forces with the national government studied strategic issues in agriculture, housing, and health, as well as legal and regulatory issues for the financial sector.

The Bank's financial assistance has been focusing on (i) broad support for fairly comprehensive transformation programs through Structural Adjustment Loans (SALs), supporting major policy and institutional measures in financial sector development and private sector development; (ii) specific programs and projects in these sectors to strengthen their development and increase the efficiency and mobility of labor and capital resources; (iii) projects to modernize and improve the efficiency of the infrastructure base in transport and telecommunications; (iv) support for policy improvements and appropriate investments for energy and environment; and (v) specific programs in the social policy area.

The International Finance Corporation (IFC), which is part of the World Bank Group, has supported joint venture investment operations and has promoted a dialogue on foreign investment laws and procedures. IFC's capital markets group has assisted in the creation of new financial sector institutions and has provided advice on the legal and regulatory infrastructure for securities markets. IFC's corporate services group has advised on restructuring and privatization in Poland, Hungary, and Czechoslovakia.

The Multilateral Investment Guarantee Agency's (MIGA), also part of the World Bank Group, facilitates foreign investment by providing political risk insurance on equity investments in these countries. Several insurance transactions have taken place in Hungary and a number of additional projects in Poland, Hungary and Czechoslovakia are under active consideration.

III. Energy Activities in Central and Eastern Europe

The energy issues facing the countries of the region include: serious distortions of energy prices; extremely high energy intensities; the poor technical, economic and financial performance of energy enterprises; high import dependency for energy, with excessive vulnerability on a single exporting country; serious health problems related to environmental pollution from energy production and consumption; and serious institutional shortcomings in the face of urgent requirements to establish a new set of energy policies, institutions, priorities and investments.

The World Bank's loans to countries in the region have tried to address these problems; recent loans and some proposed projects are described below.

Poland

Structural Adjustment Loan (SAL) -- US$ 300 million loan, Board approval given in July, 1991. Under the terms of this loan, coal prices were substantially liberalized and initial steps were taken towards the elimination of energy-related subsidies and the cross-subsidization of household energy consumers. Significant progress in energy price reform has been made, including in coal prices.

Energy Resources Development Project -- US$ 250 million loan plus US$ 60 million in cofinancing from EIB. Total project cost: US$ 648 million. Board approval: June, 1990. This project aimed to:

    (a)   increase production of natural gas and encourage fuel switiching away from coal.

    (b)   support energy price adjustments with a view to improve the structure of gas prices and to increase them to market levels by the end of 1992. The full cost of distribution to household consumers would be gradually reflected in tariffs by the end of 1995; and

    (c)   finance restructuring studies for the gas, power, district heat, and coal subsectors. The studies will serve as a basis for restructuring and significant demonopolization of all energy subsectors, and for setting up a flexible regulatory framework allowing progress towards privatization and joint venture arrangements.

Heat Supply Restructuring and Conservation Project -- US$ 340 million plus US$ 50 million in cofinancing from EBRD. Total project cost: US$ 619 million. Board approval: June, 1991. This project will:

    (a)   support the implementation of comprehensive energy sector restructuring, the commercialization and privatization of restructured enterprises and of petroleum exploration and production activities. A consistent regulatory framework between network subsectors will be introduced and the improvement of energy pricing policies will continue;

    (b)   extend the life of existing district heat systems through rehabilitation work and the introduction of modern technologies and materials, thereby significantly reducing capital expenditures and operating costs;

    (c)   encourage energy conservation in the district heating sector through appropriate investments and by supporting energy price reform; and

(d)   reduce environmental pollution through investments in energy-efficient equipment and systems as well as support for a program to replace small coal-fired boilers with gas-fired boilers.

The Cogeneration Privatization Project -- tentative loan amount: US$ 85 million, with an additional US$ 30 million from commercial lenders. Total project cost is estimated at US$ 115 million, Board approval: tentatively, by the end of 1992. This proposed project would constitute the first case in which the restructuring, privatization, pricing and regulatory aspects of the structural adjustment component of the Heat Supply Restructuring and Conservation Project would be combined and tested. Its major objectives are to:

(a)   increase the share of heat supplied in Krakow through combined heat and power (CHP) production, thereby improving energy efficiency while reducing pollution;

(b)   further reduce environmental pollution by introducing appropriate NO_x and particulate pollution control equipment at the Leg CHP plants in Krakow;

(c)   increase operating efficiency and reduce the relative cost of power and heat to consumers over the long term; and

(d)   open the door to private investment in, and ultimately ownership of, major power plants in Poland, thereby setting the framework for similar future investments in other parts of the country.

Czechoslovakia

Structural Adjustment Loan I (SAL I) -- US$ 450 million structural adjustment loan, Board approval: June, 1991. Energy related conditionalities cover energy pricing reform, energy sector regulation, power sector investment planning and preparation of a medium-term environmental action plan.

Power and Environmental Improvement Project -- US$ 246 million loan, US$ 557.5 million total project cost, Board approval: May 1992. Its primary objective is environmental: to reduce air pollution in Northern Bohemia, an area that is one of the most severely polluted in Europe, and thereby improve the environment and health of the local population. This objective will be accomplished in the context of overall reform of the energy sector. To this end, the project will: (a) reduce total consumption of pollution-causing lignite through power plant efficiency improvements; (b) curtail power plant SO_2 emissions by means of flue gas desulfurization; (c) reduce dust and fly-ash pollution from power plants, improving investment planning and corporate management and organization.

Gas Investment Project - Additional projects, related primarily to gas are being planned. One project is evaluating the construction of a new international pipeline to satisfy existing and new gas demands as well as additional gas transit to the West. Additional gas storage and distribution facilities are also being considered. Benefits would include increased use of gas and improved supply security, along with the participation of the domestic private sector in these projects.

Slovak Power Loan - This proposed project would assist SEP in improving thermal efficiency at the Vojany power station. It would also help to lower power plant pollution through the reduction of noxious emissions and effluents. Another objective would be to upgrade SEP's power system to reduce losses and prepare for eventual integration into a Europe-wide network. The project would help SEP strengthen its corporate organization, financial administration, and accounting.

Hungary

Structural Adjustment Loan II -- US$ 250 million loan. Board approval: June, 1991. Energy-related agreements cover: the elimination of government budget subsidies for energy bought by households; removal of central government controls over the prices of coal, district heating, LPG and fuelwood (controls over petroleum products were removed in January 1991); and the achievement of economic cost-based prices for electricity and natural gas.

Energy/Environment -- about US$ 125 million. Expected Board approval: Autumn 1992. The main objectives are the energy supply diversification, energy conservation, and environmental improvement. The project will also support the restructuring of the Hungarian Electricity Board. Possible components include: (a) reconstruction and conversion of several gas-fired power stations to combined-cycle cogeneration; (b) improvement of the energy management system for the electricity grid to prepare the connection of Hungary's grid to the western European power pool (the UCPTE -- Union for the Coordination of Production and Transmission of Electricity); (c) construction of a gas pipeline to Austria or Czechoslovakia in order to diversify import sources of gas supply; and (d) strengthening the Hungarian Electricity Board's environmental management and monitoring capacities.

IV. A Regional Approach

The World Bank is interested in playing a role in partnership with other international agencies, with countries in the region, and with private international investors to establish a network for a process of ongoing cooperation in the energy sector. For the moment, we have called the process, and the program of tasks, CEENERGY (Central and Eastern Europe Network for Regional Energy) -- an acronym representing the synergistic results we feel will be produced.

Under CEENERGY, we are working with key international agencies and with countries of the region to implement high-priority technical assistance and pre-investment activities in the most effective manner. The multinational agencies currently participating include the Commission of the European Communities (EC), the European Bank for Reconstruction and Development (EBRD), the European Investment Bank (EIB), the International Energy Agency (IEA), and the World Bank. Countries of the region involved in the project could include Bulgaria, Czechoslovakia, Hungary, Poland, Romania and Yugoslavia, and potentially Albania and the former Soviet Union.

As part of this process, CEENERGY cooperation is promoting analytical work both at country-specific and regional levels. At present, the regional analysis includes:

(a)   Soviet energy exports and their impact on Central and Eastern Europe

(b)   Petroleum refining and transport

(c)   Electrical power interconnection and trade

(d)   Natural gas trade

(e)   Energy efficiency and the environment

Work on the these areas will contribute to the analytical foundations for investments and policy and institutional reforms within the spirit and framework of the European Energy Charter. The World Bank is making every effort to collaborate with the other international agencies in the design, funding and implementation of this work, which we feel will benefit the countries concerned, the agencies involved, and international energy investors, and foster the efficient flow of energy trade and investment in the region.

UNDP's programme for Central and Eastern Europe in Energy and Environmental Management

Mr. Kees Wijnen
Division for Europe
United Nations Development Programme

Compared to the new programmes financed by the European Communities, the development banks, and a host of bilateral donors, UNDP's programme is quite small. UNDP's Regional Programme for Europe for the period 1992 to 1996 will have less than US$ 5 million to spend, and its funding has in fact been reduced by about 60% compared that of 1987 to 1991. This is the result of UNDP's increased priority on the least developed countries.

The comparative advantage of UNDP's programme in Europe would therefore not result from its size, but is rather based on the experience it has gained in Central and Eastern Europe prior to 1989, when UNDP sponsored several projects that resulted in effective collaboration between environmental and energy technicians in Central and Eastern Europe. Examples of programmes undertaken in the 1980s are: the Abatement of Air Pollution (assistance to countries that signed international conventions to control SO_2 and NO_x emissions); Energy Conservation in Building Design and Town Planning; Improved Efficiency in the Coal Mining Industry; Low Calorie Solid Fuel Technology; and Energy Conservation in Industry. The project on Energy Conservation in Industry provided successful networking between experts in the region, and even led to the creation of a multinational Energy Conservation Consultancy Firm "ENCONET International," created by Croatia and Hungary and later joined by the CSFR.

More recently UNDP has initiated several large-scale environmental programmes for which funding was obtained from the Global Environmental Facility (GEF): The Danube River Basin project received a contribution of US$ 8.5 million from the GEF and is now part of a much larger Danube River Basin Programme, in which riparian countries are collaborating with the European Community, EBRD, EIB, Nordic Bank, UNDP, UNEP, World Bank and bilateral donors. In addition, the GEF approved a second regional environmental programme for Europe earlier this year, aiming at the Protection and Rehabilitation of the Black Sea -- US$ 9.3 million were allocated.

Based on the recommendations of this Conference, UNDP intends to develop a new GEF proposal for environmental management and energy conservation in Central and Eastern Europe. The programme should build on the results of earlier regional networking projects in the field of energy conservation and air pollution abatement. Since the task is so enormous -- as we have seen during the this Conference -- we count on the collaboration of other assistance organizations to ensure that duplication will be avoided and coordination between programmes installed. We shall also welcome proposals that can lead to new multi-donor programmes, similar to the one developed for managing pollution in the Danube River Basin.

2. Private Sector Perspectives

FINANCING: EXTERNAL ASSISTANCE AND INVESTMENT

Wolfgang Muhlbauer
AWT International Trade and Finance AG

AWT International Trade and Finance Corporation is the trade, finance and consulting subsidiary of Creditanstalt, Austria's largest banking group. AWT operates worldwide, with 150 employees and 28 offices, but the main focus of our business is Central and Eastern Europe. Our activities include countertrade and trade finance, as well as strategy and investment consulting. Our clients are mainly international companies planning to expand their activities in Central and Eastern Europe.

1. The Role of Domestic Governments

I am convinced that everyone doing business in Central and Eastern Europe is aware that many attractive possibilities for economic cooperation have arisen with the region's great economic changes. The extent to which central and eastern European authorities take advantage of cooperation with private investors in the energy sector will strongly determine the speed of their countries' economic recovery and reintegration into the European economy.

Concerning energy consumption and production in these countries, we expect that economic behavior will quickly become more and more similar to that in western market economies. Energy will be produced only if it is profitable at given or at anticipated prices. In other words, a sufficient financial return of projects will be the crucial driving force necessary to attract foreign investment in the long term.

One question that frequently arises in this context is: "What can central and eastern European governments do to encourage the flow of investment funds to their industries?" I think that in the current transition process, government authorities can play an important role by establishing and maintaining stable market conditions and a favourable investment climate. This involves the following aspects:

- The first requirement is a legal framework that provides investment security. This includes commercial, company and tax laws and guidelines on how investors can participate in privatisation programs.

- Many governments in the region have employed or are considering incentives for foreign investment. The best known financial investment incentives are tax allowances and tax exemptions. Of course, incentives are in the interest of foreign investors, but we do not think that there are many cases where these mostly short term incentives have been decisive in investment decisions. That is, <u>financial incentives are an important but relatively small part of a favourable investment climate</u>.

- On the other hand, <u>Investment services can play a more important role</u>. In AWT's experience, the professional behaviour of government authorities in their relations with potential foreign investors is crucial for the conclusion of investment deals. In contrast, bureaucratic obstacles, wearisome negotiations with various authorities, and the lack of basic information often reduce the willingness of foreign investors to enter Eastern European markets. The establishment of a national agency to help potential investors would be very useful for encouraging foreign investment. Such an agency could provide comprehensive information services, promote investment opportunities internationally, and support the project preparation and implementation. In the energy sector, the investment center should be the switchboard between the local energy industry, foreign investors and international development banks and financial institutions.

- The <u>international marketing of investment opportunities can also play an important role</u>. I am convinced that more funds could flow to Central and Eastern Europe, especially in the energy sector, if potential investors were provided with better documentation on investment opportunities. This information should not only include data on the energy sector in general, but also describe promising projects and the investment needs of local companies in specific terms. Documentation such as pre-feasibility studies would attract the attention of potential investors.

2. The Role of Investors

Let me start by defining the goal of any foreign investor. The investor wants to generate a long-term financial return on investment and thereby increase the shareholders' value. This requires two basic inputs: capital and know-how.

AWT's belief is that international economic assistance for Central and Eastern Europe should focus more on the know-how aspect. Investment capital is not the real problem. If there are promising projects with sound documentation showing credible financial returns, funds can be raised from a number of sources.

For the region's energy sector, western know-how is needed mainly in the form of technical assistance to improve the efficiency of existing power plants, reduce the energy consumption of local industry and minimize pollution. Capital, of course, is necessary, but will not create any economic benefits without know-how.

Western investors need a strategy for evaluating opportunities in the region: a structured market selection process, the identification and evaluation of local partners and the elaboration of feasibility studies for investment projects. Those feasibility studies serve as the basis for financing decisions of international development banks and private financial institutions.

When evaluating potential markets in Central and Eastern Europe, investors should keep in mind that economic indicators such as GNP, unemployment and inflation rates only reflect the present state of an economy but do not cast light on its future potential. We suggest that potential investors evaluate the markets of countries in the region according to a set of the following fundamental criteria:

- Orientation of monetary and fiscal policy
- Degree of price liberalisation
- Budget policy
- Development of the banking system and capital markets
- Degree of currency convertibility
- Development of small and medium-size enterprises
- Progress and prospects of privatisation programs
- Political and social stability

Once one or more national markets have been selected, investors would identify promising business opportunities in the energy sector and analyse the investment needs, financial returns, environmental issues and possible forms of financing.

In order for an investor to raise capital from international development banks and private financial institutions, the investor must develop feasibility studies and business plans. The following information is necessary for banks to decide whether to proceed with funding a proposed project:

- Benefits to the local economy. The investor should describe potential benefits of the proposed energy project in the following areas:

  - Technology transfer
  - Management development
  - Job creation
  - Energy savings
  - Environmental improvements
  - Energy import substitution

- Technology and equipment issues, including:

  - Advantages of the proposed technology and equipment
  - Technical assistance to be provided by the supplier
  - Description of any modernization of existing technology

- Environmental information. In the energy sector environmental issues are a priority aspect in the appraisal of investment projects. Certain projects will require a complete assessment of anticipated environmental impacts and proposed environmental controls.

- <u>Financing plan</u>: a preliminary plan for the financing structure, listing sources of international credit, local loans, foreign loans and equity.

- <u>Financial viability</u>: This part of the feasibility study has to include information on:

    - transaction sources and uses of funds
    - disbursement schedules
    - operating assumptions (e.g. sales, costs, working capital)
    - financial projections (income statement and balance sheet)
    - debt schedules.

3. The Role of International Financial Institutions

For large energy projects, a type of loan usually referred to as *project finance* can be the most effective instrument. Project finance loans are tied as far as possible to the fortunes of a particular project, thereby minimizing the exposure of the investing parent. The basic requirement is that the project can be isolated as separate entity from the parent.

In many cases the structure of a project finance deal is combined with product-payment, also known as buy-back transactions. Here the loan is given as an advance payment to the project company against future delivery of products. When the products are delivered, specialised trading companies can sell them against hard currency and use the proceeds to repay the project loan. This can be done with energy projects, where the future products will be fuels or electricity.

A project finance deal combined with a buy-back transaction could follow the subsequent path:

1. A bank syndicate makes a loan to an international energy company.

2. The energy company makes an advance payment to its project development company in Central and Eastern Europe.

3. After completion of the project, energy is delivered to a specialised trading company and sold against hard currency.

4. The proceeds are used to repay the loan.

Let me finish by quoting Carl Hahn, the chairman of Volkswagen, on why his company is investing so heavily in Eastern Europe. He said: "We have the opportunity of history. When you don't use it, you lose it."

THE ROLE OF PRIVATE FINANCE

Robert Hart
Hart Associates, Inc.
Washington, D.C.

Four questions were raised by the IEA and OECD staff in the materials distributed to the speakers on this panel:

1.   What are the likely areas for private western investment in the energy sector in Central Europe?

2.   How will environmental issues be taken into account in private investment?

3.   What are the main obstacles for private investment in the energy sector and what can be done by various governmental bodies to overcome these obstacles?

4.   Where will private western investment not provide significant resources?

The IEA and OECD staff also indicated that they would appreciate complete and thoughtful answers to all of these questions in something less than twenty minutes (a time allowance that has since been reduced). This instruction requires that I ignore the objective of *complete* answers. However, the limited time has forced me to give greater thought to the issues.

Likely Areas for Private Western Investment

For purposes of this discussion, I will consider private western investment to mean equity investment by non-governmental institutions, thus excluding loans from the multilateral and bilateral lenders, but including equity investments from western utilities that happen to be state owned.

It is my belief that this equity investment will be restricted to what most of us now know as classic *project finance* situations. An investment opportunity suitable for project finance is one that meets three tests:

(a) Revenue from the proposed project must be <u>sufficient</u> to cover all costs of the project, including debt service, <u>and</u> provide a reasonable return on the invested equity. Simply stated, the price of the project outputs must be high enough to justify the investment.

(b) Revenue from the proposed project must be relatively <u>certain</u> over the full life of the investment. Again, simply stated, the net revenue stream must be the result of long-term contractual arrangements.

(c) Finally, no investment is risk free. Experienced investors, those inclined to even consider something in Central Europe, are realistic about risk mitigation. However, a serious, professional effort to identify and mitigate the various development, construction, and operating risks is a minimum requirement.

Project finance is as simple as that. Virtually every capital improvement proposed by the various companies in the energy sector of Central Europe is a potential candidate for private western investment. Proposed improvements must be subjected to these three straightforward tests. Those that pass the tests are <u>likely</u> areas for private western investment.

In my opinion, those capital improvements that do not meet these three simple tests should not be undertaken, whether private western investment is involved or not. The discipline of project finance is a sound approach to investment decisions.

I happen to believe that the presence of private equity investment forces a more careful adherence to project finance discipline. Every bureaucracy has investment guidelines, many of which sound very much like my three tests for project finance. However, when the money comes from the central treasury or from some other distant source, the tests are often only loosely applied.

Private Investment and the Environment

There are two issues to consider. First, how does a project's environmental impact influence the investment decision? One of the three project finance tests is risk mitigation. If there is a risk that the project will be closed down or that emission fines will be imposed, thus reducing revenue, the project is not a likely candidate for investment. For reasons unrelated to the physical environment, it is extremely difficult to <u>sell</u> Central and Eastern Europe to the western investment community. If uncertainties regarding environmental compliance are added to the other risks perceived in the area, no investor will decide in favor of a project. Full environmental compliance is an absolute requirement for investment.

Second, and perhaps more interesting, one can legitimately ask if environmental improvements qualify for private investment. Do scrubbers and precipitators pass the three project finance tests? If the scrubbers are part of a retrofit to an existing power station that has revenue below costs, the answer is obvious. However, if the revenue of the power station is sufficient to cover the additional capital and operating costs of the environmental improvement, there is no reason that private investment cannot be obtained. The legal structure of the investment is a little complex, but project finance involving private equity is an ideal way to fund environmental improvements.

Obstacles to Private Investment

We could devote several full conferences to a discussion of the obstacles to private investment. I have been working in Poland for the past three years and am reasonably clear that <u>the single largest obstacle is the inability of the various participants to communicate with each other</u>.

The language problem is well known to everyone here. Also well known are the cultural and political distances that must be traversed by central and eastern Europeans seeking investors from the west, or western investors seeking opportunities in Central and Eastern Europe. Many economic concepts are new and some find them distasteful. Profit is not very palatable. Fees are considered obscene. Development and due diligence costs are unbearable.

A similar communication problem exists with the various multilateral institutions working in Central Europe. Private equity investment in combination with World Bank or EBRD lending is still largely untested. One reason it has been so hard to combine private equity and official loans is the radically different cultures that exist at the multilateral banks, on the one hand, and in the board rooms of private investors, on the other. This culture gap often resembles the gap between east and west.

Unfortunately, the only thing I can see that governments and other public bodies can do about this communication obstacle is continue to work at it. To some extent, conferences like this help. Perhaps more helpful are project teams, meeting for the specific purpose of developing opportunities suitable for project finance. In our Krakow project, the greatest communication gains between east and west, and between public and private sectors, have come from the work sessions, when boring economic models are audited or tedious legal documents reviewed in exhaustive detail.

We need to get past the trust issue. It is not helpful for central and eastern Europeans or multilateral lenders to consider private investors as some kind of nasty group of corrupt and greedy parasites. The short list of investors who have persevered in the region thus far deserve more than that. Likewise, western investors need to recognize the great personal courage required for a government official or business manager to make an important decision in present-day Central and Eastern Europe. This mutual respect is an essential condition to communication.

Energy and Environment Areas <u>not</u> Suitable for Private Investment

As you can certainly tell from my remarks thus far, the list of energy and environmental improvements that are not potentially suitable for private investment is a very short list. While there are certainly some exceptions, including specifically relatively small projects, I have generally found that those projects that do not have secure sources of sufficient revenue are simply not very well developed. Not enough work has been done to identify and segregate a revenue stream or negotiate the contractual framework, or mitigate the risks.

For political reasons, private investment may not be <u>desirable</u> for every project. I believe enough in the discipline of project finance, however, to suggest that every project should be sound enough for private investment.

PRIVATE SECTOR FINANCING
OF DEMAND-SIDE MANAGEMENT OPPORTUNITIES

Todd D. Davis
SRC International
Copenhagen, Denmark

Western public and private sectors need to work more closely together in providing economic assistance to the European economies in transition. In the energy sector, the limited capital available combined with the many investment needs suggest that least-cost investment approaches are critical. Investments for clean coal technology, power generation resources, and demand-side options should all be evaluated in a least-cost planning framework. If western public sector organizations, such as the Commission of the European Communities, continue to promote rational pricing and least-cost planning, then western investors will more quickly move into areas such as providing more energy-efficient equipment for factories and buildings in Central and Eastern Europe.

OPPORTUNITIES FOR ENERGY SERVICE COMPANIES

There is a large potential market for energy service companies to offer performance shared savings contracts to central and eastern European businesses. Of course, as in all investment in the region, the viability of externally financed energy service companies depends strongly on the success of the macro-level political and economic changes that are now underway.

Many large, energy-intensive industrial processes in Central and Eastern Europe can benefit from energy efficiency improvements. It is estimated that on average about 50 per cent of the energy used in manufacturing in the region is needlessly wasted. Much of this inefficiency can be captured with a payback of less than three years -- although low energy prices in some countries limit the investment potential.

There are a number of barriers to promoting shared savings projects in Central and Eastern Europe. These include:

- The newness of the concept. It seems that it is a deal too good to be true -- so people suspect something must be wrong.

- The ESCO firm is new and likely to come from outside the country. Thus potential clients perceive risks associated with the new firm.

- The contracting terms of shared-savings agreement are new and sometimes complex.

- Central and eastern European firms may feel that the contract terms and the perceived returns are excessive.

Obviously, energy service companies must present the energy service concept clearly to potential customers. Also, a good working relationship has to be established. It may be useful to work with local partners in marketing the concept.

A major concern will likely surround the perceived fairness and value from energy service agreements, given the site and technical risk of the project. It may appear to the potential facility manager that there is an excessive profit going to investors. However, at the present moment, the risks to foreign investors are significant, especially as many economic changes are underway. Only after a period of trial project activity will foreign investors feel more comfortable about the region's investment climate, and be willing to accept lower returns.

It should also be noted that a shared savings program may not be the cheapest method for energy users if they have capital to invest. Nonetheless, they may prefer to support new capital investment out of operational versus capital budgets -- shared savings contracts can make this possible. Also, local interest rate financing is often high in transitional economies. Thus, companies in the region there may need to seek innovative financing arrangements.

SRC INTERNATIONAL'S EXPERIENCE IN THE CSFR

In spite of the many problems, SRC International (SRCI) and other firms are making progress in energy performance contracting. SRC International has two initiatives underway in the CSFR regarding the promotion of energy efficiency to service and industrial customers. These include a joint project with PRE, an electricity distribution utility in Prague, to offer performance contracting to its largest customers. In 1993, significant tariff increases are projected for the large power service and industrial customers. PRE agreed to initiate a pilot program whose plan is illustrated in Figure 1. The program is implemented at no significant cost or liability to PRE. SRCI at its own cost, offers to complete feasibility studies to identify electric savings opportunities. Upon agreement with the customer, SRCI will complete a technical design study or implement the measures on either a paid consulting or performance contracting basis. The goal is to initiate significant long lasting energy saving investments that are cost effective to PRE, to the utility's customers, and of course, provide a return to our investors as well.

In a separate initiative, SRCI has so far completed 20 audits of large service and industrial customers in Czechoslovakia. On average, an energy savings potential of 15 per cent was found. Currently, SRCI is negotiating shared savings ventures with a group of these customers. We are about to finalize our first agreement in Czechoslovakia. Other agreements are expected to follow shortly. (The plan for this work is also shown in Figure 1.) We hope to expand these activities

---

**Figure 1. The Planned Structures of SRC International's
ESCO Initiatives in the CSFR**

Cooperative DSM Program with PRE   SRCI's Direct ESCO Services

- PRE Identifies Largest Customers
- Joint Sales Calls are made
- The program concept is presented to the potential customer
- The customer agrees to participate
- A preliminary audit is made
- Recommendations are provided
- Customer agrees to continue in the program
- Detailed technical design is made
- Customer approves
- The project is implemented (on a contract or performance basis)
- Project management

- SRCI's sales call is made
- The Program concept is presented to the potential customer
- The customer agrees to participate
- A preliminary audit is made
- Recommendations are provided
- Customer agrees to continue in the program
- A detailed technical design is completed
- The customer approves
- The project is implemented (on a contract or performance basis)
- Project management

---

in other countries. One factor determining the pace with which we expand these services to other countries in Central and Eastern Europe is the pace of the macroeconomic reforms underway.

LESSONS TO DRAW AND PROSPECTS FOR THE FUTURE

Unfortunately, the experience in Central and Eastern Europe is too brief to draw any conclusive findings or recommendations. Some preliminary insights, however, follow:

- It is easy to sign memos of understanding and intent for energy service projects. The real challenge is to follow through and reach agreements for work.

- The ESCO must be sure that it is committed to following through with a project and that it has investors who are willing to invest in a high risk market.

- Negotiations are likely to take a long time until a contract is finalized. Persistence is needed.

- It is important to work with local contacts and experts. This helps facilitate understanding, relationships and trust.

- Cooperation with local utilities and energy suppliers can help build realism and credibility.

- It is important to identify a group of investors in order to limit individual risk. An investment pool that covers multiple investment opportunities is useful.

- There are western investors interested in energy efficiency projects in Central and Eastern Europe.

The pace of private sector investment will depend on how comprehensive and extensive official assistance is for Central and Eastern Europe. I believe that the future is bright, the market will hopefully become a little less risky, and capital markets and government sectors will be able to cooperate much more in the future.

3. Innovative Opportunities for East-West Financing

Strategic options for Energy and Environment in Central and Eastern Europe

J. van Liere
N.V. KEMA
and
J. van der Kooij
N.V. Sep (The Dutch Electricity Generating Board)
The Netherlands

INTRODUCTION

Fossil power generation emits polluting gases, dust and heat into the environment. Power plants need to reduce their emissions of pollutants: particulates, gases such as nitrogen oxides (NO_x) and sulphur dioxide (SO_2) that cause acid deposition and carbon dioxide (CO_2) that contributes to the risk of global climate change.

Utility companies in the Netherlands have introduced electrostatic precipitators to remove particulates, flue gas desulphurization equipment and low NO_x technologies in most of their new and existing power plants. Additional investments could further reduce emissions, but small additional reductions will require high costs.

The pollutants causing acid precipitation cross national boundaries, and climate change is a global problem; thus, it makes sense to consider investments in other parts of Europe to reduce acid deposition in the Netherlands and to diminish global greenhouse gas emissions. Investment in Central and Eastern Europe offers several advantages: substantial reductions in local emissions at low costs; small but not insignificant reductions in acid deposition in Western Europe; the refurbishment and improvement of power generation capacity in Central and Eastern Europe; and West-to-East knowledge transfer. Additional results will be a quicker transition to the market economy and significant world-wide emission reductions both of SO_2 and CO_2.

This approach calls for global thinking and the exploration of investment policies far different from those currently followed. The strategy is worth considering, for the sake of Europe's environment and for the future of the global environment.

SO_2 EMISSION AND ACID DEPOSITION

The environmental problem in Western Europe that has received the most attention in recent years is acid precipitation: the detrimental effects on soil, surface water, vegetation, and man-made materials caused by the deposition of acidifying substances from the air. The most important of these substances are SO_2, NO_x, and ammonia (NH_3). They are emitted from several sources -- most connected with energy generation or use -- dispersed through the ambient air, and subsequently deposited on to the earth's surface. Deposition can occur in solution during rain (wet deposition) or in the form of gaseous molecules or aerosols (dry deposition).

For some years, environmental policy in the Netherlands was guided by a limit of 3000 potential acid equivalents per hectare per year for the deposition of the acidifying substances such as SO_2, NO_x and NH_3. Recent studies indicate that ecosystem sensitivity to acidification is greater than previously assumed. In the 1989 National Environmental Policy Plan, the Government of the Netherlands lowered the deposition objective to 2400 potential acid equivalents per hectare per year for the year 2000 to protect forests and natural areas. For the year 2010, this will be reduced to 1400 acid equivalents per year and the limit may eventually be further reduced to 400 acid equivalents per year. Annual emission ceiling values for aggregate emissions in the year 2000 have been established for SO_2, NO_x and NH_3 as well as volatile organic components (which also contribute to acid deposition). Industry and the Electric power plants in the Netherlands have reduced their emissions of SO_2 emissions by 40 per cent since 1980 (when they totalled 464,000 tons per year). For the years 1994 and 2000, the country-wide emissions limits are set at 176,000 and 105,000 tons per year, respectively.

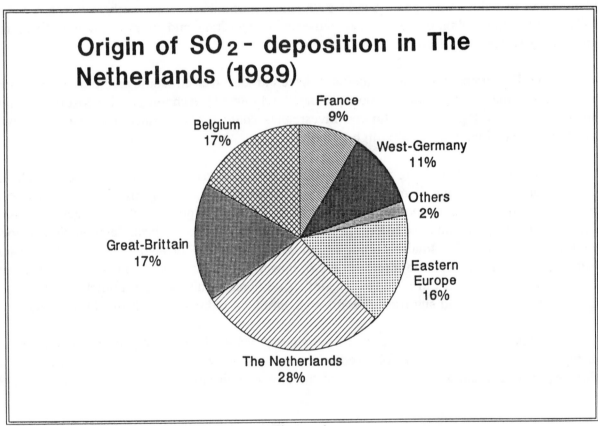

Figure 1.

The National Environmental Policy Plan called for a reduction in power plant emissions of SO_2 to 30,000 tons per year, and emissions of NO_x to 40,0000 tons, by the year 2000. However, the

Government and Sep, the Dutch Electricity Generating Board, negotiated even lower limits, and on June 12, 1990, Sep signed an agreement on behalf of power generating companies with the Government and the twelve provinces of the Netherlands to reduce SO_2 emissions to a level of 22,000 tons per year by the year 2000 and NO_x emissions to 30,000 tons per year.

Nonetheless, sources in the Netherlands account for only 28 per cent of the total deposition of acidic SO_2 in the country -- the great majority of acid precipitation in the Netherlands comes from other European countries. The break-down of SO_2 deposition in 1989 from different countries is given in figure 1. Acid precipitation originating in Central and Eastern Europe accounts for 16 per cent of the total, with Poland alone creating an estimated 2 to 3 per cent For this reason, one part of the 1990 agreement between Sep and the government involved assisting the costs of installing flue gas desulphurization equipment at a coal-fired power station abroad.

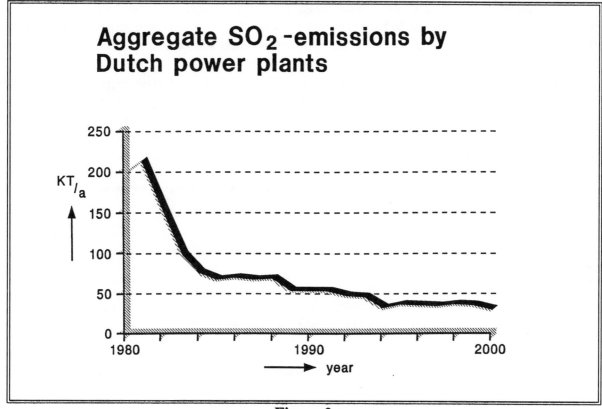

Figure 2.

The SO_2 emissions of Dutch power plants have fallen almost 80 per cent compared to 1980 levels (see Figure 2). One method to further reduce domestic emissions would be an investment in flue-gas desulphurization equipment at three old coal-fired plants that are to be decommissioned within three to seven years. This would cost US$ 60 to 70 million, and would remove about 20,000 tons of SO_2 per year -- for an average of five years of operation per plant, this makes a total of 100,000 tons in emission reductions. The same investment to refurbish existing, similarly sized power stations abroad that are expected to remain in operation for another 20 years would reduce SO_2 emission by 30,000 tons per year, and provide a total of 600,000 tons in emissions reductions over 20 years for the same investment.

Sep selected Poland for foreign investment. Emissions of SO_2 in this central and eastern European country are many times higher than in the Netherlands, and the state of the environment is severely degraded in many areas. Reducing SO_2 emissions in Poland is much more cost-effective than doing so in the Netherlands. Sep's initiative is providing technical knowledge and US$ 30 million in financing. As a result, flue-gas desulphurization (FGD) equipment has been installed at the lignite-fired Belchatow power station. Sep's initiative has acted as a catalyst for desulphurization investments in Poland. At least two and probably four FGD units will be constructed at the Belchatow power station.

CO$_2$ EMISSIONS: AN AREA FOR POSSIBLE CO-OPERATION

An international treaty on climate change was just signed at the UN Conference on Environment and Development in Rio. Carbon dioxide (CO_2) emissions contribute an estimated 60 per cent of the global warming potential from man-made sources.

Fossil fuel power plants create an important share of carbon dioxide emissions. Emission factors ranges from 56,000 tons of CO_2 per petajoule (PJ) of energy released in natural gas plants to 94,000 tons CO_2 per PJ for coal. Table 1 lists the CO_2 emissions per year worldwide and for the Netherlands. In the Netherlands, power generation accounts for only a limited part of total CO_2 emissions -- about 23 per cent.

Table 1. Carbon Dioxide Emissions

CO_2 Emissions per year (for 1990) in millions of tons

Global Emissions	26,000
Emissions -- The Netherlands	184
Emissions -- Energy Sector, the Netherlands	37

Continued man-made emissions of CO_2 have increased the concentration of this gas in the earth's atmosphere to about 365 parts per million (ppm) in 1990. By 2050, if current trends were to continue, the concentration would reach 750 ppm, and by 2100, about 1200 ppm.

The Dutch and other European governments are taking the lead to control CO_2 emissions. The goal of the Government of the Netherlands is to stabilize domestic CO_2 emissions by 1995 at 1990 levels (approximately 184 million tons per year). By the year 2000, the emissions are to be reduced to between 173 to 177 million tons per year. Dutch emissions had been estimated to grow about 2 per cent per year. Thus, to meet Government targets, a reduction of 17 million tons of yearly emissions is required by 1995, and 43 to 47 million tons by 2000 to meet current national targets (see Figure 3, lower line).

This is a significant decrease, which can only be achieved by a number of operational and strategic measures. Methods to reduce domestic CO_2 emission include: improving the efficiency of electricity use; development of renewable energy sources; the introduction of chemical or physical processes to remove carbon dioxide from coal-derived syngas or perhaps even from flue gases; the introduction of more efficient generating technologies (such as integrated coal gasification combined cycle (IGCC) plants or advanced natural gas fired combined cycle units for

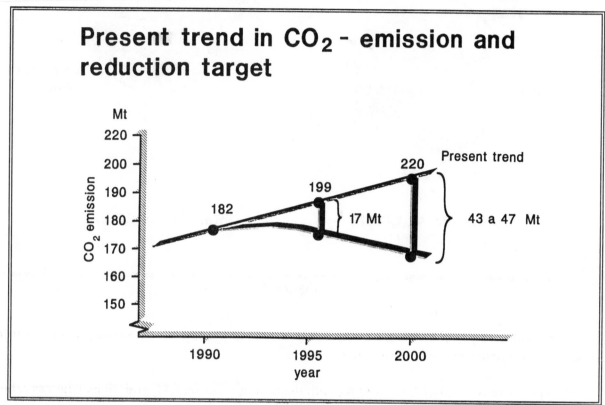

Figure 3.

cogeneration; the extension of the life of current nuclear power plants and the expansion of domestic nuclear capacity; or a new strategy based on exergy matching with the process industry and by counterbalancing CO_2 emission with afforestation. The problem with most of these solutions is, however, that they are medium-term or long-term solutions. Domestic short-term solutions will require greater energy efficiency, the introduction of wind turbines, modernization and upgrading of existing power plants with gas turbines, the construction of small combined cycle plants for industrial cogeneration and the commissioning of an IGCC demonstration plant.

In the medium term, a 1700 MW natural gas-fired high efficiency combined cycle unit will be build (thermal efficiency will be 55 per cent) as well as a number of smaller (250 MW) cogeneration units for the combined production of heat and power. An exergy strategy has been developed by Sep to reduce CO_2 emissions through increased cogeneration and replacing individual boilers with heat pumps for household heating. As a result, CO_2 emissions from the power and residential sectors could decrease about 10 per cent (figure 4).

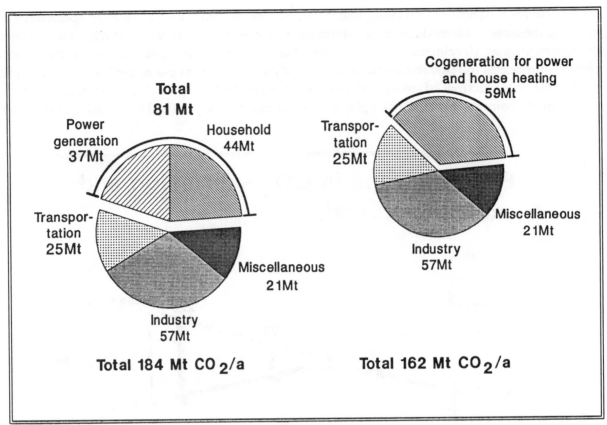

Figure 4.

In addition, preparations are being made to extend the life of the existing nuclear power plants and to further improve their safety.

The Government has discussed the introduction of a tax on CO_2 emissions whereas others prefer a so-called entropy added tax to encourage emission reductions. The utility sector strongly prefers to use voluntary measures to fulfil the objectives set by the government and to raise environmental funding from an additional percentage on electricity prices. The utility sector would use funds raised in this manner for environmental investments in the Netherlands and abroad.

Because climate change is a global problem, it is realistic to consider investments abroad to reduce CO_2 emissions. At present, Central and Eastern European countries are in the midst of a difficult transition from planned to market-based economies. From figure 5 it appears that the CO_2 emission per capita is strongly related to GDP per capita, but that planned economies have consistently higher emissions levels per GDP.

The transition to market-based economies and the introduction of economic competition will be an effective driving force for energy efficiency and CO_2 emission reduction. However, it must be expected that initially the amount of CO_2 per capita will increase due to the economic change accompanying the transition. Based on the trends shown in Figure 5, it can be estimated that the transition to a market economy will lead to a decrease in CO_2 emissions from 12 tons per capita to approximately 6 tons CO_2 per capita. For the region's population of 250 million people, this suggests a total reduction of 1500 million tons of CO_2 emissions per year. But this will be offset by eventual growth in the region's GDP per capita. Nonetheless, even if the GDP per capita in the region doubles, CO_2 emission per capita should, if they follow market-economy trends, be about 20 per cent lower than before the economic transformation. Thus, the first objective in reducing the region's carbon dioxide emissions should be to continue the transition to market-based economies.

Second, the fuel used for power generation in Eastern and Central Europe should be considered. Poland, for example, generates over 70 per cent of its electricity from coal, mostly in outdated power plants without emission control. In Czechoslovakia and Bulgaria, over 55 per cent of the power plants are coal fired. By upgrading the existing generating capacity this situation can be improved. If coal continues to be a major power generation fuel, new clean coal-fired plants with thermal efficiencies over 42 per cent should be installed to replace the old, highly polluting plants with efficiencies under 30 per cent. This will reduce CO_2 emissions in the electricity sector significantly.

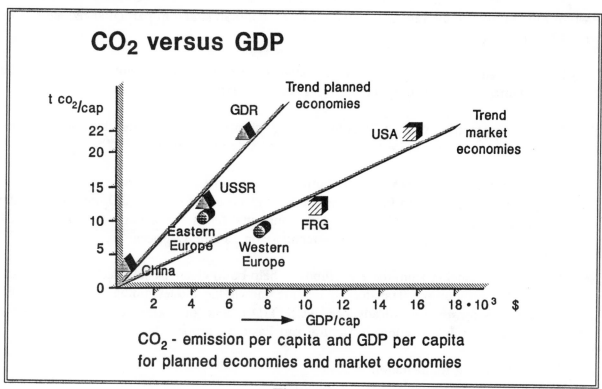

Figure 5.

Figure 5 shows that market-based countries economy such as France, Japan and Switzerland can have a high GDP per capita and low CO_2 emissions per capita. One reason is the use of non-fossil-fuel power generation: France and Sweden generate a high percentage of their electricity from nuclear power, and Switzerland and Norway from hydroelectric plants. Expansion of nuclear capacity in Central and Eastern Europe could be a strategy for reducing CO_2 emissions. In Hungary, already over 40 per cent of electricity is generated by nuclear plants. The safety of Eastern nuclear power plants, however, is a matter of concern, and a number of plants might have to be closed, modified or replaced before any expansion in nuclear power can be contemplated.

A STRATEGIC PROPOSAL FOR INTRA-EUROPEAN POWER CO-OPERATION

Another strategic option for energy saving and emission control is our proposal for "peak shaving by peak shifting": this idea -- $(PS)^2$ -- would require high-voltage lines running from western to eastern Europe, from Ireland to the Urals and from Portugal to the Caspian Sea, crossing three or four time zones. With an integrated European electricity network, it will be possible to reduce installed capacity and minimize fluctuations in demand, thus lowering the number of plants required. A strong East-West connection can help the revival of the central and eastern European economies.

The following five-step proposal shows how energy and environmental co-operation between east and west can help the development of a market-based economy in Central and Eastern Europe, reduce the region's emissions of all pollutants, and in particular reduce Europe-wide CO_2 emission.

Step 1   Arrangement of a package deal between Western governments and their utility organizations to reduce flue gas emissions domestically and abroad.

Step 2   The construction of East-West high voltage transmission lines and the foundation of a European power control system for demand side management.

Step 3   Decommission old coal-fired polluting capacity in Central Europe; at the same time providing Central and Eastern Europe with electricity from low CO_2 emitting Western European plants, as well as raising environmental funds, for example from taxes on CO_2 emissions or from an additional percentage on electricity prices.

Step 4   Use co-financing from these ecofunds to help build cleaner coal-fired plants in Central and Eastern Europe. Transfer engineering knowledge and technology from West to East with the construction of advanced PCF/FGD plants (pulverized coal-fired plants with flue-gas desulphurisation) in Central and Eastern Europe.

Step 5   Co-financing reforestation.

A hypothetical example of co-operation between Poland and the Netherlands can illustrate this strategy.

In the Netherlands, modern and highly reliable natural gas-fired plants with a capacity of 600 MW each are used as standby units. They have a thermal efficiency of 43 per cent, but new combined cycle units (52 per cent efficiency) or combiblocks (47 per cent efficiency) are now on stream. As a result these gas-fired units with 43 per cent efficiency are used less than 2000 hours per year.

In our scenario, these gas-fired power plants in the Netherlands could provide Poland with 5.5 TWh per year for four years; this electricity could partly be paid with 2.5 million tons a year of Polish coal. At the same time, about 1000 MW of old coal-fired Polish power plant capacity would be closed (these power plants consumed about 2.5 million tons of coal a year), and construction would begin on a new, advanced 1000 MW PCF/FGD power plant in Poland. Polish engineers, operators and maintenance staff for this plant could be trained in Dutch PCF plants.

The significant difference between the value of delivering 22 TWh of electricity over four years from the Netherlands for only 10 million tons of coal could be made up by the delivery of additional coal, or better yet, cheap electricity supplied from the new Polish power plant to the Netherlands over the first 10 years of its operation. Table 3 compares the CO2 savings during

The Netherlands	Poland
1000 MW gas	1000 MW coal
η = 43%	η = 30%
5500 hrs	5500 hrs
2.7 Mt CO_2/a	6.4 Mt CO_2/a
	CO_2 saving: 3.7 Mt CO_2/a

Table 3. CO$_2$ Savings During the First 4 Years of Construction

the first 4 years of construction of the new coal-fired plant.

The CO_2 emission reduction of 3.7 million tons per year corresponds to the combustion of about 1.4 million tons of hard coal per year. If a tax were placed on CO_2 emissions (at least in western Europe, initially), equivalent to between US$ 25 to US$ 50 per ton of coal, the carbon dioxide reductions in our scenario would correspond to an amount between US$ 35 to 70 million per year. If the proposed modern PCF/FGD plant in Poland is co-financed, and built in 4 years, then US$ 140 to 280 million dollars could be made available for plant construction and reforestation.

Once in operation, the new 1000 MW plant in Poland would save approximately 1.9 million tons per year of CO_2 emissions, as well as reduce SO_2 emissions by about 75,000 tons a year compared to the existing, outdated 1000 MW of power plant capacity. If there is a CO_2 tax as equivalent to between US$ 25 and US$ 50 per tons of coal, then US$ 17 to 35 million dollars per year would be saved. If the operation is just one part of a 10-year co-operation agreement between the Dutch and Polish governments, then a further US$ 170 to 350 million could be available, providing a total US$ 310 to 630 million for investment both in new, efficient power plants as well as the reforestation of about 17,000 hectares per year in Poland to restore the natural environment -- and also offset CO_2 emissions. In the meantime, older PCF power plants in the Netherlands can be replaced by 1000 MW of new IGCC capacity with very high efficiency (46 to 47 per cent) and extremely low emissions. The Polish forests would

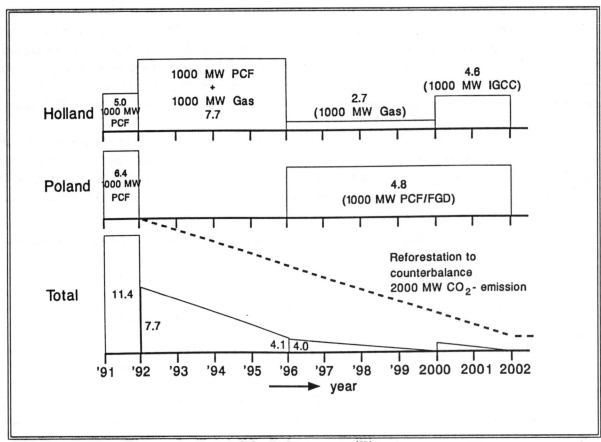

Figure 6. Total CO$_2$ Balance -- million tons per year

counterbalance the CO$_2$ emissions from the 2000 MW of new coal-fired power plants. Figure 6. shows the overall CO$_2$ balance of this co-operative strategy. In ten years time the operation would reduce CO$_2$ emissions by about 11.4 million tons a year and reduce SO$_2$ emissions about 100,000 tons a year, with benefits for both Poland and the Netherlands.

Table 4. The Advantages for Poland and the Netherlands

Poland	the Netherlands
• new efficient and reliable generating capacity	• export of engineering knowledge and supply of components to the PCF/FGD plant
• trained Polish operators and maintenance staff	• acid deposition reductions in the Netherlands; CO$_2$ abatement
• significant reduction in acid deposition and dust deposition in Poland; CO$_2$ abatement	• continuation of the fuel diversification policy
• restoration of nature by reforestation	

REFERENCES

1. *Energy operations policy.* The European Bank for Reconstruction and Development, March 1992.

2. "Strategies to meet the emissions and environmental requirements of fossil-fired plants in the Netherlands," J. van der Kooij, London, 18-20 February 1992.

3. *Energy Technology Strategy 21: Assessment of energy technology priority areas.* IEA Committee on Energy Research and Development, Paris, June 1991.

4. *Electric Power Technologies: Environmental Challenges and opportunities*, Draft Report to the Committee on Energy Research and Technology of the International Energy Agency, Paris, 16 April 1992.

5. VGB: Conference on "Power Plant Engineering 2000," Conservation of resources and CO_2 control, Essen, 21-22 February 1990.

6. R. Lubbers, European Energy Charter, Sector Protocol on Efficiency and Environmental Aspects of Energy Systems, (in preparation), The Hague, December 17, 1991.

ANNEX:

IEA ENERGY STATISTICS FOR
THE CSFR, HUNGARY, AND POLAND

Energy Indicators[1]

	1973	1974	1975	1976	1977	1978	1979	1980	1981
Czechoslovakia									
Tot. Primary Energy Supply (Mtoe)	59.090	60.655	63.643	66.579	69.036	71.253	73.031	73.336	72.661
Oil requirements (Mtoe)	14.387	14.994	16.621	17.731	18.760	19.288	19.321	18.537	18.163
Electricity generated (GWh)	53473	56026	59277	62746	66501	69097	68092	72732	73504
Population (Millions)	14.56	14.69	14.80	14.92	15.03	15.14	15.21	15.26	15.31
GDP (Billion 1985 $US)	.	.	.	.	.	.	.	36.72	36.76
TPES/GDP (Toe per 000 $US)	.	.	.	.	.	.	.	2.00	1.98
TPES/Pop. (Toe per capita)	4.06	4.13	4.30	4.46	4.59	4.71	4.80	4.81	4.74
Oil Req./GDP (Toe per 000 $US)	.	.	.	.	.	.	.	0.50	0.49
Oil Req./Pop. (Toe per capita)	0.99	1.02	1.12	1.19	1.25	1.27	1.27	1.21	1.19
Elec. gen./GDP (kWh per $US)	.	.	.	.	.	.	.	1.98	2.00
Elec. gen./Pop. (kWh per capita)	3673	3815	4005	4206	4424	4564	4476	4766	4800
Hungary									
Tot. Primary Energy Supply (Mtoe)	21.448	22.047	23.437	25.109	26.164	27.807	27.187	28.322	27.519
Oil requirements (Mtoe)	8.299	9.073	10.088	10.550	11.264	12.391	11.280	11.300	10.759
Electricity generated (GWh)	17643	18985	20472	22050	23402	25543	24519	23876	24219
Population (Millions)	10.44	10.47	10.53	10.59	10.64	10.67	10.70	10.71	10.71
GDP (Billion 1985 $US)	14.23	15.06	16.01	16.59	17.72	18.57	18.86	18.86	19.60
TPES/GDP (Toe per 000 $US)	1.51	1.46	1.46	1.51	1.48	1.50	1.44	1.50	1.40
TPES/Pop. (Toe per capita)	2.06	2.11	2.23	2.37	2.46	2.61	2.54	2.64	2.57
Oil Req./GDP (Toe per 000 $US)	0.58	0.60	0.63	0.64	0.64	0.67	0.60	0.60	0.55
Oil Req./Pop. (Toe per capita)	0.79	0.87	0.96	1.00	1.06	1.16	1.05	1.05	1.00
Elec. gen./GDP (kWh per $US)	1.24	1.26	1.28	1.33	1.32	1.38	1.30	1.27	1.24
Elec. gen./Pop. (kWh per capita)	1691	1813	1944	2082	2200	2393	2292	2229	2261
Poland									
Tot. Primary Energy Supply (Mtoe)	89.791	94.324	99.471	107.095	111.766	117.033	122.386	124.421	114.125
Oil requirements (Mtoe)	11.290	12.304	13.875	14.877	16.341	17.322	17.549	17.901	16.151
Electricity generated (GWh)	84302	91600	97169	104101	109364	115558	117468	120941	114118
Population (Millions)	33.36	33.69	34.02	34.36	34.70	35.01	35.22	35.58	35.90
GDP (Billion 1985 $US)	.	.	.	.	.	.	.	70.62	63.58
TPES/GDP (Toe per 000 $US)	.	.	.	.	.	.	.	1.76	1.80
TPES/Pop. (Toe per capita)	2.69	2.80	2.92	3.12	3.22	3.34	3.47	3.50	3.18
Oil Req./GDP (Toe per 000 $US)	.	.	.	.	.	.	.	0.25	0.25
Oil Req./Pop. (Toe per capita)	0.34	0.36	0.41	0.43	0.47	0.49	0.50	0.50	0.45
Elec. gen./GDP (kWh per $US)	.	.	.	.	.	.	.	1.71	1.79
Elec. gen./Pop. (kWh per capita)	2527	2719	2856	3030	3152	3301	3335	3399	3179

(1) GDP and Population data are from the World Bank, *World Tables 1991* (Washington, 1992)

Energy Indicators[1]

	1982	1983	1984	1985	1986	1987	1988	1989	1990
Czechoslovakia									
Tot. Primary Energy Supply (Mtoe)	72.763	72.845	75.504	75.728	77.246	78.507	73.946	72.697	69.626
Oil requirements (Mtoe)	16.899	16.288	17.318	17.057	15.780	16.238	15.560	15.222	13.395
Electricity generated (GWh)	74749	76275	78388	80627	84774	85825	87374	89201	86627
Population (Millions)	15.37	15.41	15.46	15.50	15.53	15.57	15.61	15.65	15.68
GDP (Billion 1985 $US)	37.02	37.89	38.67	39.50	40.21	40.51	41.55	42.09	40.62
TPES/GDP (Toe per 000 $US)	1.97	1.92	1.95	1.92	1.92	1.94	1.78	1.73	1.71
TPES/Pop. (Toe per capita)	4.74	4.73	4.88	4.89	4.97	5.04	4.74	4.65	4.44
Oil Req./GDP (Toe per 000 $US)	0.46	0.43	0.45	0.43	0.39	0.40	0.37	0.36	0.33
Oil Req./Pop. (Toe per capita)	1.10	1.06	1.12	1.10	1.02	1.04	1.00	0.97	0.85
Elec. gen./GDP (kWh per $US)	2.02	2.01	2.03	2.04	2.11	2.12	2.10	2.12	2.13
Elec. gen./Pop. (kWh per capita)	4865	4948	5071	5202	5457	5511	5598	5700	5525
Hungary									
Tot. Primary Energy Supply (Mtoe)	27.783	28.803	29.729	30.409	30.549	31.382	30.791	29.719	28.599
Oil requirements (Mtoe)	10.452	11.055	11.076	10.080	9.528	9.684	8.784	8.563	8.384
Electricity generated (GWh)	24775	25789	26303	26794	28063	29749	29233	29596	28411
Population (Millions)	10.71	10.70	10.68	10.66	10.64	10.62	10.60	10.58	10.55
GDP (Billion 1985 $US)	19.96	20.11	20.64	20.62	20.94	21.88	21.81	21.99	21.05
TPES/GDP (Toe per 000 $US)	1.39	1.43	1.44	1.47	1.46	1.43	1.41	1.35	1.36
TPES/Pop. (Toe per capita)	2.59	2.69	2.78	2.85	2.87	2.95	2.91	2.81	2.71
Oil Req./GDP (Toe per 000 $US)	0.52	0.55	0.54	0.49	0.46	0.44	0.40	0.39	0.40
Oil Req./Pop. (Toe per capita)	0.98	1.03	1.04	0.95	0.90	0.91	0.83	0.81	0.79
Elec. gen./GDP (kWh per $US)	1.24	1.28	1.27	1.30	1.34	1.36	1.34	1.35	1.35
Elec. gen./Pop. (kWh per capita)	2313	2410	2463	2514	2637	2801	2759	2798	2692
Poland									
Tot. Primary Energy Supply (Mtoe)	114.073	115.864	122.587	126.272	128.284	132.680	125.202	119.266	97.797
Oil requirements (Mtoe)	15.298	15.908	16.059	16.350	16.808	16.502	16.191	16.129	13.458
Electricity generated (GWh)	116517	124175	132848	135666	138094	143374	141961	143322	134315
Population (Millions)	36.23	36.57	36.91	37.20	37.46	37.66	37.86	37.85	37.97
GDP (Billion 1985 $US)	60.55	63.91	67.52	70.99	73.97	75.53	78.66	79.05	69.58
TPES/GDP (Toe per 000 $US)	1.88	1.81	1.82	1.78	1.73	1.76	1.59	1.51	1.41
TPES/Pop. (Toe per capita)	3.15	3.17	3.32	3.39	3.42	3.52	3.31	3.15	2.58
Oil Req./GDP (Toe per 000 $US)	0.25	0.25	0.24	0.23	0.23	0.22	0.21	0.20	0.19
Oil Req./Pop. (Toe per capita)	0.42	0.43	0.43	0.44	0.45	0.44	0.43	0.43	0.35
Elec. gen./GDP (kWh per $US)	1.92	1.94	1.97	1.91	1.87	1.90	1.80	1.81	1.93
Elec. gen./Pop. (kWh per capita)	3216	3395	3599	3647	3687	3807	3749	3786	3538

(1) GDP and Population data are from the World Bank, *World Tables 1991* (Washington, 1992)

Czechoslovakia 1989

Thousand toe

	Coal	Crude Oil	Petroleum Products	Gas	Nuclear	Hydro/ Other	Elec- tricity	Heat	Total
Indigenous Production	41734	144	.	634	6404	367	.	.	49283
Import	2917	16567	558	9372	.	.	892	.	30307
Export	-3291	.	-2040	-481	.	.	-665	.	-6477
Intl. Marine Bunkers	.	.	.	.	.	.	.	.	.
Stock Changes	-62	30	-36	-349	.	.	.	.	-416
TPES	41299	16740	-1519	9176	6404	367	228	.	72697
Returns and Transfers	.	.	.	.	.	.	.	.	.
Statistical Differences	112	-82	19	.	.	.	.	.	48
Public Electricity	-16126	.	-409	-397	-6404	-354	7011	.	-16679
Autoproducers of Electr.	.	.	.	.	.	-13	660	.	647
CHP Plants	-7476	.	.	-486	.	.	.	12787	4825
District Heating	-2713	.	-1449	-386	.	.	.	.	-4547
Gas Works	-526	.	.	317	.	.	.	.	-208
Petroleum Refineries	.	-16659	15984	-206	.	.	-55	.	-936
Coal Transformation	-810	.	.	.	.	.	.	.	-810
Liquefaction	.	.	.	.	.	.	.	.	.
Other Transformation	-37	.	-2427	-395	.	.	.	.	-2859
Own Use	-839	.	-49	-99	.	.	-996	.	-1983
Distribution Losses	-63	.	.	-162	.	.	-511	-353	-1089
TFC	12821	.	10149	7362	.	.	6337	12434	49104
INDUSTRY SECTOR	5564	.	4391	3385	.	.	3942	9862	27145
Iron and Steel	4843	.	.	630	.	.	681	.	6154
Chemical	.	.	1976	837	.	.	717	.	3530
(of which:Feedstocks)	.	.	.	624	.	.	.	.	624
Non-ferrous Metals	.	.	.	178	.	.	165	.	343
Non-metallic Minerals	.	.	.	1109	.	.	289	.	1398
Transport Equip. & Mach.	.	.	.	.	.	.	.	.	.
Machinery	.	.	.	263	.	.	.	.	263
Mining and Quarrying	.	.	.	142	.	.	48	.	190
Food and Tobacco	.	.	.	84	.	.	169	.	253
Paper, Pulp and Printing	.	.	.	9	.	.	.	.	9
Wood and Wood Products	.	.	.	23	.	.	276	.	299
Construction	42	.	159	77	.	.	.	.	278
Textile and Leather	.	.	.	9	.	.	194	.	202
Non-specified Industry	680	.	2257	24	.	.	1403	9862	14225
TRANSPORT SECTOR	87	.	3124	23	.	.	359	.	3593
Air	.	.	173	.	.	.	.	.	173
Road	.	.	2929	.	.	.	.	.	2929
Rail	79	.	.	.	.	.	359	.	438
Internal Navigation	.	.	.	.	.	.	.	.	.
Non-specified Transport	8	.	23	23	.	.	.	.	54
OTHER SECTORS	7170	.	2634	3955	.	.	2036	2572	18366
Agriculture	401	.	1479	1597	.	.	.	.	3478
Comm. & Pub. Services	.	.	.	.	.	.	.	.	.
Residential	4395	.	193	1596	.	.	1103	1614	8902
Non-specified Other	2373	.	962	761	.	.	933	958	5986
Non-Energy Use	.	.	.	.	.	.	.	.	.
MEMO ITEMS:									
Electricity Generated (GWh)	60353	.	.	.	24575	4273	.	.	89201
Public	52677	.	.	.	24575	4117	.	.	81525
Autoproducers	7676	.	.	.	.	156	.	.	7676

Czechoslovakia 1990

Thousand toe

	Coal	Crude Oil	Petroleum Products	Gas	Nuclear	Hydro/ Other	Elec- tricity	Heat	Total
Indigenous Production	37658	123	.	544	6416	343	.	.	45084
Import	2737	13327	589	10815	.	.	757	.	28225
Export	-2605	.	-849	-587	.	.	-367	.	-4408
Intl. Marine Bunkers	.	.	.	.	.	.	.	.	.
Stock Changes	502	184	22	17	.	.	.	.	724
TPES	38292	13634	-238	10789	6416	343	390	.	69626
Returns and Transfers	.	.	.	.	.	.	.	.	.
Statistical Differences	252	.	.	.	.	.	.	.	252
Public Electricity	-15839	.	.	-468	-6416	-343	6868	.	-16198
Autoproducers of Electr.	.	.	.	.	.	.	582	.	582
CHP Plants	-7169	.	.	-233	.	.	.	12656	5254
District Heating	-2450	.	-144	-447	.	.	.	.	-3041
Gas Works	-466	.	.	343	.	.	.	.	-123
Petroleum Refineries	.	-13634	13102	-248	.	.	-52	.	-831
Coal Transformation	-976	.	.	.	.	.	.	.	-976
Liquefaction	.	.	.	.	.	.	.	.	.
Other Transformation	.	.	-3216	-408	.	.	.	.	-3624
Own Use	-788	.	-29	-107	.	.	-1278	.	-2202
Distribution Losses	-85	.	.	-174	.	.	-501	-358	-1119
TFC	10770	.	9475	9047	.	.	6009	12298	47600
INDUSTRY SECTOR	5548	.	3756	5739	.	.	3623	9766	28432
Iron and Steel	5548	.	.	.	.	.	.	.	5548
Chemical	.	.	1720	.	.	.	.	.	1720
(of which:Feedstocks)	.	.	.	960	.	.	.	.	960
Non-ferrous Metals	.	.	.	.	.	.	.	.	.
Non-metallic Minerals	.	.	.	.	.	.	.	.	.
Transport Equip. & Mach.	.	.	.	.	.	.	.	.	.
Machinery	.	.	137	.	.	.	.	.	137
Mining and Quarrying	.	.	119	.	.	.	.	.	119
Food and Tobacco	.	.	.	.	.	.	.	.	.
Paper, Pulp and Printing	.	.	.	.	.	.	.	.	.
Wood and Wood Products	.	.	.	.	.	.	.	.	.
Construction	.	.	295	.	.	.	.	.	295
Textile and Leather	.	.	.	.	.	.	.	.	.
Non-specified Industry	.	.	1486	5739	.	.	3623	9766	20613
TRANSPORT SECTOR	.	.	2873	.	.	.	372	.	3245
Air	.	.	352	.	.	.	.	.	352
Road	.	.	2521	.	.	.	.	.	2521
Rail	.	.	.	.	.	.	372	.	372
Internal Navigation	.	.	.	.	.	.	.	.	.
Non-specified Transport	.	.	.	.	.	.	.	.	.
OTHER SECTORS	5222	.	2846	3308	.	.	2014	2533	15923
Agriculture	124	.	1176	.	.	.	.	.	1300
Comm. & Pub. Services	.	.	.	.	.	.	.	.	.
Residential	1848	.	150	1774	.	.	1144	1616	6532
Non-specified Other	3249	.	1521	1534	.	.	870	917	8091
Non-Energy Use	.	.	.	.	.	.	.	.	.
MEMO ITEMS:									
Electricity Generated (GWh)	*58017*	.	.	.	*24621*	*3989*	.	.	*86627*
Public	*51253*	.	.	.	*24621*	*3989*	.	.	*79863*
Autoproducers	*6764*	.	.	.	.	.	.	.	*6764*

Hungary 1989

Thousand toe

	Coal	Crude Oil	Petroleum Products	Gas	Nuclear	Hydro/ Other	Elec- tricity	Heat	Total
Indigenous Production	5163.5	2633.1	.	4720.1	3620.1	13.6	.	.	16150.4
Import	1928.2	6188.3	1620.8	4841.4	.	.	953.2	.	15531.9
Export	-33.6	.	-1874.4	-19.0	.	.	.	.	-1926.9
Intl. Marine Bunkers	.	.	.	.	.	.	.	.	.
Stock Changes	145.7	56.8	-61.5	-177.3	.	.	.	.	-36.4
TPES	7203.8	8878.2	-315.1	9365.2	3620.1	13.6	953.2	.	29719.0
Returns and Transfers	.	-251.4	263.3	.	.	.	.	.	11.9
Statistical Differences	-750.8	.	-226.6	.	.	.	.	.	-977.4
Public Electricity	-2071.5	.	-307.7	-956.8	-3620.1	-13.6	2463.6	.	-4506.0
Autoproducers of Electr.	-6.9	.	.	-12.9	.	.	81.6	.	61.9
CHP Plants	-608.9	.	-361.9	-206.9	.	.	.	160.0	-1017.8
District Heating	-570.8	.	-675.0	-1589.5	.	.	.	2019.6	-815.8
Gas Works	.	.	.	.	.	.	.	.	.
Petroleum Refineries	.	-8626.8	8646.9	-71.1	.	.	-41.9	.	-92.9
Coal Transformation	184.8	.	.	.	.	.	.	.	184.8
Liquefaction	.	.	.	.	.	.	.	.	.
Other Transformation	.	.	.	.	.	.	.	.	.
Own Use	-77.5	.	-27.9	-164.5	.	.	-355.6	-354.7	-980.3
Distribution Losses	-16.6	.	.	-181.6	.	.	-356.3	-155.2	-709.7
TFC	3285.6	.	6995.9	6181.7	.	.	2744.7	1669.7	20877.5
INDUSTRY SECTOR	914.8	.	1264.5	3439.0	.	.	1329.4	579.9	7527.5
Iron and Steel	787.3	.	61.7	479.9	.	.	188.1	150.0	1666.9
Chemical	.	.	5.3	939.7	.	.	289.4	329.9	1564.3
(of which:Feedstocks)	.	.	.	741.2	.	.	.	.	741.2
Non-ferrous Metals	.	.	23.0	94.7	.	.	168.2	60.0	345.9
Non-metallic Minerals	86.6	.	.	677.1	.	.	95.3	.	859.0
Transport Equip. & Mach.	.	.	.	336.9	.	.	38.2	.	375.1
Machinery	18.3	.	.	.	.	.	124.0	.	142.3
Mining and Quarrying	0.4	.	.	1.9	.	.	35.4	.	37.8
Food and Tobacco	17.2	.	.	451.3	.	.	136.6	.	605.1
Paper, Pulp and Printing	.	.	.	110.1	.	.	49.0	.	159.1
Wood and Wood Products	.	.	.	2.3	.	.	16.6	.	18.9
Construction	1.1	.	.	13.7	.	.	28.4	.	43.2
Textile and Leather	0.2	.	.	102.1	.	.	76.9	.	179.2
Non-specified Industry	3.7	.	1174.4	229.3	.	.	83.3	40.0	1530.7
TRANSPORT SECTOR	1.5	.	3198.3	0.2	.	.	100.5	.	3300.4
Air	.	.	160.8	.	.	.	.	.	160.8
Road	.	.	2828.4	0.2	.	.	.	.	2828.6
Rail	1.5	.	195.6	.	.	.	100.5	.	297.5
Internal Navigation	.	.	13.5	.	.	.	.	.	13.5
Non-specified Transport	.	.	.	.	.	.	.	.	.
OTHER SECTORS	2369.3	.	1937.0	2742.5	.	.	1314.9	1089.8	9453.5
Agriculture	35.1	.	753.0	219.7	.	.	176.0	.	1183.8
Comm. & Pub. Services	277.5	.	288.5	818.1	.	.	344.8	248.6	1977.4
Residential	2040.9	.	862.3	1522.5	.	.	744.2	841.2	6011.1
Non-specified Other	15.9	.	33.1	182.3	.	.	49.9	.	281.1
Non-Energy Use	.	.	596.2	.	.	.	.	.	596.2
MEMO ITEMS:									
Electricity Generated (GWh)	*8276*	.	*1591*	*5549*	*13891*	*158*	.	.	*29596*
Public	*8209*	.	*1244*	*5149*	*13891*	*158*	.	.	*28647*
Autoproducers	*67*	.	*347*	*404*	.	.	.	.	*949*

Hungary 1990

Thousand toe

	Coal	Crude Oil	Petroleum Products	Gas	Nuclear	Hydro/ Other	Elec- tricity	Heat	Total
Indigenous Production	4674.7	2524.3	.	3810.5	3578.4	15.3	.	.	14603.3
Import	1504.6	6283.2	1672.4	5188.6	.	.	956.9	.	15605.7
Export	-0.6	.	-1524.1	-20.0	.	.	.	.	-1544.7
Intl. Marine Bunkers	.	.	.	.	.	.	.	.	.
Stock Changes	574.8	-543.3	-28.0	-68.6	.	.	.	.	-65.2
TPES	6753.6	8264.2	120.2	8910.5	3578.4	15.3	956.9	.	28599.1
Returns and Transfers	.	-235.2	246.3	.	.	.	.	.	11.1
Statistical Differences	-571.4	.	-240.0	.	.	.	.	.	-811.4
Public Electricity	-2426.3	.	-229.9	-809.0	-3578.4	-15.3	2361.8	.	-4697.2
Autoproducers of Electr.	-8.3	.	.	-12.6	.	.	81.5	.	60.6
CHP Plants	-580.2	.	-418.6	-212.3	.	.	.	150.9	-1060.2
District Heating	-404.8	.	-601.0	-1500.0	.	.	.	1994.7	-511.0
Gas Works	.	.	.	.	.	.	.	.	.
Petroleum Refineries	.	-8029.0	8030.7	-55.4	.	.	-41.8	.	-95.4
Coal Transformation	207.7	.	.	.	.	.	.	.	207.7
Liquefaction	.	.	.	.	.	.	.	.	.
Other Transformation	.	.	.	.	.	.	.	.	.
Own Use	-66.6	.	-21.9	-151.5	.	.	-338.9	-492.2	-1071.2
Distribution Losses	-7.4	.	.	-248.4	.	.	-345.3	-130.4	-731.5
TFC	2896.2	.	6885.9	5921.3	.	.	2674.3	1523.0	19900.5
INDUSTRY SECTOR	893.3	.	889.8	3165.5	.	.	1232.2	405.8	6586.6
Iron and Steel	779.1	.	3.1	422.0	.	.	137.3	99.1	1440.6
Chemical	.	.	4.1	950.1	.	.	253.3	226.8	1434.3
(of which:Feedstocks)	.	.	.	549.7	.	.	.	.	549.7
Non-ferrous Metals	.	.	.	96.3	.	.	164.3	11.4	271.9
Non-metallic Minerals	73.2	.	.	703.8	.	.	95.2	0.4	872.6
Transport Equip. & Mach.	.	.	.	315.8	.	.	31.7	26.6	374.1
Machinery	17.5	.	.	.	.	.	126.5	.	144.0
Mining and Quarrying	0.2	.	.	4.8	.	.	29.9	1.7	36.7
Food and Tobacco	20.8	.	.	444.5	.	.	140.6	5.9	611.7
Paper, Pulp and Printing	.	.	.	101.0	.	.	48.3	15.6	164.9
Wood and Wood Products	.	.	.	2.9	.	.	18.0	1.4	22.3
Construction	1.3	.	.	10.6	.	.	32.9	1.5	46.4
Textile and Leather	.	.	.	97.6	.	.	69.7	15.4	182.6
Non-specified Industry	1.1	.	882.5	16.3	.	.	84.5	0.1	984.5
TRANSPORT SECTOR	1.2	.	3120.3	0.1	.	.	94.7	.	3216.4
Air	.	.	171.5	.	.	.	.	.	171.5
Road	.	.	2768.7	0.1	.	.	.	.	2768.9
Rail	1.2	.	170.8	.	.	.	94.7	.	266.7
Internal Navigation	.	.	9.3	.	.	.	.	.	9.3
Non-specified Transport	.	.	.	.	.	.	.	.	.
OTHER SECTORS	2001.6	.	2347.9	2755.6	.	.	1347.4	1117.1	9569.6
Agriculture	23.3	.	793.4	242.3	.	.	166.7	.	1225.7
Comm. & Pub. Services	121.9	.	395.2	785.1	.	.	340.1	287.0	1929.3
Residential	1836.0	.	948.1	1578.8	.	.	790.2	830.1	5983.2
Non-specified Other	20.4	.	211.1	149.4	.	.	50.4	.	431.4
Non-Energy Use	.	.	528.0	.	.	.	.	.	528.0
MEMO ITEMS:									
Electricity Generated (GWh)	*8295*	.	*1361*	*4846*	*13731*	*178*	.	.	*28411*
Public	*8152*	.	*1016*	*4386*	*13731*	*178*	.	.	*27463*
Autoproducers	*143*	.	*345*	*460*	.	.	.	.	*948*

- 261 -

Poland 1989

Thousand toe

	Coal	Crude Oil	Petroleum Products	Gas	Nuclear	Hydro/ Other	Elec- tricity	Heat	Total
Indigenous Production	111137	178	.	3463	.	139	.	.	114917
Import	656	14854	3275	6363	.	.	1037	.	26186
Export	-19435	.	-1013	-1	.	.	-883	.	-21332
Intl. Marine Bunkers	.	.	-1405	.	.	.	.	.	-1405
Stock Changes	964	339	-100	-303	.	.	.	.	900
TPES	93322	15372	757	9523	.	139	154	.	119266
Returns and Transfers	-2	216	1	-1	.	.	.	.	214
Statistical Differences	-1812	2	209	-38	.	.	.	1212	-428
Public Electricity	.	.	.	.	.	-139	-184	.	-323
Autoproducers of Electr.	-1302	.	-187	-14	.	.	.	.	-1504
CHP Plants	-37991	.	-186	-4	.	.	12510	.	-25671
District Heating	-15683	.	-1371	-502	.	.	.	18753	1197
Gas Works	-712	.	-1	188	.	.	.	.	-525
Petroleum Refineries	-2	-15590	14752	-57	.	.	-39	-882	-1817
Coal Transformation	-1235	.	.	.	.	.	.	.	-1235
Liquefaction	.	.	.	.	.	.	.	.	.
Other Transformation	.	.	.	-30	.	.	.	.	-30
Own Use	-1661	.	-49	-326	.	.	-2395	-1893	-6323
Distribution Losses	-82	.	-8	-214	.	.	-1114	.	-1418
TFC	32840	.	13916	8525	.	.	8932	17191	81404
INDUSTRY SECTOR	10394	.	1294	3244	.	.	4249	10905	30087
Iron and Steel	4360	.	373	1589	.	.	693	1086	8101
Chemical	329	.	167	149	.	.	1044	3522	5211
(of which:Feedstocks)	.	.	15	.	.	.	82	714	811
Non-ferrous Metals	251	.	19	139	.	.	210	96	714
Non-metallic Minerals	2859	.	188	760	.	.	332	339	4478
Transport Equip. & Mach.	2	.	.	80	.	.	.	372	454
Machinery	872	.	81	313	.	.	718	866	2849
Mining and Quarrying	155	.	59	151	.	.	311	998	1673
Food and Tobacco	849	.	84	46	.	.	267	1379	2625
Paper, Pulp and Printing	52	.	31	4	.	.	193	801	1081
Wood and Wood Products	168	.	45	3	.	.	119	275	611
Construction	255	.	232	5	.	.	112	398	1002
Textile and Leather	218	.	6	4	.	.	237	743	1208
Non-specified Industry	26	.	8	1	.	.	14	31	79
TRANSPORT SECTOR	568	.	8204	2	.	.	607	150	9530
Air	1	.	532	.	.	.	.	.	532
Road	96	.	7135	1	.	.	94	138	7464
Rail	467	.	527	1	.	.	504	.	1499
Internal Navigation	5	.	10	.	.	.	8	12	35
Non-specified Transport	.	.	.	.	.	.	.	.	.
OTHER SECTORS	21651	.	1508	3014	.	.	4076	6136	36385
Agriculture	893	.	1325	11	.	.	764	297	3290
Comm. & Pub. Services	.	.	.	.	.	.	.	.	.
Residential	362	.	181	2658	.	.	1617	5839	10656
Non-specified Other	20397	.	2	345	.	.	1695	.	22439
Non-Energy Use	227	.	2910	2265	.	.	.	.	5402
MEMO ITEMS:									
Electricity Generated (GWh)	*140229*		*1467*	*14*	.	*1612*			*143322*
Public	*140229*		*1467*	*14*		*1612*			*143322*
Autoproducers	.	.	.	.	.	.	.	.	.

Poland 1990

Thousand toe

	Coal	Crude Oil	Petroleum Products	Gas	Nuclear	Hydro/ Other	Elec- tricity	Heat	Total
Indigenous Production	94459	175	.	2378	.	113	.	.	97125
Import	393	13122	2889	6777	.	.	898	.	24078
Export	-19302	.	-1485	-1	.	.	-987	.	-21775
Intl. Marine Bunkers	.	.	-453	.	.	.	.	.	-453
Stock Changes	-176	-434	-357	-213	.	.	.	.	-1180
TPES	75374	12863	595	8941	.	113	-90		97797
Returns and Transfers	20	167	.	21	.	.	.	.	208
Statistical Differences	264	-1	232	-125	.	.	.	1179	1549
Public Electricity	.	.	.	.	.	-113	-172	.	-285
Autoproducers of Electr.	-1246	.	-182	-21	.	.	.	.	-1449
CHP Plants	-35035	.	-171	-6	.	.	11723	.	-23490
District Heating	-15098	.	-1252	-493	.	.	.	17760	916
Gas Works	-373	.	-12	108	.	.	.	.	-278
Petroleum Refineries	-1	-13029	12242	.	.	.	-34	-305	-1128
Coal Transformation	-1267	.	.	.	.	.	.	.	-1267
Liquefaction	.	.	.	.	.	.	.	.	.
Other Transformation	.	.	.	-24	.	.	.	.	-24
Own Use	-1443	.	-48	-282	.	.	-2240	-1596	-5610
Distribution Losses	-27	.	-12	-208	.	.	-908	.	-1154
TFC	21167	.	11393	7908	.	.	8279	17038	65785
INDUSTRY SECTOR	8667	.	937	2626	.	.	3676	9706	25611
Iron and Steel	3988	.	268	1289	.	.	643	1128	7317
Chemical	253	.	91	131	.	.	898	3070	4444
(of which:Feedstocks)	.	.	.	.	.	.	76	584	660
Non-ferrous Metals	160	.	18	111	.	.	186	89	564
Non-metallic Minerals	2115	.	123	655	.	.	272	279	3444
Transport Equip. & Mach.	117	.	34	36	.	.	111	322	620
Machinery	544	.	30	249	.	.	465	774	2062
Mining and Quarrying	103	.	45	94	.	.	275	962	1479
Food and Tobacco	844	.	73	48	.	.	246	1178	2388
Paper, Pulp and Printing	43	.	33	2	.	.	169	722	970
Wood and Wood Products	130	.	31	2	.	.	109	237	509
Construction	181	.	183	4	.	.	109	311	789
Textile and Leather	175	.	5	3	.	.	184	616	983
Non-specified Industry	14	.	3	1	.	.	10	17	45
TRANSPORT SECTOR	439	.	6891	2	.	.	555	145	8032
Air	1	.	212	.	.	.	.	.	213
Road	86	.	6212	1	.	.	88	120	6507
Rail	348	.	437	1	.	.	459	15	1260
Internal Navigation	5	.	30	.	.	.	7	11	52
Non-specified Transport	.	.	.	.	.	.	.	.	.
OTHER SECTORS	11874	.	1396	3347	.	.	4048	7187	27852
Agriculture	842	.	1357	11	.	.	731	237	3177
Comm. & Pub. Services	.	.	.	.	.	.	.	.	.
Residential	.	.	38	.	.	.	1739	6951	8728
Non-specified Other	11032	.	.	3336	.	.	1579	.	15947
Non-Energy Use	188	.	2170	1933	.	.	.	.	4290
MEMO ITEMS:									
Electricity Generated (GWh)	*131534*	.	*1451*	*13*	.	*1317*	.	.	*134315*
Public	*131534*	.	*1451*	*13*	.	*1317*	.	.	*134315*
Autoproducers	.	.	.	.	.	.	.	.	.

LIST OF PARTICIPANTS

Mr. J.G.A. AL
Director
Air and Energy Directorate
Ministry of Environment
PO Box 450
2260 MB
NETHERLANDS

Mr. Robert ARCHER
Deputy Chief
U.S. Agency for International
Development
 Bureau for Europe, Energy and
Infrastructure
Washington D.C. 20253
UNITED STATES

Ms. Andrea BALLA
Allami Energetikai es Energiabiztonsag
Technikai
Felugyelet Koztkrsasag ter 7
1081 Budapest
HUNGARY

Mr. Simeon BATOV
Technical University of Sofia
Nilin Kamak Str. 1
Sofia 1421
BULGARIA

Mr. Jozef BELCAK
Minister of Economy of the Slovak
Republic
MH SR
Mierova 19
827 15 Bratislava
CSFR

Ing. Vladimir BELOVIC
Slovak Commission for the Environment
Hlboka 2
Bratislava
CSFR

Mr. Olav BENESTAD
University of Oslo
0Department for Environmental Research
P.O. Box 1116 Blindern
Oslo 3
NORWAY

Mr. Giuseppe ARCELLI
President
Ansaldo Industria
Via dei Pescatori 35
16129 Genova
ITALY

Mr. Eric ASHDOWN
HESCO
Chief Financial Officer
1188 Franklin Street
San Francisco CA 94109
UNITED STATES

Mr. Bela BARNER
Energiahtekonysagi Iroda
1072 Budapest
Kiraly utca 47
HUNGARY

Mr. Klaus BAUMANN
Federal Ministry of Economy
Programme Management Unit PHARE
Nabr. Kpt. Jarose 1000
170 32 Prague
CSFR

Mr. Alexander BELOV
Ukraine Ministry of Environment
Protection
 Kreschatic Str.5
Kiev
UKRAINE

Mr. Karel BENDA
Contract Department
Skoda Praha Ltd.
Fossile Power systems and Envtl.
M. Horakové, 109,
160 00 Prague 6
CSFR

Dr. J. E. BERRY
Energy Technology Support Unit for
Dept of Energy
Harwell Lab B149
Oxfordshire OX11 ORA
UNITED KINGDOM

Ms. Livia BIELIKOVA
Ministry of Economy of the Slovak
Republic
MH SR
Mierova 19
827 15 Bratislava
CSFR

Mr. Oldrich BILIK
Federal Ministry of Economy
Natreze Kpt. Jarose 1000
170 32 Prague 7
CSFR

Dipl. Ing. Peter BOBULA
Slovensky Podnik
Hranicana 12
827 36 Bratislava
CSFR

Mrs. Henryka BOCHNIARZ
Nicom Consulting Ltd
pl. Inwalidow 10
01-552 Warszawa
POLAND

Mr. Zbigniew BOCHNIARZ
Senior Program Advisor on Energy and
Environment to UNDP
Hubert H Humphrey Institute
University of Minnesota
301 19th Avenue South
Minneapolis
55455 Minnesota
USA

Mr. Wolfgang BOGER
Director
Sales and Marketing
Deutsche Babcock Energie
UWD Umwelttechnik
AG. Oberhausen
GERMANY

Mr. Tomas BOJNICKY
Ministry of Economy of the Slovak
Republic
MH SR
Mierova 19
827 15 Bratislava
CSFR

Mr. Ronald BOWES
US Department of Energy
5224 Tooley Court
Fairfax 22032
USA

Mr. Bram BRANDS
Commission of the European
Communities
226-236 Avenue de Tervuren
1150 Brussels
BELGIUM

Mr. Bohuslav BRIX
Head of Department
CEZ Jungmannova 29
111 48 Praha 1
CSFR

Mr. Ian BROWN
Commission of the European
Communities
Energiahtekonysagi Iroda
1072 Budapest
Kiraly utca 47
HUNGARY

Mr. Giovanni CAPRIOGLIO
Federal Ministry of Economy
Programme Management Unit PHARE
Nabrezi Kpt. Jarose 1000
170 32 Prague
CSFR

Dr. David CARLESS
ETSU
Harwell Laboratories
Oxfordshire
UNITED KINGDOM

Mr. Renaud CAZETOU
Inestene
5 rue Buot
75013 Paris
FRANCE

Mr. M. CERMAK
Contract Department
Skoda Praha Ltd
Fossile Power systems and Envtl
Prague
CSFR

Mr. William CHANDLER
Director Advanced International Studies
Unit
Battelle Pacific Northwest Laboratories
370 L'Enfant Promenade
Washington D.C. 20024
USA

Mr. C. CIMPONER
Regia Autonoma A Huilei Din Romania
Petrosani Judetul Hunedoara
Str. Timisoara nr. 2
ROMANIA

Mr. R. CIZEK
VUPEK
Vladislavova 4
113 72 Praha 1
CSFR

Ing. Alexander DANO
Slovak Commission for the Environment
Hlboka 2
84235 Bratislava
CSFR

Mr. Boguslaw DEBSKI
Energy Information Centre
ul. Mysia 2, 009-950
Warsaw
POLAND

Mr. Arpad DEMKO
Slovensky Plenarensky Priemysel
c/o MHSR
Mierova 19
827 15 Bratislava
CSFR

Mr. Mark CHANDLER
Mission Energy Company UK Ltd
11/12 Buckingham Gate
London SW1E 6LB
UNITED KINGDOM

Mr. Yves CHEVALIER
BCEOM
15 Square Max Hymans
Paris
FRANCE

Dott. CLEMENTE
Area Director for Energy and
Environment
ENEA
Viale Regina Margherita
125 Rome 00198
ITALY

Mr. Alex CHRISTOFARO
US EPA
401 M. Street PM 221
Washington D.C.
USA

Mr. Todd DAVIS
Senior Vice President, SRC
Suite 12, 711 Presidential Boulevard
Bala Cynwyd
Pennsylvania 19004
USA

Mr. I. DEJMAL
Minister of Environment of the Czech
Republic
MZP CR
Vrsovicka 65
100 10 Praha 10-Vrsovice
CSFR

Mr. Bernard DEVIN
Conseiller
ADEME
27 rue Louis Vicat
75737 Paris Cedex 15
FRANCE

Ms. Tzuetana Pavlove DIMITROVA
Ecoglasnost
Douducov 39
Sofia 1000
BULGARIA

Mr. Kalensky DOBROMIL
Energoprojekt Praha
Praha 7 Bubenska c 170 05
CSFR

Mr. Joszef DUBROVAY
Ministry of Economy of the Slovak
Republic
MH SR
Mierova 19
827 15 Bratislava
CSFR

Ms. Sid EMBREE
Environment Canada
Atmospheric Envt. Services
373 Promenade Sussex
Block E Premier Etage
Ottowa
ONTARIO K1AOH3 CANADA

Mr. Pavel ERBAN
Fuel Research Institute
Vladislavova 4
113 72 Praha 1
CSFR

Prof. Boguslaw FIEDOR
Director
Institute of Economics
Oskarlonge Academy of Economics
ul. Komandorska 118/120
53-345 Wroclaw
POLAND

Mr. Duncan FISHER
Editor
East West Environment Newsletter
49 Wellington Street
London WC2E 7BN
ANGLETERRE

Mr. DLOUHY
Minister
Federal Ministry of Economy of the
Czech and Slovak Federal Republic
Nabrezi Kpt. Jarose 1000
170 32 Prague 7
CSFR

Mr. Libor DOLEZAL
Vupek, s.p., Stredisko Ostrava
Vystavni 13
709 34 Ostrava 1
CSFR

Ms. E. DYVIK
European Bank for Reconstruction and
Development
122 Leadenhall Street
London EC3V 4QL
UNITED KINGDOM

Mr. Dennis EOFF
US EPA
401 M. Street PM 221
Washington D.C.
USA

Ms. Andrea FENNESZ
G-24 Coordination V
Commission of the European
Communities
Rue de la Loi 200
B-1049 Brussels
BELGIUM

Mr. Bruzzo FILLIPPO
Ansaldo Industria SPA
Via Pierogostimi 50
16151 Genova
ITALY

Mr. Christopher R. GADOMSKI
250 East Hartsdale Avenue
Suite 26 Hartsdale NY 10530
UNITED STATES

Mr. Pavol GALVANEK
Slovensky Zapadoslovenks Energe Zavody
c/o MHSR
Mierova 19
827 15 Bratislava
CSFR

Mr. Zdravko GENTCHEV
National Centre for Regional
Development and Housing Policy
Ministry for Regional Development
14 Alabin Str
1000 Sofia
BULGARIA

Mr. Villa GIACOMO
Nuclear Division
Commercial Manager
Ansaldo Industria
Via dei Pescatori 35
16129 Genova
ITALY

Mr. Tom GRAY
Ministry of Economy of the Slovak
Republic
MH SR
Mierova 19
827 15 Bratislava
CSFR

Mr. Aef Olav GRINDE
Senior Executive Officer
Ministry of Petroleum and Energy
P.O. Box 8148 Dep
0033 Oslo
NORWAY

Mr. J. HALZL
MVMT
Vam u. 5-7
1011 Budapest
HUNGARY

Mrs. HAUSKRECHTOVA
Slovak Commission for the Environment
HIBOKA 2
84235 Bratislava
CSFR

Ing. Rudolf GELTNER
Specialist
Praha 2 Slozska
CSFR

Mr. Jean-Michel GERMING
Electrowatt Engineering Services Ltd
Bellerivestrasse 36
P.O. Box CH-8034 Zurich
SWITZERLAND

Mr. Norman GILROY
HESCO
Vice President
1188 Franklin Street
San Francisco CA 94109
UNITED STATES

Mr. Irvela GRIACOVA
Ministry of Economy of the Slovak
Republic
MH SR
Mierova 19
827 15 Bratislava
CSFR

Ms. Line Amlund HAGEN
Executive Officer
Ministry of Petroleum and Energy
P.O. Box 8148 Dep
0033 Oslo
NORWAY

Mr. Robert HART
Hart Associates
1819 H Street N.W.
RM 410
Washington D.C.
USA

Unir. Prof. Dr. Manfred HEINDLOR
Linke Wienzeile 18
1060 Wien
AUSTRIA

Mr. Stefan HERICH
The Ministry of Economy of the Slovak
Republic
19 Mierova St.
82715 Bratislava
CSFR

Mr. Greg HINOTE
Rodgers Capital International Inc.
Szentharomsag Ter 6
H-1014 Budapest 1
HUNGARY

Mr. Peter HOELLER
Economics and Statistics Directorate
(ESD)
OECD
2 rue Andre Pascal
75775 Paris
FRANCE

Mr. John G. HOLLINS
Environment Canada
Associate Science Advisor
Hull (Quebec)
K1A OH3
CANADA

Mr. Jan HORAK
VUHU-Brown Coal Research Institute
434 37 Most
CSFR

Mr. P. HORROCKS
Commission of the European
Communities DGXVII
Rue de la Loi 200
B-1049 Brussels
BELGIUM

Mr. Laszlo HUNYADI
Vattenfall R&D
S-16207 Vallingby
SWEDEN

Mr. Christopher HILZ
DG I - PHARE Programme
Commission of the European
Communities
Rue de la Loi 200
B-1049 Brussels
BELGIUM

Mr. HOEDEMAKERS
CADDET
NOVEM
Swentibold Straat 21
PO Box 17
6130 AA Sittard
NETHERLANDS

Mr. Erik HOEG
Birch & Krogboe Consultants & Planners
Foldegade 2
7100 Vejle
DENMARK

Mr. John HONTELEZ
Central and Eastern Europe Program
Minister Elandstraat 27
NL-6523 CS Nijmegen
NETHERLANDS

Mr. HORACEK
Ministry of Environment for the Czech
Republic
Vrsovicka 65
100 10 Prague 10
CSFR

Mr. G. HUGHES
The World Bank
1818 H Street N.W.
Washington D.C. 20433
USA

Mr. Bob ICHORD
Director
Energy and Infrastructure Division
Bureau for Europe US Aid
Washington D.C. 20523
USA

Mr. Tamas JASZAY
Technical University of Budapest
Muegyetem rkp. 9
Budapest H-1111
HUNGARY

Mr. Rolf JEKER
Ambassador
Office fédéral des affaires économiques
extérieures
CH-3003 Berne
SWITZERLAND

Dipl. ing. Paval JILEK
Ministry of Environment of the Czech
Republic
Air Protection Department
Kodanska 10
CS-10010 Praha 10
CSFR

Mr. Jan JURACIC
Ministry of Economy of the Slovak
Republic
MH SR
Mierova 19
827 15 Bratislava
CSFR

Mrs. KABELACOVA
Federal Committe for the Environment
Slezska 9
120 29 Praha 2
CSFR

Mr. Peter J. KALAS
Federal Office for Foreign Economic
Affairs
Federal Palais East
3003 Berne
SWITZERLAND

Mr. J. KARA
Czech Ministry of the Environment
Vrsovicka 65
1000 Prague 10
CSFR

Mr. Jaroslav JAROMERSKY
Marketing and Development Dep
ZVU Hradec Kralove Prazska ul.
501 47 Hradec Kralova
CSFR

Mr. J. JICHA
Federal Ministry of Economy of the
Czech
and Slovak Federal Republic
Nabrezi Kpt. Jarose 1000
170 32 Prague 7
CSFR

Mr. Lars JOSEPHSEN
Danish Energy Agency
11 Landemaerket
9DK-1119 Copenhagen
DENMARK

Mr. James JURACKA
Ministry of Industry of the Czech
Republic
Na Frantisku 32
110 15 Praha 1
CSFR

Mr. KADLEC
Energy Systems Division
VUPEK
Research, Engineering and Consulting
Institute
Vladislavova 4 113 72 prague 1
CSFR

Mr. Tobias KAMPET
Innotec Systemanalyse GMBH
Kurfurstendahm 180
1000 Berlin 15
GERMANY

Mr. Ceslav KARPETA
EGU - Power Research Institute
9 Bechovice
190 11 Prague
CSFR

Mr. David KEITH
Principal
RCG/Hagler, Bailly, Inc.
1530 Wilson Bivd
Suite 900
Arlington, VA 22209
UNITED STATES

Mr. Zbigniew KLIMONT
Research Fellow
Dept. of Energy Problems
Institute of Fundamental Technical
Research
ul. Swigtoknyska 21
Warsaw
POLAND

Mr. Chris KNOWLES
Banque Europeene D'investissement
100 Bld Konrad Adenauer
L-2950 LUXEMBOURG

Ing. Oto KRENC
Chemopetrol
Chemopetrol s. p.
Litvinov 436 70
CSFR

Ms. Marina KUNIS
The Wharton Business School
Hotel Kaiser Franz Joseph
Sieveringer Strasse 4
A-1190 Wien
AUSTRIA

Mr. Norbert LADOUX
CEA/DSE
29-33 rue de la Federation
75752 Paris Cedex 15
FRANCE

Mr. Gustav LAURENCIK
Ministry of Economy of the Slovak
Republic
MH SR
Mierova 19
827 15 Bratislava
CSFR

Mr. Vaclav KINDL
Design and Engineering Company
Bubenska 1
170 05 Praha 7
CSFR

Ing. Jaroslav KNAPEK
Czech Technical University
Department of Energy Economy
Praha 6 Technicka 2
CSFR

Mr. Vladimir KOSINA
Managing Director
Skoda Praha Ltd
Fossile Power systems and Envtl.
M. Horakové, 109,
160 00 Prague 6
CSFR

Mr. Dorota KRYSTKIEWICZ
Hart Associates
1819 H Street N.W.
RM 410
Washington D.C.
USA

Mr. George KVIDERA
Ministry of Privatisation
Slikova 8
160 00 Praha 6
CSFR

Mr. Vladimir LANG
Federal Energy Agency
Project Manager
nabrezi kpt
Jarose 1000
17032 Praha 7
CSFR

Mr. Mathew LEACH
Imperial College Centre for
Environmental Technology
48 Princes Gardens
London SW7 2PE
UNITED KINGDOM

Ing. Antonin LECIAN
Leiter der Abteilung fur Umweltschutz
Sprava OKD a.s. Ostrava
Prokesova nam. 6, 72830
CSFR

Mr. J. Van LIERE
Dutch Electric Utility Kema
N.V. Kema
Utrechtseweg 310
6812 Ar Arnhem
NETHERLANDS

Mr. Augustin MACHATA
Slovensky Uholne Bane
c/o MHSR
Mierova 19
827 15 Bratislava
CSFR

Mr. Nig Mala
Ministry of Economy of the Slovak
Republic
MH SR
Mierova 19
827 15 Bratislava
CSFR

Mr. A. MAJDANNIK
Ministry of Environment Protection
Kreschatic Str. 5
Kiev
UKRAINE

Mr. John MARROW
Coopers and Lybrand
Plumtree Court
London EC4A 4HT
UNITED KINGDOM

Mr. Jaroslav MAROUSEK
Executive Director Energy
Effficiency Center
Slezska 9
120 29 Prague 2
CSFR

Mr. Laszlo LENGYEL
UNECE
IT Building 54-56
Rue de Montbrillant
CH-1202 Geneva
SWITZERLAND

Mr. V. LUDVIK
Deputy Minister
Economic Policy and Development of
Czech Republic
MHP CR
Vrsovicka 65
101 60 Praha 10
CSFR

Mr. Jorgen MAGNER
Ministry of the Environment
Slots Holmsgade 12
Dk-1216 Copenhagen
DENMARK

Dr. Miroslav MALY
Energy Systems Division
VUPEK
Research, Engineering and Consulting
Institute
Vladislavova 4 113 72 prague 1
CSFR

Mr. Jerzy MAJCHER
ELEKTRIM SA
Power Plant Department
8 Chalubinskiego St
00-950 Warsaw
POLAND

Mr. Antony MARKIEWICZ
Central Office of planning
Plac Trzech Krzyzy 5
00-507 Warsaw
POLAND

Mr. W. MATLAK
Ministry of Environmental
Protection Natural Resources and Forestry
52/54 Wowelsko Str.
00-922 Warsaw
POLAND

Mr. M. MATRICA
Regia Autonoma A huilei Din Romania
Petrosani Judetul Huedoara
Str. Timisoara nr. 2
ROMANIA

Mr. Rudolf J. MINAR
500 West 123rd Street
Apartment 4
New York NY 10027
UNITED STATES

Mr. Andras MORENTH
Ministry of Industry and Trade
H-1525 Budapest, Pf. 96
HUNGARY

Mr. Karel MRAZEK
Buildinng Technical Institute
Deputy Director
Perlova 1 110 01 Praha 1
CSFR

Mr. Jaroslav MYSLIVECEK
Fuel Research Institute
190 11 Praha 9 - Bechovice
CSFR

Ms. A. Arquit NIEDERBERGER
Forests and Landscape
Federal Office of Environment
Hallwylstrasse 4
CH-3003 Bern
SWITZERLAND

Ms. Angela NEMBAVLAKIS
The Norman Patterson Carleton
 University
Ottowa Ontario
CANADA

Mr. Maciej NOWICKI
Ministry of Environmental Protection
Wawelska 52/54
00 922 Warsaw
POLAND

Mr. Alexander MAKOVETS
Managing Director
Semiplan Company Ltd
Orlovskaya Str 58
220053 Minsk
BELARUS

Mr. Petr MORAVICKY
Slovensky Slovensky Energeticky Podnik
c/o MHSR
Mierova 19
827 15 Bratislava
CSFR

Dr. Zoran MORVAJ
Econet International
Unska 3
41000 Zagreb
CROATIA

Mag. Wolfgang M. MUHLBAUER
Project Manager AWT Consulting
Concordiaplatz 2
A-1013 Vienna
AUSTRIA

Mr. Coleman J. NEE
Science Counselor
Al. Ujazdowskie 29/31
Warsaw
POLAND

Mr. Petr NIEDOBA
Vendryne 843
739 94 Trinec X
CSFR

Mr. Vladimir NOVOTNY
Ministry of Environment
Air Protection Department
Kodanska 10 100 10
Praha 10
CSFR

Mr. ODENHAL
Federal Ministry for Economy
Prague
CSFR

Mr. Dag OMRE
Ministry of Petroleum and Energy
P.O. Box 8148 Dep
N-0033 Oslo
NORWAY

Mr. Frits Van OOSTVOORN
ESC/European Studies
Netherlands Energy Research Foundation
ECN
P.O. Box 1
1755 ZG Petten
THE NETHERLANDS

Mr. Edourdo PALAZZI
Anslado
Lovohaz UTC 39
Budapest
HUNGARY

Mr. Michal PALECKO
Industrial Energetics
Ministry of Industry of the Czech
Republic
Na Frantisku 32
110 15 Praha 1
CSFR

Mr. Slawomir PASIERB
Polish Foundation for Energy Efficiency
40-024 Katowice
Powstancow 41A
POLAND

Ms. Eszeter PASZTO
Ministry of Industry and Trade
Department of Environmental
Management
15 25 Budapest 2
Martirok UTJA 85
HUNGARY

Mr. Josef PETRRILKA
Ministerstvo pro hospodarskou
 politiku a rozvoj cr
Vrsovicka 65 Praha 10
CSFR

Mr. Alfred PLOCEK
Specialist of Control and measuring
Systems
for heating and Air Conditioning
152 00 Praha 5
Barrandov Skalni 15
CSFR

Mr. Vaolav POLAK
Specialist
Praha 2 Slezska 9
CSFR

Dr. Frantisek POLASEK
Energy Services
Klipam 294
1900 Praha 9
CSFR

Mr. Mariusz POPIOLEK
Ministry of Environment
Wawelska 52/54
00-922 Warsaw
POLAND

Mr. Jan POUCEK
Programme Management Unit PHARE
Nabrezi Kpt. Jarose 1000
170 32 Prague
CSFR

Mr. Arne Faaborg POVLSEN
Danish Power consult
Elsamprojekt A/S
Kraftvaerksvej 53
DK 7000 Fredericia
DENMARK

Ing. Jan PSENICKA
Leiter der energetischen Abteilung
Sprava OKD, a.s. Ostrava
Prokesova nam. 6 72830
CSFR

Mr. Pierre RADANNE
Inestene
5 rue Buot
75013 Paris
FRANCE

Mr. Corneliu RADULESCU
Romanian Agency for Energy
Conmservation
Splaiul Independentei 202A
ROMANIA

Dipl. Ing. Ivana RAPANTOVA
Slovensky Podnik
Hranicana 12
827 36 Bratislava
CSFR

Mr. Donald B. REID
Vice President Special Ind
Westpac Banking Corp
225 West Washington
Chicago I/60022
UNITED STATES

Mr. Georg REBERNIG
Federal Ministry for Environment
Youth and Family
Radetzkystrasse 2
AUSTRIA 1031

Mrs. Anne RIALHE
INVESTENE
5 Rue Buot
75013 Paris
FRANCE

Ms. Marianne RONNEBAEK
Ministry of the Environment
Slots Holmsgade 12
DK-1216 Copenhagen
DENMARK

Mr. V. ROUCEK
VUHU-Brown Coal Research Inst.
434 37 Most
CSFR

Prof. Andrzej RUDNICKI
Krakow Polytechnical University
ul. Opolska 35/261
31-276 Krakow
POLAND

Dr. Ivo SANC
Director
Institute of Mineral Raw Materials
Vitezna 425
28403 Kutna Hora
CSFR

Dr. Manfred SCHAFER
Postbox 61 02 47
D-1000 Berlin 61
GERMANY

Mr. Thomas J. SECREST
Pacific Northwest Laboratories
Programe Manager/Energy Sciences
Department
Battelle Boulevard
Richland Washington 99352
UNITED STATES

Dr. Jorg SCHNEIDER
Federal Environmental Agency
Bismarchplatz 1
1000 Berlin 33
GERMANY

Mr. Vaclav SIMUNEK
Federal Ministry of Economy
Natreze Kpt. Jarose 1000
170 32 Prague 7
CSFR

Mr. Mara SILINA
Coordination Europeene des
Amis de la Terre
CEAT 29 Rue blanche
1050 Bruxelles
BELGIQUE

Mr. Jim SKEA
Leader, Environment Programme
Univrsity of Sussex
Mantell Building
Falmer
Brighton East Sussex BXI 9RF
UNITED KINGDOM

Mr. Vaclav SKUROVEC
Head of Department
Czech Technical University
Dept. of Energy Economics and
Management
Technicka 2
Praha 6
CSFR

Mr. Iva SLAVOTINEK
The Energy Efficiency Center
Senior Research Associate
Slezska 9
120 29 Praha 2
CSFR

Mr. Jan SPALENSKY
Vattenfall AB
Sokolska 9
120 00 Praha 2
CSFR

Ing. Tamara SPILKOVA
Director of Department
Praha 2 Slozska
CSFR

Mr. SRYMANOWSKI
ELEKTRIM
Director of Power Plant Dep
00-950 Warszawa
8 Chalubinskiego St
POLAND

Dr. Peter STEINREICH
Dynalytics Corporation
Hungary 145
Bimbo UT 159/A I/4
H-1026 Budapest
HUNGARY

Mr. Alajos STROBL
Head of the Section for Strategies
Hungarian Power Companies Ltd
1011 Budapest Vam UTCA 5-7
HUNGARY

Mr. Constantin SYNADINO
EIB
100 Bld Konrad Adenauer
L-2950 LUXEMBOURG

Mr. Imrich SZITAS
Ministry of Economy of the Slovak
Republic
MH SR
Mierova 19
827 15 Bratislava
CSFR

Mr. Waldemar R. SZYLINSKI
Tech Director PP Turow
Elektrownia Turow PL 59 916 Bogatynia
POLAND
Tel: 49 1 611202974

Mr. Dennis A. TIRPAK
Environmental Protection Agency
401 M Street
S.W. Room
3220-Mall-PM 221 Washington DC 20460
UNITED STATES

Mr. I. TIRPAK
Minister
Slovak Commission for Environment
Hlboka 2
811 04 Bratislava
CSFR

Mr. R. TOMKINS
ERL
106 Glouchester Place
London W1H 3DB
UNITED KINGDOM

Mr. Karl Z. VAVRICKA
ABB Power Generation Ltd
Sales Manager
Retrofit and Rehabilitation of Steam
Power Plants for Utilities
CH_5401 Baden
SWITZERLAND

Mr. Bart VERHAGEN
Directorate-General for Environmental
Protection
Air Directorate
dr. Reijersstraat 8
P.O. Box 450 2260 MB Leidschendam
The NETHERLANDS

Mr. Stefan VILKAY
Ministry of Economy of the Slovak
Republic
MH SR
Mierova 19
827 15 Bratislava
CSFR

Mr. Vladimir VONKA
Netherland Energy Research Foundation
ECN
P.O. Box 1 NL - 1755 ZG Petten
HOLLAND

Mr. Miroslav VLCEK
Czech Power Company
State Utility
Jungmannova 29
111 48 Praha 1
CSFR

Mr. Michael WALSH
Consultant
2800 N. Dinwiddle Street
Arlington Virginia 22207
USA

Dipl. ing Bruno VALLANCE
Enorcievbrwbrungsagbntur (BVA)
A-1010 Wien
Oprnring 1/R/3
AUSTRIA

Minister Josef VAVROUSEK
Federal Committee for the Environment
Priona 2
110 00 Prague
CSFR

Mr. Voic VEILLARD-BARON
Compagnie Generale de Chauffe
65 rue de Bercy
75012 Paris

Mr. Karol VISACKY
Ministry of Economy of the Slovak
Republic
MH SR
Mierova 19
827 15 Bratislava
CSFR

Ing. Miroslav VRBA, Csc
Institute for General Energy Research
Prague 2 Machova 7
CSFR

Mr. Josef VOTRUBA
Ministerstvo Pro Hospodarskou
 politiku a rozvoj CR
Vrsovicka 65
Praha 10
CSFR

Ing. Zdislav WANTULA
Direktor fur Technik
OKD a.s. Sprava Ostrava
Prokesova nam. 6 72830
CSFR

Ms. Ulla WEIGELT
Ministry of the environment and Natural
Resources
S-103 33 Stockholm
SWEDEN

Mr. Vladimir WILDA
Federal Energy Agency
Federal Ministry of Economy
nabr. kpt. Jarare 1000
170 32 Praha 7U1. 00-043
CSFR

Mr Ronald YOUNG
Director
EC Energy Centre
Prumstav bld
Stetkova 18
Prague 4
CSFR

Mr. Kees WIJNEN
Division for Europe
United Nations Development Programme
One United Nations Plaza
NY 10017 New York
USA

Mr. Michael WILLINGHAM
United Nations Department of Economic
 and Social Development
RM DCl-877 1 United Nations Plaza
New York NY 10017
UNITED STATES

Mr. Julian ZAHKO
Ministry of Economy of the Slovak
Republic
MH SR
Mierova 19
827 15 Bratislava
CSFR

MAIN SALES OUTLETS OF OECD PUBLICATIONS
PRINCIPAUX POINTS DE VENTE DES PUBLICATIONS DE L'OCDE

ARGENTINA – ARGENTINE
Carlos Hirsch S.R.L.
Galería Güemes, Florida 165, 4° Piso
1333 Buenos Aires   Tel. (1) 331.1787 y 331.2391
Telefax: (1) 331.1787

AUSTRALIA – AUSTRALIE
D.A. Information Services
648 Whitehorse Road, P.O.B 163
Mitcham, Victoria 3132   Tel. (03) 873.4411
Telefax: (03) 873.5679

AUSTRIA – AUTRICHE
Gerold & Co.
Graben 31
Wien I   Tel. (0222) 533.50.14

BELGIUM – BELGIQUE
Jean De Lannoy
Avenue du Roi 202
B-1060 Bruxelles   Tel. (02) 538.51.69/538.08.41
Telefax: (02) 538.08.41

CANADA
Renouf Publishing Company Ltd.
1294 Algoma Road
Ottawa, ON K1B 3W8   Tel. (613) 741.4333
Telefax: (613) 741.5439
Stores:
61 Sparks Street
Ottawa, ON K1P 5R1   Tel. (613) 238.8985
211 Yonge Street
Toronto, ON M5B 1M4   Tel. (416) 363.3171
Les Éditions La Liberté Inc.
3020 Chemin Sainte-Foy
Sainte-Foy, PQ G1X 3V6   Tel. (418) 658.3763
Telefax: (418) 658.3763

Federal Publications
165 University Avenue
Toronto, ON M5H 3B8   Tel. (416) 581.1552
Telefax: (416) 581.1743

CHINA – CHINE
China National Publications Import
Export Corporation (CNPIEC)
16 Gongti E. Road, Chaoyang District
P.O. Box 88 or 50
Beijing 100704 PR   Tel. (01) 506.6688
Telefax: (01) 506.3101

DENMARK – DANEMARK
Munksgaard Export and Subscription Service
35, Nørre Søgade, P.O. Box 2148
DK-1016 København K   Tel. (33) 12.85.70
Telefax: (33) 12.93.87

FINLAND – FINLANDE
Akateeminen Kirjakauppa
Keskuskatu 1, P.O. Box 128
00100 Helsinki   Tel. (358 0) 12141
Telefax: (358 0) 121.4441

FRANCE
OECD/OCDE
Mail Orders/Commandes par correspondance:
2, rue André-Pascal
75775 Paris Cedex 16   Tel. (33-1) 45.24.82.00
Telefax: (33-1) 45.24.85.00 or (33-1) 45.24.81.76
Telex: 640048 OCDE
OECD Bookshop/Librairie de l'OCDE :
33, rue Octave-Feuillet
75016 Paris   Tel. (33-1) 45.24.81.67
(33-1) 45.24.81.81
Documentation Française
29, quai Voltaire
75007 Paris   Tel. 40.15.70.00
Gibert Jeune (Droit-Économie)
6, place Saint-Michel
75006 Paris   Tel. 43.25.91.19

Librairie du Commerce International
10, avenue d'Iéna
75016 Paris   Tel. 40.73.34.60
Librairie Dunod
Université Paris-Dauphine
Place du Maréchal de Lattre de Tassigny
75016 Paris   Tel. 47.27.18.56
Librairie Lavoisier
11, rue Lavoisier
75008 Paris   Tel. 42.65.39.95
Librairie L.G.D.J. - Montchrestien
20, rue Soufflot
75005 Paris   Tel. 46.33.89.85
Librairie des Sciences Politiques
30, rue Saint-Guillaume
75007 Paris   Tel. 45.48.36.02
P.U.F.
49, boulevard Saint-Michel
75005 Paris   Tel. 43.25.83.40
Librairie de l'Université
12a, rue Nazareth
13100 Aix-en-Provence   Tel. (16) 42.26.18.08
Documentation Française
165, rue Garibaldi
69003 Lyon   Tel. (16) 78.63.32.23
Librairie Decitre
29, place Bellecour
69002 Lyon   Tel. (16) 72.40.54.54

GERMANY – ALLEMAGNE
OECD Publications and Information Centre
Schedestrasse 7
D-W 5300 Bonn 1   Tel. (0228) 21.60.45
Telefax: (0228) 26.11.04

GREECE – GRÈCE
Librairie Kauffmann
Mavrokordatou 9
106 78 Athens   Tel. 322.21.60
Telefax: 363.39.67

HONG-KONG
Swindon Book Co. Ltd.
13–15 Lock Road
Kowloon, Hong Kong   Tel. 366.80.31
Telefax: 739.49.75

ICELAND – ISLANDE
Mál Mog Menning
Laugavegi 18, Pósthólf 392
121 Reykjavik   Tel. 162.35.23

INDIA – INDE
Oxford Book and Stationery Co.
Scindia House
New Delhi 110001   Tel.(11) 331.5896/5308
Telefax: (11) 332.5993
17 Park Street
Calcutta 700016   Tel. 240832

INDONESIA – INDONÉSIE
Pdii-Lipi
P.O. Box 269/JKSMG/88
Jakarta 12790   Tel. 583467
Telex: 62 875

IRELAND – IRLANDE
TDC Publishers – Library Suppliers
12 North Frederick Street
Dublin 1   Tel. 74.48.35/74.96.77
Telefax: 74.84.16

ISRAEL
Electronic Publications only
Publications électroniques seulement
Sophist Systems Ltd.
71 Allenby Street
Tel-Aviv 65134   Tel. 3-29.00.21
Telefax: 3-29.92.39

ITALY – ITALIE
Libreria Commissionaria Sansoni
Via Duca di Calabria 1/1
50125 Firenze   Tel. (055) 64.54.15
Telefax: (055) 64.12.57
Via Bartolini 29
20155 Milano   Tel. (02) 36.50.83
Editrice e Libreria Herder
Piazza Montecitorio 120
00186 Roma   Tel. 679.46.28
Telefax: 678.47.51
Libreria Hoepli
Via Hoepli 5
20121 Milano   Tel. (02) 86.54.46
Telefax: (02) 805.28.86
Libreria Scientifica
Dott. Lucio de Biasio 'Aeiou'
Via Coronelli, 6
20146 Milano   Tel. (02) 48.95.45.52
Telefax: (02) 48.95.45.48

JAPAN – JAPON
OECD Publications and Information Centre
Landic Akasaka Building
2-3-4 Akasaka, Minato-ku
Tokyo 107   Tel. (81.3) 3586.2016
Telefax: (81.3) 3584.7929

KOREA – CORÉE
Kyobo Book Centre Co. Ltd.
P.O. Box 1658, Kwang Hwa Moon
Seoul   Tel. 730.78.91
Telefax: 735.00.30

MALAYSIA – MALAISIE
Co-operative Bookshop Ltd.
University of Malaya
P.O. Box 1127, Jalan Pantai Baru
59700 Kuala Lumpur
Malaysia   Tel. 756.5000/756.5425
Telefax: 757.3661

NETHERLANDS – PAYS-BAS
SDU Uitgeverij
Christoffel Plantijnstraat 2
Postbus 20014
2500 EA's-Gravenhage   Tel. (070 3) 78.99.11
Voor bestellingen: Tel. (070 3) 78.98.80
Telefax: (070 3) 47.63.51

**NEW ZEALAND
NOUVELLE-ZÉLANDE**
Legislation Services
P.O. Box 12418
Thorndon, Wellington   Tel. (04) 496.5652
Telefax: (04) 496.5698

NORWAY – NORVÈGE
Narvesen Info Center – NIC
Bertrand Narvesens vei 2
P.O. Box 6125 Etterstad
0602 Oslo 6   Tel. (02) 57.33.00
Telefax: (02) 68.19.01

PAKISTAN
Mirza Book Agency
65 Shahrah Quaid-E-Azam
Lahore 3   Tel. 66.839
Telex: 44886 UBL PK. Attn: MIRZA BK

PORTUGAL
Livraria Portugal
Rua do Carmo 70-74
Apart. 2681
1117 Lisboa Codex   Tel.: (01) 347.49.82/3/4/5
Telefax: (01) 347.02.64

OECD PUBLICATIONS, 2 rue André-Pascal, 75775 PARIS CEDEX 16

PRINTED IN ENGLAND

(61 93 04 1) ISBN 92-64-13813-7 - No. 46412 1993

THE REFERENCE SHELF (*Continued*)

THE REFERENCE SHELF

Vol. 22   No. 3

REPRESENTATIVE AMERICAN
SPEECHES: 1949-1950

Edited, and with introductions,
by
A. CRAIG BAIRD
Department of Speech, State University of Iowa

THE H. W. WILSON COMPANY
NEW YORK   1950

PREFATORY NOTE

REPRESENTATIVE AMERICAN SPEECHES: 1949-1950 is the thirteenth in this annual series. Each volume contains some twenty-five "representative" speeches, delivered by Americans, or by others temporarily here (e.g. Madame Chiang Kai-shek, Winston Churchill). The thirteen volumes include 388 addresses by some 218 orators.

The speeches are grouped according to content, such as International Policies, Hydrogen Bomb, National Defense, Industry and Labor, Education. An alternate classification, based upon speech types of occasions, is also suggested, such as speeches of introduction, those of legislative bodies, executive statements, courtroom, pulpit, radio, luncheon or dinner gatherings, political conventions, professional meetings.

These divisions, whether based on content or on speech occasions, obviously overlap. A speech on foreign policy may also have to do with national defense or the theory of democratic government. A radio talk may be also a political address, one of introduction, farewell, or eulogy. The tentative classifications help students interested in contemporary problems or those concerned with speeches as models for original compositions.

This editor, as he has done in the previous volumes, disavows any assumption that these are the "best" speeches of the year, or that the combined group are the "best" of the decade. They are, he hopes, "representative" or "typical" of the kind and quality of the American public utterances of a given period. Most are "important" in that they deal with issues that have affected millions of Americans. Some of these speeches, especially those of outstanding national leaders in periods of crisis, have probably influenced the direction of recent American history.

The Introduction to each of these thirteen volumes expounds some phase of speech criticism. Together these partial treatments constitute a well-developed body of speech theory.

A brief introduction accompanies each speech. The background and immediate occasion, issues, ideas, structure, organization, language, audience adaptation, immediate results of the speaking are suggested. These comments, without pretense of completeness, aim to stimulate the student to further research on the speech. The assumption of this critic is that speech is for social adaptation; that it springs from immediate situations; and that the attitudes and trends of American life of 1949-50 are partly revealed through the speeches of this volume.

The biographical notes in the Appendix are of necessity much condensed. The investigator should explore fully the biography of each speaker, especially his intellectual background, his experiences, his personality, and previous speaking record. Such information may well help in the proper appreciation and evaluation of a given speech of 1949 or 1950.

The Table of Contents of each edition and the Cumulated Author Index at the end of this volume are further means of surveying issues and speakers of the period of 1937-1950. Since speakers are often included in successive years (e.g. President Truman since 1945), a review of his performances as reported in the earlier collections will be most helpful.

This volume, like the earlier ones, is a reference source for the study of contemporary American problems; a partial record of the history of recent months; a collection of material for courses in debate and extempore speaking; a series of speeches for the systematic study of contemporary American public address; and a series of examples of how to proceed with one's own speech composition. Each volume, then, in addition to its service as a library reference, is especially recommended to students of extempore speaking, communication, debate, social science, history, and general public speaking.

The editor here expresses his great debt to various speakers for their uniform courtesy in supplying authentic texts and in granting permission for publication. He is also grateful to publishers and organizations that have permitted reprinting of the texts. Specific acknowledgement is made in the footnotes accompanying the speeches.

A. CRAIG BAIRD

May 1, 1950

CONTENTS

INTRODUCTION

How Shall We Judge the Oral
Language of a Speech?

How shall we judge the oral language or oral style of a speech?

Students of speechmaking have long agreed that the chief components of a speech include (1) thought, or ideas, (2) structure, or organization, (3) language or style, and (4) delivery. In previous Introductions to these annual collections I have discussed various aspects of rhetorical criticism.

The Introduction to the edition of 1948-1949, for example, includes a systematic series of suggestions concerning the criticism of ideas or thought as one of the basic elements of a speech. I propose here to summarize briefly the problem of language or style—the principles for its effective use, and the standards by which to judge its effectiveness in a given speech or speeches.

1. *The superior speaker is effective in his language usage.* His platform results may be due partly to his ideas, personality, delivery, rebuttal skill, anecdotal cleverness, or a combination of these and other factors. The more important contemporary speakers, however, including those in this volume, use language with uncommon readiness. To them words and phrases are no incidental factor in their speaking. John Foster Dulles, for example, uses much care in the composition of his speeches. He tries to state his ideas exactly. Outstanding speakers have been at home with word meanings. Webster, Phillips, Parker, Lincoln, Ingersoll, Grady, Bryan, Beveridge, Theodore Roosevelt, Wilson, and F. D. Roosevelt absorbed a good deal of the richness of the English vocabulary. Partly through their original and persuasive reflection of words and phrases, they produced powerful addresses.

2. *Language is closely related to the speaker's thought.* The thinking, we are told, is really not much wider than the thinker's vocabulary. One test of the breadth and depth of a given idea is the sharpness and completeness with which it has been form-

ulated in words. Although language is not identical with thought, the translation of mental activity into word symbols is "necessary for thinking and for communication." The words are thus an outward expression of these inner "thoughts."

3. *The speaker's language should correspond to his thought.* Obviously, your thoughts may pursue one highway; your words, another. Your inspired thoughts may soar; your language may remain below. Effective speaking, we assume, represents close identification of ideas and their expression. Sometimes, however, the wide gap is deliberate, as when a card-carrying Communist publicly rails against communism and eulogizes American democracy. Even when honest effort is made to translate ideas into equivalent language, the gulf may remain. Many meanings, as we know, attend a single word. Also each term has a different connotation to almost every hearer. Further, the limited vocabulary of a speaker may mean his failure to symbolize accurately his meanings. Nevertheless, good speaking demands that language move in the same channel with corresponding ideas. Only thus can a talker have much satisfaction in his utterances and only thus can his hearers be reasonably sure that they know what he is trying to say.

4. *Language should be for communication.* Speech aims at social control and social interaction. You are justified in talking only when you are attempting genuine communication. What are the factors of oral communication? They are (1) the initiation of an idea or ideas; (2) the formulation of the idea into symbolic equivalents—words; (3) the expression and interpretation of these word symbols through oral sounds and accompanying bodily activity; (4) the effective transmission by these visual-auditory means to an audience (one or more); (5) the appropriation by that audience of this communicated message and its reconstruction in their thinking; and (6) the completed response in belief, attitude, and action.

In such effective communication, language has a major role. Words must be no mere "blah-blah" of empty utterings. Nor must they be for mere showmanship. Rather the symbols must be selected and pronounced so as to aid in this clear broadcasting of ideas from speaker to recipient. Ideas as well as words should traverse the space and find recreation in the listener.

5. *The language should express effectively the speaker's purpose in communication.* What are the motives for communication? They are to inform; or to change belief; or to produce desired action; or to interest or entertain; or to impress and inspire; or to achieve any combination of these purposes. These aims, familiar to every student of speech, are also guiding principles for the selection and use of language. The necessity for information, for example, imposes on the vocabulary the requirement of absolute clarity; that of changing belief and conduct, or that of entertaining or impressing the auditor, calls for special skill in the selection of motivative (emotional and imaginative) language.

6. *The language should be closely adapted to the learning level, cultural background, experiences, beliefs and attitudes of the audience.* He who would address any group should be familiar with the personalities, cultural background, education, experiences, the beliefs and desires of these individuals. Such audience analysis will determine much of the speaker's vocabulary. Although the speechmaker will retain his usual habits of word selection, he will either talk only before audiences of which he is normally a part; or will either make satisfactory adjustments both in content and manner of expression, or will wisely remain silent.

The spoken language of each nationally prominent speaker has much in common with that of the others. Yet subtle differences appear as the discourse is directed to a specific audience. Note that in this volume the language employed in each case takes on somewhat the character of an audience on a specific occasion. Eisenhower at Columbia is lecturing to a Morningside Heights group; Judge Medina, in the courtroom in Foley Square, talks to the jury. President Truman, rising before five thousand Democratic diners, frames ideas so as to enlist the attention of that vast dinner party. So General Omar Bradley, Dean James McBurney, H. V. Kaltenborn, Philip Murray—each shapes his discourse to secure the maximum response from the special audience, for example, CIO unionists, speech teachers, Armed Services' Committee of the House of Representatives.

This principle does not mean that the specialist-lecturer on chemistry should abandon, before fellow chemists, his technical vocabulary. Neither does it imply that before a lay audience he should stick to his professional terms. Language, to be efficient, should be pitched to the understanding of the group, and we can judge the validity of that language only as we note its relation to the character of its hearers.

7. *The language should be accurate.* Accuracy is first of all a problem of absolute clearness. "Do I understand what the speaker is saying?" If he is wise, he will often insert repeated definitions. But beyond such clarity is a question of the reliability of the statements. Most platform orators (and lesser talkers) exaggerate in their phrasing. "The greatest crime of modern civilization is the growth of the welfare state," is ill defined (*welfare state* means what?), vague, and all-inclusive. "Since Frenchmen are defeatists, that nation should not share in America's military aid to Europe," an assertion frequently heard in early 1950, fails to qualify Frenchmen. Much of public speech, especially political persuasion, is filled with obvious exaggeration and sweeping generalizations. "All" and "every" are used when "many" and "some" would be more accurate. Words and phrases, then, should be free from these unqualified assertions that astute listeners will condemn as simply untrue or grossly overstated.

8. *The language should be concrete.* Words range from the most concrete, those that label simple objects, to the most abstract designations, such as "virtue" and "humanity." Although we need not limit our speaking vocabulary to the first few hundred words used most frequently by the general population, we should not by-pass the fact that auditors respond most readily to word symbols that suggest concrete situations and experiences. "James Jeffrey" is more meaningful and interesting than "a man." "Democracy" and other ideological political terms will also benefit if translated into more tangible equivalents.

For abstract terms, may well be substituted specific days, figures, instances, dialogues, direct quotations. Important speeches, including most of those in this volume, would be improved by a recasting for more concreteness.

9. *The language should be concise.* Herbert Spencer's argument for "economy of style"—that no more words should be used than are necessary—is to the point. Many radio talks and

debates in the House of Representatives are limited to five minutes. Not much excuse is there for long speeches elsewhere.

Conciseness is the opposite of garrulity and verbosity. Speech marathons have no justification. Compactness, nevertheless, does not imply a telegraphic style. The test of effective conciseness is, "Does the speaker say enough (but no more), in view of audience requirements, to establish his idea and the accompanying motivative responses?"

10. *The language should be varied and unhackneyed.* Audiences become bored with continual clichés. The good speaker who would keep his auditors awake and responsive will constantly prune from his style the worn out slogans, quotations, epithets, figures of speech, and threadbare words. The speeches of our day, in their effort to say things plainly, usually fall into conventionality of phrasing. The result is stylistic baldness, mediocrity, and dullness. The superior speakers are sensitive to fresh expression. Without being smartly journalistic, or obviously clever, the good talkers appeal through language that has marks of distinction from a million other speeches on the same theme.

11. *The language should be connotative as well as denotative.* The combinations of words should convey much meaning beyond the literal signification. Audiences are moved by emotion and imagination as well as by logic and fact, persuaded as well as convinced. The style, therefore, should be enlivened with analogies, similes, metaphors, personifications—forms that call up pictures and suggest much beyond the literal meanings. Here, as in other language usages, we are not implying that phrases and niceties of expression are for decorative purposes alone. The test is in the utility of language to realize the purpose of the discourse.

12. *Language should be oral.* The language should be that of talk rather than that of written literature. Platform speaking is heightened conversation. The language, like the delivery, should usually be direct, simple, lively, broken—as is good conversation. Pedantry and sentimentality are absent. Personal pronouns are frequent. The general movement is much more irregular than that of the written style. A certain rhetorical quality, repetition of phrases, balanced structure, asides, paren-

thetical interpolations, give the utterance a flavor and movement that set it off from the more orderly compositions that are chiefly designed for "permanence and beauty." Speech language is directly designed for a specific audience. The differences are those of degree rather than kind. Nevertheless these differences are well marked. Speakers, dealing with hearers, select materials and expression to that end. Word choice is controlled by the demands of an occasion. The choice will vary from audience to audience. "Essential marks of the oral style must, therefore, be determined in the light of the peculiar medium in which speech functions." [1]

13. *Effective sentence structure aids materially in securing the desired audience response.* Proper syntax as well as wise word selection is essential to effective oral style. Bad grammar and syntax are obvious blocks to satisfactory communication. Various sentence types have their function in informing and stimulating hearers. Short and long sentences, for example, both have their use in the process of defining, discriminating, emphasizing. Sentence choppiness gives thinness to the style and destroys rhythm. Periodic, loose, balanced structure, transitional and summarizing sentences properly phrased and incorporated in the text, contribute to clarity, interest, persuasiveness. Imperative, exclamatory, and interrogative types are natural modes of expressing aroused feeling. They suggest suitable conduct to the auditor, stimulate him to give answers (those desired by the questioner), and carry him along a logical emotional current.

Most speeches with rhetorical resourcefulness are more than a succession of declarative sentences. The stimulus of the audience and the orator's own platform purposes will inspire him to a variety of stylistic modes, including varied sentence structure, in keeping with the subject, the occasion, and the temper of the assembly.

14. *The larger units of the speech are to be composed with proper appreciation of the values of the speech structure.* Language and style are closely related to speech organization. Organic structure is an essential of every speech. The familiar units

---

[1] Thonssen, Lester and Baird, A. Craig. *Speech Criticism.* New York, Ronald Press, 1948. p427.

of introduction, body, and conclusion, with their subdivisions, are each to be developed with compositional skill. Unity, order, proportion, and interest govern also framing of these larger units, just as these principles help in the construction of phrases, clauses, and sentences.

Organization is an obvious mark of the good speech. To make that structure apparent and impressive is the problem of the speech composer. The introduction, for example, may or may not include personal reference, striking questions, reference to the occasion, statement of issues, quotation, or simple narrative, according to the subject, the speaker's goals, and the time, place, and other limitations of the occasion. So the main body and the conclusion will be constructed to secure stylistic appropriateness.

15. *The style is the man.* Language should be individual. Your words, if they really represent your thinking and ways of communication, will stamp your discourse as highly personal. Out of your background, education, emotional and intellectual attitudes will your language or style emerge. Your reserve, humor, informality, deductive or inductive appraisals of ideas, your tendencies to abstract thinking or to amplified illustration, your saturation in Biblical or other literature, all modify and illumine—or should—your methods of expression. Thus F. D. Roosevelt, Churchill, Hoover, Truman, Conant, Hancher, Sockman, Sheen have their style. More important than skill in using the machinery of correct English is the problem of retaining and developing individual habits of thought and expression that reveal the personality of the orator himself.

Text Authenticity and Completeness

Editors of speeches are always confronted with the problem, "Did the speaker write the speech which he delivers?" Ghost writers abound. Nevertheless it is hoped that the speeches here included were in general composed by those who gave them before audiences. Often "fact gatherers," consultants, and transscribers have contributed, but the personal quality of the document itself and other internal evidence support my assumption of originality of authorship.

A kindred problem is that of the completeness of the document. "Did the speaker say more than is reported in the text? Or did he say less (as in *Congressional Record* House or Senate debates printed in an Appendix)?" Wherever feasible, I have inserted the complete text. In Senate debates of several hours in length, for example, the Taft-Dulles debate; in court room speeches, as Judge Medina's two-hour instructions to the jury; in hearings before Senate or House Committees, for example, General Bradley's long testimony; in extended lectures, such as Dewey's four lectures at Princeton, and Eisenhower's at Columbia, I have been able to include only a part of the complete document. I can only hope that the reader of this volume will follow through, reading in the *Congressional Record*, or elsewhere, to appreciate fully the breadth and depth of the speaker's thinking.

INTERNATIONAL POLICIES

THE NORTH ATLANTIC PACT [1]

Robert A. Taft, John Foster Dulles [2]

Senator Robert A. Taft gave this Senate speech against the North Atlantic Treaty on July 11, 1949. The next day Senator John Foster Dulles replied. He had been appointed by Governor Thomas E. Dewey of New York to fill the vacancy caused by the resignation of Robert F. Wagner, and had been formally inducted into his Senate office on July 8th. To engage in a major speech within three days after entrance to the Senate was breaking with long-time precedent.

What were the specific issues in this historic debate? At Brussels, on March 17, 1948, Britain, France and the Benelux countries (Belgium, Netherlands, and Luxembourg) had signed an agreement for collective defense. Agitation for America's participation began immediately. On April 4, 1949, the foreign ministers of twelve countries, including Italy, Canada, Denmark, Norway, Portugal, and the United States, assembled in Washington, D.C., and signed a mutual defense pact of fourteen articles.

Article 3 pledged mutual aid to resist attack. Article 5 stated that "armed attack against one or more shall be considered attack against them all." In case of such attack, each was to "take such action as it deems necessary, including the use of armed force, to restore and maintain the security of the North Atlantic area."

On July 5 the Senate debate on the treaty began. Taft and others argued that (1) the treaty takes from Congress the war-making power and gives it to the President; (2) the treaty commits this country to arming the other members of the pact—the treaty and arms program are one; (3) an arms program of this kind will be a heavy drain financially; (4) it will certainly promote hostility and might lead to war with the Soviets.

Dulles, Vandenberg, and other supporters of the pact argued that (1) the instrument is one of concrete power—the only force sufficient to deter Soviet aggression; and (2) the arms program is not identical with the treaty.

Senator Taft's argument, like that of his other debates, was closely reasoned and expressed in comparatively unemotional language. He in-

[1] For the Taft speech, see *Congressional Record* (81st Congress, 2nd session) 95:9383, 9392, July 11, 1949 (daily edition); for that of Dulles, see 95:9492, 9502, July 12, 1949 (daily edition). A portion only of this extended debate is here reprinted.

[2] For biographical notes, see Appendix.

terpreted the document as a lawyer would. It meant to him a military alliance. He attempted to assess the results, financially, politically, and militarily, of the commitment.[3]

His debate speech was chiefly a refutation of the long series of arguments over the air and to the nation on this subject since April 1949. As he concluded, six of his fellow Republicans stood and applauded. The speech was one of Taft's strongest.

Senator Dulles, in his turn, accused Taft of raising "false and dangerous interpretations" of the proposed treaty. The Ohio Senator interrupted with many questions and replies. It was "one of the most heavily attended Senate debates in recent years." [4]

Like Taft, Dulles gave a scholarly analysis of the document, reviewed its history, and justified it as essential if war is to be averted. Taft accused Dulles of drawing "fine distinctions" and refusing to be candid about the obligations imposed by the treaty.

Taft's position, although logical, was held to be in contradiction to his own statements as given on February 20, 1949. His outspoken argument of July 11 was also regarded as a hard blow to the Vandenberg-Truman bipartisan foreign policy and as indicating a split in the Republican leadership. Taft's voting record on foreign policy would indicate that, as of this period, he was vacillating—"a Hamlet who cannot make up his mind." The strongest criticism of Taft was that he implied a retreat before Russian threats and a tendency, undesigned by him, to support "division and disarmament" of Western Europe.

On July 21st, the Senate, after rejecting reservation proposals, ratified the document, 82 to 13, thus with the two-thirds necessary majority. Two Democrats and eleven Republicans opposed—among them Taft, K. S. Wherry of Nebraska, E. C. Johnson of Colorado, G. H. Taylor of Idaho, W. N. Langer of North Dakota, W. E. Jenner of Indiana, R. E. Flanders of Vermont, and F. C. Donnell of Missouri.

For the first time in history, the nation was committed to the principle that its frontiers were in Europe.[5]

Later Congress ratified a bill, the Military Assistance Program (MAP), committing us during the first year to more than a billion dollars worth of equipment to increase the twelve nations' ability to resist Soviet aggression.

Taft is a mature debater rather than an orator. He speaks rapidly, sometimes tightens his voice, elevates the pitch unnecessarily, but convinces by his reasoning.[6]

Mr. Dulles, defeated in November 1949, by Herbert H. Lehman in the New York Senate campaign, prepares speeches with much care. Ob-

---

[3] See *Representative American Speeches: 1948-1949*, p 15-26.

[4] William S. White, in the New York *Times*, July 13, 1949.

[5] See *Representative American Speeches: 1948-1949*, p 15-26.

[6] For references to Taft's speeches in previous volumes of *Representative American Speeches*, consult the Cumulated Author Index at the end of this volume.

servers state that he spends many days in thought and in gathering material before he begins dictating to a secretary. He observes that he never repeats a speech. "He believes that there must be mental progression at all times and that each succeeding speech should represent an advance in thinking." [7]

His delivery and approach to an audience are those of the trained lawyer. "Seldom does he reply hastily to a new question," although he stood up very well under the sharp cross examination in the Senate on July 12th. His voice is well modulated. He uses few gestures, and is no impassioned orator.

MR. TAFT. Mr. President, I listened with great interest to the speech made today by the distinguished Senator from Iowa [Mr. Gillette]. I wish to assure the Senate that I have not consulted with the Senator from Iowa; but the arguments I shall make against the Atlantic Pact are very similar to the ones he made, and I agree thoroughly with the very effective argument and very effective speech he made on that subject. However, the same arguments have led me to the conclusion that I must vote against the pact, rather than for it, as he has announced he intends to do.

It is with great regret that I have come to my conclusion, but I have come to it because I think the pact carries with it an obligation to assist in arming, at our expense, the nations of western Europe, because with that obligation I believe it will promote war in the world rather than peace, and because I think that with the arms plan it is wholly contrary to the spirit of the obligations we assumed in the United Nations Charter. I would vote for the pact if a reservation were adopted denying any legal or moral obligation to provide arms. . . .

I have come reluctantly to the conclusion, therefore, that the arms program now presented to Congress must be considered an integral part of the Atlantic Treaty.

If that is the fact, we have a very different problem from the one which is urged upon us by the Committee on Foreign Relations, by its distinguished chairman, by the State Department, and by the distinguished Senator from Michigan.

[7] Statement from the headquarters of the Commission on a Just and Durable Peace, New York, 1950.

First. With the arms in the pact it is even more clear that the pact is a military alliance, a treaty by which one nation undertakes to arm half the world against the other half, and in which all the pact members agree to go to war if one is attacked. It cannot be described otherwise than a military alliance. Of course, it is not like some of the alliances in the past, although many of them, such as the Franco-British Alliance prior to World War I, were entirely defensive in character, or purported to be. Others were offensive and defensive alliances. I quite agree that the purpose of this alliance is not offensive, and that we have no offensive purpose in mind. But it is exactly like many defensive military alliances of the past.

Second. The pact standing by itself would clearly be a deterrent to war. If Russia knows that if it starts a war it will immediately find itself at war with the United States, it is much less likely to start a war. I see and believe in the full force of that argument. That is why I would favor the extension of the Monroe Doctrine to Europe. But if Russia sees itself ringed about gradually by so-called defensive arms, from Norway and Denmark to Turkey and Greece, it may form a different opinion. It may decide that the arming of western Europe, regardless of its present purpose, looks to an attack upon Russia. Its view may be unreasonable, and I think it is. But from the Russian standpoint it may not seem unreasonable. They may well decide that if war is the certain result, that war might better occur now rather than after the arming of Europe is completed. In 1941, Secretary Hull sent a message to Japan in the nature of an ultimatum which said, in effect, that if Japan did not withdraw from China, sooner or later they would face a war with the United States. The Japanese appear to have concluded that if ultimately there was to be such a war, it was to their interest to have it occur at once.

Third. The pact with the arms obligation, I believe, violates our obligations under the United Nations. The pact apparently is not made under articles 52 to 54 inclusive, because we do not propose to consult the Security Council as there contemplated, we do plan to take enforcement action without the authorization of the Security Council, and we do not plan to keep them fully informed. The pact must, therefore, be supported under article 51, which says:

> Nothing in the present Charter shall impair the inherent right of individual or collective self-defense if an armed attack occurs against a member of the United Nations, until the Security Council has taken the measures necessary to maintain international peace and security. . . .

Fourth. The obligation to furnish arms is either a mere token obligation, or it is one of vast extent. I do not know enough about modern military equipment to make any estimate. I have heard that to provide sixty divisions, which is said to be the very minimum necessary and perhaps completely inadequate against Russian attack, would cost a total of $24 billion. We are entering on a new lend-lease. The history of these obligations has been that once begun, they cannot be easily brought to an end. Furthermore if the Russian threat justifies arms for all of western Europe, surely it justifies similar arms for Nationalist China, for Indochina, for India, and ultimately for Japan; and in the Near East for Iran, for Syria, and for Iraq. There is no limit to the burden of such a program, or its dangerous implications.

Fifth. The justification for the arms aid rests on the necessity of defense against Russia, but remember that once these arms are provided, they are completely within the control of the nation receiving them. They are subject to the orders of those who, at the time, control the government of the country. Those governors may be Communists or Fascists, they may be peace loving, or they may be aggressors. In furture years, these arms may be used against us instead of on our side. If Russia should choose to go to war within the next year or two, they might easily be captured by the Russians and turned against us. We would be playing a dangerous game if we encouraged every country in Europe to arm itself to the teeth. Modern arms are not toys.

Sixth. By approving this pact with the arms program, I believe we are committing ourselves to a particular course of action in war which may be unwise at the time when a war may actually develop. It is one thing to agree to go to war with

Russia if it attacks western Europe. It is another to send American ground troops to defend Norway or Denmark or Holland or Italy or even France and England. I cannot assert positively that we are committing ourselves to a particular type of war, but I am inclined to think that we are. Thus, General Bradley testified before the committee:

> Finally, after studied appraisal of the future security provisions for our country, the Joint Chiefs of Staff are in unanimous agreement that our strategy, in case we are attacked—

And that means if any member country is attacked, if we ratify this pact—

> must rely on sufficient integrated forces of land, sea, and air power to carry the war back to the aggressor, ultimately subjugating the sources of his military and industrial power. Plans for the common defense of the existing free world must provide for the security of western Europe without abandoning these countries to the terrors of another enemy occupation. Only upon that premise can nations closest to the frontiers be expected to stake their fortunes with ours in the common defense.

This appears to contemplate a land war with Russia on the continent of Europe. It appears to contemplate an invasion along the lines which Napoleon and Hitler found to be impossible. It asserts clearly that the nations which signed this pact expect us to send American troops to defend their frontiers.

If this is their expectation, I think we are promising something we cannot do, as I said earlier. I see no way in which we could defend Italy, for it is not even permitted to have an army of its own. The defense of Norway and Denmark would probably be impossible and, if we are bound to do it, may result in the loss of thousands of American lives. It may be that we should conduct a war on the Continent of Europe, even though it involves again the sending of millions of American boys to fight Russians who, on land, will outnumber them four to one. But I do not think we should commit ourselves at the present time to any such program or make any such promise to our allies. We may find, if war ever comes, that our part in the war should be conducted from the air alone. We may find that the occupation of an enemy country is vain and useless if the war can be won otherwise, by the destruction of all of their military potentials. We should not commit ourselves by the ratification of this pact to the military assistance program and the plan of campaign which has apparently been promised the members of the pact.

Seventh. Finally, Mr. President, it is becoming increasingly apparent that England, at least, intends to trade extensively with Russia, and inevitably the same thing will be true of other western European nations. They have provided airplane engines for Russia, heavy machinery and other equipment which can aid the Russians' war-making potential. The more we take off their shoulders the burden of providing for their own defense, the more free they will be to ship steel and heavy machinery to the east. As a matter of fact, trade between eastern and western Europe has prevailed for thousands of years, and it is going to go on, no matter what we say about it. Of course, the recent agreement between Russia and England is very clear evidence of that fact. We are providing extensive economic assistance. To a large extent, economic assistance and aid for arms will go into the same pot. I do not think that the American people at this time desire to increase the over-all aid we are giving to western Europe with its tremendous burden on the American taxpayer.

Mr. President, since I feel that this pact is inextricably linked with the arms program, and since I believe that, so linked, the program is a threat to the welfare of the people of the United States, I shall vote against the treaty.

I am quite willing to consider the providing of assistance to particular countries, at particular times, if such aid seems at that time a real deterrent to war, and on that principle I voted for aid to Greece and Turkey. But that is a very different thing from an obligation to build up the armed forces of eleven countries, and a commitment on the American taxpayer for twenty years to give continued aid under circumstances of which we have not the slightest conception today. It is a very different thing from arming half the world against the other half.

My conclusion has been reached with the greatest discomfort. When so many disagree with that conclusion, I must admit that

I may be completely wrong. I do not claim to be an expert in questions of foreign policy. I would like to be able to vote for a policy that will commit us to war if Russia attacks western Europe. I would be glad to join in an agreement to occupy Germany indefinitely to guard against a third attack from that quarter. I would waive my other objections to the Atlantic Pact if I did not feel that it was inextricably involved with the arms program. But I cannot escape the logic of the situation as I see it, and therefore I cannot vote for a treaty which, in my opinion, will do far more to bring about a third world war than it will ever do to maintain the peace of the world.

MR. DULLES. Mr. President, I am hesitant about speaking so soon. I feel that I am still wrapped in senatorial swaddling clothes rather than in a senatorial toga. But several Senators, both Republicans and Democrats, have been good enough to suggest that I should express myself about the North Atlantic Treaty before the debate closes. Those suggestions reflect the spirit of cordial reception which has welcomed me here, for which I am profoundly grateful, and by which I have been deeply moved. I say with all sincerity that I speak very humbly before Senators who, over the recent years, have dealt so wisely and constructively with the great problems of war and peace that have come before them.

During much of this period, and almost constantly since early in 1945, I have been in attendance at international conferences, seeking to establish a just and durable peace. The task has not been easy and there have been moments when another war was perilously near. But at last there has been evolved a strategy for peace in the west which I am confident will succeed if it is pushed vigorously to its full conclusion. The North Atlantic Treaty is one of the essential ingredients of that over-all strategy for peace. I shall give my understanding of the North Atlantic Pact from that viewpoint. . . .

There are some who hesitate to accept this commitment to organize the Atlantic community, because they believe it will require us to undertake a militaristic program for rearming the nations of western Europe. Of course, Mr. President, there is not a word in the North Atlantic Treaty that expresses any such obligation. The pending military-aid program does not even purport to be an implementation of the Atlantic Treaty, as the State Department's statement, read here yesterday by the Senator from Michigan [Mr. Vanderberg] made evident. Article 3 of the treaty does contemplate developing a collective capacity to resist armed attack and mutual aid in that respect, and Article 9 of the treaty provides for a council and for a defense committee which are to make recommendations regarding implementation of Article 3. What those recommendations will be, no one here can possibly know, for there is as yet no treaty, there is as yet no council, there is as yet no defense committee, and there are as yet no recommendations.

What we do know is that when the council exists and the defense committee exists, and when the recommendations are made, they will be only recommendations. That is specific in the treaty. When those recommendations are made, they will, I assume, be considered on their merits. If the recommendations seem to be advantageous, I assume we will accept them. If they appear to be disadvantageous, we are certainly free to reject them, and I assume and hope we shall reject them. Certainly the treaty gives no other nation or group of nations a blank check on the United States. That, it seems to me, is a preposterous and dangerous interpretation of the treaty, and I think it needs to be made perfectly clear that those who vote for the treaty totally reject that interpretation.

I find in the treaty no obligation, legal or moral, to vote for any armament program or for any item of any armament program unless it be meritorious in its own right.

Mr. President, the opponents of the treaty, in addition to assuming that it gives other parties a blank check on the United States, seem also to assume that the collective defense contemplated by the treaty will be more monumental and more militaristic than the total of twelve separate defenses. I confess that I have been surprised by that argument, for I myself have assumed precisely the contrary. I have supported the treaty because, in my opinion, it will make it possible to reduce the very heavy burden of military expenditure which our nation is now carrying.

I came to that conclusion because it seemed to me that the political commitment of the treaty, one for all and all for one, would itself greatly reduce the risk of war. No nation will be likely to assault the combined resources and facilities of twelve nations and the 350 million people who make up this Atlantic community. If the risk of war is reduced, the cost of insurance against that risk should be likewise reducible; and if the 350 million people each carries a fair share of the common defense, then surely that should be less burdensome to each than for each to attempt it alone. Instead of multiplying military establishments, the treaty should reduce them to diversifying and spreading the responsibility.

I am profoundly convinced that the North Atlantic Treaty, if it be ratified, will make it possible at long last to begin to realize the Atlantic Charter promise to lighten for peace-loving peoples the crushing load of armament. That is the way the treaty should work, once it gets into operation, and that is the way I believe the proponents of the treaty intend that it shall work. They do not intend or expect that the treaty shall work in the way its opponents propose. I think it is important to disabuse the other parties to the treaty of any illusion they might have come under as a result of hearing some features of the debate, that the United States Senate interprets the treaty as giving them a right to draw freely upon the United States for their own independent military establishments.

Mr. President, I have a feeling of regret that in all this debate we deal with it so much in a spirit that assumes that under the treaty we are to be the benefactor and others the beneficiaries. We are constantly talking about what we are going to do for others, but we have talked very little about what others are, through this treaty, going to do for us.

The prime minister of one of the gallant small countries of Europe recently said to me:

If we are attacked, it will be this time because we are your allies and friends; we are no longer an important target of ourselves.

That, Mr. President, is, I think, a fair estimate of the situation, and I think it is worth something to us that there are brave people close to danger who are willing, if need be, to absorb the first shock of devastating attack because they believe in the things in which we believe and want to show solidarity with us. Mr. President, I feel that it is not right to treat such people as mendicants.

Of course, it is never possible to know in advance that legislative authority such as is given for European economic recovery or for the common defense of the Atlantic community will, in fact, be used by the Executive to the best advantage and in the spirit intended by the Congress. I think we must frankly recognize, for example, that under the European recovery program there has been little progress in achieving in Europe a broad market and the reduction of currency and customs barriers which were the great goal.

Some, notably in England, want to limit international trade to a bilateral, governmental bartering of hard goods. That is properly a matter of deep concern to us, for it strikes at the heart of our anti-Communist strategy which depends on increased unity as the fountain for increased vigor.

Despite such setbacks, which are to be expected, and which, in my opinion, can be and must be overcome, the results to date under the European Recovery Act have fully justified the initial appropriations. Future appropriations remain subject to Congressional control and to the provision of the act that the continuity of American aid is dependent upon continuity of cooperation as between the European participants.

It is conceivable that, in the future, some of the parties to the North Atlantic Treaty might seek to pervert it by building up great military establishments and bringing about an armament race. If that happened it would, in my opinion, be a grievous distortion of the intent and purpose of the pact. But—and this is vital—that cannot occur under the treaty without our consent, and the Congress, through its control of appropriations, has that situation under its control.

In any great enterprise there are risks and possibilities of abuse. Such risks have to be taken to defeat the dynamism of Soviet communism. The greatest risk of all is the risk of doing nothing, for the dynamic always prevails against the static. When I say that, I do not say it as an apology for recklessness. Of course, it devolves upon us to seek scrupulously, painstakingly, to perfect and safeguard our programs before we act. The Committee on Foreign Relations has done a great task in this respect, and it has clarified some dangerous ambiguities that were found in the text. But in the end there comes a time for action, and that is where we now are.

Mr. President, no charter, no constitution, no treaty, can be judged merely by its words. Never was there an international instrument which expressed such lofty and noble sentiments as that which created the Holy Alliance. The Soviet constitution is replete with guaranties of human rights, freedom of speech and press, and of religious worship.

This North Atlantic Treaty purports to be an undertaking by the members of the Atlantic community to work together to safeguard free institutions, individual liberty, and the rule of law. Certainly that is a noble purpose. Already, even before its ratification, the treaty has brought new hope to our friends and new discomfiture to those who wish us ill.

Of course, I know that the North Atlantic Treaty has defects and that there are possibilities of abuse. It is not drafted precisely as I would have it. I know that it could be used as an instrument of militarism or to sabotage the United Nations. I have thought of all the horrid possibilities that have been suggested here—and then some. However, at this stage the decision must be made primarily as an act of faith—or lack of faith—in the American people. It is they who will determine whether this instrument is used for good or for evil. Because there are great possibilities of good, because the need is urgent, and because I have faith in the American people, I support the treaty.

All the world is watching to see what we do here. They have seen tension mount. Means of mass destruction are being feverishly developed, and there is conceded risk that mankind may be plunged into an awful abyss. Hundreds of millions, including our own people and peoples throughout the world, look to our nation as alone possessing the combination of material and moral power needed to lead humanity out of the present peril. That places upon us a great responsibility.

There are those, some deeply devoted to the cause of peace, who would swerve away from any line of effort that is cast in a military mold. But unfortunately no program will suffice unless it provides men with a sense of security as against the menace of those who exalt ways of violence and practice the use of terror.

The North Atlantic Treaty, as I said in the beginning, is not an isolated act. The union of our States was also a measure for common defense, but it was far more than that. Common defense is a part, a necessary part, of every organized community, but it is not the whole. Admiral Mahan said that the function of force in human affairs is to give moral ideas the opportunity to take root. I am confident that the North Atlantic Treaty will never be regarded as an all-sufficient end in itself. Rather, it can provide the opportunity for our spiritual faith to reassert itself in practices that will enlarge men's equal opportunity to develop, morally, intellectually, and materially. That is the core of our new program for peace. I am confident that the individual men and women who make up our citizenry understand that, and that they, with others, can be trusted to infuse into this treaty a spirit which will make it a living instrument for righteousness and peace.

STATE OF THE UNION [8]

HARRY S. TRUMAN [9]

President Harry S. Truman read his "State of the Union" address of six-thousand words before a joint session of the Senate and the House of Representatives, in the newly refurbished chamber of the House, at one o'clock, on January 4, 1950. Present were also the cabinet, ambassadors, ministers, and other distinguished guests. When the President walked down the aisle he received a rising ovation, and when Samuel Rayburn, Speaker of the House, introduced him.

The later frequent applause was obviously more partisan than general. His reference to the "ill considered tax reduction of the Eightieth Congress" brought forth good natured protests and laughter from the Republicans and loud cheers and applause from the Democrats.

The speech repeated the usual Truman New Deal and Fair Deal recommendations concerning taxes, business, agriculture, labor, social security, health, education, housing, military service, European Recovery program, and power resources.

The President was unusually optimistic. Some Republicans called the speech "sweetness and light" and described it as having a "hearts and flowers" refrain. Widely discussed, for example, was the section in which the President envisioned the year 2000 A.D. as a time when the American standards of living could be measured by an annual famliy income of some $12,000 ("about three times what it is today").

The Democrats, for example, Senator Herbert H. Lehman of New York, pronounced it a most able state document. The proposals for social welfare led Republicans to call the address a "soak-the-rich salestalk" (Senator William E. Jenner). Two hours after the address, the Republican Congressmen issued a statement (signed by 105 of 169) denouncing the document as not one concerning "the State of the Union," but "the State of Socialism." "Here and there," remarked the statement, "he bows politely to American love for its traditional institutions, its free markets, and its free men. In reality he is embracing black reaction in new gladrags." [10]

The President when he speaks "off the cuff" is much better than when he reads from a manuscript. His delivery in his routine reading is often monotonous. He occasionally lacks a lively sense of communication. When he becomes aroused on the platform, however, his vocal emphasis

[8] Text supplied by the White House.
[9] For biographical note, see Appendix.
[10] New York *Times*, January 5, 1950, p 11.

increases, and his audience orientation and response are much more effective. He makes the best impression as a popular speaker when he becomes vocally the "fighting" leader of millions of Democratic followers.[11]

Mr. President, Mr. Speaker, Members of the Congress: A year ago I reported to this Congress that the state of the Union was good. I am happy to be able to report to you today that the state of the Union continues to be good. Our Republic continues to increase in the enjoyment of freedom within its borders, and to offer strength and encouragement to all those who love freedom throughout the world.

During the past year we have made notable progress in strengthening the foundations of peace and freedom, abroad and at home.

We have taken important steps in securing the North Atlantic community against aggression. We have continued our successful support of European recovery. We have returned to our established policy of expanding international trade through reciprocal agreement. We have strengthened our support of the United Nations.

While great problems still confront us, the greatest danger has receded—the possibility which faced us three years ago that most of Europe and the Mediterranean area might collapse under totalitarian pressure. Today, the free peoples of the world have new vigor and new hope for the cause of peace.

In our domestic affairs, we have made notable advances toward broader opportunity and a better life for all our citizens.

We have met and reversed the first significant downturn in economic activity since the war. In accomplishing this, government programs for maintaining employment and purchasing power have been of tremendous benefit. As the result of these programs, and the wisdom and good judgment of our businessmen and workers, major readjustments have been made without widespread suffering.

During the past year, we have also made a good start in providing housing for low-income groups; we have raised minimum wages; we have gone forward with the development of

[11] For other Truman speeches and comment, consult the Cumulated Author Index.

our natural resources; we have given greater assurance of stability to the farmer; and we have improved the organization and efficiency of our government.

Today, by the grace of God, we stand a free and prosperous nation with greater possibilities for the future than any people have ever had before.

We are now, in this year of 1950, nearing the midpoint of the twentieth century.

The first half of this century will be known as the most turbulent and eventful period in recorded history. The swift pace of events promises to make the next fifty years decisive in the history of man on this planet.

The scientific and industrial revolution which began two centuries ago has, in the last fifty years, caught up the peoples of the globe in a common destiny. Two world-shattering wars have proved that no corner of the earth can be isolated from the affairs of mankind.

The human race has reached a turning point. Man has opened the secrets of nature and mastered new powers. If he uses them wisely, he can reach new heights of civilization. If he uses them foolishly, they may destroy him.

Man must create the moral and legal framework for the world which will insure that his new powers are used for good and not for evil. In shaping the outcome, the people of the United States will play a leading role.

Among all the great changes that have occurred in the last fifty years, none is more important than the change in the position of the United States in world affairs. Fifty years ago, we were a country devoted largely to our own internal affairs. Our industry was growing, and we had new interests in the Far East and in the Caribbean, but we were primarily concerned with the development of vast areas of our own continental territory.

Today, our population has doubled. Our national production has risen from about $50 billion, in terms of today's prices, to the staggering figure of $255 billion a year. We have a more productive economic system and a greater industrial potential than any other nation on the globe. Our standard of living is an inspiration for all other peoples. Even the slightest changes in our economic and social life have their effect on other countries all around the world.

Our tremendous strength has brought with it tremendous responsibilities. We have moved from the outer edge to the center of world affairs. Other nations look to us for a wise exercise of our economic and military strength, and for vigorous support of the ideals of representative government and a free society. We will not fail them.

Our objective in the world is peace. Our country has joined with others in the task of achieving peace. We know now that this is not an easy task, or a short one. But we are determined to see it through. Both of our great political parties are committed to working together—and I am sure they will continue to work together—to achieve this end. We are prepared to devote our energy and our resources to this task, because we know that our own security and the future of mankind are at stake.

Our success in working with other nations to achieve peace depends largely on what we do at home. We must preserve our national strength. Strength is not simply a matter of arms and force. It is a matter of economic growth, and social health, and vigorous institutions, public and private. We can achieve peace only if we maintain our productive energy, our democratic institutions, and our firm belief in individual freedom.

Our surest guide in the days that lie ahead will be the spirit in which this great Republic was founded. We must make our decisions in the conviction that all men are created equal, that they are equally entitled to life, liberty, and the pursuit of happiness, and that the duty of government is to serve these ends.

This country of ours has experienced many blessings, but none greater than its dedication to these principles. At every point in our history, these ideals have served to correct our failures and shortcomings, to spur us on to greater efforts, and to keep clearly before us the primary purpose of our existence as a nation. They have enshrined for us, as a principle of government, the moral imperative to do justice, and the divine command to men to love one another.

These principles give meaning to all that we do.

In foreign policy, they mean that we can never be tolerant of oppression or tyranny. They mean that we must throw our weight on the side of greater freedom and a better life for all peoples. These principles confirm us in carrying out the specific programs for peace which we have already begun.

We shall continue to give our wholehearted support to the United Nations. We believe that this organization can ultimately provide the framework of international law and morality without which mankind cannot survive. It has already set up new standards for the conduct of nations in the Declaration of Human Rights and the Convention on Genocide. It is moving ahead to give meaning to the concept of world brotherhood through a wide variety of cultural, economic, and technical activities.

The events of the past year again showed the value of the United Nations in bringing about the peaceful adjustment of tense international controversies. In Indonesia and in Palestine, the efforts of the United Nations have put a stop to bloodshed and paved the way to peaceful settlements.

We are working toward the time when the United Nations will control weapons of mass destruction and will have the forces to preserve international law and order. While the world remains unsettled, however, and as long as our own security and the security of the free world require, we will maintain a strong and well-balanced organization. The Selective Service System is an essential part of our defense plans, and it must be continued.

Under the principles of the United Nations Charter, we must continue to share in the common defense of free nations against aggression. At the last session, this Congress laid the basis for this joint effort. We now must put into effect the common defense plans that are being worked out.

We shall continue our efforts for world economic recovery, because world prosperity is the only sure foundation for permanent peace.

As an immediate means to this end, we must continue our support of the European Recovery Program. This program has achieved great success in the first two years of operation, but it has not yet been completed. If we were to stop this program now, or cripple it, just because it is succeeding, we should be doing exactly what the enemies of democracy want us to do. We should be just as foolish as a man who, for reasons of false economy, failed to put a roof on his house after building the foundation and the walls.

World prosperity also requires that we do all we can to expand world trade. As a major step in this direction, we should promptly join the International Trade Organization. The purpose of this organization, which the United States has been foremost in creating, is to establish a code of fair practice, and an international authority for adjusting differences in international commercial relations. It is an effort to prevent the kind of anarchy and irresponsibility in world trade which did so much to bring about the world depression in the 1930's.

An expanding world economy requires the improvement of living standards and the development of resources in areas where human poverty and misery now prevail. Without such improvement, the recovery of Europe and the future of our own economy will not be secure. I urge that the Congress adopt this legislation now before it to provide for increasing the flow of technical assistance and capital investment to underdeveloped regions.

It is more essential now than ever, if the ideals of freedom and representative government are to prevail in these areas, and particularly in the Far East, that their people experience, in their own lives, the benefits of scientific and economic advances. This program will require the movement of large amounts of capital from the industrial nations, and particularly from the United States, to productive uses in the underdeveloped areas of the world. Recent world events make prompt action imperative.

This program is in the interest of all peoples—and it has nothing in common with either the old imperialism of the last century or the new imperialism of the Communists.

Our aim for a peaceful, democratic world of free peoples will be achieved in the long run, not by force of arms, but by an appeal to the minds and hearts of men. If the peace policy of the democratic nations is to be successful, they must demonstrate that the benefits of their ways of life can be increased and extended to all nations and all races.

In the world today, we are confronted with the danger that the rising demand of people everywhere for freedom and a better life may be corrupted and betrayed by the false promises of Communism. In its ruthless struggle for power, Communism seizes upon our imperfections, and takes advantage of the delays and setbacks which the democratic nations experience in their effort to secure a better life for their citizens. This challenge to us is more than a military challenge. It is a challenge to the honesty of our profession of the democratic faith; it is a challenge to the efficiency and stability of our economic system; it is a challenge to our willingness to work with other peoples for world peace and world prosperity.

For my part, I welcome the challenge. I believe that our country, at this crucial point in world history, will meet that challenge successfully. I believe that, in co-operation with the other free nations of the world, we shall extend the full benefits of the democratic way of life to millions who do not now enjoy them, and preserve mankind from dictatorship and tyranny.

I believe that we shall succeed in our struggle for peace, because I have seen the success we have had in our own country in following the principles of freedom. Over the last fifty years, the ideals of liberty and equal opportunity to which our nation is dedicated have been increasingly realized in the lives of our people.

The ideal of equal opportunity no longer means simply the opportunity which a man has to advance beyond his fellows. Some of our citizens do achieve greater success than others as a reward for individual merit and effort, and this is as it should be. As the same time, our country must be more than a land of opportunity for a select few. It must be a land of opportunity for all of us. In such a land, all can grow and prosper together.

The simple truth that we can all go forward together is often questioned by selfish or shortsighted persons. It is strange that this is so, for this proposition is so clearly demonstrated by our national history. During the last fifty years, for example, our nation has grown enormously in material well-being. This growth has come about, not by concentrating the benefits of our progress in the hands of a few, but by increasing the wealth of the great body of our citizens.

In the last fifty years, the income of the average family has increased so greatly that its buying power has doubled. The average hours of work have declined from sixty to forty a week, while the hourly production of the average worker has tripled. Average wages, allowing for price changes, have increased from about 45 cents an hour to $1.40 an hour.

We have accomplished what to earlier ages of mankind would have been a miracle—we work shorter hours, we produce more, and we live better.

Increasing freedom from poverty and drudgery has given a fuller meaning to American life. Our people are better educated; we have more opportunities for travel and recreation and enjoyment of the arts. We enjoy more personal liberty in the United States today than ever before.

If we can continue in the spirit of cooperative adventure which has marked the recent years of our progress, we can expect further scientific advances, further increase in our standard of living, and a still wider enjoyment of democratic freedom.

No one, of course, can foretell the future exactly. However, if we assume that we shall grow as fast in the future as we have grown in the past, we can get a good idea of how much our country should grow over the next fifty years.

At present our total national production is $255 billion a year. Our working population and our output per worker are increasing. If our productive power continues to increase at the same rate as it has increased over the past fifty years, our total national production fifty years from now will be nearly four times as much as it is today. Allowing for the expected growth in population, this would mean that the real income of the average family in the year 2000 A. D. would be about three times what it is today.

These are estimates of what we can do in the future, but we can reach those heights only if we follow the right policies. We have learned by bitter experience that progress is not automatic—that wrong policies lead to depression and disaster. We cannot achieve these gains unless we have a stable economy and avoid the catastrophes of boom and bust that have set us back in the past.

These gains cannot be achieved unless our businessmen maintain their spirit of initiative and enterprise and operate in a competitive economy. They cannot be achieved unless our working men and women and their unions help to increase productivity and obtain for labor a fair share of the benefits of our economic system. They cannot be achieved unless we have a stable and prosperous agriculture. They cannot be achieved unless we conserve and develop our natural resources in the public interest.

Our system will not work unless our people are healthy, well educated and confident of the future. It will not work unless all citizens can participate fully in our national life.

In achieving these gains, the government has a special responsibility to help create and maintain the conditions which will permit the growth we know is possible. Foremost among these conditions is the need for a fair distribution of our increasing prosperity among all the great groups of our population who help to bring it about—labor, business, agriculture. . . .

As we move forward into the second half of the twentieth century, we must always bear in mind the central purpose of our national life. We do not seek material prosperity for ourselves because we love luxury; we do not aid other nations because we wish to increase our power. We have not devised programs for the security and well-being of our people because we are afraid or unwilling to take risks. This is not the meaning of our past history or our present course.

We work for a better life for all, so that all men may put to good use the great gifts with which they have been endowed by their Creator. We seek to establish those material conditions of life in which, without exception, men may live in dignity, perform useful work, serve their communities, and worship God as they see fit.

These may seem simple goals, but they are not little ones. They are worth a great deal more than all the empires and conquests of history. They are not to be achieved by military aggression or political fanaticism. They are to be achieved by humbler means—by hard work, by a spirit of self-restraint in our dealings with one another, and by a deep devotion to the principles of justice and equality.

It should make us truly thankful, as we look back to the beginnings of this country, that we have come so far along the road to a better life for all. It should make us humble to think, as we look ahead, how much farther we have to go to accomplish, at home and abroad, the objectives that were set out for us at the founding of this nation.

As we approach the halfway mark in the twentieth century, we should ask for continued strength and guidance from that Almighty Power who has placed before us such great opportunities for the good of mankind in the years to come.

A BASIS FOR RUSSIAN-AMERICAN PEACE [12]

DEAN G. ACHESON [13]

Secretary of State Dean Acheson gave this address at a conference on International Cooperation for World Economic Development, held at the University of California, Berkeley campus, on March 16, 1950.

Eight thousand "be-sweatered and be-jeaned" students packed the men's gymnasium for the occasion. "The Secretary spoke straight through, without interruption, in his best professional manner, and when he concluded, his audience applauded until he rose a second time and bowed and waved his appreciation." [14]

The speech, according to the State Department, was three months in drafting. The speaker outlined seven steps for ending the cold war between Russia and the Western democracies, for furnishing the basis of peace treaties, and for solving the problem of atomic controls.

Recent events had obviously caused a huge shift in our policy, especially as it related to the Orient. (1) China had fallen. (2) Russia had recognized the Ho Chi Minh Communist leadership in Viet Nam, Indochina, whereas this country had decided to support the Bao Dai French-backed force. (3) Our decision to build the H-bomb had led to a considerable national demand for this country to attempt to come to terms with Russia. (4) Secretary Acheson and his Department had been accused of having no positive or consistent policy with respect to Russia. Taft, McCarthy, and others had vigorously questioned Acheson's ability for his job. (5) Bipartisan direction of foreign policy had obviously broken down with the illness of Senator Vandenberg. (6) Associated with the State Department, Owen Lattimore, Philip Jessup, and others were under attack as "Communist sympathizers."

The Berkeley address was not so much a listing of agenda for any conference between the Soviets and Americans as it was a statement of the basic philosophies that separated the two powers. The speech set up the seven major issues that would have to be faced and settled before any twentieth century Pax Romana might be established.

American public opinion recognized the thorough analysis and statesmanship that underlay the California address. The explanation no doubt strengthened—for the time—the position of the State Department. The address had wide distribution in Western Europe and in the Far East. Nationalists were said to have engineered the distribution of thousands of copies among Chinese Communists.

[12] Text furnished by the Department of State.
[13] For biographical note, see Appendix.
[14] San Francisco *Examiner*, March 17, 1950.

As the cold war increased in violence, Secretary Acheson continued to address the Americans on Russo-American relations. Part of his speaking was directed toward defense of his Department staff against the charges that they were pro-Russian. Part was to denounce Russia for her continued acts of aggression. (1) In late April 1950, for example, Russia rejected an American protest against the alleged shooting down of an American unarmed naval airplane in the Baltic, and accused the United States of attempting to photograph military installations. (2) Russia demanded that the United States, Britain, and Yugoslavia withdraw their troops from Trieste and that under the Big Four an international regime be set up there. (3) Russia demanded again from Turkey the acknowledgment of special Russian rights in the control of the Dardanelles. (4) Communist-controlled Czechoslovakia closed down the United States Information Service and proceeded with further trials of Czechs accused of spying for the United States. Acheson, in one of his speeches of late April, called the Russian moves "saber rattling." Although the cold war was hardly expected to break immediately into a full scale conflict, the Russians were obviously stepping up their bitter opposition to the Marshall Plan, the Atlantic Pact, and the other programs for strengthening the non-Communist nations.[15]

I wish to make a report to you about the tensions between the United States and the Soviet Union.

Now, the right and obligation of the Secretary of State to speak to his fellow citizens, or to the representatives of other nations, about our foreign relations is not derived from any claim on his part to special knowledge or wisdom which makes him right and other people wrong. It is derived from the fact that our forefathers by free choice worked out and approved a Constitution. This Constitution, with the amendments and interpretations which have made it a living and growing thing, has survived to this day as an expression of the will of the entire people. A President is duly elected under this Constitution with a heavy and solemn responsibility to direct the foreign relations of the American people. The President has, in accordance with law and with the advice and consent of the Senate, appointed a man to serve as Secretary of State to assist him in the conduct of our foreign affairs. This right to speak on your behalf results directly from the constitutional processes by which the American people

[15] For further comment on Dean Acheson as a speaker, see *Representative American Speeches: 1948-1949*, p 15-26.

provide a government for themselves in an orderly, clear and democratic manner.

A little over thirty years ago there came into power in one of the great countries of the world a group of people who also claim the right to speak on your behalf. That claim was based not on any Constitutional procedure, or on any expression of the will of those whose representatives they professed to be. It was based on a claim which those men made to a monopoly of the knowledge of what was right and what was wrong for human beings. They further profess that their claim is based on a body of thought taken over in large part from the writings of a mid-nineteenth century German economist and theorist, Karl Marx.

I have no desire to debate here the errors of one version or another of what is today called "Marxism." But I think it must be recognized in the light of the experience of the last hundred years that many of the premises on which Marx based his thought have been belied by the known facts of what has actually happened in the decades since Marx made his studies. Marx's law of capitalist accumulation, his law as to the rate of profit, his prediction of the numerical decline of the middle classes, and of the increase of the class struggle: none of these calculations has been borne out by the experience of the societies of the West. Marx did not foresee the possibility of democratic solutions.

Furthermore, the body of doctrine now professed by the Moscow-controlled Communists is only tenuously identified with Marx's writings and is largely overlaid with Russian imperialism. We certainly cannot accept the thesis that such a doctrine can serve as the justification for the right of a small group of individuals to speak for the great masses of human beings who have never selected them as their spokesmen and whose own opinions they have never consulted.

Now for three decades this group of people, or their successors, has carried on as the rulers of that same great country. They have always, at the same time, maintained the pretense that they are the interpreters of the aspirations of peoples far beyond their borders. In the light of that professed philosophy they have conducted, as masters of the Russian state, a foreign policy which now is the center of the most difficult and troublesome problems of international affairs, problems designed to keep the peoples of the world in a state of deepest apprehension and doubt. In addition to this, they have operated within the limits of the Soviet state on the basis of a domestic policy founded, they say, on the same philosophy.

There are many points in this philosophy, and particularly in the way in which it has already been applied in practice in the Soviet Union and elsewhere, which are not only deeply repugnant to us, but raise questions involving the most basic conceptions of good and evil—questions involving the ultimate moral nature of man. There is no use in attempting to ignore or gloss over the profundity of this conflict of view.

The free society values the individual as an end in himself. It requires of him only that self-discipline and self-restraint which make the rights of each individual compatible with the rights of every other individual. Individual freedom, therefore, implies individual responsibility not to exercise freedom in ways inconsistent with the freedom of other individuals, and responsibility positively to make constructive use of freedom in the building of a just society.

In relations between nations, the prime reliance of the free society is on the strength and appeal of its principles, and it feels no compulsion sooner or later to bring all societies into conformity with it.

It does not fear, rather it welcomes, diversity and derives its strength from freedom of inquiry and tolerance even of antipathetic ideas.

We can see no moral compromise with the contrary theses of international communism: that the end justifies the means, that any and all methods are therefore permissible, and that the dignity of the human individual is of no importance as against the interest of the state.

To our minds, these principles mean, in their practical application, the arrogation to individual human leaders, with all their inevitable frailties and limitations, of powers and pretenses which most of us would be willing to concede only to the infinite wisdom and compassion of a Divine Being. They mean the police state, with all that that implies; a regimentation of the worker which is hardly distinguishable from slave labor; a loss to society of those things which appear to us to make life worth living; a denial of the fundamental truths embodied in all the great religions of the world.

Here is a moral issue of the clearest nature. It cannot be evaded. Let us make no mistake about it.

Yet it does not follow from this that the two systems, theirs and ours, cannot exist concurrently in this world. Good and evil can and do exist concurrently in the whole great realm of human life. They exist within every individual, within every nation, and within every human group. The struggle between good and evil cannot be confined to governments. That struggle will go on, as it always has, in the wider theater of the human spirit itself.

But it also does not follow from this coexistence of good and evil that the two systems, theirs and ours, will necessarily be able to exist concurrently. That will depend largely on them, for we ourselves do not find impossibility in the prospect of coexistence with the Soviet system.

However much we may sympathize with the Soviet citizens who for reasons bedded deep in history are obliged to live under it, we are not attempting to change the governmental or social structure of the Soviet Union. The Soviet regime, however, has devoted a major portion of its energies and resources to the attempt to impose its system on other peoples. In this attempt it has shown itself prepared to resort to any method or stratagem including subversion, threats and even military force.

Therefore, if the two systems are to coexist, some acceptable means must be found to free the world from the destructive tensions and anxieties of which it has been the victim in these past years and the continuance of which can hardly be in the interests of any people.

I wish, therefore, to speak to you about those points of greatest difference which must be identified and sooner or later reconciled if the two systems are to live together, if not with mutual respect, at least in reasonable security. What is it which the leaders of international communism could do to make such coexistence more tolerable to everyone?

There are a number of things they could do, which, while leaving much yet to do, would give the world new confidence in the possibility of peaceful change, in the principle and processes of peaceful settlement as an effective means of finding workable solutions in areas of disagreement.

Let us look first at the points where we and they are perhaps most closely in contact, and where the establishment of peace in its narrowest, most limited sense is dangerously impeded by the absence of common ground.

One: *Definition of Terms of Peace.*

It is now nearly five years since the end of hostilities, and the victorious allies have been unable to define the terms of peace with the defeated countries. This is a grave, a deeply disturbing fact. For our part, we do not intend nor wish, in fact we do not know how, to create satellites. Nor can we accept a settlement which would make Germany, Japan, or liberated Austria satellites of the Soviet Union. The experience in Hungary, Rumania, and Bulgaria has been one of bitter disappointment and shocking betrayal of the solemn pledges by the wartime allies. The Soviet leaders joined in the pledge at Tehran that they looked forward "with confidence to the day when all peoples of the world may live free lives, untouched by tyranny, and according to their varying desires and their own consciences." We can accept treaties of peace which would give reality to this pledge and to the interests of all in security.

With regard to Germany, unification under a government chosen in free elections under international observation is a basic element in an acceptable settlement. With that need recognized and with a will to define the terms of peace, a German treaty could be formulated which, while not pretending to solve all of the complex and bitter problems of the German situation, would, nevertheless, go far toward a relaxation of a set of major tensions.

With regard to Austria, that unhappy country is still under occupation because the Soviet leaders do not want a treaty. The political and economic independence of Austria is being sabotaged by the determination of the Soviets, camouflaged in technicalities, to maintain their forces and special interests in Eastern Austria.

With regard to Japan, we feel that the Soviet leaders could recognize the interest which nations other than the members of the Council of Foreign Ministers have in a Japanese peace treaty and could refrain from taking positions and insisting on procedures which block progress toward a treaty.

In the Far East generally, there are many points where the Soviet leaders could, if they chose, relax tensions. They could, for example, permit the United Nations' Commission in Korea to carry out its duties by allowing the Commission's entry into North Korea and by accepting its report as the basis for a peaceful settlement of that liberated country's problems. They could repatriate Japanese prisoners of war from Siberian camps. They could refrain from subverting the efforts of the newly independent states of Asia and their native leaders to solve their problems in their own way.

Two: *Use of Force.*

With regard to the whole group of countries which we are accustomed to think of as the Satellite area, the Soviet leaders could withdraw their military and police force and refrain from using the shadow of that force to keep in power persons or regimes which do not command the confidence of the respective peoples, freely expressed through orderly representative processes. In other words, they could elect to observe, in practice, the declaration to which they set their signatures at Yalta concerning liberated Europe.

In this connection we do not insist that these governments have any particular political or social complexion. What concerns us is that they should be truly independent national regimes, with a will of their own and with a decent foundation in popular feeling. We would like to feel, when we deal with these governments, that we are dealing with something representative of the national identity of the peoples in question. We cannot believe that such a situation would be really incompatible with the security of the Soviet Union.

This is a question of elementary good faith, and it is vital to a spirit of confidence that other treaties and other agreements will be honored. Nothing would so alter the international climate as the holding of elections in the satellite states in which the true will of the people could be expressed.

Three: *Obstruction in the United Nations.*

The Soviet leaders could drop their policy of obstruction in the United Nations and could instead act as if they believe the United Nations is, as Stalin himself has recently called it, a serious instrumentality for the maintenance of international peace and security. They are simply not acting that way now.

Their policy of walk-out and boycott is a policy that undermines the concept of majority decision. Indeed, they seem deliberately to entrench themselves in a minority position in the United Nations. This was illustrated last fall when they voted against the Essentials of Peace Resolution which solemnly restated and reaffirmed the principles and purposes of the United Nations Charter and which pointed to practical steps which members should take to support the peace.

A respect for the expressed will of the majority is as fundamental to international organization as it is to democracy. We know that a majority of the General Assembly has generally not agreed with the Soviet Union, whereas we ourselves have generally been on the majority side. There is nothing artificial about this situation. It has not been the result of any sleight of hand or pressures on our part. We do not have any satellites whose votes we control. The significant fact is that proposals which have commended themselves to a majority of the members of the United Nations have also commended themselves to us.

Let the Soviet Union put forward in the United Nations genuine proposals conducive to the work of peace, respectful of the real independence of other governments, and appreciative of the role which the United Nations could and should play in the preservation of world stability and the cooperation of nations. They will then doubtless have a majority with them. We will rejoice to see them in such a majority. We will be pleased to be a member of it ourselves.

Four: *Effective Control of Atomic Energy.*

The Soviet leaders could join us in seeking realistic and effective arrangements for the control of atomic weapons and the limitation of armaments in general. We know that it is not easy for them under their system to contemplate the functioning on their territory of an authority in which people would participate who are not of their political persuasion.

If we have not hesitated to urge that they as well as we accept this requirement it is because we believe that a spirit of genuine responsibility to mankind is widely present in this world. Many able administrators and scientists could be found to operate such an authority who would be only too happy, regardless of political complexion, to take an elevated and enlightened view of the immense responsibility which would rest upon them. There are men who would scorn to use their powers for the negative purpose of intrigue and destruction. We believe that an authority could be established which would not be controlled or subject to control by either ourselves or the Soviet Union.

Five: *Attempts at Undermining Established Governments.*

The Kremlin could refrain from using the Communist apparatus controlled by it throughout the world to attempt to overthrow, by subversive means, established governments with which the Soviet Government stands in an outward state of friendship and respect. In general, it could desist from, and could cooperate in efforts to prevent, indirect aggression across national frontiers —a mode of conduct which is inconsistent with the spirit and the letter of the United Nations Charter.

Six: *Proper Treatment of Diplomatic Representatives.*

The Soviet leaders could cooperate with us to the end that the official representatives of all countries are treated everywhere with decency and respect and that an atmosphere is created in which these representatives could function in a normal and helpful manner, conforming to the accepted codes of diplomacy.

The standards of conduct of our own representatives are known from more than a century and a half of American diplomatic experience. These standards are such that all countries which have accepted our representatives in a spirit of respect and confidence over periods of many decades have certainly remained none the worse for it. The independence of those countries has not been undermined; their peoples have not been corrupted; their economies have not been scathed by sabotage.

When we now find our representatives treated as criminals, when we see great official propaganda machines reiterating that they are sinister people and that contact with them is pregnant with danger—we cannot believe that such insinuations are advanced in good faith, and we cannot be blind to the obvious implications of such an attitude.

Seven: *Distortion of Motives of Others.*

In general, the Soviet leaders could refrain, I think, from systematically distorting to their own peoples the picture of the world outside their borders, and of our country, in particular.

We are not suggesting that they become propagandists for any country or system other than their own. But the Soviet leaders know, and the world knows with what genuine disappointment and concern the people of this country were brought to the realization that the wartime collaboration between the major allies was not to be the beginning of a happier and freer era in the association between the peoples of the Soviet Union and other peoples.

What are we now to conclude from the morbid fancies which their propaganda exudes of a capitalist encirclement, of a United States craftily and systematically plotting another world war? They know, and the world knows, how foreign is the concept of aggressive war to our philosophy and our political system. They know that we are not asking to be objects of any insincere and effusive demonstrations of sentimental friendship. But we feel that the Soviet leaders could at least permit access to the Soviet Union of persons and ideas from other countries so that other views might be presented to the Russian people.

These are some of the things which we feel that the Soviet leaders could do, which would permit the rational and peaceful development of the coexistence of their system and ours. They are not things that go to the depths of the moral conflict. They are not things that promise the Kingdom of Heaven. They have been formulated by us, not as moralists but as servants of government, anxious to get on with the practical problems that lie before us, and to get on with them in a manner consistent with mankind's deep longing for a respite from fear and uncertainty.

Nor have they been formulated as a one-sided bargain. A will to achieve binding, peaceful settlements would be required of all participants. All would have to produce unmistakable evidence of their good faith. All would have to accept agreements in the observance of which all nations could have real confidence.

The United States is ready, as it has been and always will be, to cooperate in genuine efforts to find peaceful settlements. Our attitude is not inflexible, our opinions are not frozen, our positions are not and will not be obstacles to peace. But it takes more than one to cooperate. If the Soviet Union could join in doing these things I have outlined, we could all face the future with greater security. We could look forward to more than the eventual reduction of some of the present tensions. We could anticipate a return to a more normal and relaxed diplomatic atmosphere, and to progress in the transaction of some of the international business which needs so urgently to be done.

I fear, however, that I must warn you not to raise your hopes. No one who has lived through these postwar years can be sanguine about reaching agreements in which reliance can be placed and which will be observed by the Soviet leaders in good faith. We must not, in our yearning for peace, allow ourselves to be betrayed by vague generalities or beguiling proffers of peace which are unsubstantiated by good faith solidly demonstrated in daily behavior. We are always ready to discuss, to negotiate, to agree, but we are understandably loath to play the role of international sucker. We will take the initiative in the future as we have in the past in seeking agreement whenever there is any indication that this course would be a fruitful one. What is required is genuine evidence in conduct, not just in words, of an intention to solve the immediate problems and remove the tensions which divide us. I see no evidence that the Soviet leaders will change their conduct until the progress of the free world convinces them that they cannot profit from a continuation of these tensions.

So our course of action in the world of hard reality which faces us is not one that is easily charted. It is not one which this nation can adopt without consideration of the needs and views of other free nations. It is one which requires all the devotion and resolve and wisdom that can be summoned up. We have had and continue to have the assistance and advice of distinguished leaders in all walks of life. We have the benefit of the great public discussion which has been proceeding in the democratic way, by free inquiry and free expression.

It is my purpose in talking with you to point a direction and to define the choices which confront us. We need to stand before the world with our own purpose and position clear.

We want peace, but not at any price. We are ready to negotiate, but not at the expense of rousing false hopes which would be dashed by new failures. We are equally determined to support all real efforts for peaceful settlements and to resist aggression.

The times call for a total diplomacy equal to the task of defense against Soviet expansion and to the task of building the kind of world in which our way of life can flourish. We must continue to press ahead with the building of a free world which is strong in its faith and in its material progress. The alternative is to allow the free nations to succumb one by one to the erosive and encroaching processes of Soviet expansion.

We must not slacken, rather we must reinvigorate, the kind of democratic efforts which are represented by the European Recovery Program, the North Atlantic and Rio Pacts, the Mutual Defense Assistance Program, the Point IV Program for developing the world's new workshops and assistance in creating the conditions necessary to a growing, many-sided exchange of the world's products.

We must champion an international order based on the United Nations and on the abiding principles of freedom and justice, or accept an international society increasingly torn by destructive rivalries.

We must recognize that our ability to achieve our purposes cannot rest alone on a desire for peace, but that it must be supported by the strength to meet whatever tasks Providence may have in store for us.

We must not make the mistake, in other words, of using Soviet conduct as a standard for our own. Our efforts cannot be merely reactions to the latest moves by the Kremlin. The bi-partisan line of American foreign policy has been and must continue to be the constructive task of building, in cooperation with others, the kind of world in which freedom and justice can flourish. We must not be turned aside from this task by the diversionary thrusts of the Soviet Union. And if it is necessary, as it sometimes is, to deal with such a thrust or the threat of one, the effort should be understood as one which, though essential, is outside the main stream of our policy.

Progress is to be gained in the doing of the constructive tasks which give practical affirmation to the principles by which we live.

The success of our efforts rests finally on our faith in our-selves and in the values for which this Republic stands. We will need courage and steadfastness and the cool heads and steady nerves of a citizenry which has always faced the future "with malice toward none; with charity toward all; with firmness in the right, as God gives us to see the right."

WORLD PEACE: A BALANCE SHEET [16]

DWIGHT D. EISENHOWER [17]

President Dwight D. Eisenhower of Columbia University gave this lecture in McMillin Theater, at Columbia, on the evening of March 23, 1950. It was the first in a series of lectures under an endowment by Leo Silver, New Jersey industrialist, dedicated to the cause of international peace. The lectures were sponsored by the Columbia School of International Affairs. Part only of the one-hour lecture is here included.

The speech, in view of the speaker's background and of his relationship to the major problems of the "cold war" and national defense early in 1950, was highly significant.

The theme was peace—how to achieve and preserve it. As Eisenhower prepared the address, Dean Acheson and his staff of the State Department, Owen Lattimore and other "architects" of our Far Eastern policy were under strong attack by Senator McCarthy and other Republicans as "pro-Communist" in their thinking and perhaps actions. Eisenhower attempted to dissipate the foggy thinking and pessimism of the American people.

He was also concerned with the matter of the 1950-51 budget, then under consideration by Congress, for national defense. Should it be twelve, or thirteen, or fourteen billions? Was Congress too conservative in estimating the danger and too complacent in setting up powerful air, navy, and ground forces?

These issues were merely surface clues to the penetration attempted by Eisenhower as he discussed the age-old question: shall we assent to the philosophy of Christian pacifism? Or, at the other extreme, shall we measure might and estimate victory solely by the outward weapons more than by the inward resolution? Is there proper motive for any war? If so, what should be the nature of that justification?

Thus Eisenhower set up his postulates; cited graphic illustrations (Britain in 1940); defined the "peace" he would aim for, with its permanence, universality, and security; examined in detail the factors necessary for success—justice and freedom, international understanding, disarmament, and a "respected" United Nations.

The lecture has clarity and completeness of organization; refutational elements that skillfully blend with constructive propositions; concreteness of illustration; originality of phrasing, even occasional eloquence; quotable generalizations; and adaptation to his sophisticated audience.

---

[16] Permission for this reprint was given through the courtesy of President Eisenhower. The text was furnished by the President's Office, Columbia University.

[17] For biographical note, see Appendix.

The address ranks high among Eisenhower's public remarks of the period 1949-50. Others of his addresses that might well have been included in this volume were his New York *Herald Tribune* Forum address of October 25, 1949, in which he set forth his political beliefs, and his speech at the 193rd annual banquet of St. Andrew's Society of the State of New York, September 5, 1949, in which he attacked the kind of "security" that implied "slothful indolence and ease and stagnation."

President Eisenhower in 1950 was a platform leader of immense prestige, mental power, and superior speaking skill.

On behalf of Columbia University, I thank Mr. Leo Silver for the generous gift that will make the Gabriel Silver Lecture on Peace a recurring feature of the University calendar. His endowment will permit us at regular intervals to call on selected individuals for reports on peace. Perhaps there will be added new strength to the philosophical and social foundations of peace, and a stronger light thrown on the hazards within the international economy that endanger its permanence. Possibly there will be launched new attacks on inequities and injustices in which lurk some of the causes of war.

Mr. Silver has established a worthy memorial to his father and we are grateful that he has chosen Columbia University as its home. On my own behalf, I want to thank him for the honor paid me in his request that I deliver this inaugural of the series. Without his intervention, I should not be so presumptuous as to appear in this role before a distinguished gathering of Columbia faculty and graduate students because you are, in our country, part of the great body especially qualified to be the architects of world peace.

To you that classification may seem exaggeration beyond any warrant of fact. Quite the contrary. Any man who underestimates the importance of the American teacher in world affairs is misleading himself. Under our system, high governmental policy expresses the considered will of the people, and the will of the people, in the last analysis, is compounded out of the convictions, the idealisms, the purposes fostered in the classrooms of the nation's schools. What you teach is what the country does.

I come before you solely as a witness of things that have happened and of the impressions those have made upon me.

For some years, I was in the thick of war and reconstruction after war. A war that—despite all its terrors, its destruction, its cost—was, for the Allied Nations, a crusade in the best sense of an often misused word, a reconstruction after war that—despite its bickerings, its suppression of freedom in many places and its disheartening cynicism—has established in the political sphere at least a temporary—even if teetering—balance. These years and these experiences have served to ripen and enlarge my devotion to peace. I trust that they have also served to sharpen my powers of perception and judgment of the factors which seem always to balk man's efforts to close forever the doors of the Temple of Janus.

In discussing war and peace, we incline to paint one all black and the other all white. We like to repeat "There never was a good war, or a bad peace." But war often has provided the setting for comradeship and understanding and greatness of spirit —among nations, as well as men—beyond anything in quiet days; while peace may be marked by, or may even be the product of, chicanery, treachery and the temporary triumph of expediency over all spiritual values.

The pact of Munich was a more fell blow to humanity than the atomic bomb at Hiroshima. Suffocation of human freedom among a once free people, however quietly and peacefully accomplished, is more far-reaching in its implications and its effects on their future than the destruction of their homes, industrial centers and transportation facilities. Out of rubble heaps, willing hands can rebuild a better city; but out of freedom lost can stem only generations of hate and bitter struggle and brutal oppression.

Nor can we forget that, as Professor Lyman Bryson of Teachers College recently said: "There are even greater things in the world than peace." By greater things, he meant the ideals, the hopes and aspirations of humanity; those things of the soul and spirit which great men of history have valued far above peace and material wealth and even life itself.

Without these values, peace is an inhuman existence. Far better risk a war of possible annihilation than grasp a peace which would be the certain extinction of free man's ideas and ideals.

Clearly it was a choice between these two extremes that the British people were forced to make back in the dark summer of 1940. Whatever may be history's final judgment on the total war record of that nation, her people in that dire season of fear and foreboding proved themselves heroic and mighty in their spiritual greatness.

Twenty miles beyond their South coast, thinly manned by men—and women—armed with little more than their own courage, there was arrayed an invasion force of stupendous military might, hardened and flushed by sweeps from the Vistula to the Atlantic, from the Arctic to the Alps. Other members of the British Commonwealth of nations, though loyal, could do little to relieve the frightening crisis that suddenly faced the Mother Country.

In all Europe and Asia, from the Bay of Biscay far into the Pacific, men awaited the blow that would destroy the British. The multitude of millions that dwelled in those two continents— even those who lately were allies—had been corrupted into a conviction that material force was unfailingly greater than the spirit of free men.

Throughout most of the rest of the world, there seemed to be an appalling ignorance that the defeat of Britain would mean the eventual extinction of the freedom for ideas and ideals that her people had done so much to win and support for all mankind. So, in her hour of gravest trial she stood largely alone—another David to champion a righteous but apparently hopeless cause.

But the British spurned all offers of peace and their great leader asked for battle—on their beaches, in their towns, along the lanes of England. His faith was rewarded in the final and complete Allied victory of 1945.

Millions of Americans, who saw what the British endured— broken towns, years of austerity, staggering debts and near-destitution—must be witnesses all our lives to the greatness of spirit in that people. *Their decision* to fight on gave freedom a new lease on life and gave all free peoples more space in time to destroy a vicious dictator and regain an opportunity to work out an enduring peace.

Our memories are short indeed, or we have failed to read the lesson of that experience, if we in 1950 are fearful of the future and allow despair to paralyze our efforts to build a lasting peace.

By this allusion to the British record, I do not in any way belittle the wartime contributions of the other allies, including Russia; nor dull one whit the sharp fact that victory over the enemy could *not* have been accomplished without the giant strength of a united America. I dwell on the British role in 1940 and thereafter for two reasons. First, there is a tendency among us today to write off our friends in the Western nations because they are weak in numbers and weapons. Second, there is a parallel tendency to measure a possible enemy solely by the area he rules and the manpower he controls.

Many of us—even among professional soldiers—too easily accept as unfailingly true Napoleon's cynical statement: "God is on the side of the heaviest battalions." *Napoleon*, himself, lived and ruled and fought by that dictum—but his reign from coronation to final exile was shorter by months than even Hitler's; his fellow believer in the dominance of force.

Because there is one towering force in the world that often seems bent upon engulfing as much territory and as many people as it can, a great many surrender their hopes for peace as curtly as they write off our friends in Western Europe. Such pessimism invites disaster. Such an attitude, if it were founded on reason, would mean that the handful of men who dictate the policy of the Soviet system also dictate the fate of this globe. To any one ready to study the history of yesterday and the facts of today, that is a repugnant absurdity.

Granted that at any moment some one powerful nation could choose to follow a policy of world conquest by war. Nevertheless, the world has seen so many examples of this that, today, such a war would imply either an incredible stupidity, weakness, disunity and unreadiness on one side or a miscalculation equal to the insanity and moral guilt on the side of the predatory nation. Until war is eliminated from international relations, unprepared-ness for it is well nigh as criminal as war itself.

What then is the nature of the peace that we seek? What are the characteristics that distinguish it? These questions must be answered, if we are to know our objective, calculate our distance from it, decide on the measures necessary to its attainment.

Almost certainly, most men would agree that peace, to merit the name, should possess a reasonable assurance of permanence, should be the product of cooperation between all major nations, and should be secure against arbitrary violation by any power or group of powers. It is apparent, however, that we constantly use the word *"peace"* in two senses which differ sharply. One is the peace of our dreams—a peace founded in noble impulses, universally shared. It is always the ideal, the pole star that guides us on the proper path. The other peace is *something* of an armed truce; but today a half-loaf is better than none. By the improvisations, expediencies and agreements under which we strive to maintain a peace based as much upon force and power as upon concepts of justice and fair play, we hope to reach the point where this peace becomes the starting point of the *real* peace we seek.

But permanence, universality and security cannot be achieved *merely* by covenant or agreement. Treaties are too often scraps of paper; in our age the signal for two world wars was the callous repudiation of pacts and pledged word. There must be a universal urge to decency.

This fact compels the observation that they are thinking wishfully to pin their hopes of peace upon a single "high level" conference and a resulting paper that would bear the promise of governmental heads to observe all the rights of others. An agreement, though it should bear the seal and ribbon of every chancellery in the world, is worth no more than the confidence placed by each signer in the good faith and integrity of every other. We must sadly acknowledge that today such world-wide confidence does not exist.

By all means let us continue to confer—especially with the view and purpose of reaching the required level of mutual faith and confidence, or—as a substitute—of developing practical and mutually enforceable measures and reciprocal arrangements calculated to lessen the danger of war. But, equally, let us not delude ourselves that, in 1950, establishment of real peace is merely a matter of Very Important Personages signing papers or "talking tough" in Paris, Geneva, Washington or Tahiti.

It is obvious that an enduring world-wide and secure peace must be founded on justice, opportunity and freedom for all men of good will; be maintained in a climate of international understanding and cooperation; be free from militaristic menace; and be supported by an accepted and respected police power representing all nations. Critical factors in the problem of building such a peace are the needs of a human society comprised of individuals; and, further, the needs of a human society that is divided into independent nations, each sovereign within its own borders and competing with all others to promote the interests of its own citizens, often at the expense of others. There are two sides to the coin of peace, the individual and the national; if one is defective the coin is spurious.

On the side of the individual, peace requires an international society that is free from vicious provocations to strife among men. These are rooted in inequities so glaring that, to those who suffer them, they seem to make attractive any alternative. The gamble of war lures the desperate, for even overwhelming defeat can hardly worsen their state; while victory, if it gives the survivors any improvement, will be worth its cost in blood. It is possible, even probable, that hopelessness among a people can be a far more potent cause of war than greed. War—in such case—is a symptom, not the disease.

On the collective side of the coin, peace requires an international society liberated from the threat of aggression by neighbor on neighbor, a threat forever present when one or more nations are committed to the building or maintenance of gigantic military machines. No sane man will challenge, under present circumstances, the need for defensive strength designed to secure against internal or external attack the independence and sovereignty of a free state. But the continued existence of even one purely offensive force—a force for which there is no apparent need based in the logic of self-defense—denies enduring peace to the world. Those who have spawned such a force must either eventually destroy it by demobilization and find justification for the heavy cost already laid on their people; or use it, tacitly or actively, as a threat or as a weapon. There is no middle course.

Always it has been difficult to distinguish between offensive and defensive armaments. Advancing science has obliterated whatever qualitative differences that once existed; today even the atom bomb is included in defensive arsenals. But differences do exist—vital differences. They are found, partially, in the quantitative factor.

The world forms its own sound opinion of a nation's martial purposes, primarily by the size and combinations of armaments supported, and by their geographical disposition and estimated state of readiness. To be considered also is the record of the particular nation—the extent to which it observes the ordinary rules of decency, courtesy, fairness and frankness in dealing with others.

It is by such combinations of standards that we must today classify the world's armaments. For America, with whose professional security forces I have been intimately associated for almost forty years, I bear witness to peaceful intent. In all those years, I have never heard an officer of the Army, the Navy or the Air Force, or any responsible official of government, advocate, urge, discuss or even hint at the use of force by this country in the settlement of any actual or potential international problem.

And here it seems appropriate, in view of my insistent belief that the world must finally disarm or suffer catastrophic consequences, to assert my conviction that America has already disarmed to the extent—in some directions even beyond the extent—that I, with deep concern for her *present* safety, could possibly advise, until we have certain knowledge that all nations, in concerted action, are doing likewise.

I might state here also that the Baruch plan for the control of the atomic bomb was not only evidence of our peaceful intent, but was the most generous action ever made by any nation, equivalent in its field to the Marshall Plan.

Moreover, without American leadership in the search, the pursuit of a just and enduring peace is hopeless. Nowhere in the world—outside this land—is there the richness of resources, stamina and will needed to lead what at times may be a costly and exhausting effort. BUT leadership cannot be exercised by the weak. It demands strength—the strength of this great nation when its people are united in purpose, united in a common fundamental faith, united in their readiness to work for human freedom and peace; this spiritual and economic strength, in turn, must be reinforced in a still armed world by the physical strength necessary for the defense of ourselves and our friends.

Only by deliberate lies can the propagandist—foreign or domestic—stretch our arms program into more than the reasonable posture for defense that General Washington urged on his countrymen. And the heads of state everywhere, even the most suspicious and fearful, know that it is below even that level. Our processes are open to the inspection of all—we spend hardly a dollar or add a platoon to the military establishment without long and public debate.

Our twentieth century international record, the statistics of our military forces, and the open procedures of our political system—all provide proof of our peaceful purposes; they prove also that our support of programs, in which universal peace will be secure, is as honest as it is sturdy. . . .

I have spoken thus briefly of these two elements in world peace—disarmament and United Nations authority—because they are in a manner corollaries or sequels to the other two—justice, freedom, opportunity for all men of good will; and a climate of mutual understanding and cooperation among the nations. Progress is bound to come from slow, evolutionary processes rather than violent revolution in national and individual thinking.

But it is especially important that we do not fall prey to pessimism and defeatism. To describe the attitudes of many of us toward the current international scene, I give you the following quotation:

It is a gloomy moment in history. Not for many years, not in the lifetime of most men who read this paper has there been so much grave and deep apprehension; never has the future seemed so incalculable as at this time.

In France the political cauldron seethes and bubbles with uncertainty; Russia hangs as usual a cloud, dark and silent upon the horizon of Europe; while all the energies, resources and influences of the British Empire are sorely tried and are yet to be tried more sorely.

It is a solemn moment and no man can feel indifference—which happily no man pretends to feel—in the issue of events.

Of our own troubles no man can see the end.

That, ladies and gentlemen, though so vividly descriptive of today, appeared in *Harper's Weekly*, Saturday, October 10, 1857. Possibly we are wrong when we fearfully conclude that for the first time in history the governments regard each other with fear and suspicion.

What, actually, is the outlook for today? In my opinion, far better than most of us normally judge; the world of 1950 is a far brighter and better place than the world of 1850. Starvation is no longer endemic among many millions on every continent—China is the one tragic exception. Illiteracy has vastly diminished in the masses of almost every nation. In the west at least, there is a new and increased appreciation of spiritual values. Even Russia, despite its all-powerful police and purges, is for the average Russian a vast improvement compared to the Russia of 1850.

As to those countries outside the Curtain, I doubt that we can point to any era or any decade when there was as much intelligent comprehension of each other's purposes as now characterizes their relationships. And in the broader scope, the United Nations, however halting its progress may be, however much its sessions are torn by the jeers and vetoes from one sector, is a visible and working entity—substantial evidence of developing hopes and purposes, an earnest of better things to come.

All of us have come a long way in the past century; none of us should despair when we think of what our situation was, and our prospects, as recently as the summer of 1940. What then can be done now—by this University, by the United States, by the free peoples—to further the cause of peace?

The University, since its removal to Morningside Heights, has become an international center whose graduates can be found on every continent and whose influence has been a leaven for physical progress, intellectual fellowship and spiritual growth among all peoples. The purpose of this University, without over-simplification, can be epitomized in one phrase—the good of humanity.

We hope to build here on the campus a Nutrition Center in which the world's scientists will find concentrated all the knowledge, the tools, the facilities that will enable them to devise better, more productive and more effective techniques for the use of physical resources and the satisfaction of man's physical needs. We already have—and in every recent term we have further amplified—an Institute of International Affairs where we hope the political and social leaders of the world will find concentrated the materials, the information, the masses of data that will enable them to adjust the stresses and needs of one area to the strains and surpluses of another.

We hope to establish here a Chair for Peace, possibly an Institute. The purpose will be to study war as a tragic social phenomenon—its origins, its conduct, its impact, and particularly its disastrous consequences upon man's spiritual, intellectual and material progress. All this we should study in a scholarly atmosphere, free from emotional bias and the daily crises of public life. No American university, I am told, has ever undertaken this comprehensive task. For me, there is something almost shocking in the realization that, though many millions have been voluntarily donated for research in cancer of the individual body, nothing similar has been done with respect to the most malignant cancer of the world body—war.

We are presently engaged in a study of the Conservation of Human Resources—restricted, as of now, to the United States—but which will be of immeasurable benefit to all the world in furthering the dignity of man as a human being. Another hope is to conduct an exhaustive study into the ways and means of applying to every man's good, in today's intricate economy, *all* the resources of America, in such way as to maintain and enlarge every freedom that the individual has enjoyed under our system. There are other projects, under way or under discussion, that will take their places beside or even in front of these. Each of them will help Columbia University a little better to fulfill its purpose —the peace, freedom and good of America, and, therefore, of humanity.

As citizens of the United States, you and I—and all Americans in every corner of our land—must be forever mindful that the heritage of America and the strength of America are expressed in three fundamental principles: First, that individual freedom is our most precious possession; second, that all our freedoms are a single bundle, all must be secure if any is to be preserved; third, that freedom to compete and readiness to cooperate make our system the most productive on earth. Only within the framework of these principles can we hope to continue the growth that has marked our history. Only thus can our millions reach the fullness of intellectual, moral and physical welfare that is justly ours—and avoid any risk of submission to the all-powerful state. Moreover, only thus can the world have any hope of reaching the millennium of world peace—for without the example of strength, prosperity and progress in a free America, there is nothing to inspire men to victory in today's struggle between freedom and totalitarianism.

As friends of free people everywhere in the world, we can by our own example—our conduct in every crisis, real or counterfeit; our resistance to propaganda and passion; our readiness to seek adjustment and compromise of difference—we can by our own example ceaselessly expand understanding among the nations. We must never forget that international friendship is achieved through rumors ignored, propaganda challenged and exposed; through patient loyalty to those who have proved themselves worthy of it; through help freely given, where help is needed and merited. In this sense there is no great, no humble among us. In rights and in opportunity, in loyalty and in responsibility to ideals, we are and must remain equal. Peace is more the product of our day-to-day living than of a spectacular program, intermittently executed.

The best foreign policy is to live our daily lives in honesty, decency and integrity; at home, making our own land a more fitting habitation for free men; and, abroad, joining with those of like mind and heart, to make of the world a place where all men can dwell in peace. Neither palsied by fear nor duped by dreams but strong in the rightness of our purpose, we can then place our case and cause before the bar of world opinion—history's final arbiter between nations.

PEACE IN THE ATOMIC ERA [18]

ALBERT EINSTEIN [19]

Dr. Albert Einstein, in his first public statement since the decision to proceed with the hydrogen bomb, contributed to this first weekly television program, conducted by Mrs. Franklin D. Roosevelt, on Sunday, February 12, 1950. The telecast was seen (and heard) at four o'clock, Eastern Standard Time, over the Eastern and Midwestern networks of the National Broadcasting Company. The program originated in the Colonial Room of the Park Sheraton Hotel, New York. Dr. Einstein's remarks were recorded on a sound film at Princeton on the previous Friday, and inserted in the New York broadcast.

In the telecast Mrs. Roosevelt poured tea for the talking guests, Senator Brien McMahon (Connecticut), chairman of the Joint Congressional Committee on Atomic Energy; David Lilienthal, former chairman of the Commission; Dr. J. Robert Oppenheim, director of the Institute for Advanced Study of Princeton; Dr. Detev W. Bronk, president of Johns Hopkins University; Dr. Hans A. Bethe, Cornell University physicist; Harry Winne, vice president of the General Electric Company; and Allan Kline, president of the American Farm Bureau Federation.

The topic was atomic energy—whether it had gotten out of hand; whether it could now be controlled; whether its important peacetime benefits could be realized.

Critics of television and radio concluded that the topic was too broad for this thirty-minute treatment, and that too many speaking guests were "present." Each participant had at most a few minutes. Lilienthal, for example, exhibited a piece of uranium but had no time to expound its possible significance to society. The camera direction also was questioned. Each around the tea table "was too fleetingly seen and heard."

Dr. Einstein was given somewhat more time than the others. "We saw the great scientist with his wonderful, aged, inquiring face, wearing a tieless shirt and a sweater jacket, and we heard him speak quietly and with an almost dispassionate sadness, of the possible destruction of this planet." [20]

Einstein's analysis of the problem of how to secure peace was theoretical. Listeners and observers of his telecast asked, "How can we do away with the mutual fear and distrust as he proposed?" "What evi-

---

[18] Permission for this reprint given through the courtesy of Dr. Einstein and of the National Broadcasting Company. For text see also the New York *Times*, February 13, 1950.

[19] For biographical note, see Appendix.

[20] *New Yorker.* 26:88-89. February 25, 1950. "Television, Mrs. Roosevelt's Tea Party." Philip Hamburger.

dence did Einstein have that the Soviet Union and her satellite states would cooperate in the 'supranational body'?" "What hope is there to set up a supranational judicial and executive body after the preceding five years of experience with Soviet diplomatic 'road blocking'?"

The student, reviewing this speech, should examine in detail the scope and limitations of television as a medium for presenting current issues.

I am grateful to you for the opportunity to express my conviction in this most important political question.

The idea of achieving security through national armament is, at the present state of military technique, a disastrous illusion. On the part of the U. S. A. this illusion has been particularly fostered by the fact that this country succeeded first in producing an atomic bomb. The belief seemed to prevail that in the end it were possible to achieve decisive military superiority. In this way, any potential opponent would be intimidated, and security, so ardently desired by all of us, brought to us and all of humanity. The maxim which we have been following during these last five years has been, in short: Security through superior military power, whatever the cost.

This mechanistic, technical-military psychological attitude had inevitable consequences. Every single act in foreign policy is governed exclusively by one view point. How do we have to act in order to achieve utmost superiority over the opponent in case of war? Establishing military bases at all possible strategically important points on the globe. Arming and economic strengthening of potential allies. Within the country! Concentration of tremendous financial power in the hands of the military, militarization of the youth, close supervision of the loyalty of the citizens, in particular, of the civil servants by a police force growing more conspicuous every day. Intimidation of people of independent political thinking. Indoctrination of the public by radio, press, school. Growing restriction of the range of public information under the pressure of military secrecy.

The armament race between the U.S.A. and the USSR, originally supposed to be a preventive measure, assumes hysterical character. On both sides, the means to mass destruction are perfected with feverish haste—behind the respective walls of secrecy. The H-Bomb appears on the public horizon as a probably attainable goal. Its accelerated development has been solemnly proclaimed by the President. If successful, radioactive poisoning of the atmosphere and hence annihilation of any life on earth has been brought within the range of technical possibilities. The ghostlike character of this development lies in its apparently compulsory trend. Every step appears as the unavoidable consequence of the preceding one. In the end, there beckons more and more clearly general annihilation.

Is there any way out of this impasse created by man himself? All of us, and particularly those who are responsible for the attitude of the U. S. and the U.S.S.R., should realize that we may have vanquished an external enemy, but have been incapable of getting rid of the mentality created by the war. It is impossible to achieve peace as long as every single action is taken with a possible future conflict in view. The leading point of view of all political action should therefore be: What can we do to bring about a peaceful coexistence and even loyal cooperation of the nations. The first problem is to do away with mutual fear and distrust. Solemn renunciation of violence (not only with respect to means of mass destruction) is undoubtedly necessary. Such renunciation, however, can only be effective if at the same time a supra-national judicial and executive body is set up empowered to decide questions of immediate concern to the security of the nations. Even a declaration of the nations to collaborate loyally in the realization of such a "restricted world government" would considerably reduce the imminent danger of war.

In the last analysis, every kind of peaceful cooperation among men is primarily based on mutual trust and only secondly on institutions such as courts of justice and police. This holds for nations as well as for individuals. And the basis of trust is loyal give and take.

What about international control? Well, it may be of secondary use as a police measure. But it may be wise not to overestimate its importance. The times of Prohibition come to mind and give one pause.

NATIONAL DEFENSE

LONG RANGE MILITARY POLICY [1]

OMAR N. BRADLEY [2]

General Omar N. Bradley, chairman of the Joint Chiefs of Staff, gave this testimony before the House Armed Service Committee, Washington, D.C., on Wednesday, October 19, 1949. The Congressional inquiry was concerned with the bitter dispute between this country's military authorities about the strategic purposes, size, and character of the defense organization.

For the previous two weeks the Navy had stated its case, highlighted by Admiral Louis E. Denfield's criticism of alleged discrimination against the Navy in the unification of the armed services. He stated that the Navy did not object to such effort at unity, but strongly protested against the curtailing of naval aviation and the cutting down of the Marine Corps. He accused Secretary of Defense Johnson of taking "arbitrary action."

Air Secretary W. Stuart Symington, replying on October 18, stated that the Navy's testimony had been "false" and "untrue" and that the national security had been imperiled by the revealing of the "technical and operating details of our newest and latest equipment." Thus was the issued joined of Navy versus Army and Air Forces.

General Bradley denounced as "fancy Dans" the Navy officers who complained against the defense policies. He told the House committee that the Navy's attitude was "seriously wrong about our military establishment" and singled out Admiral Denfield for special criticism. General Vandenberg, head of the Air Force, offered similar criticism of the Navy.

The issues were mainly (1) What kind of unified armed defense should this nation have? (2) Should the policies of one branch of the service be overridden or vetoed by another branch? (3) What over-all military strategy should be followed in case of war?

The Navy specifically objected to the staff decision to build up the Air Force's B-36 bomber, armed with the atomic bomb, and to cut naval aviation.

[1] Text furnished by the Joint Chiefs of Staff, Pentagon Building, Washington, D.C.

[2] For biographical note, see Appendix.

General Bradley read his fifteen thousand word statement rapidly. He rarely raised his rather high-pitched voice. "Now and again there was a slight sharpening in his nasal drawl." [3]

The General stated that he had written the entire document himself, but that he was of course "helped by several aides."

His argument was a direct refutation of three principal charges given by the Navy: (1) The basic concept of our defense is wrong in that our plans for the execution of war are jeopardizing our national security; (2) the offensive power of the Navy is being destroyed; and (3) the Secretary of Defense and Joint Chiefs of Staff are underestimating the Navy's role. The student will study the methods by which Bradley attempted to refute each charge. The reply to the first of these three charges is included in this volume. In their public arguments and statements before Congressional groups, Bradley and the other military men often had to generalize without supplying the concrete but highly confidential evidence.

In this statement General Bradley frequently relied on his personal authority for proof.

The Committee adjourned on October 21. It announced that it would present its solution of the issues and recommendations to the second session of the Eighty-first Congress.

As this volume went to the publisher (May 1950), Congress was struggling with the size and distribution of the defense budget. The issues raised by Admiral Denfield and handled by General Bradley were thus being partly answered by the decisions concerning Congressional military appropriations.

Although General Bradley has had little speech training, he has had wide experience in speaking, including his service as instructor in the ROTC program at South Dakota State College immediately after World War I; his four years as instructor in mathematics at West Point, 1920-24; his instructorship in tactics and weapons at the Infantry School, 1929-1933; and his second four-year assignment at West Point as instructor in tactics, and later as plans and training officer, 1934-38. His later military career in North Africa and Europe, and his administration of the Veterans Administration, 1945-47, all involved continual speaking before military training groups, congressional committees, and many civilian audiences.[4]

Mr. Chairman, and Members of the Committee: My frequent appearances before this Committee have always been a pleasure. It would be so in this instance, if I were not adverse to public discussion of matters which might compromise our national de-

[3] New York *Times*, October 20, 1949.

[4] For this information the editor is indebted to Colonel Willis G. Matthews, Aide to General Bradley (letter of April 10, 1950).

fense. While I regret the circumstances which compel me to discuss the controversial subjects before your Committee, since they have already been discussed publicly, I welcome the opportunity to present my views.

Mr. Chairman, the testimony you have heard so far, and the remarks I am about to make emphasize war, and our war-making effort. I would like to express my gratitude to you for introducing into the record of this investigation last Thursday the article in the *Saturday Evening Post*, which I had the pleasure of writing with Mr. Beverly Smith, entitled, "This way lies peace." For in that article, I tried to emphasize the importance of a steadfast and determined effort on the part of the American people for peace. It is my sincere belief that "we [Americans] and our friends of the free world must combine our military potential and our peaceful intent in a strategy for peace— [which will ultimately make] us more secure than any strategy ever designed for war." . . .

Let's first discuss the basic concept of our defense planning. As far as I am able, without violating security, I want to discuss our plans and preparations for the execution of a war, if it is thrust upon us. As I have indicated, our basic concept for defense includes protection of the United States, and this continent, in case we are attacked. It provides for early retaliation from bases which we hope to have ready at all times.

This concept includes a decision that we shall have to be ready to seize other bases that we may need, and hold those bases against enemy attack, so that we may attack the enemy country at shorter ranges, and at the same time, deny to him bases close to this country from which he could attack us.

Ultimately, however, we will have to carry the war back to the enemy by all means at our disposal. I am convinced that this will include strategic air bombardment, and large-scale land operations.

I also believe that after the initial phases are over, there will be little need for any campaign similar to the Pacific "island hopping" that took place during the last war. And as I will develop later on in my discussion, I also predict that large-scale amphibious operations, such as those in Sicily and Normandy, will never occur again.

In addition to the concept I have just outlined, we must go back to the realization that the first prize for any aggressor in the world today is Europe, with its industrial potential and its market for goods. The American people realize this and have affirmed, in economic aid and by political tie, that we are still interested in Western Europe, which we have twice defended. Through the North Atlantic Treaty and with the Mutual Defense Assistance Act of 1949, we have indicated that our continent is linked with theirs in peace and for collective defense.

The basic defense principle of the North Atlantic Treaty, and of the mutual defense assistance program is that each nation shall contribute those things which it can best provide in the collective security plan. And in our own strategic plans, our part in this collective international security must be given its proper perspective.

Finally, our basic concept has never for a moment overlooked the primary consideration of protecting the continental United States, its coastal waters, and the key bases for this task.

At the same time, your planners have realistically assumed that the American people would never be content to sit down in confinement to this continent and suffer a long war of attrition, carried on by intercontinental bombing, and intercontinental missiles. We have realized that if we are ever attacked, our plans must include the tenacious holding of our frontiers in Europe, and the eventual defeat of the aggressor's land army.

This discussion is all too brief. There are many detailed considerations within the basic strategic concept that must be carried out. But I cannot see any jeopardy to our national security in this strategy.

Finally, if the military continues to effect more economies in defense measures, keeping constantly aware of the drain on our economy, there will be little danger of economic collapse, and our over-all risk will be less and less.

I would like to end the discussion of this accusation right here. However, in the testimony presented to the Committee, and related to this conception that our national security has been made insecure, are some specific points that I would like to deny.

First, that strategic bombing is wrong from a military standpoint, and from a moral standpoint, and that the Secretary of

Defense and the Joint Chiefs of Staff have permitted an unwarranted emphasis on strategic bombing for the best interests of national security. As a means of conducting war, I define strategic bombing as violent airborne attacks on the war-making capacity or potential of an enemy nation. I do not advocate a wanton destruction of cities or people, but it is obvious that workers live near factories, and that if you bomb the factories, you may bomb the people. From a military standpoint, any damage you can inflict on the war-making potential of a nation, and any great injury you can inflict upon the morale of that nation contributes to the victory. It has been proved that strategic bombing has such effect when properly applied. . . .

They have charged that the performance characteristics of the B-36 bomber in the eyes of the Navy make it an unsatisfactory weapon. In other words, that technically the B-36 airplane is no good for the mission of the Air Force. Without going into the technical details, I will only state that, in my opinion, it is the best bomber available for production that is capable of carrying out certain required missions in the case of emergency. I believe this opinion is substantiated by the comparative statistics as previously presented to the JCS by the Air Force on the various types of bombers available when they made their selection of the B-36 to fulfill the strategic bombing role they have been assigned.

I would also like to point out that the Joint Chiefs of Staff joined in the unanimous ratification of the Air Force investment in the B-36 last February. This ratification was not made under duress of any kind. And I raise the question, if it has become so disastrous to national security now, why did the Navy concur eight months ago?

The Navy has also made great moment of the fact that the B-36 is not the best plane for strategic bombardment, and that intercontinental bombing as such is an impracticable idea. May I point out that no member of the military establishment has said that better types won't be used when they are available, nor has any responsible individual indicated that there has been any cessation on the part of the Air Force in developing a better, faster, and longer-range bomber as soon as possible.

Meanwhile, I assure you that if war comes, we will make every effort to use bases as close as possible to the enemy for maximum effect and minimum expense of lives and material. The closer the range, the higher the speed for the run over enemy territory.

But I personally would hate to face the American people after abandoning any program for intercontinental bombing if we found ourselves suddenly devoid of bases, except for those on this continent, and we had to sit here and take it in the United States, with no means of reprisal. A long-range bomber can always be effective at shorter ranges, but a limited-range bomber is of little value beyond its distance.

The Air Force has facts and conclusions upon which they have based their judgment and belief that are at variance with some of the information presented to you by Navy personnel. However, to answer assertion with assertion would not only carry on this hearing indefinitely, it would serve no useful purpose. This is especially true when all of the services and their leaders are agreed that this weapon can best be tested by the Weapons Evaluation Group.

I would like to point out, in all fairness, that one service, the Navy, has taken this opportunity to publicly disparage a weapon—the B-36—that the Air Force, the service responsible, has chosen to perform an assigned mission. This is in direct contradiction to the Navy's own idea presented so forcefully and frequently to the public, that each service should be allowed to develop and have the weapons it feels it needs for the mission it is assigned.

Before concluding that the B-36 is unsatisfactory for the mission assigned to the Air Force, may I respectfully suggest that you await the results of the Evaluation Group report. This attack on the B-36 as a weapon included two other insinuations which I do not believe are valid charges. One was the implication *that from the B-36, our Air Force bombardiers cannot hit a target from high altitudes.*

Yet they admit that no Navy pilot has flown a B-36, nor have they participated in any tests with this bomber. On the other hand, our Air Force bombardiers have assured us that this aircraft can perform effectively under all conditions of weather, by night or day, and can deliver striking blows against their targets. These Air Force men, who will have to face the risk of the great losses that the Navy predicts, are perfectly willing to stake their reputations and their lives on their performance. Again may I suggest that you do not reach a decision on the accuracy of high level bombardment without consulting the men who are charged with doing it.

And too, *the testimony implies that the Russians—our only possible opponents for many years to come—have the capability of causing intolerable losses on any bomber engaged in mission where the Russians have adequate defenses.* They base this allegation on the creditable performance of one of the Navy's fighter-interceptor aircraft, the Banshee. However, we do not know whether or not the Russians have a "Banshee." At the same time, I might point out that the Navy is anxious to have a "flush-deck carrier" so that they can use even larger planes with longer ranges from their floating air bases. It seems to me that these larger planes would be subject to the same attack which Navy witnesses have visualized against the B-36.

This discussion of the Banshee and the B-36 does not convince me that the Russians have the capability attributed to them. It indicates only that the permanent contest between offensive and defensive weapons includes airplanes. Regardless of the planes used, I expect that some will be shot down. The number lost will be dependent upon many factors, but the fact that you may suffer *some* losses doesn't mean that you cannot still accomplish your mission.

And I must admit that I find some comfort in the fact that we have a long-range bomber that can fly from any base in the world and attack targets in the range of four thousand miles, and return home. We have accomplished a tie-up of enemy men and planes, and many millions of dollars in their radar equipment and fighter-interceptor equipment, as they look around a global circumference for any approaching attacks.

Again, I respectfully suggest that we heed the estimate of *what the enemy might do,* rather than the statistical reports of what our own Navy can perform.

Related to this entire discussion of strategic bombing is the ridiculous assertion *that the atomic bomb is effective on only a small area,* insinuating that we Americans have misplaced our confidence and our dollars in this weapon.

I believe that the insinuation that the atomic bomb is relatively ineffective as a weapon of war is refuted by every test that has been made. Contrary to many of the statements made before your Committee, the Navy case in these matters has been presented to the Joint Chiefs of Staff, and among other things, it has been the Navy's continuous argument that they should be permitted to use the atomic bomb, both strategically and tactically. If it is really so ineffective as some would have you believe, I wonder why the Navy is so anxious to use it.

And without clouding the issue, I would like to add one more relevant point on the atomic bomb. It is no secret the tests at Bikini and Eniwetok revealed that the Navy afloat is one of the most profitable targets for an enemy with an atomic bomb, and that its effect on ships is lasting. Even without sinking them, it promises to deny our use of them for many, many months after the onslaught. This, I know, contributes to the Navy's worries and indicates to some of their thinking members that surface fleets en masse might be a thing of the past.

Admiral Blandy also pointed out in his testimony, rightfully, that naval air protected the amphibious landing at Okinawa, and inferred that the success of this battle is largely dependent upon that arm, the Navy. Undoubtedly, without Navy support, any amphibious operation is impossible. However, by appraising the power of the atomic bomb, I am wondering whether we shall ever have another large-scale amphibious operation. Frankly, the atomic bomb, properly delivered, almost precludes such a possibility. I know that I, personally, hope that I shall never be called upon to participate in another amphibious operation like the one in Normandy.

If I may digress for a moment from my consideration of the atomic bomb, I would like to point out to those who hold that a tremendous Marine Corps is essential for future amphibious operations, and that naval air must be correspondingly large, that I have participated in the largest two amphibious assaults ever made in history. In neither case were any Marines present. And in neither case were any Navy carriers used.

The A-bomb is the most powerful destructive weapon known today. Personally, I hope it can be outlawed as a weapon by the adequate international control our government has recommended. But until that has been achieved, I shall not discredit its effect, nor shall I shortsightedly limit its role to purely strategic use.

As a believer in humanity I deplore its use, and as a soldier, I respect it.

And as an American citizen, I believe that we should be prepared to use its full psychological and military effect toward preventing war, and if we are attacked, toward winning it. The careless detractions of the power of this weapon have done national security no good, and may have done our collective security, in these precarious times, untold harm. Frankly, for the good of our nation, I wish that such testimony, belittling one of our great deterrents to war, had never been given.

I consider this first major charge, namely, *that the basic concept of our defense planning is wrong, and that our plans and preparations for the execution of a war are jeopardizing our national security,* the most serious detraction brought forth in this investigation.

FREEDOM AND MILITARY SECURITY [5]

W. STUART SYMINGTON [6]

W. Stuart Symington, Secretary of the Air Force, gave this address before the graduating class at Baylor University, Waco, Texas, at 9:30 A.M. (Central Standard Time) on Wednesday, February 1, 1950. The occasion was part of the University's 105 Anniversary ceremonies. The speaker received an honorary degree.

Mr. Symington, during 1946-47, had been Assistant Secretary of War, and Secretary of the Air Force in National Defense in 1947-50. He had steadily advocated a big air force, one that would comprise "seventy groups," as recommended in the Thomas K. Finletter Report of January 1, 1948. Mr. Symington made many speeches in support of vast air strength. He and Secretary of Defense Louis F. Johnson clashed sharply on the issue.

The issue specifically was whether by about 1953 the Air Force should be prepared to wage a sustained campaign, or whether it should be merely powerful enough to repel air attack from Russia. Upon analysis of air power as measured by "air frame weight," it became obvious that the Truman-Johnson force would be far inferior to that argued for by Symington and Finletter. General Eisenhower's proposed "air weight" was somewhat greater than Truman's and considerably less than that of the Symington-Finletter formula. Were we to prepare for total war? Or were we to support a military machine that would be capable only of defensive action?

The Baylor speech was a comprehensive justification of a proposed national defense budget of thirteen or fourteen billion dollars, and was timed to shake national complacency concerning military power. Symington would enlist national support for the huge military budget, especially the Air Force portion.

Note the essence of Symington's logic and his appeal through an extended analogy or comparison of conditions in 1938 with those in 1950. (1) Russia in 1950 is heavily armed. (2) The threat to our security is great. (3) We are likely to be relatively in the same position as England was in 1938-39, except that there will be no America to come to our rescue. (4) Therefore, we must arm heavily—whatever the cost and however huge the unbalanced budget.

[5] Text supplied by the Department of Defense, Office of Public Information, Washington, D.C. Permission for this reprinting given through the courtesy of Secretary W. Stuart Symington.

[6] For biographical note, see Appendix.

This obvious logic was set forth in sharp, interesting, layman's language. The persuasion was carefully managed—though no doubt naturally developed in the speech composition and without mechanical contrivance.

On March 30, 1950, the President, at Key West, Florida, announced that Mr. Symington would resign and would be made chairman of the National Security Resources Board. His successor was to be Mr. Finletter. The change was widely interpreted as a victory for Secretary of Defense Johnson—and a more moderate air arm.

Symington as speaker, although not eloquent, talks with ease and communicative directness. His absorption in his theme of adequate national defense gave his public appearances of 1949-50 much persuasive cogency and intellectual drive.

For some years now I have been a member of your national defense structure, America's team of land, sea and air; and certain observations might be of interest to you today in connection with problems incident to the future security of the United States.

In his recent message to Congress on the State of the Union, our great President outlined the position and responsibilities of our country at this turn of the mid-century. In that challenging address he said in part:

The human race has reached a turning point. Man has opened the secrets of nature and mastered new powers. If he uses them wisely, he can reach new heights of civilization. If he uses them foolishly, they may destroy him.

In the world today we are confronted with the danger that the rising demand of people everywhere for freedom and a better life may be corrupted and betrayed by the false promises of communism.

While the world remains unsettled . . . and as long as our own security and the security of the free world require, we will maintain a strong and well-balanced defense organization.

It is common knowledge that the source of the unsettled conditions to which our Commander in Chief referred is the threat of communistic aggression. Four years ago World War II ended. In 1922, four years after the close of World War I, the major powers were able to sit around the conference table in Washington, in a conciliatory atmosphere, and arrive at an agreement for the reduction of armaments. This they accomplished because no major power threatened the peace.

Ever since the end of the last war, however, America has become increasingly aware there can be no true peace while there is this threat of Communist aggression.

Indeed we may have already lived so long in this postwar cold-war atmosphere that unrest and instability are now being taken for granted, and therefore disregarded. If so, that is a very serious matter, because such lack of interest might result in loss of our freedom.

Such disregard may be natural for normal, healthy, peace-loving people. In this air-atomic age, however, it is dangerous, because the cause for this unrest—Communist aggression—is a threat not only to the preservation of the peace, but also to our existence as a nation.

Never in the history of the United States has it been more important to recognize the truth about the world we live in; to recognize that truth, and then to follow the proper course necessary for America's preservation, no matter what the sacrifices required.

As our President said, "We know now that this is not an easy task or a short one." Professor Arnold Toynbee, famed historian, recently predicted that these sacrifices might be required for the next fifty years. Toynbee assumed, of course, there would be no successful world conquest by the Communists.

Some twelve and a half years ago, in the summer of 1937, I went to the seat of a great world empire, a gay and busy city. It was the end of the London season. There were the usual number of parties. Some of the wealthy were watching their horses race; others were taking off for the continent. With the exception of very few men, always and primarily Winston Churchill, foreign affairs were viewed with but normal apprehension. Many were sympathetic with Hitler. There was fear of Communist Russia, and fear of the growth of communism in the French army, which was considered the greatest army in the world. As against these two fears, many favored Hitler's Germany as providing a balance of power and a bulwark state.

Douglas Reed of the London *Times* sounded consistent warnings from his post in Berlin. Churchill pleaded with the good people of his country, in epochal speeches which later composed a famous book, *While England Slept.*

Appeasement, however, was the order of the day. World trade, and the stock dividends from it, were important. Some were trying to "buy" security through appeasement—as if any nation can ever "buy" security through compromise with evil.

Fourteen months later came Munich. Some countries, particularly Czechoslovakia, felt they had been sold down the river. By then, however, there was no alternative, because the wolf had taken off his sheep's clothing. Hitler and his gangsters had revealed their true intent, and neither England, nor any other democracy, had adequate armament with which to trade against the war now sure to come.

In all free countries men stirred uneasily. They realized that soon they might be called upon to fight and die. They asked one another: How did we ever get into this position so soon after having won before?

How did they? That is the point of such critical importance to us today.

Less than four years later I again visited London, in early 1941. We sneaked up the coast of Portugal by air, praying for bad weather, hoping to avoid Hitler's dominant Focke-Wulf long-range bombers, as they returned over the Atlantic from their attacks on Allied shipping.

Times had changed in London. Nobody took off for the continent of Europe except in battle planes, because the Nazis controlled that continent, just twenty miles away. Horses were being eaten instead of raced, and most of the entertainment was deep in the shelter of basements, comparatively safe from the bombs raining down overhead.

One of Britain's greatest battleships, the "Hood," had been sunk. Worse to them, a large island, Crete, had just been conquered from the air.

The British people stood up with indomitable courage. Their leaders knew, nevertheless, that all which stood between them and slavery was the potential production wealth and manpower of the United States.

At this point let me ask you—in case our country in turn is caught with its defense guard down, what nation has the strength to stand behind us as we stood behind England?

At present the people on this earth are, in effect, split into two main political groups. One group is headed by an aggressive dictatorship, ruling some 285 million people directly, plus many millions indirectly through puppet, or satellite, regimes. This central Communist dictatorship has reiterated many times, to its own people and to the rest of the world, that it is conducting the modern equivalent of a holy war against all non-believers.

In every issue of Communist dogma, under the title "Problems of Leninism," published over the signature of Stalin, appears this basic Communist tenet:

> We are living not merely in a state, but in a system of states; and it is inconceivable that the Soviet Republic should continue for a long period side by side with imperialistic states. Ultimately one or the other must conquer. Meanwhile, a number of terrible clashes between the Soviet Republic and the bourgeois states will be inevitable. . .

The above statement of Communist policy has been reiterated many times, and as recently as after the close of World War II in 1945.

Furthermore, Communist leaders denounce all spiritual faiths, dictating as a substitute the cynical and materialistic doctrine of communism. As we all know, but sometimes are prone to forget, the Communist does not believe in God. That is part of the foundation of his philosophy. He has always fought to destroy religion.

The leaders of Russia have not only constantly reiterated their goal of world domination; they have also predicted the doom of all other political systems, especially capitalism. They inflamed all Communists against all non-Communists, wherever the latter may be. They have sealed off their own people behind an Iron Curtain, while taking advantage of free access in other countries to create constant distress and confusion from within.

Theirs has been a ceaseless campaign of aggression; ideological, political and economic; and wherever expedient, that campaign has been supported by guns and marching men.

In the middle thirties it was important to know what the people of France and England and Holland and Denmark and Belgium and Norway were doing. It was far more important, however, to know what the Nazis were doing. Were they really rearming? Did they really believe their marching slogan, "Today we rule Germany, tomorrow the world"?

I believe that in these United States, at this mid-century mark, the most important question for all of us today is, What are the Russians doing? Not what we are doing in the way of rearming, at some slight expense to our standard of living, but what are those other people doing—those people who say they cannot live in the same world with our way of life? What is their weapons program, and why?

Surely we Americans do not want to be caught at any future time the way the democracies were caught by Hitler in the thirties.

This we know. Those who reiterate America must be destroyed, now have: (1) A ground army greater in numbers than the combined armies of the United States and its allies; (2) An air force whose strength in nearly all categories is now the largest in the world and growing relatively larger month by month; (3) The world's largest submarine fleet; and an intensive submarine development and construction program.

It is our belief that if any democracy attempted to maintain in peacetime a comparable regular armed force, the free economy of that democracy would be wrecked. In Communist countries, however, the will of the rulers, and not the economy of the nation, is the controlling factor. People under a dictatorship do not know when great streams of national wealth, which could be used to raise their standard of living, are diverted instead to further the aggressive ambitions of their rulers

The Communist government dictators have no problems of money, because all money is owned by the state. The coin of the realm is the order of the dictator. Nor have these bosses any problem of labor, because they have millions of slaves, captive prisoners from other countries as well as their own political slaves. From our standpoint, every citizen of their state is but a slave to the handful of rulers at the top.

All men in such positions of dictatorial power, uncontrolled by the checks and balances of representative government, disdainful of the dignity and rights of the individual, and dedicated to the belief that the end justifies the means, are, and always will be, a threat to the freedom-loving peoples of the world.

Here are three facts which every American should know, because this is the world in which we live: (1) Behind the iron curtain there has been an atomic explosion. (2) Behind that curtain is the air equipment capable of delivering a surprise atomic attack against any part of the United States. (3) We have no sure defense against such an attack.

The bleak picture is that today we have a group of dictators dedicated to destroy our way of life. They are capable now of unleashing, without warning, the world's largest ground army, air force and undersea fleet. The gravity of this situation is multiplied many times by our knowledge of achievements being made by Russian scientists in the field of atomic energy.

I ask you, if these leaders want peace, why are they building their armed strength to such staggering proportions?

Today America holds the position of world economic, moral, intellectual, and in some respects, material leadership, in a struggle as bitter and fundamental as that in the Middle Ages between Islam and Christianity. In that ancient conflict the battleground was religious belief. It is with difficulty that we now understand the intensity of feelings which led to those holy wars. Many feel those dedicated to communism are, in effect, now waging a new religious war, with the dialectic materialism of communism the basis of a godless faith.

In the past the United States has been relatively safe, because our allies have given us the time necessary to build our defense against attack. Then we were at relatively safe distances from our enemies. That is no longer true. Distance is no longer any protection from the long arm and smashing fist of modern military air power. In this air-atomic age the oceans and polar wastes are not barriers against attack. Remember Russian soil is but five minutes flying time from the American soil of Alaska; and but a few hours away from our great cities. Waco is but an eighteen-hour flight from Moscow for the bombers we know Russia is now producing in quantity.

Based on these facts, are there any who would question the importance of this country maintaining as much military strength as will provide what George Washington called a "respectable posture of defense"? Would any of us like to forfeit either (1) the capacity to defend ourselves as best possible against sudden atomic air attack, or (2) the strategic air capacity necessary for instant effective retaliation against those who would make a surprise move against this country?

America is reconciled to the necessity for a peacetime defense program greater than ever required in the past. We must remain steadfast and alert until that day—God hasten it—when we can have complete assurance that any power or combination of powers which threaten peace will abandon their aggressive schemes and participate effectively in the community of nations to advance, and not destroy, civilization.

History teaches that mere races for armed might do not prevent wars. History also teaches, however, that weakness invites aggression.

Our patience in seeking peaceful solutions must not be interpreted as weakness. Rather it constitutes evidence of our own lack of aggressive designs, a manifestation of our sincere hope that as one member of a world organization, we may help to realize the aspirations of mankind for a permanent and responsible peace.

It is a basic dilemma of our time that those who menace our way of life may force arms expenditures of a magnitude that could cripple our economy and thus imperil our free institutions. I submit, however, that those who are critical of this administration for not bringing the national budget into balance may be guilty of ignoring the grim realities of the world in which we live.

I share the businessman's traditional dislike for deficits and am not unaware of the desires of the American taxpayer to have his burden made lighter. But under the circumstances of today, I am convinced that no loyal and informed American would knowingly consent to dangerous concessions in our security program in order to achieve some otherwise desirable fiscal objective. The risks involved are too great—the stakes too high, for any such false economies.

The arithmetic of the distribution of your tax dollars and mine establishes that during the current and coming fiscal year one third of that dollar, or 33c, is being allocated to the Army, Navy and Air Force. This figure does not include foreign aid, part of our payment for security, which averages 14c.

Those who say they would destroy the United States are thus forcing us to spend heavily from our resources, not only for our national defense but also for the rehabilitation and strengthening of our allies. They hope to force us into economic collapse.

This danger is always present—consequently efficiency and quality assume transcendent importance in all our preparations; and selectivity in the building of our defense structure grows increasingly vital to our solvency.

If it is more important to balance the budget than to guarantee our security, it would be a relatively simple matter for our President to do so by recommending still further reductions in appropriations for national defense.

Based on the facts presented to you above, however, I ask again, is there any American who wants to see our defense budget reduced further?

We have made the mistake more than once. Let us consider what a single mistake of this kind cost us in money alone—not to mention hundreds of thousands of American lives.

In 1913, at the start of the First World War, the national debt was a little over a billion dollars. That war heavily taxed our resources; and a few years later we went through the greatest depression of them all.

A new President came in. He helped those people who wanted work but couldn't find a job. He did so because he believed that human dignity was better for the nation than poverty and want.

At the time we started, somewhat leisurely, rearming for the Second World War, the national debt was around $40 billion. Today this debt is about $257 billion. Could there ever be clearer proof of the cost of unpreparedness?

If reports received from behind the iron curtain are correct, in a short time Russia will be at its strongest position in armaments; and under their present program that position will increase steadily year by year. So, I say today that further reduction in our payment for national security is unthinkable.

Our able and conscientious Secretary of Defense, Louis Johnson, is doing everything possible to promote true unification of the services which will guarantee the taxpayer maximum security at minimum cost. He is doing a fine job. But, it was Mr. Johnson himself who said recently that our "watchword should be military security first, economy second."

Both he and our President were front-line fighters in one war waged to preserve our way of life. They know that peace can be lost—but they know also, and you know, that the current price to America of losing any modern war is slavery.

I remind you that there is little, if any, peace in the world today. We don't have peace just because the guns are silent. Tragically, we do have "fronts" where the shooting could begin at any time; and no one knows when or where!

The history of Texas is the history of a battle for independence. May you in this great state, and in all our other states, remember the cost of such battles. When those who want to represent us in the halls of our government consistently close their request for votes with the stressing of two words—peace and prosperity—let us remember the long rows of those who have passed on to us another heritage, and who believed that we in turn would pass that heritage on to our children, and our children's children. Let us ask our statesmen to add a third word to the appeal of "peace" and "prosperity." From Sam Houston to Sam Rayburn one word is engraved on the heart of every Texan, every true American. That word is freedom.

NATIONAL DEFENSE [7]

LOUIS A. JOHNSON [8]

Mr. Louis Johnson, Secretary of Defense, gave this address before the Overseas Press Club of America, at the Waldorf-Astoria Hotel, New York, on Friday evening, March 3, 1950.

The problems which Secretary Johnson dealt with included: (1) Has our program to develop postwar military and political strength among our allies against Russia been successful? (2) Is our program of developing national defense with respect to the Navy, Air Force and Army and military equipment sufficient to meet all emergencies? (3) Is our political and military policy as it relates to China and Southeastern Asia a satisfactory one?

The student of this speech should weigh its statements and its evident persuasive techniques against the contemporary facts and subsequent developments. Critics, alarmed at the expansion of Soviet Russia and her satellites, especially the Communist victory in China and threat of further territorial inroads, condemned the Johnson speech as filled with confident and unwarranted generalizations. Some of the wide adverse criticism offered against Johnson at this time stemmed from the responsibilities piled upon him during the year 1949. He was required to enforce the unification of military services; to cut the combined budget (Congress and the people so demanded), and to determine what share each branch of service should have of that budget. The opponents of Johnson were charging that the armed might of Soviet Russia was much greater than that of the United States and its allies. This disparity, it was held, was due to the sharp cut of our defense budget from some $22 billion to $15 billion, with some $13 billion recommended for the coming fiscal year. This last-named figure, the critics charged, would not give us the minimum necessary defense in any sudden war. It was in this atmosphere of indictment and against such charges that Johnson spoke. He would reassure, mollify, and, if possible, further establish for the press and American opinion his personal leadership and that of his administrative colleagues.

The speaker, forceful on his feet, ready in extempore debate or discussion, always communicative, has had much earlier speech experience. He was president of the class of 1912 at the University of Virginia; president of the Johnson Literary Society, a debating club; winner of the intercollegiate oratorical contest of the University of Virginia in 1911;

[7] Text furnished by the Department of National Defense, Office of Public Information.

[8] For biographical note, see Appendix.

represented the University of Virginia at the Southern Intercollegiate Division contest in 1911 at the University of Alabama; and was elected to membership in Delta Sigma Rho. His later career in law, the Army, his national presidency of the American Legion, and his various government posts all called for continual speaking and contributed to his maturing as a highly capable public speaker.

A year ago today I became to the members of the Overseas Press Club, and to reporters everywhere, a commodity, an intangible commodity that you newspapermen dignify under the name "news." I became "news" on that day when President Truman announced at his press conference that he would nominate me for Secretary of Defense.

On practically every one of the 365 days that have passed since that day, some reporter, some editorial writer, some columnist, some commentator, or some cartoonist has found some opportunity to express himself on the Department of Defense. Tonight the tables are reversed. You are giving me the chance to express myself on the American press.

Let me say at the outset that I share with the American people a profound respect for our press and for your right to report and interpret news as you see it. That is your right—your freedom. Under "press" I include the radio, the pictures, television, and all other media of expression that report news and influence public opinion. On the whole, you have been eminently fair to me. True, you may not always have looked at the news as it appeared to me, and there have been times when I wondered whether both of us were looking at the same thing. Such differences are inherent to our democratic process.

Well, tonight I am a reporter myself—by command of your own President, Frank Kelley.

When Mr. Kelley came to the Pentagon to invite me to speak tonight I asked him what he would like to have me talk about.

"Why not report?" he asked, "Why not report where we stand, what problems lie ahead? Why not?"

Well, you asked for it, so for tonight, at least, I am a reporter —a reporter among reporters and their friends of the Overseas Press Club of America.

Let me open my report in the form of a lead paragraph. If I tried to sum up in a few words the answers to the questions, where do we stand, what problems lie ahead, I might perhaps put it in this way:

Off to a slow start and almost left standing at the post, the United States is now making substantial gains toward the achievement of its goal of peace through strength. America's condition is sound and is getting stronger. In Europe, the situation is improving. In Asia, it bears watching.

Now let us spell out this summary in greater detail.

Let's go back to V-J Day. The United States and her Allies had just won a terrific life-and-death struggle. Our margin of victory was so pronounced, and the possible rise of a contender to challenge our position was so remote that we planned to rest on our gains and relax. Our armed forces, we demobilized. Our war production machine, we shifted in gear to meet peace requirements. To friend and foe, we extended in all sincerity a warm heart and a firm hand. We poured out billions to hasten their economic recovery and strengthen their political stability. Our most precious military secrets, acquired by us through sweat and at tremendous cost, we stood ready to convert to the service of peace. Never in the history of mankind did a people manifest a more noble spirit of good will to all. Never was there a finer demonstration of altruism by a nation toward all of civilization.

We had every reason to be proud of our demonstration of good will to all mankind and our readiness to support it by action. Some of our erstwhile friends, however, even though they benefited most from our help when they most desperately needed it, chose to scorn our nation. They laughed at our losses, mocked at our gains, and deliberately did everything in their power to impugn our honorable motives. Wherever we came to help, they intervened to hinder. While we marched toward peace, they threw up road blocks and tossed around vetoes. At first we were patient. But realizing the state of such an international environment, we finally reacted in characteristic American fashion. We did something about it.

In succession, we created the Truman Doctrine and the Marshall Plan. We set up the Economic Cooperation Administration. We signed with eleven other nations the North Atlantic Pact. We embarked on a Mutual Defense Assistance Program with our friends under the North Atlantic Pact. In the challenge of the Berlin Airlift we showed that the American stamina, courage, and resourcefulness are forces still to be conjured with. We have strengthened our ramparts. We are carrying out the mandate of the Congress and the President backed by the will of the American people to unify our forces. We are determined to be strong and through strength to maintain peace for ourselves and for all the world.

We would have preferred to spend our money and our energies differently. There is no human gain developing hydrogen bombs or stockpiling the atomic variety for destruction when an equal amount of energy in a similar effort toward production for peace could make life so much more secure and happy for ourselves and for everybody else. Unfortunately, we have no alternative at the moment but to be prepared.

Where do we stand? Farther ahead than ever in our peacetime history. We are alert to the dangers of our times. We are girding our loins accordingly. We are getting into condition. We are removing waste. We are eliminating fancy trimmings. We are converting fat to muscle. We are releasing civilians and men in uniform whose jobs do not contribute directly to national defense. By getting rid of what we no longer need for national defense, we get that much more money with which to meet our pressing requirements in men and munitions. We are taking officers away from desks and assigning them to the field for combat training. We are approaching the problem of reserves realistically, and are setting up a strong nucleus capable of orderly, rapid expansion in an emergency. We are getting more defense value out of every appropriated dollar than ever before. We are getting deliveries on weapons and equipment. We are ordering the manufacture of items now which will keep us up to date.

We may not have all the bombs, or all the planes, or all the submarines, or all the carriers, or all the tanks, or all the guns to carry on a war today; and we never will have enough to satisfy everybody concerned with national defense. The jaws of Mars are traditionally wide open and his appetite is insatiable.

We are tailoring our defense to fit today's situation. We face danger from one source. And we are determined to make ourselves strong in the most effective ways to thwart his aggressive intentions and capabilities.

I can say to you tonight, that the Air Force today is in its best state of combat readiness since the war.

Secretary Symington and General Vandenberg, the latter having only recently returned from an extensive tour of foreign stations, advise me that the esprit of officers and men is high. General Vandenberg states the combat readiness of the Air Force units he inspected was unexcelled at any time since the demobilization at the end of the war.

As for the United States Navy, let me repeat what Admiral Forrest P. Sherman, Chief of Naval Operations, has just put in a special message to all Navy personnel:

Navy Department is exerting every effort to translate available appropriations into maximum fighting strength and mobilization potential. Savings made are generally available for increasing the state of readiness of authorized forces. Economies already effected have permitted increasing previously planned fleet strength by one large carrier and one cruiser, to provide additional equipment for antisubmarine warfare, and to augment general readiness. Planned economies are an important contributing factor in retaining two additional Marine battalions.

And as for the Army, this is what General J. Lawton Collins, Chief of Staff, said to a New Orleans audience only a few days ago:

We have units that are ready to move right now in case of aggression; we have the best men in the Army today that we have ever had in peacetime and, although we have a number of critical equipment problems yet to solve, I can assure you that our troops, with the equipment that they have, would give a good account of themselves if we were attacked.

The recent reduction of our occupation commitments has enabled us to concentrate more of our efforts upon strengthening the combat units which form the hard core of our fighting force. We are giving our divisions and other combat units more officers and men, some items of better weapons and equipment, and improved training under field conditions.

Let me add for the benefit especially of all Army men that our success in converting fat into muscle enables us to allot to the Army approximately $150 million for new postwar models in tanks and anti-aircraft equipment, and for the modernization of other existing weapons.

In the meantime, the dread of being caught with inadequate supplies is real, and it rises to torment all of us responsible for the production and distribution of munitions. I know what it is myself. I sympathize with it. I experienced it as an infantry officer on the western front in the First World War when it looked as though my outfit would run out of rations or ammunition. And then again, between 1937 and 1940, when I was the Assistant Secretary of War responsible for current procurement and industrial mobilization, the dread of shortages gave me constant concern. I had many sleepless nights worrying about the acute need for bombers and fighters for the growing Army Air Force, which was my special concern. I understood the struggle of the Chief of Ordnance, the Quartermaster General, and the heads of other departments for larger shares of the national defense pie.

I have that same concern today, and I understand the worries of the Secretaries of the Army, the Navy, and the Air Force. I am sure, too, that the President of the United States understands them. He, too, had sleepless nights on the Western Front in 1918 worrying about food and ammunition for the artillerymen of his beloved Battery "D". When I now stand before him to plead for a larger share of the national budget to meet the defense needs, I know he understands. He wishes, and so do all of us, that we could meet all of the demand of our armed forces.

If we did, we would certainly feel a lot happier about our ability to hasten an enemy's defeat. But, unfortunately, if we gave our Army, our Navy, and our Air Force all the equipment that they felt they needed, our budget would have to be greatly increased; and there is a limit to expenditures beyond which we dare not go without destroying the very free American system which enables us to have the strength with which to maintain peace.

Hence, to keep adequately prepared, we must always be alert to the intentions and the capabilities of a possible foe, and a most convenient yardstick in gauging this is a comparison of relative strengths. How many long-range bombers do we have? How many does he have? How many submarines do we have? How many does he? What can ours do? What can his do? How many divisions do we have? How many does he? And what are the relative capabilities of the respective tanks?

Comparisons such as these are very important, but there are other factors in the measurement of a nation's ability to wage war successfully, and they, too, must be considered. What of the relative capabilities of mass production, of industrial know-how, of national morale, and of potential allies and their capabilities? When all these factors are considered and added to the defense programs now under way, it must make an aggressor hesitate to start an attack, if he is at all prudent.

The forces we already have in being, plus what our potential allies are developing, should tend to discourage aggressive action. For the security and the peace of the world look not only to American manpower, American industry, and American weapons, but also to the formidable British Navy and the Royal Air Force. They count also on a French Army and a French Marine now growing in strength. They count on the potential of all of our partners under the North Atlantic Pact who, with their own efforts plus our aid, are arming for the defense of our common ideal.

We took calculated risks in aiding Europe when it looked as though the spread of communism could not be halted. Our investment is now paying off. The hunger, the disorder, and the frustration in which communism is fostered no longer prevail. There is a new hope and a new confidence.

The situation is more encouraging than at any time since V-J Day. While there is no warrant for complacency yet it is an occasion for some satisfaction. We have held communism at bay in Western Europe. We have gained partners in Europe to help maintain a free world.

While Russia has been making satellites, we have been adding partners, and there is the big difference between their ways and ours. It has always been our attitude to support the rights of states, large and small, to determine for themselves, without external pressure, how they wish to be governed. It is the doctrine of the inalienable rights of the individual stated so forcefully in our own Declaration of Independence applied to peoples. It is the inalienable right of peoples to enjoy security, freedom and a decent standard of living. These are rights we recognize. We will not be pushed around, and we do not like to see others pushed around.

Woodrow Wilson had this in mind when he proposed that "No nation should seek to extend its policy over any other nation or people, but that every people should be left free to determine its own policy, its own way of development, unlimited, unthreatened, unafraid, the little along with the great and powerful."

Franklin D. Roosevelt reiterated it when he insisted that "The rights of every nation, large or small, must be respected and guarded as jealously as are the rights of every individual within our own Republic."

Finally, President Truman implemented this ideal into action when he declared: "I believe that we must assist free peoples to work out their own destinies in their own way."

We have not always lived up to our own ideals, but beginning with the administration of Franklin D. Roosevelt we have consistently adhered to them. This doctrine of the equality of states and the recognition of their legitimate national aspirations has been approved whole heartedly by the American people and is now basic to the policy that guides us in our present relationship with other peoples. It is especially important that we keep these principles in mind when we look at the present situation in Asia.

In Asia we are confronted with formidable dynamic movements of human forces. First is the old Russian imperialist design under a new red cloak. It would control the strategic areas of North Asia and penetrate into every part of South Asia. The attempt at domination of Asia by any one country, if successful, would be a most serious threat to our security.

Second is the awakening of the national consciousness of millions of people in the Orient now determined to govern themselves. All of Southeast Asia is alive with national hopes and aspirations. It is a spirit that we as Americans should certainly understand. It is our example of 1776 and our Declaration of Independence which so greatly inspire this movement. Much depends on these new nations of Asia, their peoples, and their governments. They will have difficulty in standing alone, and require the help of friends just as we did in our early days to set us on our course.

The chief obstacle to our efforts to help is the spread of communism. In and of itself, communism is foreign to the progressive minds emerging in the Orient. These public leaders who chafed under the yokes of foreign exploitation and helped cast it off would hardly substitute the more loathsome saddle of the Soviet. Unfortunately, these peoples face misery and want. They lack experience in self-government. What may be but a momentary success may leave a permanent mark on their national pattern; and the spread of Communist powers in China is an example of the dangers inherent in the situation.

Faced with the full implications of these movements, we are following these general principles. We are trying to maintain a quarantine of Soviet communism wherever we feel that our efforts have a reasonable chance of success. We are judiciously applying our resources to help build a healthy, strong community of free Indo-Pacific nations founded on equality and friendship. We are developing the security and the well-being of Japan, the Ryukyus, and the Philippines. Our specific actions will depend upon time and circumstances.

Our specific actions in the future as in the past, will involve certain risks, calculated risks, that a strong, reasonable and confident people dare take and must take in a dangerous age. Risks will be taken only when the promise for the success of the venture is more than reasonably good. We do not promise the unattainable.

We do not and cannot promise, for instance, full immunity to all of America against atomic attack. There is a risk to living in the middle of the twentieth century instead of an earlier age which all of us must share. It is a risk that every community must take in an atomic age. We must reconcile ourselves to the fact that in case of war, some atomic raids might penetrate our cordon of defense, no matter how strong we make it. Some enemy pilot with the zeal and the fanaticism of a Kamikaze might get through our net on a one-way suicide mission, and the

United States might get hurt. No amount of money appropriated for national defense can prevent this possibility. We are spending $13 billion a year, and that is a terrific outlay. If we put all that money in air defense to the exclusion of all other forces needed for victory, we still could not guarantee against the possibilities of bombs falling on an American city. No one could honestly guarantee against the possibility of a suicide pilot eluding our air defense even if we spent twice or three times that amount, or even $50 billion a year.

This is what we can do and will do: We can build a strong air defense. We can make enemy raids costly—so costly that the attrition rate will destroy so many of his bombers that he will find himself unable to continue his attack. We can make retribution so deadly that he will wish he had never started. These will be the objectives of our defensive system. These are the goals of our present plans.

There are risks in these plans. Each is the risk of a prudent and energetic people whose economy is sound, whose courage is firm, and who faces the future unafraid; a people dedicated to peace and justice who today see no surer way to realize their ideals than through strength. Peace through strength is the goal of our defense program. To its achievement, I pledge you the full support of the unified national defense team.

And that, Gentlemen of the Press, is my story—my report to you.

HYDROGEN BOMB

THE HYDROGEN BOMB AND INTERNATIONAL GOVERNMENT [1]

HAROLD C. UREY [2]

Professor Harold C. Urey, of the University of Chicago Institute for Nuclear Studies, gave this address at the annual Roosevelt Day Dinner, at the Waldorf-Astoria Hotel, New York City, on January 27, 1950. The speech was broadcast by Columbia Broadcasting Company at 11:15 to 11:30 P.M. (EST). The dinner, one of eighteen throughout the country, was sponsored by the Americans for Democratic Action, to commemorate President Franklin D. Roosevelt's birthday anniversary, January 30.

Paul A. Porter, former Price Administrator, was toastmaster. Senator Frank P. Graham, of North Carolina, also spoke. A sketch, written by Marc Connelly and Howard Lindsay, recreating historic broadcasts of Roosevelt's White House career, was given.

Dr. Urey was the "first atomic scientist to speak out publicly about the hydrogen bomb." [3] His prestige as winner of the Nobel Prize in chemistry for his discovery of heavy hydrogen, and as key member of the atomic development program, gave immense prestige to his remarks.

On January 31, 1950, President Truman announced that this country would proceed with the making of the hydrogen bomb. General debate and discussion followed in the Senate and over the national networks.

Dr. Urey, widely experienced as a speaker, is unusually effective before popular, as well as scientific audiences. On December 29, 1949, for example, he participated with much speaking ability in a panel discussion on "the philosophy of speech in a democratic society," at a general session of the 1949 Convention of the Speech Association of America, at Chicago. He is an able extemporizer. [4]

I am happy to be addressing the members and friends of Americans for Democratic Action especially on the occasion of your Second Annual Roosevelt Day. The courage and daring of

[1] Text supplied by the Americans for Democratic Action. Permission for this reprint through the courtesy of Dr. Urey.

[2] For biographical note, see Appendix.

[3] William L. Laurence. New York *Times*. January 28, 1950.

[4] For further comment on Dr. Urey, see *Representative American Speeches*, 1945-46, p95-108.

Franklin D. Roosevelt made possible the long gamble that led to the development of atomic power. It is appropriate then, on this occasion, to discuss further developments in this field. I trust as well that these views of mine will be helpful to the ADA when it considers this whole question at its April convention in Washington.

Recently a very great service has been done for the people of the United States by Senator Johnson [Democrat of Colorado]. Quite unwittingly, and I believe unwillingly, he has brought to the attention of the people of the United States a problem which should have been considered by them a very long time ago, but because of the unwillingness of the United States officials to take the people into their confidence had not previously been brought before us. Most of the facts in regard to this have appeared occasionally in the newspapers, but most people have believed that the discussions were on a par with a great deal of the hysteria in regard to atomic bombs. I refer to the so-called hydrogen bomb. The Alsop brothers are my authority for the statement that this problem was considered in 1945 by President Truman, and on the advice of two prominent scientists it was decided that no development of this weapon should be made. I was not aware that such a decision had been made, and I think few people in the United States were aware of it.

These decisions in regard to the hydrogen bomb have been made in an almost unbelievable atmosphere. These people who decided we should not develop it believed that the USSR could not get the ordinary atomic bomb in less than ten or fifteen years. Time has proved them incorrect on this point. Moreover, due to some curious prejudice which I think I understand, the advisers to the United States government have not wished to follow certain lines of development in regard to this problem. No such prejudice exists among the Canadians, British, French and presumably the USSR, and this has put the United States in a very unfavorable position relative to what might have been, even though we decided not to build the bomb. I cannot be more specific without disclosing technical information, which it is not my intention to do at all. The result of this is a situation highly dangerous to the United States, in fact, we may have already lost the armaments race.

The question before us is this: Should the hydrogen bomb be built? First of all, it has been publicly reported for several years that such bombs would have a capacity of the order of one thousand times the capacity of the atomic bomb which has been developed in the past. It has been reported that if such bombs were dropped off the Pacific Coast of the United States the prevailing winds would carry the radioactivity over this country and would result in the extinction of all forms of life. I cannot vouch for the accuracy of this statement, but the effects of the radioactivity would certainly be far greater than those so dramatically exhibited at the Bikini Baker-Day bomb test. It is unnecessary to emphasize the great undesirability of such bombs in the world. I think it is something we all hope very much cannot in the nature of things be done. I personally hope very much that the bombs will not explode, no matter how much effort is put into the project. However, nature does not behave in the way I should like at times, and so there is no use in engaging in wishful thinking. I think we should assume that the bomb can be built.

The Alsop brothers say that the cost would be two to four billion dollars for the development of these bombs. This I doubt seriously. I am not connected with this project in any way, but it is difficult to see how the development itself should cost more than a hundred million dollars exclusive of the cost of materials. It would of course involve a considerable scientific and engineering talent, which I would much prefer to see employed on peacetime developments.

But let us turn to what the situation is in the world today. I think we should not be complacent in regard to what other countries can do in this respect, as many people were in connection with the development of the ordinary atomic bomb. To be specific, let us assume that the USSR is developing this bomb; and suppose that she should get it first. Then it seems to me that there is nothing in the temperament of the present negotiations between east and west that would lead us to believe that the rulers of the USSR would not reason approximately as follows:

It is true that the bomb is exceedingly dangerous, and we would not wish to produce so much radioactivity in the world as to endanger ourselves and the people of Russia, but the explosion of a few of these bombs will win us the world. Therefore we will build these bombs and issue ultimata to the western countries, and the millenium of communism will be with us immediately. After this the universal government of the USSR will abolish all stocks of bombs and no more will ever be made in the world.

This is a very good argument. In fact, I doubt if any bombs would need to be exploded. The atomic bomb is a very important weapon of war, but hardly decisive, as everybody has emphasized from the beginning. But I wonder if the hydrogen bomb would not be decisive, so that ultimata would be accepted and it would be unnecessary to deliver the bombs. This seems to me to be the situation.

In view of such a situation the United States can decide to intentionally lose the armaments race, which is what our decisions to date have amounted to. Suppose instead of deciding this, we decide we will build the hydrogen bomb. Suppose that we get the hydrogen bomb first. Then what do we do? Do we merely wait until the USSR also has it and we have a stalemate? It is quite out of character for the democracies to deliver ultimata with the philosophy I have ascribed to the Russian government. This is one of the things which I cannot answer, and which I merely put before you. Suppose we develop the hydrogen bomb, and suppose we get it first. Then what do we do next?

Suppose that two countries have the hydrogen bomb. Is it not believable that sooner or later an incident may occur which would make these bombs be used? This is a question again which I cannot answer definitely. I would say, however, that the probability that a war will start is increased if two groups each believe that they can win the war. This is true regardless of weapons and their magnitude. It is very difficult to get an exact balance of power. This is what we know in physical sciences as a situation of unstable equilibrium; one like balancing an egg on its end. The slightest push topples the egg in one direction or another. I have maintained, and many of my friends have maintained, that the only constructive way to solve the present situation is by adopting the Atlantic Union Resolution now in the Senate and House of the Congress of the United States, looking forward to a federal union of the democratic countries. Only in this way will we be able to maintain an overpowering political, commercial, military and ideological strength relative to the east. Only in this way do we have an enormous unbalance of power, so that perhaps the one side does not attempt to start a war because they recognize that they cannot win, and the other side does not need to start a war because the weaker side cannot attack. If this organization were perfected in the next few years there would be no question about the strength of the west, and this, regardless of the existence of any type of bombs in the world, might lead to a peaceful solution of the problem.

My own conclusion in regard to this problem is, first, I am very unhappy to conclude that the hydrogen bomb should be developed and built. I do not think we should intentionally lose the armaments race; to do this will be to lose our liberties, and with Patrick Henry, I value my liberties more than I do my life. It is important that the spirit of independence and liberty should continue to exist in the world. It is much more important that this spirit continue to exist than that I or you or any group should continue this mortal existence for a few years more. Second, there is no constructive solution to the world's problems except eventually a world government capable of establishing law over the entire surface of the earth. It is necessary to take whatever steps we possibly can in that direction, and to take them as rapidly as possible—any steps of any kind whatever that move in this direction, including the United Nations, all of the international organizations sponsored by the UN, the establishment of an Atlantic Union over the democratic countries of the world which understand each other from the standpoint of political institutions, general philosophy of life, and religions, and the extension of any such organization to as much of the rest of the world as possible and in as short a time as possible. May I emphasize, this is the only constructive direction in which to work in connection with the whole problem.

I wish to say in conclusion that I am much indebted to Senator Johnson for having dramatized this situation so that you and I can discuss it intelligently. Now, if he or someone else will only do the same thing for peacetime uses of atomic energy I shall be very grateful indeed. In fact, if we would only forget secrecy and regard it as the wholly unimportant subject that it is, progress in all lines of scientific activity of benefit to the United States and to the world would be enormously increased.

HOW CAN WE SECURE PEACE IN A HYDROGEN BOMB WORLD? [5]

George V. Denny, Jr., Senator Brien McMahon, and H. V. Kaltenborn [6]

Senator Brien McMahon, chairman of the Joint Congressional Committee on Atomic Energy, and H. V. Kaltenborn, "dean of American commentators," participated on Thursday evening, February 14, 1950, in one of the regular Town Hall debates. The program which originated in the Town Hall, New York, was released over the network of the American Broadcasting Company, and was telecast.

These Town Hall programs, given continuously since May 30, 1935, have several million listeners each week. Crucial issues are frankly debated or discussed. The speakers are invariably authorities on the topic and are excellent speakers. George V. Denny has used good judgment in developing the weekly programs and is himself a highly acceptable radio and face-to-face speaker.

The topic was a highly disturbing and controversial one in February 1950. Senator McMahon, for example, had addressed the Senate on the subject on February 2, and Kaltenborn in his radio commentaries had already discussed the problem several times.

In the Town Hall debate each speaker presented his case compactly and concretely. Kaltenborn's reply is largely a series of specific questions, which, however, go to the heart of the problem.

This Town Hall program is to be studied for the techniques of radio composition and for its demonstration of debating methods. The critic, judging the analysis, structure, language, audience adjustment, and refutation will attempt to answer the question, "Who won the debate?"

Senator McMahon is recognized as one of the outstanding Senate speakers. Mr. Kaltenborn continues with great success his long established career as radio news commentator. [7]

McMahon, both in Norwalk High School and at Fordham University, participated in forensic activities. He states: "My method of speech preparation is, I suppose, quite commonplace. Where a major address is concerned, I find it necessary to go through several rough drafts before

[5] Reprinted from the *Bulletin of America's Town Meeting of the Air*, vol. 15, no. 42, February 14, 1950. By permission of the speakers and by special arrangement with Town Hall, Inc., and through the courtesy of the American Broadcasting Company.

[6] For biographical notes, see Appendix.

[7] For further comment on H. V. Kaltenborn, consult the Cumulated Author Index in this volume.

the speech begins to please me. I am definitely a member of the blood, sweat, and tears school. Whatever pleasure I may derive from a satisfying phrase resides in looking at the finished product rather than going through the tortuous process of composition." [8]

ANNOUNCER: Of course, you've heard the press referred to as the fourth estate, but do you know how the name originated? So far as we know, the first reference to the press as the fourth estate was made by Thomas Carlyle about the reporters' gallery in the English Parliament. The three estates were the legislative, executive, and judicial departments of the government. "But," said Carlyle, "in the reporters' gallery yonder sits a fourth estate more important far than all."

Radio has been referred to, for much the same reason, as the "fifth estate," for its power and influence have already been used to elect and defeat candidates for public office, to stage revolutions, and to help hold the people of a police state in subjugation.

Wisely used, this fifth estate may inform and keep a nation free. Your Town Meeting is dedicated to this high purpose. You can help achieve this purpose by reminding your friends and neighbors to listen to Town Meeting each week.

Now to preside over our discussion, here's your moderator, the President of Town Hall, founder of America's Town Meeting, Mr. George V. Denny, Jr. Mr. Denny.

MODERATOR DENNY: Good evening, neighbors. On that fateful day in August 1945, when the atomic bomb destroyed the city of Hiroshima in Japan, we were at war. A feeling of elation spread over the country then. We felt sure that this would mean the end of World War II, and it did.

But when President Truman announced last week that we would attempt to build a hydrogen bomb one thousand times more destructive than the one used at Hiroshima, a feeling of fear and a sort of numbness gripped the hearts of men as they pondered the meaning of this step.

In desperate awareness of its meaning, Senator Brien McMahon, chairman of the Joint Committee on Atomic Energy, rushed to the floor of the Senate with a challenging plan to curb the armament race by devoting $50 billion [to peace], at the

[8] Letter to this editor, May 1, 1950.

rate of $10 billion a year, by reducing two thirds of our expenditures on armaments on condition that Russia do the same, and with the understanding that these funds would be administered by the United Nations for relief and rehabilitation around the world and including the people of the Soviet Union.

Obviously, Senator McMahon believes that this plan will promote peace. It's the first plan to receive nationwide recognition since the announcement that we would make a hydrogen bomb. So we invited the Senator from Connecticut to discuss it here tonight in company with Mr. H. V. Kaltenborn, dean of American radio commentators and a distinguished foreign correspondent, who has some questions to raise about the Senator's plan.

We hear first from Senator Brien McMahon, Democrat of Connecticut, member of the Senate Foreign Relations Committee, and chairman of the Joint Committee on Atomic Energy. Senator McMahon.

SENATOR McMAHON: Thank you, Mr. Denny. Ladies and gentlemen, I'm very happy to be here before this fine audience tonight and particularly to be in the company of a most distinguished American, Mr. Hans Kaltenborn, to discuss this very grave question with him.

To understand what the hydrogen bomb means as a weapon, we should consult the scientists. They are the best qualified witnesses on this subject.

Dr. Urey, a Nobel prize winner, says that the hydrogen bomb will be one thousand or more times as powerful as the atomic bomb.

Dr. Hans Bethe, one of the foremost scientists of our time, declares that the H-bomb will exceed the A-bomb in destructive power as tremendously as the A-bomb exceeds old-fashioned TNT explosives.

Dr. Albert Einstein, the most famous scientist in the world, declares that the hydrogen bomb brings destruction of all life on earth "within the range of technical possibilities." Dr. Einstein adds, "There beckons more and more clearly general annihilation."

This, ladies and gentlemen, is what the scientists say about hydrogen warfare. Their words drive home and underscore in red what some of us have known and said all along.

A world which contains ever-growing stocks of atomic weapons, a world which tolerates a mad atomic-armaments race is not the kind of world in which human freedom can flourish or even hold its own. We Americans want peace with all our hearts. We seek a just peace whose terms and conditions will appeal to the consciences of all mankind, including the large fraction of mankind walled off behind Russia's iron curtain.

We have tried and tried and tried again to get a just agreement for international control of the atom. Why have all our earnest efforts to achieve atomic peace been stymied?

The Kremlin and the Communist iron curtain are responsible. The people of Russia, I am sure, want peace as sincerely and heartily as we do, but they have not been allowed to know the facts. The iron curtain has been used to keep them in ignorance of the danger from atomic energy.

The Russian people have not been allowed to know that our hand is extended in friendship. This is why I say that we must create a window in the iron curtain and through it deliver our message of peace and good will to the people whose minds have been poisoned against us.

At present, we transmit "Voice of America" radio broadcasts behind the iron curtain, but these should be called the "whisper of America." We spend less money on them than we do in the mere advertising of cosmetics.

I am confident that a bold and strenuous effort can pierce the curtain, can bring to the imprisoned Russian people the knowledge that we seek to be their friends and to join hands with them amidst the blessings of atomic control. But if we are to gain the ear of the Russian people, we must prepare a special, worthwhile, dramatic, and sincere message to send them.

In a speech before the Senate, I suggested the kind of message which might be sent. My suggestion is that we offer to take two thirds of the money we now spend upon armaments and use it through the United Nations to help all other nations, including Russia, provided that all other nations would agree to dependable atomic control and also agree to spend two thirds of their own armaments budgets for peace.

Such an American offer would give visible proof that we stand ready to do our share—and more than our share—in the great task of directing all our efforts, and particularly our efforts in the field of atomic energy, toward human welfare and ennoblement.

Such an offer might prove to be the prelude to a new spirit of cooperation among the nations. Such an American offer might set off a worldwide and irresistible moral crusade for peace.

The response of plain people throughout America to this speech has been truly amazing. I have received thousands of letters and telegrams expressing strong approval. They show that Americans everywhere are hungry for peace and eager to support any effort aimed toward peace, however bold and unconventional.

Ladies and gentlemen, we are engaged in a desperate race to fend off global disaster, with unimaginable benefits and blessings as our reward if we win that race. We cannot stand still and let disaster overtake us. We must act and act now through a daring new approach to atomic control.

MODERATOR DENNY: Thank you, Senator McMahon. Well, Mr. Kaltenborn, it's been your business since you started your newspaper work thirty-five years ago to analyze and appraise and sometimes criticize such plans as Senator McMahon has advanced. Will you give us the benefit of your counsel on this proposal? Mr. H. V. Kaltenborn, dean of American commentators.

MR. KALTENBORN: I join all true lovers of peace in thanking Senator McMahon for his challenging contribution to a momentous discussion. But let us not forget the important conditions that underlie his peace proposals.

In his Senate address, he told us that we cannot be less well armed than Russia. Hence, we must build the hydrogen bomb.

He admits that even the possession of this frightful weapon cannot give us positive security. But he labors under the delusion that we could live at peace with communism if the Kremlin would sign some kind of an agreement to reduce arms by two thirds.

His positive program has two parts: He would transform what he calls the present "whisper of America" into a resounding

"Voice of America," that would penetrate the iron curtain and sway the hearts and minds of the Russian people. Let us agree that this is worth trying. He would also offer $50 billion at the rate of $10 billion a year in return for a two thirds reduction in world armaments. Russia, of course, is to get her full share of the $50 billions if she will join.

The one solid feature of this arresting McMahon proposal is that it seeks to reduce *all* armaments. It admits that to limit only atomic warfare is futile. Germs, rockets, fire bombs, gasses, guided missiles can be just as deadly or destructive as atom bombs.

We killed more people in Tokyo in one two-hour fire raid than by dropping the atom bomb on Hiroshima. Let us not be so foolish as to believe that the mere elimination of atomic war would give us any positive security.

Will Russia sell us a guaranteed peace for X billion dollars? Would we believe her if she pretended to accept? Has the past taught us anything about the mentality of the Kremlin leaders?

Was the risk of war reduced when, at Teheran, we gave Russia Manchuria? At Yalta, when we gave her Poland? At Potsdam, when we gave her East Germany?

Did we promote peace in China when we sought to appease the Chinese Communists or was the risk of war reduced when we fought back and broke the Communist grip on Greece with American arms and American leadership?

Was the risk of war reduced or increased when we withdrew all military help from China, from her Nationalists, at a crucial moment because their government refused to share power with communism?

Was the risk of war increased or reduced when we broke the starvation blockade of Berlin by a proud demonstration of American air power?

If we buy off the Russians now, will they stay bought?

If we finally get an agreement by letting Russia whip us into more and more concessions, have we secured something that really binds the Kremlin?

Do Communists ever keep an oath, pledge, treaty, or agreement when they wish to break it?

As Senator McMahon told the Senate, an ineffective agreement is worse than no agreement at all. Look at Russia's record in the United Nations. Over a four-year period, she has vetoed every constructive proposal.

No, you can't buy peace from the Soviet Union. But we need not despair. We are strong and growing stronger. We have brought the major Atlantic powers into a pact of peace. That pact can be expanded to include other powers.

We are now providing the democratic powers with arms to halt aggression. We have rescued them from postwar depressions through the Marshall Plan. All the Communist powers, including Russia, were invited to share the benefits of the Marshall Plan. They can do so tomorrow if Russia has a change of heart.

I would have no objection to asking Russia once more if she wants to participate with us in European reconstruction, but we know from bitter experience that, in dealing with the Kremlin autocrats, we have only postponed peace by being too eager to buy peace. Yet, we have advanced the cause of peace whenever and wherever we showed ourselves prepared to fight for it.

Let us always be ready to lead the way whenever a new chance for peace is open, but let us always remain strong in arms, strong in allies among the world's free peoples, strong in generous dealing with those who need our help, and above all, strong in the justice of our cause—the defense of human freedom against those who challenge it.

MODERATOR DENNY: Thank you, Mr. Kaltenborn. Well, Senator McMahon, you can't answer all the editorial comments on your plan, but here is Mr. Kaltenborn who has laid himself open to your questions. Senator McMahon.

SENATOR MCMAHON: Well, I would like first, Mr. Denny, to comment on the theme that seems to run through Mr. Kaltenborn's remarks that I suggested that we offer a bribe to the Russians. Now I contend, of course, that I didn't do any such thing. There were some editorial writers, a few of them, in fact I know, that wrote that headline who hadn't even read the speech.

Now what is the definition of a bribe? I looked in the dictionary for it the other day and it says "a bribe is a price or a gift given to corrupt the conduct of a person in a position of trust." I didn't know that I had suggested anything to corrupt the Kremlin. (*Laughter*)

MR DENNY: It might be a good thing if you did, Senator. (*Laughter*)

SENATOR MCMAHON: Well, if you would define corruption as the effort to get them to see some reason, it would be an unusual use of the word, but then I would agree with you. But, frankly, you see what I have suggested, I believe, is evidence to all of the world as to what we really intend—what is in our hearts. There is no bribe in that, no more than when we offered the Marshall Plan to the whole world. Was that denominated as a bribe?

In any international agreement when offers are made from one nation to another or one nation to the world—take the ill-fated Kellogg-Briand Pact—was that a bribe that we gave to one another when we pledged our words that aggression should be outlawed? Of course, it was broken, but that you would hardly denominate—the offer that was made—as a bribe.

Don't you see, too, Mr. Kaltenborn, that in addition to that, I suggested that the Russians put their two thirds ino a common pot to be put into the United Nations fund for the purpose of doing what? For the purpose of advancing mankind's welfare; for the purpose of—through this great agency which we could make to live—bringing hope, and bringing bread to men everywhere—bringing that instead of destruction. Do you want me to continue to comment, or shall I give Mr. Kaltenborn a chance?

MR DENNY: I think we'd better give Mr. Kaltenborn a chance, and then these people out here in the audience are ready to hop—hop on both of you.

SENATOR MCMAHON: Fine, fine.

MR. DENNY: Thank you, very much, Senator. Mr. Kaltenborn.

MR. KALTENBORN: Well, obviously, Senator, I am not afraid that you're going to corrupt the masters of the Kremlin. I am afraid that you are going to corrupt the American people into believing that when the Kremlin, perhaps, responds to some sort of an appeal that that means that we've gotten anywhere.

What I tried to point out was that, on the basis of our experience, we cannot rely on what the Kremlin says. We can only rely on what the Kremlin does, and we must judge that by what the Kremlin has done.

Now if you honestly believe that the Kremlin will agree to reduce its entire armament by two thirds and keep it reduced, well, you believe something that I don't believe and that I hope you couldn't persuade the American people to believe.

MR. DENNY: Thank you, Mr. Kaltenborn. The Senator has a rejoinder here for just a moment.

SENATOR MCMAHON: Mr. Kaltenborn, I think it would be very unfortunate if we should confuse the scheme for the reduction of armaments with mere written pieces of paper. I am not so naive—and I'm sure that the American people do not believe that I am—that I would take the Kremlin's word for anything. That is why I suggested that we should condition the proposal which I made upon the Kremlin agreeing to a control plant that would have as its basis an inspection system—an inspection system which would serve the value of letting us know when a fire was going to start. This way, we are going to spend all our time watching for a fire to break out and spending all of our efforts to do it, too.

No, I am for a self-policing agreement which is the only kind of an agreement that the Russians, of course, can be trusted with.

GOVERNMENT AND POLITICS

PARTY CONFLICT AND THE MODERN DILEMMA [1]

THOMAS E. DEWEY [2]

This lecture was the second in a series of four on "The American Political System," given by Governor Thomas E. Dewey of New York, in Alexander Hall, Princeton University, under the auspices of the Woodrow Wilson School of Public and International Affairs.

The first two lectures, given on February 8 and 9, were entitled "The Two-Party System" and "Party Conflict and the Modern Dilemma"; the next two, given on April 12th and 13th, were "Making Foreign Policy Under a Two-Party System" and "Domestic Policies Under a Two-Party System."

Some thousand Princeton students listened on each occasion. Each speech was followed by an extended rough-and-tumble period of question and answer, in which the New York Governor, without evasion, gave further clarification of his hour-long exposition of applied political theory.

The four lectures were of a high order in thought and composition. The Governor drew on his wide background of political experience for enforcement of his general theses. Political critics found in these lectures highly intelligent and statesmanlike exposition of our past political patterns and equally mature and plausible statements concerning the wisest course of action in both domestic and foreign policies.

The section of the lecture included in this volume should be examined in relation to the entire series. Aware that in the 1948 campaign Dewey was judged, perhaps necessarily so, on the record of the Republicans in the Eightieth Congress, Dewey at Princeton made plain that the voter should gauge that party by its record in those states—for example, New York, New Jersey, Minnesota—where Republicans had been in control and had produced much responsible legislation. He thus lined up with the progressive Republican wing that supported "welfare" legislation.

The New York Governor at Princeton was a "new Dewey." He thought and talked at a level distinctly above that of the seasoned politician of national leadership who has his eye on future national conven-

[1] The text was furnished by Paul E. Lockwood, secretary to Governor Thomas E. Dewey. Reprinted through the courtesy of Governor Dewey.

[2] For biographical note, see Appendix.

tions. Dewey's intellectual insight combined with organizational and compositional clarity and interest give these lectures lasting distinction—whether or not they meant "burning the political bridges" of their author.[3]

One of the standard weapons of party conflict both between conventions and during campaigns is the effort to pin labels on individuals or movements, attractive or sinister, depending upon the point of view. On the whole, the Democratic Party in recent years has been more successful, but less scrupulous, than the Republicans in their use of political semantics.

One of the most intriguing words in the political lexicon is the word "liberal." It is a touchstone eagerly sought by almost every political group. After a long and useful life, it still has warmth and confers a kind of pleasant aura upon those who garb themselves in its benign appeal. The trouble is that the word has been used to describe widely differing views and objectives and it has been greatly corrupted.

The traditional meaning of the word "liberal" described a movement to restrict the power of government over the lives of people. It came into active use in the new age ushered in by the eighteenth century when the Western world was striking off the shackles of royal absolutism. Society was to be governed by new concepts of individual freedom, equality under the law, limited government, and the rule of law instead of the rule of men.

Two hundred years later, the transmutation of the word, as the alchemist would say, has become one of the wonders of our time. Part of the change has come from a broadly based movement to use the powers of government for humanitarian ends.

It is evident that over the last hundred years there has been some loss of control by the individual over his own life. The swift advances of technology, the shift from rural to urban life, the rise of great corporate enterprise and of great unions of labor, the increasing sensitivity and interdependence of our economy—all these have stemmed from the industrial society we have built. While the industrial revolution has brought a far higher standard of living for the individual it has also brought him new kinds

---

[3] For other comment on Dewey as speaker and examples of Dewey's former speeches, see the Cumulated Author Index at the end of this volume.

of insecurity. This, in turn, has bred a collective sense of need for wider control of the forces which everyone now recognizes are far beyond the control of any individual.

After the Western world had achieved freedom from absolutism in government, the industrial revolution developed great economic powers in private hands. In the name of liberalism, the power of the state has quite properly been used to limit abuses by the strong and to protect the individual from hazards entirely beyond his control.

While our devotional words politically are still "freedom," "liberty," "independence," "self-reliance," and "individual initiative," many of us find that their meaning has become less clear since the machine came of age. People have looked for a new way to make the old and beloved words fit the new time.

This is the opportunity which Big Government and its advocates have seized. To resolve the dilemma inherent in their desire to claim the name "liberal," they have changed its meaning along with the meaning of the word "freedom." According to the new meaning employed by the neo-liberals of Big Government, freedom in its classic sense meant only freedom to starve. The new meaning says that freedom really means freedom to receive from government all the comforts and security of life. In exchange the individual is expected to do the bidding of government.

The higher purpose of the modern collectivists teaches that the legal liberty of the Western world is "formal liberty" without substance and that "actual liberty," as they call it, must be substituted for the traditional freedoms. The practitioners of Big Governmen say that the old kind of liberty was "license for the few and economic serfdom for the many."

Not only in America, but all over the world, we see men use the word "liberalism" to promote the very policies of government which liberals rose up to destroy. This sinister distortion of the word has led many well-meaning and genuine liberals into a state of confusion. The really disturbing thing about it is that it leads to the unwitting acceptance by an increasing number of people of the instruments of totalitarianism.

In addition to warping the basic concept of liberalism, the corrupters have gone further. I have already indicated that technical advances have prepared people to accept modified concepts of liberty. The supercharged word which Big Government uses to induce them to go further is "welfare." The Big Government people have taken it over as a latter-day Ark of the Covenant. Moreover, they have succeeded in tricking a lot of Republicans into appearing to attack all welfare and that, of course, seems to a good many Americans like something akin to firing on the flag.

It must have been some very clumsy Republican—I do not know the origin of the phrase or who perpetrated it—who tried to pin the label, "welfare state," on Mr. Truman's government. Others joined in the clamor and, of course, the apologists for Big Government joyously accepted the epithet as a new instrument of party warfare. They admit they are running a welfare state. They are proud of it!

Of course, they are running a welfare state. There has never been a responsible government which did not have the welfare of its people at heart. I am proud of the fact that we in the State of New York have made great social welfare advances, as have most of the states.

Anybody who thinks that an attack on the fundamental idea of security and welfare is appealing to people generally, is living in the Middle Ages. Everybody wants welfare and security in one form or another. It makes no difference whether he is a day laborer who wants his social security or a small business man who wants the value of his savings.

Here, in the words of a great Democrat, is the hard core of the Republican position today. It is the basic issue between the parties. It is not the issue between all Republicans and all Democrats. There are Republicans and Democrats who believe every social advance we have made toward personal security in the last twenty years should be abolished. There are Republicans and Democrats who believe we should rush headlong toward total government security and supervision from the cradle to the grave and some even include nationalization of industry as part of the program.

Disregarding the minority views within the parties, and judging preponderant sentiment by the standards I set up in last night's lecture, the essential difference between the parties lies in the way "to protect liberty when the government's purposes are beneficent." Or, to put it another way, the issue lies in the means of achieving objectives without injury to other objectives. . . .

I reach four basic conclusions: First, Big Government denies the great fundamental that the primary purpose of all government is to preserve liberty. By asserting that security is the chief aim of our society, it seeks to turn our people to the lotus and away from the basic truth that without working and producing we perish.

Second, Big Government requires a special kind of permanent control and continuity and therefore inevitably moves in the direction of the one-party system. It seeks to collect and pay out such a large share of the people's income that any interruption of its multifarious activities would produce hardship and crisis. To carry out this purpose will require the transfer of the power of the public purse from the Congress to the Executive.

Third, Big Government, like dictatorships, can continue only by growing larger and larger. It can never retrench without admitting failure. It feeds on the gradual obliteration of state and local governments as elements of sovereignty and tends to transform them into districts and prefectures. By absorbing more than half of all the taxing power of the nation, Big Government now deprives the states and local governments of the capacity to support the programs they should conduct. In place of their own taxing powers, it offers them in exchange the counterfeit currency of federal subsidy.

Fourth, Big Government gradually destroys the mainspring of our society. It offers no incentives to those who must create the goods and services which provide the security. In the words of the ancient writer, it sings a siren song: "Cast in thy lot among us; let us have one purse." It levels all down and throttles the source of our strength which lies in the restless ambitions of the ten million centers of initiative in our individual businesses and on our farms.

In its debut in this country Big Government has enjoyed considerable success. That is because it has been living on past accumulations of capital and techniques in a period of prosperity growing out of the postwar, worldwide demand for everything America can produce.

It is a fair weather system. One of two perils will catch up with it. The first peril is in the high taxes, oppressive regulations, delays and frustrations due to massive bureaucracies, inflation of prices and the ominous threat to adequate production. Each of these factors has an obviously destructive effect. Price inflation is especially virulent because it nullifies the value of the security programs which Big Government uses to justify its existence. It also falls hardest on those in the middle income range—the white collar groups—the people with moderate, fixed incomes, such as teachers, scholars, clergy and engineers. No free society has ever survived without a successful middle group.

The other peril that will catch up with Big Government is that, like all governments, it will make mistakes. Whenever government is so powerful that its mistakes can destroy the nation, then you may be sure the nation will be destroyed. To this truth the people of Germany, Italy and Japan bear eloquent and tragic witness.

Human freedom demands that we develop a better way than that of Big Government. First of all we must begin by agreeing among ourselves what the goal of our society should be. I propose that our goal should be the same today as it has been for 175 years: to foster individual liberty as the only means to a society of opportunity and abundance.

For government to act against the insecurities of life in our modern society is not at all inconsistent with a system based on individual competition and reward for everything above those minimum security levels. We can build a floor under the uncertainties of life in our industrial economy without putting a ceiling on the height of our building.

Our time is faced with the problems of unemployment, old age, medical care, housing, discrimination and agricultural price stabilization. Each of these problems can and will be met. But the road to Washington is not the only road.

We can believe in traffic control without agreeing that all traffic regulations should be promulgated from Washington.

We can practice our religion without agreeing that the Federal Government should appoint and pay the clergy.

We can approve of marriage without having all marriage licenses issued by the Department of the Interior.

We must have a tougher and wiser view of the modern dilemma than Big Government offers to us. I propose that we set up criteria by which to judge government action as we seek to reconcile the deep-rooted individualism of our country with the problems of the machine age.

Does the particular welfare measure of government build up the independence and responsibility of the individual citizen or does it make him dependent and subservient?

Does a particular intervention by government widen or narrow the bounds of personal liberty?

Does the proposal deprive any group or segment of our people of any legitimate individual freedom of action they now enjoy?

Does it do by governmental action what people can and should do for themselves by voluntary action?

Does it remove to a distant seat of government power or responsibility that belong in the locality?

Does it remove from productive work a substantial number of people in order to administer the program?

Does it have a sound fiscal basis?

Not all of these criteria may be relevant in each case. But they all stand as signposts of the right road.

Our only battleship in service recently showed what happens when the channel course is not kept. It happens more quickly to battleships but it happens just as surely to governments and their people.

In a later lecture I shall attempt to apply these criteria across the broad range of public issues today.

The central problem of twentieth century politics remains unsolved. No nation, no system of government has yet succeeded in reconciling the age-old conflict between liberty and authority.

It is our great responsibility, as a people, to press for the solution of that conflict within the framework of our free system.

THE DEMOCRATIC PARTY [4]

HARRY S. TRUMAN [5]

President Harry S. Truman gave this address at the Jefferson Day dinner at Washington, D.C., on the evening of February 16, 1950. The dinner, held in the National Guard Armory, the largest hall in the capitol, was attended by some 5,300 Democrats who had paid $100 a plate. After expenses, some $450,000 would go to the party treasury.[6]

The speech was broadcast and telecast over nationwide outlets.

Vice President Alben W. Barkley, Sam Rayburn, Charles Luckman, the dinner chairman, and others in addition to the President, spoke. Eleven Democratic governors, labor union leaders, members of the judiciary, members of the cabinet, and many other municipal, state, and Federal office holders attended.

The speech was the utterance of a strong party man rather than a statesman. Many of the stylistic turns that marked the Truman campaign speeches of 1948 were present. The substance was not too original or closely reasoned. Plenty of attention-getting-and-holding elements were used and expertly blended with the frame of logical continuity.

The usual types of personal proof were followed. The Republicans were identified with everything bad, and the Democrats, their ancestors and present friends and conduct, were splendid. The Republicans were users of scare words like welfare and state and socialism. They belonged to the Union League Club. They were of the 80th, the do-nothing Congress. In 1934, '36, '40, '44 and '50 they made absurd predictions that failed to scare or be borne out. The Democrats, on the contrary, were (1) inheritors of the Jefferson-Jackson tradition, (2) frank, (3) truthful, (4) constructive, (5) interested also in balancing the budget, (6) responsible for present prosperity, (7) non-socialistic, (8) determined to protect economic and other freedoms. There was no mention of the Taft-Hartley law, no eulogy of the 81st Congress. Rather the generalizations were skillfully calculated to appease many of the industrialists present.

The audience received the speech with applause and laughter, but hardly with the unrestrained enthusiasm evoked so often by Roosevelt and sometimes by Truman.

The Jefferson Day dinner speech should be compared in method and content with Truman's political speech at Kansas City on Thursday, September 29, 1949, honoring William M. Boyle, Jr., new chairman of the

[4] Text furnished by the White House.
[5] For biographical note, see Appendix.
[6] Carl Levin, in the New York *Herald Tribune,* February 17, 1950.

Democratic National Committee; and with the President's Labor Day speech at Pittsburgh on Monday, September 5, 1949. The Washington address echoes much of the sentiment of these earlier and more intimate utterances, but lacks some of the cleverness.

The President has become increasingly effective as a speaker since 1945. His constant formal speaking and press conferences, especially his "fighting" political speeches and rear platform talks, have given him fluency, confidence, and ample skill in audience adaptation.[7]

Fellow Democrats: This is a most remarkable dinner. This dinner and others like it throughout the land are evidence of the growing strength of the Democratic Party. They show that our party is determined, more than ever before, to carry its message to the voters of this country.

It is very significant that such great interest and enthusiasm are being shown in a Congressional election year. We know that Congressional elections are as important as presidential elections. We found out in 1946 how much harm can be done to our country when a Congressional election goes wrong. We are not going to let that happen again. We don't want another do-nothing 80th Congress.

These dinners carry forward a great tradition. The original Jefferson-Jackson dinner was held in this city in 1830, one hundred and twenty years ago. It was given in memory of Thomas Jefferson, and its guest of honor was President Jackson. At that first Jefferson-Jackson dinner, President Jackson gave his famous toast—"Our Federal Union, it must be preserved!"

Tonight, we meet again to think of our Federal Union, to be thankful that it has been preserved, and that it has grown in strength and in service to the people. As in Jackson's time, we meet to discuss some of the probems that our country faces.

We have some very serious problems today. We are living in a troubled period of the world's history. Our responsibilities, as a nation, have never been so great, and the decisions we face have never been more difficult. We confront serious questions of foreign policy. We have the problem of maintaing an adequate national defense. We have the task of maintaining prosperity

[7] For further comment on Truman as a speaker, see the introduction to and text of the "Madison Square Garden address," *Representative American Speeches: 1948-1949*, p110-21.

and protecting our economy from depression. We have the question of handling the nation's finances and the national debt.

These are grave issues. And the Democratic Party is meeting them squarely. We do not believe in trifling with the people about these issues. We do not offer to solve them with vague generalities or worn-out slogans. We know that the solution of these problems requires all the wisdom and energy we possess as a nation. We know that their solution requires heavy expenditures. The Democratic Party does not propose to deceive the people either about the problems we face or the cost of solving them.

The Democratic Party has confidence that the United States will meet these great responsibilities. It knows that the United States is a dynamic, growing nation. We believe that this country will make as much progress in the next fifty years as it has made in the last fifty years.

But we cannot meet the responsibilities of today or the challenge of the future by following the outmoded concepts of fifty years ago. The promise of the twentieth century cannot be fulfilled by those who would like to return to the days of McKinley.

We must go forward with our programs for peace through defense and foreign aid. We must proceed with our domestic programs for health, education, social security, and economic stability. Both our foreign programs and our domestic programs are necessary to answer the demands which this critical period of history makes upon us. We cannot have prosperity at home unless we play our full part in the defense and the revival of other free nations. We cannot have peace abroad unless we increase the strength, the freedom, and the well-being of our people at home.

There are some who would like to see us turn our backs upon the rest of the world and drop our efforts to strengthen our domestic economy. At the present time, they are spreading the mistaken idea that we can save money by going backward. They advocate slashing our expenditures for peace and for our domestic programs. These people are blind to the problems that confront us. They can see that a tax cut would help their own pocketbooks temporarily. They fail to see that in the long run false economy would endanger not only their pocketbooks but their lives and the continuation of civilization itself.

It is true that our present expenditures are large. But the Democratic administration is working toward a balance in the Federal budget. I wish we could balance the budget immediately by the simple expedient of cutting expenses. But that is out of the question. More than 70 per cent of our Federal budget goes to pay for past wars and to work for peace in the future. Anyone who says that these expenditures are extravagant does not understand the kind of world we live in. Our other expenditures are less than one third of the budget, and less in proportion to the national income than they were ten years ago.

I would like to cut expenditures further, and I intend to do so at every opportunity. But I do not propose to weaken the strength and security of this country. I do not propose to place the peace of the world in jeopardy to satisfy the advocates of false economy.

In this difficult world situation, some people are talking about general tax reductions. I regard this as political hypocrisy. We had one recent experience with an ill-timed, irresponsible tax cut. Much of our present financial difficulty is the result of the sweeping tax reduction which was enacted in 1948 over my veto—at a time when expenditures for defense and foreign policy were inevitably rising. We must not make the same mistake again.

In this election year, the Democratic Party will not play politics with the Federal budget. We will state the honest truth about the budget, just as we will about all other issues. We believe that the people are entitled to the plain facts about every issue, so that they can make up their own minds.

The Democratic Party can afford to be frank and truthful, because it is working for the general welfare of all our citizens. It does not serve any narrow group or clique. This makes it easy for the Democratic Party to put its program before the country openly and completely. We have nothing to hide from the people. Our strength lies in explaining our program and our policies to the people. And the more thoroughly we explain to them what the Democratic Party is trying to do, the more certain we can be of their continued support.

There are many differences between the Democratic and the Republican Parties. But I think the greatest difference is that the Democratic Party is the party of affirmative action—it is for measures to achieve prosperity and progress. The Republican Party is the party of negative inaction—it is always against things.

The principal thing that Republicans are against, of course, is the Democratic Party. But they can't win on that plank alone. They must try to find reasons for being against the Democratic Party. They must persuade people to vote against the Democratic Party. And that is getting harder and harder to do.

One reason it is hard to do is that the Republican Party has no affirmative program of its own. It refuses to face the problems of our economy. It refuses to take thought and make plans for the future. Instead of presenting a positive program of their own, the Republicans sit around waiting for us to make a proposal. Then they react with an outburst of scare words. They are like a cuttlefish that squirts out clouds of black ink whenever its slumber is disturbed.

Right now, the main problem of the Republican leaders seems to be to find some new scare words. They have not had much luck along that line, lately. They tried using the phrase "welfare state" as a scare word for a while, but they discovered that the people are in favor of a government that promotes their welfare. So they dropped that scare word. Then they tried "statism." But my good friend Governor Lehman took care of that one in the New York election—so they had to drop it, too.

Now, the Republican leaders have had to go back to an old standby. Frankly, I don't think it's as good as some of the others, but it appears to be the best they can think of. Their current scare word is "socialism."

It's perfectly safe to be against "socialism." The difficult thing is to make the country believe that the Democratic Party stands for socialism. How in the world can the Republicans persuade people that all you Democrats at all these dinners are Socialists?

It can't be done. But the Republicans will try it just the same. That's what they've been trying to do ever since 1933. For the last seventeen years they have called every new Democratic measure "socialism" or "communism," and they have made constant predictions of doom and disaster. The plans and proposals that we have advanced for improving the condition of the people of this country have been greeted with these same old scare tactics during all these years.

And I'm going to prove that to you. Let us take it step by step.

In 1933, this country faced some of the greatest problems in its history—the problems of providing food and work for millions of jobless persons and their families, of saving millions of farms and homes from foreclosure, of restoring a banking system that had collapsed, of placing the entire economy on the way to recovery.

The Democratic Party rolled up its sleeves and went to work. It took steps to provide relief and jobs, to save farms and homes, to restore banks and businesses. Bit by bit the economy responded to those vigorous measures. Income began to grow, confidence returned, business activity mounted. This was the response of the economy to our farm and labor and business programs—our programs for resource development and public works and the building of homes.

As this miracle of recovery unfolded, what was the attitude of the Republican Party?

In 1934, the Republican National Committee issued a policy statement. And in that statement they said: "American institutions and American civilization are in greater danger today than at any time since the foundation of the republic."

That sort of talk may have frightened the members of the Union League Club. But it didn't frighten the people who had been saved by the New Deal from bread lines and bankruptcy.

In 1936, the Republicans thought the danger was worse. In that year, the Republican platform cried out: "America is in peril. The welfare of American men and women and the future of our youth are at stake. . . The New Deal Administration"— this is from the 1936 Republican platform—"has bred fear and hesitation in commerce and industry, thus discouraging new enterprises, preventing employment, and prolonging the depression."

People weren't scared by that one either. They knew it just didn't make sense, because the national income had risen more than 50 per cent in the previous four years, and it was still rising.

In 1940, the Republicans tried to scare us again. This time their platform said: "The Administration has imposed upon us a regime of regimentation which has deprived the individual of his freedom and has made of America a shackled giant. . . . The New Deal administration has failed America."

That's what the Republicans said, but the America that the New Deal had saved—the economy that the New Deal had freed and made productive again—became the arsenal of democracy that overwhelmed the forces of totalitarian aggression.

But that still didn't teach the Republicans anything. In 1944, when we stood at the peak of our wartime production—the economic bulwark of the free world—the Republican Party platform proclaimed: "The fact remains that under the New Deal, American economic life is being destroyed." That's what they said in 1944—"American economic life is being destroyed."

Apparently, they never learn anything. Today, when we have a national output of over $250 billion a year and a higher standard of living than ever before, the Republican Party still cannot see anything good about the situation. In their policy statement issued ten days ago, the Republican National Committee declared: "The major domestic issue today is liberty against socialism. . . Basic American principles"—they said—"are threatened by the Administration's program. . . ."

It's the same old story—the same old words and music—the same empty and futile attempt to scare the American people—in complete contradiction of the plain facts that are visible to every citizen in his daily life.

For the past seventeen years, the same outcry has greeted every proposal advanced by the Democratic Party—whether it was for better housing, social security, rural electrification, farm price supports, minimum wages, or any other program for the general welfare.

In 1944, Representative Joseph W. Martin, Jr., summarized the Republican attitude toward all these progressive steps in one brief paragraph when he said: "For eleven years we have been steadily drifting into a regimented nation, with absolute control vested in a power-mad group of bureaucrats and social planners. Unless there is a change in government this year"—that was in 1944—"we can be reconciled to some kind of totalitarian, Socialist government."

That is what the Republicans said about our programs in 1944. That is the way they talked about them in 1948. That is what they are saying about them now.

Today, we are proposing further development of our resources, further strengthening of our economy, new measures for the welfare of the people. And what do we hear? The same old story. It is all repeated in that latest statement of the Republican National Committee: "This program"—they said, and they were talking about the program of the Democratic Party—"This program is dictated by a small but powerful group of persons who believe in socialism, who have no concept of the true foundation of American progress, and whose proposals are wholly out of accord with the true interests and real wishes of the workers, farmers and businessmen."

Well, let's look at the record. What is our program? Where did it come from? Our program is the platform adopted by the Democratic Party in its Convention of 1948. And it has been voted on by the people of this country, including the workers, farmers, and businessmen.

If our program was dictated, as the Republicans say, it was dictated at the polls in November 1948. It was dictated by a "small but powerful group" of twenty-four million voters. And I think they knew more than the Republican National Committee about the real wishes of the workers, farmers, and businessmen.

Of course, this program is not socialism. It is based upon a firm faith in the strength of free enterprise. It is designed to strengthen the markets of free enterprise and to expand the investments of free enterprise. It will make our citizens economically secure, well educated, and confident of the future. Only in a nation of such citizens can free enterprise grow and expand and reach its full possibilities.

The program of the Democratic Party is aimed to promote the prosperity and welfare of the American people. It is aimed to increase the freedom of the American people.

Freedom is not an abstraction. Freedom is a reality in our daily lives. The programs of our party have freed workers from economic subjection to their employers. They have freed farmers from the fear of bankruptcy. They have released farm wives from the bondage of ceaseless drudgery. They have freed older people from the fear of a dependent old age.

Our programs look forward to the day when our people will be freed from the fear of inadequate medical care and crushing medical expenses. They are aimed at freeing our young people from ignorance and poor education. And on these foundations for greater freedom for all our people, we are going forward to break down the barriers to economic opportunity and political liberty that have been created by prejudice and discrimination.

This is the record and the promise of the Democratic Party in expanding the freedom of the American people. And when the Republican Party proclaims that we are engaged in restricting freedom—that we are the enemies of freedom—I ask, "Whose freedom?" Let the American people look into their own lives and ask themselves whether they enjoy greater freedom or less than they did eighteen years ago.

About the only freedom we have limited is the freedom of Republicans to run the country. Maybe that is what they are complaining about.

For the Republicans to drag out the same old moth-eaten scraecrow of "socialism" again in 1950—after having used it, or something very like it, in opposition to every progressive step the nation has taken since 1933—is an insult to the intelligence of the American people. Out of the great progress of this country, out of our great advances in achieving a better life for all, out of our rise to world leadership, the Republican leaders have learned nothing. Confronted by the great record of this country, and the tremendous promise of its future, all they do is to croak— "Socialism!"

The Democratic Party is going right ahead to meet the needs and carry out the aspirations of the American people.

Our objective is to advance in freedom—to create a system of society that is ever more responsive to the needs of the people —to establish democratic principles so firmly in the hearts of the people that they can never be uprooted.

In the present anxieties and troubles of the world, the real strength of our country lies not in arms and weapons, important as they may be, but in the freedom of our citizens and their faith in a democratic society. Among the nations of the world, we stand as an example of what free men can do when they are in control of their own affairs and dedicated to the concept of a better life for all.

To work for the prosperity, the welfare, and the freedom of the American people is to work for the vindication of democratic institutions everywhere. And it is only through the growth of democratic institutions that a just and lasting peace can finally be achieved.

In this troubled world, it is more than ever important that the Democratic Party remain steadfast in its devotion to these ideals. It is more than ever important this year that the Democratic Party present its program to the people so plainly that it cannot be misunderstood. If we do that, I am confident that the people will again voice their approval of the principles which lead to increased prosperity, welfare, and freedom—not only for this country, but for free nations everywhere.

THE WELFARE STATE [8]

JAMES ROOSEVELT [9]

James Roosevelt gave this address before the Commonwealth Club at San Francisco, on December 2, 1949.

On November 15, 1949, the speaker had announced his candidacy for nomination on the Democratic ticket for the California governorship.

In that formal announcement the candidate had stressed (1) the development of California resources accompanied by the declaration that "we will not permit them to be wastefully dissipated for the profit of the few," (2) full employment, (3) the spread of tolerance, (4) extension and strengthening of social security laws, (5) the development of the Central Valley project, (6) the further protection of the interests of farmers and fruit growers, (7) the promotion of public education, and (8) extension of health services. These matters were, of course, familiar politico-social aims, and were generally subscribed to by California citizens. The question had to do with the extent to which the liberal approach of Franklin D. Roosevelt would shape the implementation of aid to labor, agriculture, and so on.

In the San Francisco speech, the younger Roosevelt delineated his New Deal, Fair Deal position, and elaborated on the political philosophy implicit in the earlier declarations.

Note the care and detail with which *individualism* and *welfare state* are defined and illustrated. Are his interpretations satisfactory? What was the extent of unemployment in California that led Roosevelt to note at length that problem?

Note the completeness with which Roosevelt meets the objections to the welfare state. What refutatory methods does he use for each of the six points to be refuted? Would his techniques be apparently adequate for an audience of economic conservatives? Are the arguments to be refuted arranged in the best order? Does he give undue space and attention to any one of them? What, of these arguments to be refuted, are most important? What, if any, major objections to the welfare state does the speaker ignore?

Early in February 1950, Governor Earl Warren announced his candidacy for a third term. Twice he had been elected by large majorities, running as he had been on both major party tickets.

Young Roosevelt, arriving in California in 1938, became a Los Angeles insurance broker. Later he entered politics, deplored the Old Guard

[8] Text and permission to reprint were furnished through the courtesy of James Roosevelt.

[9] For biographical note, see Appendix.

leadership of the Democratic party, and became a Democratic National Committeeman. The "invisible" leader of that Old Guard was allegedly E. W. Pauley, Jr., wealthy oil operator and close friend of Harry Truman. Other powerful Democratic leaders of California vigorously opposed the liberal leadership of James Roosevelt.

Warren's success in California politics was attributed to his popular personal qualities, the freedom of his administration from machine party politics, and his financial skill in balancing the state's billion dollar budget at a lower tax level than previously, in spite of a sudden population expansion from seven to ten million.

Roosevelt, after January 1950, made hundreds of speeches throughout the state. As speaker and campaigner he had had much experience earlier in supporting and often speaking for his father's candidacy in the campaigns of 1932, 1936, and 1940. The son closely resembles the father in gestures, smile, voice quality, and vocal inflections. Observers were still wondering to what extent James could produce the political wisdom and persuasive oral style of Franklin D. Roosevelt.

It is a pleasure and an honor once again to appear before the Commonwealth Club. For nearly half a century this organization has demonstrated the value of open-minded inquiry, of unbiased discussion, and of a hard-headed determination to get the facts. These things must be preserved if we are to retain the key to progress.

I am particularly grateful for the opportunity to discuss the subject which is before us today. Reactionaries are telling ghost stories again. They are trying to frighten the American electorate with a new bogey. They have even given it a name—the "Welfare state."

Today I propose to put that ghost to rest. I propose to show why the American people, who have never been notably subject to fears in the night, will not be frightened by this synthetic apparition. In short I shall defend the welfare state—the proposition that our government should work for the general welfare—and I shall do so without apology.

Yet I cannot refrain from expressing wonder and indignation that it should be necessary for *any* American to stand before his fellow citizens and defend an idea which has been written from the beginning into our Constitution, which has been reaffirmed throughout our history, and which has served more than anything else to distinguish our American society from societies based on caste and special privilege. From its very birth this nation has been committed to the proposition that welfare must be general, and that it is the business of the state to promote it.

Those who have chosen thus to draw the lines of battle, who cheapen the word "welfare" and say it with a sneer, have made, I think, a tactical blunder. They have led with their right. They have betrayed their weakness. They have shown their hand. They have demonstrated their ignorance of what American history means. They have misunderstood human nature. And the weakness of their principles is equaled only by the shortcomings of their logic.

For it is obvious, is it not, that this is no battle over the meaning of a mere word. The issue can't be settled by consulting a dictionary. It goes far deeper than that. It is a moral issue. It involves the whole question of the aims of society, of the function of government, and of the relation of the citizen to his government.

It has been said many times that our democratic government rests on a basis of individualism. This certainly is true. But what does individualism in this context mean? Surely it stands for something other than an inalienable right to drive through a red light or to refuse with a show of melodrama to pay a withholding tax to the treasurer of the United States. The moral history of Western civilization suggests a more profound and fruitful answer. It is an answer which has its basis in religion— in the moral insights of the prophets and in the social teaching of Jesus. It was deeply rooted in the minds of the men who brought this nation into being and who wrote the most glorious pages of our history.

For individualism means the principle that each human being is uniquely valuable; that he is a child of God; that he is endowed therefore with dignity and sacredness. His highest good consists in developing the best powers that lie within him. He is an end in himself. And, because he is an end in himself, he should always be so treated, and never be regarded as a mere commodity. This view of man is the moral foundation on which our democracy rests.

I emphasize this point because it is essential to the question before us today. This principle of individualism, this belief that every human being is an end, is not universally accepted. Throughout history and throughout the world today men have been used as means or commodities merely, and their unique value as ends is lost sight of.

Individualism, conceived in this way, is no empty platitude. There follow from it consequences of the greatest significance. If *men* are ends in themselves, if the *individual* has the highest value, then the *state* cannot be supreme. The state is a *means* and not an end. This is the reason we Americans and all freedom-loving men everywhere detest totalitarianism. To elevate the state to supremacy, to endow it with a sanctity of its own, to permit *its* demands to override the welfare of the individuals who make it up—this violates the deepest moral convictions that we have. This is why both fascism and communism are evil.

Now if these things are true, and I profoundly believe that they are, I think we can derive a more definite idea as to what the function of the state really is. Its business is to foster and maintain that kind of economic and social environment in which the *individual* has a real opportunity to develop his full stature as a *man*. This gives us a principle, a criterion by which to judge the rightness of proposed courses of action: Every collective action, every piece of legislation, should contribute toward the perfecting of a society in which the *individual* can be really free to develop his higest capabilities.

Obviously this is not a matter of material well-being merely. It has to do with the development of the total individual, whose motives and goods are not exclusively economic. I certainly do not maintain that government can or should concern itself directly with every aspect of human life. Spiritual, intellectual, and artistic values lie completely outside the proper sphere of direct legislation. In this country we don't establish truth in science, or critical standards in music, for example, by passing laws. But it cannot be doubted that this economic and social environment of which I have spoken *affects* every aspect of human life. It imposes conditions and limitations; it is an inescapable, bed-rock fact, it can either stifle human aspirations or it can help make their achievement possible.

The "general welfare," then, means the establishment and preservation of those conditions which give real, substantial freedom to individuals. If the people, through the democratic process, choose, as they have always done in this country, to use their instrument, the state, for this purpose, I maintain that they are using it properly. This is why I hold that to contrast the welfare state with what is called the "opportunity state," and to say that the two are opposed, is completely false. Welfare, on American principles, *means* opportunity; it means *real* opportunity; and it means opportunity for *all*.

It is for these reasons that the American people have approved measures for unemployment insurance, old-age security, minimum wages, insurance of bank deposits, low-cost housing, and emergency loans to home owners—and incidentally, gentlemen, emergency loans for business. It is for these reasons that they will approve further expansion of social security, extension of employment opportunities, the planned development of natural resources, the passage of civil rights legislation, the restoration of more workable rules of collective bargaining, and provision for medical care within the reach of the middle and lower income groups. . . .

Such measures as unemployment insurance, social security, commissions for fair employment practices, and adequate labor legislation are intended to adjust the admittedly imperfect machinery of our economy. They are not handouts. They are designed to help provide the conditions under which men and women can work in honor and in decent security. The American people as a whole understand this, even if people like Senator Taft don't. And they will reject the libellous charge that they merely want something for nothing. When the reactionaries say—as they do—that we are trying to eat our cake and have it too, let us remind them that the American people own the bakery.

Another common argument against recent legislative measures for the general welfare is that such legislation robs us of our freedom and is leading us ultimately into dictatorship. The electorate is being bribed, it is said; the people are selling their birthright of freedom for a mess of pottage. This is the charge.

Now of course this is another libel against the American people, but apart from that, it doesn't even make good sense.

One writer for an Eastern financial publication recently put it into a neat formula which gave the whole thing a mathematical flavor. "As welfare expands," he wrote, "freedom dwindles." Let's examine this for a minute. Welfare and freedom on this view are inversely related. As one increases, the other diminishes. Thus it must follow that as welfare diminishes, freedom increases. The conclusion is inescapable, is it not?—the country is most free when the people are most destitute, most poorly housed and fed, most disease ridden, and most illiterate. Can you wonder, gentlemen, that I sometimes question even the intelligence of the opposition?

Further, this sort of argument completely ignores the true causes of dictatorship. Dictatorship thrives on mass poverty and insecurity. A society whose members make ample provision for their own security through the democratic process is in no danger of becoming a dictatorship. Those who find the threat of "statism" in every effort of the people through their government to promote their general welfare are themselves inviting some form of dictatorship. By reducing democratic government to impotence, by denying it the power to cope with the problems which face it, they would subject it to the very strains and tensions which would-be dictators shrewdly exploit. A people which has known democracy will not willingly surrender it until it has lost faith in the power of democracy to act.

Still another argument of the anti-welfare faction is that the government has no business tinkering with our economic machinery. But hasn't the American government, in order to promote the general welfare, always concerned itself with how our economic machinery runs? Such powers were given it in the Constitution and have been repeatedly confirmed by decisions of the Supreme Court. The very first Congress of the United States adopted a protective tariff for the purpose of aiding manufactures and promoting the development of industry. This came about on the recommendation of Alexander Hamilton. Later the railroads were given subsidies in the form of public lands—lands which finally equalled in total size the area of the whole state of Texas. The government has provided funds for roads, canals, and harbors. More recently it has subsidized shipping and the airlines. The Reconstruction Finance Corporation has lent millions to American industries. The list of similar measures could go on for pages.

It is when the government concerns itself with measures which more directly benefit the people that the reactionaries really protest. They don't literally believe the principle they invoke. They conveniently forget such measures as the Homestead Act, which was passed during the administration of President Lincoln. What they really appear to believe in is a kind of trickle-down theory of general welfare. This is illustrated in their opposition to the public housing measure which finally passed the 81st Congress only after a long and bitter fight. The difficulty with the trickle-down theory is that not enough trickles down.

Let me turn to a final objection. It emphasizes our already great tax burden and our alleged inability to afford a comprehensive program of direct measures for the general welfare. First of all we must balance the cost of such a program against the cost of failure to provide it. For example we must weigh the cost of decent housing for everyone against the heavy cost of not having it. The costs of delinquency and expenditures for mental institutions, for example, are directly related to this social failure.

But also we must consider the cost of a welfare program in light of our total national income and our total national production before we predict that the welfare state will spend us into bankruptcy. Not only is our national income rising—and our national productivity,—but so is the per capita productivity of our workers. For example, the output in manufacturing per man-hour more than doubled in the twenty-year period between 1919 and 1939. There can be no doubt that we have the resources and the productive skill to create an economy in which every citizen has security and an opportunity to work. To maintain otherwise is to take a pessimistic view of our economic system which the facts do not warrant.

The Director of the United States Bureau of the Budget reminded this organization in a recent address that approximately

80 per cent of the money we pay in taxes goes to meet the cost of past wars, and to pay for insurance against future wars. The current needs of national defense and international affairs consume more than 50 cents out of each dollar we spend. I am convinced that if our democracy in America can demonstrate to the world that it can and will enable the just needs of all Americans to be met, the millions of people in Western Europe, India and China will turn to democracy. That is the only way to reduce the threat of Soviet Russia and eliminate the necessity of spending for war.

I should like to conclude, gentlemen, with some general observations. The Republican Party has chosen to make the welfare state the issue of the coming elections. In doing so I fear it has chosen to fight again the campaigns of the 1930's instead of the 1950's. The real issue before us is not whether in fact we shall have the welfare state. The American people have already decided that. They want more than freedom in the abstract. They have already decided that a society as fabulously wealthy and productive as our own can and must make adequate provision for *all* of its members. Such provision must come, not as a grudging concession, but as a forthright recognition of the rights of free people.

As a Democrat I might rejoice over what is assuredly a major strategic error on the part of the opposition. But as a citizen I must regret that we are diverted from the issues that ought really to concern us. We ought to be in agreement on the goals and devote our effort to the measures necessary to achieve them. One thing, for example, that certainly is required is a productive and continuously expanding economy. In the end, welfare for all the people depends upon production and continued full employment. This is the practical issue which should most concern the American people. This is the issue to which the parties should be addressing themselves.

The achievement of a genuine welfare society, whose government chosen by the people acts in the interest of *all* of them, may be delayed and hindered. But it cannot be averted. The American people have decided this. The certainty of this achievement is not a calamity, as the reactionaries would have us believe. Rather it is an assurance of the fulfillment of the American ideal. The achievement will not come without heroic effort. But it will be a righteous struggle—a struggle, in the words of Abraham Lincoln, "for maintaining in the world that form and substance of government whose leading object is to elevate the condition of men—to lift artificial weights from all shoulders; to clear the paths of laudable pursuits for all; to afford to all an unfettered start." This is our best hope for justice, security, and peace.

CHARGE TO JURY [10]

HAROLD R. MEDINA [11]

Federal Judge Harold R. Medina gave this charge to the jury, on October 13, 1949, at the conclusion of the nine-month Communist trial, in the Federal Court House, Foley Square, New York City. The charge occupied two hours.

Eleven members of the Communist Party's American Politburo were charged with criminal conspiracy to organize the party, under orders from Moscow, to "teach and advocate the overthrow of the government and destruction of American democracy, by force and violence."

The judge's instructions called for a verdict of (1) guilty for all eleven, or (2) acquittal for all, or (3) guilty for some, or (4) disagreement.

The judge agreed with the prosecution that the right of free speech is not absolute. The issue was whether the defendants were advocating governmental change by peaceful means or by violence and revolution. The jury was thus urged to weigh carefully the testimony that would answer this issue. Said the judge, the case required "calm, cool, deliberate consideration of the evidence." The jurors must not be governed by "conjecture, passion, prejudice, public opinion, or public feeling."

The judge read his charge swiftly, clearly, calmly, and dispassionately. "In his black robe he leaned back in his chair and rocked back and forth gently under the American flag and the great seal of the United States in the high ceiling of the court room." [12]

The jury followed him closely.

On the next day, the jury declared the eleven guilty. Would such decision mean the end of the Communist Party in this country? General opinion so concluded—provided the Federal Court of Appeals and the Supreme Court sustained the verdict. The Constitutional question was whether the Smith Act of New York State, as applied to Communists, violated the first Amendment to the Constitution with its safeguarding of freedom of speech. The question at stake (to echo the language of Justice Oliver Wendell Holmes) was in this case, "whether the words used are used in such circumstances and are of such nature as to create a clear and present danger."

On October 21, Judge Medina sentenced ten of the eleven to a term of five years in prison and a fine for each of $10,000. Robert G. Thomp-

[10] Text and permission for this reprint furnished through the courtesy of Judge Medina.

[11] For biographical note, see Appendix.

[12] New York *Times*, October 14, 1949.

son received only three years because of his army record—he had won the Distinguished Service Cross in World War II.

The Judge denied bail; the verdict was appealed.

Judge Medina has practiced at the bar for almost forty years, where his time has been devoted almost entirely to the argument of appeals and the trial of cases. He also has had experience on the faculty of the Columbia Law School for some twenty-five years.

LADIES AND GENTLEMEN OF THE JURY: You now approach the performance of one of the most sacred duties of citizenship, the meting out of justice. Just after you were sworn in as jurors I took occasion to make a few remarks which I shall now repeat in somewhat different form, as the thoughts I then expressed are peculiarly applicable to the period of your deliberations in order to reach a just and true verdict. I then told you to be patient and said that there are few qualities in life so important. I said that if you once get yourself in the frame of mind where you know that you have a task ahead and it has to be done carefully and it has to be done just right and you know that it will be wrong to let little things disturb you, then there comes a certain calm and peace of mind which are of the essence in the administration of justice. When you get yourself in that frame of mind, you find not only that the task ahead becomes much easier, but in addition that the quality of your work in the administration of justice is of the quality that it should be. Justice does not flourish amidst emotional excitement and stress.

The rich and the poor, and persons of every race, creed and condition stand alike before the bar of justice; and you must consider and weigh the evidence carefully, calmly and dispassionately, without the slightest trace of sympathy or prejudice for or against any party to the proceeding. The very importance of the case makes it all the more urgent that you heed these words of caution. In this connection you will bear in mind at all times that these eleven men are charged here as eleven individuals. The guilt or innocence of each of which must be passed on by you separately, pursuant to and in accordance with the instructions which I am about to give you. . . .

And so I come to the construction and interpretation of the statute. You will have noticed that, to infringe this law, a defendant must not only have conspired to organize as the Communist Party of the United States of America a society, group and assembly of persons who teach and advocate the overthrow or destruction of the Government by force and violence, and to advocate and teach the duty and necessity of overthrowing or destroying the Government by force and violence. The statute makes such conduct unlawful only when persons have so conspired "wilfully" or "knowingly"; and the indictment so charges these defendants.

Thus the question of intent also enters into the offense charged. If you find that the defendants, or any of them, participated in the conspiracy charged in the indictment, one of the questions for you to consider and determine is whether they acted wilfully. This is a question of their intent. You must be satisfied from the evidence beyond a reasonable doubt that the defendants had an intent to cause the overthrow or destruction of the Government of the United States by force and violence, and that it was with this intent and for the purpose of furthering that objective that they conspired both (1) to organize the Communist Party of the United States as a group or society who teach and advocate the overthrow or destruction of the Government of the United States by force and violence and (2) to teach and advocate the duty and necessity of overthrowing or destroying the Government of the United States by force and violence. And you must further find that it was the intent of the defendants to achieve this goal of the overthrow or destruction of the Government of the United States by force and violence as speedily as circumstances would permit it to be achieved.

In further construction and interpretation of the statute I charge you that it is not the abstract doctrine of overthrowing or destroying organized government by unlawful means which is denounced by this law, but the teaching and advocacy of action for the accomplishment of that purpose, by language reasonably and ordinarily calculated to incite persons to such action. Accordingly, you cannot find the defendants or any of them guilty of the crime charged unless you are satisfied beyond a reasonable doubt that they conspired to organize a society, group and assembly of persons who teach and advocate the overthrow or destruction of the Government of the United States by force and violence and to advocate and teach the duty and necessity of overthrowing or destroying the Government of the United States by force and violence, with the intent that such teaching and advocacy be of a rule or principle of action and by language reasonably and ordinarily calculated to incite persons to such action, all with the intent to cause the overthrow or destruction of the Government of the United States by force and violence as speedily as circumstances would permit.

No such intent could be inferred from the open and aboveboard teaching of a course on the principles and implications of communism in an American college or university, where everything is open to the scrutiny of parents and trustees and anyone who may be interested to see what is going on. That is why it is so important for you to weigh with scrupulous care the testimony concerning secret schools, false names, devious ways, general falsification and so on, all alleged to be in the setting of a huge and well-disciplined organization, spreading to practically every State of the Union and all the principal cities, and industries.

It is obviously impossible to ascertain or prove directly what were the operations of the minds of the defendants. You cannot look into a person's mind and see what his intentions are or were. But a careful and intelligent consideration of the facts and circumstances shown by the evidence in any given case enables us to infer with a reasonable degree of accuracy what another's intentions were in doing or not doing certain things. With a knowledge of definite acts we may draw definite logical conclusions. We are in our affairs continually called upon to decide from actions of others what their intentions or purposes are. And experience has taught us that frequently actions speak more clearly than spoken or written words. You must therefore rely in part on circumstantial evidence in determining the guilt or innocence of any of these defendants.

Circumstantial evidence may be received and is entitled to such consideration as you may find it deserves depending upon the inferences you think it necessary and reasonable to draw from such evidence. No greater degree of certainty is required when the evidence is circumstantial than when it is direct, for in either case the jury must be convinced beyond a reasonable doubt of the guilt of the defendants. Circumstantial evidence consists of facts proved from which the jury may infer by process of reasoning other facts sought to be established as true.

Different inferences, however, may be drawn from the facts and circumstances in the case, whether proved by direct or circumstantial evidence. The prosecution asks you to draw one set of inferences while the defendants ask you to draw another. It is for you to decide and for you alone, which inferences you will draw. If all the circumstances taken together are consistent with any reasonable hypothesis which includes the innocence of the defendants, or any of them, the prosecution has not proved their guilt beyond a reasonable doubt, and you must acquit them. On the other hand, if you find that all of the circumstances established by the evidence in this case, taken together, satisfy you beyond a reasonable doubt of the guilt of the defendants, in accordance with these instructions, it is your duty to find the defendants guilty.

Thus, if you find that the evidence has established to your satisfaction beyond a reasonable doubt that any defendant has violated the statute as thus construed by me, you will find such defendant guilty. Otherwise you will acquit him by a verdict of not guilty. Under these instructions you may find all the defendants guilty or all of them not guilty or you may find one or more of them guilty and the others not guilty.

If you are satisfied that the evidence establishes beyond a reasonable doubt that the defendants, or any of them, are guilty of a violation of the statute, as I have interpreted it to you, I find as a matter of law that there is sufficient danger of a substantive evil that the Congress has a right to prevent to justify the application of the statute under the First Amendment of the Constitution.

This is matter of law about which you have no concern. It is a finding on a matter of law which I deem essential to support my ruling that the case should be submitted to you to pass upon the guilt or innocence of the defendants. It is the duty of counsel for both sides to present by way of objections, motions, and similar procedural devices, matters of law affecting the case for my consideration and determination. All such matters of law and their presentation by counsel, including motions of every name, nature and description, challenges, questions relating to the admissibility of evidence and things of that sort must be entirely disregarded by you. These are matters of procedure with which you have no concern. Neither the presentation of such matters by counsel for either side, nor any argument made in support or in opposition to any of them, has any bearing upon your deliberations. Put all such matters out of your minds. They should not influence you in any way in arriving at your verdict.

I charge you that in arriving at your verdict you must not consider anything which the court has said with respect to the conduct of either the prosecution or counsel for the defense in the course of this trial as being any indication or suggestion or direction of the court to you as to what your verdict should be, nor shall you be influenced thereby in arriving at your verdict. . . .

Now, ladies and gentlemen of the jury, one last word. If you find that the evidence respecting the defendants or any of them is reasonably consistent with innocence, such defendant or defendants should be acquitted. If you find that the law has not been violated, you should not hesitate for any reason to render a verdict of not guilty. But, on the other hand, if you find, in accordance with these instructions, that the law has been violated as charged you should not hesitate because of sympathy or any other reason to render a verdict of guilty.

The exhibits will be gathered together by counsel and will be available for the jury if the jury wish to have them.

SOCIO-ECONOMIC RELATIONS

THE CHALLENGE OF HUMAN RELATIONS [1]

RALPH J. BUNCHE [2]

Dr. Ralph J. Bunche, acting assistant Secretary General, Department of Trusteeship and Information from Non-Self-Governing Territories, United Nations, gave this address at an Abraham Lincoln celebration, sponsored by the City Club of Rochester (New York), at the Eastman Theater, on the evening of February 11, 1950. On the same program was Mrs. Franklin D. Roosevelt. Earlier that day these two speakers had addressed a student conference on human rights at the University of Rochester, part of a program to celebrate that University's 100th Anniversary.

Dr. Bunche at Rochester carried the prestige of his United Nations success as Acting Mediator for Palestine in the war between Israel and its neighbors. On the island of Rhodes, in 1949, he succeeded in setting up an armistice between Israel, on one hand, and Egypt, Iraq, Saudi Arabia, Lebanon, and Transjordan on the other. For his splendid results in ending hostilities and effecting an armistice until permanent peace terms could be signed, Dr. Bunche was awarded the Spingarn Medal in 1949, given annually since 1915 "for the highest achievement of an American Negro."

Dr. Bunche was educated at Michigan, Harvard, Northwestern, the London School of Economics, and the University of California. He has been head of the Department of Political Science at Harvard University since 1929.

His addresses show mature thinking and wide research. His language is original and forceful.

His diagnosis of the problems of race relations and his fresh affirmation of his own faith in American democracy were timely. After a scheduled concert by the Negro baritone Paul Robeson, at Peekskill, New York, in August 1949, had ended in a riot, many Americans looked to Dr. Bunche for leadership in stemming the tide of racial prejudice.

We are gathered here tonight to pay tribute to a man of rare greatness—one of the most stalwart figures of our nation's history. But it is not within our feeble power to do honor to

[1] Text furnished by the United Nations Department of Public Information. Permission to reprint given through the courtesy of Dr. Bunche.
[2] For biographical note, see Appendix.

Abraham Lincoln except as we may dedicate ourselves to the fulfilment of the imperative objectives which he sought.

Lincoln, the man, was mortal, and being mortal was fallible. History records his moments of indecision, his groping, his bows to political expediency. But in the crucial hours of decision, he found a boundless strength which flowed from his unwavering faith in the "plain people," from the equalitarianism of the West in which he was born and reared, from his undecorated belief in the equality and dignity of man.

I am impelled to deviate for a moment and to say that on this platform tonight there is another great American personality, whose greatness history will also record, and from whose untiring efforts posterity will reap an abundantly rich harvest. A great lady, who walks unerringly in the hallowed tracks of Jefferson and Lincoln, and whose greatness, like theirs, is grounded in the dedication of her life to the high principles of true democracy. Mrs. Roosevelt, herself identified with a group —women—which is still not fully emancipated from traditional and unjust inequalities, is, in her own right, a twentieth century emancipator.

I have been chosen to speak tonight to the topic—The Challenge of Human Relations—for two reasons.

In the first place, it seems to me to be a rather appropriate subject for this occasion. Lincoln, himself, was called upon to save this nation from as great a crisis and conflict in human relations as has ever confronted any nation. And though he met the challenge and saved the nation, even Lincoln could not avert a cruel, tragic, devastating internecine war. Indeed, eighty-five years later, that war is still not fully liquidated, and at times it may seem not entirely clear who won it.

In the second place, the greatest danger to mankind today, in my view, is to be found in the sordid human relations which everywhere prevail.

Were Lincoln alive today, he could scarcely avoid taking a dark view of the relations among peoples the world over, not by any means excluding his own country. It would be understandable if even a quick view of the situation should induce in him one of those occasional moods of melancholia which some historians have attributed to him.

For what is the situation? The relations among peoples are broadly characterized by dangerous animosities, hatreds, mutual recriminations, suspicions, bigotries and intolerances. Man has made spectacular progress in science, in transportation and communication, in the arts, in all things material. Yet, it is a matter of colossal and tragic irony that man, in all his genius, having learned to harness nature, to control the relations among the elements and to direct them as he sees fit—even to the point where he now has the means readily at hand for his own complete self-destruction—has never yet learned how to *live* with himself; has not mastered the art of human relations. In the realm of human understanding the peoples of the world remain shockingly illiterate. This has always been and today remains man's greatest challenge: how to teach the peoples of the world the elemental lesson of the essential kinship of mankind and man's identity of interest.

We live in a most dangerous age—an age of supersonic airspeeds, of biological warfare, of atomic and hydrogen bombs, and who knows what next. In no exaggerated sense, we all today exist on borrowed time. If we of this generation deserve no better fate, surely our children do. They, certainly, can never understand why we could not do at least as well as the animal kingdoms.

We need peace desperately. But the world has always needed peace. Today, however, the question is not peace or war, as it has been in the past. The question now is sheer survival—survival of civilization, survival of mankind. And time is short, frighteningly short.

How is the question to be answered! We may improvise, we may build diplomatic dams, we may pile pact upon pact. The United Nations, as it is doing, may scurry about valiantly with its fire-fighting machinery and put out a war-fire in Indonesia today, in Palestine tomorrow, and in Korea or Kashmir or Greece the next day. But new war-fires will continue to flare up, and one day one of them, fanned by a furious windstorm of human conflict, may very well get out of hand. And then the final havoc will be upon us. Indeed, it is a sign of the deplorable state of human affairs in our time that unless we blind ourselves to the realities we must always think and speak of the future in terms of sound and fury, of fire and brimstone. Yet I do not believe that either the present or the future is by any means irretrievably lost, that all is hopeless.

No strength is ever to be gained from sheer imaginings and escapisms. Let us be not like the figures in Plato's parable of mankind in the dark cave. We must see and face reality and truth rather than shadows and images, distortions and illusions on the wall of the cave. The truth is that there can be but one really secure foundation for peace in the world. And that foundation must be in the attitudes which reflect the state of the hearts and minds of man. Without great changes in human attitudes, without massive strides toward human understanding and brotherhood, the most perfect international machinery for peace will ultimately be unavailing. No mechanical device, no international charters or pacts, no diplomacy however ingenious, can serve to save mankind from itself if man in his relations with man remains mean and brutish.

It is ourselves that we must fear more than the atomic or hydrogen bomb. It is in man's perversities, in his brooding suspicions, in his arrogances and intolerances, in his false self-righteousness and in his apathy that the real danger is to be found. In the final analysis, there is but one road to peace and that is the road of human understanding and fellow-feeling, of inflexible determination to achieve peaceful relations among men. That, clearly, is a long, hard road, and today it is too little travelled.

I repeat that the fundamental weakness and danger of the world today is the universality of bad human relations. If these relations were everywhere, or let us even say *almost* everywhere, internationally and domestically, good, there would be little to fear. For then the free peoples of the world would have unassailable strength, and more than that, unwavering confidence in their ability to protect themselves collectively and fully against any maverick who might go on the loose. On the other side of the coin, bad human relations are, indeed, an encouragement and stimulus to the adventures of mavericks. It is on the disunity of peoples that Hitlers prey.

By "human relations" I mean simply the ability—or inability —of mankind to live with itself in peace and order, in harmony and understanding, in honor and mutual respect.

I am optimistic enough about my fellow beings to believe that it is human *attitudes,* not human nature, that must be feared —and changed. On the international scene, it is these attitudes which have brought the world to the menacing state of affairs of today—the "cold war," the maneuverings for power and dominance, the dangerous rivalries, the propaganda battles— cannibalistic struggles in which ethical principles, and moral law are often callously jettisoned. If peoples could not be induced to suspect, to fear, and finally to hate one another, there could be no wars, for governments, from whatever motivations, can only lead peoples into wars—the peoples must fight them. And in these wars, countless numbers of human beings—by nature essentially good, whatever their immediate attitudes—must be sacrificed solely because the peoples of one society or another embark, or permit themselves to be embarked, upon fatal adventures of conquest or domination. On the domestic scene, it is human attitudes, not human nature, which nurture the racial and religious hatreds and bigotries which today permeate many soceities, and even in democracies thrive in the fertile soil of complacency.

The picture is foreboding and the future looms ominously. But perhaps there lies the hope. Can man, a thinking animal, capable of both emotion and cool calculation with regard to his self-interest, be brought to his senses in time? Can he see the black doom which awaits him at the end of the path he now follows? I have enough faith in the potentiality of mankind for good to believe that he can save himself.

Certainly, there is nothing in human nature which renders it impossible for men to live peacefully and harmoniously with one another. Hatred, intolerance, bigotry, chauvinism are never innate—they are the bad lessons taught in society. Despite the fact that in recorded history, mankind has been as much at war as at peace, it cannot be concluded that war is inevitable—a natural state of mankind. Nor do I believe that because hatreds, bigotries, intolerances and prejudices loom large in the pages of history, these are the natural conditions of man's societal existence on earth.

I am under no illusions about mankind and I do not for a moment underestimate his capacity for evil doing. All of us, no doubt, are painfully aware of some individuals who live up to the hilt—and then some—to the Hobbesian characterization of man as "nasty, poor, mean and brutish." Yet, I am persuaded that such persons are the exception rather than the rule, and in any case, they are the unfortunate end-products of society. I believe, with Julian Huxley, that there is a sharp distinction between human nature and the *expression* of human nature. War and bigotry are not reflections of human nature but rather collective expressions of it in the particular circumstances in which man finds himself at a given time. Ironically enough, modern man has given some of the best demonstrations of how peoples can work together in a close bond of understanding during the adversities of war itself. Human nature may be relatively constant, but its expression is subject to change. That man has the *ability* to change the circumstances which influence the expression of his nature and lead him down disastrous paths is undoubted. The great decision involves his *will* to do so.

It may be that man's will can be activated only by an impending sense of catastrophe; that only on the brink of disaster may he turn to human solidarity as his last chance for salvation. If so, he finds himself today precariously on that brink.

I think it no exaggeration to say that unfortunately, throughout the ages, organized religion and education have failed miserably in their efforts to save man from himself. Perhaps they have failed because so often they have merely reflected the mean and narrow attitudes of the very peoples they were striving to save.

Human understanding, human brotherhood and solidarity, will be achieved, if at all, only when the peoples of many lands find a common bond through a compelling sense of urgency in achieving common goals. The purposes and principles of the United Nations—with peace as the universal common denominator—afford that bond and the common goals. The implements of modern warfare afford the urgency, if people once understand the frightful implications and elect to survive.

Lincoln, instinctively a true democrat, believed deeply in the essential justice of the plain people, whose better impulses and good will he trusted ultimately to prevail. Given half a chance, I believe that the peoples of the world today, in their collectivity, will justify Lincoln's faith.

It is not necessary to seek to transform people into saints in order that impending disaster may be averted.

Throughout the world today, thinking and psychology have not kept pace with the times. That people inevitably think in terms of their self-interest is something very little can be done about. But is it not equally tenable that a great deal can be done about influencing people to think and act in terms of their *true* self-interest? In this dangerous age, notions of exalted and exaggerated nationalism, of chauvinism, of group superiority and master race, of group exclusiveness, of national self-righteousness, of special privilege, are in the interest of neither the world nor of any particular group in it. They are false views of self-interest and carry us all toward the disaster of war. And in the war of tomorrow there can be no victor; at best there will be only survivors. The old concepts and values are no longer valid or realistic. The future may well belong to those who first realign their international sights.

I sincerely believe that the generality of peoples throughout the world really long for peace and freedom. There can be no doubt that this is true of the American people. If this is true, it is the one great hope for the future. The problem is how to crystallize this longing, how to fashion it into an overpowering instrument for good. The United Nations recognizes acutely the desperate need, but has not yet found the ways and means of mobilizing the peace-loving attitudes of the peoples of the world over the stubborn walls of national egoisms.

I sincerely believe that the generality of peoples throughout the world really long for peace and freedom. There can be no doubt that this is true of the American people. If this is true, it is the one great hope for the future. The problem is how to crystallize this longing, how to fashion it into an overpowering instrument for good. The United Nations recognizes acutely the desperate need, but has not yet found the ways and means of mobilizing the peace-loving attitudes of the peoples of the world over the stubborn walls of national egoisms.

Every nation, every government, every individual, has a most solemn obligation to mankind and the future of mankind in the fateful effort to rescue the world from the morass in which it is now entrapped and to underwrite a future of peace and freedom for all. This is a time of gravest crisis. Constructive, concerted actions—not negativism and recrimination—are called for. There are many motes in many eyes. There is no nation which can stand before the ultimate bar of human history and say: We have done our utmost to induce peoples to live in peace with one another as brothers.

It must be very clear that what the world needs most desperately today is a crusade for peace and understanding of unparalleled dimension; a universal mobilization of the strong but diffused forces of peace and justice. The collective voice of the peoples of the world could be so irresistible as to dwarf into insignificance both A and H bombs and to disperse and discourage the warlike and war minded.

In the existing state of affairs, societies admittedly owe it to themselves to be prepared and protected against any eventuality. With that, given the international circumstances, reason and reality might perceive no quarrel. But it would also appear that reason and reality would dictate that since armament is never an end in itself and must expand itself, if at all, only in war, the only way peace-loving societies might cover their mounting losses from the tremendous expenditures on armaments would be to exert an effort of at least equal magnitude for peace—to the end that the armaments would never have to be used. This, it seems to me, would be at once good economics, good humanitarianism, and good self-interest.

And now, if I may take advantage of my nationality and speak for a moment simply as an American citizen, I may ask where do we, as Americans, stand with regard to the challenge of human relations?

The United States is in the forefront of international affairs today. The eyes of the world are focussed upon us as never before in our history. A great part of the world looks to us for a convincing demonstration of the validity and the virility of the democratic way of life as America exalts it. It would be catastrophic if we should fail to give that demonstration. We cannot afford to fail.

But it is only too apparent that our democratic house is not yet in shipshape order. There are yawning crevices in our human relations; the gap between our democratic profession on the one hand, and our daily practices of racial and religious intolerance on the other, while less wide than formerly, is still very wide.

Race relations is our number one social problem, perhaps our number one problem. It is no mere sectional problem; it is a national—indeed an international—problem. For any problem today which challenges the ability of democracy to function convincingly, which undermines the very foundations of democracy and the faith of people in it, is of concern to the entire peace and freedom loving world. Surely, it must be abundantly clear that it is only through the triumph of democracy and the determined support of peoples for it as an imperative way of life that secure foundations for world peace can be laid.

That race relations are gradually improving, both in the South and elsewhere in the nation, cannot be doubted. But neither can it be doubted that these relations remain in a dangerous state, that they are a heavy liability to the nation, and constitute a grave weakness in our national democratic armor.

Certainly the costs of anti-racial and anti-religious practices are enormously high. Attitudes of bigotry, when widely prevalent in a society, involve staggering costs in terms of prestige and confidence throughout the rest of the world, not to mention the contamination and degradation resulting from the presence of such psychological diseases in the body of the society.

Throughout the nation, in varying degree, the Negro minority —almost a tenth of the population—suffers severe political, economic and social disabilities solely because of race. In Washington, the nation's capital, Lincoln, the Great Emancipator, sits majestically in his great armchair behind the marble pillars, and overlooks a city which does not yet admit his moral dictum that the Negro is a man; a city in which no Negro can live and work with dignity; a city which, administered by Congress itself, subjects one fourth of its citizens to segregation, discrimination and daily humiliation. Washington is this nation's greatest shame precisely because it is governed by Congress and is the capital of a great democracy. Washington, of all American cities, should symbolize and vitalize that democracy.

Lincoln saw that slavery had to be abolished not only because as an institution it was contrary to human morality, but also because it was inimical to the interests of the "plain people" of America. By the same token, present-day practices of racial segregation and discrimination should be outlawed as inimical to the interests of all who believe in and derive benefit from democracy, whatever their race or religion.

The most valuable resources of any country are its people. But in our country today, and in the South particularly, our human resources, white and black alike, are being recklessly squandered. They are being squandered in interracial conflict, in prejudices and animosities among two groups of citizens— Americans all—which prevent that unity of purpose and that cooperative effort which alone could insure the full realization of the nation's potential in its human resources; and this at a time when it vitally requires its maximum strength.

The vitality of this great country derives from the unity of purpose and the devotion to its democratic ideals of the diversified peoples—by race, religion and national origin—who make up its population. Disunity and group conflict constantly sap that vitality.

As a nation we have also found strength in the fact that we have always been able and willing to face our shortcomings frankly and attack them realistically. It is in this spirit and in this knowledge that I, as an American, take occasion to point to our shortcomings. I do not imply, in any sense, that the rest of the world is free of such imperfections, or in given instances, even greater ones.

To enjoy our maximum strength, we need more *applied* democracy. We need to live up to the principles which we believe in and for which we are hailed by the world. We too need a mobilization—a mobilization throughout the country of men and women of good will, of men and women who are determined to see American democracy fulfill its richest promise, and who will ceaselessly exert their efforts towards that end.

This nation, by its traditional philosophy, by its religious precepts, by its Constitution, stands for freedom, for the brotherhood of man, and for full respect for the rights and dignity of the individual. By giving unqualified expression to these ideals in our daily life we can and will achieve a democratic society here so strong in the hearts and minds of its citizens, so sacred to the individual, that it will be forever invulnerable to any kind of attack.

Because I believe in the reason and essential goodness of human beings; because I have deep respect for and faith in my fellow man, I look to the future of race relations in our country with reasonable optimism. I know that there are very many men and women of good will in the North, South, East and West, that their ranks increase daily, that their influence is being widely felt, and that this influence is gradually clearing away the race-relations fog which has enshrouded us. But I must add that where rights and birthrights are concerned, gradual progress can never be rapid enough for those deprived, since rights and birthrights can never be enjoyed posthumously.

If I may be pardoned for a personal reference, I am proud to be an American and I am proud of my origin. I believe in the American way of life, and believing in it, deplore its imperfections. I wish to see my country strong in every way—strong in the nature and practice of its democratic way of life; strong in its world leadership; strong in both its material and spiritual values; strong in the hearts and minds of all of its people, whatever their race, color or religion, and in their unshakable devotion to it. I wish to see an America in which both the fruits and the obligations of democracy are shared by *all* of its citizens on a basis of full equality and without qualification of race or creed.

The United Nations ideal is a world in which peoples would "practice tolerance and live together in peace with one another as good neighbors." If this ideal is far from realization it is only because of the state of mind of mankind. Man's reason and calculated self-interest can be powerful forces for changes in that state of mind. No ideal could be more rewarding. Every individual today has it in his power—in his daily living, in his attitudes and practices—to contribute greatly to the realization of that ideal. We must be strong in our adherence to ideals. We must never lose faith in man's potential power for good.

FOR THE FEDERAL FAIR EMPLOYMENT
PRACTICES ACT [3]

ADAM CLAYTON POWELL, JR. [4]

Congressman Adam C. Powell, Jr., gave this short debate before the House of Representatives, on February 22, 1950. This speech should be reviewed in conjunction with that of Congressman Sims which follows.[5]

The proposed Federal Fair Employment Practices bill was a highly controversial one. More than a hundred Southern Democrats met in caucus on February 21 to map out their opposition strategy. The Administration bill, sponsored by Congressman Lesinski of Michigan, Chairman of the Educational Labor Committee, was scheduled for floor consideration under a House rule that provides for "Calendar Wednesdays," days on which chairmen of many bills, blocked by other House procedures, might call up their measures. Alphabetically the Committee on Education and Labor was entitled to its turn on this Wednesday. A House rule also stipulated that a measure at issue must be brought to a final vote before that legislative day ends. Each side was to be given an equal amount of time—with speeches usually limited to five minutes. A filibuster, as often developed in Senate debate, was thus hardly possible.

The bill would make it illegal for any employer of fifty or more persons to discriminate in hiring because of a job applicant's race, color, religion, ancestry, or national origin.

The setting for the debate was dramatic. Crowds packed the galleries and, in long lines on the floor below, more people waited admission.

Involved parliamentary tactics occupied five hours after the House convened at twelve o'clock. There was reading of Washington's Farewell Address, followed by eight roll calls on one pretext or another, including motions to adjourn. Reading the bill in full, for example, was resorted to "as a road block."

It was one of the most turbulent House sessions in years. Language and delivery were bitter. There were constant shouts. "Southerners interrupted with rebel yells."

Congressman Lesinski opened the debate with a brief statement and then yielded to Congressman Powell, who controlled the debate, and who, after his argument in support of the motion, recognized in turn many affirmative speakers. His argument was a compact debater's brief.

[3] *Congressional Record* (81st Congress, 2nd session). 96:2211-14. February 22, 1950 (daily edition).

[4] For biographical note, see Appendix.

[5] See below, p159.

It exemplifies the condensed argument given in the House when time limitations are imposed.

Powell, a graduate of Colgate with an advanced degree from Columbia, has been since 1937 a minister of the Abyssinian Baptist Church of Harlem, New York City, and since 1945 a member of Congress. As speaker he is fluent, physically and emotionally highly active. In his Congressional speeches, he usually adheres closely to argument without much rhetorical embellishment.

Toward the end of the debate many amendments were offered and at 3:14 A.M., on February 23, fifteen hours after the debate started, by a vote of 221 to 178, the House accepted amendments that defeated the Lesinski measure. Later that day, 240 to 177, the House passed and sent to the Senate a "voluntary" fair employment practice program. For enforcement reliance would be placed on conciliation, education, and public opinion. The outcome was regarded as a major defeat for the Administration. The measure, scheduled to be introduced in the Senate, was expected to result in a filibuster. Even the "voluntary" bill had little chance of passage in the Eighty-second Congress.

Mr. Chairman, I would like to express my thanks to the members of the FEPC [Fair Employment Practice Committee] subcommittee for the cooperation they gave me in the hearings on this bill. I would like to publicly thank our colleague from Ohio [MR. BREHM], whose cold has been plaguing him and developed into laryngitis. His actions on the subcommittee were greater than any words he could utter today. Also I want to thank members of the full committee on Education and Labor, and I refer to Members on both sides, those who agreed and disagreed, for the cooperation and understanding that we had in committee. I trust that further debate on this bill will be in an atmosphere of dignity, even though we may oppose it bitterly or we may be in favor of it wholeheartedly.

I have allotted myself only five minutes because there are scores of members who want to talk and I do not want to cover myself with any personal glory.

I would like to say one or two things concerning the bill so that we can remove from our minds anything that we may not know concerning the details. . . .

I. Does job discrimination exist? There can be no serious question that employment discrimination is widespread. In its final report, the wartime FEPC predicted that even such gains as it had made were dissipating and predicted further, accelerated dissipation. . . .

II. Should it be eliminated? Without going into the vast wealth of detail available in answer to this question, it should suffice here to indicate briefly some of the areas adversely affected by employment discrimination.

(a) The democratic principles on which the nation was founded are flaunted by discrimination. Any violation of these principles has an adverse effect. Futhermore, the general moral code to which we pay allegiance, demands that all men be considered as individuals and rated according to their individual worth. As the bill states, "it is essential that this gap between principle and practice be closed."

(b) Our foreign relations are hampered by the publicity our enemies give to our discriminatory practices. Secretary of State Acheson describes discrimination as "a handicap in our relations with other countries." Senator Dulles when a United States delegate to the UN said that FEPC is necessary to "erase what today is the worst blot on our national escutcheon." The United States is bound by its international agreements to eliminate discrimination—for example, the Inter-American Conference in Mexico City, 1945; the Charter of the UN; and the Universal Declaration of Human Rights proclaimed by the General Assembly.

(c) The economic waste of discrimination cannot be totally computed. One economist estimated before the House subcommittee that we send at least $15 billion annually down the drain because of discrimination. Contributing to this total is the cost of training those whom we will not allow to use their training; the cost to industry of using artificially limited pools in selecting what should be the most skilled manpower; the creation, in minority populations, of a disproportionate degree of unemployment, resulting in an island of depression which affects its surroundings—"a man who can't earn can't buy"; the breakdown in morale among those who know that no matter what their skills, they cannot compete on an equal basis with those whom they are taught to believe are their equals; the personality difficulties resulting from lack of home life when mothers are forced to work to supplement inadequate income brought in by fathers.

The only remaining question, then, is—

III. Can S.-1728 [the FEPC bill] properly do the required job? Since the testimony at the various hearings in support of FEPC, combined with the analysis of the S. 1728 above, seems to make out a prima facie case for an affirmative answer to this question, it would appear sensible to put the burden on the objections raised.

The chief ones are as follows:

(a) "The bill is unconstitutional; it violates States' rights."

But, first, the Federal Government has the right to impose any reasonable regulations regarding its own employment relations, including regulations against discrimination—United Public Workers against Mitchell.

Second, it can do likewise re employment relations of those who contract with it—Perkins against Lukens Steel Co.

Third, it may regulate the employment relations of private businesses engaged in commerce—NLRB against Jones & Laughlin Steel Corp.

Fourth, it can therefore impose regulations against discrimination in such businesses, (i) logically, from first, second, and third above, and (ii) on the basis of cases like New Negro Alliance against Sanitary Grocery Co.

(b) "Even if constitutional, this matter should be left to the states; it is a Southern problem."

But, first, the problem is not a Southern problem—nor a Negro, or Jewish, or Catholic, or Mexican problem. Discrimination exists in the North, South, East, West, and middle of America; it is an American problem.

Second, cutting across State lines as it does, discrimination is of national legislative concern.

Third, in general, the greater number of discriminators in a given area, the more difficult to enact local antidiscrimination laws; so the areas which do practice the most discrimination will be just those with no statutory inhibition.

Fourth, many large businesses have their affairs spread out into many states; where one sells may not be where it hires. Federal legislation is the only feasible way to meet this problem.

As an impartial study made by the Library of Congress states, education alone is not sufficient to do the job.

These various studies, together with the testimony presented during the hearings on H. R. 4453, demonstrate all too strikingly that in virtually every section of this country qualified workers are being denied an opportunity of making a living—and a life—solely because of their race, color, religion, or national origin.

Gentlemen, let us conduct this debate in dignity. Let us now proceed to the business of restoring integrity to this body. Both parties and presidential nominees pledged this in their platforms and we will now show the world that at least the House of Representatives is a place that keeps its word.

AGAINST THE FEDERAL FAIR EMPLOYMENT
PRACTICES ACT [6]

HUGO S. SIMS, JR. [7]

Representative Hugo Sims, Jr., of South Carolina, gave this speech in the House of Representatives, at Washington, D.C., on February 22, 1950.

Through the late hours of that day and far into the night determined debaters argued for the passage of the Fair Employment Practices Act. Equally vigorous opponents of the measure replied. Each side was given its proper allotment of the limited time allowed for the debate. And each speaker was usually restricted to not more than five minutes.[8]

Prominent supporters were T. H. Nurke of Ohio, Helen Douglas of California, Chet Holifield of California, Jacob Javits of New York, John Lesinski of Michigan, Vito Marcantonio of New York, Mary Norton of New Jersey, Adam C. Powell of New York, John M. Vorys of Ohio, John Walsh of Indiana, and Sidney Yates of Illinois. Important negative debaters were Thomas Abernathy of Mississippi, Paul Brown of Georgia, Donald Jackson of California, Wingate Lucas of Texas, Samuel McConnell of Pennsylvania, John Rankin of Mississippi, Hugo Sims of South Carolina, William Whittington of Mississippi, and Arthur Winstead of Mississippi.

Congressman Sims, whose short speech was among the more impressive for his side, had been a high school debater at Orangeburg, South Carolina, and at Wofford College, Spartansburg, South Carolina.

Sims had also studied law (LL.B., University of South Carolina, 1947); had considerable experience as a columnist; had practiced law and had served one term in the State legislature of South Carolina; and during his war experience had made many speeches as company commander. In his candidacy for nomination and election to Congress, he had campaigned widely and ably. Thus, although young in years and in Congress, he had established his reputation as an effective speaker.

Of his methods of speech preparation he writes: "I have no set plan for preparing a speech. Sometimes I write out a whole speech word for word, then throw the speech away, make an outline of it, throw the out-

---

[6] *Congressional Record* (81st Congress, 2nd session). 96:2225-6. February 22, 1950 (daily edition). Text furnished through the courtesy of Congressman Sims.

[7] For biographical note, see Appendix.

[8] For details of the speaking situation, see the Introduction to Congressman Powell's speech, p154.

line away and then make the speech. On other occasions I make speeches without any preparation at all. Except for radio speeches, I do not use notes of any kind." [9]

Mr. Chairman, I am opposed to this legislation; I am opposed to any legislation of this type, because I do not believe that civil rights is an end in itself. I do not believe there is anything sacred about civil rights legislation; I think that whether civil rights legislation is right or wrong depends entirely on whether it accomplishes its ultimate end of attaining and preserving human rights. As I understand it, the enactment of civil rights is merely putting human rights into law; consequently, if by passing the law you do not attain and preserve human rights then I feel that civil rights legislation is wrong. . . .

If the proponents of FEPC really want to give the Negroes in America equal opportunity, if the proponents of FEPC accept the minority problem as a national problem (and I agree with you, it is a national problem), then the proponents of this legislation should step boldly forward with a program for providing basic needs to this minority group—basic needs so that they can properly develop their personalities.

The argument is used by proponents of FEPC that we cannot sell democracy and the idea of equal opportunity to the world if we do not practice it at home—that we must close the gap between principles and practices. I agree with them completely that solving the race problem and providing equal opportunity is a national problem. Let us face it realistically.

Let us not make the same mistake that we made in America back in the nineteenth century when slavery was abolished. The problem then was exactly the same problem as it is today; that is, two races living together harmoniously with human rights for all. What was the situation then? We had many people from outside of the South shouting, "Pass a law that makes all people equal and then we will have political freedom and human rights." And on the other hand, within the South you had an equally loud group that were so busy shouting "States rights" that they did not have time to try and solve the race problems that did exist in the South. Neither group recognized the problem of the South for what it was, an economic problem.

[9] Letter to this editor, April 5, 1950.

Perhaps the War Between the States could have been avoided, if, instead of abolishing slavery, the slaves had been bought by the government, and freed, and had been given education, and training, and land, and an opportunity to be economically independent individually. But Congress then did not recognize the problem as an economic one. They thought that by passing laws they would secure political freedom and human rights for the Negro. Let us not make that same mistake again.

Fair employment practice legislation will not give to the Negro an opportunity to become economically independent. Let us give the Negro the opportunity to develop his personality and his capabilities. After all, the Christian religion uses as a standard the development of the personality, to determine right from wrong. The Christian religion is not nearly as concerned with the rewards that one receives on this earth, even if that reward be fair employment, as it is with the opportunity to develop one's personality.

Education is certainly one way toward solving this problem. But education is not enough. Education should be coupled with legislation and that legislation should be designed toward providing those basic needs for all people. Actually, legislation designed toward lifting up those people on the bottom rungs of the economic ladder will, in the long run, eliminate most of the causes for prejudice and will provide opportunities for millions and millions of Negroes who are not given an opportunity to develop their abilities.

However, if the proponents of FEPC legislation feel that we cannot wait on legislation designed to lift up all people who are on the bottom rungs of the economic ladder because of our position as the leading advocate of democracy in the world, I suggest that we pass legislation designed specifically to provide these opportunities to the Negro minorities.

I suggest, first, that we make a huge federal appropriation to the states on the basis of their Negro population for the purpose of providing adequate educational, health, housing, and recreational facilities for the Negro. I suggest, secondly, that we establish a minority employment agency for the purpose of finding jobs for Negroes all over the United States. In other words, it would encourage voluntary migration of Negroes from the South to those parts of the United States where better employment opportunities exist. And, thirdly, that a national education program should be conducted with the objective of eliminating discrimination by education and publicity.

My suggestion of legislation to eliminate the causes of prejudice would help the common man within the Negro race. It is not designed like FEPC to help only a small percentage of the Negroes, perhaps 3 to 5 per cent who could be classified as the elite members of that race.

My objection to FEPC is, first, that the Commission will, in my opinion, use its authority in an effort to end segregation in the South. Secondly, FEPC legislation, or the consideration of FEPC legislation, stirs bitterness and hatred among the races in the South. It does not work toward harmonious race relations and the rank and file of the people will not accept it—consequently, it will be unenforceable.

If this FEPC law were passed it is reasonable to assume that the President of the United States in appointing members for the Commission would appoint people genuinely interested in the success of the legislation. I think that it is also reasonable to assume that all of the members of the commission would feel that segregation is discrimination in itself and that, consequently, they would have no sympathy at all with the people in Southern states who are opposed to ending segregation. I think it is entirely reasonable to assume that these people would agree with the report of President Truman's civil rights committee that the nation should force the South to end segregation and they would use what authority they have toward furthering this aim. I think that the activity of the wartime FEPC justifies these expectations.

President Truman's Committee on Civil Rights recommended that the nation force the South to end segregation by withholding federal funds. And, since the South would not end segregation, it would be bled economically—just as it has been bled by discriminatory freight rates, high protective tariffs, and so forth. This would destroy human rights by lowering per capita income, lowering ability to meet basic needs in a section of the country with an already low per capita income.

A vote for FEPC is not a liberal vote—it is a vote against human rights. I refuse to vote to throw a sop to minority agitators not genuinely interested in the Negroes in South Carolina. I shall continue to oppose vigorously this and similar legislation.

INDUSTRY, LABOR, AGRICULTURE

DETOUR AHEAD [1]

BENJAMIN F. FAIRLESS [2]

Benjamin F. Fairless, President of the United States Steel Corporation, gave this address before the Baltimore Association of Commerce, Baltimore, Maryland, April 21, 1950. The address is a clever, well-reasoned argument, buttressed by specific instances, of capital's defense against the charges of "big business," "monopoly," and "concentration." Because of the investigations of big business and monopoly early in 1950, under Senator Joseph C. O'Mahoney, chairman of the Senate Committee on Interior and Insular Affairs, and those under Emmanuel Cellar, of the House Judiciary Committee, United States Steel was under special scrutiny. Its raising of the price of steel after the end of the strike of 1950 produced much new criticism of that company as monopolistic.

President Fairless' speech is highly personal, informal, humorous, at times sarcastic, and certainly interesting and lacking in stuffiness.[3]

Gentlemen, I am about to deliver a critical speech, and at the outset I want to make it clear that I am neither attacking nor defending either political party as such. Neither am I attacking nor defending any individual or individuals of either political party. I am, however, attacking anyone who, in my opinion, is attempting to destroy the free competitive American industrial system which has made our country the greatest on earth. I offer this statement for clarification purposes only and it is not in any way to be construed as an apology for what I am about to say.

This visit to the Free State of Maryland is a pleasure which I have been promising myself for a long time. In fact, I had planned to be with you months ago, but unfortunately I hit a

---

[1] Text supplied by J. Carlisle MacDonald, assistant to the Chairman of the United States Steel Corporation, with permission for this reprinting.

[2] For biographical note, see Appendix.

[3] For details concerning the CIO Steel Strike of 1949 and President Fairless' leadership in negotiations, see Introduction to Philip Murray's "CIO Labor Policies," p179.

detour and wound up in a notorious suburb of yours, over near Bladensburg—a place called Washington, I believe.

I guess that's what always happens to people these days when they start heading for a free state. Some traffic cop shunts them off on a rough and bumpy road they did not want to travel, and they end up at an unhappy destination they never wanted to reach at all.

It is about detours that I want to talk to you today—and about Washington. I had expected, of course, to talk about the steel business, and some day I hope to get back to Pittsburgh long enough to find out what's happened to it. But during the past few months, I have been specializing in our National Capital, and our National Capital has certainly been specializing in me. Up to now, as you know, I've spent most of my time in O'Mahoney's doghouse; but next week I move to Emmanuel's cellar.

So it is a pleasant relief indeed to escape for a few hours and to enjoy your hospitality here in Baltimore.

I have already spent a most interesting morning. Mr. Charles E. McManus took me over to the Crown Cork and Seal Company to see the fine new cold reducing mill they have installed there. To me there is something really beautiful about machines like that. They have majesty, dignity and grace of motion; and I never cease to be fascinated by the miracles they perform.

The magician who first produced a live rabbit from a silk hat had a great deal of ingenuity and skill, and people of every age still marvel at the trick; but to me it is not nearly as mystifying or as breath taking as the process by which modern American industry produces even such seemingly simple things as bottle caps.

My visit to this plant today, however, was not merely a pleasure; it was definitely a matter of business as well—not that I am thinking of going into the bottle-closing business; and not that Crown is a customer of ours, either. They are not. They buy their steel from one of our rivals. I hate to say that, because I know what a shock it will be to some of our Washington critics who insist that there is no competition in the steel industry. Apparently they never heard of Bethlehem—or a couple of hundred other competitors of ours who are doing very nicely, thank you. You know, sometimes I wish these critics could join our sales force for a few weeks and try to sell a little steel. I think they would find out for themselves what competition really is.

When I say that my visit was a matter of business, I mean that I think it is part of my job—and the biggest part of my job, perhaps—to know how American industry produces and engineers the millions of intricate things that it turns out—to study the ingenious processes that it has devised and to see how it meets and solves the hundreds of operating problems that it has to face.

I do not believe that any man who has not seen these things for himself can hope to understand our American industrial machine. I do not see how he can hope to discuss our American enterprise system intelligently, factually, or even honestly.

If you happen to detect a note of feeling in my voice as I say that, it is because of my recent experiences in Washington. From the time it was organized fifty years ago, U. S. Steel has been subjected to almost constant investigation by various agencies of the government and for the past ten years and more, I myself have been on the business end of most of these investigations. Gentlemen, I have been through so many Congressional inquisitions that no self-respecting skeleton would hide in my closet on a bet.

So far this year, Senator O'Mahoney has already had me on the griddle once, and Congressman Celler starts dissecting me next week. After that, O'Mahoney wants me back again, it seems; and Representative Macy is proposing that I become the permanent victim of a continuing investigation. I shall never know why.

What with the T N E C [Temporary National Economic Committee] report, the voluminous records which we file regularly with various government agencies, the frequent Congressional inquiries we have faced, the proceedings before the Federal Trade Commission, and the evidence we have presented in numerous court actions, I don't suppose there is a single statistic about United States Steel which could possibly be of any real interest or significance to anyone, that is not already a matter of public record. And yet to this day, most of our inquisitors remain blissfully ignorant of the most important fact of all—how steel is made.

Among all the members of all the public bodies we have faced in the past dozen years, I don't suppose that more than two or three, at the outside, have even been inside a steel plant, or have ever seen for themselves what a gigantic opration steel making is. Yet until he *has* seen these things for himself, I do not believe that anyone has any right to tell anybody how big a steel company should be; for any views he may hold on the subject can hardly be regarded as the reasoned opinion of a qualified and competent authority.

During the hearings next week, I intend to invite Mr. Celler and the members of his committee to visit our steel plants. I hope most earnestly that they will accept that invitation; for, by doing so, I believe they could add richly to public knowledge and public understanding of this whole controversial issue of "bigness."

I am aware, however, that such action by them would constitute a radical departure from established Congressional practice as I have seen it. So far as I can discover from personal experience, Congressional investigations of businessmen follow a standardized pattern that has not been in vogue in America since the old days of the western frontier, when the established procedure was to shoot first and ask questions afterwards.

Nowadays, the Chairman sends you a letter "inviting" you to appear before his committee on a certain date. Then he starts issuing a barrage of statements to the newspapers telling the world what a dangerous and nefarious character you are. When you no longer have a friend left in the world, the hearing begins, and the chairman starts out by reading a statement in which he finds you guilty and pronounces sentence upon you. Then he announces that the committee will proceed to a full and "impartial" investigation of the facts, which seems to be a great waste of everybody's time, because when the evidence has been fully presented, the chairman ignores it completely, writes a report setting forth all of his preconceived notions, and quotes at length from his opening statement to prove he was right all the time.

Throughout the proceedings, of course, there is a great deal of talk about the "public interest," but I cannot help wondering what "public interest" a committee is serving when it conceals, distorts, and openly misstates the facts—the basic, all-important facts—which the American people must have if they are to plan their economic future intelligently and wisely.

Now, gentlemen, I am not an alarmist. I don't run around crying "wolf." I never see bogeys under the bed—and seldom see them on a golf course, these days. But I am gravely and sincerely disturbed by what I have seen in Washington.

In my opinion, our American economic system is in deadlier peril today than it has ever been in my lifetime. I say that knowing that it has always defended itself successfully against its enemies abroad; but I honestly do not know how it can be protected against its self-styled "friends" in Washington who would literally hack it to death on the pretext of saving its immortal soul. I am convinced that if these misguided planners and politically ambitious officeholders have their way, three of our most precious liberties—freedom of opportunity, freedom of initiative, and freedom of enterprise, will vanish from this earth.

I have always had great faith in the plain, cracker-barrel, common sense of the American people, and so long as they are permitted to know the facts, I have no fear that they will ever allow their economic system to be engulfed by foreign "isms" and ideologies.

I do not fear communism because every passing day proves its utter failure. The American people know that if communism were really working successfully there would be no need for police state oppression, phony trials and slave labor camps behind the iron curtain.

I do not fear fascism because it has killed the three great nations which adopted it. The American people want no part of any economic system that feeds only upon war and conquest.

I do not fear outright socialism because, in Europe today, socialism itself is living on the dole, and America is the only country on earth that is able to foot the bill for it. No American taxpayer is likely to fall for that kind of an economic system, at least until he has found some other nation that is rich enough and generous enough to indulge him in his folly.

But when somebody in Washington starts telling me how much he loves the free enterprise system and how he proposes to save it from itself, I shake in my very shoes. I wonder why it is that these self-appointed saviours of our national welfare always seem to miss the point—the one magnificent lesson that should be apparent to anyone who looks about him at the world today.

The point is, gentlemen, that our American system of free competitive enterprise is the only one left in the world that is NOT controlled by power-hungry politicians; and whether you call it the Square Deal, the Fair Deal, the New Deal or just plain federal regulation, the fact remains that once the dead hand of politics gets its convulsive grip on American business and industry, free competition will be strangled, and our economic system will be no different—and no more successful—than those noble experiments which are crumbling into dust in Europe.

Of one thing, I am convinced. The American people will never knowingly travel that foreign road to economic disaster. They have built the most magnificent industrial machine this world has ever seen and they are certainly not going to wreck it *that* way as long as the road itself is clearly marked by signposts which honestly reveal its destination.

But in Washington today there are theorists and bureaucrats and economists and Congressmen who are switching the signs. They are trying to take down all the honest guideposts and put up others reading: "Detour—to Utopia."

To my way of thinking, gentlemen, that is nothing less than economic murder; and it is hard for me to believe that all of these signpost-jugglers are so innocent and so credulous that they can sincerely suppose they are pointing the way to salvation.

We are all riding in the same machine, and we are all going to end up in the same place whether we like it or not. So I think it might be wise indeed to examine the signposts closely. Now it seems to me that the most dangerous deception which has been practiced upon us is the fallacy that our whole economy can be divided into two parts labelled "big" and "little" business. This deception has been used so long and has become so familiar to us that we have begun to accept it, unthinkingly, and without question. Because some statistician has arbitrarily drawn an entirely imaginary line between companies employing more or less than five hundred persons, we argue about big business and little business as though they were two hostile armies warring against each other. And so we fall into the trap that Washington has set for us, by creating class distinction in the industrial world.

How silly that concept is, if we stop to analyze it. There are four million individual business units in this country and they are all part and parcel of one great industrial machine. They are very much like the parts of that cold reducing mill I was watching this morning. Some of them were big and some of them were little. There were tiny electrical contacts and huge steel rolls that weighed several tons each. Some parts ran at high speed, while others ran slower; but all of them were intricately fitted together, and each had a particular job to do. So this mechanical giant went grinding along, rolling the hard, tough steel into strips, as smoothly and as easily as grandmother used to roll piecrust.

But of what use would that machine be to anybody if our Washington theorists once went to work on it? Our economists would cut it up into half a dozen pieces because it is so big. Our statisticians would sort out all the parts into neat piles according to size. Some members of Congress would pass a law decreeing that all the parts must be the same size, or that all must run at exactly the same speed. And in the end, there would be no machine at all. All the parts—the big parts and the little parts—would be junk.

So before the jugglers start taking our American industrial machine apart, there is one simple question I want to address to them. I just want to know *who* is going to put Humpty-Dumpty together again.

Of course, no one *ought* to understand all of this better than our government because never, probably, has the complete interdependence of so-called "big" and "little" business been as clearly demonstrated as it was during the recent war when this great industrial machine of ours shattered all records, and when every part and gear and piston in it was running at breakneck speed.

That was the first time our jugglers had ever had any real opportunity to put their theories to the test and to try to drive the wedge of class distinction into the machinery. They did their best.

They persuaded Congress to set up a special agency whose job it was to funnel war contracts into the hands of "small business." On many items, the Army and Navy agreed to pay small businessmen as much as 15 per cent more than they paid "big business" for the same work. And some government planners so far forgot themselves as to look with favor upon the idea of a *merger*. Heresy of heresies! They proposed to consolidate the efforts of all the small machine shops in an entire region in the hope of creating an industrial establishment big enough to handle large prime contracts.

So what happened?

You gentlemen know the answer as well as I do. When the shooting was over, we found that in spite of all the futile efforts of all the theorists in Washington, 75 per cent of the prime contracts had gone—of necessity—to the hundred largest manufacturing companies in the land.

The theorists were terribly unhappy about it, of course, and great were their lamentations. They could only see it one way, and without bothering even to consult the facts, they jumped despondently to the conclusion that the big had gotten richer and the small had gotten poorer.

They were wrong.

Over in the Department of Commerce and in the Federal Reserve Board, research experts went quietly to work with their calculating machines and came up with some amazing facts.

It was true, they found, that "big business" had been handed the lion's share of the war contracts; but it was *small business* that ended up by scoring the greatest increase in sales, in profits, and in assets. Small business had gained in size and it had gained in wealth at a vastly greater rate than the so-called industrial giants.

The explanation, of course, was all very simple. Big business had merely succeeded in doing what the government had failed to do. It had loaded up small business with contracts—just as it always does, in peace or in war.

It did the biggest jobs on its big machines in its own big plants; but it subcontracted the other jobs that could be done on smaller machines in smaller plants. It took a big company to deliver a finished B-29, but it took hundreds of companies of every conceivable size to make it—to make all the parts and materials that went into it. Which of these companies did the most important part of the job? . . . The big ones? . . . The little ones? Gentlemen, you might as well ask which soldier won the war.

So let us beware of the dangerous and deceptive signpost that would send big and little business down two separate and divergent roads. It is just as dishonest as the second of these fatal frauds that the jugglers would perpetrate upon us—the one they call "monopoly."

Now "monopoly" is a common, and highly unsavory word that all of us understand. Properly employed, it is a useful noun meaning the exact opposite of competition; but our jugglers do not use it as a noun—they use it as an epithet which they hurl freely and with great abandon at any large and successful enterprise on which they may hope to move in.

With impeccable logic, they declare that it is the inalienable right of any man to try to establish himself in any business he wants—even the steel business.

And that is undeniably true.

But then, with fallacious cunning, they insist that he can't go into the steel business because "the monopoly" won't let him. And that is utterly, completely, absolutely and ridiculously false.

What is this "monopoly power" that big business is supposed to possess? What power does United States Steel have, for example, to prevent some intrepid small businessman from setting up shop in the steel business? How could we go about it? What could we do?

Those are questions which our Washington critics, I notice, conveniently ignore; and until somebody answers them for me, I frankly confess that I haven't the slightest idea how I can keep any would-be competitor out of the field. I know of no way to keep him from getting the raw materials he will need or from buying the furnaces, mills and plants he must have. And if he can beat us out on quality, price, or service, I know of no power whatever that can keep him from taking our customers away from us.

No, gentlemen, it isn't "monopoly power" that keeps any small businessman from making steel today. It is simply a little matter of money.

A blast furnace alone will cost him about $12 million, and when he gets his coke ovens, open hearths, his mills, his power and fuel lines and all his auxiliary equipment, he might start turning out hot-rolled bars for an investment of $50 million or so. If he wants to make light plates and cold-reduced sheets, his plant will cost him something over $200 million at today's prices.

And if any businessman has that kind of money, there is nothing "small" about him—not in my book, at least, for he would be one of the world's richest men, and his business would be one of the very largest manufacturing companies in the United States.

Even a large new corporation, with plenty of capital behind it, might hesitate prudently before venturing into the business of making steel—not because "monopoly" exists in the industry, but for exactly the opposite reason—because of the competition which prevails in it today.

In the face of this competition, any newcomer would be at a great disadvantage, because his plant and equipment will cost him from two to three times as much as his competitors had to pay for the same facilities ten years ago—before a quarter-trillion dollar national debt, and a governmental weakness for deficit spending, transformed the almighty dollar into the not-so-almighty sixty-cent piece.

But just because a small businessman may not be able to go into the business of *making* steel, that does not mean that he cannot go into the steel business. Not at all. He can set himself up in the business of *fabricating* steel whenever and wherever he wishes, and for a relatively small capital investment, he can turn out any one or more among thousands of useful, salable, profitable products.

Sometimes I think our Washington theorists ought to turn back to their own governmental records and find out what has really been happening in the steel industry during the past generation. Thirty-three years ago, it is true, there were nearly twice as many establishments *making* steel as there are now, but their product was so crude by comparison with today's steels, that the opportunities for *fabricating* it were limited. Today fewer companies make the steel, but 12,000 more establishments are able to fabricate it. For every steel-making company that has disappeared, sixty new metal-fabricating plants have been successfully established. And for every wage earner who had a job in the industry thirty-three years ago, three are employed today. Now, is that bad? Is that "monopoly"?

Well, let's look at another trick word the jugglers have been palming off on us—"giantism." It's a beauty. It's effective. Nobody loves a giant, and why should they? From the earliest days of our childhood we have thought of giants as monstrous, wicked, bloodthirsty creatures. So, naturally, a giant corporation must be evil. It's all very simple; but what are the facts? How many big companies are there?

According to the government's latest count there are nearly 7,500 of them in America today. A century ago there were none. But wait a minute! For every single company that has grown big in this country during the past hundred years, 440 healthy new enterprises have been born. And, gentlemen, that didn't just *happen*. The truth is that had it not been for the fact that there *are* giants, most of these small establishments could never have existed at all, and could not, today, survive.

No, there is nothing sinful about size, and there should be nothing unlawful about it either.

The *size* of any company depends, in the first instance, upon the product which it intends to manufacture—upon the amount of money it is going to take to buy the plants, machines and tools that will be necessary to produce that product efficiently and competitively. From that point on, the *growth* of the company depends on its customers. If they like the product and want to buy more of it, the company will have to expand in order to meet their demands. If they don't like the product there is no way on earth that the company can force them to buy, no matter how big and how powerful it may be.

That is why today's giant must be useful, helpful, and necessary or he simply goes out of business because he failed to serve his customers to their satisfaction, and therefore failed to serve the public interest.

So when our Washington theorists attempt to place an arbitrary limit on size, they are saying, in effect, that certain products shall not be manufactured at all—except, perhaps, by the government. And when they try to put a limit on growth, they are denying to the American people the right to buy as much as they want of a particular company's product.

For my part, I don't believe that the American people will ever stand for that kind of a restricted, second-class economy.

Finally, there is one more treacherous signpost which we see everywhere these days and which menaces all of us far more seriously than many of us may suppose. The jugglers call it "concentration." It is based on the fallacy that there is something evil and dangerous about the fact that four, or eight, or sixteen, or fifty companies, do 40 or 60 or 80 per cent of the business in their particular industry.

Well, of course they do—and they always will as long as free and honest competition exists in our American economy. In industry or in the field of sports, concentration is the *result* of competition. If the top teams in any baseball league don't win the highest percentage of the games, how are they going to stay on top? And when the top companies in any industry win the highest percentage of the customers, they naturally are going to have the highest percentage of the business.

Any time you see any league or any industry where everybody has come out even, you can be reasonably sure that somehow and somewhere the boys got together in the back room, plugged up the keyhole, and indulged in a little high-handed conspiracy, otherwise known as the "fix." How else could it happen?

That's why there always is and always must be a certain amount of this so-called "concentration" in every American industry; but our inquisitors in Washington insist that "concentration" is especially marked in the steel industry. And gentlemen, I want to take that one apart right here and now, because I think the facts will amaze you.

In the first place, let me say that the steel industry has no special characteristics that could conceivably justify its classification as a public utility, or that could possibly warrant this feverish desire on the part of our Washington bureaucrats to subject it to federal regulation.

Now of *course* steel is vitally necessary to our people and our national economy. So are oil and coal and automobiles, and rubber and lumber and glass, and refrigerators and cookstoves and radios. But certainly steel is no more necessary than clothing, and it is even less necessary than food. If the Washington jugglers are going to regulate every product that is necessary to our national economy, *then, gentlemen, they are going to regulate every single business in America.* Including yours!

And if they are going to break up every industry which is as highly "concentrated" as the steel industry, *nearly half of the units in our American industrial machine will be torn apart.*

Yes. That is the exact, indisputable fact.

The United States Census Bureau has recently completed its latest count of more than four hundred American industries, and has reported on the degree of so-called "concentration" in each. And remember, I am speaking of entire *industries*—not individual companies.

Now how many of these industries do you think are more highly "concentrated" than the steel industry? Three? . . . Ten? . . . Fifty?

Well, guess again. The Census Bureau's own report on "steel works and rolling mills" shows that this industry is not anywhere near the top at all. It is in the great middle, along with the great body of all American industries. In fact, it stands 174th on the list. *So there are 173 entire industries which are more highly concentrated than steel.*

Now what are some of these industries where the "concentration of power" in the hands of the "big four" is so great as to menace our national welfare and to arrest the pursuit of happiness?

You'd never guess.

There is the pretzel industry for one. Honestly, that's right. I mean it.

And there are the candle-makers too.

Then there are straw hats, and streetcars, breakfast foods and chewing tobacco, wallpaper and cigar boxes, lead pencils and pianos. Then we have women's neckwear and boys' underwear. And, oh yes—window shades and garters.

Now if every one of these—plus 159 other industries—is more highly "concentrated" than steel, and if "concentration" is really as wicked as our theorists tell us it is, I can't for the life of me, understand why all these high-priced Congressional committees are wasting their time on me.

Seriously, gentlemen, make no mistake about it. U. S. Steel has been singled out as the target for this present attack on "bigness"—but only temporarily, and if our Washington jugglers now succeed in placing U. S. Steel on trial before the court of public opinion, then they also will have managed to put every successful, growing business in America on trial beside it.

So I wonder if it isn't time to have an entirely new Congressional investigation—one that will hale before it all the other government agencies and Congressional investigating committees which seem to be trying so desperately to destroy the finest and the only successful economic system that exists in the world to-day.

I wonder if it isn't time someone took these gentlemen aside and found out just what public interest *they* are serving—and why?

In short, I wonder if it isn't time to get back on our high-speed highway to progress and growth and production, before we get mired and lost forever on a detour to Utopia!

CIO LABOR POLICIES [4]

PHILIP MURRAY [5]

President Philip Murray, of the Congress of Industrial Organizations, gave this address at the opening of the eleventh annual convention of that organization, in the Public Hall, Cleveland, Ohio, on Monday, October 31, 1949.

Two major issues confronted the convention: (1) Should the strike against United States Steel, then in progress, be prosecuted by labor until its demands should be accepted in full? (2) Should left wing "Communist dominated" unions be expelled from the CIO?

President Murray's address reviewed the strike situation. On June 15 the steel industry flatly rejected the proposal for negotiating with the union the questions of wages, non-contributory pension plans, and the development of related social insurance programs. On July 7th negotiations broke off. President Truman intervened on July 13 and appointed a fact-finding body to report and recommend. On September 10 the Board gave its findings and recommendations. On the 13th the steelworkers accepted, but the next day the steel industry rejected the proposals. The strike started on October 1.

Benjamin F. Fairless of United States Steel was spokesman for the steel industry, comprising some sixty major concerns. The United Steelworkers had a membership of almost a million.

The issues were: (1) Should the steel industry accept a plan costing six cents per hour per worker for pensions and four cents per hour per worker for other social security? (2) Should the management pay all the costs of such pension and social security program?

On the day of Murray's speech, Bethlehem Steel agreed to a "non-contributing" pension plan providing for at least $100 per month for workers retiring at the age of sixty-five after twenty-five years of service. The pension would include old-age benefits payable under the Federal Social Security System. A contributing social insurance plan was also agreed to that would provide for life insurance and other benefits, the company and worker each to pay 2½ cents per hour for such program. On November 13, the United States Steel agreed to similar terms, and the strike was thus ended as a Philip Murray victory.

An aftermath was that "Big Steel" boosted prices of steel on the average of $4 a ton. Labor vigorously denounced the price increases and

---

[4] *Daily Proceedings of the Eleventh Constitutional Convention of the Congress of Industrial Organizations*, Monday, October 31, 1949, Cleveland, Ohio. Permission for this reprinting given through the courtesy of President Murray.

[5] For biographical note, see Appendix.

pointed to U. S. Steel profits for nine months of 1949 as $133,233,409 larger than for any previous comparable period. As Murray in his speech put it: "This giant industry . . . will be able to report . . . profits of approximately one billion dollars, the highest in the entire history of that great industry."

The second great issue raised by President Murray concerned left-wing unions. On November 8, 1935, eight unions of the AFL joined together to promote industrial unionism and established the CIO. Its membership rose from 900,000 to some 6,000,000.

During President Murray's speech most of the 620 delegates vigorously applauded his denunciations of the "Commies" and his recommendations for their expulsion. The left-wing delegates "sat on their hands." Whereas the CIO pressed for the "Fair Deal," the Marshall Plan, the North Atlantic Pact, and similar measures, the left wing (after 1945) allegedly followed the "Moscow-Stalin" line of obstructing these moves.

The Convention voted (1) to bar from membership on the CIO Executive Board all Communists, (2) to expel the United Electrical and the Farm Equipment Workers and to set up a new International Union of Electrical Workers (IUE), and (3) grant to the Executive Board power to expel other left-wing unions.

As speaker, Mr. Murray has accomplished much in round table negotiations. He has believed that most problems can be settled in such conferences, where his considerable storehouse of facts concerning industry and economics can be brought into play. On the platform he speaks quietly, earnestly, with occasional humor. He has excellent voice control. He is little given to overwhelming oratory. He is at his best in open forums and in extempore give-and-take.[6]

I desire to take advantage of this opportunity to express to the Mayor of the City of Cleveland, Archbishop Hoban and others, the sincere appreciation of the delegates participating in this convention, to the City of Cleveland and all of its citizens for their very splendid manifestations of hospitality to the officers and delegates attending this, the Eleventh Constitutional Convention of the CIO.

I should like also to take advantage of this occasion to express to our organizations affiliated with the Congress of Industrial Organizations, the appreciation of the President of this Union for the manner in which most of them have cooperated with me in the promotion of our organization's affairs during the past year. Your Union, the CIO, has taken a leading part

[6] For further comment on Murray as a speaker, see *Representative American Speeches: 1946-47*, p 177-89.

in the conduct of fights, if I may refer to them in such language, in the halls of Congress for the enactment of progressive legislation designed to promote and to protect the wellbeing of not only the members of our own Union but also of our entire citizenry. This mighty organization has won for itself the respect and admiration of all right-thinking people throughout our great land for the courageous, intelligent and constructive manner in which it has fought for the protection of our people and the welfare of our country.

Beginning with the Ninth Constitutional Convention of the Congress of Industrial Organizations in the City of Boston, your organization gave its unanimous approval to the adoption of the European Recovery Program. We loaned our influences in securing through Congress the enactment of this most important piece of legislation. Your organization, through its Executive Board, has given approval to the adoption of the North Atlantic Pact as a necessary adjunct to the furtherance of the work of the European Recovery Program.

In conformity with the expressed desire of the Tenth Constitutional Convention of the CIO your International Executive Board, meeting in the City of Washington last May, adopted a resolution authorizing the accredited officers of this organization to disaffiliate membership in the World Federation of Trade Unions.

We expect to have this convention give approval to the action of your Executive Board upon these all-important matters. Together with our great departed leader, Sidney Hillman, I assumed a substantial measure of responsibility for the formation of the original World Federation of Trade Unions. In so doing I, together with other members of the CIO Executive Board, expressed the hope at that time that the World Federation of Trade Unions would promote the wellbeing of the peoples of the universe, would promote peace, and would promote the healthy development of true democratic trade union movements throughout the world.

Contrary to our expectations the World Federation of Trade Unions was used by certain elements within its structure, to propagandize the world for the purpose of spreading diabolical, subversive communism. Because of our experience as representatives of the CIO within the World Federation of Trade Unions, as well as those of other unions in democratic countries, it became necessary to sever our relationship with the World Federation of Trade Unions this year. In pursuit of our desire to secure the formation of a truly democratic world trade union movement we have joined with the British Trades Union Congress, the American Federation of Labor, and other democratic trade unions in an effort to form a new world labor movement. We hope by the end of the present month, as a result of conferences which are scheduled to begin in London on or about November 26th, to frame a constitution and to create all of the necessary mechanisms incident to the formation of a new democratic world trade union movement.

Since your convention last met in the City of Portland the workers of the United States of America have experienced what I have commonly referred to as a man-made recession in employment. I have consistently contended, since the beginning of the present recession during the spring of the present year, that the unemployment situation in the United States grew out of a desire on the part of leading industrialists to force upon our country widespread unemployment. There was no necessity for the prevalence of unemployment in the United States of America. The extreme and extraordinary demand for American products, not only here in the United States but all over the world, made it quite obvious to all of those of us who had an understanding of our situation here at home that our country should continue to enjoy prosperity—and, if I may add, prosperity of an unprecedented nature. It has been the goal, therefore, of the Congress of Industrial Organizations to correct the evils growing out of this man-made recession by deliberately charging that the responsibility for the creation of unemployment in our country lay directly at the door of the leading manufacturers and industrialists and bankers in this country.

Marvelous changes have taken place in our economic system in the course of the past four or five years—the introduction of new technological devices designed to increase productivity, per capita productivity, lower costs of manufacture and production are evident in almost every line of endeavor. It is particularly notable in a few of the major industries. Witness the giant steel industry, during the year 1948, establishing a record of unprecedented profits, which, in the course of the year 1949, will undoubtedly be surpassed. These tremendous profits are attributable to two factors: one, the great technological improvements that have taken place in the steel industry; and two, the extortion practiced by the employers in the steel industry in charging American consumers extremely and extraordinarily high prices for goods.

It is anticipated that for the present year, although we have had a strike in the basic steel industry for a period of approximately one month, that this giant industry, if it gets back to work quickly, will be able to report to its stockholders and the American people profits of approximately one billion dollars, the highest in the entire history of that great industry. . . .

The presidential fact-finding board, in its recommendations, recommended to the industry and to the Union that the first charge against revenues of the industry should be the investment of moneys for the wear and tear on the human machine, the human being. The Board said so, the President said so, the Union said so, and I believe the American people say so.

I addressed a great meeting in the City of Homestead just about two weeks ago. Homestead is a great steel center, and there were some 25,000 or 30,000 steelworkers there. At that meeting I endeavored to express in graphic form the real, true meaning of this issue. There was an old man there 67 years of age. Forty-four out of those 67 years had been spent in the service of the United States Steel Corporation. He stood beside me, broken down, no money, in a state of complete poverty. He could not pay his rent, he could not buy his medicine, could not provide himself with clothing or purchase his food——44 years of loyal service to that Corporation. I asked him to tell that great crowd of steelworkers what kind of a pension the Steel Corporation was paying him, after 44 years of service, and he said, "The Steel Corporation, Mr. Murray, is paying me 29 cents a month." Twenty-nine cents a month! His frame broken, in a state of complete destitution——and 29 cents expended on that man, that human being who bears the dignity of a man and the dignity of God! Twenty-nine cents, and right across the hill, in a great modern plant, where the machinery is carefully nursed and protected, the same industry had expended in the year 1948 $146,-000,000 to maintain the health and the efficiency of its machine —the inanimate machine, a piece of metal.

That is an issue of major consequence. The industry at the moment is resisting the recommendations of the presidential fact-finding board that has said to the industry: "It is your bounden, God-given responsibility to arise now to your social consciousness, to a position where you might meet the needs of a human being"—like the man I have just referred to.

The Steelworkers are fighting to support the recommendations of the Board, and let me say this to you, this is the first time in the history of our government that any governmental agency or board has recommended to industry the institution of non-contributory pension plans. This is the first time, and we are fighting for it, and we are going to fight for it until we get it.

Wall Street is fighting our Union—we know that. The steel industry is fighting our Union. The President of the American Federation of Labor, in the course of the American Federation of Labor Convention over in the city of St. Paul a few weeks ago, took occasion to castigate me personally because we accepted the recommendations of the presidential fact-finding board. Old Bill! Need I say anything more there? He joined the procession of Wall Streeters and barons of the steel industry.

When the presidential board's recommendations were made to the Steel Union, Wall Street not only attacked us, the steel industry not only attacked us and forced us into a strike, but the Communist Party attacked us as well. I observed when the original attack was made upon us by the Communist Party and by Wall Street that perhaps that is where they both belonged, they ought to get together and sleep in the same bed. They both have the same objectives in mind—totalitarian dictatorship in some form or other; American business on the one hand, communism on the other and decent American labor caught between them fighting, fighting, fighting every day of their lives to improve the lot of people whom they are privileged to represent.

That is the type of strike we have been engaged in. Why, just after the steelworkers had accepted the Presidential Fact-Finding Committee's report, to show you the far-reaching repercussions of the union's decisions in matters of this description, there were transmitted over the shortwave radio system from the City of Moscow three radio addresses. Each of them charged me with being a Wall Streeter, claiming that I was not a fighter, I did not defend my people, criticized the policies of our union —all the way out of Moscow, a distant and remote land. And the same radio addresses transmitted overseas were proclaiming to the universe the militancy of some of our left-wing unions, naming them.

We have had a combination of interests to contend with in the conduct of this strike. But with this combination of interests at work, as they have been until very recently, to undermine the Steelworkers in their strike, like they did the Mine Workers in 1928, these interests, big interests, big money interests, and the Communist Party joined hands in 1928 to destroy the United Mine Workers of America, and they attempted just recently to carry out the same program in 1948. What do they care about trade unionism? Their interests are the interests of the Soviet Government. If that means the disruption of the democratic trade union movement in the United States, the Communist Party will say to you tomorrow, "To hell with trade unionism, I am going to support the Soviets." No devotion to their union.

At meetings of my own Executive Board and the CIO Executive Board, in recent months I have taken occasion to say that I didn't know whether I could talk freely to the members of my own Board or not, I didn't know whether I was talking to a Fink, a Commie, or an FBI man. Now I can't tell you, if I had to take an oath before God Almighty on this platform this morning, whether the fellow I meet who proclaims to be a Communist or serves the Communist Party's interests is an agent of the FBI or the agent of a corporation.

They have said that if we in the CIO are going to cleanse this movement—which, by the way, we are going to do in this convention—it has been surreptitiously scattered around, at least the reports indicate that they might go underground. I don't know where that hole in the ground is they are talking about going to, but I am going to make quite sure that hole in the ground is not under the CIO.

This is a fundamental question that touches the lives of not only the members of the labor movement in the United States of America, but its effects are felt in the home of almost every citizen. No subtlety that might be engaged in by representatives of these organizations to the effect that they are not serving the interests of the Communist Party in this convention will be sufficient to meet the requirements of this delegation.

I became the President of this organization in November 1940. I was ushered into this office against my will. Throughout the early part of 1941 I was treated with a great deal of reserve by certain of the leaders of some of the organizations affiliated with CIO. There was a question mark as to whether or not the new President of the CIO was reliable. The 7th day of December 1941, Japan attacked our country, resulting in a Congressional declaration of war against Japan, which eventually brought our country into this great big international holocaust, World War II, and from December 1941 on to August of 1945, when Japan capitulated or surrendered, almost everything within the family of CIO unions was serene. Some of the extremists who purported to represent the Communist-type of thinking during those days went to the greatest extremes, even to the point of almost abjectly surrendering their trade union principles. For a period of four years I had a great amount of co-operation while there was a war on. The nation needed its production, it had to win a war, it was fighting a war against Hitler and all that Hitler stood for.

And then along came the capitulation of Japan and the ending of the war, and before the end of 1945 the line had changed —the line had changed, there was no longer any unanimity in the Board on matters of policy.

In 1946 we endeavored to correct some of the misgivings in the organization by writing up some new rules for the regulation of our councils, eliminating so far as humanly possible the evil propaganda of the Communist Party in our state and city councils.

In 1947 we reviewed the Communist situation within the CIO, and there was a Convention declaration to the effect that we were definitely and unalterably opposed by communism or any other kind of totalitarianism, including fascism. And the convention adopted that. But that was not sufficient to meet the requirements of our situation.

During the Portland convention in 1948, we again reexamined our situation, and at that time the convention carefully reviewed the situation and gave greater emphasis in its pronunciamentos to the effect that this organization of ours could no longer tolerate the infiltration and propaganda of the Communist Party into the trade union movement of America.

In May of the present year the CIO Executive Board met in the city of Washington. In pursuance to instructions given it by the last National Convention of the CIO, it adopted another resolution, and that resolution proclaimed to our membership the fact that no one who adhered to the communistic philosophy and propagated communism to the detriment of our trade union movement in this country could hope to serve in office or be a member of our International Executive Board. The May declaration of the CIO Executive Board was fought bitterly by certain elements within the Board. This servile process of serving the interests of the Communist Party continued following the May declaration of the CIO Executive Board.

We come around now to another convention, the 11th Constitutional Convention of the Congress of Industrial Organizations. As the President of your organization I have exhausted every measure of tolerance and patience in an effort to compose the difference between those groups who serve our organization as members of the CIO Executive Board. I find it impossible for the President of your organization to resolve the issues. I am, so far as I am concerned, just as far apart from the philosophy of those who advocate support of the communistic cause as the two poles might be, just as far apart. There is no way, no decent way by which we can hope to resolve these issues in the International Executive Board. It cannot be done. The issues have their roots, and those roots are deep, and they are fundamental, and there will therefore be recommended to this convention certain definite, constructive, constitutional changes designed to put an end to these practices within the Congress of Industrial Organizations.

It is my hope that this convention will respond to the recommendations of your committees when they are placed before you on this all-important subject.

I have covered a number of the more important aspects of problems which in due course will be presented to the convention and acted upon by you.

I do express the hope—I always do—that we will have a good convention, a constructive convention, a convention designed to serve the best interests of the millions we represent.

We have thrust upon our shoulders great and very grave responsibilities, obligations that not only run to the membership of our own unions, but grave obligations and responsibilities which run to our people and to our country. This convention has a prime interest in protecting the welfare and the well-being of our people and our nation. We seek the preservation of the CIO as a forward-looking, militant, constructive, democratic trade union movement. We will lend our services in that direction to not only the members of our own organization here at home, but to the new world labor movement which will undoubtedly be created before the end of the present year.

I wish at this juncture, therefore, to express to you my appreciation for the patience which you have exercised while I have taken the liberty to express my point of view to you on some of the more important issues to come before this convention. I thank you.

UNITED AUTOMOBILE WORKERS:
AIMS AND PROGRAM [7]

WALTER P. REUTHER [8]

President Walter Reuther of the United Automobile Workers, Congress of Industrial Organizations, gave this address at the opening of the Twelfth Constitutional Convention, at Milwaukee, Wisconsin, on July 10, 1949.

The speech aimed to stir the delegates to unwavering support of the coming showdown concerning wages and pensions with the Ford, Chrysler, and other automobile companies.

The address enunciated vigorously the labor philosophy of Reuther. To him and his million-member union, government legislative programs and policies favored big business; industry's profits, although necessary for the continued prosperity of labor, were unduly swollen. A disproportionate share of these earnings and profits was going to stockholders and management, or reserved for future dividends. To labor, demanding a larger percentage of these profits, it was clear that wage increases and pension provisions could be effected without increasing prices. General prosperity, to Reuther and his UAW, depended on full employment at relatively high wages and in a market with sufficiently low prices to ensure general purchasing power and thus wide distribution of goods and services. Reuther had been a Socialist, an organizer of automobile workers, and a powerful spokesman in negotiations with management since 1935.[9]

President Reuther, in this speech, closely articulates with the needs, attitudes, and stereotypes of his audience. He uses freely personal references, specific examples of his points, detailed evidence, occasional colorful and idiomatic language (e.g., "twilight period," "hifalutin'"), sarcasm and invective ("They are sitting there in Wall Street on their fat money bags. . . . The people in Wall Street who are doing these things that drive us down the road to depression are Joe Stalin's real fifth-column agents in America").

Reuther is a vigorous debater, intelligent in his analysis of a problem, in marshalling of facts and in quick reply. Many conservatives who fear labor domination look to Walter Reuther and to his brother Victor as stabilizing agents.

[7] Text supplied by the public relations department of the United Automobile Workers, CIO, Frank Winn, director, and by permission of President Walter Reuther.

[8] For biographical note, see Appendix.

[9] For introductory comment on Reuther and for examples of his speeches, see *Representative American Speeches: 1945-1946*, p165-79; *1947-1948*, p103-17.

In November 1949, UAW negotiations with the Ford Company resulted in an agreement generally regarded as a victory for labor. That company was to contribute 8¾ cents an hour per worker to provide a pension at the age of 65 of $100 per month, including Social Security benefits. The company was to continue a contribution of 1¼ cents per hour for social welfare. Thus the plan and settlement gave the UAW a strong lever in its effort to exact similar terms from other automobile companies during 1950.

Mr. Chairman, distinguished guests, delegates to the twelfth Constitutional Convention, fellow workers and friends:

I want first to thank Mayor Ziedler, in behalf of this convention for his words of welcome. Milwaukee truly is a progressive community, but Mayor Zeidler is a modest citizen, he did not advise you of the most important function that he has performed with respect to this convention.

When he learned that 2,400 thirsty Automobile, Aircraft and Agricultural Implement Workers were going to convene in the hot days of July he called an emergency conference over at the City Hall, and who do you think he invited? Mr. Pabst, Mr. Blatz, and Mr. Schlitz, and he said, "You don't know these guys in the UAW; they have capacities that are unlimited." And Mr. Schlitz, Mr. Blatz and Mr. Pabst put on a third shift in every plant in Milwaukee, and we thank the good Mayor for that special service, because we will need it before the convention is over. I speak as a guy who knows.

Twelve years ago we met in this same auditorium. We were a young organization. We had just come out of the sit-down strikes. Since that day twelve years ago the UAW-CIO has been in the vanguard of the struggle of American labor to move forward in the building of that kind of world in which the people, whose sweat and skill and labor create the wealth, can realize their full equity of the fruits of their labor.

In those twelve years we can be proud of the fact that we wrote some glorious and militant chapters in labor's struggle.

We meet today in a difficult period, a period of great decision, a period when, throughout the world, there is fear and anxiety in the hearts and minds of men, because they are uncertain and afraid of what tomorrow will bring.

This is a kind of twilight period in the world. We have neither war nor peace. We have neither prosperity nor depression. But we can't stay balanced in that middle position; we are either going forward to peace and freedom and abundance, or we are going to slide back to depression and war and disaster. And what this convention does during this week—how effectively we mobilize our power to implement the current contract negotiations, how effectively the steelworkers fight on their front, and the coal diggers on their front, and how effectively labor fights in every aspect of the economic struggle—will be decisive in determining whether we go forward or backward.

As the banner says, we can drift to depression and war and disaster. But we have to plan and work and fight for peace and security and freedom and abundance.

They tell the story that when the Marines were storming the beachheads in the South Pacific one group of Marines, after they had made themselves secure on the beachhead, put up a sign that read: "Golden Gate in '48; Breadline in '49."

The atomic bomb changed the calendar date of the first item, but the atomic bomb will not solve the problem of growing breadlines in 1949. That will be solved only if you and I and millions of other Americans who believe that we fought a war in order to have an opportunity for free men to work out their economic and political destinies, will mobilize the productive power for building the peace as we did for war and destruction. If we fail we lose all. We will shatter the common hopes and aspirations of people everywhere.

This convention has got to speak out in clear and unmistakable language. We have got to ask the same question which those Marines asked, the same question that five million unemployed Americans are asking, the same question that hungry people all over the world are asking. That is this question: if they could give us a gun to fight in war, if they could give us a job producing for destruction, producing to kill life in achieving the negative ends of war, why can't they give us employment and a job making the good things in life for people in peacetime?

You can dress up the problems of the world, you can put them into hifalutin' sounding language in the United Nations, or you can write them in noble resolutions, but fundamentally the struggle in the whole world is for men to find the answer to the age-old problem, how do you solve the basic economic problems and get economic security for the great mass of people without at the same time robbing them of their basic political freedoms? That is the problem we have to find an answer to, and people all over the world are looking to America for the answer, because we have everything it takes to find the answer. The American economy, our human and material resources, our technical know-how, our tremendous productive capacity—these are freedom's greatest asset. But they will not find the answer unless we help them intelligently in finding that answer. And unless we can find the answer in America it cannot be found any place in the world. We say to the world, we are going to find that answer, and that is part of the job of this convention.

We know that the answer will not be found in the magic formulas of totalitarianism, Fascist or Communist. They offer a promise of economic security at the price of freedom and spiritual enslavement. Nor will the answer of America—and we have got to make this clear—nor will the answer be found in the kind of reckless socially irresponsible Wall Street economics of "boom and bust," which offer you freedom at the price of security.

We take the position in America that we want both bread and freedom, and it is possible to have both bread and freedom living in democracy's house side by side. You don't have to trade one for the other; we can have both. . . .

We have lost $23 billion in the first half of 1949. If we had full employment we could be making about $273 billion in production in goods, but we are only getting $250 billion, so we are losing $23 billion worth. That is enough to pay for all these things we are asking for. But the boys down in Washington who are beating the economic drums just don't understand these elementary things, or they don't want to.

The world is going to judge America, and we in America must judge ourselves, not by our technical progress, not by our ability to split the atom or make a jet ship go seven hundred miles an hour. We have got to judge ourselves as the world would judge us, by our ability to translate technical progress into human progress, human security, human dignity and human happiness.

It is of little consolation if you happen to be among the five million unemployed in America, to sit down in your kitchen with a bare table and tell your kids, Mary and Johnny and Susie, "Don't feel too badly about the fact daddy is unemployed and we can't get you all the things you want and need to eat. Remember America is a great country, we know how to split the atom, and down in Oak Ridge at the Atomic Energy plant, they are building a bigger and bigger stockpile of atomic bombs every day." I say that will not feed the hungry stomachs of the kids in America. Human needs have to be taken care of. That is what we are fighting for when we talk about these things in this convention. I say the hour is getting late, and if we let things slip we can lose everything, and labor has the opportunity to take the lead in America and demonstrate that leadership, that vision and courage and that imagination necessary to formulate democratic solutions to our complicated economic and political problems and translate those solutions into programs of action.

That is the challenge before us. We have all the tools in America to conquer human insecurity. We have the material resources and everything. It is a question of whether the people are going to use them or whether we are going to be blocked by the powers that be in Wall Street. You hear a lot of talk about planning in America, and the Wall Street boys would have you believe they don't plan. Well, they plan, but it's the wrong kind of planning. The conflict in America is between two kinds of planning. It is privately planned economic scarcity by companies for profits or publicly planned economic abundance for people. That is really the struggle. I say the challenge can be met. We have to build a broad coalition of labor and farmers in America and weld a joint political and economic program. With a program that makes sense, these forces, welded together in America, can be the architects of tomorrow. It is a big job, but we in the UAW-CIO come into this convention better equipped than ever before to discharge our broad responsibilities. During the past several months we have had more than a million dues-paying members. Since the last convention we have organized

366 new shops, with more than 200,000 new members, the biggest peacetime increase in our membership in the history of our union. Financially we are stronger, but we are not strong enough, and this convention must address itself to that problem.

Internally we are in the healthiest condition we have ever been. By and large we have broken up the destructive power of factional political blocs. We have tried to weld together the forces in this union around a militant, democratic program, around the slogan that we raised at last convention, "Teamwork in the Leadership and Solidarity in the Ranks." We still have a little more progress to make on that, but we have gone a long way in welding together the forces of this union—not on a personal or political basis, but on the basis of a sound, democratic, militant trade union program.

We have got to go out and complete the organization of the unorganized in every segment of our jurisdiction. We have got to work to build, first a practical working unity among American labor unions, and some day to have organic unity, one powerful union in America representing all the workers, and when we do that we will be in a position to do something that has to be done. We have got to take steps to see to it that we get a national labor daily newspaper with regional supplements in every community in America. We have got to have these things.

Since the last convention we have taken a step forward in our radio program. Some months ago we dedicated WDET, the first UAW-CIO radio station in Detroit. Two weeks ago we dedicated the second UAW-CIO radio station, WCUO in Cleveland. We ought to urge at this convention that every labor union that can get the money, every farm group, every co-op group that can get the money, do so and build a radio station, so that we can tie together a national labor-farm-co-op hookup covering the whole country. We have got to get the tools to fight this battle with, because we are up against powerful opposition. We have to work with the farm groups, we have to support their basic program to get security in our economy, and we have got to build the co-ops.

There are many other problems that I will not discuss now, but which we will discuss in detail at the various committees on them. I only want to say that this convention can be an important milestone in the forward march of our great union. Let us work together, plan together and act together in this convention in the spirit and in the tradition of our great union. And I say, working together, planning together, acting together for the great, broad sections of America with the people of goodwill in America, with the help of God we can go forward and build that better world where men can be free and secure, where they can live in dignity and brotherhood and peace with the rest of the world.

I thank you.

A LONG RANGE FARM PROGRAM [10]

ALLAN BLAIR KLINE [11]

Mr. Allan Kline, President of the American Farm Bureau Federation, and Charles F. Brannan, Secretary of the United States Department of Agriculture, debated before the National Farm Institute, Des Moines, Iowa, in the KRNT Theater, on February 18, 1950. The four thousand members of the audience often cheered or booed.

The Institute was sponsored by the Agricultural Department of the Des Moines Chamber of Commerce in cooperation with the Iowa Farm Press and farm organizations. J. S. Russell, farm editor of the Des Moines *Register and Tribune,* presided over the debate. The purpose of the Institute was "to promote free discussion and objective study of farm questions as related to national and world economy."

Mr. Kline gave the opening address, and Mr. Brannan followed. The debate took almost two hours. Professor T. W. Schultz, of the University of Chicago, afterward conducted a turbulent panel.

The issue of the debate was: "Shall the Brannan plan be adopted?" Secretary Brannan proposed his plan early in 1949 as a method of dealing with farm surpluses. The government would support farm income at "relatively high levels" by crop purchases, loans, and direct payments to farmers. Farm prices would be allowed to reach their own levels in the open market, to the advantage of the consumer. The government would pay the farm producer the difference between this open market price and the "support" level. The government would determine the acreage to be permitted to each farmer for a given crop.

The Farm Bureau, representing some 1,400,000 farmers, at their 31st annual convention in Chicago on December 12, 1949, denounced the plan as "regimentation" and "nationalization of agriculture."

The Des Moines debate developed into a personal and bitter clash. Kline as speaker is forceful and even eloquent. He had public speaking courses at Morningside College, Iowa, but most of his experience, as he states, "has been with actual public speaking. My objective has been rather uniformly to create understanding of problems, and also to create both desire and intention to act on issues which listeners might confront." [12]

Mr. Brannan was vocally less relaxed, tended to elevate unduly his pitch and tighten his voice. He gesticulated frequently and often at ran-

[10] *Proceedings of the Twelfth National Farm Institute, 1950.* Text supplied by the Des Moines, Iowa, Chamber of Commerce, and permission to reprint given through the courtesy of Allan Kline.

[11] For biographical note, see Appendix.

[12] Letter to this editor, March 11, 1950.

dom. He resorted to personalities and sarcasm more than did his opponent.

Professor Schultz criticized both speakers for by-passing important issues. According to him, both arguers completely ignored the discussion of basic commodities—tobacco, cotton, peanuts and wheat. Both proposed to retain acreage allotments, marketing quotas, and marketing controls. "Neither is prepared to abandon them in good times. Why not?" "Neither debated the problem of poverty in agriculture." "More than a million farm families have been by-passed by the economic programs." [13]

The Brannan plan, supported by President Truman, continued to be a major domestic issue in the political speaking of 1950.

It is under rather peculiar auspices that I am here today. I have been on the National Farm Institute program for many years, and have assisted in a good many ways. But I have been reading in the papers and hearing on the radio that this session is a sort of contest—a peculiar sort of contest. That makes it a little difficult for me, and I want to take a few minutes to explain why.

For one thing, you have also on the program a fellow who is a recognized political exponent. He is a member of the President's cabinet. He is frankly, honestly, aggressively partisan and political in his approach to this question. That makes it difficult to have a contest, because I am president of the American Farm Bureau Federation. I was elected by Farm Bureau members— 1,409,000 of them. They set the policies and they are half Republicans and half Democrats. All of them are agreed that we should decide agricultural policy on a nonpartisan basis, that we should make every possible effort to consider issues on their merits and decide them on the basis of what is right and what is wrong. That makes it difficult for me.

I will give you an illustration—one peculiarly pertinent to this state in which many of you live. During the past year there has been much national publicity to the effect that during the last presidential campaign I campaigned for Mr. Dewey in Iowa, and that in spite of my efforts I was unable to switch the farmers of Iowa to Mr. Dewey. Some of you may have said, "It must have been over in some other part of the state." But the people who live there thought it was in your part of the state. Because I

[13] Des Moines *Register and Tribune*, February 19, 1950.

wasn't in your state, I didn't make a speech. I didn't write a speech, I didn't make a telephone call, I didn't send anybody out, and nobody came to see me. It is that sort of thing that I want to get out of your minds.

I am going to roll up for you some ideas. All I want you to do is to twist them, turn them, look at them from both sides, and see whether they stand up. Let's think together on this proposition of agricultural policy as it fits into the present scene and see whether we can make up our minds about the direction in which we would like to go.

As a representative of farmers and as a farmer myself, I think I know what farmers want. What they want is prosperity and all the things that go with it, all the advantages created by the sort of situation in agriculture that we think we must have and to which we think we are entitled. . . .

The approach of the farmers who are members of the American Farm Bureau Federation is based on the philosophy that the American system of regulated free enterprise really works, that it has been as peculiarly successful as it is peculiarly American, and that we ought to make whatever we do consistent with that kind of economy.

At the same time, of course, we ought not lose sight of the necessity of preventing monopoly in business and out of business, nor of the necessity for maintaing a high production per man in agriculture. The only chance you will have of getting a high standard of living—build a new house, buy new furniture, landscape the front yard, or plant a tree and sit in the shade and tell the world to go rest—the only chance you will have depends on the service you render to society. Whenever you lose sight of that fact, or allow something to come in and restrict your capacity to render service, look out! You are the people with the most to lose, and if you lose, America loses, too, because it has been that pattern of progress which has made possible what we have done in the past.

There was a time when you went 'way out to the well to get water. We made a great improvement when we put a pump in the back yard. How did we get the job done? We did it by improving the capacity of farmers to earn—the most fundamental requirement of all. Any price support program must be fitted into that kind of a proposition. That is the reason, for instance, why we are in favor of flexible price supports.

Some of you who were at this meeting last year remember that I said there was faulty economics in the notion of some farmers that loans on corn were all pure gain. It might not have been too bad an idea if we had fed more corn—if we had fed a few more cattle and if they had not reached $41.50—because then the corn would have been used up. Any time you take a half billion bushels of corn off the market, you have added to demand. But any time you put that corn back on the market, you subtract from demand. There is an equal and contrary effect. You have to keep that in mind if you want to think straight—and we need desperately to think straight because we are dealing with the question of whether agriculture is going to continue to be more prosperous or whether we are going to give up.

Now there is another philosophy—the philosophy that you can't afford to take a chance, that you can't afford to depend on yourself, that you have to depend on a guaranteed fair price, or alleged fair price, set by the government. As much as I regret it, I suppose I have to identify that philosophy as the Brannan plan.

In considering that plan, I have two choices: First, I can assume it means exactly what it says; second, I can assume it does not. If I take the second choice, then I am assuming it is pure hokum. I don't assume that. I take it for granted that it means what it says, that it is the idea presented by Secretary Brannan to the agricultural committee of the house, that it is the plan being presented by employees of the Department of Agriculture to farmers here and there over the country. I take it for granted that it is a proposal to support prices until they reach the income support standard.

I want to refer to my business. I raise pigs. I have raised pigs all my life since I was old enough to raise anything. Long before I was able to raise hell I raised pigs. That is my business. Now here is a proposition which says that we will be guaranteed $19 for pigs and $1.46 for corn. That is a 13-to-1 corn-hog ratio, and I don't need to tell you what that means. Everybody decides to raise more pork, and a lot of people who didn't raise any pork before now decide to keep two sows. Here is a profitable level, a supposedly guaranteed profit. So you get a lot of pork.

Presumably that is a good idea. But let's look at what would happen. Over the past two months you fellows have been selling hogs for about $15. If they had been supported at $19, it would have cost the taxpayer $4 a hundred plus the costs of administration. And, mind you, if we went ahead and produced still more and they went on down in price—and demand for most food products is such that if you increase supplies by 20 per cent you get more than a 20 per cent reduction in price—the tax would still be up there, plus the cost of administration.

I have said that we must live with big government and we do, because there are a lot of things that you and I want government to do for us. But we have the problem of keeping it responsive to the people. When you have the expansion in production I have described, you have not only the problem of cost but also the difficulties caused by a very large, centrally administered government. When you have an expansion in uneconomic production and then start controlling—and you must control because you couldn't get the appropriations required if you don't—you soon get into the ridiculous. . . .

Finally, there is this question: Is it appropriate and proper for farmers and others to build on the record of the past—to use the means which have been successful in America? Or must we go over to a system of letting the government figure out on a statistical basis who is to produce what for whom and how much each is to produce? You may think we aren't heading that way. The best example I know is the tobacco program. I recommend a little compulsory reading of the debate on the Chapman amendment to the Agricultural Act of 1949—an amendment sponsored, not by people against the tobacco program, but by congressmen from Kentucky and Tennessee. The proposal was that minimum tobacco allotments were reduced from 9/10ths of an acre to 5/10ths of an acre, with everybody entitled to the minimum. And, as Senator McKellar pointed out, 72 per cent of all tobacco allotments are at the minimum of 9/10ths of an acre. Is that the direction in which you want to go? Where would America be if we did that? With everybody trying to get an allotment of 5/10ths of an acre of tobacco because there is a guaranteed profitable price, you would, of course, squeeze economic production. And you don't get plenty that way.

Is our peculiarly successful regulated free enterprise worth fooling with any more? Maybe we ought to discard the blooming thing and start over. Maybe we ought to copy another pattern. After all, we are in a period of great confusion following a great world war, and we are cutting the pattern for the future today. Maybe we ought to cut out a new one. Maybe we ought to base it on some new plan. Maybe we ought to say that we shouldn't let these things be decided by too many people. Maybe we ought to have more controls so we can guarantee more to everybody.

Or we can increase opportunity, then restrain ourselves and keep the rest of the money to do with as we please. That is my philosophy and the philosophy of the American Farm Bureau. Has it worked? I recommend that you read, in the January issue of the *Atlantic Monthly* the article by Sumner Slichter, a great business and management-labor analyst, recognized not only in this country but throughout the world.

Suppose someone had told you in 1900 that this country was going to have to fight two great wars in the next fifty years. Suppose he had described those wars and had said: "We are going to take out all the men, materials and production necessary to fight those wars to a successful conclusion, and at the same time we are going to cut working hours from 58 to 40 a week, increase consumption of goods per capita by 250 per cent, increase the percentage of kids in college three times as fast as the population grows, and have three out of four of all children of high school age in school." You would have said: "You're crazy. That can't be done. It is ridiculous." But it is in the record: That is what we did do in America.

I think I know why we did it. I think it was because there was something fundamentally right about America—something which said to every individual citizen: "This is the land of opportunity. We are going to try to help you and you are going to help yourself. If you render an unusual service to society— whether you raise pigs, cattle, corn or cotton, or whether you are a worker in a factory, a schoolteacher, coal miner, ditch digger or whatever you are—we are going to try to create opportunity, we are going to try to make it possible for you to use your imagination, and you will get paid on the basis of the service you render to society." Look at the record. Did it work? The whole world is coming to America's door to see how we got it done. The only people who would sell America short are Americans. (Applause.)

We have done another thing. I confidently believe that Americans are better than before. If they are, it is because this kind of system encouraged a man to use what he had, to be a little better each generation than in the generation before, to somehow fan the little spark of divinity in every man, and we had millions of people doing it. What it did was to create a great light. It is the light of the whole world here in the middle of the twentieth century. It shows up over the horizon of tomorrow, and it is the only possible light that shows to free men any place in the world the capacity or possible capacity to dispel the dismal gloom of a philosophy that is completely opposite—a philosophy which says, "Man is nothing; the state is everything," a philosophy which has a ruthless recklessness about it which submerges the individuality of every citizen and denies the existence of God.

This thing we have is a different thing. This is the proposition that it is the citizen that counts—that the important question is: Are we better today than we were yesterday? This is the time to stick out your chest, take a full breath, and say that you have the same kind of courage as did the men who left you the most magnificent heritage in the history of the world.

A FARM PLAN FOR THE FUTURE [14]

CHARLES F. BRANNAN [15]

Charles F. Brannan, Secretary of Agriculture, gave this speech at Des Moines, on February 18, 1950, as a continuation of the debate on the Brannan plan for agriculture. For detailed comment see the introduction to Kline's speech, p 196.

These kinds of programs going on over this country and participated in by farmers—by the people who are directly and immediately affected—are as fundamental expressions of our democracy as can be found anywhere. I believe that out of American agriculture have come many of the roots of American democracy. We got cooperatives and we got the cooperative spirit; we got the method of working together to develop and improve the things we were doing; and I believe that the residual depository of that influence in America is still among the farmers. It is there more so—as demonstrated by our farm cooperatives, as demonstrated by our committee system—than you will find in any place else in the country.

In his opening, Mr. Kline made the personal reference to the fact that I am a politician. Ladies and gentlemen, I plead guilty. (Laughter and applause.) I thought that in a democracy people expressed their point of view about what was going on and about what had gone on. So last year when Mr. Kline, as he eloquently told us, maintained hands off of everything mildly suggesting politics, I confess that I was out telling the American people in my inadequate way that I thought there was a threat to farmers' cooperatives in legislation which had been proposed to the Congress, and that the threat was coming from people who called themselves politicians because they were members of the House

[14] *Proceedings of the Twelfth National Farm Institute, 1950.* Text supplied through the courtesy of the Agricultural Department of the Des Moines Chamber of Commerce. Permission to reprint given through the courtesy of Charles F. Brannan. Because of the extreme length of the debate, it has been possible to include here only a part of the argument.
[15] For biographical note, see Appendix.

and Senate and who perhaps were under the influence of people outside.

I went about this country telling American farmers that there had been a group in Congress which had taken away the right of your government to assist you in providing adequate storage for the ever-increasing crops we have been able to produce. I went about this country telling the people of America that I thought the gentleman then in the White House was a great human being and that he was entitled to your consideration for the position of President—and that is a political position if there ever was politics in this country.

Ladies and gentlemen, I am guilty of being a politician. And I say to you that again this year I shall go to the American people and I shall tell them that cooperatives are being threatened again. I shall tell them that there is another attempt to deprive us of the right to have adequate storage facilities. I shall tell them all the rest of the things that I think should be known by citizens with the right to vote—and this is one of the few countries on the face of the earth with that right. I shall exhort them to cast their ballots—I don't care how—but to cast them intelligently. And I say above all that I shall not sit back in a holier-than-thou attitude and say that I do not participate in politics. (Applause and whistles.)

We have before us for consideration today some serious problems of farm policy—problems which demand an early solution, not only in the farmer's interest but for the welfare of the entire nation. There are undoubtedly a number of approaches that would help us try to get at this problem, but I would like to suggest today—because we are objectively trying to reach some understanding as to where we ought to be going from here—that we take this approach:

At my request a bushel of corn has been placed on the platform. If you will assume that this bushel of corn is the first extra bushel beyond our assumed domestic need, beyond export requirements, and beyond even the safe reserves required to protect the nation against crop failure or other emergency, then it is a symbol of our major national farm problem.

It is the extra bushel. It is the bushel for which a satisfactory market must be found if the men who produced it are to get a fair price and if it is to do anybody any good. Its counterpart is to be found in many other kinds of crops whether measured in bushels or bales or tons or in any other fashion. Yet it is no different from any other bushel of corn. Time and effort and money are required to produce it, and it contains the same essential feed values as does all the rest of our corn.

Farmers may accidentally produce it in good faith as part of their effort to earn a living for their families and to help feed our nation adequately and properly. They can produce many like it through more efficient use of their resources, through new and better farm practices, through better care of the soil, through new varieties developed by long and painstaking research, and through mechanization to cut down man-hours of labor.

What are we going to do with that extra bushel of corn? In my opinion, there are just two alternatives: We must either consume it by transforming it into meat, milk, eggs or poultry and by getting that extra food eaten; or we will have to lock up that extra bushel of corn and go back to the American farmer and say, "Next year, don't produce quite so much."

Of course, there are some industrial uses for a small portion of that extra bushel of corn. But the alcohol manufacturer who is one of those industrial users could not pay the American farmer more than fifty cents for that bushel and still produce alcohol and stay in business. He has to compete with sorghum from Cuba and with potatoes from a lot of places. (Applause and laughter.)

So that is all the choices we have, unless I don't understand this economy. That is all the choices we have and that about sums up our farm problem today. There it is—that extra bushel of corn. The future course of our farm policies will determine what shall happen to it, whether we use its potential nutritional values for better diets or whether we stop producing it—if it is possible to stop. Making use of it will benefit both farmers and consumers. Abandoning its production will be a sacrifice for both of us. . . .

Nor do I believe that the farmers or the rest of the American people are willing to concede that more efficient use of resources is a waste because it produces that extra bushel, or that we should give up the know-how for producing that abundance. We want to learn, and must learn, to live with our abundance. That is why I have advocated a farm program aimed at making use of that abundance rather than shackling it.

I want to discuss some of those recommendations with you today. I want to point out to you that we have not suggested that you abandon a single one of the things that have been put into legislation since 1935, when we first began to get good, sound farm legislation in this country. But just as any other program must be dynamic or adapted to the new things we know, learn and have done, so must we make in our farm program the necessary improvements required by changing conditions.

There still appears to be some misconception—and I have been listening to another evidence of it—and lack of understanding of our recommendations and even of my motives for having made them. Some of this is the natural result of insufficient information, but I say to you in complete candor and without any feeling of malice at all that some of the misinformation and misconception has been intentionally manufactured by the leadership of a great farm organization. (Applause, boos and whistles.)

But whatever the cause, let's do a little objective study about it. Let's get down to some of the basic concepts. (Applause.) I am for parity. I am for the original concept of parity and a standard of equality for agriculture—a fair share of the national income for the farmers who contribute so greatly to creating that income. I am thinking in terms of people rather than just in terms of commodities. I want parity of opportunity for the farmers to earn a fair return from investment of capital, of labor and of skill, and of their management ability—not just parity for the bushel of corn. I want parity of living opportunity for the farm family and for all of the farm families.

I am against any form of regimentation. (Applause.) I am against any form of controls that can reasonably be avoided and which may not have the affirmative support of a large majority of the producers affected. I am for the widest possible freedom of choice by the farmer himself in the management of his enterprise. I am for the farm programs that will make the maximum use of our farm production so we can avoid the strict controls that will be inevitable if we fail to provide profitable and useful outlets for the extra bushel of corn. I am for efficiency of production and for constantly increasing it. But I do not agree with those who hold that the only path to efficient production is industrialized mass farming.

I want to see no collectives taking over the farms of America, whether of the Soviet design or of the corporate pattern. (Applause.) I believe that the family-type farm can be efficient, and I believe we should concentrate our efforts for increased efficiency upon the family-size farm and the family-size farm unit, because of the important human value it contributes to our society, if for no other reason. I am for encouraging, strengthening and preserving it as the backbone of American agriculture, not for turning our backs upon it and destroying it in the false name of increased efficiency.

I am for government economy—for economy by eliminating the uneconomic practices . . . (Laughter.)

Now let me speak to the hecklers a moment: Do you remember the summation of Mr. Kline a few moments ago when, if I understood it, he even accused anybody who didn't follow the program he sponsors of being un-Godlike? Is that what he said? (Applause, cries of "yes" and "no".) Who was he talking about? He had been talking about me all afternoon, so you can't say it was a gross assumption. But let's get down to the hecklers: Come right on any time; this is a grand America where everybody has a right to say what they want to say. I don't know whether the radio will hold out, but if you will be patient with me—those of you who did not come to heckle—I am going to try to say what I intended to say. (Applause.)

I want to remind you again that I am your servant. I am your employee; you pay my salary. I do in the Department of Agriculture what I conscientiously think is my best. It may not be good enough. But I do say to you that when I come out here to talk to you about these problems and to express what is in my heart and mind—and I sat quietly while my opponent made considerable light of the serious recommendations we have made—it occurs to me that in line with something we used to call "American" you might hear the guy out. (Applause.)

Now for the benefit of the hecklers I say again: I am for government economy. I am for economy eliminating the un-economical practices of present price support methods that waste good food and penalize the consumers by making them pay the costs twice—first in their tax bill and second in their food bill. I am for doing everything in our power now to avoid the tremendous cost to government of another disastrous depression, and to avoid its cost in human misery to the people of our nation. . . .

But just what is our situation today? Are we making progress toward our objective? Are we slipping backward or are we on the right track? Unfortunately, both farm prices and incomes are headed in the wrong direction. Farm prices have dropped an average of almost one fourth in less than two years. They are still going down, but farmers still have to pay within 5 per cent as much for what they buy as they paid two years ago. In 1947, farm operators had a net income of nearly $18 billion. Last year it was down to around $14 billion. The forecast for 1950 is for a net income of under $12 billion. That is a net decline of almost one third in net farm income at a time when national income is at its all-time peak.

Is this the way to parity? Is this a desirable trend? The gap between farm and non-farm income is widening instead of closing. Even at the peak of agricultural income total per capita income of persons on farms—and I am talking about both commercial and non-commercial farmers—was only 60 per cent as high as for persons not on farms. In 1949 this income gap widened and in 1950 it is expected to widen still more.

The people on farms constitute one fifth of the total population, yet the year before last they got from their farms less than 10 per cent of the national income and last year they got only 7.8 per cent of the total national income. We are headed away from, instead of toward, our real concept of parity—which in my opinion is equality of opportunity for agriculture.

Should we not be disturbed about this? Should we not seek its cause and should we not offer some kind of remedies and suggestions which might reverse that trend? Must those in public office whose duty it is to be particularly sensitive to these trends be attacked as "stupid," "dishonest," or as "nuts" because they speak out about such trends and seek to offer some kind of remedy?

Behind and around all the pros and cons, the underlying conflict is in the very philosophy of our farm policy itself. You are confronted with two entirely different ways of thinking about what objectives we should seek for the American farmer.

One group, of which the present administration is a part, believes it is in the best interests of the entire nation to use price supports as a means for providing agriculture the opportunity to earn a fair income. It does not propose to guarantee that income to anybody. But it does propose to assure diligent farmers the opportunity of achieving a level of income that would bring them closer to the goal of equality with other groups.

On the other hand, there are those who preach that the only role of price support is to protect the farmer against bankruptcy. In other words, they see no reason for stopping price and income declines until the farmer's back is against the wall.

The Farm Bureau's present national leadership, if I understand it correctly, may fall in that category. It advocates "stop-loss" price supports—whatever they are. Sometimes it uses that terminology and sometimes it uses more exact language. Sometimes they say they are only against "unreasonable" price declines. What do you mean by "unreasonable" price declines? Farm prices already have dropped 23 per cent. How much farther must they fall before we begin to call the decline "unreasonable"? Must the farmer almost go broke before he can expect the steadying hand of his own government to be extended? And where is the fine line between being almost broke and just plain broke? For my part, I can't fix that line.

If I understand it correctly, and if that quotation I gave you was correct, then the Farm Bureau's leadership at this moment has turned its back on the historic position of its own great organization, when it so often declared—and I quote again from its own former statements of policy: "The fight of organized agriculture has been and is now for equal opportunity and parity position with the other great groups." Why aren't those words still true today? Will somebody tell me? (Applause.)

Now, because the gentleman who now heads the American Farm Bureau is here today, I would like to take the opportunity, for just this once, of addressing him directly, in the hope of reaching a better understanding of his attitude and perhaps of the attitude of some of us in the Department of Agriculture. I would like to ask the president of the American Farm Bureau Federation in all seriousness: Does it aid agriculture in any way to say of the administration's proposals, "People who propose such a program to farmers are very dumb or downright dishonest?" How will that kind of attack help us to solve the hog-price-support problem?

I would like to ask the gentleman: Do you actually expect to halt the decline in farm prices by calling the administration's recommendations a "statement of politico-economic philosophy, not a farm program"? Or by calling those recommendations "a supreme delusion"? Or, as you have also done, by saying that the proposals are "nuts"? (Applause.)

And I would like to ask in all sincerity: Do you think it fair to farmers in your membership to be openly favoring still lower price supports for farmers in the hope of forcing some of them out of business so that farming can be more profitable for the big-scale farmers with large cash reserves who are able to survive? (Applause.)

I would like to ask if you really feel that the Farm Bureau is fulfilling a constructive role in behalf of agriculture by having its spokesmen spend their time tearing down the recommendations of others with such abusive remarks as, "It shines and stinks and stinks and shines like rotten mackerel in the moonlight?"

Ladies and gentlemen, again I say to you that I am a public official; I realize that all public officials are entitled to or must expect abusive language addressed to them, and I assure you that I am neither offended nor bothered by the laughter and applause. As a matter of fact, if it gives some release to the feeling of frustration at not having an adequate program, I am for their doing it and I want them to. (Applause and laughter.) . . .

Let's keep that bushel of corn in mind. What do you want to do with it? Shall we find a way to get it used—fully used and into the stomachs of the American people? Do you know that the Irish eat more meat per capita than the people of the United States? We are not eating all the meat we can eat. So we can convert that corn into meat and get it into the marketplace and get it consumed, and then we won't have to come back to the American farmer and say, "Quit producing corn."

There are just two ways you can go: Find a good use for the things we can produce—get them into the marketplace at attractive prices and keep the government out of the channels of trade; or go back to this thing called regimentation and ask American farmers to cut down production. I don't want to go to the American farmer and ask him to cut off the production of anything until I have satisfied myself beyond any reasonable doubt that we have exhausted every effort to get that corn converted into the things people want to eat and into the marketplace at prices which are attractive. And I think we have a long, long way to go.

We ate eight eggs less per person this year than last and five to six less pounds of meat. We have eaten a lot less of everything these past few years because we have priced ourselves out of the marketplace. And we have a lot of things down in the cave and potatoes down in the ground.

Thank you for hearing me out. This has been a grand audience. I was told when I came to Iowa, the home state of Mr. Kline, that the going would be tough. But I don't think it is tough anywhere. People are people and human beings, and the problems in Iowa are no different than the problems anywhere else. I think there is so much of good human Americanism in every one of us that I will be happy to talk or accept an invitation to talk to any audience anytime anywhere.

EDUCATION

THE PLIGHT OF THE CONSERVATIVE IN PUBLIC DISCUSSION [1]

JAMES H. McBURNEY [2]

James H. McBurney, Dean of the School of Speech, Northwestern University, and President of the Speech Association of America during 1949, gave this address at the first general session of the thirty-fourth annual conference of that organization, in the Grand Ball Room, Stevens Hotel, Chicago, Illinois, on December 28, 1949. This conference was held in conjunction with the annual meeting of the American Speech and Hearing Association (Silver Anniversary) and the American Educational Theatre Association (fourteenth annual meeting).

The theme of this first session was "Areas of the study of speech—what do they have in common?" Horace G. Rahskopf, University of Washington, First Vice President (and President-elect) of the Speech Association of America, presided. On the program also were the Honorable Ralph E. Church, Representative of the 13th Illinois District in the United States Congress; President Delyte W. Morris of Southern Illinois University, President of the American Speech and Hearing Association; and Hubert Heffner of Stanford University, President of the American Educational Theatre Association. More than a hundred registered for the convention, and some one thousand, including teachers, research specialists, graduate and undergraduate students of speech, and other educational groups, were in the audience.

The convention, a three day conference, included sectional meetings on oral interpretation, semantics, business communication, secondary and college teaching, preaching, experimental phonetics, forensics, public address, voice and diction, television and radio, debate and discussion philosophy and techniques, library and the speech teacher, speech and human relations, clinical procedures, discussion, rhetoric, listening, history of speech education, British oratory, stuttering, acting, play production, and new trends in theatre education.

The address reflects the speech philosophy of its author; is closely adjusted to the immediate listeners; conveys much of the speaker's personality; is well organized.

[1] Permission for this reprint through the courtesy of Dean James H. McBurney. Text supplied by the author. See also *Quarterly Journal of Speech*. 36:164-8. April 1950.
[2] For biographical note, see Appendix.

Only indirectly is it addressed to the business conservatives themselves, few of whom obviously were in the audience. The language is oral, unhackneyed, personal, animated.

Mr. McBurney has been dean of the School of Speech, Northwestern University, since 1942. Previously he had taught speech at Northwestern, the University of South Dakota, University of Michigan, Columbia University, and at several secondary schools. At the University of Michigan McBurney was awarded the doctorate in speech. The chairman of his doctoral committee was professor J. M. O'Neill, one of the two or three national leaders in speech education.

The speaker, a former school and college debater, is an excellent platform speaker and discussion leader. He has demonstrated the principles of effective discussion in his widely used *The Principles and Methods of Discussion* (with Kenneth Hance), and in his more recent *Discussion in Human Affairs* (also with Hance).

The plight of the conservative in American public life is a fact which hardly needs documentation. An analysis of this plight was presented in a recent issue of the Chicago *Daily News* in which opinions from grass-root voters to political and educational leaders were reported. Says the *News*: "Whether it was called a 'welfare state,' 'creeping socialism,' 'fascism,' 'a regimented state,' or something else, it boiled down to a belief that individual freedom and initiative are being threatened by the government." When queried by the *News*, Franklyn B. Snyder, President Emeritus of Northwestern University, added this: "Complacency today is the greatest foe of the conservative."

I think this hits the nail on the head. Complacency it is! And this complacency affects public discussion in America in ways which are good for no one, least of all the conservatives.

I have the temerity to argue that the conservatives in America have become inarticulate to a point where their voice does not do credit to their ideas and often does their cause a positive disservice. I think my analysis is not a partisan one. I confess to a conservative bias, but my concern here is a professional interest in public discussion and debate. In a very real sense, discussion is the essence of the democratic process. Whatever weakens discussion in America, weakens America. A monolithic society is not conducive to vigorous discussion of public questions. We need differing points of view, and we need articulate spokesmen for these points of view.

For the past eight years, I have had charge of the Northwestern University Reviewing Stand, a national radio forum originating in radio station WGN, Chicago, and carried by the Mutual network. We are on the air each week with discussions of contemporary problems, mainly social, economic, and political questions. Our speakers are members of the University faculty and distinguished guests from business, industry, labor, government, and the press. As moderator of these discussions, I am the recipient of an amazing volume of letters and comments from all over America. One of the most persistent criticisms is the charge that we are radicals, reds, and even Communists. To be sure, we are often labeled radicals and reactionaries on the same program, but the charge of radicalism far outruns any other single criticism.

Why this persistent charge of radicalism? I am sure the answer does not lie in the sponsorship and management of our radio forum. Even our critics express surprise that we should be the ones to commit this indiscretion. What is more, precisely the same charge is directed against the other leading radio forums. The answer must be sought in the discussions themselves.

In the first place, we usually discuss changes in the status quo —questions of public policy. That is an important function of discussion. All kinds of social, economic, and political changes are analyzed in the interest of better understanding. The conservative, by definition, opposes change; he supports the status quo; he usually takes "the traditional position." The very fact that discussion concerns itself with change may suggest that discussion supports such change. Actually, of course, it does not. Properly conceived, discussion is a method for analyzing problems and considering solutions to these problems. It is not even a good vehicle for propaganda.

More important are the persons who take part in these programs. In organizing discussions of controversial questions, we naturally try to secure the most competent spokesmen available for all points of view. We have little trouble getting the advocates of change, the liberals, the radicals. These people invariably accept our invitations with pleasure and alacrity; but not so with the gentlemen on the right, the representatives of business and industry, the conservatives. More often than not, they are too busy, have other commitments, or refuse to appear on the same platform with other speakers we have invited. Sometimes they say quite frankly that they are afraid of give-and-take discussion.

As moderator of these discussions, I frequently find myself wanting to come to the aid of the conservative spokesmen. Often they are nervous and inarticulate. Especially is this true when their basic assumptions are challenged. They lack facility in verbal analysis and synthesis, in give-and-take argument, in rebuttal and refutation. More often than not they are no match for rhetorically seasoned liberals, with long experience on every kind of platform from a cracker barrel to a radio microphone. There are notable exceptions, but my description is faithful to the rule.

I think this is the reason why our radio forum is charged with radicalism—the conservative spokesmen do not come through! It is either this or the less charitable explanation that the conservative position in America today is not tenable in public discussion. Whether or not the conservative position, or any other position, is tenable is precisely what public discussion is designed to test. Given spokesmen of high competence and reasonably equal competence, it provides one of the best tests democracy has been able to devise. Unless these conditions are met, we run the risk of serious distortions in public policy.

If this problem were confined to radio forums, I would not take your time with it. It most emphatically is not so confined. These forums are just a small sample of the kind of discussion that goes on all over America—in homes, schools, churches, places of business, legislative assemblies, and deliberative bodies of all kinds. In this larger arena, we can witness the full measure of the rhetorical bankruptcy of the conservative.

For many years past in America, the conservative has been in the saddle. The industrialists, the banker, the businessman have been the backbone of America—respected, accepted, and looked to for leadership. Whether this reputation was deserved is neither here nor there. It is a fact. But this long, unchallenged tenure has not been an unmixed blessing. The conservative grew soft under it. He came to take his position for granted. He became complacent. And he lost his voice, except for occasional ceremonial chants and cries of distress. In the meantime, the little fellow on the outside grew in strength and lung power, until one day there appeared on the scene a great spokesman for the ill fed, the ill housed, and the ill clothed. Since that time we have lived under New Deals and Fair Deals.

How have the conservatives responded to this rude unseating? Not too well, I fear. The National Association of Manufacturers invited a number of students to attend their annual convention in New York this month. *Time* magazine reports some of the reactions of these young observers:

> Too many of the NAMsters, the students felt, talked in such platitudes and generalities about the drift towards socialism, the welfare state, taxes, that what they had to say lost its effect. What was needed, said one student, was a clear, fresh exposition "to the man in the street in terms of the simple why and wherefore of the price of his bread."
> A further student criticism was that, in panel discussions, the NAMsters "were often unqualified to answer our questions."
> One student put his finger on NAM's biggest trouble: its failure to capitalize on opportunities to catch the public's ear.

Quite obviously the answer to this problem is not a simple one. Indeed, there may be no answer which the conservatives will like. Whether or not an intransigent liberalism is good for America must be ground out in countless discussions and debates all over America. My hope is that the conservatives will find the means of developing an effective voice in these discussions and debates. I think they are lost unless they do. And I think America stands to lose without their best counsel. I would say exactly the same of the liberals were the situation reversed.

I realize that this thesis comes easily from a teacher of discussion and debate and a moderator of public forums. Some will say the plight of the conservative is dictated by economic, social, and cultural realities in the American scene which have little or nothing to do with "talk" about these realities. I do not propose to assess these realities in this paper, but I do profess to know something about the influence of talk in building attitudes and shaping events. Talk influences men, and men influence events. The case for making good sense and good taste articulate is a familiar one to most teachers of speech. We have substantial experimental data to support this thesis.

In the first place, we know that attitudes toward social problems do change significantly as a result of discussion. In other words, something is accomplished in discussion; people do change their positions on public questions as a result of listening to discussions and participating in them. Secondly, we know that the initial or pre-discussion dispersion of attitudes is significantly reduced as a result of discussion. People get closer together. There is a significant tendency toward consensus. Thirdly, we know that people develop superior attitudes toward public questions through discussion, as measured by the opinions of experts. In other words, discussion has the effect of developing sound positions on social questions. Finally, we know the greatest influence in discussion is exerted by the more competent people, as measured by standard tests of personal competence, such as personality inventories, intelligence tests, social maturity scales, and the like.

I cite these data to make the point that public discussion is a democratic tool which no segment of American society interested in social attitudes can afford to neglect; and by the same token, it is a matter of great importance to American society that all social groups be competently represented in public discussion.

Several suggestions for developing effective spokesmen in deliberative councils are implicit in what I have already said. I should like to spell these out in greater detail.

In the first place, men in executive positions in business and industry must be willing to participate in public discussion. As the President of the United States Rubber Company put it last June:

> The eleventh hour is here for business to speak for itself. Now, and from now on, the men who run American business must devote as much —if not more—time and effort to the public relations of their business as they spend on finance, production, and distribution. Unless they do, they will not need to worry about the latter problems. Government will be glad to handle them all.

In the second place, the paid spokesmen of the conservatives, the public relations officers of business and industry, must be selected with careful attention to their qualifications for serious intellectual discussion and vigorous public debate. The main job of such officers is developing relations with the public rather than with their brothers in the bond. This requires social, political, and economic literacy of a high order and top-notch dialectical ability.

Thirdly, the conservatives urgently need to develop greater sensitivity to the changing pattern of communication in America. This pattern is characterized by a growing emphasis on logical values in place of high pressure mumbo-jumbo; by simple, direct statement rather than verbal obfuscation; and by a sense of relativity in language usage in place of arbitrary, dogmatic assertion. These changes are inevitable in a democratic society which is becoming more conscious of the processes of communication and more sophisticated in their use. Any speaker ignores them at his own peril.

Fourthly, the conservatives must rid themselves of some unfortunate stereotypes. In this co-called "era of the common man," the conservative is depicted as the foe of the common man. Unfortunately, this role can easily be given specious plausibility because the conservative does have vested interests in the status quo. In a society in which men are living longer and specialized economic functions tend to draw class lines, it is easy to think of the conservative as an old man who has lost the common touch. Actually, the interests of the common man on any given issue at any given time and place may be just as completely identified with the conservatives as with the liberals. Most certainly it begs the question to assume otherwise. The lines between conservatives and liberals in America need not, and should not, be drawn on the basis of age or class. They should be determined in free and widespread discussion, and the conservatives must learn how to conduct themselves in such discussions in ways which will enlist the sympathy and undertanding of common men.

The conservatives have also succeeded in alienating many of the intellectuals in America. Witch hunts in the colleges and universities, journalistic caricatures of the mortar board, and frantic name calling are hardly designed to win the understanding of men who place a high premium on objectivity in discourse. Moreover, there are echelons in the intellectual hierarchy in which there are fashions in ideas just as there are in goods. In some of these quarters, I fear, the conservative position has lost caste for reasons which have very little or nothing to do with its merit.

A minimum program of education and training for the kind of public discussion I am talking about should include: (1) a broad understanding of social, political, and economic issues in American life and culture; (2) clear insight into personal and social values as they affect these issues; and (3) specific training in the philosophy and method of democratic participation.

On this last point may I add with some feeling that such training is not to be secured in classes in after-dinner speaking and polite elocution. What is needed is sound education in discussion, debate, persuasion, and semantics under conditions which provide opportunities for realistic experiences in participation and leadership under the direction of competent teachers.

In conclusion, I wish again to make it clear that I do not present this analysis to plead the cause of the conservative, nor do I mean to question the ability and integrity of the conservative. It is my purpose rather to point out that conservatives generally are not doing their cause justice in public discussion and debate, explain why this is the case, and suggest some of the ways in which this weakness can be corrected. I believe this to be a problem of more than ordinary importance in American public life, and certainly one of great significance to students and teachers of speech.

As Aristotle put it, over two thousand years ago, "Truth and justice are by nature more powerful than their opposites; when decisions are not made as they should be, the speakers with the right on their side have only themselves to thank for the outcome."

THE SCHOLAR AND THE TWENTIETH CENTURY [3]

GEORGE P. RICE, JR.[4]

George P. Rice, Jr., professor of speech at Butler University, Indianapolis, gave this address at the twenty-seventh annual dinner of the honor society, Phi Kappa Phi, at that institution, on May 13, 1949.

Steeped in rhetoric and the humanities, the speaker composed and presented a discourse rich in rhetorical and literary allusion; clear in its recognition of the attributes of a scholar who is also a teacher; comprehensive in its summary of the problems to be solved; constructive in its delineation of the principles by which such solutions can be effected.

The speech is weighted with propositions—syllogistic enthymemes. Some of the representative ideas invite more leisurely analysis, illustration, and explication (for example, the criteria to be used as a measuring rod for the successful solution of the problems) than the thirty-minute address would permit.

Mr. Rice was graduated *cum laude* at the State College, Albany, New York, and there later earned an A.M. degree. At Cornell University he was awarded a doctorate in speech and rhetoric, under the direction of Lane Cooper, Herbert Wichelns, and Frederick G. Marcham. For four years at Albany he was in intercollegiate debate; he was elected to Delta Sigma Rho. He also "coached" the Cornell women. He was a member of the New York State Speakers' Bureau, was chief of the Speakers' Bureau of the Indiana State Mental Hygiene Association, educational director of the National Foundation for Education in American Citizenship. Previous to going to Butler, he taught speech at Pennsylvania State, Cornell, City College of New York, and Columbia University.

Professor Rice states, "The ideal public speaker is a man of intelligence and good will who exercises his powers to lead his fellows to think, to judge, and to act in matters of public concern, that the ends of truth and justice may be served. In America today this means stimulating men to understand their rights and duties under the Constitution and relating these to the newer concepts of 'One World.' " [5]

One of the masterpieces of eloquence of the Golden Age of Greece is a noble panegyric pronounced by Pericles in 431

---

[3] Text and permission for this printing supplied by the author. See also *Vital Speeches of the Day*. 15:574-6. July 1, 1949.
[4] For biographical note, see Appendix.
[5] Letter to this editor, March 17, 1950.

B.C. upon the civic virtues and valor of Athenians. In it the orator-statesman reminded listeners that great deeds were independent of praise and that he spoke only in obedience to a law which demanded utterance to mark the occasion. It is so with us tonight. Words of approval in this hour can neither add to the magnitude of your accomplishment nor increase the deep satisfaction which accompanies it. However, academicians cherish tradition and ceremony; hence it is altogether appropriate that your society should have called upon a speaker to express those deep sentiments you share and even allow him to suggest certain lines of thought and standards of conduct in keeping with your new privileges and responsibilities. It is a source of singular satisfaction to me that a rhetorician should have the honor of addressing the chapter on its anniversary. The invitation reveals a discerning regard for an ancient discipline whose twenty-five centuries of recorded history merit your respect upon very substantial grounds. Moreover, most men and women who have to do with teaching and learning take pleasure in discussing their way of life in its several aspects with colleagues and friends. I may even claim, like Herodotus, to have a story to tell, and like him, I hope no god or hero will take offense at what I have to say.

This gathering is, of course, no isolated instance of recognition of men and women of superior intellectual abilities. Sister chapters of this society and other groups devoted to similar ideals are meeting during these weeks throughout the United States. We are part of a far-flung brotherhood whose membership stretches across years and miles, for associations which identify and unify the ranks of the fit though few are not modern in origin. The Italian scholar of the Renaissance wore the Ring of Pythagoras as proudly as you now wear the shining symbol which declares your allegiance to intellect. And the Socratic Circle has its modern counterpart in the learned academies of France, England, and the United States. There is a bond which binds this university in unbroken continuity to Oxford, to Paris, to Rome, to Alexandria, and to Athens. We begin, therefore, by offering our homage and admitting our very great debt to the revered band of seekers after Truth in each generation, small in numbers but gigantic in strength, which has drawn and will draw its recruits from the first minds of every age without regard for creed, nation, color, or tongue. Your new status is proof that those who are qualified to judge think you may one day be of this great company. It is at the least a guarantee of your serious interest in the privileges and duties of talented intelligence. It is upon this assumption that I address myself to you upon the thesis of "the scholar and the twentieth century."

I would first define the general attributes of scholars and of scholarship, and then attempt to show the man of learning in relation to some of the pressing problems of our time. Let us begin with definitions. Who is a scholar? What does he do? The word "schole" is Greek and means "leisure." My colleagues at this board would qualify the noun by inserting before it the adjective "industrious," for the scholar is preeminently a gifted person who makes industrious use of his hours for the advancement of the common welfare. By "twentieth century" is intended the present time and the next four or five decades. By "humanism" is meant a mode of thought or action in which the highest aspirations of humanity predominate.

The position of the scholar in any society is exemplified by the Platonic figure of the "body politic." Members of each generation are given special tasks in their community. We may say that to the thinker is assigned the role of eye in this body. His life is one of studious contemplation, and he is the observer and critic of what he sees, the discriminating instrument of the rest. A foremost American Hellenist, Cornell's Lane Cooper, classes the scholar with the poet, the philosopher, the painter, and the composer of music. Those chiefs of state who are wise men secure the future by making suitable provision for colleges and universities and the intellects they house. Emerson thought that "in the ideal state the scholar is man thinking." Such a one devoted his life to gaining and holding new areas on the frontiers of knowledge. He formed hypotheses; he assembled evidence; he judged; and he shared the harvest of his studies. In these and other ways he proved his value to his fellows. But he was and is, as Emerson claimed also, a man of action at need. The Homeric ideal was a "doer of deeds and a speaker of words." This concept is generally approved and admired today. We recall Plato at Syracuse. We celebrate this year the bicentennial of the birth of Johann Wolfgang von Goethe and are reminded of his services to the duchy of Weimar. The dependence of Winston Churchill upon the Oxford professor, Lindemann, is generally known. And there are notable instances in which colleges and universities have turned to diplomacy, professions, business, and even the armed forces for their heads, bringing the combination of doer and thinker to the campus community.

There are certain other qualifications which mark a man of good will who is also intelligent. He knows that true perspective of men and events comes only to him who is happy, because freedom from care brings wisdom in its train through release from many distorting pressures. He cultivates many areas besides the one in which he speaks with the authority of knowledge. He is one who in his early years gives promise and possesses convictions. You will remember the idealism of Thomas Mann who returned a doctorate granted him *in honoris causa* by a great German university because he disapproved strongly its failure to oppose tyranny. He is a philosopher in the true sense of that word, a "lover of wisdom" before he seeks to possess encyclopedia. He is aware of two audiences —the immediate which hears his lectures or reads his books or learns his discoveries, and the remote—the as yet unborn judges before the bar of whose opinion he will stand one day through his works. The learned man's progress is marked by indications of his obligation to predecessors and contemporaries, without whose assistance he could not have made his way. Important among his concerns is that of selecting, training, and encouraging gifted young men and women. He examines their ethical and intellectual qualifications with painstaking care. Nor will he assemble large numbers of learners about him. The opinions of Scaliger, Boeckh, Agassiz, and Lang, among many, stress that *only the opportunity for education is democratic and that not all who are eligible can benefit by instruction to the same degree.* Such men know that the state is wisely guided by those who have great natural parts supplemented by artful instruction at the hands of capable teachers. And our scholar is a good teacher. Those who assert it is possible to be an effective teacher without being a good scholar speak hastily. Aristotle tells us that the pleasure of recognition through learning is a basic drive in human conduct. Who shall deny that the best teaching takes place when teacher and learner share the same experience, though on different levels?

Nor is mere transfer of fact and theory from one academic generation to the next the chief function of the scholar. He must inspire his charges to think and to act and to make discoveries for themselves, cultivating independence of action and judgment alike. And he will encourage in them the development to those traits of individuality which so peculiarly distinguish nobility of intellect: the awful patience of the discoverers of radium; the self-denial and persistence which enabled Marie Sklodovska to live in Paris in 1892 on three francs a day while she studied chemistry and physics at the Sorbonne; the capacity for broad vision supported by minute investigation practiced by Schleiermacher and Gaston Paris; the acumen to discern the limits of his powers and to undertake good and useful tasks within them. Thus, George Saintsbury, professor of Rhetoric and English Literature in the University of Edinburgh: "At a very early time of my life it was, as the old phrase goes, borne in upon me that I was not destined to create great literature but that I had perhaps some faculty of appreciation for it, and might even to some extent assist that appreciation in others." That "appreciation in others" was assisted through great numbers of books and numerous articles and addresses over a long span of years; his tasteful industry earned for Saintsbury an enduring measure of fame.

Let us endow our scholar finally with the idealism and high-minded courage of Fichte. Recall his words at Erlangen: "I am a Priest of Truth; I am in her pay; I have bound myself to do all things, to venture all things, to suffer all things for her. If I should be persecuted and hated for her sake, if I should even meet death in her service, what wonderful thing shall I have done?—what but that which I greatly ought to do?"

The modes of thought and action expressed by the qualities I have enumerated are extraordinary and they mark the exceptional man. But it is time that some importance be assigned to the gifted and that a little of the emphasis on the mediocre be lifted. Too much has been said and written to the effect that this is the "century of the common man," another name for the cult of mediocrity. Hear Somerset Maugham on this: "That nation is proudest and noblest and most exalted which has the greatest number of really great men."

The representative scholar is not without a sense of humor. And upon some occasions he goes abroad, a bird of rare and colorful plumage in academic processions, displaying the bright scarlet of theology, the deep green of medicine, the pure white of humanities, moving through all colors of the spectrum, rising finally to the cloth of gold robe for the honorary doctorate of the University of Dublin. I shall tell several tales which stand in contrast to what has been said and show our man in lighter vein.

Among the vast body of fact and apocrypha extant is the story of the great chemist, Chandler, who says of himself "no chemist enjoyed a more oleaginous career." He was brought up on the proceeds of the whale oil industry in New Bedford. In grammar school he was punished with a whale-bone switch. The vessel which carried him to a German university for graduate study bore also a cargo of oil. His first scientific article, rejected for publication on the ground it was too fantastic, dealt with the possibilities of obtaining illuminating oil from the earth. His early career exemplifies the German axiom that "a professor is a man who thinks otherwise." Chandler applied for a position as assistant in chemistry at Union College. He was informed that there was no vacancy, but that a janitor was needed at $500 a year. Chandler took the job, teaching chemistry *gratis*. But in ten years he had a chair in a great university and a national reputation.

And one remembers with amusement an incident involving Columbia's noted professor of dramatic literature, Brander Matthews. He had submitted an article to the *Forum* when that journal was edited by Walter Hines Page. Several weeks went by without word as to the fate of the manuscript, whereupon Matthews, not accustomed to such cavalier treatment, descended upon the *Forum* for purposes of inquiry. He was informed by Page that the article was not acceptable, that material for the *Forum* must be like a rifle shot, whereas Matthews' paper was like a shotgun discharge—smooth spray of no great weight cast in many directions. "You say the *Forum* is like a rifle?" asked Matthews. "Yes," replied Page, "that is how we like to think of it." "Well, then," replied Matthews, "That explains why it has such a smooth bore for an editor."

The same man was an irrepressible wit in faculty meetings and often lightened the somber deliberations of his colleagues by his mirth. Then as now the doctoral candidate in humanities had to pass an oral examination in Latin. This rule could be waived in special cases. Such an instance, it was urged, occurred with an Arab student whose adviser requested the Latin requirement be dropped and Arabic substituted. He remarked at the conclusion of the argument that, in any case, the Arab had recently had all his teeth removed and could hardly pronounce Latin at all. Matthews listened carefully, then rose and said: "Mr. Dean, I move that this man be permitted to substitute gum-Arabic."

There is finally the tale of a piece of literary criticism by Saintsbury on *Twelfth Night*. The line under discussion was, "Then come kiss me, sweet and twenty." "Ideas differ as to the interpretation of this line," said the lecturer. "Some think that both 'sweet' and 'twenty' refer to the lady; others think that only 'sweet' refers to the lady and that 'twenty' refers to the number of kisses. For myself, I prefer to think that both 'sweet' and 'twenty' refer to the lady and that the number of kisses is quite unlimited."

But it is in order now to return to the thesis of this discourse —the relation of the scholar to the main problems of his era. To his usual functions of discovery and dissemination the twentieth century has especially given him the task of applying his own acumen and knowledge to public affairs. Not since the emergence of Europe from the Middle Ages into the bright light of the Renaissance has there been so great a need for his aid in so many directions. The arrival of Atomic Age has stressed these fields of inquiry: the intelligent control of a new and immense source of power; the vital decision of whether conflict or cooperation is to be the pattern of the struggle between capitalism and communism; the subordination of technical to humanistic values in modern society; the maintenance of a proper balance between the interests of management and labor on the one hand and those of the commonwealth on the other; the spiritual and material regeneration of Europe, especially the shattered German state; the practice of the four freedoms by all men; the management of an enormous public debt which bestrides the national economy like a colossus; the eradication of gross political immorality in some of our civic units; and the encouragement of instruments and processes designed to make the present nebulous force we call public opinion an effective and vigorous factor in the control and direction of local and world affairs.

To meet these problems with success we need more groups like the Institute for Advanced Studies at Princeton and a resurgence of the spirit and practice of the old New England town meeting. We need more stress on the value of the spoken word in exchanges of opinion. Remember these words of an Oxford Chancellor addressed to a graduating class of that University a half century ago: "Public address can flourish only where intellectual civilization has made some progress, where the force of reasoning and the connection of sentences can be comprehended, and where the manner of presentation of thought is considered as well as the matter. Further, oratory that is political can occur only in a nation where there are, first, politics to discuss, and in the second, liberty to discuss them; and the opportunities for eloquence of the highest order will be in proportion to the issues at stake. . . . We must find a nation politically free, with high and noble aspirations, endowed with great and widely diffused culture, so that its leading spirits may be able to think lofty thoughts, and its common people may be able to understand and appreciate them; and we must look for a time when the fullest intellectual development coincides with some decisive moment of political life, when the best minds of the country are bent to some issue of the supremest importance. . . ."

The measuring-rod for successful solution of these problems may be found among the following criteria, several of which were suggested by a congregation of scholars at Princeton three years ago.

1. An awareness of the premanence of the Greek tradition in our life.
2. The ultimate mastery of external nature by man through the application of science.
3. The need for a common language to serve as a medium of communication for all men to promote peace, understanding, and good will.
4. The preeminence of truth in human affairs.
5. The primary of divine and human justice under the law.
6. The desire of all men for freedom.
7. The predominance of certain intellectual and emotional sanctions in the oral and written literature of many cultures: the concept of equality; the concern with justice; the subordination of expediency to ethics; a respect for the wisdom and ancestors; reverence for the word of God; the value of reflective thinking of an objective sort; the love of country; an obedience to the laws of logic; and the human tendency to prefer the delightful to the useful.

The scholarly intellect which applies these standards to our common problems will bring to his task a final asset. He will display a love of the language and literature of his native country and an appreciation of those of others. He will extol the power of noble and elevated conceptions powered by the drive of vehement and sustained passion. He will speak and write a clear and appropriate diction and endow his compositions with tasteful forms of support. He will display a good understanding of the architectonics of excellent prose and oral communication. In sum, he will be the possessor of a style which represents truly what he is himself.

The humanist who adopts the historical approach to determine his relation to the present will examine and apply the values in enduring concepts of truth, justice, love, and beauty with the aid of Plato, Virgil, Dante, Shakespeare, Milton, and Goethe. He will appreciate and understand the past—the great ages of Greece, of Rome, of Italy, and England—because they are a part of the greater whole. He knows they form a useful and even indispensable guide to the future, an explanation of the present. The re-creation of a milieu is no easy task. But before one can know and apply the wisdom of the past, be *gemuetlich* with its climate of opinion, he must carefully explore the history of ideas in a long and unbroken continuum. If one understands a culture able to produce an Isocrates, a Cicero, a Peter Abelard, a Lord Chesterfield, an Abraham Lincoln, or a Winston Churchill, he can better appreciate the wisdom of John Donne's *Devotion*, "No man is an island." We have a common humanity. We have common goals and aspirations. This is not the time to insist upon fragmentation of disciplines preserving archaic dichotomies. There is need for a design to provide unity among subject matter, method, and governing philosophy in the humanistic process. To deny this need, I submit, is to be monoptic in an age where clear vision and the widest possible perspective is imperative.

These are distrait and perilous times beyond peradventure, but they are also times of discovery and decision. And it may be the dawn of a new and wonderful epoch. Let us face it with the high courage and optimism John Milton felt in another era of uncertainty and conflict. "Methinks I see in my mind a noble and puissant Nation rousing herself like a strong man after sleep, and shaking her invincible locks. Methinks I see her as an Eagle muing her mighty youth, and kindling her undazzled eyes at the full midday beam, purging and scaling her long abused sight at the fountain itself of heavenly radiance."

Let me finish with the classic peroration recommended by the First Rhetorician: "I have spoken; you have heard; you know the facts; now give your decision."

WHAT SHOULD A COLLEGE PRESIDENT BE? [6]

WILLIAM HAROLD COWLEY [7]

Dr. William Harold Cowley gave this address at the luncheon at the Lubbock Country Club for delegates and honored guests attending the inauguration of Dossie Marion Wiggins as fifth president of Texas Technological College, at Lubbock, on May 10, 1949.

W. P. Clement, Registrar, introduced the speaker as follows:

"In planning for this occasion the committee sought to secure an outstanding leader of higher education in America, and immediately our thoughts turned to the speaker of today, Dr. William H. Cowley of Stanford University. He graciously accepted the invitation to be present and we are signally honored.

"Dr. Cowley is a graduate of Dartmouth College and holds the degree Doctor of Philosophy from the University of Chicago. He has been the recipient of a number of honorary degrees from leading colleges and universities of America. For some time he was President of Hamilton College in New York, but gave up that work to return to his first love, teaching and writing.

"He is today outside the realm of the college presidency by choice, as in 1941 he was elected President of the University of Minnesota and since that time has been approached regarding the presidency of several colleges and universities of the country, but in each instance he has declined in order to give his time to his chosen field. For some time he was editor of a journal of higher education and is at present a member of its editorial board. He is a specialist in student personnel work and an authority on the history and philosophy of higher education. Throughout the modern educational world there are, perhaps, only five or six men who are giving their time exclusively as professors of higher education. Dr. Cowley is one of that group.

"Those of us who have had the privilege of hearing Dr. Cowley on other occasions have been deeply impressed by his insight into the problems of higher education in various areas. Not only is he an authority on the work and problems of a college president, but he is equally at home in discussing the administrative problems of the dean, registrar, and personnel director. The committee, therefore, is delighted to share with you the experience of hearing one of America's outstanding leaders in the realm of higher education. It is, therefore, my honor and privilege

---

[6] *Bulletin of the Texas Technological College.* 25 no. 4:9-23. August 1949. Permission to reprint granted by Texas Technological College, through the courtesy of Professor W. H. Cowley.

[7] For biographical note, see Appendix.

to present to you Dr. William Harold Cowley, Professor of Higher Education, Leland Stanford University."

This address, as became its luncheon setting, was both thought provoking in its statement of educational philosophy, and highly interesting in its personal reminiscence, anecdote, and congeniality.

Cowley "has an animated delivery, forceful, yet he is fully aware of the audience reaction to his ideas. His appearance is dignified, scholarly, and carries with it an enthusiasm and vitality which one associates with executive ability. The forcefulness of the delivery is related to the strength and vividness of his ideas rather than to the beauty of his language." [8]

Last week I had a letter from an old friend of mine who is the president of a well-known college. Among other things it told of his introduction at a recent banquet by a prominent alumnus:

> In introducing me and reciting some of my multifarious, not to say nefarious, duties and activities, he asked his audience how it is that colleges are still able to persuade people to assume the presidency. For himself, he said that he could only reply that it is something like flagpole sitting: there are just those who go for it.

A few days earlier I had another letter from the president of a leading university commenting on an article I had written, and among other things he wrote:

> When presidents of universities have to deal with questions of high policy, they are forced to call upon others—usually professors—to appraise the issues involved. Isn't there something rather dangerous in the fact that college presidents are so involved in their endless duties that they are not able to do some of these things for themselves?

The title of my talk is "What should a college president be?" Is he really a flagpole sitter? Are his duties so endless and so exacting that he seldom has time to think about the meaning of what he does? The presidents I have quoted imply, if not directly say, these things; and if they are true, then clearly there *is* "something rather wrong" with the position not only for the incumbents but also for their institutions and for society at large. The occasion of the inauguration of a new president seems to provide an appropriate opportunity for taking a critical look at

[8] Letter from David Grant, Stanford University, to this editor, May 1, 1950.

the college president and for suggesting what ideally he ought to be.

May I observe, President Wiggins, that I address myself not only to you but also—and even more pointedly—to your associates on your Board of Directors and on your faculty. In most institutions members of the governing board and of the faculty have only the vaguest of notions about what a college presidency is and what a college president does. My hope is that I may help enlarge the knowledge and understanding of both groups so that you may have their help in conducting your office under better circumstances than most college presidents have yet achieved.

Eleven years ago I sat as you sit today listening to good wishes and advice, and five years ago I resigned after deciding that I didn't like being a college president. Now I am a professor of higher education, and I devote a good part of my time to studying the college presidency. It seems to me to be one of the most important positions in American society, and I discuss today some of the conclusions about it to which I have come during my years in it and my study of it.

Before tackling the question of what a college president should be, we ought first to describe what in general he is now. In my judgment, the answer is that he is one of the most burdened, one of the most harrased, one of the most put-upon people in American life. He is a hewer of wood and a drawer of water, a dray horse, a gallery slave, a bellhop, a hack, and a nursemaid all wrapped up in one. He may seem to be the top brass of an educational institution, but actually he spends most of his time polishing other people's brass—and breaking his back in the process.

He is expected to be an educator, a scholar, an administrator, a businessman, a public speaker, a writer, a money-raiser, a politician, a giver of dinners, a charmer at receptions, a moral force in the community, a commentator on national and international affairs, and popular with students, alumni, faculty, and readers of newspapers. If you think that I'm exaggerating, let me quote a statement made some years ago by President Dodds of Princeton:

I once saw a complete job specification drawn by the trustees of a university in search of a president. Talk about dual personalities! The gifts of a financier, businessman, scholar, preacher, salesman, diplomat, politician, administrator, Y.M.C.A. secretary, were some of the qualifications enumerated in addition to high moral character and a happy marriage to a charming wife.

Obviously no one can meet these specifications, and of course no one does. Yet we go on deluding ourselves that such men are to be found when we ought properly to be deciding what it is possible for a college president to be. Failing to do this, the position becomes more and more impossible, more and more hazardous, more and more subject to criticism.

The criticism began early in this century, and it has been mounting ever since. At first college presidents were accused of being too able, too strong; and groups of professors organized over the country to take power away from them. As one of the most vociferous of these professorial critics put it, "the president is the black beast in the academic jungle." These complaints were directed at that powerful group of presidents who, beginning about 1870 and continuing until about 1910, organized American higher education as we know it today: Eliot of Harvard, Gilman of Johns Hopkins, Harper of Chicago, Low of Columbia, Thomas of Bryn Mawr, and their mighty fellows. The professors largely succeeded in their campaigns to cut down the stature of presidents, and then after the First World War complaints began to be heard that the character and capacity of presidents had deteriorated. One editorial writer in a widely read magazine even went so far as to say that weaklings chiefly held presidential posts and that their small-visioned leadership had led to "the decay of the intellectual life of the nation." In the same vein another non-academic critic last August published this bitter verse in the *American Mercury* entitled "Last words of a college president":

> I walked and sat erect for thirty years,
> A proud merchant of correct ideas,
> Cold gladness and unsullied decorum,
> I fashioned cautious men without souls
> And brittle women with measured passion.
> Behold a traitor
> To his Creator.

This is pushing criticism to its ultimate, but even such un-reasonable blasts will almost certainly grow in number until we face the clear fact that college presidents are expected to be and to do too many things. No one has the capacity to be so able, so energetic, and so versatile. We must promptly quit thinking that they should even try to be such paragons, and we must give attention to the question of what they should be in terms of what they *can* be.

What today can a college president reasonably be expected to be? I suggest that he should be three things—three and no more —and that he can be these things only if he is not expected to spread himself thin in other directions. These three things are: first, an organizer; second, a coordinator; and third, an educational philosopher.

I shall discuss each of these abilities in turn, but may I first point out that I have not included an ability which most college presidents and most students of educational administration, as well as most trustees and faculty members, put first, that is, executive ability. Indeed, I am asserting that a college president should *not* be an executive. This is such strange doctrine that I must explain myself.

An executive is a doer, and I am declaring that a college president should not do most of the things that he now does. His doing should be limited to organizing, coordinating, and seeking to understand the place in society of his institution. These responsibilities are so crucially important that he cannot give attention to the myriads of details that now clutter the typical college president's desk and take up most of the hours of his days and his nights.

Let me illustrate what I mean by recalling an experience I had just after I graduated from college a quarter of a century ago. The father of one of my classmates was the president of one of the country's larger corporations, and he invited me to come to his office about a possible position in his organization. By appointment I arrived at nine-thirty on a Monday morning; and I remember how on the way to his office I thought that at the beginning of a busy week such an important businessman would probably be able to give me only two or three minutes of his time. He surprised me, however, by giving me an hour and a half during which not a paper lay upon his desk or crossed it, not a single telephone call came in, and not once did his secretary disturb us. As we talked, I grew more and more interested in what seemed to me to be a strange situation; and when the interview ended, I asked if I might put to him a question that had been developing in my mind while we talked.

The question was this: "How is it, Mr. Du Bois, that at the beginning of a week you have so little to do that you can give me an hour and a half of your time, time which must have cost your company, at your salary, at least a hundred dollars?" I pointed to the fact that his desk had remained totally bare during the entire period, that his phone had not rung once, and that his secretary had not come near him.

My question interested him, and he took another fifteen minutes to answer it. His chief point was this: he considered it his job not to be a doer but rather the organizer, planner, and philosopher of the company. I remember him saying, "You can hire executives or doers by the hundreds, but only the head of the business can see the organization as a whole. Only the president has all the facts necessary to plan for the future. If he wastes his time on routines, he loses his opportunity for rangy understanding of what the company ought to be doing and how it should go about doing it."

He took me over to a case of charts at one side of his office and showed graphs into the future that he spent a good deal of his time working on, and then he opened a drawer of his as-yet-unsullied desk and brought out manuscripts of proposals he was preparing for the discussion of his vice presidents and his board of directors. He ended by suggesting that if ever I became an executive I should never do any routine job that I could get someone else to do, that I should concentrate on thinking through the basic problems of the enterprise and planning for the future.

That incident of twenty-five years ago had not a little to do with my resigning my college presidency twenty years later. I discovered that no one in my institution had any such conception of a college presidency. Everyone expected me to be involved in the details of the institution, to see them whenever they wanted to be seen, to attend innumerable committee meetings, to introduce every visiting speaker, to greet every returning alumnus and, to boot, to entertain all faculty members and their wives at lunch or dinner at least once a year.

Most college presidents continue to live this kind of a harried, routine-full life with the result that they are always hurried, always weary, always short of time to do the crucial business which they alone can do, that is, to organize, to coordinate, and to carry forward the institution to new intellectual and social fronts.

Fortunately, some administrators have been able to persuade their boards and their faculties that they should have personal assistants of high competence, administrative or executive vice presidents, and a full complement of administrative officers to handle routines. These men—and as yet their numbers are few—are able to handle their positions properly and to put their energies where they ought to be put. The rest comment upon their lives as do the two men whose letters I have quoted.

A college president, I am asserting, should not be a routinist; and he can avoid routine only by being the first of the three things that I have listed, to wit, an organizer. You may remark that organizing constitutes a preeminent kind of executive ability, and you would be right. The point that I would stress, however, is that setting up a plan of operations does not involve being engrossed in the detailed functioning of the plan. In general college presidents are expected not only to plan the organizational structure of the institution, but also to be functionaries carrying innumerable routines. These housekeeping duties I would rule out as completely as possible. I would set up the ideal that President Du Bois of the Western Electric Company described to me in that interview in 1924, an ideal, by the way, that I have found honored by most of the higher business executives that I have since come to know.

What does being an organizer mean? Two things preeminently, I suggest: building and perfecting, first, an organizational structure; and second, a system of communications. In other words, an organizer must establish the procedures that make it possible for people to work together in effective cooperation: and he must also establish methods for the exchange of ideas both within the organization and with those associated with the organization.

Let me give an illustration of what a president not overladen with executive responsibilities can do as a planner. Until a few years ago it took the students of a well-known university five or six hours to register at the beginning of each term, and they spent those boresome, line-standing hours sneering at their Alma Mater's inefficiency. A new president decided to put an end to such stupidity and bad blood. He studied the problem carefully, and after experimenting for two or three terms he reduced the time required to fifteen minutes. I submit that if the president in question had allowed himself to get bogged down in details, he would not have been able to achieve the vast saving of student time and tempers that his planning made possible. To be a planner, I repeat, is a major responsibility of a college president, a responsibility which he can neglect only at great risk to the well-being of his institution. Such planning, I shall point out in a few minutes, should not be limited to material considerations, but of that in due course. Here I emphasize planning university administrative machinery.

The other day I had an experience illustrating the importance of the second element of sound organization, that is, a good system of internal communications. I was driving about the campus of a large university with a full professor and with a second-line administrator of the institution. Several new buildings were being erected, but neither of my companions knew anything about them except their names. They had heard some gossip about the new buildings, but they knew nothing authoritatively or of any importance. I commented on their ignorance, and they replied to the effect that the central administration never took the trouble to tell anyone anything, that the president and his immediate associates treated the faculty and most of the administrative staff as mere employees who didn't need to be informed of what was going on. I asked if that didn't mean that the morale of the institution was low, and they replied, "Of course."

This situation isn't unusual in the colleges and universities of the United States. By and large academic administrators haven't yet learned the crucial significance in staff morale of good systems of internal communications, and the result is that antagonisms born of ignorance exist much more frequently in academic communities than in any other social enterprise of which I know. Obviously this ruins cooperation and good will. Many presidents know that it does; but, snowed under with details of administrative mingle-mangle, they neglect their communications. The college president who spends his time fussing with papers on his desk and who neglects to develop his communications gambles with both his own career and with the destinies of his institution.

The second function that I have listed is coordination. Planning is a type of coordination, but here I am discussing the coordination of ideas and of the people who hold them. The proper word for this kind of coordination is politics, but most people think of politics as an underhanded manipulation and double-dealing, and so in the describing of the essential duties of the college president I use the word coordination. But I mean politics, that is getting people to work together, compromising opposing ideas, persuading recalcitrants to come to a middle ground, negotiating differences of opinion; in sum, coordinating the energies of a people.

One of the best definitions of a college president that I know of is this: he is a man who makes compromises—for a living. The writer of the definition made it in derogation, but it's really a high compliment even though those who habitually insist upon having all or nothing sneer at the compromiser. To these men I quote Edmund Burke's statement in his famous speech recommending that the British Crown work out the differences with the colonies rather than seek to discipline them:

All government—indeed, every human benefit and enjoyment, every virtue and every prudent act—is founded on compromise and barter.

If you don't like the word compromise, then employ the euphemism consultation or the euphemism negotiation. All that I am saying is that the well-advised college president gives a good deal of his time to bringing opposing points of view together and that he cannot do this if he is saddled with administrative minutia. Working out compromises requires leisure, that is, plenty of time for turning over in one's mind many courses of action and choosing the one that best fits the situation in hand. Harassed men never make good compromisers. They are too busy to get the illuminations, the hunches, that point roads out of difficulties.

In my judgment the college president needs more time to work on his political problems than any other administrator of whom I can think in American life. This is true because the college president administers an institution permanently peopled by one of the most difficult kinds of human beings extant today. I mean the college professor. The professor is the individualist *par excellence,* perhaps even more individualistic than operatic prima donnas. And the more gifted he is as a scholar or scientist, the more the individualist he is likely to be.

Consider the psychology of the professor. He is the master of a sector of knowledge, and he is not used to being questioned about his field of competence. Yet he is so completely specialized that he seldom sees his specialty in broad perspective. He is too busy digging deep to look very often at the horizon. He has his experiment to finish, his article to publish, his book to write. He lives in an important world, but it is usually a very small and specialized world. He does not have time for educational thinking in the broad, and thus whatever he may be in politics he is usually a conservative in education who doesn't like to be disturbed by new educational ideas. As one commentator put it a few years ago, "every educational improvement in the history of American higher education has been accomplished over the dead bodies of countless professors." And this is not seriously overstating the historical facts. A nineteenth century German philosopher who knew professors well defined a professor as "a man who thinks otherwise." Certainly in educational matters this defines him almost perfectly.

Presidents who have ideas about education are therefore usually highly unpopular with professors, and thus today most presidents avoid educational discussions and stick to administrative routines. Yet I am proposing that through political skill presidents must rise above the limitations that professors would put upon him. And the political skill required here is of the highest order as will become obvious, I think, when I review the campaign waged beginning forty years ago against presidents being educators as well as administrators.

The movement began about 1909 under the leadership of a professor of psychology at Columbia University, the late James McKeen Cattell. Cattell was the editor of several important learned journals including *Science,* and for a number of years he conducted a vigorous and even vicious campaign against college presidents having anything to do with educational policy. He even went so far as to advocate the abolition of the office and also the abolition of boards of trustees. He wanted professors to have all the authority with no check from anyone.

Cattell's father had been President of Lafayette College, and I suppose that the psychoanalysts would explain his antagonism for college presidents by insisting that he must have hated his father. In any event, the story is told that when one day Cattell's young daughter asked him what to call her new rag doll, he proposed the name "President." "Why?" queried his daughter. "Because," responded Cattell, "rag dolls and college presidents have a lot in common. For example, either will lie naturally in any position."

Obviously, a college president cannot negotiate easily with professors who think as Cattell did. Nor can he get on happily with professors like the distinguished University of Chicago scientist who is reported to have walked by President Judson's home "each evening so that he could spit on that gentleman's sidewalk." President Judson's current successor, Robert Maynard Hutchins, has had even worse experiences; and he recently observed that "academic communities, whatever their protestations to the contrary, really prefer anarchy to any form of government." Sometimes it is hard not to agree with him.

Only those presidents can get on with their faculties who either have no educational programs worthy of the name or who are skilled politicians in the sense of being able in counsel and brilliant in compromise. In a recent article in *Life* Professor

Arthur M. Schlesinger of Harvard reported that every one of the six presidents of the nation considered by historians to be the greatest in our history were men with positive ideas about the directions the country should take, but they were also and paramountly skilled political negotiators or compromisers.

Professor Schlesinger first emphasizes the point that I have been stressing about the relative unimportance of presidents being good executives, and he writes that "as administrators, the six great presidents did not distinguish themselves." Then he goes on to describe their skill in compromising:

> They had to work experimentally within the framework of the democratic tradition. . . . Political considerations permitted them to be idealists if they liked, but not doctrinaires. "What is practical must often control what is pure theory," wrote Jefferson, the political theorist. As James Russell Lowell put it in his essay on Lincoln, the ultimate test of statesmanship is not a "conscientious persistency in what is impractical" but rather, "loyalty to ends, even though forced to combine the small and opposing methods of selfish men to accomplish them."

In other words, the president with an educational program must be a master in negotiations, a skilled compromiser, a brilliant politician in the best sense of that abused word. He must also be able to take abundant criticisms without serious psychic damage; and the more positive his program, the more numerous and bitter will be the criticism from those whose comfortable arrangements he upsets. On this score Professor Schlesinger has also written pointedly:

> Strong leaders arouse strong opposition. . . . Even the comparatively sacrosanct Washington was not immune. As he remarked, he was assailed "in such exaggerated and indecent terms as could scarcely be applied to a Nero, a notorious defaulter or even to a common pickpocket." When he retired an opposition paper rejoiced that "the man who is the source of all the misfortunes of our country . . . is no longer possessed of power to multiply evils upon the U.S."

Your efforts as a compromiser, President Wiggins, will of course not be limited to the faculty. You will also need to use your political abilities with the alumni and also with your Board of Directors. You will often be impatient with them both, and you will perhaps sometimes find comfort in the knowledge that other presidents have had their troubles with both groups. If you are inclined, now and then, to recall General Goethals' remark that "all boards are long, narrow, and wooden," take comfort in the thought that board members and alumni aren't around very often.

We come now to the final and most important of the functions of a college president—being an educational philosopher. By this I do not of course mean theoretical dreaming. Rather I mean formulating and defining institutional purposes, and I would recall again my interview with the President of the Western Electric Company and his statement that he considered his chief responsibility to be philosophizing, that is, seeing the work of his company as a whole and plotting the course to be followed into the future. This, and not a dreamer, is what I mean by a philosopher; and I suggest that if business needs such philosophers, education needs them even more.

A business corporation produces goods and services for the well-being of society, but a college has considerably more important work. It exists for the discovery of new knowledge, for the interpretation of that knowledge in the lives of peoples, and for forming the minds and the moral standards of the rising generation. If business corporations need philosophers at their helms, then colleges and universities need them infinitely more.

Being an educational philosopher means working on *educational* problems. These are the core questions of colleges and universities; and even at the risk of faculty disapproval and opposition, college presidents must wrestle with educational questions. Organizational structures, systems of communication, political negotiations are only means to the end of education. Hence college presidents must be educators primarily; to be an educator means to be an educational philosopher.

Unfortunately most college presidents seem to have forgotten this; and if they haven't forgotten it, they have allowed themselves to be frightened away from their main jobs by opposition or to become so burdened with routines and machinery that they have little if any time to think about what the routines and the machinery are for. Thus while colleges and universities grow in the numbers of their students, in the sizes of their budgets, and in the grandeur of their plants, most of them lack direction.

They recall the cartoon, described by President Hopkins of Dartmouth at my inaugural luncheon, of two motorcyclists speeding down a road. One turned to the other and said, "I think we've lost the way." "Never mind," said the other, "we're making such good time, let's keep right on."

President Wiggins, I am declaring to you that beyond doubt the cardinal, the paramount, the most insistent part of your job is being an educational philosopher, that is, the man who should be continuously interpreting the educational directions of this institution. If Texas Technological College is to have a large social aim, then you must discover and state it. You alone will be seeing the institution as a whole. Professors are specialists who see only their small though important sectors, and the same is true of second-line administrators. Your board of directors will have ideas, but they are busy men in other walks of life. Only you will see the complete institution. Only you will have all the facts necessary for developing the pattern of the college.

To drive home this point, let me quote from a little book that President A. Lawrence Lowell of Harvard wrote a few years after he retired from the presidency of Harvard in 1933. It is entitled, *What a University President Has Learned*, and I recommend, President Wiggins, that you own it and read it periodically. The passage I would have you think about now reads as follows:

> For distinguishing the essential elements of a plan from accessories, for perceiving the differences between the whole of a part and a part of the whole, the benefit of a pattern . . . is great. Such a pattern is by no means rigid; the final objective is perfectly definite, but the details are fluid and must be kept so throughout. . . . With a pattern of this kind it is comparatively easy to discern quickly the value of any proposal made; for one has not to consider it by itself as a distinct thing on its own merits alone, but in its relations to the whole, whether it fits or can be made to fit into the pattern.

The pattern that President Lowell has written about is not a pattern of buildings and administration machinery. It is a pattern of *education*. It is a pattern which defines the purposes of education first, and only after the purposes of education have been defined does it move on to the means necessary for the accomplishment of those purposes.

It must be obvious to you that by a philosopher I do not mean a man of theory living in an ivory tower. Instead I mean a very practical man living in the midst of buzzing activity who seeks to make directions clear. Such a practical philosopher above all things needs leisure: leisure to talk with many people, leisure to read the thoughts of our best minds living and dead, leisure to think calmly and deeply.

College presidents are called the leaders of their institutions, and undoubtedly during these ceremonies President Wiggins will frequently be referred to as the leader of Texas Technological College. May it be so, but it cannot be so unless he develops a pattern, an educational philosophy. A leader is a man who is going somewhere and who had the ability to persuade people to follow him. Not to have a pattern, a plan, or philosophy is to be lost on a stormy sea without a chart or a rudder.

President Wiggins, I have been attempting to answer the question, "What should a college president be?" and I have suggested that he should be three things preeminently: an organizer, a coordinator of men and their ideas, and chiefly an educational philosopher. To be these things, I have urged, he must not permit himself to be a routinist swamped in executive trivia. These he must assign to others and give his energies to the large and long-range development of his institution. Today you enter officially upon the presidency of a very young but potentially great institution. You begin in troublous times, in times of great world-wide perplexity and fear. Each of us must make his contributions to the making of a better world; and you are in a strategic position, in a strategic state, and in a strategic nation. You have a tremendous opportunity, and when in some distant year you lay down the burdens of office, may it be said of you: "Wiggins was no flagpole sitter. Not he. He dreamed dreams, and he had the ability to make them into realities because he knew how to organize the work of the college and to deal happily with people. He knew what a college president should be and he turned his knowledge into brilliant fact." Power to you, President Wiggins!

UNIVERSITY ASSEMBLY [9]

HAROLD W. STOKE [10]

President Harold W. Stoke, of the State University of Louisiana, gave this address at a University Assembly Meeting, at the Agricultural Auditorium, at 4:15 P.M. on Monday, September 19, 1949.

The speech is a sort of "state of the Union" applied to the Louisiana campus. In the beginning the President reports on the physical state of the campus and refers to faculty changes. He, for example, introduces the new deans—Dean C. G. Taylor of the College of Liberal Arts, Henry George McMahon of the Law School, and Dr. William W. Frye of the Medical School. The speech throughout is personal, interesting, and intellectually stimulating.

Concerning his speech experiences and methods of preparation, he states, "I did some debating in college, but suspect that such public speaking as I am capable of doing was learned for the most part as teacher, talking to large lecture sections of classes in government.

"In preparing speeches, I generally try to decide as clearly as possible just what it is I am trying to say. I then try to make it as simple as possible, keeping in mind the fact that an audience usually has no intrinsic interest in what I am about to say unless I can create that interest in them." [11]

I am told that one of the fascinations of golf is the opportunity it gives to begin anew at every tee, that no matter how dissatisfied we were with our last score, the next hole will surely be made in par. This is no less true in opening a new school year. We now stand at the tee.

Many of you have continued to work steadily through the summer and to you I extend deep sympathy. Some others have been fortunate enough to have had vacations, study, travel or other interesting variations. A larger number than usual are completing sabbatical leaves of absence. We have missed you while you were gone and we are very happy to welcome you back. We shall all profit vicariously from your experiences. . . .

The operation of a university, especially of a state university

[9] Text and permission for this reprint furnished through the courtesy of President Harold W. Stoke.
[10] For biographical note, see Appendix.
[11] Letter to this editor, April 21, 1950.

is conditioned very largely by the atmosphere prevailing in the society in which it exists. It shares in the prevailing prosperity or stringency. Even more, it shares in the prevailing climate of ideas, of preoccupations. If a nation is at war, its universities are at war. If a nation is unhappy, if it is suffering some disillusionment and uncertainty, its universities will reflect that fact. I do not mean to say that as a university we have no independence of life and mind but that the life and mind we have will be powerfully shaped by the dominant interests of our society.

Perhaps the most difficult period for a university is when there *is* no strong and dominant force to give it direction and to shape its activities. When the prevailing interests of a society are patriotic, religious, scientific, or revolutionary, the universities have missions that are clear and convincing, resolving our doubts and channeling our energies. But what happens when we do not have such compulsions, when we must rely upon our own philosophies and resources to give meaning and value to our work?

This is currently our situation. The clear and present compulsions of war under which we have worked so long have passed. The bustling excitements of postwar accommodations, with their subtle flattery as to our usefulness and indispensability, have passed their peak. Our ship is entering quieter waters. As a crew we have become conditioned to storms. Have we lost our skill in more precise navigation?

This year our enrollment is less than that of a year ago. Our opportunity to examine our work, to redirect our time and energy, to reach decisions as to the value of some of our activities is something we have looked forward to. Next year our entering class will again be large. Our chance to achieve perspective this year is unique.

A few years ago, on a visit to London, I was invited to tea by Mr. Charles Galton, the long-time secretary of the Fabian Society. He told me many amusing stories of the early Fabian days, of Graham Wallas, George Bernard Shaw, the Webbs and many others. Among these stories was one of H. G. Wells. When Wells first started his journalistic career, he became very much interested in the achievements of a certain headmaster of one of England's most famous public schools. Beatrice and Sidney Webb had become interested in young Wells and decided to help him with his career by inviting him to their home, a center where many great and near-great gathered. They asked Wells whom they might invite who might be of interest to him. He had become very much interested in the achievements of a certain headmaster in one of England's most famous public schools, and he promptly named this great schoolmaster. The evening came and so did the educator, but the results were sad. The schoolmaster seized the floor and held it. He pontificated and solioquized. He was opinionated and stuffy. Wells' hero-worship visibly evaporated.

"Wells wrote many books after that," Galton chuckled, "and in them he turned to the engineer, the statesman, the scientist and even the military as the future hope of society. But never in all of his later works could he bring himself to turn again to the schools as the source of social salvation."

I have pondered that story many times searching for solid ground for refuting or affirming Wells' opinion. Whether justified or not, more millions are turning to the schools as the future hope of society than have ever turned to them before. In the words of Robert Hutchins, words with the solemn overtones of a Jeremiah, "Education may not save us, but it is the only hope we have."

These are portentous words. It is more than a little appalling if the world has no hope save education and we are the trustees of that hope. Our society looks upon the universities now as something more than mere places of formal teaching and learning. We are that, yes, but we are more. We are now part of a social system, a part of a method by which that system solves its problem of unemployment, rewards its warriors, improves its technological development, bolsters up the pillars of national sentiment and is even an important factor in redistributing the national income. Never have the schools played the role in national life which they are playing today, and their part in the future will be greater if we play it well.

Our students, too, are at the stage in their own lives where they need us most. If we have asked ourselves at what period of human life are aspirations highest and beliefs most idealistic, I think we should say it is at the college age. It is then that the unrealism of childhood has been corrected, but the discouragements and disillusionments which come from the revelations of self-limitations and from the discovery of the depths of social resistence are not yet dominant. It is a period in which energy needs channels, ambition needs worthy objectives, idealism needs faith. These things it is our opportunity and obligation as teachers to provide. I am convinced that our students will respond to far more exacting challenges than we have yet asked them to meet.

Nor does our intellectual responsibility as a university stop with what we can do for our students. Did you ever stop to think that each of us today can no longer be adequately described by the term "teacher." Rather we are called historians, psychologists, chemists, political scientists, biologists and by these very designations the world is informed that we are not only teachers but trustees for important bodies of knowledge upon which our society depends. Where shall our hungry, yearning society turn if not to us for its answers? Where, more logically, than to the universities, operating in atmospheres of thoughtfulness and detachment, shall the world look for the formulation of the satisfying ethical principles it needs so badly, for fresh insight into human nature, for its new canons of social justice, for its knowledge of nature and of art? The burden of expectation which each of us bears upon his shoulders today is enormous. I hope that by the end of the year each of us may honestly say that we have met, at least in part, that expectation. I am sure I can wish for each of you nothing more satisfying.

APPENDIX

BIOGRAPHICAL NOTES [1]

ACHESON, DEAN G. (1893-   ). Born in Middleton, Connecticut; B.A., Yale, 1915; LL.B., Harvard, 1918; honorary M.A., Yale, 1936; honorary LL.D., Wesleyan, 1947; private secretary to Louis D. Brandeis, 1919-21; practiced law, 1921-33; Under Secretary of Treasury (resigned), 1933; practiced law, 1934-41; Assistant Secretary of State, 1941-45; Under Secretary of State, 1945-47; practiced law, 1947-48; Secretary of State since January 1949; Ensign, U.S. Navy, World War I; member, Delta Kappa Epsilon, Scroll and Key. (See also *Current Biography: 1949.*)

BRADLEY, OMAR NELSON (1893-   ). Born, Clark, Missouri; B.S., United States Military Academy, 1915; Command and General Staff School, 1929; Army War College, 1934; honorary LL.D., University of Missouri, Drury College, Harvard, Dartmouth, Princeton, and many other colleges and universities; commander, 2nd lieutenant, infantry, U.S. Army, 1915, advanced through the grades to general, 1945; in Tunis, Sicily, Normandy, France, Germany campaigns, 1944-45; administrator, veteran's affairs, 1945-47; chief of staff of U.S. Army, 1948-49; chairman, Army-Navy-Air Force Joint Chiefs of Staff since August 1949; awarded many military honors and decorations. (See also *Current Biography: 1943.*)

BUNCHE, RALPH JOHNSON (1904-   ). Born in Detroit, Michigan; A.B., University of California, 1927; A.M., Harvard University, 1928, Ph.D., 1934; post-doctoral studies in anthropology and colonial policy, Northwestern University, London School of Economics, and University of Capetown, South Africa,

---

[1] The chief sources of these notes are *Who's Who in America, Current Biography, Religious Leaders in America, Who's Who in American Education, Directory of American Scholars,* and the *Congressional Directory.*

1936-37; Rosenwald Fellowship, Europe and Africa, 1931-32;
Social Science Research Council Fellowship, 1936-38; on Carnegie Corporation's Survey of Negro in America, Southern United
States, 1939; assistant, political science department, University of
California, 1925-27; teacher of political science, Howard University, since 1928 (head of department since 1929); senior
social science analyst in charge of research on Africa and other
colonial areas, Office of Strategic Services, 1941-44; territorial
specialist, division of territorial studies, Department of State,
1944-45; adviser, United States delegation Dunbarton Oaks,
1944; adviser, other United States Delegations connected with
the United Nations; director, Department of Trusteeship, United
Nations, since 1946; on United Nations Palestine Commission,
1948; personal representative of Secretary General with the
United Nations mediator on Palestine, 1948; acting United
Nations Mediator on Palestine since 1948. (See also *Current
Biography: 1948.*)

COWLEY, WILLIAM HAROLD (1899-   ). Born at Petersburg, Virginia; A.B., Dartmouth College, 1924; Ph.D., University of Chicago, 1930; honorary degrees, including LL.D., Hamilton, 1938, L.H.D., Hobart, 1939, Litt.D., Union College, 1940;
with New York business corporations, 1913-18; Bell Telephone
Laboratories, 1924-25; University of Chicago, 1927-29; research
associate and assistant professor of psychology, Bureau of Educational Research, Ohio State University, 1929-34; associate professor, 1934-35; professor, 1935-38; president of Hamilton College, 1938-44; professor of higher education, Stanford University since 1945; member, Phi Beta Kappa; contributor of articles
to magazines and journals.

DENNY, GEORGE VERNON, JR. (1899-   ). Born in
Washington, North Carolina; B.S., University of North Carolina, 1922; LL.D., Temple University, 1940; instructor in dramatic production, University of North Carolina, 1924-26; actor,
1926-27; manager of W. B. Feakins, Inc., 1927-28; director,
Institute of Arts and Sciences, Columbia University, 1928-30;
associate director, League of Political Education, 1931-37; founder
and director, America's Town Meeting of the Air; president of

Town Hall, Inc., since 1937; treasurer, Economic Club of New York; member of executive board, American Association for Adult Education; served Students' Army Training Corps, 1918. (See also *Current Biography: 1940.*)

DEWEY, THOMAS EDMUND (1902-   ). Born in Owosso, Michigan; A.B., University of Michigan, 1923, LL.M., 1937; LL.B., Columbia University, 1925; honorary degrees at Tufts, Dartmouth, and other institutions; admitted to New York bar, 1926; chief assistant, United States Attorney, 1931-33; special prosecutor, Investigation of Organized Crime, New York City, 1935-37; elected District Attorney, New York County, 1937; Republican Governor of New York since 1942; defeated as candidate for the presidency, Republican ticket, November 1944 and 1948; author, *The Case Against the New Deal*, 1940. (See also *Current Biography: 1944.*)

DULLES, JOHN FOSTER (1888-   ). Born in Washington, D.C.; B.A., Princeton, 1908, LL.D., 1946; Sorbonne, Paris, 1908-09; LL.B., George Washington University, 1911; LL.D., Tufts, Wagner, Northwestern and other colleges; began law practice, New York City, 1911; director, Bank of New York; trustee, Rockefeller Foundation; chairman, Carnegie Endowment for International Peace; chairman, Federal Council of Churches Commission on a Just and Durable Peace; secretary, The Hague Peace Conference, 1907; captain and major, United States Army, 1917-18; counsel, American Commission to Negotiate Peace, 1918-19; member, Reparations Commission and Supreme Economic Council, 1919; member, United States delegation, San Francisco Conference on World Organization, 1945; Council of Foreign Ministers, London, 1945; General Assembly, United Nations, 1946; Meeting of Council of Foreign Ministers, Moscow, 1947; London meeting of "Big Four," 1947; United States Senator from New York, appointed July 1949 (to complete term of Senator Wagner); defeated by Herbert Lehman, November 1949, for election as United States Senator; appointed counsellor, Department of State, April 1950; Phi Beta Kappa; writer and speaker on international affairs. (See also *Current Biography: 1944.*)

EINSTEIN, ALBERT (1879-   ). Born at Donau, Germany; educated at Luitpold Gymnasium (Munich), Aarauer Kantonsschule (Switzerland); Technische Hochschule (Zurich); Doctor, *honoris causa*, Geneva, Oxford, Cambridge, Paris, Princeton, Harvard, London, Brussels, and elsewhere; Professor at Universitat Zurich,   Preuss. Akademie d. Wissenschaft (Berlin); came to United States in 1933, became citizen, 1940; appointed life member of Institute for Advanced Study, Princeton, N.J., 1933; discoverer and exponent of the theory of relativity; Nobel Prize, 1922; author, *Meaning of Relativity*, 1923; (with others) *Living Philosophies*, 1931; *On the Method of Theoretical Physics*, 1933; *The World As I See It*, 1934; also other books, brochures and magazine articles. (See also *Current Biography: 1941*.)

EISENHOWER, DWIGHT DAVID (1890-   ). Born in Denison, Texas; B.S., United States Military Academy, 1915; Army Tank School, 1921; graduate, War College, 1929; 2nd Lieutenant, U. S. Army, 1915; Lt. Colonel, Tank Corps, World War I; advanced through grades to General of the Army, December 1944; Chief of Operations Division, Office of Chief of Staff, 1942; Commanding General, European Theatre of Operations, June 1942; Allied Commander in Chief, North Africa, November 1942; Supreme Commander of Allied land, sea, and air forces in Western Europe, November 1943; Chief of Staff, United States Army, 1945-48; elected President of Columbia University, 1948; author of *Eisenhower Speaks*, 1948; *Crusade in Europe*, 1948. (See also *Current Biography: 1948*.)

FAIRLESS, BENJAMIN F. (1890-   ). Born at Pigeon Run, Ohio; student, Wooster College; graduated in civil engineering, Ohio Northern University, 1913; honorary D.Sc., Kent State University, University of Pittsburgh; D.Eng., Ohio Northern, Stevens Institute; civil engineer, Wheeling and Lake Erie Railroad, 1913; with Central Steel Company, successively civil engineer, mill superintendent, general superintendent, vice president in charge of operations, 1913-26; vice president and general manager, United Alloy Steel, 1926-28; president and general manager, 1928-30; executive vice president, Republic Steel Corporation, 1930-35; president Carnegie Illinois Steel Corporation, 1935-37; president and director, United States Steel Corporation since 1938.

JOHNSON, LOUIS ARTHUR (1891-   ). Born in Roanoke, Virginia; LL.B., University of Virginia, 1912; LL.D., Salem College, 1938, Kenyon College, 1939; began practice of law, Clarksburg, West Virginia, 1912; director, various banks, Consolidated Vultee Aircraft Corporation, and other corporations; Secretary of Defense, Washington, D.C., since March 1949; member, Federal Advisory Council, United States Employment Service; Assistant Secretary of War, 1937-40; Captain, infantry overseas, First World War; decorated Commander, Legion of Honor (France); National Commander, American Legion, 1932-33; Chairman, National Finance Committee, Democratic National Committee; member Delta Chi, Delta Sigma Rho, Tau Kappa Alpha. (See also *Current Biography: 1949.*)

KALTENBORN, HANS V. (1878-   ). Born in Milwaukee, Wisconsin; A.B., cum laude, Harvard, 1909; reporter, Brooklyn *Eagle*, 1902-05, dramatic editor, editorial writer, assistant managing editor, associate editor, 1910-30; radio news analyst since 1922; news editor of the Columbia Broadcasting System, 1929-40; with the National Broadcasting Company since 1940; radio reporter, Republican and Democratic Conventions, summer, 1932, London Economic Conference, summer, 1933, League of Nations, Geneva, 1935; author of *We Look at the World*, 1930, *I Broadcast the Crisis*, 1938. (See also *Current Biography: 1940.*)

KLINE, ALLAN BLAIR (1895-   ). Born at Waterbury, Nebraska; A.B., Morningside College, Iowa, 1915; B.S., Iowa State College, 1936; farm operator, Iowa, 1920-44; president, Iowa Life Insurance Company, (1945-47), Iowa Farm Mutual Insurance Company (1944), Iowa Farm Serum Company (1944-47), Iowa Plant Food Company (1945-47), Benton County Farm Bureau (1928-37), Iowa Farm Bureau (1944-47); president, American Farm Bureau, since 1947; director, Federal Reserve Bank of Chicago; sergeant, medical corps, World War I;

member, National Planning Board and various other economic and agricultural councils or commissions. (See also *Current Biography: 1948.*)

MCBURNEY, JAMES HOWARD (1905-   ). Born in Tyndall, South Dakota; Yankton College, 1925; A.M., University of South Dakota, 1929; Ph.D., University of Michigan, 1935; student, Columbia, 1935-36; instructor in speech, Norfolk (Nebraska) High School, 1925-26, Fremont, Nebraska, 1926-27, East High, Sioux City, Iowa, 1927-28; University of South Dakota, 1928-29, University of Michigan, 1929-35; assistant professor, Columbia, 1936; associate professor of speech, Northwestern University, 1936-41, professor, 1941-42, professor and dean of school of speech since 1942; moderator, Northwestern University Reviewing Stand, Mutual Broadcasting System; president, Speech Association of America, 1949; member of Phi Beta Kappa, Delta Sigma Rho; author, *The Working Principles of Argument* (with J. M. O'Neill), 1932; *The Principles and Methods of Discussion* (with K. G. Hance), 1938; *Foundations of Speech* (with others), 1941; *Speech: A High School Course* (with Lew Sarett and W. T. Foster), 1943; *Discussion in Human Affairs* (with K. G. Hance), 1950.

MCMAHON, BRIEN (1903-   ). Born in Norwalk, Connecticut; A.B., Fordham University, 1924; LL.D., 1946; LL.B., Yale, 1927; practiced law, Norwalk, Connecticut, since 1927; Assistant United States Attorney General, in charge of Criminal Division, 1936; elected U. S. Senator from Connecticut, November 1944 for term expiring January 1951; author, *McMahon Act for Control of Atomic Energy*; chairman, Special Committee on Atomic Energy, U. S. Senate, 1945-47; chairman, Joint Congressional Committee on Atomic Energy, since 1948. (See also *Current Biography: 1945.*)

MEDINA, HAROLD R. (1888-   ). Born in Brooklyn, New York; A.B., Princeton University, 1909; LL.B., Columbia University, 1912; honorary LL.D., St. Johns, 1947; with Davies, Auerbach, and Cornell law firm, 1912-18; senior member of law firm, Medina and Sherpick, 1918-47; lecturer in law, Columbia

University, 1915-17, associate in law, 1917-25, associate professor of law, 1925-47; Judge, U. S. District Court, Southern District of New York, since July 1, 1947; presided in New York City over trial of eleven Communists, January-October, 1949; served on many legal commissions and committees; Phi Beta Kappa; author, *Pleading and Practice Under New Civil Practice Act,* 1922; (with Carr and Finn) *Civil Practice Manual,* 1936-42; and other legal books; contributor to legal reviews. (See also *Current Biography: 1949.*)

MURRAY, PHILIP (1886-   ). Born in Blantyre, Scotland; came to the United States, 1902, naturalized, 1911; member, International Board of United Mine Workers of America, 1912, international vice president, 1926-42; president of Congress of Industrial Organizations since 1940; president of United Steel workers since 1942; member of numerous governmental commissions related to labor problems. (See also *Current Biography: 1949.*)

POWELL, ADAM CLAYTON, JR. (1908-   ). Born in New Haven, Connecticut; A.B., Colgate, 1930; M.A., Columbia, 1932; LL.D., Virginia Union University, 1947; Minister, Abyssinian Baptist Church, New York City, since 1937; first Negro elected to City Council of New York, 1941; elected to Congress, November 1945; member of 79th-80th-81st Congress (1945-51), 22nd New York District; chairman board of directors, Powell-Buchanan Publishing Corporation; author: *Is This a White Man's War?* 1942; *Stage Door Canteen,* 1944; *Marching Blacks,* 1945. (See also *Current Biography: 1942.*)

REUTHER, WALTER PHILIP (1907-   ). Born in Wheeling, West Virginia; apprentice tool and diemaker, Wheeling; employee, Briggs Manufacturing Company, Ford Motor Company (a foreman), Detroit; attended Wayne University for three years; traveler, by bicycle, through Germany, Russia, China, Japan; student of auto plants and machine shops, 1933-35; organized auto workers in Detroit, 1935; member of the executive board, International Union of Automobile Workers, 1936-46; vice president of the International Union, United Automobile, Aircraft and

Agricultural Workers of America of the Congress of Industrial Organizations, 1942-46, president, since March 1946; led General Motors strike, 1945-46; severely wounded by assailant, 1948. (See also *Current Biography: 1949.*)

RICE, GEORGE P., JR. (1911-   ). Born in Albany, New York; B.Sc., cum laude, State College, Albany, 1932, M.A., 1936; Ph.D., Cornell University, 1944; student at Cornell under Lane Cooper, Herbert Wichelns and Frederick G. Marcham; teacher of speech successively at Pennsylvania State, Cornell University, City College of New York, Columbia University, and professor of speech at Butler University, Indianapolis; educational director, National Foundation for Education in American Citizenship; contributor to *Quarterly Journal of Speech, Classical Journal, School and Society*, and other professional publications.

ROOSEVELT, JAMES (1907-   ). Born in New York; graduate of Groton School, 1926; A.B., Harvard, 1930; with Roosevelt and Sargent, Inc., Boston, insurance broker, 1930-38; removed to Los Angeles, California, and entered the motion picture industry, 1938-40; west coast representative of Roosevelt and Sargent after 1946; captain (later colonel) U. S. Marines, 1941-45; decorated, Navy Cross, Silver Star; candidate for Governor of California, 1950.

SIMS, HUGO SHERIDAN, JR. (1921-   ). Born, Orangeburg, South Carolina; A.B., Wofford College, South Carolina, 1941; LL.B., University of South Carolina, 1947; Editor, *The Times and Democrat*, Orangeburg, 1941-42; Columnist, *Editor's Copy*, newspaper syndicate, 1941-42; admitted to South Carolina State Bar, 1947; House of Representatives, State of South Carolina, 1947-48; member 81st Congress, 2nd District of South Carolina, 1949-51; entered Army, 1942, advanced from private to captain; Commander Company A, 501st Parachute Infantry, 101st Airborne Division overseas, 1944-45, awarded D.S.C., Silver star and citations from France, Belgium, and Netherlands; war service recorded in "The Incredible Patrol," *Life Magazine*, January 15, 1945. (See also *Current Biography: 1949.*)

STOKE, HAROLD W. (1903-   ). Born at Bosworth, Missouri; A.B., Marion (Indiana) College, 1924; M.A., University of Southern California, 1925; Ph.D., Johns Hopkins, 1930; associate professor of history and political science, Berea College, 1926-28; assistant, associate, and professor of political science, University of Nebraska, 1930-37; principal supervisor of training in public administration, Tennessee Valley Authority, lecturer in political science, University of Pennsylvania, 1937-39; dean of graduate school, University of Nebraska, 1939-40; professor of political science, University of Wisconsin, 1940-43; president, University of New Hampshire, 1944-47; president, Louisiana University since September 1947; consultant on military training, office of Provost Marshal General, 1943-44; member, Classification Committee Association of American Universities, 1940-44; author, *The Foreign Relations of the Federal State,* 1931; *The Background of European Governments* (with Norman L. Hill), 1935.

SYMINGTON, WILLIAM STUART (1901-   ). Born, Amherst, Massachusetts; served in United States army, 1918; at Yale, 1919-23; International Correspondence School; with Symington Companies, Rochester, N. Y., 1923-35; Rustless Iron and Steel Company, Baltimore, Md., 1935-37, President, Emerson Electric Manufacturing Company, St. Louis, Mo., 1938-45; surplus property administrator, Washington, 1945-46; Assistant Secretary of War for Air, 1946-47; Secretary of Air Force, National Defense 1947-50; chairman, National Security Resources Board, 1950. (See also *Current Biography: 1945.*)

TAFT, ROBERT ALPHONSO (1889-   ). Born in Cincinnati, Ohio; attended public schools of Cincinnati and the Taft School, Watertown, Connecticut; A.B., Yale University, 1910; LL.B., Harvard University, 1913; admitted to the bar, 1913; assistant counsel for the United States Food Administration, 1917-19; counsel for the American Relief Administration, 1919; Republican member of the Ohio House of Representatives, 1921-26, speaker, 1926; Ohio State Senate, 1931-32; United States Senate, since 1939; candidate for presidential nomination on Republican ticket, 1948. (See also *Current Biography: 1940, 1948.*)

TRUMAN, HARRY S. (1894-   ). Born in Lamar, Missouri; student, Kansas City School of Law, 1923-25; captain, Field Artillery, World War I; judge, Jackson County Court, 1922-24; presiding judge, 1926-34; United States Senator from Missouri, 1935-41, reelected for the term 1941-47; elected Vice President of the United States on the Democratic ticket, November 1944; sworn in as President on the death of President Roosevelt, April 1945; elected President in 1948. (See also *Current Biography: 1945*.)

UREY, HAROLD CLAYTON (1893-   ). Born, Walkerton, Indiana; B.S., University of Montana, 1917; Ph.D., University of California, 1923; at University of Copenhagen, 1923-24; D.Sc., Montana, Princeton, and other universities; chemist, Barret Chemical Company, Philadelphia, 1917-19; instructor in chemistry, University of Montana, 1919-21; associate in chemistry, Johns Hopkins, 1924-29; associate professor, chemistry, Columbia, 1929-34, professor, 1934-45; professor of chemistry, University of Chicago, since 1945; prominent in development of atomic bomb, World War II; member of many learned societies; author (with A. E. Ruark) of *Atoms, Molecules and Quanta*, 1930; editor, *Journal of Chemical Physics*, 1933-40; contributor to scientific journals; specialized in structure of atoms and molecules; discoverer of hydrogen atom of atomic weight two; awarded the Nobel prize in chemistry, 1934. (See also *Current Biography, 1941*.)

CUMULATED AUTHOR INDEX

An author index to the volumes of *Representative American Speeches* for the years 1937-1938 through 1949-1950. The date following the title of each speech indicates the volume in which it appears.

9662